P 360

YIELD CURVE ANALYSIS:

The Fundamentals of Risk and Return

Livingston G. Douglas, C.F.A.

New York Institute of Finance

Library of Congress Cataloging-in-Publication Data

Douglas, Livingston G.
  Yield curve analysis.

  Includes index.
  1. Bonds—Prices—United States. 2. Risk—United
States. I. Title.
HG4936.D68 1988   332.63′23   87–31499
ISBN 0–13–972456–7

This publication is designed to provide accurate and authoritative information in regard to the subject matter covered. It is sold with the understanding that the publisher is not engaged in rendering legal, accounting, or other professional service. If legal advice or other expert assistance is required, the services of a competent professional person should be sought.

From a Declaration of Principles Jointly Adopted by
a Committee of the American Bar Association and a
Committee of Publishers and Associations

New York Institute of Finance
(NYIF Corp.)
70 Pine Street
New York, NY 10270–0003

In memory of
Livingston Douglas and Mildred Snyder Douglas

Contents

Section IV
Applications of the Fundamentals

Preface

Yield Curve Analysis: The Fundamentals of Risk and Return is intended to provide a broad and comprehensive review of the techniques and strategies that emanate from the most basic representation of the tradeoff between bond risk and bond return: the yield curve. This book is an outgrowth of a seminar on yield curve analysis that I conduct at the New York Institute of Finance. Students have expressed a strong desire for an up-to-date, clear, and concise text on this important topical area. The market lacks a practitioner-oriented book on the basics and the complexities of bond risk and bond return. The preponderance of available texts on fixed-income subjects are compendiums of contributed chapters that tend to be overspecialized and somewhat disjointed in presentation.

Yield Curve Analysis: The Fundamentals of Risk and Return is designed to address both the general and specific aspects of yield curve analysis in a practical and understandable manner. The most basic concepts are carefully explained through illustration. These examples form the basis for the more complex applications of this subject matter, which are discussed in subsequent chapters. A logical and coherent progression through the ideas and methods of analyzing bond risk and bond return permeate the book.

Fixed-income investing is predicated on two basic fundamentals:

risk and return. The yield curve is a simplistic representation of the inherent tradeoff between these critical variables. After providing a review of the underlying mathematics, *Yield Curve Analysis: The Fundamentals of Risk and Return* delves into the variety of risk measures that are employed in the fixed-income marketplace. The book then illustrates the types of return proxies that are commonly utilized by bond market participants. Approximately one-half of the text is devoted solely to applications of the risk and return concepts to real-life investing and bond portfolio management.

Yield Curve Analysis: The Fundamentals of Risk and Return is organized into four sections:

I. The Fundamentals of Bond Mathematics (Chapters 1–3)
II. The Fundamentals of Bond Risk (Chapters 4–7)
III. The Fundamentals of Bond Return (Chapters 8–11)
IV. Applications of the Fundamentals (Chapters 12–15)

Each chapter begins with a *chapter outline* and an *introductory paragraph* that provide the reader with an overview of the material to be discussed. The body of each chapter is dotted with *observations* that act as brief summaries of the concepts and applications presented. These *observations* have two purposes. First, they assist the reader in maintaining sight of the *forest* in spite of the *trees* often encountered in a specialized subject matter such as yield curve analysis. Second, they provide an excellent mechanism for review of the chapter material. Further pursuit of a particular issue can be made within the subsection summarized by the *observation* comment. *Footnotes* are used sparingly, but are an important contribution to the full understanding of the chapter contents and should not be overlooked. A myriad of *tables* and *figures* support the explanations of the concepts presented in the chapters. Each chapter concludes with a brief *summary* of the major topics covered in the chapter. A total of eight *appendixes* investigate some of the intricacies of bond risk and bond return in more detail. A *glossary* of important terms and a *subject index* are provided at the back of the book to facilitate in the full usage of the text material.

Section I reviews the *Fundamentals of Bond Mathematics*. Chapter 1 presents the time value of money concept. The appendix to Chapter 1 details the specifics of simple interest and compound interest. These primary underpinnings of bond mathematics form the basis for Chapter

2's discussion of the relationship between bond prices and bond yields. The yield-to-maturity concept, a critical element in yield curve analysis, is introduced in Chapter 2. The appendix to Chapter 2 illustrates the calculation of accrued interest, an integral part of the yield-to-maturity derivation. Chapter 3 extends Chapter 2's findings to the calculation of a series of yield measures commonly encountered in the bond marketplace: current yield, yield to maturity, yield to call, crossover yield, call-adjusted yield, yield to average life, discounted cash flow (DCF) yield, and realized compound yield. Section I covers the basic mathematics requisite to comprehending the risk and return discussions of the subsequent sections.

Section II analyzes the *Fundamentals of Bond Risk*. In yield curve analysis, a risk measure is positioned on the *X*-axis of a graphical presentation. The variety of bond risk measures is broad. Chapter 4 commences this section with an observation of the volatility of bond prices. This chapter lays the groundwork for finding a risk measure that adequately describes the underlying price risk of a bond investment. Chapter 5 looks at the traditional measures of bond risk: term to maturity, weighted average maturity, and weighted average cash flow. The contemporary proxies for bond risk include duration, convexity, and the yield value of a 32nd. These concepts are analyzed in Chapter 6. Chapter 7 is forward-looking in nature. This chapter explains the futuristic measures of bond risk that, although currently in limited use, are gaining advocates in the fixed-income community. These measures include standard deviations and bond betas. Regression line analysis is introduced in Chapter 7.

Section III turns to the *Y*-axis of yield curve analysis, that is, representations of *Bond Return*. Chapter 8 focuses on measures of total return and its counterpart, the realized compound yield (RCY). The components of a bond's return are carefully dissected and the influences on a bond's return are explained. The appendixes to Chapter 8 elaborate on the concepts of reinvestment rates and total return attribution. Chapter 9 contrasts the concept of bond yield and the reality of bond return. This differentiation is critical to making appropriate investment decisions in a risk:return context. Chapter 10 looks at the calculation of gains, losses, and returns. The deceiving nature of book gains/(losses) is revealed through illustration. Chapter 11 concludes the *Fundamentals of Bond Return* section with a discussion of a relative newcomer to the scene of bond returns, the risk-adjusted return. Capital market line analysis, security market line analysis, and risk:return quadrant analysis are used in addressing the issue of risk-adjusted return. The appendix to Chapter

11 illustrates the use of security market line analysis as a total return enhancement tool.

Section IV, the final section of the book, integrates the comprehensive coverage of the first three sections in an *Applications Framework.* Chapter 12 applies the concepts of bond mathematics, bond risk, and bond return to the traditional methods of yield curve analysis. Chapter 13 introduces the concept of a total return curve, a *new and improved yield curve* that is slowly gaining wider recognition. Chapter 14 discusses the broad array of bond swaps that can be undertaken with the analytical tools presented in Chapters 1–13 of the text. Many of these swaps are designed to take advantage of yield curve shifts/twists and anomalies in specific market sectors. The appendix to Chapter 14 delves into the specifics of risk-neutralizing swaps. Chapter 15 wraps up the book with an extensive foray into the realities of bond mathematics, bond risk, and bond return in the context of a portfolio of fixed-income securities. Benchmark comparisons are a critical component in the process of managing bond portfolios in today's performance-oriented world. The two appendixes to Chapter 15 reveal the structure of the major bond market indexes and the danger of portfolio averages, respectively.

In sum, *Yield Curve Analysis: The Fundamentals of Risk and Return* is designed to provide a comprehensive and coherent coverage of the critical concepts underlying this most important subject matter. The book is geared toward fixed-income practitioners and business school students desiring a solid grounding in the basics of bond mathematics, bond risk, and bond return. The book is not an academic exercise permeated with formulas and mathematical derivations. Rather, *Yield Curve Analysis: The Fundamentals of Risk and Return* concentrates on the development and application of sound theoretical principles in a real-world context. The highly quantitative and highly specialized aspects of bond portfolio management are reserved for the more technically oriented manuals and the academic journals.

Yield Curve Analysis: The Fundamentals of Risk and Return is refreshing and forward-looking in its approach. It applies the techniques of yield curve analysis to the new developments of bond indexation and active bond management oriented toward outperforming a specified benchmark. The book is not afraid to challenge the accepted norms of fixed-income investing. It proposes better methods for dealing with the commonly encountered realities of bond portfolio management.

Acknowledgments

Many individuals make the undertaking of a book such as *Yield Curve Analysis: The Fundamentals of Risk and Return* possible. My thanks extend to two of my colleagues at MacKay-Shields Financial Corporation, Ravi Akhoury and Don Mesler, for their patience and assistance in the review of the text chapters. David Kroon, Steve Edelman, and Bill Budd all deserve recognition for their valuable inputs in my previous money management endeavors. I am grateful to Ron Ryan and Boyce Greer of the Ryan Financial Strategy Group for their insights in both the basics of bond risk and bond return as well as in the more complex elements of bond mathematics.

The cooperation of the fixed-income research departments at several Wall Street firms—particularly First Boston, Merrill Lynch, Salomon Brothers Inc., and Shearson Lehman Brothers—has made the task of gathering supporting data a manageable one. Merrill Lynch's Bloomberg Financial Markets system aided in the derivation of durations and total returns. Ed Bishop of Drexel Burnham Lambert and Jack Breaks of Merrill Lynch provided important contributions in the specifics of yield curve analysis. Special thanks go to Greg Parseghian of First Boston for his tireless review of the many memoranda which formed the basis for this book. I am indebted to Bob Kuberek of Wilshire Associates (Santa Monica, California) for his thoroughness in explicating the quanti-

tative aspects of yield curve analysis and bond portfolio analysis. Jim
Kaplan, Brig Belvin, and Sonia Dixon of Capital Management Sciences
(Los Angeles, California) have assisted in the portfolio applications of
yield curve analysis in both a comprehensive and intelligible fashion.

My publisher and good friend, Fred Dahl, is deserving of more
than simple thanks. Fred, you have made what can be an arduous task
into an enjoyable and fulfilling endeavor. The many hours of manuscript
preparation and revision have finally come to fruition. I also must acknowl-
edge the assistance of my production editor, Jeanmarie Brusati, whose
professional expertise in organization and design of the text has proved
most beneficial to the final product.

My colleagues at the New York Institute of Finance have been
most gracious in allowing me to participate in their educational programs.
Finally, the students in my Yield Curve Analysis seminars at the NYIF
have been an invaluable source of inspiration for this text. I hope that
Yield Curve Analysis satisfies your thirst for an understandable, up-to-
date book on this complex subject. This one is truly for you.

SECTION I
THE FUNDAMENTALS
OF BOND MATHEMATICS

The Time Value of Money

This chapter begins the section of the text on the *Fundamentals of Bond Mathematics* by discussing the time value of money concept. Simple interest, compound interest, present values, and future values emanate from this underpinning of bond mathematics. Chapter 2 focuses on the present value concept by analyzing the inverse relationship between bond prices and bond yields. The chapter details the cash flow discounting process and introduces the yield to maturity. Chapter 3 concludes this section with a review of the yield measures commonly encountered in the bond market. The strengths and weaknesses of each measure are provided through illustrations.

The basic features of a bond

A *bond* is a financial instrument backed by an issuer who promises to pay a specified stream of future cash flows to the bondholder. These cash flows include periodic interest payments, called *coupons*, and a repayment of the *principal amount*, generally in a lump sum at final maturity. A bond is termed a *fixed-income security* because its periodic income flows are fixed by the specified coupon rate of interest on the bond. The principal amount of a bond is typically $1,000.00, and is also referred to as the *par value* or *face value* of the bond. For purposes of this book, all bonds are assumed to carry $1,000.00 par values. Interest payments are calculated as a percentage of this amount.

The mathematics of bonds is rooted in the concept of the *time value of money*. A dollar received today is worth more than a dollar promised at some future point in time because today's dollar can be invested in financial instruments which provide a positive return on that initial investment over time. From an investor's viewpoint, *interest* is the compensation, or enticement, for deferring consumption to a future period. To a borrower, the *interest rate* is the price of money.

Simple interest

There are two basic approaches to accumulating interest: simple interest and compound interest. *Simple interest* is the interest earned on the principal amount. In the bond world, simple interest is the coupon cash flow generated by a bond. Over time, the accumulation of simple interest becomes significant. Exhibit 1–1 illustrates the amount of simple interest earned over various holding periods for a 7%, 10%, and 14% coupon bond, respectively. This table leads to two general observations.

First, simple interest is tied directly to the coupon size. In high interest rate environments (14%), simple interest is more appreciable than in low interest rate environments (7%). Over a 10-year investment

Exhibit 1–1. Simple interest on a 7% coupon bond purchased at par.

Holding Period (Years)	Cumulative Simple Interest		
	7% Bond	*10% Bond*	*14% Bond*
1	$ 70	$ 100	$ 140
2	140	200	280
3	210	300	420
4	280	400	560
5	350	500	700
10	700	1,000	1,400
20	1,400	2,000	2,800
30	2,100	3,000	4,200
40	2,800	4,000	5,600
50	3,500	5,000	7,000

Exhibit 1–2. Relationship between simple interest and the length of the holding period. (Data from Exhibit 1–1.)

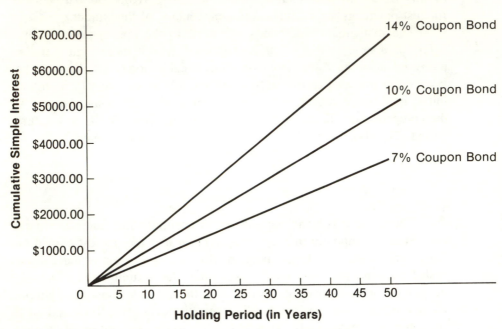

period, for example, the 14% coupon bond generates $1,400.00 in simple interest versus only $700.00 in simple interest for the 7% coupon issue. Second, for a given bond, simple interest accumulates at a constant rate and at a constant dollar amount per year. A 10% coupon bond, for example, creates $100.00 in simple interest each year. The cumulative amount reflects this $100.00 annual add-on. At the end of 50 years, the simple interest sums to $5,000.00. Graphically speaking, simple interest grows in a linear fashion over time (see Exhibit 1–2).

Compound interest

In all likelihood, an investor will reinvest the periodic coupon cash flows generated by a bond. *Compound interest* is predicated on this notion. Interest is earned on both the principal amount and on the coupon receipts. The *interest-on-interest* component differentiates compound interest from simple interest. Interest-on-interest is also termed *reinvestment return*.[1] Exhibits 1–3 through 1–5 calculate the compound interest accu-

---

[1] Chapter 8 discusses reinvestment returns in detail.

Exhibit 1–3. Simple interest and compound interest on a 7% coupon bond purchased at par, with reinvestments made at a 7% annual rate.

Holding Period (Years)	Cumulative Simple Interest*	Cumulative Compound Interest*
1	$ 70	$ 70
2	140	145
3	210	225
4	280	311
5	350	403
10	700	967
20	1,400	2,870
30	2,100	6,612
40	2,800	13,975
50	3,500	28,457

* Figures rounded to the nearest dollar.

mulations for the 7%, 10%, and 14% coupon bonds of earlier illustration. Several conclusions flow from these tables.

First, compound interest is magnified over longer investment horizons. For example, a $1,000.00, 10% coupon bond investment compounded at 10% accumulates $611.00 in compound interest by the end of 5 years. The same bond is responsible for $16,449.00 in compound interest over a 30-year time span and a staggering $116,391.00 over a 50-year period. Second, compound interest flourishes in high interest rate environments. For example, in a 7% interest rate environment, a

Exhibit 1–4. Simple interest and compound interest on a 10% coupon bond purchased at par, with reinvestments made at a 10% annual rate.

Holding Period (Years)	Cumulative Simple Interest*	Cumulative Compound Interest*
1	$ 100	$ 100
2	200	210
3	300	331
4	400	464
5	500	611
10	1,000	1,594
20	2,000	5,728
30	3,000	16,449
40	4,000	44,259
50	5,000	116,391

* Figures rounded to the nearest dollar.

Exhibit 1–5. Simple interest and compound interest on a 14% coupon bond purchased at par, with reinvestments made at a 14% annual rate.

Holding Period (Years)	Cumulative Simple Interest[*]	Cumulative Compound Interest[*]
1	$ 140	$ 140
2	280	300
3	420	482
4	560	689
5	700	925
10	1,400	2,707
20	2,800	12,744
30	4,200	49,950
40	5,600	187,884
50	7,000	699,233

[*] Figures rounded to the nearest dollar.

Exhibit 1–6. Relationship between compound interest and the length of the holding period. (Data from Exhibits 1–3, 1–4, and 1–5.)

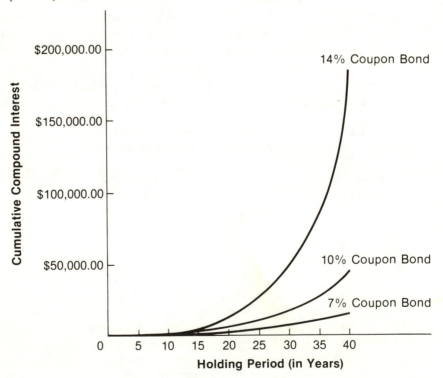

par (i.e., $1000.00) bond investment can be expected to generate compound interest of $6,612.00 over 30 years. A par bond investment in a 14% yield environment balloons into a $50,950.00 value over the same 30-year time span ($1,000.00 principal + $49,950.00 compound interest = $50,950.00, per Exhibit 1–5). The compound interest under 14% interest rate conditions ($49,950.00) far exceeds the compound interest accumulated in a 7% interest rate environment ($6,612.00) given a 30-year holding period.

Third, compound interest dwarfs both the principal investment and the accumulated simple interest, most decisively over long-term horizons. For example, Exhibit 1–4 illustrates that a 10% coupon bond records $16,449.00 in compound interest over a 30-year investment horizon. This figure makes the principal amount ($1,000.00) and the simple interest ($3,000.00) appear small. Exhibit 1–6 displays the dominance of compound interest by graphing the data from Exhibits 1–3 through 1–5. Exhibit 1–7 overlays the compound interest graph for the 10% coupon issue on the simple interest graph for the same bond. The Appendix to this chapter provides a more detailed comparison of the simple interest and compound interest concepts.

> **Observation:** *Simple interest is the coupon cash flow generated by a bond investment. Compound interest includes both the coupon cash flow and the interest earned on these coupons (i.e., interest-on-interest). High interest rate environments and long investment horizons lead to greater accumulations of simple interest and, particularly, of compound interest.*

Future values and the compounding process

Using hand calculations

Exhibit 1–8 shows the compounding process in a timeline format. In this case, a bond is purchased at par with interest compounded at 10% annually. Each year, the investment base grows by 10% such that at the end of Year 1, the value of the investment is $1,100.00. By the end of Year 2, the investment grows to a $1,210.00 value; the end of Year 3 finds the investment worth a total of $1,331.00, etc. A series of additional calculations leads to a $2,593.74 value at the end of the tenth year. This approach requires a total of ten calculations to arrive at the final answer, or one at the end of each compounding period.

Exhibit 1–7. Dominance of compound interest over simple interest on a 10% coupon bond purchased at par, with reinvestments made at a 10% annual rate. Simple interest increases at a constant rate in a linear fashion; compound interest increases at a geometric rate in a nonlinear fashion. (Data from Exhibit 1–4.)

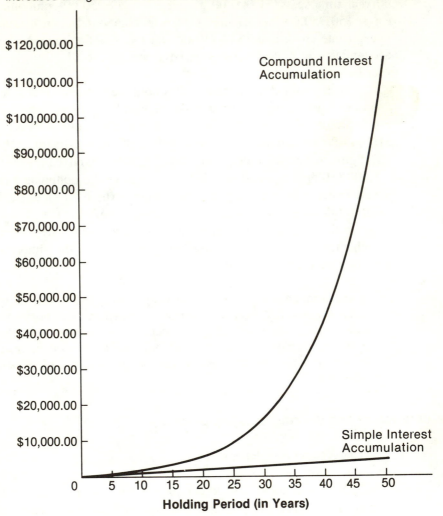

Using formulas

The individual calculations outlined in Exhibit 1–8 are very similar. Each subsequent compounding period requires an additional *multiplication* by an identical compounding factor (in this case, 1.10). Indeed, the arduous sequence of multiplications can be summarized in a general

Exhibit 1–8. Timeline of the creation of a future investment value. In this case, a 10% coupon bond grows to $2593.70 over 10 years, assuming annual compounding at a 10% interest rate. (*Note:* Totals are subject to rounding error.)

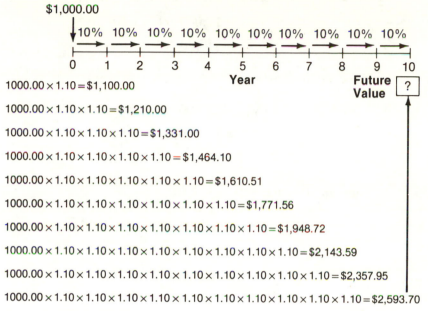

$1,000.00

10% 10% 10% 10% 10% 10% 10% 10% 10% 10%

0   1   2   3   4   5   6   7   8   9   10
Year   Future
                                          Value [?]

$1000.00 \times 1.10 = \$1,100.00$

$1000.00 \times 1.10 \times 1.10 = \$1,210.00$

$1000.00 \times 1.10 \times 1.10 \times 1.10 = \$1,331.00$

$1000.00 \times 1.10 \times 1.10 \times 1.10 \times 1.10 = \$1,464.10$

$1000.00 \times 1.10 \times 1.10 \times 1.10 \times 1.10 \times 1.10 = \$1,610.51$

$1000.00 \times 1.10 \times 1.10 \times 1.10 \times 1.10 \times 1.10 \times 1.10 = \$1,771.56$

$1000.00 \times 1.10 \times 1.10 \times 1.10 \times 1.10 \times 1.10 \times 1.10 \times 1.10 = \$1,948.72$

$1000.00 \times 1.10 \times 1.10 \times 1.10 \times 1.10 \times 1.10 \times 1.10 \times 1.10 \times 1.10 = \$2,143.59$

$1000.00 \times 1.10 \times 1.10 \times 1.10 \times 1.10 \times 1.10 \times 1.10 \times 1.10 \times 1.10 \times 1.10 = \$2,357.95$

$1000.00 \times 1.10 \times 1.10 \times 1.10 \times 1.10 \times 1.10 \times 1.10 \times 1.10 \times 1.10 \times 1.10 \times 1.10 = \$2,593.70$

formula for an investment compounded at interest rate i over n compounding periods:

$$\text{future value}_n = \text{present value} \times (1 + i)^n$$

$$FV_n = PV \times \underbrace{(1 + i)^n}_{\substack{\text{compound interest} \\ \text{factor}}}$$

where

FV_n = future value of an investment; its value at the future time period n

PV = present value of an investment; its value in today's dollars, or its current market price

$(1 + i)^n$ = compound interest factor; the multiplier that translates the current value of the investment into a future value, as compounded at interest rate i for n periods

1. Value in 1 year:

$$FV_1 = \$1{,}000.00 \times (1 + 0.10)^1$$
$$= \$1{,}000.00 \times 1.10$$
$$= \$1{,}100.00$$

2. Value in 10 years:

$$FV_{10} = \$1{,}000.00 \times (1 + 0.10)^{10}$$
$$= \$1{,}000.00 \times 2.5937$$
$$= \$2{,}593.70$$

3. Value in 30 years:

$$FV_{30} = \$1{,}000.00 \times (1 + 0.10)^{30}$$
$$= \$1{,}000.00 \times 17.4494$$
$$= \$17{,}449.40$$

While the results are subject to a few pennies in rounding error, the time savings from boiling down a series of calculations to a single one is substantial.

Using tables

An interest factor table makes the derivation of future investment values less burdensome. Exhibit 1–9 compiles the compound interest factors for a variety of interest rates and compounding periods. The table shows the future values of $1.00. Multiplying the amount of dollars invested by the appropriate compound interest factor gives the future value of the specific investment. The compound interest factors of Exhibit 1–9 provide a quick solution to the determination of a future wealth position. For example, a $1,000.00 investment compounded annually at 10% for 10 years grows to $2,593.70. A 2.5937 compound interest factor is found at the intersection of the "$n = 10$ periods" row and the "$i = 10\%$" column. The future investment value is estimated as $2,593.70 ($1,000.00 × 2.5937 factor = $2,593.70). This result is consistent with both the hand and the formula calculations completed earlier.

Exhibit 1–9. Compound interest factors $(1 + i)^n$ for a variety of interest rates and compounding periods.

Number of Periods, n	*Periodic Interest Rate*, i					
	2.00%	*3.50%*	*5.00%*	*7.00%*	*10.00%*	*14.00%*
1	1.0200	1.0350	1.0500	1.0700	1.1000	1.1400
2	1.0404	1.0712	1.1025	1.1449	1.2100	1.2996
3	1.0612	1.1087	1.1576	1.2250	1.3310	1.4815
4	1.0824	1.1475	1.2155	1.3108	1.4641	1.6890
5	1.1041	1.1877	1.2763	1.4026	1.6105	1.9254
6	1.1262	1.2293	1.3401	1.5007	1.7716	2.1950
7	1.1487	1.2723	1.4071	1.6058	1.9487	2.5023
8	1.1717	1.3168	1.4775	1.7182	2.1436	2.8526
9	1.1951	1.3629	1.5513	1.8385	2.3579	3.2519
10	1.2190	1.4106	1.6289	1.9672	2.5937	3.7072
11	1.2434	1.4600	1.7103	2.1049	2.8531	4.2262
12	1.2682	1.5111	1.7959	2.2522	3.1384	4.8179
13	1.2936	1.5640	1.8856	2.4098	3.4523	5.4924
14	1.3195	1.6187	1.9799	2.5785	3.7975	6.2613
15	1.3459	1.6753	2.0789	2.7590	4.1772	7.1379
16	1.3728	1.7340	2.1829	2.9522	4.5950	8.1372
17	1.4002	1.7947	2.2920	3.1588	5.0545	9.2765
18	1.4282	1.8575	2.4066	3.3799	5.5599	10.5752
19	1.4568	1.9225	2.5270	3.6165	6.1159	12.0557
20	1.4859	1.9900	2.6533	3.8697	6.7275	13.7435
21	1.5157	2.0594	2.7860	4.1406	7.4003	15.6676
22	1.5460	2.1315	2.9253	4.4304	8.1403	17.8610
23	1.5769	2.2061	3.0715	4.7405	8.9543	20.3616
24	1.6084	2.2833	3.2251	5.0724	9.8497	23.2122
25	1.6406	2.3632	3.3864	5.4274	10.8347	26.4619
26	1.6734	2.4460	3.5557	5.8074	11.9182	30.1666
27	1.7069	2.5316	3.7335	6.2139	13.1100	34.3899
28	1.7410	2.6202	3.9201	6.6488	14.4210	39.2045
29	1.7758	2.7119	4.1161	7.1143	15.8631	44.6931
30	1.8114	2.8068	4.3219	7.6123	17.4494	50.9502
40	2.2080	3.9593	7.0400	14.9745	45.2593	188.8835
50	2.6916	5.5849	11.4674	29.4570	117.3909	700.2330
60	3.2810	7.8781	18.6792	57.9464	304.4816	2595.9187

Observation: *The calculations of compound interest and future values of an investment are made easier by the use of future value formulas. Compound interest factors, as summarized in a format such as Exhibit 1–9, make the task even simpler.*

The power of compound interest

Exhibit 1–9 clearly illustrates the power of the compounding process. For example, $1.00 invested at 3½% per annum grows into $7.88 in 60 years ($i = 3½\%$, $n = 60$). The same dollar invested at 7% annually accumulates to $57.95 in 60 years ($i = 7\%$, $n = 60$). At a 10% annual interest rate, $1.00 grows to a whopping $304.48 60 years hence ($i = 10\%$, $n = 60$). Compounding $1.00 for 60 years at 14% creates an ending wealth position of a staggering $2,595.92 ($i = 14\%$, $n = 60$)!

A doubling of the compounding rate has a greater impact than a mere doubling of the terminal wealth position. For example, doubling the interest rate from 3½% to 7% leads to a sevenfold increase in wealth ($57.95 versus $7.88). Doubling the compounding rate again, this time from 7% to 14%, creates an ending portfolio of approximately 45 times the size of the portfolio compounded at 7% ($2,595.92 versus $57.95)! The relative impacts are not as dramatic over shorter holding periods, but they are still noticeable (see Exhibit 1–10).

Intrayear compounding

Most bonds make coupon payments on a semiannual basis. A 10% coupon bond, for example, pays $50.00 every 6 months rather than a single annual payment of $100.00. Semiannual pay bonds require the use of semiannual compounding of interest. Semiannual compounding adds some incremental return since an investor can earn interest-on-interest

Exhibit 1–10. Selected compound interest factors (from Exhibit 1–9). The power of compounding is directly related to (1) the length of the time horizon and (2) the compounding rate.

Time Horizon	Interest Rate		
(Years)	3½%	7%	14%
1	1.0350	1.0700	1.1400
5	1.1877	1.4026	1.9254
10	1.4106	1.9672	3.7072
30	2.8068	7.6123	50.9502
60	7.8781	57.9464	2,595.9187

halfway through the year rather than having to wait until year-end to reinvest.

The mathematics of semiannual compounding is tedious, requiring twice as many calculations as annual compounding. However, the formula approach to finding future investment value simply requires that the periodic interest rate and the number of compounding periods be adjusted to reflect the shorter compounding interval. For semiannual compounding, the i interest rate is a semiannual rate and n the number of semiannual periods in the investment horizon. Relative to annual compounding, the periodic interest rate is halved and the number of compounding periods is doubled.

For example, a 10% coupon bond is purchased at par and is held for 10 years. The value of the investment in 10 years is a function of how often the compounding process occurs (using factors from Exhibit 1–9):

1. 10% interest, compounded annually:

$$FV_{10} = \$1,000.00 \times (1 + 0.10)^{10}$$
$$= \$1,000.00 \times 2.5937$$
$$= \$2,593.70$$

2. 10% interest, compounded semiannually:

$$FV_{20} = \$1,000.00 \times (1 + 0.05)^{20}$$
$$= \$1,000.00 \times 2.6533$$
$$= \$2,653.30$$

It is clear that the table factor for "10%, 10" is not interchangeable with the table factor for "5%, 20" because of the compounding process. The ability to compound semiannually adds \$59.60 (\$2,653.30 − \$2,593.70) to the investment's terminal value, or 5.96% more return given a \$1,000.00 initial investment. In general, the more frequent the compounding period, the greater the added return. The example can easily be extended to quarterly compounding and monthly compounding.

> **Observation:** *Compound interest exercises its power over longer invest-*
> *ment horizons. Intrayear compounding further amplifies the accumula-*
> *tion of interest-on-interest.*

Present values and the discounting process

Compound interest plays a key role in the determination of a bond's
price. A *bond* is simply a series of future cash flows promised by the
issuer of the bond.[2] Up to this point, the focus has been on carrying a
present value (i.e., an investment) forward into the future. The valuation
of a bond is conducted in the opposite direction: discounting the future
back to the present.

In bond mathematics, *compounding* involves moving from a present
value to a future value; *discounting* entails moving from a future value
back to a present value. Mathematically, discounting is exactly the opposite of compounding. The discounting process can be analyzed in the
three methods presented earlier: hand calculation, formula, and the use
of table factors.

Using hand calculations

Exhibit 1–11 diagrams the discounting process in a timeline format.
In this illustration, a zero-coupon bond that matures in 10 years is valued
in today's dollars by discounting back to the present the single cash
flow ($1,000.00 par amount) to be received 10 years hence. A 10%
annual interest rate is assumed with interest compounded annually. Notice
that each discounting period requires an additional *division* to be made.
Each divisor is identical (in this case, 1.10), and the investment value
declines at the same rate in each subsequent discounting period. At the
end of Year 9, the investment is valued at $909.09; the end of Year 8
finds the investment worth $826.45. In today's dollars (beginning of

---

[2] Technically speaking, U.S. Treasury obligations issued with 1 year or less to maturity
are termed *bills;* U.S. Treasury bonds issued with 2 to 10 years to maturity are labeled *notes;*
U.S. Treasury bonds issued with maturities exceeding 10 years are called *bonds.* Corporate obligations
use the same time criteria for designating notes and bonds. The focus of this book is on the
concept of a bond as a series of promised future cash flows. Therefore, a semantic difference
between a note and a bond is not made. For simplicity, all issues are called bonds. Money market
instruments such as Treasury bills are not a subject of discussion in this text.

Exhibit 1–11. Timeline of the creation of a present value. In this case, a zero-coupon bond maturing in 10 years is today valued at $385.54, assuming 10% interest rates and annual compounding. (*Note:* Totals are subject to rounding error.)

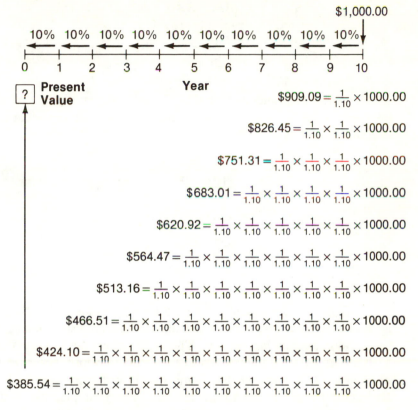

$$\$909.09 = \frac{1}{1.10} \times 1000.00$$

$$\$826.45 = \frac{1}{1.10} \times \frac{1}{1.10} \times 1000.00$$

$$\$751.31 = \frac{1}{1.10} \times \frac{1}{1.10} \times \frac{1}{1.10} \times 1000.00$$

$$\$683.01 = \frac{1}{1.10} \times \frac{1}{1.10} \times \frac{1}{1.10} \times \frac{1}{1.10} \times 1000.00$$

$$\$620.92 = \frac{1}{1.10} \times \frac{1}{1.10} \times \frac{1}{1.10} \times \frac{1}{1.10} \times \frac{1}{1.10} \times 1000.00$$

$$\$564.47 = \frac{1}{1.10} \times \frac{1}{1.10} \times \frac{1}{1.10} \times \frac{1}{1.10} \times \frac{1}{1.10} \times \frac{1}{1.10} \times 1000.00$$

$$\$513.16 = \frac{1}{1.10} \times \frac{1}{1.10} \times \frac{1}{1.10} \times \frac{1}{1.10} \times \frac{1}{1.10} \times \frac{1}{1.10} \times \frac{1}{1.10} \times 1000.00$$

$$\$466.51 = \frac{1}{1.10} \times \frac{1}{1.10} \times \frac{1}{1.10} \times \frac{1}{1.10} \times \frac{1}{1.10} \times \frac{1}{1.10} \times \frac{1}{1.10} \times \frac{1}{1.10} \times 1000.00$$

$$\$424.10 = \frac{1}{1.10} \times \frac{1}{1.10} \times \frac{1}{1.10} \times \frac{1}{1.10} \times \frac{1}{1.10} \times \frac{1}{1.10} \times \frac{1}{1.10} \times \frac{1}{1.10} \times \frac{1}{1.10} \times 1000.00$$

$$\$385.54 = \frac{1}{1.10} \times \frac{1}{1.10} \times \frac{1}{1.10} \times \frac{1}{1.10} \times \frac{1}{1.10} \times \frac{1}{1.10} \times \frac{1}{1.10} \times \frac{1}{1.10} \times \frac{1}{1.10} \times \frac{1}{1.10} \times 1000.00$$

Year 1), the bond is worth only $385.54. A total of ten divisions is required to derive the present value, one division for each discounting period encountered.

Using formulas

Similar to the future value computation, the mathematics of deriving present values is repetitious. Each subsequent discounting factor [in this case, $1/(1.10)$] is identical. The series of divisions can be captured in a single formula for an investment discounted at interest rate i over n discounting periods:

$$\text{present value} = \text{future value}_n \times \frac{1}{(1 + i)^n}$$

$$PV = FV_n \times \underbrace{\frac{1}{(1 + i)^n}}_{\substack{\text{discount interest} \\ \text{factor}}}$$

where the discount interest factor $1/(1 + i)^n$ is the multiplier that reduces the future value to a current dollar equivalent. For the zero-coupon bond of Exhibit 1–11:

$$PV = \$1,000.00 \times \frac{1}{(1 + 0.10)^{10}}$$

$$= \$1,000.00 \times 0.3855$$

$$= \$385.50$$

Using tables

Discount interest factor tables enhance the efficiency of the formula approach. Exhibit 1–12 lists the discount factors for a selection of interest rates and compounding periods. The table shows the present values of $1.00 received at various points in the future. To find the present value of a multidollar future cash flow, simply multiply the appropriate discounting factor by the stated future amount. For example, the $1,000.00 zero-coupon bond maturing in 10 years is worth $385.50 today if a 10% annual interest rate is applied and interest is compounded annually ($1,000.00 × 0.3855 factor). The 0.3855 factor is found at the intersection of the "$n = 10$ periods" row and the "$i = 10\%$" column of Exhibit 1–12. This result agrees with the earlier findings by both hand calculation and formula usage.

Implications of the discounting process

The discounting process makes two general statements regarding the present value of a future cash flow. First, the present value of a specified future cash flow is inversely related to the length of the investment

Exhibit 1–12. Discount interest factors (i.e., present value factors) $1/(1 + i)^n$ for a variety of interest rates and discounting periods.

Number of Periods, n	Periodic Interest Rate, i					
	2.00%	3.50%	5.00%	7.00%	10.00%	14.00%
1	0.9804	0.9662	0.9524	0.9346	0.9091	0.8772
2	0.9612	0.9335	0.9070	0.8734	0.8264	0.7695
3	0.9423	0.9019	0.8638	0.8163	0.7513	0.6750
4	0.9238	0.8714	0.8227	0.7629	0.6830	0.5921
5	0.9057	0.8420	0.7835	0.7130	0.6209	0.5194
6	0.8880	0.8135	0.7462	0.6663	0.5645	0.4556
7	0.8706	0.7860	0.7107	0.6228	0.5132	0.3996
8	0.8535	0.7594	0.6768	0.5820	0.4665	0.3506
9	0.8368	0.7337	0.6446	0.5439	0.4241	0.3075
10	0.8203	0.7089	0.6139	0.5083	0.3855	0.2697
11	0.8043	0.6849	0.5847	0.4751	0.3505	0.2366
12	0.7885	0.6618	0.5568	0.4440	0.3186	0.2076
13	0.7730	0.6394	0.5303	0.4150	0.2897	0.1821
14	0.7579	0.6178	0.5051	0.3878	0.2633	0.1597
15	0.7430	0.5969	0.4810	0.3624	0.2394	0.1401
16	0.7284	0.5767	0.4581	0.3387	0.2176	0.1229
17	0.7142	0.5572	0.4363	0.3166	0.1978	0.1078
18	0.7002	0.5384	0.4155	0.2959	0.1799	0.0946
19	0.6864	0.5202	0.3957	0.2765	0.1635	0.0829
20	0.6730	0.5026	0.3769	0.2584	0.1486	0.0728
21	0.6598	0.4856	0.3589	0.2415	0.1351	0.0638
22	0.6468	0.4692	0.3419	0.2257	0.1228	0.0560
23	0.6342	0.4533	0.3256	0.2109	0.1117	0.0491
24	0.6217	0.4380	0.3101	0.1971	0.1015	0.0431
25	0.6095	0.4231	0.2953	0.1842	0.0923	0.0378
26	0.5976	0.4088	0.2812	0.1722	0.0839	0.0331
27	0.5859	0.3950	0.2678	0.1609	0.0763	0.0291
28	0.5744	0.3817	0.2551	0.1504	0.0693	0.0255
29	0.5631	0.3687	0.2429	0.1406	0.0630	0.0224
30	0.5521	0.3563	0.2314	0.1314	0.0573	0.0196
40	0.4529	0.2526	0.1420	0.0668	0.0221	0.0053
50	0.3715	0.1791	0.0872	0.0339	0.0085	0.0014
60	0.3048	0.1269	0.0535	0.0173	0.0033	0.0004

period. The longer the time transpiring until the future cash flow is received, the greater the amount of interest that can be earned in the interim waiting period and, consequently, the lower the present value of the investment. For example, $1.00 received in 2 years is worth approximately 83 cents today if interest rates are at a 10% level (0.8264 per Exhibit 1–12 for "$i = 10\%, n = 2$"). Under the same interest rate assumption, $1.00 received in 20 years is worth only 15 cents today (0.1486 per Exhibit 1–12 for "$i = 10\%, n = 20$").

Second, the present value of a future cash flow is inversely related to the level of the interest rate (i.e., the discount rate of interest). Higher interest rates lead to lower present values. For example, $1.00 received 10 years hence is currently valued at 71 cents if interest rates are at a 3½% level (0.7089 per Exhibit 1–12 for "$i = 3\frac{1}{2}\%, n = 10$"). With interest rates at 14%, however, that same dollar is worth only 27 cents today (0.2697 per Exhibit 1–12 for "$i = 14\%, n = 10$").

> **Observation:** *The present value of a promised future cash flow is inversely related to both the length of the investment period and the level of interest rates.*

The relationship of compounding factors and discounting factors

The compound interest factors of Exhibit 1–9 transport cash flows into the future. The discount interest factors of Exhibit 1–12 bring future cash flows back to the present. Recall from the formula presentations that compounding factors and discounting factors are reciprocals of each other:

$$\text{compound interest factor}_{i,n} = (1 + i)^n$$

$$\text{discount interest factor}_{i,n} = \frac{1}{(1 + i)^n}$$

Therefore,

$$\text{discount interest factor}_{i,n} = \frac{1}{\text{compound interest factor}_{i,n}}$$

Exhibits 1–9 and 1–12 make this fact clear. For example, at a 10% interest rate and a 20-period horizon, the compound interest factor is 6.7275 (Exhibit 1–9) and the discount interest factor is 0.1486 (Exhibit 1–12). Mathematically,

$$0.1486 = \frac{1}{6.7275}$$

Pragmatically, one can see that $148.60 grows into a $1,000.00 value over 20 periods at a 10% interest rate by using Exhibit 1–9 ($148.60 × 6.7275 factor = $1,000.00) or Exhibit 1–12 ($1,000.00 in 20 periods at a 10% interest rate is worth $148.60 today; $1,000.00 × 0.1486 factor = $148.60). Exhibit 1–12 can be used to assess how a fractional amount grows into a whole dollar over time. The two tables are very much alike in this sense except that a compound interest table begins with a $1.00 investment and a discount interest table ends with a $1.00 investment.

> **Observation:** *Compound interest factors and discount interest factors are reciprocals of each other.*

Summary

The time value of money is the fundamental underpinning of bond mathematics. An investor demands a return called *interest* to compensate him for the usage of his funds over a period of time. The investment process deems today's dollar to be worth more than a dollar received at some future point in time. *Simple interest* is interest earned on the principal amount of an investment. *Compound interest* includes interest-on-interest as well as interest on principal. The interest compounding phenomenon is powerful over long-term horizons and in high interest rate environments. Through the use of compound interest factors, one can calculate the accumulation of wealth for a given initial investment. An investment with a specified set of future cash flows, such as a *bond,* can be valued in today's dollars by discounting the future cash flows back to the present. Financial calculators and tables of discount interest factors simplify the task of determining the present value of the investment.

Simple Interest and Compound Interest

Simple interest is interest earned on the principal or face amount of a bond. Compound interest includes interest-on-interest in addition to the interest payments generated by the principal amount. The calculation of simple interest is straightforward:

$$\text{simple interest} = \text{principal amount} \times \text{coupon rate of interest}$$

As noted in this chapter, the simple interest amount is earned at a constant rate and at a constant dollar amount per year. Compound interest, however, is an accumulation phenomenon. The calculation of compound interest requires an updating of the accumulated amount subject to interest:

$$\begin{matrix} \text{compound} \\ \text{interest} \end{matrix} = \underbrace{\begin{matrix} \text{simple} \\ \text{interest} \end{matrix}}_{\text{coupons}} + \underbrace{\left(\begin{matrix} \text{compound interest} \\ \text{accumulation} \end{matrix} \times \begin{matrix} \text{reinvestment rate} \\ \text{of interest} \end{matrix} \right)}_{\text{interest-on-interest}}$$

Exhibit 1A–1. Compound interest calculations on a 10% coupon bond purchased at par, with reinvestments made at a 10% annual rate.

Year	(1) *Compound Interest Accumulation (Beginning of Year)*	(2) = (1) × 10% *Interest-on- Interest*	(3) *Annual Coupon*	(4) = (1) + (2) + (3) *Compound Interest Accumulation (End of Year)*
1	$ 0.00	$ 0.00	$100.00	$ 100.00
2	100.00	10.00	100.00	210.00
3	210.00	21.00	100.00	331.00
4	331.00	33.10	100.00	464.10
5	464.10	46.41	100.00	610.51
6	610.51	61.05	100.00	771.56
7	771.56	77.16	100.00	948.72
8	948.72	94.87	100.00	1,143.59
9	1,143.59	114.36	100.00	1,357.95
10	1,357.95	135.80	100.00	1,593.75
20	5,115.90	511.59	100.00	5,727.49
30	14,863.10	1,486.31	100.00	16,449.41

Comments: *Assumes an annual-pay bond with the annual coupon received at year-end.*

Exhibit 1A–1 walks through the machinations of compound interest for a 10% coupon, annual-pay bond with reinvestments made at a 10% annual rate. Interest-on-interest arises from the reinvestment of coupon cash flows as well as any previous interest-on-interest captured. In Year 1, the bond investment grows to a $1,100.00 value:

$1,000.00	investment value at the beginning of Year 1
100.00	coupon received during Year 1 ($1,000.00 × 10%)
0.00	interest-on-interest
$1,100.00	investment value at the end of Year 1

Since the coupon is received at year-end, there is no potential for reinvestment return during the first year. Year 2 finds the investment progressing to a $1,210.00 value:

$1,100.00	investment value at the beginning of Year 2
100.00	coupon received during Year 2 ($1,000.00 × 10%)
10.00	interest-on-interest ($100.00[*] × 10%)
$1,210.00	investment value at the end of Year 2

[*] Coupon received during Year 1.

The interest-on-interest is calculated as the product of the compound interest accumulation (coupons plus previous reinvestment returns) and the assumed rate of reinvestment (in this case, 10%). For Year 2, the only funds subject to reinvestment are the $100.00 coupon received at the end of the first year. Hence, the interest-on-interest is $10.00 ($100.00 × 10%).

Year 3 follows the same path, and the investment climbs to the $1,331.00 level:

$1,210.00	investment value at the beginning of Year 3
100.00	coupon received during Year 3 ($1,000.00 × 10%)
21.00	interest-on-interest ($210.00[*] × 10%)
$1,331.00	investment value at the end of Year 3

In this instance, the interest-on-interest is earned on two annual coupons and a small amount of reinvestment return from Year 2. Year 4 sees the investment value rise to $1,464.10 as the result of an additional $100.00 coupon and $33.10 in interest-on-interest:

$1,331.00	investment value at the beginning of Year 4
100.00	coupon received during Year 4 ($1,000.00 × 10%)
33.10	interest-on-interest ($331.00[†] × 10%)
$1,464.10	investment value at the end of Year 4

During Year 5, the interest-on-interest component of return expands to $46.41, helping propel the investment to a $1,610.51 position:

$1,464.10	investment value at the beginning of Year 5
100.00	coupon received during Year 5 ($1,000.00 × 10%)
46.41	interest-on-interest ($464.10[‡] × 10%)
$1,610.51	investment value at the end of Year 5

It becomes clear that the coupon cash flow is a stable amount per year ($100.00) whereas the interest-on-interest contribution grows sizably over time.

---

[*] Coupons from Years 1 and 2 ($200.00) plus interest-on-interest from Year 2 ($10.00).

[†] Coupons from Years 1, 2, and 3 ($300.00) plus interest-on-interest from Years 2 and 3 ($31.00).

[‡] Coupons from Years 1, 2, 3, and 4 ($400.00) plus interest-on-interest from Years 2, 3, and 4 ($64.10).

In general terms, simple interest and compound interest can be differentiated as follows:

simple interest = coupon return

compound interest = coupon return + reinvestment return

The reinvestment return, or interest-on-interest, accounts for the explosive growth in compound interest vis-à-vis simple interest, particularly over long investment horizons.

Recall from Exhibit 1–4 that a 10% coupon bond creates sizable return differences under simple interest and compound interest assumptions. For example, a 5-year investment horizon awards a reinvestment return of a modest $111.00 ($611.00 compound interest − $500.00 simple interest = $111.00 reinvestment return). This return component expands to $594.00 over 10 years, to $13,449.00 over 30 years, and to $111,391.00 over 50 years. Clearly, longer investment horizons accelerate reinvestment returns and create wider gaps between simple interest returns and compound interest returns (recall Exhibit 1–7).

Higher interest rate levels also magnify the differential. For example, a 5-year investment horizon finds a $53.00 accumulation of reinvestment

Exhibit 1A–2. Ending wealth positions of an investor who purchases a 10% coupon bond at par and (1) fails to reinvest the coupons or (2) reinvests the coupons at a 10% annual rate. (Data from Exhibit 1A–1)

Year	Wealth Position at End of the Year Assuming:	
	Simple Interest	*Compound Interest*
1	$1,100.00	$ 1,100.00
2	1,200.00	1,210.00
3	1,300.00	1,331.00
4	1,400.00	1,464.10
5	1,500.00	1,610.51
6	1,600.00	1,771.56
7	1,700.00	1,948.72
8	1,800.00	2,143.59
9	1,900.00	2,357.95
10	2,000.00	2,593.75
20	3,000.00	6,727.49
30	4,000.00	17,449.41

return in a 7% interest rate environment ($403.00 compound interest −
$350.00 simple interest = $53.00, per Exhibit 1–3). At 14% yields,
however, the reinvestment return over the same 5-year period increases
to $225.00 ($925.00 compound interest − $700.00 simple interest =
$225.00, per Exhibit 1–5). Longer horizons find this advantage even
greater.

Compound interest returns tend to far outweigh the principal value
and the simple interest accumulations. Interest-on-interest is the primary
cause. Using the 10% coupon bond of Exhibit 1–4 as an example, a
30-year investment horizon finds the compound interest accumulation
at $16,449.00, of which $13,449.00 is interest-on-interest. This reinvestment return is over 4 times the coupon return of $3,000.00 and over
13 times the size of the $1,000.00 principal value.

Exhibit 1A–3. Ending wealth positions of an investor who purchases a 10% coupon bond
at par under a simple interest case and a compound interest case. (Data per Exhibit
1A–2.)

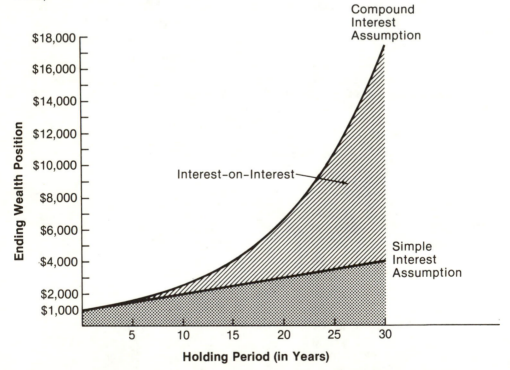

Comments: *The incremental wealth accumulation attributable to inter-*
est-on-interest is significant over long-term investment periods.

Exhibit 1A–2 shows the importance of reinvestment returns by calculating the ending wealth position of an investor who (1) fails to reinvest coupons or (2) reinvests coupons at a 10% rate. Exhibit 1A–3 plots the data of Exhibit 1A–2 and highlights the importance of interest-on-interest. Exhibit 1A–1 looks at the same 10% coupon bond on a year-by-year basis. This table reveals that at a 10% interest rate level, the annual amount of interest-on-interest surpasses the annual coupon return in only 9 years ($114.36 versus $100.00 coupon).

The annual returns from interest-on-interest become the dominant influence on a bond's total return over long investment horizons. The bottom portion of Exhibit 1A–1 vividly captures this effect by portraying the interest-on-interest in Year 20 and Year 30 of the bond's life. The interest-on-interest is 5 times the annual coupon amount in Year 20 and, by Year 30, it amounts to almost 15 times the annual coupon. As a result, the reinvestment component of total return assumes a greater and greater proportion of a bond's total return over progressively longer time horizons. The relative importance of the components of a bond's total return is discussed at greater length in Chapter 8.

Observation: *Compound interest is differentiated from simple interest by the interest-on-interest, or reinvestment, component of return. This return component becomes a significant factor over longer investment horizons and in higher interest rate environments.*

CHAPTER 2

The Relationship between Bond Prices and Bond Yields

The time value of money concepts presented in Chapter 1 form the basis for bond price and bond yield calculations. A bond is simply a series of promised future cash flows. A bond's value is the sum of the bond's future cash flows, expressed in today's dollars (i.e., current dollar equivalents). Each future cash flow must be individually adjusted for the time value of money. As noted in Chapter 1, a dollar received at some point in the future is worth less than a dollar in hand today. *How much less* is a function of the discounting process, which is, in turn, influenced by the discount rate of interest and the length of time elapsing before the cash flow is received.[1] All other things held equal, the present value of a future cash flow is smaller (1) the higher the discount rate of interest, and (2) the longer the maturity of the cash flow under consideration.

The formula for calculating a bond price

The formula for deriving the present value of a single cash flow was given in Chapter 1 as

[1] The terms *discount rate of interest, discount rate, interest rate, market rate of interest,* and *yield* are used interchangeably.

$$PV = FV_n \times \frac{1}{(1 + i)^n}$$

The present value (i.e., price) of a zero-coupon bond is calculated as follows:

$$\text{zero-coupon bond value} = \frac{CF_n}{(1 + i)^n}$$

where CF_n is the cash flow received at maturity, n the number of compounding periods to maturity, and i the discount rate of interest.

A coupon-bearing bond is a *stream* of future cash flows, not simply a single payment obligation. The price of a bond is the sum of the present values of all of its individual cash payments:

$$\text{bond price} = \sum_{t=1}^{n} \frac{CF_t}{(1 + i)^t}$$

where CF_t is the cash flow received at the end of period t, i the periodic discount rate of interest, and n the number of compounding periods to final maturity. For an *annual-pay bond*, CF_t is the amount of cash flow received at the end of the year t, i represents the annual discount rate of interest, and n symbolizes the number of years remaining until final maturity. For the more typical case of a *semiannual-pay bond*, CF_t is the amount of cash flow received at the end of the semiannual period t, i the semiannual discount rate of interest (exactly one-half the annual rate), and n the number of semiannual periods remaining until final maturity (exactly double the number of annual periods). Interest rates are generally stated in annual form and require that semiannual-pay bond price derivations reflect a halving of the annual rate of interest. Unless otherwise stated, the remainder of the illustrations in this book are based on semiannual-pay bonds.[2]

The price of a coupon-bearing bond reflects both the coupon cash flows generated by the bond as well as the principal repayment at maturity. In formal terms, the bond price can be derived in the following two ways:

---

[2] The phrases *annual pay* and *semiannual pay* simply refer to the frequency of coupon payments. Most bonds pay coupons on a semiannual basis and are, therefore, termed *semiannual-pay bonds*.

$$\text{bond price} = \sum_{t=1}^{n} \frac{CF_t}{(1 + i)^t}$$

where CF_t is the total cash flow received at the end of period t.

$$\text{bond price} = \underbrace{\sum_{t=1}^{n} \frac{CPN_t}{(1 + i)^t}}_{\substack{\text{coupon} \\ \text{cash flows}}} + \underbrace{\frac{P_n}{(1 + i)^n}}_{\substack{\text{principal} \\ \text{repayment}}}$$

where CPN_t is the coupon cash flow received at the end of period t and P_n is the principal cash flow received at final maturity (i.e., period n).

The latter formulation is useful in differentiating the relative contribution of coupon cash flow and principal cash flow to the bond's price. Both approaches will be used in this book with the appropriate choice a function of the specific illustration.

Calculating a bond price: Applications

Assuming a discount rate of 10%, the value of a 7% coupon, 5-year U.S. Treasury bond is $884.17:

$$\text{bond price}_{7\% \text{ coupon}} = \sum_{t=1}^{10} \frac{CF_t}{\left(1 + \dfrac{0.10}{2}\right)^t}$$

$$= \sum_{t=1}^{10} \frac{CPN_t}{(1 + i)^t} + \frac{P_n}{(1 + i)^n}$$

$$= \underbrace{\sum_{t=1}^{10} \frac{\$35.00}{(1.05)^t}}_{\substack{\text{coupon} \\ \text{cash flows}}} + \underbrace{\frac{\$1,000.00}{(1.05)^{10}}}_{\substack{\text{principal repayment} \\ \text{at the end of 5 years}}}$$

$$= (\$33.33 + 31.75 + 30.23 + 28.79 + 27.42 + 26.12 + 24.87 + 23.69 + 22.56 + 21.49) + \$613.90$$

$$= \$270.27 + \$613.90$$

$$= \$884.17$$

Exhibit 2–1. Calculation of the price of a 7% coupon, 5-year U.S. Treasury bond using a 10% discount rate.

End of Period t	(1) Cash Flow, CF_t	(2) PV Factor	(3) = (1) × (2) $PV(CF_t)$
1	$ 35.00	0.9524	$ 33.33
2	35.00	0.9070	31.75
3	35.00	0.8638	30.23
4	35.00	0.8227	28.79
5	35.00	0.7835	27.42
6	35.00	0.7462	26.12
7	35.00	0.7107	24.87
8	35.00	0.6768	23.69
9	35.00	0.6446	22.56
10	35.00	0.6139	21.49
10	1,000.00	0.6139	613.90
		Total PV →	$884.17

↑
Bond price

Comments: *Cash flows are semiannual coupons of $35.00 ($1,000.00 par × 0.07 × ½) and a final principal repayment of $1,000.00 par. The present value factors are calculated as 1/(1 + 0.10/2) or 1/(1 + 0.05). PV(CF$_t$) represents the present value of the cash flow received in time period* t. *Totals are subject to rounding error.*

Notice that the denominator of the price formula divides the annual interest rate (10%) in half to arrive at a semiannual interest rate (0.10/ 2 = 0.05). One can verify the $884.17 figure by using a financial calcula-tor. Exhibit 2–1 shows the individual calculations comprising the $884.17 result. The present value factors (i.e., discount interest factors) come from Exhibit 1–12 in Chapter 1.[3] The contents of Exhibit 2–1 are presented in a timeline format in Exhibit 2–2. Both the table and the figure make it clear that cash flows received at more distant future points are worth a lesser amount in today's dollars. For example, a $35.00 coupon received in 1 year is worth $31.75 today. A $35.00 coupon received in 5 years is equivalent to only $21.49 in current dollars, almost 39% less than

_____

[3] Now that the reader is familiar with the present value concept, the discount interest factors of Exhibit 1–12 will be called, more simply, present value (PV) factors.

Exhibit 2–2. Timeline of the discounting process for a 7% coupon, 5-year U.S. Treasury bond.

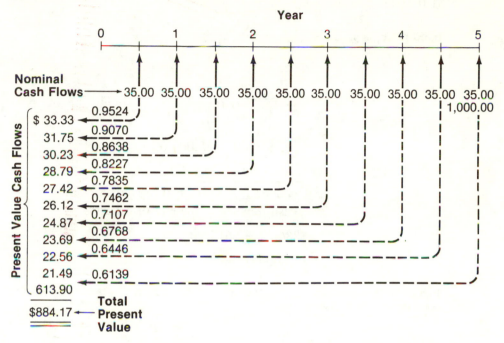

its face value. The principal repayment of $1,000.00 contributes $613.90, or 69.43%, to the bond's price.

> **Observation:** *A bond's price is simply the present value of the bond's future cash flows. The more distant a future cash flow of a given amount, the less value it has in today's dollars.*

Influences on a bond price

The impact of the coupon rate

The price of a bond is directly related to the bond's coupon rate of interest. Holding the discount rate constant, a higher coupon bond sells at a higher price than a lower coupon issue of the same maturity. This is logical since the size of the cash flow stream is increased while holding all other factors stable. In formula terms, the numerator of the summation is larger while the denominator is left unchanged.

Recall that in a 10% yield environment, a 7% coupon, 5-year U.S. Treasury bond sells for $884.17 (see Exhibit 2–1). Raising the bond's coupon rate from 7% to 10% increases the bond's value to $1,000.00:

$$\text{bond price}_{10\% \; coupon} = \sum_{t=1}^{10} \frac{CF_t}{\left(1 + \dfrac{0.10}{2}\right)^t}$$

$$= \sum_{t=1}^{10} \frac{CPN_t}{\left(1 + \dfrac{0.10}{2}\right)^t} + \frac{P_{10}}{\left(1 + \dfrac{0.10}{2}\right)^{10}}$$

$$= \underbrace{\sum_{t=1}^{10} \frac{\$50.00}{(1.05)^t}}_{\substack{\text{coupon} \\ \text{cash flows}}} + \underbrace{\frac{\$1,000.00}{(1.05)^{10}}}_{\substack{\text{principal repayment} \\ \text{at the end of 5 years}}}$$

$$= \$386.10 + \$613.90$$

$$= \$1,000.00$$

Exhibit 2–3. Calculation of the price of a 10% coupon, 5-year U.S. Treasury bond using a 10% discount rate.

End of Period t	*(1)* *Cash Flow,* CF_t	*(2)* *PV Factor*	*(3) = (1) × (2)* $PV(CF_t)$
1	$ 50.00	0.9524	$ 47.62
2	50.00	0.9070	45.35
3	50.00	0.8638	43.19
4	50.00	0.8227	41.14
5	50.00	0.7835	39.18
6	50.00	0.7462	37.31
7	50.00	0.7107	35.54
8	50.00	0.6768	33.84
9	50.00	0.6446	32.23
10	50.00	0.6139	30.70
10	1,000.00	0.6139	613.90
		Total PV →	$1,000.00
			↑ Bond price

Comments: *Cash flows are semiannual coupons of $50.00 ($1,000 par × 0.10 × ½) and a final principal repayment of $1,000 par. The present value factors are calculated as 1/(1 + 0.10/2) or 1/(1 + 0.05).*

Exhibit 2–4. Calculation of the price of a 14% coupon, 5-year U.S. Treasury bond using a 10% discount rate.

End of Period t	(1) Cash Flow, CF_t	(2) PV Factor	(3) = (1) × (2) $PV(CF_t)$
1	$ 70.00	0.9524	$ 66.67
2	70.00	0.9070	63.49
3	70.00	0.8638	60.47
4	70.00	0.8227	57.59
5	70.00	0.7835	54.85
6	70.00	0.7462	52.23
7	70.00	0.7107	49.75
8	70.00	0.6768	47.38
9	70.00	0.6446	45.12
10	70.00	0.6139	42.97
10	1,000.00	0.6139	613.90
		Total PV →	$1,154.43
			↑ Bond price

Comments: *Cash flows are semiannual coupons of $70.00 ($1,000.00 par × 0.14 × ½) and a final principal repayment of $1,000.00 par. The present value factors are calculated as 1/(1 + 0.10/2) or 1/(1 + 0.05).*

The enhanced value of the coupon stream ($386.10 − $270.27 = $115.83) fully accounts for the increase in price from $884.17 on the 7% coupon issue to $1,000.00 on the 10% bond. The principal repayment in 5 years is currently worth $613.90, regardless of the coupon rate of interest. Exhibit 2–3 summarizes the arithmetics related to the 10% coupon issue.

Exhibit 2–4 applies present value computations to a 14% coupon, 5-year U.S. Treasury bond, once again using a discount rate of 10%. The value of the 14% coupon bond is $1,154.43, summarized as follows:

$$\text{bond value}_{14\% \ coupon} = \sum_{t=1}^{10} \frac{CF_t}{\left(1 + \dfrac{0.10}{2}\right)^t}$$

$$= \sum_{t=1}^{10} \frac{CPN_t}{\left(1 + \dfrac{0.10}{2}\right)^t} + \frac{P_{10}}{\left(1 + \dfrac{0.10}{2}\right)^{10}}$$

$$= \sum_{t=1}^{10} \underbrace{\frac{\$70.00}{(1.05)^t}}_{\substack{\text{coupon} \\ \text{cash flows}}} + \underbrace{\frac{\$1,000.00}{(1.05)^{10}}}_{\substack{\text{principal repayment} \\ \text{at the end of 5 years}}}$$

$$= \$540.53 + \$613.90$$

$$= \$1,154.43$$

Once again, the higher present value of the coupon payments ($540.53) warrants the higher bond value of $1,154.43 (versus $1,000.00 for the 10% coupon issue and $884.17 for the 7% coupon issue). The coupon stream on the 14% issue accounts for almost half of the bond's value ($540.53/$1,154.43), whereas it accounts for only one-third of the 7% coupon bond's worth ($270.27/$884.17). It is evident that, all other things held equal, higher coupon bonds command higher prices.

Exhibit 2–5. Calculation of the price of a 10% coupon, 5-year U.S. Treasury bond using a 7% discount rate.

End of Period t	(1) *Cash Flow,* CF_t	(2) *PV* *Factor*	(3) = (1) × (2) *PV(CF*$_t$*)*
1	$ 50.00	0.9662	$ 48.31
2	50.00	0.9335	46.68
3	50.00	0.9019	45.10
4	50.00	0.8714	43.57
5	50.00	0.8420	42.10
6	50.00	0.8135	40.68
7	50.00	0.7860	39.30
8	50.00	0.7594	37.97
9	50.00	0.7337	36.69
10	50.00	0.7089	35.45
10	1,000.00	0.7089	708.90
		Total PV →	$1,124.75
			↑ Bond price

Comments: *Cash flows are semiannual coupons of $50.00 ($1,000.00 par × 0.10 × ½) and a final principal repayment of $1,000.00 par. The present value factors are calculated as 1/(1 + 0.07/2) or 1/(1 + 0.035).*

The impact of the discount rate of interest

The price of a bond is inversely related to the discount rate of interest. As the discount rate increases, the bond's value falls. Conversely, the bond's value rises as the discount rate is reduced. In terms of the general formula for bond valuation, as the discount rate rises/(falls), the denominator rises/(falls), which, in turn, decreases/(increases) the value of each individual cash flow and, consequently, the bond's total value:

$$\text{bond price} = \sum_{t=1}^{n} \frac{CF_t}{(1 + i)^t}$$

For example, a 10% coupon, 5-year U.S. Treasury bond is valued at par ($1,000.00) in a 10% interest rate environment (see Exhibit 2–3). The same issue is worth $1,124.75 when the discount rate is lowered to 7% (see Exhibit 2–5). A rise in the discount rate to 14% drives the

Exhibit 2–6. Calculation of the price of a 10% coupon, 5-year U.S. Treasury bond using a 14% discount rate.

End of Period t	(1) Cash Flow, CF_t	(2) PV Factor	(3) = (1) × (2) PV(CF_t)
1	$ 50.00	0.9346	$ 46.73
2	50.00	0.8734	43.67
3	50.00	0.8163	40.82
4	50.00	0.7629	38.15
5	50.00	0.7130	35.65
6	50.00	0.6663	33.32
7	50.00	0.6228	31.14
8	50.00	0.5820	29.10
9	50.00	0.5439	27.20
10	50.00	0.5083	25.42
10	1,000.00	0.5083	508.30
		Total PV →	$859.53
			↑
			Bond price

Comments: *Cash flows are semiannual coupons of $50.00 ($1,000.00 par × 0.10 × ½) and a final principal repayment of $1,000.00 par. The present value factors are calculated as 1/(1 + 0.14/2) or 1/(1 + 0.07).*

value of a 10% coupon, 5-year bond down to $859.53 (see Exhibit 2–6).

The price of a bond of a given maturity is a function of the coupon rate and the discount rate. If the coupon rate is lower than the discount rate, the bond will be valued below par (i.e., less than $1,000.00). In other words, the bond sells at a discount to par value. A bond of this nature is commonly referred to as a *discount bond*. A bond with a coupon rate set exactly equal to the discount rate will sell at par (i.e., $1,000.00) and is termed a *par bond*. A bond offering a coupon rate in excess of the discount rate will trade at a price above par value (i.e., greater than $1,000.00). These bonds are dubbed *premium bonds*. In sum:

Coupon Rate:Discount Rate Relationship	*Bond Type*
Coupon rate < Discount rate	Discount bond
Coupon rate = Discount rate	Par bond
Coupon rate > Discount rate	Premium bond

Observation: *Bond prices are positively related to the coupon rate of interest but are inversely related to the discount rate of interest. Discount bonds are bonds trading at prices below par value and premium bonds are bonds trading at prices exceeding par value. Par bonds are issues trading at exactly the par value.*

The nomenclature of bond prices and the consideration of accrued interest

Bond prices are quoted as a percentage of par value. For example, a bond trading at a price of 86 is valued at $860.00 (i.e., 86% of $1,000.00 par). An issue priced at 119.50 costs the investor $1,195.00 (i.e., 119.50% of $1,000.00 par). The fractional terms of the prices of U.S. Treasury bonds, federal agency bonds, and mortgage passthrough securities are typically quoted in 32nds. For example, a U.S. Treasury bond trading at 104–16 is selling at 104.50 in decimal form (i.e., $104^{16}/_{32} = 104.50$), or 104.50% of par value (i.e., $1,045.00).[4] This pricing method arises from the convention of the 1/32nd point as the minimum price move in

---

[4] Alternatively, one may see the quote as 104.16. Typical usage, however, finds the fractional amount preceded by a dash (–) for 32nd quotes and by a period (.) for decimal quotes.

these types of bonds; 1/32nd point is equivalent to 0.03125 point in decimal parlance. Exhibit 2–7 provides a translation of 32nd fractions into decimal equivalents. The aforementioned bond types can be priced in decimal form.

Corporate bonds and most other securities are traded in eighths of a point and/or in decimal terms. For example, a telephone utility bond

Exhibit 2–7. The decimal equivalents of 32nds of a point.

Fraction	Typical Format	Decimal Equivalent
1/32	−01	0.03125
2/32	−02	0.06250
3/32	−03	0.09375
4/32	−04	0.12500
5/32	−05	0.15625
6/32	−06	0.18750
7/32	−07	0.21875
8/32	−08	0.25000
9/32	−09	0.28125
10/32	−10	0.31250
11/32	−11	0.34375
12/32	−12	0.37500
13/32	−13	0.40625
14/32	−14	0.43750
15/32	−15	0.46875
16/32	−16	0.50000
17/32	−17	0.53125
18/32	−18	0.56250
19/32	−19	0.59375
20/32	−20	0.62500
21/32	−21	0.65625
22/32	−22	0.68750
23/32	−23	0.71875
24/32	−24	0.75000
25/32	−25	0.78125
26/32	−26	0.81250
27/32	−27	0.84375
28/32	−28	0.87500
29/32	−29	0.90625
30/32	−30	0.93750
31/32	−31	0.96875

quoted at 96¼ (or 96.25) sells for $962.50 ($1,000.00 par × 96.25%). A corporate bond traded at 104.16 costs the investor $1,041.60 ($1,000.00 par × 104.16%). In this book, the reader can easily differentiate between bond prices and the actual dollar value of the bond at that price. Bond price quotes are devoid of dollar signs and tend to vary around the 100.00 level, which corresponds to par value. For simplicity, most of the price quotes in this book are made in decimal form. The actual dollar value of the bond is accompanied by a dollar sign and is expressed in magnitudes that tend to gravitate around the $1,000.00 level, which corresponds to a bond's par value.

Bond prices are stated *net* of accrued interest. Bonds purchased between coupon payment dates require the addition of an *accrued interest* amount to the quoted price. Since the issuer of the bond pays the semi-annual coupon to the bondholder of record on the interest payment date, the buyer must pay the seller for the interest earned since the last coupon payment date. The buyer is then *reimbursed* by the issuer on the upcoming coupon payment date. A *full purchase price*, or *full price*, includes accrued interest. The present value discounting process derives a full purchase price. The Appendix to this chapter illustrates the mechanics of calculating accrued interest on a bond.

Accrued interest is positively related to the coupon rate of interest and the length of time since the last coupon payment date. Accrued interest builds up as time passes and drops off as coupon payments are made. The resulting alteration in the full price has an impact on the inherent price sensitivity of the bond (see Chapter 6 for a discussion of the impact of accrued interest on a bond's duration). For purposes of clarity, the book illustrations utilize bonds purchased/(sold) on either the date of issuance or on a coupon payment date. In these cases, the bonds have no accrued interest and the *bond price* and *full price* are synonymous. In the *Applications of the Fundamentals* section of this book (Chapters 12–15), the examples incorporate all of the complexities of a typical bond investment, with bonds traded between interest payment dates and subject to accrued interest.

Observation: *Bond prices are quoted as percentages of par value (e.g., 86.50, 94³/₃₂, 100, 120¹/₈). Fractional amounts are expressed in 32nds, 8ths, or in decimal form. A bond's full price is the bond's stated price plus accrued interest.*

The concept of yield to maturity

A bond's *price* is the market value at which the bond currently trades. A bond's *yield to maturity* is the single discount rate that forces the present value of all future cash flows to exactly equal the bond's current market price:

$$\text{bond price} = \sum_{t=1}^{n} \frac{CF_t}{\left(1 + \dfrac{YTM}{2}\right)^t}$$

The YTM, or yield, is typically stated as an annual rate of interest and, therefore, requires a division to arrive at the semiannual compounding rate necessary for a semiannual-pay bond. Essentially, the YTM is a special case of the many potential discount rates available. One might think of the YTM as the market consensus discount rate for a particular security. Just as a bond's price is inversely related to the discount rate chosen, so is a bond's price inversely related to its yield to maturity.

A bond's YTM is found by an iterative, trial-and-error procedure. Given the bond's price, one can solve for the YTM rate. For example, if a 10% coupon, 5-year U.S. Treasury bond is selling at a 110.00 price (i.e., a $1,100.00 value), what is its YTM? Given that the bond is trading above par value, the YTM rate must lie below the coupon rate of 10%. Let's try a 7% discount rate:

$$\$1,100.00 = \sum_{t=1}^{10} \frac{\$50.00}{\left(1 + \dfrac{0.07}{2}\right)^t} + \frac{\$1,000.00}{\left(1 + \dfrac{0.07}{2}\right)^{10}}$$

$$\neq \$1,124.75 \qquad \text{[per Exhibit 2–5]}$$

The initial guess creates a $1,124.75 price—too high. Let's raise the discount rate to 8%:

$$\$1,100.00 = \sum_{t=1}^{10} \frac{\$50.00}{\left(1 + \dfrac{0.08}{2}\right)^t} + \frac{\$1,000.00}{\left(1 + \dfrac{0.08}{2}\right)^{10}}$$

$$\neq \$1,081.17 \qquad \text{[per Exhibit 2–8]}$$

Exhibit 2–8. Calculation of the price of a 10% coupon, 5-year U.S. Treasury bond using an 8% discount rate.

End of Period t	*(1)* Cash Flow, CF_t	*(2)* PV Factor	*(3) = (1) × (2)* $PV(CF_t)$
1	$ 50.00	0.9615	$ 48.08
2	50.00	0.9246	46.23
3	50.00	0.8890	44.45
4	50.00	0.8548	42.74
5	50.00	0.8219	41.10
6	50.00	0.7903	39.52
7	50.00	0.7599	38.00
8	50.00	0.7307	36.54
9	50.00	0.7026	35.13
10	50.00	0.6756	33.78
10	1,000.00	0.6756	675.60
		Total PV →	$1,081.17
			↑ Bond price

Comments: *Cash flows are semiannual coupons of $50.00 ($1,000.00 par × 0.10 × ½) and a final principal repayment of $1,000.00 par. The present value factors are calculated as 1/(1 + 0.08/2) or 1/(1 + 0.04).*

The second guess is $1,081.17—too low. After a few more trials, the YTM solves to 7.56%:

$$\$1,100.00 = \sum_{t=1}^{10} \frac{\$50.00}{\left(1 + \dfrac{0.0756}{2}\right)^t} + \frac{\$1,000.00}{\left(1 + \dfrac{0.0756}{2}\right)^{10}}$$

$$= \$1,100.00 \qquad \text{[per Exhibit 2–9]}$$

Exhibit 2–10 shows the bond prices for the 10% coupon, 5-year issue across a range of yields. A *basis point* (BP) is ¹⁄₁₀₀th of 1%. Using a 10BP increment in yield, one can narrow the yield into a 7.50–7.60% range (110.27–109.83 price range) for the bond priced at 110.00. Indeed, in the earlier days of bond management, *yield books* were used to estimate the YTM of a bond rather than an arduous trial-and-error

Exhibit 2–9. Calculation of the price of a 10% coupon, 5-year U.S. Treasury bond using a 7.56% discount rate.

End of Period t	(1) Cash Flow, CF_t	(2) PV Factor	(3) = (1) × (2) PV(CF_t)
1	$ 50.00	0.9636	$ 48.18
2	50.00	0.9285	46.43
3	50.00	0.8947	44.74
4	50.00	0.8621	43.11
5	50.00	0.8307	41.54
6	50.00	0.8004	40.02
7	50.00	0.7713	38.57
8	50.00	0.7432	37.16
9	50.00	0.7161	35.81
10	50.00	0.6900	34.50
10	1,000.00	0.6900	690.00
		Total PV →	$1,100.00
			↑ Bond price

Comments: *Cash flows are semiannual coupons of $50.00 ($1,000.00 par × 0.10 × ½) and a final principal repayment of $1,000.00 par. The present value factors are calculated as $1/(1 + 0.0756/2)$ or $1/(1 + 0.0378)$.*

approach [see Publication #63, *Expanded Bond Values Table* (Boston, MA: Financial Publishing Company, 1970)]. Fortunately, a financial calculator can perform the tedious iterations quickly and automatically.

Observation: *A bond's yield to maturity is the discount rate that equates the present value of the bond's future cash flows to the bond's current market price.*

The curvilinear relationship between bond prices and bond yields

A bond's price varies inversely with its yield to maturity. Exhibit 2–11 compiles the price and yield data for a 10% coupon, 30-year U.S. Treasury bond over a range of interest rate levels. The price : yield relationship

Exhibit 2–10. The bond prices for a 10% coupon, 5-year U.S. Treasury issue across a wide range of yields. The bond's price is found between the 7.50% and 7.60% yield levels.

YTM (%)	Bond Price	YTM (%)	Bond Price
6.00	117.06	8.00	108.11
6.10	116.59	8.10	107.69
6.20	116.13	8.20	107.26
6.30	115.66	8.30	106.84
6.40	115.20	8.40	106.43
6.50	114.74	8.50	106.01
6.60	114.28	8.60	105.59
6.70	113.83	8.70	105.18
6.80	113.37	8.80	104.77
6.90	112.92	8.90	104.36
7.00	112.48	9.00	103.96
7.10	112.03	9.10	103.55
7.20	111.59	9.20	103.15
7.30	111.14	9.30	102.75
7.40	110.70	9.40	102.35
7.50	110.27	9.50	101.95
7.60	109.83	9.60	101.56
7.70	109.40	9.70	101.17
7.80	108.97	9.80	100.78
7.90	108.54	9.90	100.39
8.00	108.11	10.00	100.00

is nonlinear in nature. In other words, for a given change in yield, the price of a bond does not change by a uniform amount. Exhibit 2–12 illustrates the price:yield relationship for a 10% coupon, 30-year U.S. Treasury. The price:yield pairings form a curve that is convex to the origin of the graph.[5]

The price:yield curve originates at the bond price corresponding to a 0% interest rate. At a 0% yield, the bond's present value is simply the sum of its nominal cash flows; no discounting factors are applied to the cash flows. For the 10% coupon, 30-year bond of Exhibit 2–11, the price is 400.00:

---

[5] The impacts of this *convexity* are discussed in Chapter 6.

$$\text{bond price}_{0\% \ yield} = \sum_{t=1}^{n} \text{coupons} + \text{principal value}$$

$$= (\$50.00 \times 60) + \$1,000.00$$

$$= \$3,000.00 + \$1,000.00$$

$$= \$4,000.00 \ (\text{or } 400.00 \text{ in price terms})$$

Theoretically, if interest rates drop to 0%, the bond trades at a maximum price of 400.00. On the other end of the yield spectrum, the price: yield curve approaches, but fails to touch, the x-axis. That is, the bond's price falls toward, but never reaches, a zero value.

Exhibit 2–13 plots the price:yield trade-offs for a high coupon (14%), low coupon (7%), and a zero-coupon (0%) bond. Exhibit 2–14 provides supporting data. The graph demonstrates that the prices of lower

Exhibit 2–11. Price and yield data for a 10% coupon, 30-year U.S. Treasury bond.

Yield to Maturity (%)	Bond Price[*]
0.00	400.00
1.00	332.77
2.00	279.82
3.00	237.83
4.00	204.28
5.00	177.27
6.00	155.35
7.00	137.42
8.00	122.62
9.00	110.32
10.00	100.00
11.00	91.28
12.00	83.84
13.00	77.45
14.00	71.92
15.00	67.10
16.00	62.87
17.00	59.13
18.00	55.81
19.00	52.84
20.00	50.16

[*] Prices rounded to the nearest two decimal places.

Exhibit 2–12. Price:yield relationship for a 10% coupon, 30-year U.S. Treasury bond. (Data per Exhibit 2–11.)

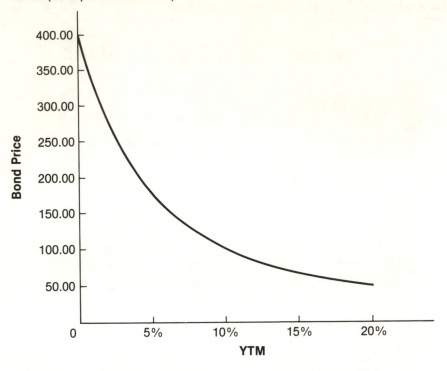

Exhibit 2–13. Price:yield relationships for 30-year U.S. Treasury bonds of various coupon rates. (Data per Exhibit 2–14.)

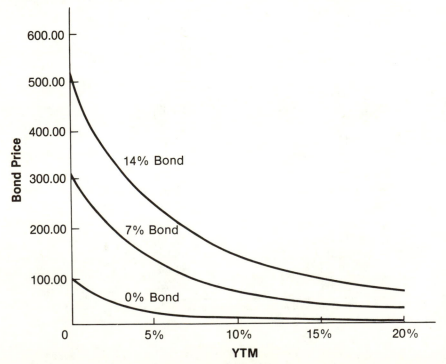

Exhibit 2–14. Price and yield data for a high coupon (14%), low coupon (7%), and no-coupon (0%) bond. Each bond matures in 30 years.

Yield to Maturity (%)	Bond Price for the:[*]		
	14% Bond	7% Bond	0% Bond
0.00	520.00	310.00	100.00
1.00	436.22	255.18	74.14
2.00	369.73	212.39	55.04
3.00	316.59	178.76	40.93
4.00	273.80	152.14	30.48
5.00	239.09	130.91	22.73
6.00	210.70	113.84	16.97
7.00	187.31	100.00	12.69
8.00	167.87	88.69	9.51
9.00	151.60	79.36	7.13
10.00	137.86	71.61	5.35
11.00	126.17	65.10	4.03
12.00	116.16	59.60	3.03
13.00	107.52	54.90	2.29
14.00	100.00	50.86	1.73
15.00	93.42	47.36	1.30
16.00	87.62	44.31	0.99
17.00	82.49	41.62	0.75
18.00	77.90	39.24	0.57
19.00	73.80	37.11	0.43
20.00	70.10	35.21	0.33

[*] Prices rounded to the nearest two decimal places.

Comments: *At a 0% yield, the bonds trade at prices reflecting the nominal value of their future cash flow streams (i.e., no discounting process).*

coupon bonds are more sensitive to changes in yield than higher coupon issues. Zero-coupon bonds exhibit the greatest degree of price volatility.[6] For example, the price of a 14% coupon bond rises by just over 50% if yields fall to 6% from 10% (210.70 price versus 137.86 price). For the same change in yield, a 30-year zero-coupon bond more than triples in value, surging to 16.97 from 5.35 (see Exhibit 2–14).

Shorter maturity issues have flatter price:yield curves, revealing that these issues are less price sensitive than their longer maturity counter-

[6] Bond price volatility is the subject of Chapter 4.

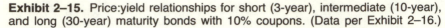

Exhibit 2–15. Price:yield relationships for short (3-year), intermediate (10-year), and long (30-year) maturity bonds with 10% coupons. (Data per Exhibit 2–16.)

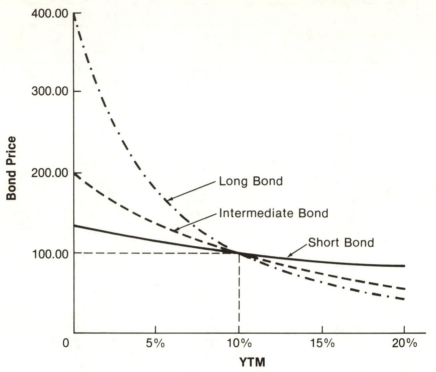

parts. Exhibit 2–15 illustrates this phenomenon using 10% coupon U.S. Treasury bonds maturing in 3, 10, and 30 years, respectively, and initially priced at par. As an illustration, the price of a 30-year bond surges by over 50% if yields decline to 6% from 10% (155.35 price versus 100.00 price). A 3-year issue experiences only an 11% appreciation in price under the same market conditions (110.83 price versus 100.00 price). Supporting data are given in Exhibit 2–16. In general, the lower the coupon rate and the longer the maturity, the steeper (and more cup-shaped) the price:yield curve of a bond and, consequently, the more volatile is its inherent price behavior.

> **Observation:** *Bond prices vary inversely with bond yields. The price: yield relationship plots a curve that is more convex, or cup-shaped, for low coupon issues and long maturity issues. Higher coupon, short maturity bonds render flatter price:yield curves, reflecting their lesser degree of price sensitivity.*

Exhibit 2–16. Price and yield data for short (3-year), intermediate (10-year), and long (30-year) maturity bonds with 10% coupons.

Yield to Maturity (%)	Bond Price for the:[*]		
	3-Year Issue	*10-Year Issue*	*30-Year Issue*
0.00	130.00	200.00	400.00
1.00	126.53	185.44	332.77
2.00	123.18	172.18	279.82
3.00	119.94	160.09	237.83
4.00	116.80	149.05	204.28
5.00	113.77	138.97	177.27
6.00	110.83	129.75	155.35
7.00	107.99	121.32	137.42
8.00	105.24	113.59	122.62
9.00	102.58	106.50	110.32
10.00	100.00	100.00	100.00
11.00	97.50	94.02	91.28
12.00	95.08	88.53	83.84
13.00	92.74	83.47	77.45
14.00	90.47	78.81	71.92
15.00	88.27	74.51	67.10
16.00	86.13	70.55	62.87
17.00	84.06	66.88	59.13
18.00	82.06	63.49	55.81
19.00	80.11	60.34	52.84
20.00	78.22	57.43	50.16

[*] Prices rounded to the nearest two decimal places.

Comments: *At a 0% yield, the bonds trade at prices reflecting the nominal value of their future cash flow streams (i.e., no discounting process).*

Summary

A *bond's value* can be estimated by a discounting of all of the bond's future cash flows into current dollar equivalents. The market consensus discount rate is termed the bond's *yield to maturity*. The YTM is the discount rate that equates the present value of the bond's future cash flows to the bond's current market price.

Bond prices are influenced by *coupon rates* and *discount rates*.

Higher coupon rates warrant higher bond prices as the present value of the cash flow stream is increased. Higher discount rates lead to lower bond prices as future dollar receipts are deemed lower present values. The price:yield relationship resembles a curvature that is more severely cup-shaped for low coupon bonds and long maturity issues.

The Calculation of Accrued Interest

Accrued interest is calculated on an *actual/actual basis* for U.S. Treasury bonds and is computed on a *30/360 basis* for federal agency and corporate bonds. Actual/actual calculations simply divide the actual number of days transpiring since the last coupon payment date by the actual number of days in the interval between the last coupon payment date and the next coupon payment date. 30/360 calculations assume a 30-day month and a 360-day year. Sample calculations of accrued interest for both a U.S. Treasury bond and a corporate bond are provided as follows:

Settlement date:	July 15, 1987	Settlement date:	July 15, 1987
Bond type:	U.S. Treasury	Bond type:	Corporate
Coupon rate:	10.00%	Coupon rate:	10.00%
Maturity date:	May 15, 1992	Maturity date:	May 15, 1992
Accrued interest:	1.6576[a] *or*	Accrued interest:	1.6667[b] *or*
	$16.58 per bond		$16.67 per bond

$$^a \frac{(16 + 30 + 15)^*}{184^\dagger} \times 10.00\% \times \frac{1}{2} = 1.6576$$

$$^b \frac{(15 + 30 + 15)}{360} \times 10.00\% = 1.6667$$

As noted in this chapter, the amount of accrued interest attached to a bond is a function of the bond's coupon rate of interest and the period of coupon accrual. Higher coupon bonds are subject to a greater degree of buildup in accrued interest and commensurately larger drops in full price as coupon payments are made. Exhibits 2A–1 and 2A–2 illustrate these phenomena for U.S. Treasury bonds and corporate bonds.

Exhibit 2A–1. The accrued interest (expressed in points) on U.S. Treasury bonds and corporate bonds of various coupon rates. A July 15, 1987 settlement date is assumed.

	Coupon Rate		
Issue	*7%*	*10%*	*14%*
U.S. Treasury bond due May 15, 1992	1.1603	1.6576	2.3207
Corporate bond due May 15, 1992	1.1667	1.6667	2.3333

Comments: *Higher coupon bonds require a larger payment of accrued interest and, therefore, a higher full purchase price.*

---

* Actual days in the May 15–July 15 period (first day excluded, last day included) is 61 days (16 + 30 + 15).

† Actual days in the May 15–November 15 period (first day excluded, last day included) is 184 days (16 + 30 + 31 + 31 + 30 + 31 + 15).

Exhibit 2A–2. The accrued interest (expressed in points) on a 10% coupon U.S. Treasury bond and a 10% coupon corporate bond of identical maturity. A variety of settlement dates are illustrated.

Settlement Date	Accrued Interest on a 10% Coupon Issue with a May 15 Maturity Date	
	U.S. Treasury	*Corporate Bond*
February 27, 1987	2.8729	2.8333
February 28, 1987	2.9006	2.8611
March 1, 1987	2.9282	2.9444
March 2, 1987	2.9558	2.9722
.	.	.
.	.	.
.	.	.
May 14, 1987	4.9724	4.9722
May 15, 1987	5.0000	5.0000
May 16, 1987	0.0272	0.0278
.	.	.
.	.	.
.	.	.
May 29, 1987	0.3804	0.3889
May 30, 1987	0.4076	0.4167
May 31, 1987	0.4348	0.4444
June 1, 1987	0.4620	0.4444

Comments: *U.S. Treasuries and corporate bonds with identical coupons accrue interest at different rates (actual/actual basis versus 30/360 basis). The actual coupon payment is the same (i.e., 5 points in this case), but the roads to the full coupon accrual differ, particularly around month-ends.*

CHAPTER 3

Bond Yield Measures

Chapter 2 introduced the concept of a bond's yield to maturity. There are several additional bond yield measures that deserve attention. They include current yield, yield to call, yield to average life, cash flow yield, call-adjusted yield, and realized compound yield. This chapter investigates these alternative yield proxies, explains how to calculate them, and discusses the circumstances under which they are most useful.

Current yield

Current yield (CY) is a measure of a bond's annual coupon income. CY is expressed as a percentage of the bond's current market price[1]:

$$\text{current yield (in \%)} = \left(\frac{\text{annual coupon}}{\text{bond price}}\right) \times 100$$

$$= \left(\frac{\text{annual coupon cash flow (dollars)}}{\text{bond price (dollars)}}\right) \times 100$$

[1] In calculating a bond's current yield, the bond price excludes accrued interest.

55

Exhibit 3–1. Calculation of the current yield on 3-year U.S. Treasury bonds of various coupon rates. Each bond is priced to yield 7.00% to maturity.

(1) *Coupon Rate* (%)	(2) *Annual Coupons*	(3) *Bond Price*	(4) = (2)/(3) *Current Yield* (%)
0.00	0.00	81.35	0.00
4.00	4.00	92.01	4.35
7.00	7.00	100.00	7.00
10.00	10.00	107.99	9.26
14.00	14.00	118.65	11.80

Current yield is, in essence, that portion of a bond's return attributable to the coupon component. The emphasis on coupon return per dollar invested tends to give higher coupon bonds noticeably higher current yields. Exhibit 3–1 underscores this fact by analyzing a series of 3-year U.S. Treasuries with varying coupons, while holding the YTM on the bonds constant at 7.00%. A par bond has a current yield equal to its YTM. A premium bond sports a current yield in excess of its YTM— 480BP higher for a 14% coupon, 3-year issue (11.80% CY versus 7.00% YTM, per Exhibit 3–1). A 4% coupon issue of similar maturity offers only 4.35% in current yield, 265BP less than its YTM of 7.00%.

In general, since the coupon rate on a bond is fixed, a bond's CY rises/(falls) as the bond's price falls/(rises).[2] The price changes experienced by a bond may arise from changes in yield levels or from the passage of time and the related scientific amortization of the bond's premium or discount.[3] As an example, a 14% coupon U.S. Treasury bond priced to yield 7.00% offers increments of current yield over progressively shorter remaining terms to maturity. Exhibit 3–2 shows the 14% coupon issue over a wide span of maturities. Its current yield is dramatically higher as a 1-year bond (CY = 13.13%) than as a 10-year bond (CY = 9.35%) or as a 30-year bond (CY = 7.47%). As the premium bond's price falls over time, its current yield advances commensurately. A discount bond experiences the opposite effect: as the bond approaches maturity, its price rises inexorably toward par and its current yield declines.

---

[2] This text does not delve into the complexities of floating rate debt.

[3] Scientific amortization is also termed *effective interest amortization*. This concept is discussed in Chapter 8.

Exhibit 3–2. Behavior of current yield as a bond approaches maturity. The illustrative issue is a 14% coupon U.S. Treasury bond priced to yield 7.00% to maturity.

(1) Years Remaining to Maturity	(2) Annual Coupons	(3) Bond Price	(4) YTM (%)	(5) = (2)/(3) Current Yield (%)
30	14.00	187.31	7.00	7.47
29	14.00	186.40	7.00	7.51
28	14.00	185.43	7.00	7.55
27	14.00	184.40	7.00	7.59
26	14.00	183.29	7.00	7.64
25	14.00	182.09	7.00	7.69
24	14.00	180.82	7.00	7.74
23	14.00	179.45	7.00	7.80
22	14.00	177.99	7.00	7.87
21	14.00	176.42	7.00	7.94
20	14.00	174.74	7.00	8.01
19	14.00	172.94	7.00	8.10
18	14.00	171.02	7.00	8.19
17	14.00	168.95	7.00	8.29
16	14.00	166.74	7.00	8.40
15	14.00	164.37	7.00	8.52
14	14.00	161.83	7.00	8.65
13	14.00	159.12	7.00	8.80
12	14.00	156.20	7.00	8.96
11	14.00	153.08	7.00	9.15
10	14.00	149.74	7.00	9.35
9	14.00	146.16	7.00	9.58
8	14.00	142.33	7.00	9.84
7	14.00	138.22	7.00	10.13
6	14.00	133.82	7.00	10.46
5	14.00	129.11	7.00	10.84
4	14.00	124.06	7.00	11.28
3	14.00	118.65	7.00	11.80
2	14.00	112.86	7.00	12.40
1	14.00	106.65	7.00	13.13
Maturity	14.00	100.00	7.00	14.00

Comments: *Scientific amortization of the bond premium accounts for the gradual decline in price over time.*

Observation: *The current yield of a bond is simply the annual coupon return generated by the bond, expressed as a percentage of the bond's current market price. Premium bonds offer higher current yields than discount bonds of similar maturity.*

Internal rate of return measures

An *internal rate of return* (IRR) is the single discount rate that when applied to a bond's expected future cash flows, equates those future cash flows with the price at which the bond is currently traded in the marketplace. There are four yield measures that act as internal rates of return:

1. Yield to maturity (YTM).
2. Yield to call (YTC).
3. Yield to average life (YTAL).
4. Cash flow or discounted cash flow (DCF) yield.

Yield to maturity

The *yield to maturity* (YTM) is the single discount rate that equates the present value of all the bond's cash flows *to maturity* with the bond's current market price:

$$\text{bond price} = \sum_{t=1}^{n} \frac{\text{CF}_t}{\left(1 + \dfrac{\text{YTM}}{2}\right)^t}$$

As its name implies, the YTM assumes that the bond is held to maturity and that all cash flows are received as scheduled through final maturity. Any interruption of the cash flow scheme renders the YTM measure faulty. Premature call/refunding, sinking fund payments, or an early sale of the security alter the yield that the investor actually realizes. For illustrative purposes, if an investor purchases a 10% coupon, 5-year U.S. Treasury bond at 112.48, the YTM of the bond is calculated as 7.00%:

$$\text{bond price} = \sum_{t=1}^{n} \frac{\text{CF}_t}{\left(1 + \dfrac{\text{YTM}}{2}\right)^t}$$

$$= \sum_{t=1}^{n} \frac{\text{CPN}_t}{\left(1 + \dfrac{\text{YTM}}{2}\right)^t} + \frac{P_n}{\left(1 + \dfrac{\text{YTM}}{2}\right)^n}$$

$$\$1{,}124.80 = \sum_{t=1}^{10} \frac{\$50.00}{\left(1 + \dfrac{\text{YTM}}{2}\right)^t} + \frac{\$1{,}000.00}{\left(1 + \dfrac{\text{YTM}}{2}\right)^{10}}$$

The YTM solves to 0.070 or 7.00%. Refer to Exhibit 3–3 for the calculations verifying the 7.00% discount rate.

The YTM measure is useful as an indicator of relative price. All

Exhibit 3–3. Calculation of the value of a 10% coupon, 5-year U.S. Treasury bond using a 7% discount rate.

End of Period t	(1) Cash Flow, CF$_t$	(2) PV Factor	(3) = (1) × (2) PV(CF$_t$)
1	$ 50.00	0.9662	$ 48.31
2	50.00	0.9335	46.68
3	50.00	0.9019	45.10
4	50.00	0.8714	43.57
5	50.00	0.8420	42.10
6	50.00	0.8135	40.68
7	50.00	0.7860	39.30
8	50.00	0.7594	37.97
9	50.00	0.7337	36.69
10	50.00	0.7089	35.45
10	1,000.00	0.7089	708.90
		Total PV →	$1,124.75
			↑
			Bond price

Comments: *Cash flows are semiannual coupons of $50.00 ($1,000.00 par × 0.10 × ½) and a final principal repayment of $1,000.00 par. The present value factors are calculated as 1/(1 + 0.07/2) or 1/(1 + 0.035).*

other things held equal, a higher yielding bond sells at a lower price. Troubles arise when an investor attempts to rely on the YTM as a proxy for the bond's expected rate of return.[4] As an internal rate of return, YTM assumes that all cash flows are reinvested at the YTM rate and that the bond is held to maturity. Over long horizons, reinvestment rates can be very unpredictable. For active bond managers, issues are often sold prior to maturity. In both cases the YTM measure may not accurately reflect the realized yield on the investment.

> **Observation:** *A bond's yield to maturity is the discount rate that equates the present value of the bond's future cash flows promised through final maturity to the bond's current market price.*

Yield to call

The *yield to call* (YTC) is the single discount rate that equates the present value of a bond's cash flows *received through the call date* to the bond's current market price:

$$\text{bond price} = \sum_{t=1}^{c} \frac{\text{CF}_t}{\left(1 + \dfrac{\text{YTC}}{2}\right)^t}$$

$$= \sum_{t=1}^{c} \frac{\text{CPN}_t}{\left(1 + \dfrac{\text{YTC}}{2}\right)^t} + \frac{\text{P}_c}{\left(1 + \dfrac{\text{YTC}}{2}\right)^c}$$

where CF_t is the total cash flow received at the end of period t, CPN_t the coupon cash flow received at the end of period t, P_c the principal value received on the call date (i.e., the call price), and c the number of semiannual periods remaining until the call date. The YTC is expressed as an annual figure and, therefore, must be divided by 2 to arrive at a semiannual rate applicable to the price calculation for semiannual-pay bonds.

The YTC calculation differs from the YTM derivation in two important respects. First, the call date precedes the maturity date; therefore, the discounting period is shorter. Second, the call price is generally above par value; therefore, the final principal payment may be larger than if the bond was retired at par at final maturity.

---

[4] The differences between yields and returns are discussed at length in Chapter 10.

As an illustration, assume that an investor can purchase a 10% coupon, 10-year General Motors Acceptance Corporation (GMAC) bond at 116.00. The bond is callable at 105.00 in 5 years. The bond's yield to call works out to 7.00%:

$$\text{bond price} = \sum_{t=1}^{10} \frac{\text{CF}_t}{\left(1 + \dfrac{\text{YTC}}{2}\right)^t}$$

$$= \sum_{t=1}^{10} \frac{\text{CPN}_t}{\left(1 + \dfrac{\text{YTC}}{2}\right)^t} + \frac{P_{10}}{\left(1 + \dfrac{\text{YTC}}{2}\right)^{10}}$$

$$\$1,160.00 = \sum_{t=1}^{10} \frac{\$50.00}{\left(1 + \dfrac{\text{YTC}}{2}\right)^t} + \frac{\$1,050.00}{\left(1 + \dfrac{\text{YTC}}{2}\right)^{10}}$$

The YTC solves to 0.070 or 7.00%. Exhibit 3–4 summarizes the mathematics behind the 7.00% discount rate calculation. For comparative purposes, Exhibit 3–5 shows that at a 116.00 price, the bond bears a YTM of 7.68%. The YTM rate assumes, of course, that the bond will not be called away 5 years hence and that the bond's premium can be amortized over the (longer) 10-year maturity period.

The YTC measure is valuable in assessing the relative prices of callable bonds that are traded at dollar prices above the *crossover price*. At this price, the bond's YTM and YTC are identical. The yield corresponding to the crossover price is appropriately termed the *crossover yield*. Given that the call price (105.00) lies above the par value (100.00), the crossover price exceeds the call price by a modest margin. The bond trades to the *worst case* (i.e., the lower) yield. In sum:

Bond Price	*Yield Relationship*
Above crossover price	YTC < YTM
At crossover price	YTC = YTM
Below crossover price	YTC > YTM

Given that the bond trades to the lower yield, at prices above the crossover mark, the bond is treated on a YTC basis. At prices below the crossover threshold, the bond is regarded as a maturing issue and is traded on a YTM basis.

Exhibit 3–4. Calculation of the price of a 10% coupon, 10-year GMAC bond (callable in 5 years at $1,050.00) assuming early call and a 7.00% YTC rate.

End of Period t	(1) Cash Flow, CF_t	(2) PV Factor	(3) = (1) × (2) $PV(CF_t)$
1	$ 50.00	0.9662	$ 48.31
2	50.00	0.9335	46.68
3	50.00	0.9019	45.10
4	50.00	0.8714	43.57
5	50.00	0.8420	42.10
6	50.00	0.8135	40.68
7	50.00	0.7860	39.30
8	50.00	0.7594	37.97
9	50.00	0.7337	36.69
10	50.00	0.7089	35.45
10	1,050.00	0.7089	744.35
		Total PV →	$1,160.00
			↑ Bond price

Comments: *Cash flows are semiannual coupons of $50.00 ($1,000.00 par × 0.10 × ½) and a final principal repayment of $1,050.00 (call price). The present value factors are calculated as 1/(1 + 0.07/2) or 1/(1 + 0.035).*

For example, the 10% coupon, 10-year GMAC bond of earlier reference carries a crossover price of 108.25 and a corresponding crossover yield of 8.745% (see Exhibit 3–6). At prices below 108.25, the bond is traded to the maturity date at a (worst case) YTM rate. At prices in excess of 108.25, the bond is viewed on a call date basis and is traded on a (worst case) YTC assumption.[5] As time passes, of course, the crossover price falls. For example, with 7 years remaining to maturity (2 years remaining to call), the crossover price is 106.50 (crossover yield = 8.74%).

---

[5] In reality, market participants may treat the bond differently as a result of the level of market volatility and the sentiment regarding the future direction of interest rates. Additionally, option valuation techniques can be applied to callable bonds to assess the relative attractiveness of the issue. Rather than assigning a discrete "yes" or "no" to the occurrence of an early call, an option model uses a *probability* of early call, which can range between 0 and 100% (see the discussion of call-adjusted yield later in this chapter).

Exhibit 3–5. Calculation of the price of a 10% coupon, 10-year GMAC bond (callable in 5 years at $1,050.00) at a 7.68% YTM rate.

End of Period t	(1) Cash Flow, CF_t	(2) PV Factor	(3) = (1) × (2) $PV(CF_t)$
1	$ 50.00	0.9630	$ 48.15
2	50.00	0.9274	46.37
3	50.00	0.8931	44.66
4	50.00	0.8601	43.01
5	50.00	0.8283	41.42
6	50.00	0.7976	39.88
7	50.00	0.7682	38.41
8	50.00	0.7397	36.99
9	50.00	0.7124	35.62
10	50.00	0.6860	34.30
11	50.00	0.6607	33.04
12	50.00	0.6362	31.81
13	50.00	0.6127	30.64
14	50.00	0.5901	29.51
15	50.00	0.5682	28.41
16	50.00	0.5472	27.36
17	50.00	0.5270	26.35
18	50.00	0.5075	25.38
19	50.00	0.4887	24.44
20	50.00	0.4707	23.54
20	1,000.00	0.4707	470.70
		Total PV →	$1,160.00
			↑ Bond price

Comments: *Cash flows are semiannual coupons of $50.00 ($1,000.00 par × 0.10 × ½) and a final principal repayment of $1,000.00 par. The present value factors are calculated as 1/(1 + 0.0768/2) or 1/(1 + 0.0384).*

Observation: *A bond's yield to call is the discount rate that equates the present value of the bond's future cash flows received through a specified call date to the bond's current market price.*

Yield to average life

Yield to average life (YTAL) can be used to analyze bonds with a series of principal repayments (e.g., sinking fund bonds, mortgage-

Exhibit 3–6. YTM and YTC on a 10% coupon, 10-year GMAC bond with a 5-year call at 105.00. The YTM and YTC are equal at the *crossover price.*

	Bond Price	YTM (%)		YTC (%)
	100.00	10.00		10.78
	101.00	9.84		10.52
	102.00	9.68		10.27
	103.00	9.53		10.02
	104.00	9.38		9.77
	105.00	9.22		9.52
	106.00	9.08		9.28
	107.00	8.93		9.04
	108.00	8.78		8.80
Crossover Price	108.25	8.745	=	8.745
	109.00	8.64		8.57
	110.00	8.50		8.34
	111.00	8.36		8.11
	112.00	8.22		7.89
	113.00	8.08		7.66
	114.00	7.95		7.44
	115.00	7.81		7.22
	116.00	7.68		7.00
	117.00	7.55		6.79
	118.00	7.42		6.58
	119.00	7.29		6.37
	120.00	7.17		6.16

Comments: *A callable bond trades to the lower yield in each pairing represented. The yield at which the YTM and YTC are equal is called the crossover yield, and the corresponding price at that yield is called the crossover price.*

backed securities). For simplicity, all principal repayments are assumed to occur on the average life date. The *average life* of a bond is the *weighted average maturity* (WAM) of the bond's principal repayments[6]:

---

[6] In future chapters, the average life will be referred to as the weighted average maturity (WAM). The average life (i.e., WAM) calculation should not be confused with the *weighted average life* (WAL) computation used with mortgage-backed securities. The WAL *does* consider the coupon cash flows in addition to the principal cash flows. The WAL derivation is discussed in Chapter 5 in the guise of a *weighted average cash flow* (WACF).

$$\text{average life (years)} = \sum_{t=a}^{n} \left(\frac{P_t}{\text{TPCF}} \times t \right)$$

where

P_t = principal cash flow received (per bond) in year t

TPCF = total principal cash flow to be repaid per bond (typically, $1,000.00)

t = time period (years)

a = date of the first principal repayment (years)

n = final maturity (years)

The YTAL measure is intended to allow comparability between a sinking fund bond (or mortgage-backed security) and a typical *bullet bond* that repays principal in one lump sum at maturity.[7] The YTAL views the average life date as the final maturity date for the bond. That is, the YTAL is simply an IRR to the average life date:

$$\text{bond price} = \sum_{t=1}^{n} \frac{\text{CF}_t}{\left(1 + \dfrac{\text{YTAL}}{2}\right)^t}$$

$$= \sum_{t=1}^{n} \frac{\text{CPN}_t}{\left(1 + \dfrac{\text{YTAL}}{2}\right)^t} + \frac{P_n}{\left(1 + \dfrac{\text{YTAL}}{2}\right)^n}$$

where n is the number of semiannual periods to the average life date. All principal repayments (P_n) are assumed to be made on the average life date.

For example, assume that an investor can purchase a 4% coupon, 10-year IBM sinking fund debenture at 87.07. The issue has a 90% sinker, with sinking fund payments commencing at the end of the first year and paying down 10% of the bonds annually through the ninth year. In the final year (Year 10), IBM redeems the remaining 10% of

---

[7] A *bullet bond* is a noncallable bond devoid of any sinking fund provisions. It should be noted that a cash flow yield measure is always preferable to a YTAL measure. A *cash flow yield* is the representative internal rate of return (IRR) of a sinking fund or mortgage-backed bond. For sinking fund bonds with market, rather than pro-rata, sinkers, additional considerations must be made regarding the timing of sinking fund receipts.

the bonds. All principal repayments are made at par value.[8] The investor calculates the average life on the IBM issue as follows:

$$\text{average life}_{IBM} = \sum_{t=1}^{10} \left(\frac{P_t}{\text{TPCF}} \times t \right)$$

$$= \left(\frac{\$100.00}{\$1,000.00} \times 1 \right) + \left(\frac{\$100.00}{\$1,000.00} \times 2 \right)$$

$$+ \left(\frac{\$100.00}{\$1,000.00} \times 3 \right) + \cdots + \left(\frac{\$100.00}{\$1,000.00} \times 10 \right)$$

$$= 0.10 + 0.20 + 0.30 + 0.40 + 0.50 + 0.60$$
$$+ 0.70 + 0.80 + 0.90 + 1.00$$

$$= 5.50 \text{ years}$$

The time periods of cash receipt are weighted according to the relative size of the principal repayment in that time period. Notice that the coupon cash flows generated by a bond play no role in the average life computation. The yield to average life (YTAL) is calculated as

$$\text{bond price} = \sum_{t=1}^{11} \frac{CF_t}{\left(1 + \dfrac{\text{YTAL}}{2} \right)^t}$$

$$= \sum_{t=1}^{11} \frac{CPN_t}{\left(1 + \dfrac{\text{YTAL}}{2} \right)^t} + \frac{P_n}{\left(1 + \dfrac{\text{YTAL}}{2} \right)^n}$$

$$= \frac{\$20.00}{\left(1 + \dfrac{\text{YTAL}}{2} \right)^1} + \frac{\$20.00}{\left(1 + \dfrac{\text{YTAL}}{2} \right)^2} + \cdots + \frac{\$20.00}{\left(1 + \dfrac{\text{YTAL}}{2} \right)^{10}}$$

$$+ \frac{\$1,020.00}{\left(1 + \dfrac{\text{YTAL}}{2} \right)^{11}}$$

[8] The *percentage sinker* (in this case, 90%) is simply the total percentage of the bonds retired prior to the final maturity date. The principal payment at maturity is commonly called the *balloon payment*, or simply, the *balloon*. Unless otherwise indicated, all sinking fund payments are made at par (face) value.

Exhibit 3–7. Calculation of the price of a 4% coupon, 10-year IBM sinking fund debenture priced to yield 6.86% to its 5½-year average life.

End of Period t	(1) Cash Flow, CF_t	(2) PV Factor	(3) = (1) × (2) $PV(CF_t)$
1	$ 20.00	0.9668	$ 19.34
2	20.00	0.9348	18.70
3	20.00	0.9038	18.08
4	20.00	0.8738	17.48
5	20.00	0.8448	16.90
6	20.00	0.8168	16.34
7	20.00	0.7897	15.79
8	20.00	0.7635	15.27
9	20.00	0.7382	14.76
10	20.00	0.7137	14.27
11	20.00	0.6901	13.80
11	1,000.00	0.6901	690.10
		Total PV →	$870.70
			↑ Bond price

Comments: *Cash flows are semiannual coupons of $20.00 ($1,000.00 par × 0.04 × ½) and a final principal repayment of $1,000.00 par. The present value factors are calculated as $1/(1 + 0.0686/2)$ or $1/(1 + 0.0343)$.*

The YTAL solves to 0.0686 or 6.86% (verified in Exhibit 3–7). In essence, the IBM 4% issue is roughly comparable to a bullet bond trading at a 6.86% YTM and maturing in 5½ years.

A current-coupon IBM 7% sinking fund debenture with a similar 90% sinking fund schedule trades at 100.00 for a 7.00% yield to a 5½-year average life (see Exhibit 3–8). A high coupon IBM 10% issue maturing in 10 years with the same sinking fund provisions is priced at 112.92. The 10% coupon issue bears a 7.12% yield to its 5½-year average life (see Exhibit 3–9). In all three cases, the YTAL assumes that all principal repayments occur on the average life date.

Observation: *The yield to average life measure can be applied to sinking fund bonds and mortgage-backed securities. The YTAL is, essentially, a YTM to the average life date. An assumed maturity date serves as the point at which all principal repayments are made.*

Exhibit 3–8. Calculation of the price of a 7% coupon, 10-year IBM sinking fund debenture priced to yield 7.00% to its 5½-year average life.

End of Period t	(1) *Cash Flow,* CF_t	(2) *PV Factor*	(3) = (1) × (2) $PV(CF_t)$
1	$ 35.00	0.9662	$ 33.82
2	35.00	0.9335	32.67
3	35.00	0.9019	31.57
4	35.00	0.8714	30.50
5	35.00	0.8420	29.47
6	35.00	0.8135	28.47
7	35.00	0.7860	27.51
8	35.00	0.7594	26.58
9	35.00	0.7337	25.68
10	35.00	0.7089	24.81
11	35.00	0.6849	23.97
11	1,000.00	0.6849	684.90
		Total PV →	$1,000.00
			↑ Bond price

Comments: *Cash flows are semiannual coupons of $35.00 ($1,000.00 par × 0.10 × ½) and a final principal repayment of $1,000.00 par. The present value factors are calculated as $1/(1 + 0.07/2)$ or $1/(1 + 0.035)$.*

Cash flow yield

A *cash flow yield* is the single discount rate that equates the present value of all of a bond's future cash flows to final maturity (e.g., coupons, sinking fund payments, mortgage prepayments) to the bond's current market price. The cash flow yield is also called the *discounted cash flow (DCF) yield*. For a sinking fund bond, the DCF yield is a more accurate reflection of the bond's yield than the YTM or the YTAL of the issue. The DCF yield is calculated as

$$\text{bond price} = \sum_{t=1}^{n} \frac{CF_t}{\left(1 + \dfrac{DCF}{2}\right)^t}$$

Exhibit 3–9. Calculation of the price of a 10% coupon, 10-year IBM sinking fund debenture priced to yield 7.12% to its 5½-year average life.

End of Period t	(1) Cash Flow, CF_t	(2) PV Factor	(3) = (1) × (2) PV(CF_t)
1	$ 50.00	0.9656	$ 48.28
2	50.00	0.9324	46.62
3	50.00	0.9004	45.02
4	50.00	0.8694	43.47
5	50.00	0.8395	41.98
6	50.00	0.8107	40.54
7	50.00	0.7828	39.14
8	50.00	0.7559	37.80
9	50.00	0.7299	36.50
10	50.00	0.7048	35.24
11	50.00	0.6806	34.03
11	1,000.00	0.6806	680.60
		Total PV →	$1,129.20
			↑ Bond price

Comments: *Cash flows are semiannual coupons of $50.00 ($1,000.00 par × 0.10 × ½) and a final principal repayment of $1,000.00 par. The present value factors are calculated as 1/(1 + 0.0712/2) or 1/(1 + 0.0356).*

The DCF yield for a bullet bond is simply its YTM. For a bond with principal repayments received over a period of time, rather than at one point in the future, the DCF yield is the internal rate of return of the bond. The computation of DCF yield differs from the YTM calculation in that the periodic cash flows lack uniformity. Exhibit 3–10 walks through the DCF yield calculation for the 4% coupon, 10-year IBM sinking fund debenture alluded to earlier and priced at 87.07. The DCF yield solves to 7.00%. Exhibit 3–11 confirms the 7.00% DCF yield for the current-coupon 7% IBM bond priced at par. Exhibit 3–12 provides a similar review for the 10% coupon, 10-year IBM sinking fund bond priced at 112.92. Once again, a DCF yield of 7.00% is obtained.

Exhibit 3–13 examines the misleading nature of the YTAL by comparing the YTAL and DCF yields of the three IBM issues of earlier example. The table shows that the use of an average maturity can lead to spurious results. The YTAL of 6.86% for the low coupon 4% bond

Exhibit 3–10. Calculation of the price of a 4% coupon, 10-year IBM sinking fund debenture trading at a 7% DCF yield. The sinking fund retires 10% of the bonds annually, commencing at the end of the first year.

End of Period t	(1) P_t	(2) CPN_t	(3) = (1) + (2) Total Cash Flow, CF_t	(4) PV Factor	(5) = (3) × (4) $PV(CF_t)$
1		$20.00	$ 20.00	0.9662	$ 19.32
2	$100.00	20.00	120.00	0.9335	112.02
3		18.00	18.00	0.9019	16.23
4	100.00	18.00	118.00	0.8714	102.83
5		16.00	16.00	0.8420	13.47
6	100.00	16.00	116.00	0.8135	94.37
7		14.00	14.00	0.7860	11.00
8	100.00	14.00	114.00	0.7594	86.57
9		12.00	12.00	0.7337	8.80
10	100.00	12.00	112.00	0.7089	79.40
11		10.00	10.00	0.6849	6.85
12	100.00	10.00	110.00	0.6618	72.80
13		8.00	8.00	0.6394	5.12
14	100.00	8.00	108.00	0.6178	66.72
15		6.00	6.00	0.5969	3.58
16	100.00	6.00	106.00	0.5767	61.13
17		4.00	4.00	0.5572	2.23
18	100.00	4.00	104.00	0.5384	55.99
19		2.00	2.00	0.5202	1.04
20	100.00	2.00	102.00	0.5026	51.27
				Total PV →	$870.70
					↑ Bond price

Comments: *Cash flows are semiannual coupons of 4% of the remaining principal balance and sinking fund payments of 10% of the original principal annually for 10 years. The present value factors are calculated as $1/(1 + 0.07/2)$ or $1/(1 + 0.035)$.*

underestimates the true yield by 14 basis points; the YTAL of the higher coupon 10% bond is a 12-basis-point overestimate of the true yield. These differences become more significant (1) the more dispersed the principal repayments, and (2) the more the bond's price deviates from par.

Exhibit 3–11. Calculation of the price of a 7% coupon, 10-year IBM sinking fund debenture trading at a 7% DCF yield. The sinking fund retires 10% of the bonds annually, commencing at the end of the first year.

End of Period t	(1) P_t	(2) CPN_t	(3) = (1) + (2) Total Cash Flow, CF_t	(4) PV Factor	(5) = (3) × (4) $PV(CF_t)$
1		$35.00	$ 35.00	0.9662	$ 33.82
2	$100.00	35.00	135.00	0.9335	126.02
3		31.50	31.50	0.9019	28.41
4	100.00	31.50	131.50	0.8714	114.59
5		28.00	28.00	0.8420	23.58
6	100.00	28.00	128.00	0.8135	104.13
7		24.50	24.50	0.7860	19.26
8	100.00	24.50	124.50	0.7594	94.55
9		21.00	21.00	0.7337	15.41
10	100.00	21.00	121.00	0.7089	85.78
11		17.50	17.50	0.6849	11.99
12	100.00	17.50	117.50	0.6618	77.76
13		14.00	14.00	0.6394	8.95
14	100.00	14.00	114.00	0.6178	70.43
15		10.50	10.50	0.5969	6.27
16	100.00	10.50	110.50	0.5767	63.73
17		7.00	7.00	0.5572	3.90
18	100.00	7.00	107.00	0.5384	57.61
19		3.50	3.50	0.5202	1.82
20	100.00	3.50	103.50	0.5026	52.02
			Total PV →		$1,000.00
					↑
					Bond price

Comments: *Cash flows are semiannual coupons of 7% of the remaining principal balance and sinking fund payments of 10% of the original principal annually for 10 years. The present value factors are calculated as $1/(1 + 0.07/2)$ or $1/(1 + 0.035)$.*

Observation: *A cash flow yield is the internal rate of return of a bond. This yield measure is commonly applied to sinking fund bonds and mortgage-backed securities. When applied to the bond's future cash flow stream, the cash flow yield generates a total present value equal to the bond's current market price.*

Exhibit 3–12. Calculation of the price of a 10% coupon, 10-year IBM sinking fund debenture trading at a 7% DCF yield. The sinking fund retires 10% of the bonds annually, commencing at the end of the first year.

End of Period t	(1) P_t	(2) CPN_t	(3) = (1) + (2) Total Cash Flow, CF_t	(4) PV Factor	(5) = (3) × (4) $PV(CF_t)$
1		$50.00	$ 50.00	0.9662	$ 48.31
2	$100.00	50.00	150.00	0.9335	140.03
3		45.00	45.00	0.9019	40.59
4	100.00	45.00	145.00	0.8714	126.35
5		40.00	40.00	0.8420	33.68
6	100.00	40.00	140.00	0.8135	113.89
7		35.00	35.00	0.7860	27.51
8	100.00	35.00	135.00	0.7594	102.52
9		30.00	30.00	0.7337	22.01
10	100.00	30.00	130.00	0.7089	92.16
11		25.00	25.00	0.6849	17.12
12	100.00	25.00	125.00	0.6618	82.73
13		20.00	20.00	0.6394	12.79
14	100.00	20.00	120.00	0.6178	74.14
15		15.00	15.00	0.5969	8.95
16	100.00	15.00	115.00	0.5767	66.32
17		10.00	10.00	0.5572	5.57
18	100.00	10.00	110.00	0.5384	59.22
19		5.00	5.00	0.5202	2.60
20	100.00	5.00	105.00	0.5026	52.77

Total PV → $1,129.20
↑
Bond price

Comments: *Cash flows are semiannual coupons of 10% of the remaining principal balance and sinking fund payments of 10% of the original principal annually for 10 years. The present value factors are calculated as 1/(1 + 0.07/2) or 1/(1 + 0.035).*

Modified versions of the yield to maturity

Call-adjusted yield

A *callable bond* can be thought of as a combination of a *noncallable bond* and a short position in a *call option*. When an investor purchases

Exhibit 3–13. Yield comparison of three IBM sinking fund issues (data compiled from Exhibits 3–7 through 3–12).

Issue	Yield Measure (%)	
	YTAL	DCF Yield
4% coupon IBM issue	6.86	7.00
7% coupon IBM issue	7.00	7.00
10% coupon IBM issue	7.12	7.00

a callable bond, the investor gives the issuer the right (i.e., the option) to call the bond away at a specified price (or series of prices) over a specified period. If interest rates decline significantly, the issuer will exercise that right and leave the investor in the unfavorable position of reinvesting the redemption proceeds in a lower yielding environment. Consequently, an investor is willing to pay more for a noncallable issue than for a callable issue that implicitly sells the early redemption privilege to the issuer:

$$\begin{matrix} \text{noncallable bond's} \\ \text{price} \end{matrix} = \begin{matrix} \text{callable bond's} \\ \text{price} \end{matrix} + \begin{matrix} \text{value of} \\ \text{the call option} \end{matrix}$$

Alternatively,

$$\begin{matrix} \text{callable bond's} \\ \text{price} \end{matrix} = \begin{matrix} \text{noncallable} \\ \text{bond's price} \end{matrix} - \begin{matrix} \text{value of} \\ \text{the call option} \end{matrix}$$

A callable bond, therefore, requires a price (and yield) adjustment in order to allow a proper comparison to a noncallable issue such as a U.S. Treasury bond.

For example, assume that Illinois Bell Telephone (IBT) can issue a 40-year debenture at an 8.00% YTM. The bond is callable in 5 years at 108.00, and the bond bears an 8% coupon and is priced at par. A comparable long-term U.S. Treasury bond yields 7.00%. It appears that the investor receives a 1% (100BP) premium for assuming the credit risk of IBT. If the call option is valued at 7.50 points, however, the investor garners only 41BP in incremental yield for the credit risk under-taken in holding the non-U.S. Treasury issue:

$$\text{noncallable bond's price} = \frac{\text{callable bond's}}{\text{price}} + \frac{\text{value of}}{\text{the call option}}$$

$$= 100.00 + 7.50$$

$$= 107.50$$

YTM at a 100.00 bond price = 8.00%   (quoted yield)

YTM at a 107.50 bond price = 7.41%   (call-adjusted yield)

Adjusting the callable bond's price upward by the amount of the call option value allows one to create the equivalent price of a noncallable issue.[9] The *call-adjusted yield* (CAY) is simply the YTM at the *grossed-up,* noncallable equivalent bond price. The CAY lies below the YTM because of the value of the call option to the issuer. In this case the option is worth 7.50 and a 40-year, 8% coupon noncallable IBT issue would, theoretically speaking, trade at 107.50.

The CAY shows the investor the true incremental yield advantage offered for the added credit risk implicit in a non-Treasury issue. In the IBT example, the investor receives only 41 basis points in additional yield (7.41% CAY versus 7.00% YTM on U.S. Treasuries), which may or may not be an adequate compensation for the incremental risk incurred. Clearly, the CAY measure casts a whole new light on corporate bond valuation assessments.

> **Observation:** *A call-adjusted yield is the YTM of an equivalent non-callable bond of identical features. The callable bond's price is grossed up to a noncallable bond equivalent price in order to derive the CAY figure. The upward price adjustment is simply the value of the call option as derived by an option pricing model.*

Realized compound yield

As an internal rate of return, the YTM assumes that all coupon cash flows are reinvested at the YTM rate and the bond is held to maturity and redeemed at par. The *realized compound yield* (RCY) measure relaxes

---

[9] The reader is encouraged to consult texts on option pricing for further elaboration. The intent here is merely to make the reader aware of the limited usefulness of the YTM as a yield measure for callable bonds. Putable bonds require that the value of the put option be *subtracted* from the bond price in order to calculate an *adjusted yield* comparable to a security devoid of put features.

Exhibit 3–14. Realized compound yields on a 7% coupon, 30-year U.S. Treasury bond under several reinvestment rate assumptions and a 30-year holding period. The bond is originally purchased at par to yield 7.00% to maturity.

Actual Reinvestment Rate (%)	Realized Compound Yield (%)
4.00	5.43
7.00	7.00
10.00	8.83

the rigid assumptions underlying the YTM concept. The RCY is, essentially, the YTM rate adjusted for:

1. The actual reinvestment rate(s) realized.

2. The actual sale price of the bond, if sold prior to maturity.

The YTM is a special version of the RCY where the bond is held to maturity (and retired at par) and the coupons are all reinvested at the same rate (the YTM rate).

The RCY can be defined as the discount rate that equates the total future value of a bond's stream of cash flows [using a specified reinvestment rate(s) and ending bond price] to the bond's current market price. The RCY is the bond's expected future total return expressed in a semiannually compounded fashion to allow comparability between various issues.[10]

As an illustration, Exhibit 3–14 examines the difference between YTM and RCY for a long maturity U.S. Treasury bond. By altering the actual reinvestment rate experienced, the actual YTM (or RCY) gravitates toward the reinvestment rate. For a 30-year, 7% coupon U.S. Treasury bond purchased at par, the RCY is only 5.43% if coupons are reinvested at 4%. The RCY surges to 8.83% in an environment of 10% reinvestment rates. At a 7% reinvestment rate, the RCY coincides with the YTM rate of 7.00%. For a bond held to maturity, the RCY must lie between the YTM and the reinvestment rate. The longer the investment horizon, the more the RCY is tugged toward the reinvestment rate. This phenomenon occurs because of the dominance of the reinvestment component of total return over long holding periods.[11]

---

[10] The calculations underlying realized compound yield are detailed in Chapter 8.

[11] The components of total return are discussed in Chapter 8.

Exhibit 3–15. Realized compound yields on a 7% coupon, 30-year U.S. Treasury bond held for 1 year under several interest rate environments. The bond is originally purchased at par to yield 7.00% to maturity.

Interest Rate Environment	Interest Rate Level at Year-End (%)	Assumed Reinvestment Rate (%)	Bond Price at Year-End	RCY (%)
Falling rates	6.00	6.50	113.67	19.80
Stable rates	7.00	7.00	100.00	7.00
Rising rates	8.00	7.50	88.79	−4.13

Exhibit 3–15 summarizes the RCYs for the same 30-year U.S. Treasury bond under an early sale arrangement. Over shorter holding periods, the terminal bond price has a strong influence on the RCY. If interest rates rise, the bond price is pulled downward and the RCY is adversely affected. For example, if yields rise from 7% to 8% over a 1-year time horizon, the 30-year U.S. Treasury bond incurs a −4.13% RCY, a far cry from the bond's 7.00% starting yield. A 100BP decline in rates instills a positive bias in the RCY, and it surges to 19.80%. Only under a stable interest rate environment does the RCY offer no surprises.

> **Observation:** *A realized compound yield is the compounded total return of a bond. The RCY reflects the actual cash flows generated by the bond over the assumed investment period.*

Summary

A variety of bond yield measures are encountered by bond market participants. Each yield concept applies to a slightly different cash flow structure or investment situation. A bond's *current yield* is simply the annual percentage return attributable to the bond's coupon cash flow. *Yield to maturity* is used on noncallable bonds and on callable bonds trading on a maturity date basis. The *yield to call* measure is applicable to callable bonds trading on a call date basis. The *yield to average life* serves as an estimate of the internal rate of return on a sinking fund bond or a mortgage-backed security. A *cash flow yield* represents the internal rate of return of a bond with sinking fund or other principal prepayment features. A *call-adjusted yield* is applied to callable bonds. The CAY is the implied YTM of an equivalent noncallable bond. The CAY is intended to allow comparability between callable and noncallable issues. The *realized compound yield* measure relaxes the rigid assumptions of an IRR (e.g., the YTM) in order to arrive at a more representative proxy of a bond's total return in either historical or projected form.

THE FUNDAMENTALS OF BOND RISK

The Volatility of Bond Prices

This chapter introduces the section of the book on the *Fundamentals of Bond Risk*.[1] Chapter 4 examines the causal factors explaining bond price volatility.[2] Chapters 5 and 6 outline the commonly used measures of bond risk from the past and from the present, respectively. Chapter 7 introduces several new proxies for bond risk that may eventually supplant the measures currently in vogue.

Analysis of bond price volatility stems from Chapter 2's discussion of the inverse relationship between bond prices and bond yields.[3] Exhibit

---

[1] The focus of these chapters is on a bond's price risk given an instantaneous change in yield. There are other risks that should be considered, such as credit risk, call risk, liquidity risk, and sector risk. These risks are addressed in Chapters 14 and 15.

The book illustrations typically cover interest rate levels ranging from 4 to 10%. Although not observed in the U.S. markets for over 20 years, 4% bond yields are found in some of the foreign bond markets. In this sense, the book is applicable to a reasonably wide range of interest rate environments and a broad spectrum of financial markets.

[2] Throughout the text, *volatility* is used in a *price sensitivity* sense. The terms volatility and sensitivity are used interchangeably. The sensitivity of a bond's price to an absolute basis point change (not a percentage change) in yield is the focus of discussion. If nonparallel yield shifts occur, volatility and price sensitivity may diverge. However, given the general assumption of parallel yield shifts underlying the preponderance of bond risk measures, the nonparallel aspects are deferred to Chapters 14 and 15.

[3] Unless otherwise indicated, the terms *yield* and *yield to maturity* are used interchangeably.

Exhibit 4–1. Inverse relationship between a bond's price and a bond's yield to maturity.

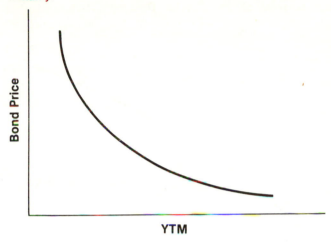

4–1 displays the typical shape of a price:yield curve. Recall the formula relating a bond's price to its yield:

$$\text{bond price} = \sum_{t=1}^{n} \frac{CF_t}{\left(1 + \dfrac{YTM}{2}\right)^t}$$

It naturally follows that there are only three factors that can affect a bond's price:

1. The term to maturity of the bond (n compounding periods).
2. The coupon rate of the bond. The coupon rate dictates the size of the periodic cash flows (CF_t) received.[4]
3. The yield to maturity of the bond (YTM). The YTM rate determines the present value of the bond's future cash flows.

Each of these factors is discussed in terms of the magnitude of its effect on a bond's price given a general movement in the level of interest rates.

---

[4] For sinking fund or mortgage-backed bonds, the distribution of the principal repayments must also be considered in the assessment of the stream of periodic cash flows.

Exhibit 4–2. Bond price volatility as a function of a bond's term to maturity. Issues displayed are 7% coupon U.S. Treasuries priced initially at par to yield 7.00%. Interest rates fall 300BP to 4.00%. (Data per Exhibit 4–4.)

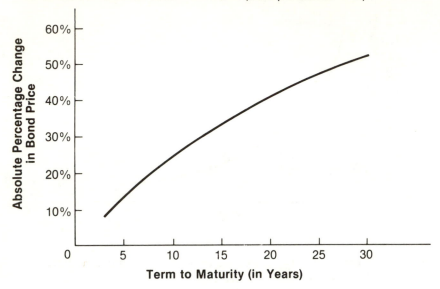

The impact of the term to maturity

A bond's price volatility and its term to maturity are directly linked.[5] Exhibit 4–2 provides a graphical presentation of this relationship for 7% coupon U.S. Treasury bonds of short (3-year), intermediate (10-year), and long (30-year) maturities in an environment of falling interest rates. Exhibit 4–3 illustrates the same issues in a scenario of rising interest rates. Both figures show that for a given change in yield level (300BP in this case), longer maturity bonds experience greater percentage price changes than do shorter maturity issues.

Exhibit 4–4 summarizes the supporting data for 3-year, 10-year, and 30-year maturity U.S. Treasury bonds in a 7.00% yield environment. Given a 300BP decline in yields to the 4.00% level, the 3-year bond garners an 8.40% price return. The 10-year issue registers almost three times as much return (24.53%) and the 30-year security provides a sizable 52.14% return. The volatility knife is double-edged, however. In an environment of rising rates of comparable magnitude (+300BP), long

---

[5] For sinking fund or mortgage-backed issues, the weighted average maturity is a more appropriate measure of a bond's representative *maturity*.

Exhibit 4–3. Bond price volatility as a function of a bond's term to maturity. Issues displayed are 7% coupon U.S. Treasuries priced initially at par to yield 7.00%. Interest rates rise 300BP to 10.00%. (Data per Exhibit 4–4.)

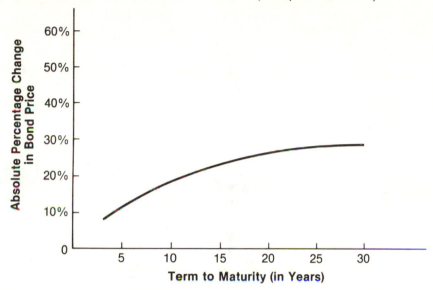

maturity bonds endure sizable price declines of 28.39%, while 10-year issues decline 18.69% and short maturity issues suffer only modest depreciations of 7.61%. In both environments, the absolute amount of price volatility is greater for longer maturity bonds. Graphically speaking, the price:yield curve is steeper for longer maturity issues than for shorter maturity issues (see Exhibit 4–5).[6]

> **Observation:** *Long maturity bonds are more price sensitive than short maturity bonds.*

The rationale behind bond price sensitivity: A 3-year bond

The time value of money concepts presented in Chapter 1 explain why longer maturity issues have more price volatility than shorter maturity issues. Exhibit 4–6 derives the price of a 3-year maturity bond at a YTM of 7.00%. Given a coupon rate of 7%, the price is calculated to

---

[6] Long maturity issues own price:yield curves that are more convex, or cup-shaped, than shorter maturity issues. Convexity is discussed in Chapter 6.

Exhibit 4–4. Bond price volatility as a function of the term to maturity, using 7% coupon U.S. Treasury bonds priced initially at par to yield 7.00%.

Issue	YTM (%)	Bond Price	Percent Change in Price
	4.00	108.40	+ 8.40
	5.00	105.51	+ 5.51
	6.00	102.71	+ 2.71
3-Year Bond	**7.00**	**100.00**	
	8.00	97.38	− 2.62
	9.00	94.84	− 5.16
	10.00	92.39	− 7.61
	4.00	124.53	+24.53
	5.00	115.59	+15.59
	6.00	107.44	+ 7.44
10-Year Bond	**7.00**	**100.00**	
	8.00	93.20	− 6.80
	9.00	86.99	−13.01
	10.00	81.31	−18.69
	4.00	152.14	+52.14
	5.00	130.91	+30.91
	6.00	113.84	+13.84
30-Year Bond	**7.00**	**100.00**	
	8.00	88.69	−11.31
	9.00	79.36	−20.64
	10.00	71.61	−28.39

Comments: *Long maturity bonds are more volatile than short maturity bonds; under smaller magnitudes of yield change, the effects are less dramatic.*

be $1,000.00. The present value of the principal payment at maturity (column 5) accounts for 81.35% of the bond's price.

Exhibit 4–7 illustrates the impact of a yield decline to 4.00%: the 3-year bond increases $84.00 in price to $1,084.00. The surge in principal value from $813.50 to $888.00 accounts for 90% of the price appreciation. This specific benefit can be attributed to the more dramatic rise in the long PV factor (for $t = 6$, $PV_{2\%} = 0.8880$ versus $PV_{3\frac{1}{2}\%} = 0.8135$) over the marginal change in shorter PV factors (e.g., for $t = 1$, $PV_{2\%} = 0.9804$ versus $PV_{3\frac{1}{2}\%} = 0.9662$).

Exhibit 4–8 analyzes a rising interest rate environment, pricing the 3-year bond to yield 10.0%. Once again, the longer PV factors experience the greatest degree of change. For $t = 6$, the PV factor

Exhibit 4–5. Price:yield curves for 3-year, 10-year, and 30-year maturity U.S. Treasury bonds. (Data per Exhibit 4–4.)

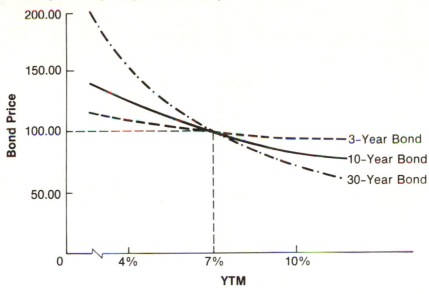

falls from 0.8135 to 0.7462 as rates rise from 7 to 10%. For $t = 1$, the PV factor falls from 0.9662 to 0.9524 given the same market conditions. The loss (in present value terms) incurred by the (long) principal cash flow is the primary culprit behind the bond price decline from $1,000.00 to $923.90.

Exhibit 4–6. Calculation of the price of a 7% coupon, 3-year U.S. Treasury bond yielding 7.00% to maturity.

(1)	*(2)*	*(3)*	*(4) = (2) × (3)*	*(5) = (4)/Price*
				Relative
End of	*Cash Flow,*	*PV*		*Contribution*
Period t	*CF*$_t$	*Factor*	*PV(CF*$_t$*)*	*to Bond Price (%)*
1	$ 35.00	0.9662	$ 33.82	3.38
2	35.00	0.9335	32.67	3.27
3	35.00	0.9019	31.57	3.16
4	35.00	0.8714	30.50	3.05
5	35.00	0.8420	29.47	2.95
6	35.00	0.8135	28.47	2.85
6	1,000.00	0.8135	813.50	81.35
		Total PV →	$1,000.00	100.00
			↑	
			Bond price	

Exhibit 4–7. Calculation of the price of a 7% coupon, 3-year U.S. Treasury bond yielding 4.00% to maturity.

(1)	*(2)*	*(3)*	*(4) = (2) × (3)*	*(5) = (4)/Price*
				Relative
End of	*Cash Flow,*	*PV*		*Contribution*
Period t	CF_t	*Factor*	$PV(CF_t)$	*to Bond Price (%)*
1	$ 35.00	0.9804	$ 34.31	3.17
2	35.00	0.9612	33.64	3.10
3	35.00	0.9423	32.98	3.04
4	35.00	0.9238	32.33	2.98
5	35.00	0.9057	31.70	2.92
6	35.00	0.8880	31.08	2.87
6	1,000.00	0.8880	888.00	81.92
		Total PV →	$1,084.00	100.00

↑
Bond price

Indeed, if one observes a series of present value factors for a variety of interest rate scenarios (see Exhibit 4–9), one can easily conclude that longer factors (for large *n* discounting periods) are more sensitive than shorter factors to changes in yield (see Exhibit 4–10). It is not surprising, therefore, that a long maturity bond, having most of its cash

Exhibit 4–8. Calculation of the price of a 7% coupon, 3-year U.S. Treasury bond yielding 10.00% to maturity.

(1)	*(2)*	*(3)*	*(4) = (2) × (3)*	*(5) = (4)/Price*
				Relative
End of	*Cash Flow,*	*PV*		*Contribution*
Period t	CF_t	*Factor*	$PV(CF_t)$	*to Bond Price (%)*
1	$ 35.00	0.9524	$ 33.33	3.61
2	35.00	0.9070	31.75	3.44
3	35.00	0.8638	30.23	3.27
4	35.00	0.8227	28.79	3.12
5	35.00	0.7835	27.42	2.97
6	35.00	0.7462	26.12	2.83
6	1,000.00	0.7462	746.20	80.77
		Total PV →	$923.90	100.00

↑
Bond price

Exhibit 4–9. Present value factors under several interest rate environments (4%, 7%, 10%) assuming semiannual compounding.

Period t	*Present Value Factors for:*		
	i = 2.00%	i = 3.50%	i = 5.00%
1	0.9804	0.9662	0.9524
2	0.9612	0.9335	0.9070
3	0.9423	0.9019	0.8638
4	0.9238	0.8714	0.8227
5	0.9057	0.8420	0.7835
6	0.8880	0.8135	0.7462
.	.	.	.
.	.	.	.
.	.	.	.
18	0.7002	0.5384	0.4155
19	0.6864	0.5202	0.3957
20	0.6730	0.5026	0.3769
.	.	.	.
.	.	.	.
.	.	.	.
58	0.3171	0.1360	0.0590
59	0.3109	0.1314	0.0562
60	0.3048	0.1269	0.0535

flow weight occurring *after* the maturity of a short-term bond, is more price sensitive than the short maturity issue.

The rationale behind bond price sensitivity: A 10-year bond

Exhibits 4–11, 4–12, and 4–13 extend the analysis to a 10-year bond. The 7% coupon bond's price in a 7% yield environment is calculated at $1,000.00 in Exhibit 4–11. The 10-year bond's final principal payment, which accounts for just over 50% of the bond's price in a 7% rate scenario, surges to a 54.04% weight if rates fall to 4% (see Exhibit 4–12), and falls to a 46.35% contribution if rates rise to 10% (see Exhibit 4–13). Given the constancy of the $1,000.00 nominal principal repayment at the end of Year 10, the PV factor fluctuation lies behind the bond price surges and contractions. Additionally, the fact that only 18% of the 10-year bond's price is composed of cash flow received by the end of Year 3, it is hardly shocking that the 10-year bond is more volatile than the 3-year bond, whose entire cash flow stream is exhausted by the end of the third year. A greater proportion of cash flow received

Exhibit 4–10. Percentage change in PV factors for various compounding periods *t* if interest rates (1) fall by 300BP and (2) rise by 300BP from an initial yield level of 7.00%.

	Percent Change in PV Factor if:	
Period t	Rates Fall 300BP	Rates Rise 300BP
1	+ 1.47	− 1.43
2	+ 2.97	− 2.84
3	+ 4.48	− 4.22
4	+ 6.01	− 5.59
5	+ 7.57	− 6.95
6	+ 9.16	− 8.27
.	.	.
.	.	.
.	.	.
18	+ 30.05	−22.83
19	+ 31.95	−23.93
20	+ 33.90	−25.01
.	.	.
.	.	.
.	.	.
58	+233.16	−56.62
59	+236.61	−57.23
60	+240.19	−57.84

Exhibit 4–11. Calculation of the price of a 7% coupon, 10-year U.S. Treasury bond yielding 7.00% to maturity.

(1)	(2)	(3)	(4) = (2) × (3)	(5) = (4)/Price
				Relative
End of	Cash Flow,	PV		Contribution
Period t	CF_t	Factor	$PV(CF_t)$	to Bond Price (%)
1	$ 35.00	0.9662	$ 33.82	3.38
2	35.00	0.9335	32.67	3.27
3	35.00	0.9019	31.57	3.16
.	.	.	.	.
.	.	.	.	.
.	.	.	.	.
18	35.00	0.5384	18.84	1.88
19	35.00	0.5202	18.21	1.82
20	35.00	0.5026	17.59	1.76
20	1,000.00	0.5026	502.60	50.26
		Total PV →	$1,000.00	100.00
			↑	
			Bond price	

Exhibit 4–12. Calculation of the price of a 7% coupon, 10-year U.S. Treasury bond yielding 4.00% to maturity.

(1) End of Period t	(2) Cash Flow, CF_t	(3) PV Factor	(4) = (2) × (3) $PV(CF_t)$	(5) = (4)/Price Relative Contribution to Bond Price (%)
1	$ 35.00	0.9804	$ 34.31	2.76
2	35.00	0.9612	33.64	2.70
3	35.00	0.9423	32.98	2.65
.	.	.	.	.
.	.	.	.	.
.	.	.	.	.
18	35.00	0.7002	24.51	1.97
19	35.00	0.6864	24.02	1.93
20	35.00	0.6730	23.56	1.89
20	1,000.00	0.6730	673.00	54.04
		Total PV →	$1,245.30	100.00

Bond price

Exhibit 4–13. Calculation of the price of a 7% coupon, 10-year U.S. Treasury bond yielding 10.00% to maturity.

(1) End of Period t	(2) Cash Flow, CF_t	(3) PV Factor	(4) = (2) × (3) $PV(CF_t)$	(5) = (4)/Price Relative Contribution to Bond Price (%)
1	$ 35.00	0.9524	$ 33.33	4.10
2	35.00	0.9070	31.75	3.90
3	35.00	0.8638	30.23	3.72
.	.	.	.	.
.	.	.	.	.
.	.	.	.	.
18	35.00	0.4155	14.54	1.79
19	35.00	0.3957	13.85	1.70
20	35.00	0.3769	13.19	1.62
20	1,000.00	0.3769	376.90	46.35
		Total PV →	$813.10	100.00

Bond price

Exhibit 4–14. Calculation of the price of a 7% coupon, 30-year U.S. Treasury bond yielding 7.00% to maturity.

(1)	(2)	(3)	(4) = (2) × (3)	(5) = (4)/Price
				Relative
End of	*Cash Flow,*	*PV*		*Contribution*
Period t	*CF*$_t$	*Factor*	*PV(CF*$_t$*)*	*to Bond Price (%)*
1	$ 35.00	0.9662	$ 33.82	3.38
2	35.00	0.9335	32.67	3.27
3	35.00	0.9019	31.57	3.16
.	.	.	.	.
.	.	.	.	.
.	.	.	.	.
58	35.00	0.1360	4.76	0.48
59	35.00	0.1314	4.60	0.46
60	35.00	0.1269	4.44	0.44
60	1,000.00	0.1269	126.90	12.69
		Total PV →	$1,000.00	100.00

Bond price ↑

further into the future, combined with sizable increases in PV factor volatility, leads to greater price sensitivity in longer maturity issues.

The rationale behind bond price sensitivity: A 30-year bond

Exhibits 4–14, 4–15, and 4–16 further confirm the foregoing findings by assessing the price volatility of a 30-year bond. Since the 30-year issue receives approximately 50% of its cash flow (in present value terms) after 10 years, it is subject to a greater degree of price fluctuation than the shorter, 10-year maturity issue (recall Exhibit 4–4). Exhibit 4–14 details the price contributions made by the cash flows attached to the 30-year bond. The final principal repayment accounts for only 12.69% of the bond's price at a 7% yield. As rates decline, however, the longer cash flows surge in relative importance. Conversely, as interest rates rise, the longer cash flows suffer sizable declines in present value terms, dragging down the bond's price (Exhibit 4–16). The examples using short (3-year), intermediate (10-year), and long (30-year) maturity bonds drive home the underlying importance of the time value of money and the power of compounding/discounting in the pricing and repricing of fixed-income securities.

Exhibit 4–15. Calculation of the price of a 7% coupon, 30-year U.S. Treasury bond yielding 4.00% to maturity.

(1)	*(2)*	*(3)*	*(4) = (2) × (3)*	*(5) = (4)/Price*
				Relative
End of	*Cash Flow,*	*PV*		*Contribution*
Period t	*CF_t*	*Factor*	*$PV(CF_t)$*	*to Bond Price (%)*
1	$ 35.00	0.9804	$ 34.31	2.26
2	35.00	0.9612	33.64	2.21
3	35.00	0.9423	32.98	2.17
.	.	.	.	.
.	.	.	.	.
.	.	.	.	.
58	35.00	0.3171	11.10	0.73
59	35.00	0.3109	10.88	0.72
60	35.00	0.3048	10.67	0.70
60	1,000.00	0.3048	304.80	20.03
		Total PV →	$1,521.40	100.00

↑
Bond price

Exhibit 4–16. Calculation of the price of a 7% coupon, 30-year U.S. Treasury bond yielding 10.00% to maturity.

(1)	*(2)*	*(3)*	*(4) = (2) × (3)*	*(5) = (4)/Price*
				Relative
End of	*Cash Flow,*	*PV*		*Contribution*
Period t	*CF_t*	*Factor*	*$PV(CF_t)$*	*to Bond Price (%)*
1	$ 35.00	0.9524	$ 33.33	4.65
2	35.00	0.9070	31.75	4.43
3	35.00	0.8638	30.23	4.22
.	.	.	.	.
.	.	.	.	.
.	.	.	.	.
58	35.00	0.0590	2.07	0.29
59	35.00	0.0562	1.97	0.28
60	35.00	0.0535	1.87	0.26
60	1,000.00	0.0535	53.50	7.47
		Total PV →	$716.10	100.00

↑
Bond price

Observation: *The extreme sensitivity of long PV factors to changes in yield level is largely responsible for the higher degree of price volatility inherent in a long maturity bond. The extended maturities of a 30-year bond's cash flows explain the bond's inherently price-sensitive nature.*

The impact of the coupon rate

Bond price volatility is inversely related to a bond's coupon rate of interest. Exhibit 4–17 aggregates the price volatility figures for low coupon (4%), current-coupon (7%), and high coupon (10%) 30-year U.S. Trea-

Exhibit 4–17. Bond price volatility as a function of coupon rate, using 30-year maturity U.S. Treasury bonds priced initially to yield 7.00%.

Issue	*YTM (%)*	*Bond Price*	*Percent Change in Price*
	4.00	100.00	+59.80
	5.00	84.55	+35.11
	6.00	72.32	+15.56
4% Coupon Bond	**7.00**	**62.58**	
	8.00	54.75	−12.51
	9.00	48.40	−22.66
	10.00	43.21	−30.95
	4.00	152.14	+52.14
	5.00	130.91	+30.91
	6.00	113.84	+13.84
7% Coupon Bond	**7.00**	**100.00**	
	8.00	88.69	−11.31
	9.00	79.36	−20.64
	10.00	71.61	−28.39
	4.00	204.28	+48.65
	5.00	177.27	+29.00
	6.00	155.35	+13.05
10% Coupon Bond	**7.00**	**137.42**	
	8.00	122.62	−10.77
	9.00	110.32	−19.72
	10.00	100.00	−27.23

Comments: *For a given maturity, low coupon bonds are more volatile than high coupon bonds. Under smaller magnitudes of yield change, the effects are less dramatic.*

Exhibit 4–18. Bond price volatility as a function of a bond's coupon rate. Issues displayed are 30-year U.S. Treasuries priced initially to yield 7.00%. Interest rates fall 300BP to 4.00%. (Data per Exhibit 4–17.)

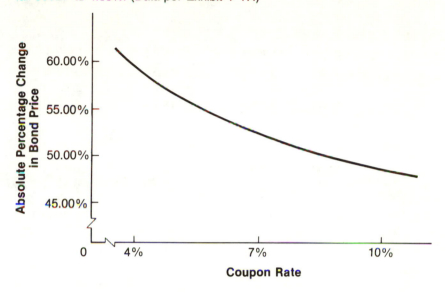

Exhibit 4–19. Bond price volatility as a function of a bond's coupon rate. Issues displayed are 30-year U.S. Treasuries priced initially to yield 7.00%. Interest rates rise 300BP to 10.00%. (Data per Exhibit 4–17.)

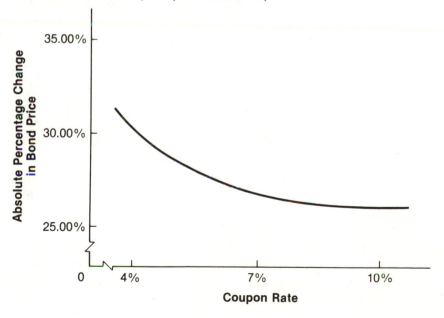

Exhibit 4–20. Calculation of the price of a 4% coupon, 30-year U.S. Treasury bond yielding 7.00% to maturity.

(1)	(2)	(3)	(4) = (2) × (3)	(5) = (4)/Price
				Relative
End of	Cash Flow,	PV		Contribution
Period t	CF$_t$	Factor	PV(CF$_t$)	to Bond Price (%)
1	$ 20.00	0.9662	$ 19.32	3.09
2	20.00	0.9335	18.67	2.98
3	20.00	0.9019	18.04	2.88
.	.	.	.	.
.	.	.	.	.
.	.	.	.	.
58	20.00	0.1360	2.72	0.43
59	20.00	0.1314	2.63	0.42
60	20.00	0.1269	2.54	0.41
60	1,000.00	0.1269	126.90	20.28
		Total PV →	$625.80	100.00

79.72% Coupon Component

20.28% Principal Component

↑
Bond price

sury bonds initially priced to yield 7.00%. Under a 300BP change in yields, the higher coupon (10%) bond exhibits less price volatility than that portrayed by the lower coupon issue. For example, if rates decline 300BP to 4%, the 10% coupon bond's 48.65% appreciation trails the 4% coupon bond's 59.80% price surge. Concomitantly, if rates rise 300BP to 10%, the 10% coupon security experiences a 27.23% decline in price, while the low coupon 4% issue suffers almost a 31% price fall. Exhibits 4–18 and 4–19 display the inverse relationship between coupon rate and bond price volatility for falling and rising interest rate scenarios, respectively.

The rationale behind the lesser price volatility of a high coupon issue is fairly straightforward. Coupon payments account for a greater proportion of a high coupon issue's total cash flow, in both nominal and present value terms, vis-à-vis a low coupon bond. The shorter maturity of these coupon cash flows (relative to the principal repayment) renders them inherently less price volatile.

Exhibits 4–20, 4–21, and 4–22 summarize the cash flow and discounting data for 4% coupon, 7% coupon, and 10% coupon 30-year U.S. Treasury bonds priced to yield 7.00%. The present value of future coupon cash flows accounts for 79.72% of the 4% bond's value and

Exhibit 4–21. Calculation of the price of a 7% coupon, 30-year U.S. Treasury bond yielding 7.00% to maturity.

(1)	*(2)*	*(3)*	*(4) = (2) × (3)*	*(5) = (4)/Price*	
				Relative	
End of	*Cash Flow,*	*PV*		*Contribution*	
Period t	CF_t	*Factor*	$PV(CF_t)$	*to Bond Price (%)*	
1	$ 35.00	0.9662	$ 33.82	3.38	
2	35.00	0.9335	32.67	3.27	
3	35.00	0.9019	31.57	3.16	
.	.	.	.	.	87.31%
.	.	.	.	.	Coupon
.	.	.	.	.	Component
58	35.00	0.1360	4.76	0.48	
59	35.00	0.1314	4.60	0.46	
60	35.00	0.1269	4.44	0.44	12.69%
60	1,000.00	0.1269	126.90	12.69 }	Principal
		Total PV →	$1,000.00	100.00	Component

↑
Bond price

Exhibit 4–22. Calculation of the price of a 10% coupon, 30-year U.S. Treasury bond yielding 7.00% to maturity.

(1)	*(2)*	*(3)*	*(4) = (2) × (3)*	*(5) = (4)/Price*	
				Relative	
End of	*Cash Flow,*	*PV*		*Contribution*	
Period t	CF_t	*Factor*	$PV(CF_t)$	*to Bond Price (%)*	
1	$ 50.00	0.9662	$ 48.31	3.52	
2	50.00	0.9335	46.68	3.40	
3	50.00	0.9019	45.10	3.28	
.	.	.	.	.	90.77%
.	.	.	.	.	Coupon
.	.	.	.	.	Component
58	50.00	0.1360	6.80	0.49	
59	50.00	0.1314	6.57	0.48	
60	50.00	0.1269	6.35	0.46	9.23%
60	1,000.00	0.1269	126.90	9.23 }	Principal
		Total PV →	$1,374.20	100.00	Component

↑
Bond price

over 90% of the higher coupon 10% bond's value. Given that coupon cash flows are received at earlier points in time than the principal repayment, the 10% coupon bond is less susceptible to dramatic price swings than the 4% coupon bond, which is a more principal-dependent issue. Interim coupon cash flows tend to moderate the severely price-sensitive nature of the principal cash flow. Put another way, the average PV discounting factor is longer and more volatile for low coupon bonds.

Observation: *High coupon bonds are less volatile than lower coupon issues of similar maturity.*

Exhibit 4–23. Bond price volatility as a function of the initial yield level. The issues illustrated are current-coupon, 30-year maturity U.S. Treasury bonds priced initially at par.

Issue	YTM (%)	Bond Price	Percent Change in Price
	4.00	152.14	+52.14
	5.00	130.91	+30.91
	6.00	113.84	+13.84
7% Coupon Bond	**7.00**	**100.00**	
	8.00	88.69	−11.31
	9.00	79.36	−20.64
	10.00	71.61	−28.39
	7.00	137.42	+37.42
	8.00	122.62	+22.62
	9.00	110.32	+10.32
10% Coupon Bond	**10.00**	**100.00**	
	11.00	91.28	− 8.72
	12.00	83.84	−16.16
	13.00	77.45	−22.55
	10.00	128.39	+28.39
	11.00	117.45	+17.45
	12.00	108.08	+ 8.08
13% Coupon Bond	**13.00**	**100.00**	
	14.00	92.98	− 7.02
	15.00	86.84	−13.16
	16.00	81.44	−18.56

Comments: *For a given BP change in yield, bond prices are more volatile the lower the initial yield level. Under smaller magnitudes of yield change, the effects are less dramatic.*

Exhibit 4–24. Bond price volatility as a function of initial yield level. Issues displayed are 30-year, current-coupon U.S. Treasuries priced at par. Interest rates are assumed to fall 300BP. (Data per Exhibit 4–23.)

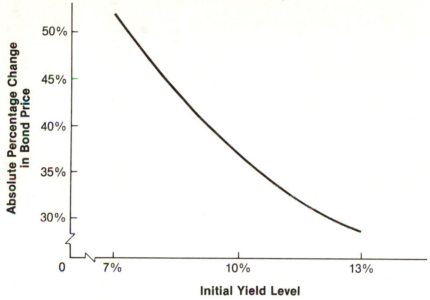

Exhibit 4–25. Bond price volatility as a function of initial yield level. Issues displayed are 30-year, current-coupon U.S. Treasuries priced at par. Interest rates are assumed to rise 300BP. (Data per Exhibit 4–23.)

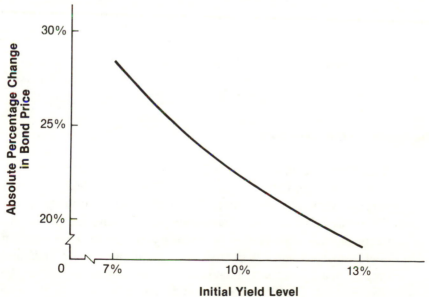

Exhibit 4–26. Bond price volatility as a function of the initial yield level. The issues illustrated are 10% coupon, 30-year maturity U.S. Treasury bonds priced initially at 7%, 10%, and 13% yield levels.

Issue	YTM (%)	Bond Price	Percent Change in Price
	4.00	204.28	+48.65
	5.00	177.27	+29.00
	6.00	155.35	+13.05
10% Coupon Bond	**7.00**	**137.42**	
	8.00	122.62	−10.77
	9.00	110.32	−19.72
	10.00	100.00	−27.23
	7.00	137.42	+37.42
	8.00	122.62	+22.62
	9.00	110.32	+10.32
10% Coupon Bond	**10.00**	**100.00**	
	11.00	91.28	− 8.72
	12.00	83.84	−16.16
	13.00	77.45	−22.55
	10.00	100.00	+29.12
	11.00	91.28	+17.86
	12.00	83.84	+ 8.25
10% Coupon Bond	**13.00**	**77.45**	
	14.00	71.92	− 7.14
	15.00	67.10	−13.36
	16.00	62.87	−18.83

Comments: *For a given BP change in yield, bond prices are more volatile the lower the initial yield level. Under smaller magnitudes of yield change, the effects are less dramatic.*

The impact of the yield level

The general level of yields is inversely related to bond price volatility. For a given absolute change in yield level, low yield environments are inherently more price volatile than high yield environments. Exhibit 4–23 verifies this inverse relationship by assessing the price volatility of current-coupon 30-year U.S. Treasury bonds in 7%, 10%, and 13% yield environments. A 300BP decline in rates has significantly more impact in a 7% scenario than in a 13% rate environment (52.14% versus 28.39%). A 300BP surge in yields has a more negative implication from a 7% starting point than from a 13% base (−28.39% versus

Exhibit 4–27. Calculation of the price of a 0% coupon, 3-year U.S. Treasury STRIPS yielding 7.00% to maturity.

(1)	*(2)*	*(3)*	*(4) = (2) × (3)*	*(5) = (4)/Price*
				Relative
End of	*Cash Flow,*	*PV*		*Contribution*
Period t	CF_t	*Factor*	$PV(CF_t)$	*to Bond Price (%)*
1	$ 0	0.9662	$ 0	0
2	0	0.9335	0	0
3	0	0.9019	0	0
.	.	.	.	.
.	.	.	.	.
.	.	.	.	.
6	1,000.00	0.8135	813.50	100.00
		Total PV →	$813.50	100.00
			↑	
			Bond price	

−18.56%). Exhibits 4–24 and 4–25 plot the numerics. Similar results are obtained when a single 10% coupon bond is used in the comparison (see Exhibit 4–26). These findings concur with the shape of the price: yield curve, which is steep in the lower yield range and flattens out in the higher yield area (recall Exhibit 4–1).

> **Observation:** *For a given BP change in interest rates, low yield environments are more price volatile than high yield environments.*

The price volatility of zero-coupon bonds

Zero-coupon bonds exemplify the inherent sensitivity of low coupon bonds to changes in yield level. A zero-coupon bond, as its name implies, makes no interest payments during its life. The final principal payment at maturity accounts for the bond's price in its entirety. For example, a 3-year zero priced to yield 7.00% sells for 81.35, or $813.50 for each $1,000.00 par amount (see Exhibit 4–27). A 30-year STRIPS yielding 7.00% is priced at 12.69, or $126.90 per $1,000.00 par value (see Exhibit 4–28).[7] Combining the earlier discovery that long PV factors are more volatile than short PV factors (Exhibit 4–16) with the fact

---

[7] STRIPS stands for Separately Traded Registered Interest and Principal Securities. STRIPS are the component parts (coupons, principal) of U.S. Treasury debt quite literally "stripped" from designated notes and bonds.

Exhibit 4–28. Calculation of the price of a 0% coupon, 30-year U.S. Treasury STRIPS yielding 7.00% to maturity.

(1)	(2)	(3)	(4) = (2) × (3)	(5) = (4)/Price
				Relative
End of	*Cash Flow,*	*PV*		*Contribution*
Period t	*CF*$_t$	*Factor*	*PV(CF*$_t$)	*to Bond Price (%)*
1	$ 0	0.9662	$ 0	0
2	0	0.9335	0	0
3	0	0.9019	0	0
.	.	.	.	.
.	.	.	.	.
.	.	.	.	.
60	1,000.00	0.1269	126.90	100.00
		Total PV →	$126.90	100.00

↑
Bond price

Exhibit 4–29. Price volatility of a 3-year, current-coupon U.S. Treasury bond versus a 3-year STRIPS. Each issue is priced initially to yield 7.00%.

Issue	YTM (%)	Bond Price	Percent Change in Price
	4.00	108.40	+8.40
	5.00	105.51	+5.51
	6.00	102.71	+2.71
3-Year U.S. Treasury Bond	**7.00**	**100.00**	
	8.00	97.38	−2.62
	9.00	94.84	−5.16
	10.00	92.39	−7.61
	4.00	88.80	+9.16
	5.00	86.23	+6.00
	6.00	83.75	+2.95
3-Year STRIPS	**7.00**	**81.35**	
	8.00	79.03	−2.85
	9.00	76.79	−5.61
	10.00	74.62	−8.27

Comments: *STRIPS are more volatile than their coupon-bearing counterparts. Under smaller magnitudes of yield change, the effects are less dramatic.*

Exhibit 4–30. Price volatility of a 30-year, current-coupon U.S. Treasury bond versus a 30-year STRIPS. Each issue is priced initially to yield 7.00%.

Issue	YTM (%)	Bond Price	Percent Change in Price
	4.00	152.14	+ 52.14
	5.00	130.91	+ 30.91
	6.00	113.84	+ 13.84
30-Year U.S. Treasury Bond	**7.00**	**100.00**	
	8.00	88.69	− 11.31
	9.00	79.36	− 20.64
	10.00	71.61	− 28.39
	4.00	30.48	+140.19
	5.00	22.73	+ 79.12
	6.00	16.97	+ 33.73
30-Year STRIPS	**7.00**	**12.69**	
	8.00	9.51	− 25.06
	9.00	7.13	− 43.81
	10.00	5.35	− 57.84

Comments: *STRIPS are more volatile than their coupon-bearing counterparts, particularly with longer maturity issues. Under smaller magnitudes of yield change, the effects are less dramatic.*

that a zero-coupon bond's price sensitivity is completely dependent on the longest PV factor (i.e., the PV factor to maturity date) leads to the conclusion that for a given maturity, a zero-coupon bond is the most price-volatile instrument.

Exhibit 4–29 illustrates the high degree of price sensitivity of zeros by comparing a 3-year STRIPS to a 3-year current-coupon U.S. Treasury bond. The STRIPS gains more in a 300BP market rally (+9.16%) and loses more in a 300BP bear market (−8.27%) than does its current-coupon counterpart (+8.40% and −7.61%, respectively). These figures translate into approximately 9% incremental price volatility for the STRIPS issue. Longer maturity zeros are far more price sensitive than are their coupon-bearing cohorts. For example, a 30-year STRIPS displays more than twice the volatility of a 30-year current-coupon U.S. Treasury (see Exhibit 4–30). The 30-year STRIPS garners an impressive 140.19% return in a 300BP market rally, whereas the 30-year, coupon-bearing instrument captures a 52.14% prize. A downmarket damages the long zero disproportionately as well, with a 57.84% price depreciation versus the 28.39% suffrage of the current-coupon issue.

Exhibit 4–31. Bond price volatility of zero-coupon bonds versus their similar maturity, current-coupon counterparts. Interest rates are assumed to fall 300BP from a 7.00% initial yield level.

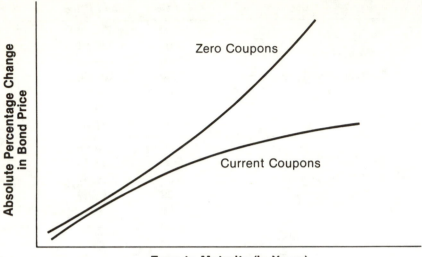

Exhibits 4–31 and 4–32 demonstrate the volatility differences between STRIPS and current coupons of like maturity in a graphical format. Expressed another way, the price:yield curves for STRIPS are more convex, or cup-shaped, than are coupon-bearing issues of similar maturity (see Exhibit 4–33). Exhibit 4–34 reflects the fact that within the STRIPS

Exhibit 4–32. Bond price volatility of zero-coupon bonds versus their similar maturity, current-coupon counterparts. Interest rates are assumed to rise 300BP from a 7.00% initial yield level.

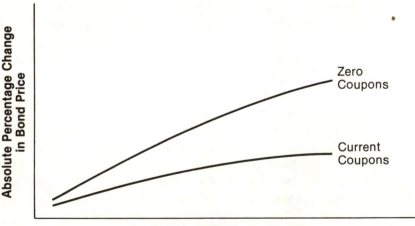

Exhibit 4–33. Price:yield curves for a 7% coupon, 30-year U.S. Treasury bond and a 30-year STRIPS.

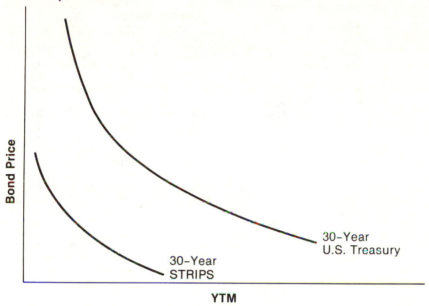

Exhibit 4–34. Price volatility of a short STRIPS (3-year) versus a long STRIPS (30-year). Each issue is priced initially to yield 7.00%.

Issue	*YTM (%)*	*Bond Price*	*Percent Change in Price*
	4.00	88.80	+ 9.16
	5.00	86.23	+ 6.00
	6.00	83.75	+ 2.95
3-Year STRIPS	**7.00**	**81.35**	
	8.00	79.03	− 2.85
	9.00	76.79	− 5.61
	10.00	74.62	− 8.27
	4.00	30.48	+140.19
	5.00	22.73	+ 79.12
	6.00	16.97	+ 33.73
30-Year STRIPS	**7.00**	**12.69**	
	8.00	9.51	− 25.06
	9.00	7.13	− 43.81
	10.00	5.35	− 57.84

Comments: *Long maturity STRIPS are more volatile than short maturity STRIPS. Under smaller magnitudes of yield change, the effects are less dramatic.*

Exhibit 4–35. Bond prices of a 3-year maturity issue for a variety of coupon rates and yield levels.

YTM(%)	Coupon Rate										
	0%	1%	2%	3%	4%	5%	6%	7%	8%	9%	10%
0.0	100.00	103.00	106.00	109.00	112.00	115.00	118.00	121.00	124.00	127.00	130.00
0.5	98.51	101.49	104.46	107.43	110.41	113.38	116.36	119.33	122.30	125.28	128.25
1.0	97.05	100.00	102.95	105.90	108.84	111.79	114.74	117.69	120.64	123.59	126.53
1.5	95.62	98.54	101.46	104.38	107.31	110.23	113.15	116.08	119.00	121.92	124.84
2.0	94.20	97.10	100.00	102.90	105.80	108.69	111.59	114.49	117.39	120.28	123.18
2.5	92.82	95.69	98.56	101.44	104.31	107.18	110.06	112.93	115.80	118.67	121.55
3.0	91.45	94.30	97.15	100.00	102.85	105.70	108.55	111.39	114.24	117.09	119.94
3.5	90.11	92.94	95.76	98.59	101.41	104.24	107.06	109.89	112.71	115.53	118.36
4.0	88.80	91.60	94.40	97.20	100.00	102.80	105.60	108.40	111.20	114.00	116.80
4.5	87.50	90.28	93.06	95.83	98.61	101.39	104.17	106.94	109.72	112.50	115.27
5.0	86.23	88.98	91.74	94.49	97.25	100.00	102.75	105.51	108.26	111.02	113.77
5.5	84.98	87.71	90.44	93.17	95.90	98.63	101.37	104.10	106.83	109.56	112.29
6.0	83.75	86.46	89.17	91.87	94.58	97.29	100.00	102.71	105.42	108.13	110.83
6.5	82.54	85.23	87.91	90.60	93.28	95.97	98.66	101.34	104.03	106.72	109.40
7.0	81.35	84.01	86.68	89.34	92.01	94.67	97.34	100.00	102.66	105.33	107.99
7.5	80.18	82.82	85.47	88.11	90.75	93.39	96.04	98.68	101.32	103.96	106.61
8.0	79.03	81.65	84.27	86.89	89.52	92.14	94.76	97.38	100.00	102.62	105.24
8.5	77.90	80.50	83.10	85.70	88.30	90.90	93.50	96.10	98.70	101.30	103.90
9.0	76.79	79.37	81.95	84.53	87.11	89.68	92.26	94.84	97.42	100.00	102.58
9.5	75.70	78.25	80.81	83.37	85.93	88.49	91.05	93.60	96.16	98.72	101.28
10.0	74.62	77.16	79.70	82.24	84.77	87.31	89.85	92.39	94.92	97.46	100.00
10.5	73.56	76.08	78.60	81.12	83.64	86.15	88.67	91.19	93.71	96.22	98.74
11.0	72.52	75.02	77.52	80.02	82.52	85.01	87.51	90.01	92.51	95.00	97.50
11.5	71.50	73.98	76.46	78.94	81.41	83.89	86.37	88.85	91.33	93.80	96.28
12.0	70.50	72.95	75.41	77.87	80.33	82.79	85.25	87.71	90.17	92.62	95.08
12.5	69.51	71.95	74.39	76.83	79.26	81.70	84.14	86.58	89.02	91.46	93.90
13.0	68.53	70.95	73.37	75.79	78.22	80.64	83.06	85.48	87.90	90.32	92.74
13.5	67.58	69.98	72.38	74.78	77.18	79.58	81.99	84.39	86.79	89.19	91.59
14.0	66.63	69.02	71.40	73.78	76.17	78.55	80.93	83.32	85.70	88.08	90.47
14.5	65.71	68.07	70.44	72.80	75.17	77.53	79.90	82.26	84.63	86.99	89.36
15.0	64.80	67.14	69.49	71.84	74.18	76.53	78.88	81.22	83.57	85.92	88.27
15.5	63.90	66.23	68.56	70.89	73.22	75.54	77.87	80.20	82.53	84.86	87.19
16.0	63.02	65.33	67.64	69.95	72.26	74.57	76.89	79.20	81.51	83.82	86.13
16.5	62.15	64.44	66.74	69.03	71.32	73.62	75.91	78.21	80.50	82.79	85.09
17.0	61.29	63.57	65.85	68.12	70.40	72.68	74.96	77.23	79.51	81.79	84.06
17.5	60.45	62.71	64.97	67.23	69.49	71.75	74.01	76.27	78.53	80.79	83.05
18.0	59.63	61.83	64.11	66.36	68.60	70.84	73.08	75.33	77.57	79.81	82.06
18.5	58.81	61.04	63.27	65.49	67.72	69.94	72.17	74.40	76.62	78.85	81.08
19.0	58.01	60.22	62.43	64.64	66.85	69.06	71.27	73.48	75.69	77.90	80.11
19.5	57.22	59.42	61.61	63.80	66.00	68.19	70.39	72.58	74.77	76.97	79.16
20.0	56.45	58.63	60.80	62.98	65.16	67.34	69.51	71.69	73.87	76.05	78.22

market, long STRIPS are more price volatile than short STRIPS. Although low coupon bonds reflect, to some extent, the "tail wagging the dog" syndrome (i.e., the principal repayment fluctuating the bond price), zero-coupon issues epitomize this effect since the "tail" *is* the dog!

Observation: *Zero-coupon bonds are more price volatile than similar maturity, coupon-bearing instruments. Long maturity zeros are more volatile than short maturity zeros.*

Exhibit 4–35 (con't).

YTM (%)					Coupon Rate					
	11%	12%	13%	14%	15%	16%	17%	18%	19%	20%
0.0	133.00	136.00	139.00	142.00	145.00	148.00	151.00	154.00	157.00	160.00
0.5	131.23	134.20	137.17	140.15	143.12	146.10	149.07	152.04	155.02	157.99
1.0	129.48	132.43	135.38	138.33	141.27	144.22	147.17	150.12	153.07	156.02
1.5	127.77	130.69	133.61	136.53	139.46	142.38	145.30	148.23	151.15	154.07
2.0	126.08	128.98	131.88	134.77	137.67	140.57	143.47	146.36	149.26	152.16
2.5	124.42	127.29	130.17	133.04	135.91	138.79	141.66	144.53	147.40	150.28
3.0	122.79	125.64	128.49	131.33	134.18	137.03	139.88	142.73	145.58	148.43
3.5	121.18	124.01	126.83	129.66	132.48	135.31	138.13	140.96	143.78	146.60
4.0	119.61	122.41	125.21	128.01	130.81	133.61	136.41	139.21	142.01	144.81
4.5	118.05	120.83	123.61	126.38	129.16	131.94	134.72	137.49	140.27	143.05
5.0	116.52	119.28	122.03	124.79	127.54	130.29	133.05	135.80	138.56	141.31
5.5	115.02	117.75	120.48	123.22	125.95	128.68	131.41	134.14	136.87	139.60
6.0	113.54	116.25	118.96	121.67	124.38	127.09	129.79	132.50	135.21	137.92
6.5	112.09	114.77	117.46	120.15	122.83	125.52	128.21	130.89	133.58	136.26
7.0	110.66	113.32	115.99	118.65	121.31	123.98	126.64	129.31	131.97	134.64
7.5	109.25	111.89	114.53	117.18	119.82	122.46	125.10	127.75	130.39	133.03
8.0	107.86	110.48	113.11	115.73	118.35	120.97	123.59	126.21	128.83	131.45
8.5	106.50	109.10	111.70	114.30	116.90	119.50	122.10	124.70	127.30	129.90
9.0	105.16	107.74	110.32	112.89	115.47	118.05	120.63	123.21	125.79	128.37
9.5	103.84	106.40	108.95	111.51	114.07	116.63	119.19	121.75	124.30	126.86
10.0	102.54	105.08	107.61	110.15	112.69	115.23	117.76	120.30	122.84	125.38
10.5	101.26	103.78	106.29	108.81	111.33	113.85	116.36	118.88	121.40	123.92
11.0	100.00	102.50	105.00	107.49	109.99	112.49	114.99	117.48	119.98	122.48
11.5	98.76	101.24	103.72	106.20	108.67	111.15	113.63	116.11	118.59	121.06
12.0	97.54	100.00	102.46	104.92	107.38	109.83	112.29	114.75	117.21	119.67
12.5	96.34	98.78	101.22	103.66	106.10	108.54	110.98	113.42	115.86	118.30
13.0	95.16	97.58	100.00	102.42	104.84	107.26	109.68	112.10	114.52	116.94
13.5	94.00	96.40	98.80	101.20	103.60	106.00	108.41	110.81	113.21	115.61
14.0	92.85	95.23	97.62	100.00	102.38	104.77	107.15	109.53	111.92	114.30
14.5	91.72	94.09	96.45	98.82	101.18	103.55	105.91	108.28	110.64	113.01
15.0	90.61	92.96	95.31	97.65	100.00	102.35	104.69	107.04	109.39	111.73
15.5	89.52	91.85	94.18	96.51	98.84	101.16	103.49	105.82	108.15	110.48
16.0	88.44	90.75	93.07	95.38	97.69	100.00	102.31	104.62	106.93	109.25
16.5	87.38	89.68	91.97	94.26	96.56	98.85	101.15	103.44	105.74	108.03
17.0	86.34	88.62	90.89	93.17	95.45	97.72	100.00	102.28	104.55	106.83
17.5	85.31	87.57	89.83	92.09	94.35	96.61	98.87	101.13	103.39	105.65
18.0	84.30	86.54	88.79	91.03	93.27	95.51	97.76	100.00	102.24	104.49
18.5	83.30	85.53	87.76	89.98	92.21	94.43	96.66	98.89	101.11	103.34
19.0	82.32	84.53	86.74	88.95	91.16	93.37	95.58	97.79	100.00	102.21
19.5	81.35	83.55	85.74	87.93	90.13	92.32	94.52	96.71	98.90	101.10
20.0	80.40	82.58	84.76	86.93	89.11	91.29	93.47	95.64	97.82	100.00

Bond price volatility: A recap

Bond price volatility can be observed in a set of bond price tables.
Exhibits 4–35, 4–36, and 4–37 present a series of bond prices for 3-
year, 10-year, and 30-year maturity issues, respectively. The coupon
rate of interest varies from 0 to 20% in increments of 1%. The YTM
ranges from 0 to 20% in increments of 0.5%. These tables provide
support for some of the conclusions made in this chapter and prior chapters.

Exhibit 4–36. Bond prices of a 10-year maturity issue for a variety of coupon rates and yield levels.

YTM (%)	0%	1%	2%	3%	4%	5%	6%	7%	8%	9%	10%
0.0	100.00	110.00	120.00	130.00	140.00	150.00	160.00	170.00	180.00	190.00	200.00
0.5	95.13	104.87	114.61	124.36	134.10	143.84	153.58	163.32	173.07	182.81	192.55
1.0	90.51	100.00	109.49	118.99	128.48	137.97	147.47	156.96	166.46	175.95	185.44
1.5	86.12	95.37	104.63	113.88	123.14	132.39	141.64	150.90	160.15	169.41	178.66
2.0	81.95	90.98	100.00	109.02	118.05	127.07	136.09	145.11	154.14	163.16	172.18
2.5	78.00	86.80	95.60	104.40	113.20	122.00	130.80	139.60	148.40	157.20	166.00
3.0	74.25	82.83	91.42	100.00	108.58	117.17	125.75	134.34	142.92	151.51	160.09
3.5	70.68	79.06	87.44	95.81	104.19	112.56	120.94	129.32	137.69	146.07	154.45
4.0	67.30	75.47	83.65	91.82	100.00	108.18	116.35	124.53	132.70	140.88	149.05
4.5	64.08	72.06	80.05	88.03	96.01	103.99	111.97	119.95	127.94	135.92	143.90
5.0	61.03	68.82	76.62	84.41	92.21	100.00	107.79	115.59	123.38	131.18	138.97
5.5	58.13	65.74	73.35	80.97	88.58	96.19	103.81	111.42	119.03	126.65	134.26
6.0	55.37	62.81	70.25	77.68	85.12	92.56	100.00	107.44	114.88	122.32	129.75
6.5	52.75	60.02	67.29	74.56	81.83	89.10	96.37	103.63	110.90	118.17	125.44
7.0	50.26	57.36	64.47	71.58	78.68	85.79	92.89	100.00	107.11	114.21	121.32
7.5	47.89	54.84	61.79	68.73	75.68	82.63	89.58	96.53	103.47	110.42	117.37
8.0	45.64	52.43	59.23	66.02	72.82	79.61	86.41	93.20	100.00	106.80	113.59
8.5	43.50	50.15	56.79	63.44	70.09	76.73	83.38	90.03	96.68	103.32	109.97
9.0	41.46	47.97	54.47	60.98	67.48	73.98	80.49	86.99	93.50	100.00	106.50
9.5	39.53	45.89	52.26	58.63	64.99	71.36	77.72	84.09	90.45	96.82	103.18
10.0	37.69	43.92	50.15	56.38	62.61	68.84	75.08	81.31	87.54	93.77	100.00
10.5	35.94	42.04	48.14	54.24	60.34	66.44	72.54	78.65	84.75	90.85	96.95
11.0	34.27	40.25	46.22	52.20	58.17	64.15	70.12	76.10	82.07	88.05	94.02
11.5	32.69	38.54	44.39	50.25	56.10	61.95	67.81	73.66	79.51	85.37	91.22
12.0	31.18	36.92	42.65	48.39	54.12	59.86	65.59	71.33	77.06	82.80	88.53
12.5	29.75	35.37	40.99	46.61	52.23	57.85	63.47	69.09	74.71	80.33	85.95
13.0	28.38	33.89	39.40	44.91	50.42	55.93	61.44	66.94	72.45	77.96	83.47
13.5	27.08	32.48	37.88	43.28	48.69	54.09	59.49	64.89	70.29	75.69	81.09
14.0	25.84	31.14	36.44	41.73	47.03	52.33	57.62	62.92	68.22	73.51	78.81
14.5	24.66	29.86	35.05	40.25	45.45	50.64	55.84	61.03	66.23	71.42	76.62
15.0	23.54	28.64	33.74	38.83	43.93	49.03	54.12	59.22	64.32	69.42	74.51
15.5	22.47	27.47	32.48	37.48	42.48	47.48	52.48	57.49	62.49	67.49	72.49
16.0	21.45	26.36	31.27	36.18	41.09	46.00	50.91	55.82	60.73	65.64	70.55
16.5	20.49	25.30	30.12	34.94	39.76	44.58	49.40	54.22	59.04	63.86	68.68
17.0	19.56	24.29	29.02	33.76	38.49	43.22	47.95	52.68	57.41	62.15	66.88
17.5	18.68	23.33	27.98	32.62	37.27	41.92	46.56	51.21	55.86	60.50	65.15
18.0	17.84	22.41	26.97	31.54	36.10	40.66	45.23	49.79	54.36	58.92	63.49
18.5	17.04	21.53	26.01	30.50	34.98	39.46	43.95	48.43	52.92	57.40	61.89
19.0	16.28	20.69	25.09	29.50	33.91	38.31	42.72	47.13	51.53	55.94	60.34
19.5	15.56	19.89	24.22	28.55	32.88	37.21	41.54	45.87	50.20	54.53	58.86
20.0	14.86	19.12	23.38	27.63	31.89	36.15	40.41	44.66	48.92	53.18	57.43

First, the price:yield relationship is an inverse one (recall Chapter 2). For a selected coupon rate, one can scan down a column of the table and notice the bond price decline as yields are progressively raised. For example, a 10% coupon, 10-year maturity bond's price ranges from 200.00 at a 0% yield to 57.43 at a 20% yield.

Second, at a 0% YTM, the bond is valued at a price that reflects the nominal (face) amount of the bond's future cash flows (recall Chapter

Exhibit 4–36 (con't).

YTM (%)	Coupon Rate									
	11%	12%	13%	14%	15%	16%	17%	18%	19%	20%
0.0	210.00	220.00	230.00	240.00	250.00	260.00	270.00	280.00	290.00	300.00
0.5	202.29	212.04	221.78	231.52	241.26	251.00	260.75	270.49	280.23	289.97
1.0	194.94	204.43	213.92	223.42	232.91	242.41	251.90	261.39	270.89	280.38
1.5	187.91	197.17	206.42	215.68	224.93	234.18	243.44	252.69	261.95	271.20
2.0	181.20	190.23	199.25	208.27	217.30	226.32	235.34	244.36	253.39	262.41
2.5	174.80	183.60	192.40	201.20	210.00	218.80	227.60	236.39	245.19	253.99
3.0	168.67	177.26	185.84	194.43	203.01	211.60	220.18	228.76	237.35	245.93
3.5	162.82	171.20	179.58	187.95	196.33	204.71	213.08	221.46	229.83	238.21
4.0	157.23	165.41	173.58	181.76	189.93	198.11	206.28	214.46	222.64	230.81
4.5	151.88	159.86	167.85	175.83	183.81	191.79	199.77	207.76	215.74	223.72
5.0	146.77	154.56	162.36	170.15	177.95	185.74	193.53	201.33	209.12	216.92
5.5	141.87	149.49	157.10	164.72	172.33	179.94	187.56	195.17	202.78	210.40
6.0	137.19	144.63	152.07	159.51	166.95	174.39	181.83	189.26	196.70	204.14
6.5	132.71	139.98	147.25	154.52	161.79	169.06	176.33	183.60	190.87	198.14
7.0	128.42	135.53	142.64	149.74	156.85	163.96	171.06	178.17	185.27	192.38
7.5	124.32	131.27	138.21	145.16	152.11	159.06	166.01	172.96	179.90	186.85
8.0	120.39	127.18	133.98	140.77	147.57	154.36	161.16	167.95	174.75	181.54
8.5	116.62	123.27	129.91	136.56	143.21	149.85	156.50	163.15	169.80	176.44
9.0	113.01	119.51	126.02	132.52	139.02	145.53	152.03	158.54	165.04	171.54
9.5	109.55	115.91	122.28	128.64	135.01	141.37	147.74	154.11	160.47	166.84
10.0	106.23	112.46	118.69	124.92	131.16	137.39	143.62	149.85	156.08	162.31
10.5	103.05	109.15	115.25	121.35	127.46	133.56	139.66	145.76	151.86	157.96
11.0	100.00	105.98	111.95	117.93	123.90	129.88	135.85	141.83	147.80	153.78
11.5	97.07	102.93	108.78	114.63	120.49	126.34	132.19	138.05	143.90	149.75
12.0	94.27	100.00	105.73	111.47	117.20	122.94	128.67	134.41	140.14	145.88
12.5	91.57	97.19	102.81	108.43	114.05	119.67	125.29	130.91	136.53	142.15
13.0	88.98	94.49	100.00	105.51	111.02	116.53	122.04	127.55	133.06	138.56
13.5	86.50	91.90	97.30	102.70	108.10	113.50	118.91	124.31	129.71	135.11
14.0	84.11	89.41	94.70	100.00	105.30	110.59	115.89	121.19	126.49	131.78
14.5	81.82	87.01	92.21	97.40	102.60	107.79	112.99	110.18	123.38	128.58
15.0	79.61	84.71	89.81	94.90	100.00	105.10	110.19	115.29	120.39	125.49
15.5	77.49	82.49	87.50	92.50	97.50	102.50	107.50	112.50	117.51	122.51
16.0	75.45	80.36	85.27	90.18	95.09	100.00	104.91	109.82	114.73	119.64
16.5	73.50	78.31	83.13	87.95	92.77	97.59	102.41	107.23	112.05	116.87
17.0	71.61	76.34	81.07	85.80	90.54	95.27	100.00	104.73	109.46	114.20
17.5	69.80	74.44	79.09	83.34	88.38	93.03	97.68	102.32	106.97	111.62
18.0	68.05	72.61	77.18	81.74	86.31	90.87	95.44	100.00	104.56	109.13
18.5	66.37	70.85	75.34	79.82	84.31	88.79	93.27	97.76	102.24	106.73
19.0	64.75	69.16	73.56	77.97	82.38	86.78	91.19	95.59	100.00	104.41
19.5	63.19	67.52	71.85	76.18	80.51	84.84	89.17	93.50	97.83	102.17
20.0	61.69	65.95	70.20	74.46	78.72	82.97	87.23	91.49	95.74	100.00

2); no discounting factors are applied. For example, a 10% coupon, 10-year bond sells at a 200.00 price (i.e., $2,000.00) if yields are 0%. Although it is unlikely that yields would ever reach the zero level, it is interesting to note the "upside limit" in a bond's price behavior.

Third, long maturity bonds are more price sensitive than short maturity issues. For a selected coupon rate and a specified range in yield, the 30-year bond shows a wider range of prices than either the 10-year or the 3-year bond. For example, over a 5–15% YTM range, a

Exhibit 4–37. Bond prices of a 30-year maturity issue for a variety of coupon rates and yield levels.

YTM (%)	Coupon Rate										
	0%	1%	2%	3%	4%	5%	6%	7%	8%	9%	10%
0.0	100.00	130.00	160.00	190.00	220.00	250.00	280.00	310.00	340.00	370.00	400.00
0.5	86.09	113.91	141.74	169.57	197.39	225.22	253.04	280.87	308.70	336.52	364.35
1.0	74.14	100.00	125.86	151.73	177.59	203.45	229.31	255.18	281.04	306.90	332.77
1.5	63.87	87.96	112.04	136.13	160.22	184.30	208.39	232.48	256.56	280.65	304.74
2.0	55.04	77.52	100.00	122.48	144.96	167.43	189.91	212.39	234.87	257.34	279.82
2.5	47.46	68.47	89.49	110.51	131.53	152.54	173.56	194.58	215.60	236.61	257.63
3.0	40.93	60.62	80.31	100.00	119.69	139.38	159.07	178.76	198.45	218.14	237.83
3.5	35.31	53.80	72.28	90.76	109.24	127.72	146.20	164.69	183.17	201.65	220.13
4.0	30.48	47.86	65.24	82.62	100.00	117.38	134.76	152.14	169.52	186.90	204.28
4.5	26.31	42.69	59.06	75.44	91.81	108.19	124.56	140.94	157.31	173.69	190.06
5.0	22.73	38.18	53.64	69.09	84.55	100.00	115.45	130.91	146.36	161.82	177.27
5.5	19.64	34.25	48.86	63.47	78.08	92.69	107.31	121.92	136.53	151.14	165.75
6.0	16.97	30.81	44.65	58.49	72.32	86.16	100.00	113.84	127.68	141.51	155.35
6.5	14.68	27.80	40.93	54.06	67.18	80.31	93.44	106.56	119.69	132.82	145.94
7.0	12.69	25.17	37.64	50.11	62.58	75.06	87.53	100.00	112.47	124.94	137.42
7.5	10.98	22.85	34.72	46.59	58.46	70.33	82.20	94.07	105.93	117.80	129.67
8.0	9.51	20.82	32.13	43.44	54.75	66.06	77.38	88.69	100.00	111.31	122.62
8.5	8.23	19.03	29.82	40.62	51.42	62.21	73.01	83.81	94.60	105.40	116.19
9.0	7.13	17.45	27.77	38.09	48.40	58.72	69.04	79.36	89.68	100.00	110.32
9.5	6.18	16.05	25.93	35.81	45.68	55.56	65.43	75.31	85.19	95.06	104.94
10.0	5.35	14.82	24.28	33.75	43.21	52.68	62.14	71.61	81.07	90.54	100.00
10.5	4.64	13.72	22.81	31.89	40.97	50.05	59.13	68.21	77.30	86.38	95.46
11.0	4.03	12.75	21.48	30.20	38.93	47.65	56.38	65.10	73.83	82.55	91.28
11.5	3.49	11.88	20.28	28.67	37.06	45.45	53.84	62.24	70.63	79.02	87.41
12.0	3.03	11.11	19.19	27.27	35.35	43.44	51.52	59.60	67.68	75.76	83.84
12.5	2.63	10.42	18.21	26.00	33.79	41.58	49.37	57.16	64.95	72.74	80.53
13.0	2.29	9.80	17.32	24.84	32.35	39.87	47.38	54.90	62.41	69.93	77.45
13.5	1.99	9.25	16.51	23.77	31.03	38.29	45.55	52.81	60.07	67.33	74.59
14.0	1.73	8.75	15.76	22.78	29.80	36.82	43.84	50.86	57.88	64.90	71.92
14.5	1.50	8.29	15.09	21.88	28.67	35.47	42.26	49.05	55.84	62.64	69.43
15.0	1.30	7.88	14.46	21.04	27.62	34.20	40.78	47.36	53.94	60.52	67.10
15.5	1.13	7.51	13.89	20.27	26.65	33.03	39.41	45.78	52.16	58.54	64.92
16.0	0.99	7.18	13.36	19.55	25.74	31.93	38.12	44.31	50.49	56.68	62.87
16.5	0.86	6.87	12.88	18.89	24.89	30.90	36.91	42.92	48.93	54.94	60.94
17.0	0.75	6.59	12.43	18.26	24.10	29.94	35.78	41.62	47.46	53.29	59.13
17.5	0.65	6.33	12.01	17.68	23.36	29.04	34.71	40.39	46.07	51.75	57.42
18.0	0.57	6.09	11.62	17.14	22.66	28.19	33.71	39.24	44.76	50.28	55.81
18.5	0.50	5.87	11.25	16.63	22.01	27.39	32.77	38.15	43.52	48.90	54.28
19.0	0.43	5.67	10.91	16.15	21.39	26.63	31.87	37.11	42.36	47.60	52.84
19.5	0.38	5.49	10.59	15.70	20.81	25.92	31.03	36.14	41.25	46.36	51.47
20.0	0.33	5.31	10.30	15.28	20.26	25.25	30.23	35.21	40.20	45.18	50.16

10% coupon bond in the 3-year maturity sector experiences prices varying from 113.77 to 88.27. An identical bond in a 10-year maturity version generates prices ranging from 138.97 to 74.51. A 10% coupon, 30-year bond is more volatile, with prices ranging from 177.27 (5% YTM) to 67.10 (15% YTM).

Fourth, higher coupon bonds are less volatile than low coupon

Exhibit 4–37 (con't).

YTM (%)	Coupon Rate									
	11%	*12%*	*13%*	*14%*	*15%*	*16%*	*17%*	*18%*	*19%*	*20%*
0.0	430.00	460.00	490.00	520.00	550.00	580.00	610.00	640.00	670.00	700.00
0.5	392.17	420.00	447.83	475.65	503.48	531.31	559.13	586.96	614.78	642.61
1.0	358.63	384.49	410.35	436.22	462.08	487.94	513.80	539.67	565.53	591.39
1.5	328.82	352.91	377.00	401.08	425.17	449.26	473.34	497.43	521.52	545.60
2.0	302.30	324.78	347.25	369.73	392.21	414.69	437.16	459.64	482.12	504.60
2.5	278.65	299.66	320.68	341.70	362.72	383.73	404.75	425.77	446.79	467.80
3.0	257.52	277.21	296.90	316.59	336.28	355.97	375.66	395.35	415.04	434.73
3.5	238.61	257.10	275.58	294.06	312.54	331.02	349.51	367.99	386.47	404.95
4.0	221.66	239.04	256.42	273.80	291.18	308.57	325.95	343.33	360.71	378.09
4.5	206.43	222.81	239.18	255.56	271.93	288.31	304.68	321.06	337.43	353.80
5.0	192.73	208.18	223.63	239.09	254.54	270.00	285.45	300.91	316.36	331.81
5.5	180.36	194.97	209.58	224.20	238.81	253.42	268.03	282.64	297.25	311.86
6.0	169.19	183.03	196.86	210.70	224.54	238.38	252.22	266.05	279.89	293.73
6.5	159.07	172.20	185.32	198.45	211.58	224.70	237.83	250.96	264.09	277.21
7.0	149.89	162.36	174.83	187.31	199.78	212.25	224.72	237.20	249.67	262.14
7.5	141.54	153.41	165.28	177.15	189.02	200.89	212.76	224.62	236.49	248.36
8.0	133.94	145.25	156.56	167.87	179.18	190.49	201.81	213.12	224.43	235.74
8.5	126.99	137.79	148.58	159.38	170.18	180.97	191.77	202.57	213.36	224.16
9.0	120.64	130.96	141.28	151.60	161.91	172.23	182.55	192.87	203.19	213.51
9.5	114.81	124.69	134.57	144.44	154.32	164.19	174.07	183.95	193.82	203.70
10.0	109.46	118.93	128.39	137.86	147.32	156.79	166.25	175.72	185.18	194.65
10.5	104.54	113.62	122.70	131.79	140.87	149.95	159.03	168.11	177.19	186.28
11.0	100.00	108.72	117.45	126.17	134.90	143.62	152.35	161.07	169.80	178.52
11.5	95.80	104.20	112.59	120.98	129.37	137.76	146.16	154.55	162.94	171.33
12.0	91.92	100.00	108.08	116.16	124.24	132.32	140.40	148.48	156.56	164.65
12.5	88.32	96.11	103.89	111.68	119.47	127.26	135.05	142.84	150.63	158.42
13.0	84.97	92.48	100.00	107.52	115.03	122.55	130.07	137.58	145.10	152.62
13.5	81.85	89.11	96.37	103.63	110.89	118.15	125.41	132.67	139.93	147.19
14.0	78.94	85.96	92.98	100.00	107.02	114.04	121.06	128.08	135.10	142.12
14.5	76.22	83.02	89.81	96.60	103.40	110.19	116.98	123.78	130.57	137.36
15.0	73.68	80.26	86.84	93.42	100.00	106.58	113.16	119.74	126.32	132.90
15.5	71.30	77.68	84.05	90.43	96.81	103.19	109.57	115.95	122.32	128.70
16.0	69.06	75.25	81.44	87.62	93.81	100.00	106.19	112.38	118.56	124.75
16.5	66.95	72.96	78.97	84.98	90.99	97.00	103.00	109.01	115.02	121.03
17.0	64.97	70.81	76.65	82.49	88.32	94.16	100.00	105.84	111.68	117.51
17.5	63.10	68.78	74.45	80.13	85.81	91.48	97.16	102.84	108.52	114.19
18.0	61.33	66.86	72.38	77.90	83.43	88.95	94.48	100.00	105.52	111.05
18.5	59.66	65.04	70.42	75.80	81.17	86.55	91.93	97.31	102.69	108.07
19.0	58.08	63.32	68.56	73.80	79.04	84.28	89.52	94.76	100.00	105.24
19.5	56.57	61.68	66.79	71.90	77.01	82.12	87.23	92.34	97.45	102.55
20.0	55.15	60.13	65.11	70.10	75.08	80.07	85.05	90.03	95.02	100.00

bonds. In the 10-year maturity sector, for example, a 20% coupon bond surges from a 125.49 to a 216.92 price (a 72.86% increase) as yields fall from 15 to 5%. For a similar yield decline, a 10% coupon bond of similar maturity moves from a 74.51 price to a 138.97 level (an 86.51% increase). The tables include a column for 0% (i.e., zero-coupon) bonds. As noted earlier in this chapter, these issues experience the greatest degree of price volatility. The table data serve to confirm this notion.

Finally, bond price volatility is inversely related to the general level of yields. For example, a 10% coupon, 10-year maturity bond suffers lesser degrees of price loss as yields are raised:

Yield Change	Price Change	Percent of Price Loss
0% YTM → 5% YTM	200.00 → 138.97	(30.52)
5% YTM → 10% YTM	138.97 → 100.00	(28.04)
10% YTM → 15% YTM	100.00 → 74.51	(25.49)
15% YTM → 20% YTM	74.51 → 57.43	(22.92)

Exhibits 4–35 through 4–37 allow the reader to tailor specific examples to the investment situation encountered. The general concepts outlined will permeate all of the applications.

Special applications of bond price volatility

The price volatility of sinking fund bonds

As discussed in Chapter 3, a sinking fund (SF) bond requires special treatment because of its unique cash flow characteristics.[8] A traditional bullet bond repays its entire principal at maturity. A sinking fund bond returns the principal in specified allotments called sinking fund payments.[9] Conceptually, the YTM equivalent (i.e., internal rate of return) of a SF bond is its DCF yield.

For example, a GMAC 7% coupon, 10-year SF debenture has its principal repaid annually, commencing at the end of the sixth year. The sinker retires 20% of the bonds in each of the final 5 years. At a 7% DCF yield, the issue is priced at par (refer to Exhibit 4–38). If rates decline to 4%, the bond trades at 120.28 (Exhibit 4–39). If rates rise to 10%, the bond's price declines to 83.87 (Exhibit 4–40). The bond's observed price volatility is more like that of an 8-year U.S. Treasury than a similar maturity, 10-year U.S. Treasury issue (see Exhibit

---

[8] Mortgage-backed securities deserve similar treatment based upon their expected principal repayment schedule.

[9] As noted in Chapter 3, pro-rata sinking funds are assumed for illustrations in this book. Market sinkers can introduce a high degree of subjectivity into the analysis.

Exhibit 4–38. Calculation of the price of a 7% coupon, 10-year GMAC sinking fund debenture trading at a 7% DCF yield. The sinking fund retires 20% of the bonds annually, commencing at the end of the sixth year.

End of Period t	(1) P_t	(2) CPN_t	(3) = (1) + (2) Total Cash Flow, CF_t	(4) PV Factor	(5) = (3) × (4) $PV(CF_t)$
1		$35.00	$ 35.00	0.9662	$ 33.82
2		35.00	35.00	0.9335	32.67
3		35.00	35.00	0.9019	31.57
4		35.00	35.00	0.8714	30.50
5		35.00	35.00	0.8420	29.47
6		35.00	35.00	0.8135	28.47
7		35.00	35.00	0.7860	27.51
8		35.00	35.00	0.7594	26.58
9		35.00	35.00	0.7337	25.68
10		35.00	35.00	0.7089	24.81
11		35.00	35.00	0.6849	23.97
12	$200.00	35.00	235.00	0.6618	155.52
13		28.00	28.00	0.6394	17.90
14	200.00	28.00	228.00	0.6178	140.86
15		21.00	21.00	0.5969	12.53
16	200.00	21.00	221.00	0.5767	127.45
17		14.00	14.00	0.5572	7.80
18	200.00	14.00	214.00	0.5384	115.22
19		7.00	7.00	0.5202	3.64
20	200.00	7.00	207.00	0.5026	104.04
				Total PV →	$1,000.00
					↑ Bond price

Comments: *Cash flows are semiannual coupons of 7% of the remaining principal balance and sinking fund payments of 20% of the original principal annually for 5 years, commencing at the end of Year 6. The present value factors are calculated as $1/(1 + 0.07/2)$ or $1/(1 + 0.035)$.*

Exhibit 4–39. Calculation of the price of a 7% coupon, 10-year GMAC sinking fund debenture trading at a 4% DCF yield. The sinking fund retires 20% of the bonds annually, commencing at the end of the sixth year.

End of Period t	(1) P_t	(2) CPN_t	(3) = (1) + (2) Total Cash Flow, CF_t	(4) PV Factor	(5) = (3) × (4) $PV(CF_t)$
1		$35.00	$ 35.00	0.9804	$ 34.31
2		35.00	35.00	0.9612	33.64
3		35.00	35.00	0.9423	32.98
4		35.00	35.00	0.9238	32.33
5		35.00	35.00	0.9057	31.70
6		35.00	35.00	0.8880	31.08
7		35.00	35.00	0.8706	30.47
8		35.00	35.00	0.8535	29.87
9		35.00	35.00	0.8368	29.29
10		35.00	35.00	0.8203	28.71
11		35.00	35.00	0.8043	28.15
12	$200.00	35.00	235.00	0.7885	185.30
13		28.00	28.00	0.7730	21.64
14	200.00	28.00	228.00	0.7579	172.80
15		21.00	21.00	0.7430	15.60
16	200.00	21.00	221.00	0.7284	160.98
17		14.00	14.00	0.7142	10.00
18	200.00	14.00	214.00	0.7002	149.84
19		7.00	7.00	0.6864	4.80
20	200.00	7.00	207.00	0.6730	139.31
				Total PV →	$1,202.80
					↑ Bond price

Comments: *Cash flows are semiannual coupons of 7% of the remaining principal balance and sinking fund payments of 20% of the original principal annually for 5 years, commencing at the end of Year 6. The present value factors are calculated as $1/(1 + 0.04/2)$ or $1/(1 + 0.02)$.*

Exhibit 4–40. Calculation of the price of a 7% coupon, 10-year GMAC sinking fund debenture trading at a 10% DCF yield. The sinking fund retires 20% of the bonds annually, commencing at the end of the sixth year.

End of Period t	(1) P_t	(2) CPN_t	(3) = (1) + (2) Total Cash Flow, CF_t	(4) PV Factor	(5) = (3) × (4) $PV(CF_t)$
1		$35.00	$ 35.00	0.9524	$ 33.33
2		35.00	35.00	0.9070	31.75
3		35.00	35.00	0.8638	30.23
4		35.00	35.00	0.8227	28.79
5		35.00	35.00	0.7835	27.42
6		35.00	35.00	0.7462	26.12
7		35.00	35.00	0.7107	24.87
8		35.00	35.00	0.6768	23.69
9		35.00	35.00	0.6446	22.56
10		35.00	35.00	0.6139	21.49
11		35.00	35.00	0.5847	20.46
12	$200.00	35.00	235.00	0.5568	130.85
13		28.00	28.00	0.5303	14.85
14	200.00	28.00	228.00	0.5051	115.16
15		21.00	21.00	0.4810	10.10
16	200.00	21.00	221.00	0.4581	101.24
17		14.00	14.00	0.4363	6.11
18	200.00	14.00	214.00	0.4155	88.92
19		7.00	7.00	0.3957	2.77
20	200.00	7.00	207.00	0.3769	78.02

Total PV → $838.70

↑
Bond price

Comments: *Cash flows are semiannual coupons of 7% of the remaining principal balance and sinking fund payments of 20% of the original principal annually for 5 years, commencing at the end of Year 6. The present value factors are calculated as $1/(1 + 0.10/2)$ or $1/(1 + 0.05)$.*

Exhibit 4–41. Price volatility of a 10-year, 7% coupon GMAC sinking fund debenture versus a similar maturity (10-year) U.S. Treasury bond and a similar average life (8-year) U.S. Treasury bond.

Issue	DCF Yield (%)	Bond Price	Percent Change in Price
7% Coupon, 10-Year GMAC SF Bond	4.00	120.28	+20.28
	5.00	112.99	+12.99
	6.00	106.24	+ 6.24
	7.00	**100.00**	
	8.00	94.21	− 5.79
	9.00	88.85	−11.15
	10.00	83.87	−16.13
7% Coupon, 10-Year U.S. Treasury	4.00	124.53	+24.53
	5.00	115.59	+15.59
	6.00	107.44	+ 7.44
	7.00	**100.00**	
	8.00	93.20	− 6.80
	9.00	86.99	−13.01
	10.00	81.31	−18.69
7% Coupon, 8-Year U.S. Treasury	4.00	120.37	+20.37
	5.00	113.06	+13.06
	6.00	106.28	+ 6.28
	7.00	**100.00**	
	8.00	94.17	− 5.83
	9.00	88.77	−11.23
	10.00	83.74	−16.26

Comments: *Sinking fund debentures have price volatilities more similar to those of a U.S. Treasury bond of similar average life than that of a U.S. Treasury bond of similar maturity.*

4–41). This is not surprising given that the GMAC debenture has a weighted average maturity (WAM) of 8 years.[10] Since its principal cash flow is received at earlier points in time, the SF debenture is less volatile than its final maturity suggests. All other factors held equal, the larger the SF bond's balloon payment (i.e., the lower the percentage of bonds

[10] The WAM, or average life, is calculated as follows:

$$(6 \times 20\%) + (7 \times 20\%) + (8 \times 20\%) + (9 \times 20\%) + (10 \times 20\%) = 8.0 \text{ years}$$

The percentage of the principal repaid is multiplied by the year in which the repayment occurs. The factors are then summed to obtain the weighted average (recall the Chapter 3 discussion).

sunk prior to final maturity), the longer the WAM and the more price volatile the bond.

> **Observation:** *A sinking fund bond offers a lesser degree of price volatility than a similar maturity bullet bond. The final principal payment at maturity contributes less to the bond's price, thus having less impact on the bond's price volatility. A sinking fund bond exhibits price volatility similar to that of a bullet bond maturing on the WAM date.*

The price volatility of callable bonds

The price volatilities analyzed up to this point have been associated with noncallable bonds. Callable bonds carry features that make the volatility assessment a more difficult one. Corporate bonds are traditionally callable in nature, with standard structures applied in the industrial, electric utility, and telephone utility sectors.[11] As opposed to its noncallable counterparts, a callable bond offers limited upside appreciation potential and a somewhat *cushioned* downside performance. For example, assume that an investor can purchase the following issues:

1. A 10% coupon, 30-year noncallable Public Service Electric and Gas (PSEG) bond priced at par to yield 10.00%.
2. A 10% coupon, 30-year PSEG bond with a current cash call at 109.50 and a 5-year refunding call at 108.50. The bond is priced at 97.70 to yield 10.25%.
3. A 13% coupon, 30-year PSEG bond with a current cash call at 112.00 and a 5-year refunding call at 110.75. The bond is currently trading at 115.00.

Exhibits 4–42 and 4–43 summarize the expected price behavior of the utility issues under falling yields (a 300BP decrease to 7.00%), stable yields (at 7.00%), and rising yields (a 300BP increase to 10.00%).[12]

---

[11] As a general rule, new-issue long maturity corporate bonds are of four types:

a. *Industrial bonds:* 30-year maturity, 10 years nonrefundable, immediate cash call at a premium.

b. *Electric utility bonds:* 30-year maturity, 5 years nonrefundable, immediate cash call at a premium.

c. *Telephone utility bonds:* 40-year maturity, 5 years nonrefundable and noncallable.

d. *Noncallable industrial and finance bonds.*

[12] The reader should not be concerned about the necessity of subjective estimates of the price changes of callable bonds. The purpose here is to illustrate the dulling effect of call features on a bond's price volatility.

Exhibit 4–42. Price volatility of three 30-year maturity utility bonds with differing call features and initial dollar prices.

Issue	*Interest Rate Environment*	*Bond Price(e)**	*Percent Change in Price*
10% Coupon, Noncallable	Fall 300BP	137.42	+37.42
	Stable	100.00	0
	Rise 300BP	77.45	−22.55
10% Coupon, Callable	Fall 300BP	112.00	+14.64
	Stable	97.70	0
	Rise 300BP	77.15	−21.03
13% Coupon, Callable	Fall 300BP	112.00	− 2.61
	Stable	115.00	0
	Rise 300BP	98.15	−14.65

* (e), estimated. The derivation of the estimated prices is given in Exhibit 4–43.

Exhibit 4–43. Derivation of the estimated bond prices used in Exhibit 4–42.

Issue	*Estimated Price*	*Explanation*
10% Coupon, Noncallable	137.42	Bond is priced to yield 7.00%.
	100.00	Bond is priced to yield 10.00%.
	77.45	Bond is priced to yield 13.00%.
10% Coupon, Callable	112.00	Bond trades at, but not above, cash call as investors expect the call to be exercised.*
	97.70	Bond is priced to yield 10.25% (+25BP to noncall issue).
	77.15	Bond is priced to yield 13.10% (+10BP to noncall issue).
13% Coupon, Callable	112.00	Bond trades at, but not above, cash call as investors expect the cash call to be exercised.*
	115.00	Bond trades a few points above cash call price as some investors anticipate that the cash call will not be exercised.
	98.15	Bond is priced to yield 13.25% (+25BP to noncall 10% issue).

* This is a subjective estimate based on expected perceptions given a surrounding environment of 7.00% interest rates.

Several conclusions emanate from these tables. First, noncallable corporate bonds are apt to behave like noncallable U.S. Treasury bonds. Second, callable issues currently trading close to par experience a modest degree of appreciation in a bull market and provide only a small degree of cushioning in a bear market. Third, high coupon callable bonds currently trading at a substantial premium to par participate little, if at all, in a bull market (and can actually lose value), but offer a sizable price cushion in a bear market. The 13% coupon bond has a truncated price:yield curve as a result of its call features (see Exhibit 4–44).

In general, the price of a callable bond fluctuates to a lesser degree than a noncallable bond of like maturity. In a bull market, the upside appreciation is limited by the issuer's right to call the bond from the investor at a prespecified price. The likelihood of call increases as general yield levels fall. The price declines experienced in a rising interest rate environment are mitigated somewhat by the reduced fear of issuer call and the related support of the bond price as high coupon, defensive instruments are sought by investors.

> **Observation:** *Callable bonds exhibit less price volatility than their similar maturity noncallable counterparts.*

Exhibit 4–44. Price:yield curve for a high coupon callable bond.

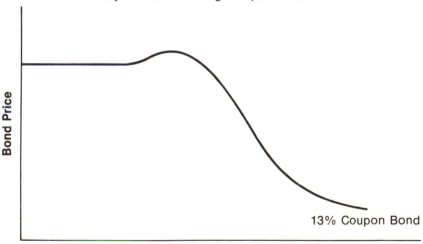

Summary

A bond's price varies inversely with its yield to maturity. A bond's sensitivity to interest rate fluctuations is a function of the bond's term to maturity, coupon rate of interest, sinking fund features, and call provisions. The current level of market interest rates is also an important influence to be considered. Bond price volatility is enhanced by long maturities, low coupon rates, minimal call and sinking fund features, and an initial environment of low yields. Long maturity, zero-coupon bonds offer the greatest potential for price volatility.

CHAPTER 5

Bond Risk Measures: The Past

This chapter reviews the older, more traditional measures of a bond's risk: term to maturity and weighted average maturity. The chapter concludes with a look at the weighted average cash flow, an extension of the weighted average maturity concept. The discussion of the weighted average cash flow construct forms a smooth transition to Chapter 6, which focuses on the risk measures currently in vogue. Chapter 6 analyzes the contemporary bond risk proxies: duration, convexity, and the yield value of a 32nd. Chapter 7 entertains the potential new entrants into the bond risk family, including the standard deviation of total return and the bond beta, and discusses the application of these new members to the bond portfolio management arena of today.

A bond risk measure is intended to capture the volatility characteristics of a particular issue or set of issues. The sophistication and rigor of the risk assessor in vogue has risen dramatically over the past 10 years. A review of the most primitive constructs of bond risk is a necessary prerequisite to an understanding of today's risk measures and to a projection of how today's measures will evolve in the future. The most basic bond risk proxies are term to maturity, weighted average maturity, and weighted average cash flow.

Term to maturity

The concept

The *term to maturity* (TTM) is simply the number of years remaining until the bond's final maturity date. Longer maturity bonds have traditionally been viewed as riskier instruments, and rightly so. The examples of bond price volatility in Chapter 4 affirm this common perception. All other factors held equal, long-term bonds exhibit greater degrees of price volatility than short-term bonds. However, the term to maturity, by focusing solely on the final maturity date of a bond, ignores several critically important influences on a bond's risk.

> **Observation:** *The term to maturity assesses a bond's risk from a final maturity date perspective. Long maturity bonds are riskier than short maturity issues.*

Problems with the term to maturity as a risk measure

First, even if "all other factors are held equal" (coupon rate, principal repayment distribution), the TTM tends to overestimate the risk inherent in long maturity bonds. For example, a 30-year issue is assumed to be 3 times as risky as a 10-year issue and 10 times as risky as a 3-year issue. Recall that the actual observed volatility of a 30-year noncallable bond is only twice that of a 10-year bond and approximately 5 times that of a 3-year bond, assuming a 7% yield environment (refer to Exhibit 4–4). In higher yield surroundings, the added risk of a long-term bond is even less dramatic.[1]

Second, all other factors are generally *not* held equal. Given the sizable surges and declines in interest rate levels since the mid-1970s, an investor is confronted with a myriad of available coupon rates, call features, and cash flow structures. Ignoring the explicit and unique cash flow payment stream of a bond (most cash flows are received prior to maturity) and failing to consider the impact of the time value of money on that specified payment stream leads to errors in the risk assessment process.

Exhibit 5–1 plots cash flow timelines for three 10-year maturity bonds. The exclusive focus of TTM on the final maturity date payment

---

[1] The influence of the market yield level on a bond's inherent riskiness is discussed at greater length in Chapter 6 under the duration concept.

Exhibit 5–1. Cash flow timelines for three 10-year maturity bonds.

(a) GMAC 7% coupon sinking fund debenture maturing in 10 years. The sinking fund retires 20% of the bonds annually, commencing at the end of the sixth year. (Data per Exhibit 5-3.)

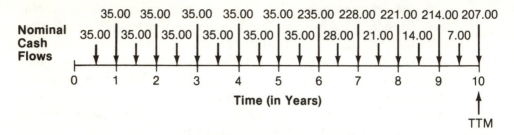

(b) 7% coupon, 10-year U.S. Treasury bond.

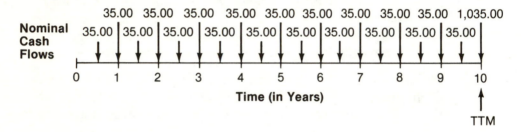

(c) 10-year STRIPS.

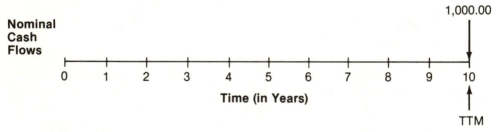

Comments: *Term to maturity focuses solely on the final maturity cash flow.*

is emphasized. The expanding list of new product offerings by investment banking firms requires a greater depth of analysis than a generic, noncallable bullet U.S. Treasury bond. The typical fluctuations in interest rate levels observed in today's markets are of a magnitude demanding that

Exhibit 5–2. Bond price volatilities of issues with similar terms to maturity. The initial market yield level is 7.00%. (Data from Exhibits 4–30, 4–41, and 4–42.)

Issue	Term to Maturity (Years)	Percent Change in Price if Yields:	
		Fall 300BP	Rise 300BP
GMAC 7% coupon SF bond	10	+ 20.28	−16.13
7% coupon U.S. Treasury bond	10	+ 24.53	−18.69
STRIPS	10	+ 33.90	−25.01
13% coupon utility bond	30	− 2.61	−14.65
7% coupon U.S. Treasury bond	30	+ 52.14	−28.39
STRIPS	30	+140.19	−57.84

factors other than simply the final maturity payment be considered in assessing a bond's underlying price risk.

Finally, the faultiness of the TTM is highlighted in Exhibit 5–2. The upper half of the table compares three bonds which, on a TTM basis, have equivalent risk (TTM = 10 years). In actuality, however, the observed price behaviors of the three issues are appreciably different. A market rally of 300BP leads to a 33.90% price return on the 10-year STRIPS but only a 20.28% rise for the GMAC 7% sinking fund bond. In the investment world, a 1,362BP difference in return (33.90% − 20.28%) is significant! A bear market portends a sizable decline in price for the STRIPS (−25.01%) and a more modest depreciation for the GMAC issue (−16.13%). The 7% coupon, 10-year U.S. Treasury bond experiences volatility in between that of the STRIPS and the GMAC debenture.

The lower half of Exhibit 5–2 extends the example to 30-year maturity bonds. Once again, TTM sees no risk differential between the three issues (TTM = 30 years). The observed variation in price movements is, however, large. The long-term STRIPS outreturns the high coupon utility bond by over 140% (i.e., 14,000 basis points) in a bull market. Conversely, the utility bond outdoes the zero by over 43% (i.e., 4,300 basis points) in a bear market. It is quite evident that the TTM measure, in and of itself, is a very questionable indicator of bond risk.

> **Observation:** *The term to maturity is a weak proxy for a bond's inherent risk. The primary cause of the term to maturity's shortcomings is its failure to consider the cash flows received prior to final maturity.*

Weighted average maturity

The concept

The *weighted average maturity,* or *average life,* of a bond is a measure of the average point in time at which half of the principal repayments have been collected.[2] A longer (i.e., higher) WAM implies a riskier security. For a sinking fund bond, the WAM is a function of the distribution of sinking fund payments. The WAM attempts to improve on the TTM by providing a measure of the average maturity of a bond that pays principal across a period of time rather than solely at maturity. The formula for calculating a WAM is:

$$\text{WAM}_{years} = \sum_{t=a}^{n} \left(\frac{\text{P}_t}{\text{TPCF}} \times t \right)$$

$$= \sum_{t=a}^{n} \left(\frac{\text{P}_t}{\$1,000.00} \times t \right)$$

where

P$_t$ = principal cash flow received (per bond) in year t

TPCF = total principal cash flow to be repaid per bond (i.e., \$1,000.00)

t = time period (years)

a = date of the first principal repayment (years)

n = final maturity (years)

Applications of the WAM concept

As an example, the GMAC 7% coupon, 10-year sinking fund debenture illustrated in Chapter 4 has a sinking fund that pays down 20% of the bonds annually, commencing at the end of the sixth year. The issue has a WAM of 8.0 years:

$$\text{WAM}_{years} = \sum_{t=6}^{10} \left(\frac{\text{PCF}_t}{\text{TPCF}} \times t \right)$$

---

[2] The weighted average maturity is not to be confused with a bond's *half-life.* A half-life is the exact, not the average, point in time at which the 50th percent of the principal reinvestment is recouped. The half-life occurs on an actual cash flow date (i.e., a sinking fund payment date).

$$= \left(\frac{\$200.00}{\$1,000.00} \times 6 \right) + \left(\frac{\$200.00}{\$1,000.00} \times 7 \right) + \left(\frac{\$200.00}{\$1,000.00} \times 8 \right)$$
$$+ \left(\frac{\$200.00}{\$1,000.00} \times 9 \right) + \left(\frac{\$200.00}{\$1,000.00} \times 10 \right)$$

$$= 1.20 + 1.40 + 1.60 + 1.80 + 2.00$$

$$= 8.00 \text{ years}$$

Each time period (t) in which a principal cash flow occurs is deemed a weighting based on the contribution of that principal cash flow to the total of all the principal repayments. In this sense the result generated is a *weighted* average. Exhibit 5–3 (left-hand side) presents the same calculation in a columnar format. Notice that the coupon cash flows are completely ignored in the WAM computation. As a result, a similar GMAC issue with a 4% coupon rate bears an identical 8.00-year WAM (see Exhibit 5–4). A 10% coupon GMAC with a similar sinking fund structure provides a WAM of 8.0 years as well (see Exhibit 5–5).

As another illustration, a 7% coupon, 8-year U.S. Treasury bond has a WAM of 8.0 years. The principal is paid entirely at maturity and, therefore, the term to maturity and the weighted average maturity coincide. Exhibit 5–6 provides a complete breakdown of the WAM calculation for the 8-year U.S. Treasury. The table results concur with the findings by the use of the WAM formula:

$$\text{WAM}_{years} = \sum_{t=8}^{8} \left(\frac{P_t}{\text{TPCF}} \times t \right)$$
$$= \frac{\$1,000.00}{\$1,000.00} \times 8$$
$$= 8.00 \text{ years}$$

The coupon cash flows emanating from the bond are completely ignored. Consequently, the WAMs of a 4% coupon, 8-year U.S. Treasury bond and a 10% coupon, 8-year U.S. Treasury bond are an identical 8.00 years (refer to Exhibits 5–7 and 5–8). Exhibit 5–9 shows that an 8-year zero-coupon bond also carries an 8-year WAM. Exhibit 5–10 plots cash flow timelines for the GMAC 7% coupon bond; the 7% coupon, 8-year U.S. Treasury; and the 8-year STRIPS. Notice how the WAM

Exhibit 5–3. Calculation of the WAM and WACF of a 7% coupon, 10-year GMAC sinking fund debenture. The sinking fund retires 20% of the bonds annually, commencing at the end of the sixth year.

	(a) Calculation of WAM			(b) Calculation of WACF		
(1) t (Years)	(2) Principal Cash Flow	(3) = (2)/$1,000 CF Weight	(4) = (1) × (3) Weighted t	(5) Total Cash Flow	(6) = (5)/TCF CF Weight	(7) = (1) × (6) Weighted t
0.5	$ 0	0	0	$ 35	0.0224	0.0112
1.0	0	0	0	35	0.0224	0.0224
1.5	0	0	0	35	0.0224	0.0336
2.0	0	0	0	35	0.0224	0.0448
2.5	0	0	0	35	0.0224	0.0560
3.0	0	0	0	35	0.0224	0.0672
3.5	0	0	0	35	0.0224	0.0784
4.0	0	0	0	35	0.0224	0.0896
4.5	0	0	0	35	0.0224	0.1008
5.0	0	0	0	35	0.0224	0.1120
5.5	0	0	0	35	0.0224	0.1232
6.0	200	0.20	1.20	235	0.1506	0.9036
6.5	0	0	0	28	0.0179	0.1164
7.0	200	0.20	1.40	228	0.1462	1.0234
7.5	0	0	0	21	0.0135	0.1013
8.0	200	0.20	1.60	221	0.1417	1.1336
8.5	0	0	0	14	0.0090	0.0765
9.0	200	0.20	1.80	214	0.1372	1.2348
9.5	0	0	0	7	0.0045	0.0428
10.0	200	0.20	2.00	207	0.1327	1.3270
	$1,000	1.00	8.00	$1,560	1.0000	6.7000
	↑ TPCF		↑ WAM	↑ TCF		↑ WACF

Exhibit 5–4. Calculation of the WAM and WACF of a 4% coupon, 10-year GMAC sinking fund debenture. The sinking fund retires 20% of the bonds annually, commencing at the end of the sixth year.

	(a) Calculation of WAM			(b) Calculation of WACF		
(1) t (Years)	(2) Principal Cash Flow	(3) = (2)/$1,000 CF Weight	(4) = (1) × (3) Weighted t	(5) Total Cash Flow	(6) = (5)/TCF CF Weight	(7) = (1) × (6) Weighted t
0.5	$ 0	0	0	$ 20	0.0152	0.0076
1.0	0	0	0	20	0.0152	0.0152
1.5	0	0	0	20	0.0152	0.0228
2.0	0	0	0	20	0.0152	0.0304
2.5	0	0	0	20	0.0152	0.0380
3.0	0	0	0	20	0.0152	0.0456
3.5	0	0	0	20	0.0152	0.0532
4.0	0	0	0	20	0.0152	0.0608
4.5	0	0	0	20	0.0152	0.0684
5.0	0	0	0	20	0.0152	0.0760
5.5	0	0	0	20	0.0152	0.0836
6.0	200	0.20	1.20	220	0.1667	1.0002
6.5	0	0	0	16	0.0121	0.0787
7.0	200	0.20	1.40	216	0.1636	1.1452
7.5	0	0	0	12	0.0091	0.0683
8.0	200	0.20	1.60	212	0.1606	1.2848
8.5	0	0	0	8	0.0061	0.0519
9.0	200	0.20	1.80	208	0.1576	1.4184
9.5	0	0	0	4	0.0030	0.0285
10.0	200	0.20	2.00	204	0.1545	1.5450
	$1,000	1.00	8.00	$1,320	1.0000	7.1200
	↑ TPCF		↑ WAM	↑ TCF		↑ WACF

Exhibit 5-5. Calculation of the WAM and WACF of a 10% coupon, 10-year GMAC sinking fund debenture. The sinking fund retires 20% of the bonds annually, commencing at the end of the sixth year.

	(a) Calculation of WAM			(b) Calculation of WACF		
(1) t (Years)	(2) Principal Cash Flow	(3) = (2)/$1,000 CF Weight	(4) = (1) × (3) Weighted t	(5) Total Cash Flow	(6) = (5)/TCF CF Weight	(7) = (1) × (6) Weighted t
0.5	$ 0	0	0	$ 50	0.0278	0.0139
1.0	0	0	0	50	0.0278	0.0278
1.5	0	0	0	50	0.0278	0.0417
2.0	0	0	0	50	0.0278	0.0556
2.5	0	0	0	50	0.0278	0.0695
3.0	0	0	0	50	0.0278	0.0834
3.5	0	0	0	50	0.0278	0.0973
4.0	0	0	0	50	0.0278	0.1112
4.5	0	0	0	50	0.0278	0.1251
5.0	0	0	0	50	0.0278	0.1390
5.5	0	0	0	50	0.0278	0.1529
6.0	200	0.20	1.20	250	0.1389	0.8334
6.5	0	0	0	40	0.0222	0.1443
7.0	200	0.20	1.40	240	0.1333	0.9331
7.5	0	0	0	30	0.0167	0.1253
8.0	200	0.20	1.60	230	0.1278	1.0224
8.5	0	0	0	20	0.0111	0.0944
9.0	200	0.20	1.80	220	0.1222	1.0998
9.5	0	0	0	10	0.0056	0.0532
10.0	200	0.20	2.00	210	0.1167	1.1670
	$1,000	1.00	8.00	$1,800	1.0000	6.3900
	↑ TPCF		↑ WAM	↑ TCF		↑ WACF

Exhibit 5–6. Calculation of the WAM and WACF of a 7% coupon, 8-year U.S. Treasury bond.

(1) t (Years)	(a) Calculation of WAM			(b) Calculation of WACF		
	(2) Principal Cash Flow	(3) = (2)/$1,000 CF Weight	(4) = (1) × (3) Weighted t	(5) Total Cash Flow	(6) = (5)/TCF CF Weight	(7) = (1) × (6) Weighted t
0.5	$ 0	0	0	$ 35	0.0224	0.0112
1.0	0	0	0	35	0.0224	0.0224
1.5	0	0	0	35	0.0224	0.0336
2.0	0	0	0	35	0.0224	0.0448
2.5	0	0	0	35	0.0224	0.0560
3.0	0	0	0	35	0.0224	0.0672
3.5	0	0	0	35	0.0224	0.0784
4.0	0	0	0	35	0.0224	0.0896
4.5	0	0	0	35	0.0224	0.1008
5.0	0	0	0	35	0.0224	0.1120
5.5	0	0	0	35	0.0224	0.1232
6.0	0	0	0	35	0.0224	0.1344
6.5	0	0	0	35	0.0224	0.1456
7.0	0	0	0	35	0.0224	0.1568
7.5	0	0	0	35	0.0224	0.1680
8.0	1,000	1.00	8.00	1,035	0.6635	5.3080
	$1,000	1.00	8.00	$1,560	1.0000	6.6500
	↑ TPCF		↑ WAM	↑ TCF		↑ WACF

131

Exhibit 5–7. Calculation of the WAM and WACF of a 4% coupon, 8-year U.S. Treasury bond.

(1) t (Years)	(a) Calculation of WAM			(b) Calculation of WACF		
	(2) Principal Cash Flow	(3) = (2)/$1,000 CF Weight	(4) = (1) × (3) Weighted t	(5) Total Cash Flow	(6) = (5)/TCF CF Weight	(7) = (1) × (6) Weighted t
0.5	$ 0	0	0	$ 20	0.0152	0.0076
1.0	0	0	0	20	0.0152	0.0152
1.5	0	0	0	20	0.0152	0.0228
2.0	0	0	0	20	0.0152	0.0304
2.5	0	0	0	20	0.0152	0.0380
3.0	0	0	0	20	0.0152	0.0456
3.5	0	0	0	20	0.0152	0.0532
4.0	0	0	0	20	0.0152	0.0608
4.5	0	0	0	20	0.0152	0.0684
5.0	0	0	0	20	0.0152	0.0760
5.5	0	0	0	20	0.0152	0.0836
6.0	0	0	0	20	0.0152	0.0912
6.5	0	0	0	20	0.0152	0.0988
7.0	0	0	0	20	0.0152	0.1064
7.5	0	0	0	20	0.0152	0.1140
8.0	1,000	1.00	8.00	1,020	0.7727	6.1816
	$1,000	1.00	8.00	$1,320	1.0000	7.0900
	↑ TPCF		↑ WAM	↑ TCF		↑ WACF

Exhibit 5–8. Calculation of the WAM and WACF of a 10% coupon, 8-year U.S. Treasury bond.

(1) t (Years)	(a) Calculation of WAM			(b) Calculation of WACF		
	(2) Principal Cash Flow	(3) = (2)/$1,000 CF Weight	(4) = (1) × (3) Weighted t	(5) Total Cash Flow	(6) = (5)/TCF CF Weight	(7) = (1) × (6) Weighted t
0.5	$ 0	0	0	$ 50	0.0278	0.0139
1.0	0	0	0	50	0.0278	0.0278
1.5	0	0	0	50	0.0278	0.0417
2.0	0	0	0	50	0.0278	0.0556
2.5	0	0	0	50	0.0278	0.0695
3.0	0	0	0	50	0.0278	0.0834
3.5	0	0	0	50	0.0278	0.0973
4.0	0	0	0	50	0.0278	0.1112
4.5	0	0	0	50	0.0278	0.1251
5.0	0	0	0	50	0.0278	0.1390
5.5	0	0	0	50	0.0278	0.1529
6.0	0	0	0	50	0.0278	0.1668
6.5	0	0	0	50	0.0278	0.1807
7.0	0	0	0	50	0.0278	0.1946
7.5	0	0	0	50	0.0278	0.2085
8.0	1,000	1.00	8.00	1,050	0.5833	4.6664
	$1,000	1.00	8.00	$1,800	1.0000	6.3300
	↑ TPCF		↑ WAM	↑ TCF		↑ WACF

133

Exhibit 5–9. Calculation of the WAM and WACF of an 8-year STRIPS.

(1) t (Years)	(a) Calculation of WAM			(b) Calculation of WACF		
	(2) Principal Cash Flow	(3) = (2)/$1,000 CF Weight	(4) = (1) × (3) Weighted t	(5) Total Cash Flow	(6) = (5)/TCF CF Weight	(7) = (1) × (6) Weighted t
0.5	$ 0	0	0	$ 0	0	0
1.0	0	0	0	0	0	0
1.5	0	0	0	0	0	0
2.0	0	0	0	0	0	0
2.5	0	0	0	0	0	0
3.0	0	0	0	0	0	0
3.5	0	0	0	0	0	0
4.0	0	0	0	0	0	0
4.5	0	0	0	0	0	0
5.0	0	0	0	0	0	0
5.5	0	0	0	0	0	0
6.0	0	0	0	0	0	0
6.5	0	0	0	0	0	0
7.0	0	0	0	0	0	0
7.5	0	0	0	0	0	0
8.0	1,000	1.00	8.00	1,000	1.00	8.00
	$1,000	1.00	8.00	$1,000	1.00	8.00
	↑ TPCF		↑ WAM	↑ TCF		↑ WACF

134

Exhibit 5–10. Cash flow timelines for three 8-year WAM bonds.

(a) GMAC 7% coupon sinking fund debenture maturing in 10 years. The sinking fund retires 20% of the bonds annually, commencing at the end of the sixth year. (Data per Exhibit 5–3.)

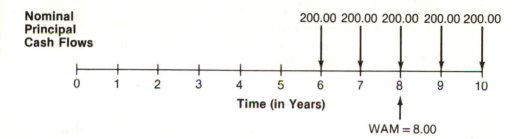

(b) 7% coupon, 8–year U.S. Treasury bond. (Data per Exhibit 5–6.)

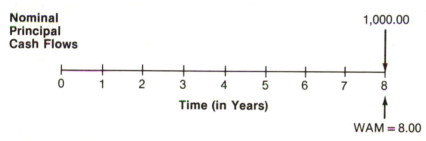

(c) 8-year STRIPS. (Data per Exhibit 5-9.)

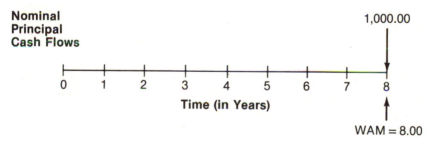

Comments: *Weighted average maturity (WAM) considers all principal cash flows, but ignores coupon cash flows.*

focuses on the principal repayments of a bond, taking little note of the coupon cash flows.

> **Observation:** *The weighted average maturity uses the average date of principal redemption as the measure of bond price risk. For sinking fund and mortgage-backed securities, the WAM is a revised version of the term to maturity construct. For bullet bonds, the WAM is identical to the term to maturity. Longer WAMs are associated with greater degrees of bond price volatility.*

Problems with the WAM as a risk measure

The WAM bond risk measure is a step above the TTM risk proxy to the extent that the WAM considers the distribution of principal repayments rather than simply the final principal payment at maturity. However, the WAM fails to incorporate all of a bond's cash flows into the analysis and neglects to consider the time value of money. Coupon payments are glossed over and market yield levels have no impact on the WAM computation. In reality, however, both the coupon rate and the market yield level affect a bond's inherent riskiness.[3]

The weaknesses of WAM as a bond risk proxy can be observed from three perspectives. First, the size of the coupon rate on a bond, while leaving the WAM untouched, changes the bond's price volatility. Second, the principal repayment distribution on a sinking fund bond may affect the bond's price volatility and yet leave the WAM intact. Third, different types of securities (sinking fund bonds, bullet bonds, STRIPS) may share the same WAM but exhibit dramatically different volatility characteristics. Each of these points is discussed in turn.

The coupon rate effect. The WAM of a bond is insensitive to coupon differentials. As an illustration, the WAM of the GMAC 10-year sinking fund debenture of several previous examples is 8.00 years, regardless of the attached coupon rate. The identical 8-year WAMs suggest equivalent riskiness among the sample issues. However, the actual price volatilities indicate otherwise. For example, Exhibit 5–11 shows that a 4% GMAC issue has more inherent price volatility than a current-coupon 7% GMAC or a premium-coupon 10% GMAC. The bond price calculation *does* consider all of the bond's cash flows and *does* consider the time

---

[3] The impact of coupon rate and market yield level on a bond's price volatility was addressed in Chapter 4. The reader is encouraged to review the material in that chapter before proceeding.

Exhibit 5–11. Bond price volatilities of a series of GMAC sinking fund debentures maturing in 10 years with sinking funds retiring 20% of the bonds annually, commencing at the end of the sixth year. The initial yield level is at a 7.00% DCF yield.

		Percent Change in Bond Price if DCF Yields:	
Issue	*WAM (Years)*	*Fall 300BP*	*Rise 300BP*
GMAC 4% SF bond	8.0	+21.98	−17.36
GMAC 7% SF bond	8.0	+20.28	−16.13
GMAC 10% SF bond	8.0	+19.09	−15.28

value of money (through PV factors), creating the incongruence in volatility between issues of varying coupon rate.

The price calculations for the 7% coupon GMAC were given in Chapter 4 in Exhibits 4–38, 4–39, and 4–40. Exhibits 5–12, 5–13, and 5–14 provide the pricing data for the 4% coupon GMAC issue; Exhibits 5–15 through 5–17 compile the price derivations for the 10% coupon GMAC issue. Yields are initially at a 7% level and are moved down 300BP (to a 4% DCF yield) and up 300BP (to a 10% DCF yield) for each issue in order to assess their true volatility characteristics. As noted above, the results are aggregated in Exhibit 5–11.

The 4% GMAC issue rises by 21.98% if yields decline to 4% from a 7% level, as its price appreciates from 81.98 to 100.00. On the other hand, the 10% GMAC bond experiences a price surge of only 19.09% under the same bull market conditions (a 289BP return differential vis-à-vis the 4% coupon issue). In a bear market, the higher coupon 10% GMAC outperforms the lower coupon 4% issue by 208BP (−15.28% versus −17.36%), once again a sizable difference that the WAM measure fails to discern.

The sinking fund distribution effect. The WAM, as its name suggests, is an *average*. As an average, a given WAM can have a myriad of potential cash flow combinations behind it. For example, a GMAC 7% coupon sinking fund debenture may have these alternative structures:

1. 10-year final maturity with a sinking fund commencing at the end of Year 6 and paying down 20% of the bonds annually through Year 10 (as discussed previously).

2. 15-year final maturity with a sinking fund paying down half of the bonds at the end of Year 1 and paying off the remainder at maturity.

Exhibit 5–12. Calculation of the price of a 4% coupon, 10-year GMAC sinking fund debenture trading at a 7% DCF yield. The sinking fund retires 20% of the bonds annually, commencing at the end of the sixth year.

End of Period t	(1) P_t	(2) CPN_t	(3) = (1) + (2) Total Cash Flow, CF_t	(4) PV Factor	(5) = (3) × (4) $PV(CF_t)$
1		$20.00	$ 20.00	0.9662	$ 19.32
2		20.00	20.00	0.9335	18.67
3		20.00	20.00	0.9019	18.04
4		20.00	20.00	0.8714	17.43
5		20.00	20.00	0.8420	16.84
6		20.00	20.00	0.8135	16.27
7		20.00	20.00	0.7860	15.72
8		20.00	20.00	0.7594	15.19
9		20.00	20.00	0.7337	14.67
10		20.00	20.00	0.7089	14.18
11		20.00	20.00	0.6849	13.70
12	$200.00	20.00	220.00	0.6618	145.60
13		16.00	16.00	0.6394	10.23
14	200.00	16.00	216.00	0.6178	133.44
15		12.00	12.00	0.5969	7.16
16	200.00	12.00	212.00	0.5767	122.26
17		8.00	8.00	0.5572	4.46
18	200.00	8.00	208.00	0.5384	111.99
19		4.00	4.00	0.5202	2.08
20	200.00	4.00	204.00	0.5026	102.53
				Total PV →	$819.80
					↑ Bond price

Comments: *Cash flows are semiannual coupons of 4% of the remaining principal balance and sinking fund payments of 20% of the original principal annually for 5 years, commencing at the end of Year 6. The present value factors are calculated as $1/(1 + 0.07/2)$ or $1/(1 + 0.035)$.*

Each of these two cash flow schedules creates a WAM of 8 years (consult Exhibit 5–18 for the WAM calculation on the 15-year GMAC). The expected price volatility under rising and falling yields, however, varies materially between the two issues.

Exhibits 5–19 through 5–21 provide supporting price data for the

Exhibit 5–13. Calculation of the price of a 4% coupon, 10-year GMAC sinking fund debenture trading at a 4% DCF yield. The sinking fund retires 20% of the bonds annually, commencing at the end of the sixth year.

End of Period t	(1) P_t	(2) CPN_t	(3) = (1) + (2) Total Cash Flow, CF_t	(4) PV Factor	(5) = (3) × (4) $PV(CF_t)$
1		$20.00	$ 20.00	0.9804	$ 19.61
2		20.00	20.00	0.9612	19.22
3		20.00	20.00	0.9423	18.85
4		20.00	20.00	0.9238	18.48
5		20.00	20.00	0.9057	18.11
6		20.00	20.00	0.8880	17.76
7		20.00	20.00	0.8706	17.41
8		20.00	20.00	0.8535	17.07
9		20.00	20.00	0.8368	16.74
10		20.00	20.00	0.8203	16.41
11		20.00	20.00	0.8043	16.09
12	$200.00	20.00	220.00	0.7885	173.47
13		16.00	16.00	0.7730	12.37
14	200.00	16.00	216.00	0.7579	163.71
15		12.00	12.00	0.7430	8.92
16	200.00	12.00	212.00	0.7284	154.42
17		8.00	8.00	0.7142	5.71
18	200.00	8.00	208.00	0.7002	145.64
19		4.00	4.00	0.6864	2.75
20	200.00	4.00	204.00	0.6730	137.29
				Total PV →	$1,000.00
					↑ Bond price

Comments: *Cash flows are semiannual coupons of 4% of the remaining principal balance and sinking fund payments of 20% of the original principal annually for 5 years, commencing at the end of Year 6. The present value factors are calculated as $1/(1 + 0.04/2)$ or $1/(1 + 0.02)$.*

15-year GMAC issue. Exhibit 5–22 summarizes the volatility results. The 10-year GMAC exhibits more volatility than the 15-year GMAC bond. For example, in a rising interest rate environment, the 10-year issue registers a 16.13% price loss, 320BP more detrimental than the 15-year bond's 12.93% price decline. A bull market favors the 10-year

Exhibit 5–14. Calculation of the price of a 4% coupon, 10-year GMAC sinking fund debenture trading at a 10% DCF yield. The sinking fund retires 20% of the bonds annually, commencing at the end of the sixth year.

	(1)	(2)	(3) = (1) + (2)	(4)	(5) = (3) × (4)
End of Period t	P_t	CPN_t	Total Cash Flow, CF_t	PV Factor	$PV(CF_t)$
1		$20.00	$ 20.00	0.9524	$ 19.05
2		20.00	20.00	0.9070	18.14
3		20.00	20.00	0.8638	17.28
4		20.00	20.00	0.8227	16.45
5		20.00	20.00	0.7835	15.67
6		20.00	20.00	0.7462	14.92
7		20.00	20.00	0.7107	14.21
8		20.00	20.00	0.6768	13.54
9		20.00	20.00	0.6446	12.89
10		20.00	20.00	0.6139	12.28
11		20.00	20.00	0.5847	11.69
12	$200.00	20.00	220.00	0.5568	122.50
13		16.00	16.00	0.5303	8.48
14	200.00	16.00	216.00	0.5051	109.10
15		12.00	12.00	0.4810	5.77
16	200.00	12.00	212.00	0.4581	97.12
17		8.00	8.00	0.4363	3.49
18	200.00	8.00	208.00	0.4155	86.42
19		4.00	4.00	0.3957	1.58
20	200.00	4.00	204.00	0.3769	76.89
				Total PV →	$677.50

↑
Bond price

Comments: *Cash flows are semiannual coupons of 4% of the remaining principal balance and sinking fund payments of 20% of the original principal annually for 5 years, commencing at the end of Year 6. The present value factors are calculated as $1/(1 + 0.10/2)$ or $1/(1 + 0.05)$.*

issue by 203BP in return (20.28% versus 18.25%). It is obvious that WAM, although an improvement over TTM, is still deficient in the task of risk assessment.

The effect of alternative security types. In the term to maturity section, Exhibit 5–2 illustrated that the TTM is misleading when used across

Exhibit 5–15. Calculation of the price of a 10% coupon, 10-year GMAC sinking fund debenture trading at a 7% DCF yield. The sinking fund retires 20% of the bonds annually, commencing at the end of the sixth year.

	(1)	*(2)*	*(3) = (1) + (2)*	*(4)*	*(5) = (3) × (4)*
End of Period t	P_t	CPN_t	*Total Cash Flow,* CF_t	*PV Factor*	$PV(CF_t)$
1		$50.00	$ 50.00	0.9662	$ 48.31
2		50.00	50.00	0.9335	46.68
3		50.00	50.00	0.9019	45.10
4		50.00	50.00	0.8714	43.57
5		50.00	50.00	0.8420	42.10
6		50.00	50.00	0.8135	40.68
7		50.00	50.00	0.7860	39.30
8		50.00	50.00	0.7594	37.97
9		50.00	50.00	0.7337	36.69
10		50.00	50.00	0.7089	35.45
11		50.00	50.00	0.6849	34.25
12	$200.00	50.00	250.00	0.6618	165.45
13		40.00	40.00	0.6394	25.58
14	200.00	40.00	240.00	0.6178	148.27
15		30.00	30.00	0.5969	17.91
16	200.00	30.00	230.00	0.5767	132.64
17		20.00	20.00	0.5572	11.14
18	200.00	20.00	220.00	0.5384	118.45
19		10.00	10.00	0.5202	5.20
20	200.00	10.00	210.00	0.5026	105.55

Total PV → $1,180.30

↑

Bond price

Comments: *Cash flows are semiannual coupons of 10% of the remaining principal balance and sinking fund payments of 20% of the original principal annually for 5 years, commencing at the end of Year 6. The present value factors are calculated as $1/(1 + 0.07/2)$ or $1/(1 + 0.035)$.*

different types of securities. The same concept holds true for securities with identical WAMs. Exhibit 5–23 organizes the bond price volatility data for the GMAC 7% coupon, 10-year sinking fund (SF) debenture and two alternative investments with 8-year WAMs: an 8-year, current-coupon U.S. Treasury bond and an 8-year STRIPS. The WAMs were calculated earlier in Exhibits 5–3, 5–6, and 5–9. The 8-year STRIPS is

Exhibit 5–16. Calculation of the price of a 10% coupon, 10-year GMAC sinking fund debenture trading at a 4% DCF yield. The sinking fund retires 20% of the bonds annually, commencing at the end of the sixth year.

End of Period t	P_t (1)	CPN_t (2)	Total Cash Flow, CF_t (3) = (1) + (2)	PV Factor (4)	$PV(CF_t)$ (5) = (3) × (4)
1		$50.00	$ 50.00	0.9804	$ 49.02
2		50.00	50.00	0.9612	48.06
3		50.00	50.00	0.9423	47.12
4		50.00	50.00	0.9238	46.19
5		50.00	50.00	0.9057	45.29
6		50.00	50.00	0.8880	44.40
7		50.00	50.00	0.8706	43.53
8		50.00	50.00	0.8535	42.68
9		50.00	50.00	0.8368	41.84
10		50.00	50.00	0.8203	41.02
11		50.00	50.00	0.8043	40.22
12	$200.00	50.00	250.00	0.7885	197.13
13		40.00	40.00	0.7730	30.92
14	200.00	40.00	240.00	0.7579	181.90
15		30.00	30.00	0.7430	22.29
16	200.00	30.00	230.00	0.7284	167.53
17		20.00	20.00	0.7142	14.28
18	200.00	20.00	220.00	0.7002	154.04
19		10.00	10.00	0.6864	6.86
20	200.00	10.00	210.00	0.6730	141.33
				Total PV →	$1,405.60
					↑ Bond price

Comments: *Cash flows are semiannual coupons of 10% of the remaining principal balance and sinking fund payments of 20% of the original principal annually for 5 years, commencing at the end of Year 6. The present value factors are calculated as $1/(1 + 0.04/2)$ or $1/(1 + 0.02)$.*

a more volatile instrument, performing approximately 600BP better than its counterparts in an upmarket and just over 400BP worse than its equivalent-WAM cohorts in a downmarket (Exhibit 5–23). It is interesting to note the similarity in volatility between the two 7% coupon bonds: the GMAC 7% bond and the U.S. Treasury 7% bond perform almost

Observation: *Conceptually, duration can be thought of as (1) a sophisti-cated average maturity of the bond's cash flows, (2) the fulcrum of the bond's present value cash flow stream, or (3) the bond's zero-coupon equivalent.*

The influences on duration

Duration as a function of maturity. *Duration is positively related to a bond's term to maturity.* All other factors held equal, the longer the term to maturity, the higher the bond's duration. Exhibit 6–7 summa-rizes the durations for a wide variety of current-coupon U.S. Treasury issues, ranging in maturity from 1 to 50 years. A 3-year bond, for example, has a 2.76-year duration. A 10-year issue carries a duration of 7.36 years. Tripling the term to maturity from 10 years to 30 years creates only a 75% increase in duration, from 7.36 years to 12.91 years. Although it is clear that duration rises in concert with the term to maturity, it does so at a decreasing rate for coupon-bearing bonds (see Exhibit 6–8). Zero-coupon bond durations have a direct, one-to-one relationship

Exhibit 6–7. Duration as influenced by a bond's term to maturity. Issues illustrated are 7% coupon U.S. Treasury bonds priced at par to yield 7.00% to maturity.

Term to Maturity (Years)	Duration (Years)
1	0.98
2	1.90
3	2.76
4	3.56
5	4.30
6	5.00
7	5.65
8	6.26
9	6.83
10	7.36
15	9.52
20	11.05
25	12.14
30	12.91
40	13.84
50	14.31

Comments: *Duration is positively related to the term to maturity. Duration increases at a decreasing rate as maturity is extended.*

Exhibit 5–17. Calculation of the price of a 10% coupon, 10-year GMAC sinking fund debenture trading at a 10% DCF yield. The sinking fund retires 20% of the bonds annually, commencing at the end of the sixth year.

End of Period t	(1) P_t	(2) CPN_t	(3) = (1) + (2) Total Cash Flow, CF_t	(4) PV Factor	(5) = (3) × (4) $PV(CF_t)$
1		$50.00	$ 50.00	0.9524	$ 47.62
2		50.00	50.00	0.9070	45.35
3		50.00	50.00	0.8638	43.19
4		50.00	50.00	0.8227	41.14
5		50.00	50.00	0.7835	39.18
6		50.00	50.00	0.7462	37.31
7		50.00	50.00	0.7107	35.54
8		50.00	50.00	0.6768	33.84
9		50.00	50.00	0.6446	32.23
10		50.00	50.00	0.6139	30.70
11		50.00	50.00	0.5847	29.24
12	$200.00	50.00	250.00	0.5568	139.20
13		40.00	40.00	0.5303	21.21
14	200.00	40.00	240.00	0.5051	121.22
15		30.00	30.00	0.4810	14.43
16	200.00	30.00	230.00	0.4581	105.36
17		20.00	20.00	0.4363	8.73
18	200.00	20.00	220.00	0.4155	91.41
19		10.00	10.00	0.3957	3.96
20	200.00	10.00	210.00	0.3769	79.15
				Total PV →	$1,000.00
					↑ Bond price

Comments: *Cash flows are semiannual coupons of 10% of the remaining principal balance and sinking fund payments of 20% of the original principal annually for 5 years, commencing at the end of Year 6. The present value factors are calculated as $1/(1 + 0.10/2)$ or $1/(1 + 0.05)$.*

identically in up- and downmarkets. A U.S. Treasury of similar WAM, but not of identical maturity, bears a similar degree of price risk to the sinking fund issue. This observation makes it clear that the WAM measure is superior to the TTM measure since the WAM includes all of the principal repayments in its calculation, not simply the final one.

Exhibit 5–18. Calculation of the WAM and WACF of a 7% coupon, 15-year GMAC sinking fund debenture. The sinking fund retires 50% of the bonds at the end of the first year, with the balance retired at maturity.

(1) t (Years)	(a) Calculation of WAM			(b) Calculation of WACF		
	(2) Principal Cash Flow	(3) = (2)/$1,000 CF Weight	(4) = (1) × (3) Weighted t	(5) Total Cash Flow	(6) = (5)/TCF CF Weight	(7) = (1) × (6) Weighted t
0.5	$ 0	0	0	$ 35.00	0.0224	0.0112
1.0	500	0.50	0.50	535.00	0.3429	0.3429
1.5	0	0	0	17.50	0.0112	0.0168
2.0	0	0	0	17.50	0.0112	0.0224
2.5	0	0	0	17.50	0.0112	0.0280
3.0	0	0	0	17.50	0.0112	0.0336
3.5	0	0	0	17.50	0.0112	0.0392
4.0	0	0	0	17.50	0.0112	0.0448
4.5	0	0	0	17.50	0.0112	0.0504
5.0	0	0	0	17.50	0.0112	0.0560
5.5	0	0	0	17.50	0.0112	0.0616
6.0	0	0	0	17.50	0.0112	0.0672
6.5	0	0	0	17.50	0.0112	0.0728
7.0	0	0	0	17.50	0.0112	0.0784

7.5	0	0	0	17.50	0.0112	0.0840
8.0	0	0	0	17.50	0.0112	0.0896
8.5	0	0	0	17.50	0.0112	0.0952
9.0	0	0	0	17.50	0.0112	0.1008
9.5	0	0	0	17.50	0.0112	0.1064
10.0	0	0	0	17.50	0.0112	0.1120
10.5	0	0	0	17.50	0.0112	0.1176
11.0	0	0	0	17.50	0.0112	0.1232
11.5	0	0	0	17.50	0.0112	0.1288
12.0	0	0	0	17.50	0.0112	0.1344
12.5	0	0	0	17.50	0.0112	0.1400
13.0	0	0	0	17.50	0.0112	0.1456
13.5	0	0	0	17.50	0.0112	0.1512
14.0	0	0	0	17.50	0.0112	0.1568
14.5	0	0	0	17.50	0.0112	0.1624
15.0	500	0.50	7.50	517.50	0.3317	4.9755
	$1,000	1.00	8.00	$1,560.00	1.0000	7.7500
	↑	↑	↑	↑		↑
	TPCF		WAM	TCF		WACF

145

Exhibit 5–19. Calculation of the price of a 7% coupon, 15-year GMAC sinking fund debenture trading at a 7% DCF yield. The sinking fund retires 50% of the bonds at the end of the first year, with the balance retired at maturity.

End of Period t	(1) P_t	(2) CPN_t	(3) = (1) + (2) Total Cash Flow, CF_t	(4) PV Factor	(5) = (3) × (4) $PV(CF_t)$
1		$35.00	$ 35.00	0.9662	$ 33.82
2	$500.00	35.00	535.00	0.9335	499.42
3		17.50	17.50	0.9019	15.78
.		.	.	.	.
.		.	.	.	.
.			.	.	.
29		17.50	17.50	0.3687	6.45
30	500.00	17.50	517.50	0.3563	184.39
				Total PV→	$1,000.00

↑
Bond price

Comments: *Cash flows are semiannual coupons of 7% of the remaining principal balance and two sinking fund payments of 50% of the original principal, one payment at the end of the first year and one payment at final maturity. The present value factors are calculated as 1/(1 + 0.07/2) or 1/(1 + 0.035).*

In sum, the WAM is a better bond risk proxy than the TTM. However, by ignoring the coupon cash flows attached to a bond and by failing to incorporate the impact of the time value of money in its derivation, the WAM concept is not a comprehensive measure of a bond's inherent price risk.

Observation: *As an average, the WAM fails to discern the full impact of a bond's cash flow distribution on the bond's riskiness. By focusing solely on principal repayments and by viewing a bond's principal cash flows on a nominal basis rather than on a present value basis, the WAM does not act as a complete measure of a bond's risk.*

Exhibit 5–20. Calculation of the price of a 7% coupon, 15-year GMAC sinking fund debenture trading at a 4% DCF yield. The sinking fund retires 50% of the bonds at the end of the first year, with the balance retired at maturity.

End of Period t	*(1)* P_t	*(2)* CPN_t	*(3) = (1) + (2)* *Total Cash Flow,* CF_t	*(4)* *PV Factor*	*(5) = (3) × (4)* $PV(CF_t)$
1		$35.00	$ 35.00	0.9804	$ 34.31
2	$500.00	35.00	535.00	0.9612	514.24
3		17.50	17.50	0.9423	16.49
.		.	.	.	.
.		.	.	.	.
.				.	.
29		17.50	17.50	0.5631	9.85
30	500.00	17.50	517.50	0.5521	285.71
				Total PV→	$1,182.50
					↑ Bond price

Comments: *Cash flows are semiannual coupons of 7% of the remaining principal balance and two sinking fund payments of 50% of the original principal, one payment at the end of the first year and one payment at final maturity. The present value factors are calculated as $1/(1 + 0.04/2)$ or $1/(1 + 0.02)$.*

Weighted average cash flow

The concept

The *weighted average cash flow* (WACF) measure is calculated similarly to the WAM except that the WACF considers *all* of the bond's cash flows, not exclusively its principal repayments, in its derivation:

$$\text{WACF}_{years} = \sum_{t=0.50}^{n} \left(\frac{CF_t}{TCF} \times t \right)$$

where

CF_t = cash flow received in year t

TCF = total cash flow generated by the bond (coupon flows + principal payback)

t = time period (years)

n = final maturity (years)

Exhibit 5–21. Calculation of the price of a 7% coupon, 15-year GMAC sinking fund debenture trading at a 10% DCF yield. The sinking fund retires 50% of the bonds at the end of the first year, with the balance retired at maturity.

End of Period t	*(1)* P_t	*(2)* CPN_t	*(3) = (1) + (2)* Total Cash Flow, CF_t	*(4)* PV Factor	*(5) = (3) × (4)* $PV(CF_t)$
1		$35.00	$ 35.00	0.9524	$ 33.33
2	$500.00	35.00	535.00	0.9070	485.25
3		17.50	17.50	0.8638	15.12
.		.	.	.	.
.		.	.	.	.
.		.	.	.	.
29		17.50	17.50	0.2429	4.25
30	500.00	17.50	517.50	0.2314	119.75
				Total PV→	$870.70
					↑ Bond price

Comments: *Cash flows are semiannual coupons of 7% of the remaining principal balance and two sinking fund payments of 50% of the original principal, one payment at the end of the first year and one payment at final maturity. The present value factors are calculated as $1/(1 + 0.10/2)$ or $1/(1 + 0.05)$.*

Exhibit 5–22. Bond price volatilities of two GMAC issues similar in all respects except for the structure of the sinking fund schedule. The initial yield level is at a 7.00% DCF yield.

Issue	WAM (Years)	*Percent Change in Bond Price if DCF Yields:* Fall 300BP	Rise 300BP
GMAC 7% coupon SF bond maturing in 10 years and retiring 20% of the bonds annually, starting at the end of the sixth year	8.0	+20.28	−16.13
GMAC 7% coupon SF bond maturing in 15 years and retiring 50% of the bonds at the end of the first year, with the balance paid at final maturity	8.0	+18.25	−12.93

Exhibit 5–23. Bond price volatilities of several issues with similar WAMs. The initial yield level is at a 7.00% DCF yield.

Issue	WAM (Years)	Percent Change in Bond Price if DCF Yields:	
		Fall 300BP	Rise 300BP
GMAC 7% coupon SF bond maturing in 10 years and retiring 20% of the bonds annually, starting at the end of the sixth year	8.0	+20.28	−16.13
7% coupon, 8-year U.S. Treasury	8.0	+20.37	−16.26
8-year STRIPS	8.0	+26.30	−20.57

The WACF can be defined as the point in time at which, on average, half of the bond's total cash flows have been received. A longer (i.e., higher) WACF implies a greater degree of risk.

Observation: *The weighted average cash flow assesses a bond's volatility risk by finding the average maturity of the bond's cash flows, considering coupons as well as principal repayments. Longer WACFs suggest higher levels of bond risk.*

Applications of the WACF concept

The computation of WACFs is completed on the right-hand side of Exhibits 5–3 through 5–9 and Exhibit 5–18 for the sample issues discussed earlier in this chapter. The side-by-side comparison is helpful in showing how similar WAMs and WACFs are in concept. The inclusion of all cash flows in the calculation makes the task a more tedious one.

Exhibit 5–24 presents cash flow timelines to illustrate the location of WACF from the perspective of a bond's life span. The WACF is a step above the WAM in accuracy because the WACF incorporates all of the bond's future cash flows into its calculation. However, the WACF is insufficient as a bond risk proxy because it fails to consider the impact of the time value of money on bond price volatility. The duration risk measure, discussed in Chapter 6, closes this final gap.

Exhibit 5–24. Cash flow timelines for three sample issues.

(a) GMAC 7% coupon sinking fund bond maturing in 10 years. The sinking fund retires 20% of the bonds annually, commencing at the end of the sixth year. (Data per Exhibit 5–3.)

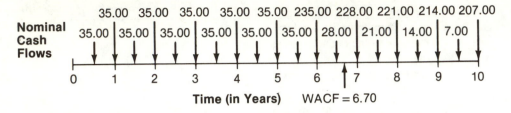

(b) 7% coupon, 8–year U.S. Treasury bond. (Data per Exhibit 5–6.)

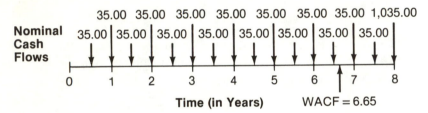

(c) 8-year STRIPS. (Data per Exhibit 5-9.)

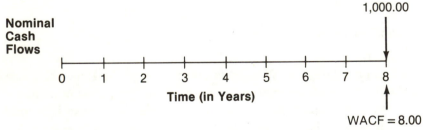

Comments: *Weighted average cash flow (WACF) considers all of a bond's cash flows.*

Comparing the traditional risk measures

Exhibit 5–25 summarizes the results of the term to maturity, the weighted average maturity, and the weighted average cash flow calculations pre-

Exhibit 5–25. Summary of the three traditional bond risk measures as applied to a series of alternative investments.

	Risk Measure (Years)		
Issue	*TTM*	*WAM*	*WACF*
GMAC 4% coupon SF bond	10	8.0	7.12
GMAC 7% coupon SF bond	10	8.0	6.70
GMAC 10% coupon SF bond	10	8.0	6.39
GMAC 7% coupon SF bond	15	8.0	7.75
4% coupon, 8-year U.S. Treasury bond	8	8.0	7.09
7% coupon, 8-year U.S. Treasury bond	8	8.0	6.65
10% coupon, 8-year U.S. Treasury bond	8	8.0	6.33
8-year STRIPS	8	8.0	8.00

sented in the chapter illustrations. The table reveals that the TTM, WAM, and WACF measures are related as follows:

Bond Type	*Relationship*
Coupon-bearing bullet bond	WAM = TTM WACF < WAM
Sinking fund bond	WAM < TTM WACF < WAM
Zero-coupon bond	WACF = WAM = TTM

TTMs and WAMs are unaffected by coupon size. However, all other factors held equal, WACFs are shorter for high coupon bonds and are longer for low coupon bonds. As a result, WACFs render low coupon bonds as riskier instruments, a general conclusion that was noted in Chapter 4's observation of price volatility differences between low coupon and high coupon bonds.

For example (from Exhibit 5–25), the 10-year GMAC sinking fund bonds appear equally risky from TTM and WAM viewpoints; however, the WACF measure differentiates the riskiness of the three issues. The WACF on the 4% coupon issue is 7.12 years. The 7% coupon bond's WACF is 6.70 years, and the 10% coupon issue bears an even shorter 6.39-year WACF. Higher coupon bonds are deemed less risky according to the WACF measure. Similarly, the 8-year U.S. Treasury bonds are riskier as discounts (WACF = 7.09) than as premiums

Exhibit 5–26. Summary of the advantages and disadvantages of three traditional bond risk measures.

Risk Measure	Advantages	Disadvantages
1. Term to maturity	No calculations necessary	Fails to consider any cash flows received prior to final maturity Ignores the time value of money
2. Weighted average maturity	Relatively easy to calculate Considers all principal cash flows	Fails to consider coupon cash flows Ignores the time value of money
3. Weighted average cash flow	Considers all cash flows	Cumbersome calculation Ignores the time value of money

(WACF = 6.33). Exhibit 5–26 summarizes the relative advantages and disadvantages of the three traditional risk measures explained in this chapter.

Summary

The traditional proxies for bond risk include the *term to maturity* and the *weighted average maturity*. The TTM focuses on the date of final maturity, ignoring the timing and magnitude of all other cash flow receipts. The WAM considers the specific timing and relative size of all principal repayments, but fails to incorporate coupon payments into its derivation. The *weighted average cash flow* is an extension of the WAM measure. The WACF assesses the complete cash flow stream of a bond on a weighted average basis, but neglects to adjust the individual cash flows for valuation differences created by the time value of money. The duration concept, presented in Chapter 6, extends the WACF measure to a present value weighted basis. The traditional measures of bond risk fail to adequately represent a bond's inherent volatility. The contemporary and futuristic risk proxies in the forthcoming two chapters attempt to better explain the observed fluctuations in bond prices.

CHAPTER 6

Bond Risk Measures: The Present

The contemporary bond risk measures attempt to build on the traditional measures discussed in Chapter 5. The current measures are designed to capture the inherent volatility of bond prices as observed in Chapter 4. The bond risk proxies popularized in today's fixed-income market include duration, convexity, and the yield value of a 32nd. This chapter analyzes these three contemporary risk measures and addresses their attendant strengths and weaknesses through illustration.

Duration

The formula for duration

The concept of duration is an extension of the weighted average cash flow (WACF). Recall that the WACF is the most sophisticated of the traditional risk measures, lacking only in that it fails to consider the impact of the time value of money on future cash flow receipts. Like the WAM, the WACF relies on nominal cash flows in its derivation:

$$\text{WACF (years)} = \sum_{t=0.50}^{n} \left(\frac{\text{CF}_t}{\text{TCF}} \times t \right)$$

where

CF_t = cash flow received in year t

TCF = total cash flow generated by the bond

t = time period (years)

n = final maturity (years)

Chapters 1 and 4 argue that all future cash flows are not created equal. Viewing a 20-year coupon cash flow as equivalent in relative importance to that of a 2-year cash flow is inconsistent. Duration eliminates the inherent weakness of the WACF by incorporating a present value treatment of future cash flows into its calculation:

$$\text{duration (years)} = \sum_{t=0.50}^{n} \left(\frac{PV(CF_t)}{TPV} \times t \right)$$

$$= \sum_{t=0.50}^{n} \left(\frac{PV(CF_t)}{\text{bond price}} \times t \right)$$

where

TPV = total present value of the bond (i.e., the bond's price)

$PV(CF_t)$ = present value of the cash flow received in year t

This formulation is commonly called *Macaulay's duration*.[1] The computation employs the internal rate of return (IRR) of the bond as the discount rate for all future cash flows.[2] Recall that the IRR of a noncallable bond is its YTM; sinking fund bonds and mortgage-backed securities require the use of a DCF yield. The present value of all of a bond's future cash flows discounted at the IRR is, by definition, the bond's current market price.

Observation: *Duration is an advanced version of a WACF that uses present values, rather than nominal values, as the cash flow weights.*

---

[1] Consult Frederick Macaulay's *Some Theoretical Problems Suggested by the Movements of Interest Rates, Bond Yields, and Stock Prices in the United States Since 1865* (New York: National Bureau of Economic Research, 1938) for further elaboration.

[2] If the *yield curve,* or *term structure of interest rates,* is not flat, the implied *spot rate curve* supplies a series of discount rates (rather than a single one) applicable to the bond's future cash flows, generating a duration figure that differs from the Macaulay's derivation (refer to Chapter 12 for a discussion of spot rate curves).

Exhibit 6-1. Calculation of the WACF and duration of a 7% coupon, 10-year GMAC sinking fund debenture priced to yield 7.00% DCF. The sinking fund retires 20% of the bonds annually, commencing at the end of the sixth year.

		(a) Calculation of WACF			(b) Calculation of Duration		
(1) t (Years)	(2) Total Cash Flow	(3) = (2)/TCF CF Weight	(4) = (1) × (3) Weighted t	(5) PV Factor	(6) = (2) × (5) PV(CF$_t$)	(7) = (6)/Price CF Weight	(8) = (1) × (7) PV-Weighted t
0.5	$ 35	0.0224	0.0112	0.9662	$ 33.82	0.0338	0.0169
1.0	35	0.0224	0.0224	0.9335	32.67	0.0327	0.0327
1.5	35	0.0224	0.0336	0.9019	31.57	0.0316	0.0474
2.0	35	0.0224	0.0448	0.8714	30.50	0.0305	0.0610
2.5	35	0.0224	0.0560	0.8420	29.47	0.0295	0.0738
3.0	35	0.0224	0.0672	0.8135	28.47	0.0285	0.0855
3.5	35	0.0224	0.0784	0.7860	27.51	0.0275	0.0963
4.0	35	0.0224	0.0896	0.7594	26.58	0.0266	0.1064
4.5	35	0.0224	0.1008	0.7337	25.68	0.0257	0.1157
5.0	35	0.0224	0.1120	0.7089	24.81	0.0248	0.1240
5.5	35	0.0224	0.1232	0.6849	23.97	0.0240	0.1320
6.0	235	0.1506	0.9036	0.6618	155.52	0.1555	0.9330
6.5	28	0.0179	0.1164	0.6394	17.90	0.0179	0.1164
7.0	228	0.1462	1.0234	0.6178	140.86	0.1409	0.9863
7.5	21	0.0135	0.1013	0.5969	12.53	0.0125	0.0938
8.0	221	0.1417	1.1336	0.5767	127.45	0.1275	1.0200
8.5	14	0.0090	0.0765	0.5572	7.80	0.0078	0.0663
9.0	214	0.1372	1.2348	0.5384	115.22	0.1152	1.0368
9.5	7	0.0045	0.0428	0.5202	3.64	0.0036	0.0342
10.0	207	0.1327	1.3270	0.5026	104.04	0.1040	1.0400
	$1,560	1.0000	6.7000		$1,000.00	1.0000	6.2200
	↑ TCF		↑ WACF		↑ Bond price		↑ Duration

Sample calculations of duration

As an illustration, Exhibit 6–1 calculates the WACF and duration of the 7% coupon, 10-year GMAC sinking fund debenture analyzed in Chapter 5. The bond has a WACF of 6.70 years and a duration of 6.22 years. In the duration derivation, the weight assigned to an individual cash flow is the relative contribution of that cash flow to the bond's price. A bond's duration must be shorter than its WACF because of the discounting process. Earlier cash flows have more relative weight, and later cash flows less relative weight, than under a nominal weighting scheme.[3] Using the GMAC bond as an example, the semiannual coupon received in one year has a 3.27% weight in the duration computation as opposed to a 2.24% weight in the WACF calculation. A long-term cash flow, such as the final principal and interest payment, bears less relative importance in the duration calculation (10.40% versus 13.27%, per Exhibit 6–1).

The duration of a 7% coupon, 10-year U.S. Treasury bond priced at par works out to 7.36 years (see Exhibit 6–2). Once again, the calculations are many and the process tedious. Fortunately, computer software programs and financial calculators generate durations effortlessly. Not surprisingly, the duration of a zero-coupon bond equals its term to maturity since the bond's entire cash flow weight rests on that single date. For comparative purposes, Exhibit 6–3 solves for the duration of a 10-year STRIPS.

Duration as a concept

What does duration really mean? Duration is often defined along the following lines: *the weighted average cash flow of a bond, where the present values of the cash flows serve as the weights*. This definition appears as ominous as the calculations behind it! Perhaps an easier way to think about duration is as follows:

Duration is the future point in time at which, on average, the investor has received exactly half of the original investment, in present value terms.

---

[3] Zero-coupon bonds are the exception, where the duration and WACF are equal because there are no *early* or *late* cash flows: the cash flow occurs on a single date.

Exhibit 6–2. Calculation of the WACF and duration of a 7% coupon, 10-year U.S. Treasury bond priced to yield 7.00% to maturity.

		(a) Calculation of WACF		(b) Calculation of Duration			
(1) t (Years)	(2) Total Cash Flow	(3) = (2)/TCF CF Weight	(4) = (1) × (3) Weighted t	(5) PV Factor	(6) = (2) × (5) PV(CF$_t$)	(7) = (6)/Price CF Weight	(8) = (1) × (7) PV-Weighted t
0.5	$ 35	0.0206	0.0103	0.9662	$ 33.82	0.0338	0.0169
1.0	35	0.0206	0.0206	0.9335	32.67	0.0327	0.0327
1.5	35	0.0206	0.0309	0.9019	31.57	0.0316	0.0474
2.0	35	0.0206	0.0412	0.8714	30.50	0.0305	0.0610
2.5	35	0.0206	0.0515	0.8420	29.47	0.0295	0.0738
3.0	35	0.0206	0.0618	0.8135	28.47	0.0285	0.0855
3.5	35	0.0206	0.0721	0.7860	27.51	0.0275	0.0963
4.0	35	0.0206	0.0824	0.7594	26.58	0.0266	0.1064
4.5	35	0.0206	0.0927	0.7337	25.68	0.0257	0.1157
5.0	35	0.0206	0.1030	0.7089	24.81	0.0248	0.1240
5.5	35	0.0206	0.1133	0.6849	23.97	0.0240	0.1320
6.0	35	0.0206	0.1236	0.6618	23.16	0.0232	0.1392
6.5	35	0.0206	0.1339	0.6394	22.38	0.0224	0.1456
7.0	35	0.0206	0.1442	0.6178	21.62	0.0216	0.1512
7.5	35	0.0206	0.1545	0.5969	20.89	0.0209	0.1568
8.0	35	0.0206	0.1648	0.5767	20.18	0.0202	0.1616
8.5	35	0.0206	0.1751	0.5572	19.50	0.0195	0.1658
9.0	35	0.0206	0.1854	0.5384	18.84	0.0188	0.1692
9.5	35	0.0206	0.1957	0.5202	18.21	0.0182	0.1729
10.0	1,035	0.6088	6.0880	0.5026	520.19	0.5202	5.2020
	$1,700	1.0000	8.0500		$1,000.00	1.0000	7.3600
	↑ TCF		↑ WACF		↑ Bond price		↑ Duration

Comments: *Duration is simply a present value-weighted version of a WACF.*

Exhibit 6–3. Calculation of the WACF and duration of a 10-year STRIPS priced to yield 7.00% to maturity.

		(a) Calculation of WACF		(b) Calculation of Duration			
(1) t (Years)	(2) Total Cash Flow	(3) = (2)/TCF CF Weight	(4) = (1) × (3) Weighted t	(5) PV Factor	(6) = (2) × (5) $PV(CF_t)$	(7) = (6)/Price CF Weight	(8) = (1) × (7) PV-Weighted t
0.5	$ 0	0	0	0.9662	$ 0	0	0
1.0	0	0	0	0.9335	0	0	0
.	.	.	.	.	.	.	.
.	.	.	.	.	.	.	.
9.5	0	0	0	0.5202	0	0	0
10.0	1,000	1.0000	10.0000	0.5026	502.60	1.0000	10.0000
	$1,700	1.0000	10.0000		$502.60	1.0000	10.0000
	↑ TCF		↑ WACF		↑ Bond price		↑ Duration

Comments: *A STRIPS always bears a WACF and a duration equal to its term to maturity.*

Exhibit 6–4. Plotting of the cash flows of a 7% coupon, 10-year GMAC sinking fund debenture, in present value terms (data from Exhibit 6–1).

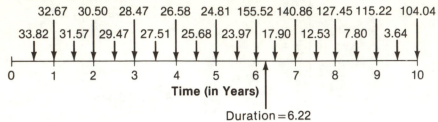

Duration = 6.22

Two phrases are key in this definition: *on average* and *in present value terms*. *On average* means that the future point is a weighted average point in time. A cash flow may or may not actually occur on that date.[4] For example, the 10-year U.S. Treasury bond with a duration of 7.36 years (Exhibit 6–2) has no cash flows paid at exactly 7.36 years in the future. *In present value terms* suggests that future dollars are worth less than dollars paid today; therefore, the 50% payback is, in a sense, the *real* return of half of the original principal invested.

A timeline is helpful in capturing the essence of duration. Exhibit 6–4 plots the cash flows of the GMAC bond where the cash flows are made comparable by converting them into today's present value equivalents. If one thinks of the timeline as a scale, the duration is the point at which the entire scale is in perfect balance. Engineers refer to this balancing point as the fulcrum. For example, the GMAC bond has a duration of 6.22 years. To balance the 20 different GMAC cash flows on the timeline, one places a beam directly underneath the 6.22-year mark on the scale. If the fulcrum is positioned to the left of 6.22, this timeline tilts to the right. If placed to the right of 6.22, the left side dominates and tilts the scale its way. Only at exactly 6.22 years is the cash flow scale perfectly level.

Exhibit 6–5 provides a cash flow timeline for the 10-year U.S. Treasury bond of earlier illustration. The balancing point (i.e., duration) for this bond is 7.36 years. It logically follows that the fulcrum of a zero-coupon bond's cash flow timeline is at its maturity date. Exhibit 6–6 displays this fact for a 10-year STRIPS. Since all of the bond's cash flow occurs at one point in time, the fulcrum of the scale can be nowhere else.

---

[4] This distinguishes duration from the *half-life* concept, which seeks the actual date (not the average date) on which the 50% return of investment is attained.

Exhibit 6–5. Plotting of the cash flows of a 7% coupon, 10-year U.S. Treasury, in present value terms (data from Exhibit 6–2).

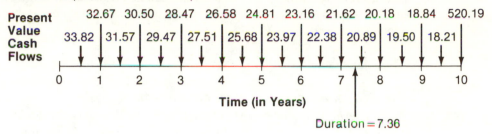

Exhibit 6–6. Plotting of the cash flows of a 10-year STRIPS, in present value terms (data from Exhibit 6–3).

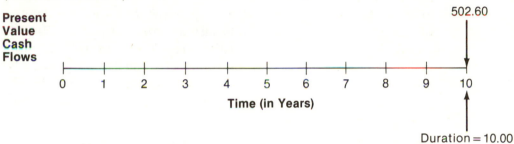

The timeline analyses lead to another simplified definition of the duration concept:

> If one had to describe a bond as, rather than a series of future cash flows, a single future cash flow, that single cash flow would occur on the duration date. In other words, *the duration of a bond is its zero-coupon bond equivalent.* In risk terms, an investor is indifferent between a coupon-bearing bond investment and a zero-coupon instrument maturing on the duration date of the coupon-bearing issue.[5]

The duration of a bond is a function of the bond's term to maturity, coupon rate, accrued interest, sinking fund features, call features, and market yield. Accrued interest is included because it is part of the cost of the bond investment.

---

[5] In addition, there are risk differences that stem from convexity, reinvestment rate assumptions, and nonparallel yield curve shifts. These risk factors are discussed in subsequent sections of the text. There are other considerations to make, including liquidity needs, income requirements, and tax considerations. At this point, grasping the concept of duration is of more importance.

Exhibit 6–8. Relationship between duration and term to maturity (data from Exhibit 6–7).

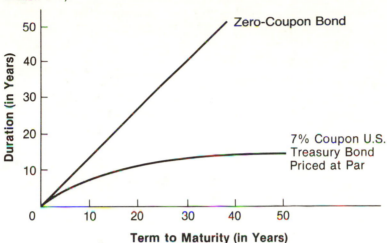

with their terms to maturity. Graphically speaking, the relationship is linear (see Exhibit 6–8).

On a cash flow timeline, the duration fulcrum moves to the right as maturity is lengthened and additional cash flows are appended to the right-hand side of the scale. The final principal payment tugs the duration along with it. The relative influence of the longer cash flows diminishes in present value terms as the maturity is sequentially extended; consequently, the duration increases at a decreasing rate.

> **Observation:** *Longer maturity bonds have longer durations. However, as maturity extends, duration increases at a decreasing rate. A zero-coupon bond has a duration that exactly matches its term to maturity.*

Duration as a function of coupon rate. *Duration is inversely related to a bond's coupon rate of interest.* As the coupon rate is increased, the bond's duration falls as the coupon cash flows account for a greater percentage of the present value of the bond (recall Exhibits 4–20, 4–21, and 4–22 from Chapter 4). The earlier occurrence of coupon payments vis-à-vis the principal repayment drags the duration down, or leftward in a timeline schematic.

Exhibit 6–9 assesses the durations of a series of long-term U.S. Treasury bonds of varying coupon rates (0 to 20%). Exhibit 6–10 plots these findings in a graphical format. The results indicate that duration

Exhibit 6–9. Duration as influenced by a bond's coupon rate of interest. Issues illustrated are 30-year U.S. Treasury bonds priced to yield 7.00% to maturity.

Coupon Rate (%)	Duration (Years)
0	30.00
1	20.30
2	17.03
3	15.38
4	14.40
5	13.74
6	13.26
7	12.91
8	12.63
9	12.41
10	12.23
11	12.08
12	11.95
13	11.85
14	11.75
15	11.67
16	11.60
17	11.53
18	11.47
19	11.42
20	11.37

Comments: *Duration is inversely related to the coupon rate of interest. Progressively higher coupons lead to a fall-off in duration, but at a diminishing rate.*

is very sensitive to low coupon rates but is relatively unaffected by high coupon rates. For example, a 7% coupon, 30-year bond has a 12.91-year duration. In moving down 500BP in coupon to a 2% issue, the bond's duration surges to 17.03 years. A 500BP rise in coupon to 12% lowers the duration by only 1 year, to 11.95 years. While the inverse relationship between duration and coupon rate is confirmed, duration decreases at a decreasing rate as the coupon rate is raised (see Exhibit 6–10). The zero-coupon bond bears the highest possible duration for a bond of a given maturity, in this case 30 years.

The influence of a change in coupon rate is a function of the maturity of the bonds involved. Exhibit 6–11 shows that the durations of long maturity bonds are more sensitive than short maturity issues to coupon

Exhibit 6–10. Relationship between duration and coupon rate (data from Exhibit 6–9).

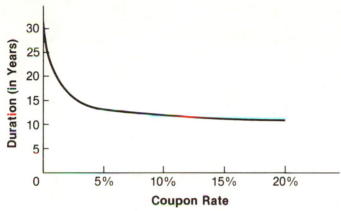

rate alterations. For example, a 3-year bond undergoes a 0.09-year increase in duration (2.85 versus 2.76) as its coupon is lowered to 4% from 7%. A 30-year bond experiences a 1½-year surge in duration under the same conditions (14.40 years versus 12.91 years). In percentage terms the duration of the long-term bond increases by 11.54% versus only a 3.26% movement by the short-term bond, a sizable difference. Exhibit 6–12 graphs the findings of Exhibit 6–11.

Exhibit 6–11. Duration as influenced by a bond's coupon rate of interest (across maturities). Issues illustrated are U.S. Treasury bonds priced to yield 7.00% to maturity.

Issue	Coupon Rate (%)	Price	Duration (Years)
3-year bond	4.0	92.01	2.85
	7.0	100.00	2.76
	10.0	107.99	2.68
10-year bond	4.0	78.68	8.08
	7.0	100.00	7.36
	10.0	121.32	6.89
30-year bond	4.0	62.58	14.40
	7.0	100.00	12.91
	10.0	137.42	12.23

Comments: *Lower coupon bonds bear higher durations. This effect is particularly pronounced for long maturity issues.*

Exhibit 6–12. Relationship between duration and coupon rate for various maturity issues (data from Exhibit 6–11).

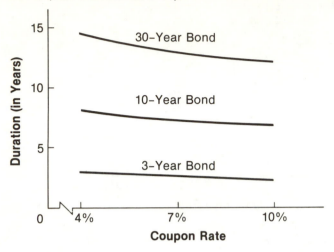

Observation: *Lower coupon bonds have longer durations than higher coupon bonds of similar maturity. As the coupon rate rises, duration falls at a decreasing rate. Coupon changes have more impact on duration the lower the initial coupon rate and the longer the term to maturity.*

Duration as a function of accrued interest. *Duration is inversely related to the amount of accrued interest attached to a bond.* The accrued interest amount is added to the price of a bond purchased between interest payment dates to arrive at the full purchase price.[6] The incremental *cost* of accrued interest is quickly returned to the investor on the first coupon payment date. Consequently, the duration of this marginal investment is very low. The greater the relative amount of this low duration investment, the lower the duration of the security in question. In other words, accrued interest tends to tug a bond's duration downward.

As an illustration, Exhibit 6–13 displays the durations of 3-, 10-, and 30-year maturity, 7% coupon U.S. Treasuries in both *full accrued*

---

[6] Refer to the Appendix to Chapter 2 for further amplification on the calculation of accrued interest and full purchase prices. Since the cost of a bond investment must include any attendant accrued interest, the impact of accrued interest on a bond's riskiness is a factor that should not be overlooked. All duration calculations in this text consider the bond's accrued interest. The reader is advised to use caution in relying on published duration figures. Unfortunately, there are a surprising number of instances in which durations are calculated with complete disregard for the bond's accrued interest.

Exhibit 6–13. Duration as influenced by a bond's accrued interest. Issues illustrated are 7% coupon U.S. Treasury bonds priced at par to yield 7.00% to maturity.

Issue	Duration (Years) if:	
	6 Months Accrued	No Accrued
3-year bond	2.67	2.76
10-year bond	7.11	7.36
30-year bond	12.48	12.91

Comments: *Duration is inversely related to the buildup of accrued interest. A bond's duration naturally extends on coupon payment date as the accrued interest drops off. This effect is particularly noticeable in long maturity issues.*

and *no accrued* states. The *coupon payment or drop* extends duration by 0.09 year, 0.25 year, and 0.43 year for 3-, 10-, and 30-year bonds, respectively. Careful attention is warranted around coupon payment dates, particularly for long maturity issues.

Observation: *The buildup of accrued interest lowers a bond's duration. The semiannual coupon drops temporarily lengthen a bond's duration. These effects are especially pronounced for high coupon issues and for long maturity bonds.*

Exhibit 6–14 Duration as influenced by the market yield level. Issues illustrated are (1) 30-year, current-coupon U.S. Treasury bonds priced at par, and (2) 30-year, 10% coupon U.S. Treasury bonds.

Issue	YTM (%)	Price	Duration (Years)
4% coupon bond	4.0	100.00	17.73
7% coupon bond	7.0	100.00	12.91
10% coupon bond	10.0	100.00	9.94
13% coupon bond	13.0	100.00	8.01
16% coupon bond	16.0	100.00	6.68
	4.0	204.28	14.98
	7.0	137.42	12.23
10% coupon bond	10.0	100.00	9.94
	13.0	77.45	8.16
	16.0	62.87	6.82

Comments: *Duration is inversely related to the surrounding yield environment.*

Exhibit 6–15. Relationship between duration and market yield level for current-coupon, 30-year U.S. Treasury bonds (data from Exhibit 6–14).

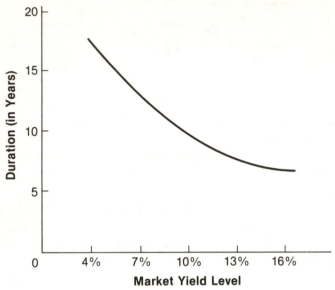

Duration as a function of market yield level. *Duration is inversely related to the general level of interest rates.* High yield environments create short durations and low yield environments are associated with longer duration tendencies (see Exhibit 6–14). The recently achieved 7% rate level is inherently riskier than the 16% yield level attained in 1981. For example, a 16% coupon, 30-year U.S. Treasury bond priced at par bears a duration of 6.68 years. A similar maturity current-coupon U.S. Treasury bond in a 7% rate environment is almost twice as risky, carrying a 12.91-year duration. A 4% interest rate level raises durations to 17.73 years on current-coupon, long maturity U.S. Treasuries.

Exhibit 6–14 further confirms that, holding the coupon rate constant, durations naturally lengthen as interest rates fall and contract as interest rates rise. For example, a 10% coupon, 30-year U.S. Treasury bond offers 9.94 years of duration at issuance. As rates decline to 4%, the bond's duration surges to 14.98 years, a 50% increase. If yields rise to the 16% level, the duration of the bond falls to 6.82 years, a 31% decrease. Duration behaves in a nonsymmetric fashion. As interest rates fall, duration increases at an accelerating rate. Conversely, as yields rise, duration falls at a decreasing rate (see Exhibits 6–15 and 6–16).

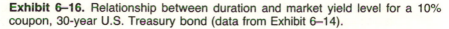

Exhibit 6–16. Relationship between duration and market yield level for a 10% coupon, 30-year U.S. Treasury bond (data from Exhibit 6–14).

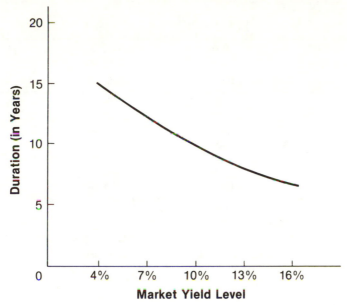

Observation: *Lower yield environments create longer durations. As yields decline, duration extends at an increasing rate. Long maturity issues are particularly susceptible to large shifts in duration as yield levels rise and fall.*

The rationale behind the duration:yield relationship. The fact that duration varies inversely with market yield level stems from the time value of money concepts outlined and applied in earlier sections of this book. Duration lengthens as yields decline because the longer cash flows gain more in present value terms than do their shorter cash flow counterparts. The lower discounting rate and the substantially higher present value factors (recall Exhibits 4–9 and 4–10 from Chapter 4) increase the relative contribution of the longer cash flows to the bond's price. In a timeline framework, the present value cash flows become heavier on the long end, requiring the duration fulcrum to move farther to the right (i.e., longer). Conversely, rising yield levels dramatically reduce the present value of long cash flows and only modestly lower the present value of short cash flows. The lesser weight of the longer

Exhibit 6–17. Duration as influenced by the market yield level (across maturities). Issues examined are 7% coupon U.S. Treasury bonds.

Issue	*YTM (%)*	*Price*	*Duration (Years)*
	4.0	108.40	2.77
3-year bond	7.0	100.00	2.76
	10.0	92.39	2.75
	4.0	124.53	7.67
10-year bond	7.0	100.00	7.36
	10.0	81.31	7.02
	4.0	152.14	15.88
30-year bond	7.0	100.00	12.91
	10.0	71.61	10.39

Comments: *The inverse relationship between duration and the surrounding yield environment is especially pronounced in longer maturity issues. The durations of short maturity bonds are little affected by major shifts in yield level.*

cash flows demands that the duration fulcrum be moved leftward (i.e., shorter) to maintain a balance.

Given the power of compounding, it is not surprising to find that longer maturity issues experience larger nominal and percentage changes in duration for a given shift in market yields. Exhibit 6–17 shows that the duration of a 3-year bond is virtually insensitive to yield levels. A 300BP yield change alters the bond's duration by only 1/100 of a year. A similar yield shift affects a 10-year bond's duration by 1/3 of a year and a 30-year bond's duration by a full 3 years.

Observation: *Changes in present value discounting factors and the shifting relative weights of short and long maturity cash flows explain the natural tendency of duration to vary inversely with the market yield level.*

The duration risk of extending maturity in differing yield environments. *The relative risk of extending maturity is greater in a low yield environment than in a high yield environment.* Exhibit 6–18 compares the durations of 3-, 10-, and 30-year U.S. Treasury bonds in a variety of yield environments (4%, 7%, 10%, and 14%). The bottom panel of the table calculates ratios of the durations of the *10-year bond*

Exhibit 6–18. Relative risk of extending out the maturity spectrum in various yield environments as illustrated by duration figures.

Issue	Duration in a Yield Environment of:			
	4%	*7%*	*10%*	*14%*
3-year bond	2.86	2.76	2.67	2.55
10-year bond	8.34	7.36	6.54	5.67
30-year bond	17.73	12.91	9.94	7.51
Ratio of:				
10-year/3-year	2.9X	2.7X	2.5X	2.2X
30-year/10-year	2.1X	1.8X	1.5X	1.3X

Comments: *Lower yield environments portend a higher degree of risk for extending out the maturity spectrum.*

versus 3-year bond and the *30-year bond versus 10-year bond.* In a high yield 14% scenario, the 10-year bond is 2.2 times as risky as the 3-year bond and the 30-year bond, in turn, is 30% riskier than the 10-year issue (ratio of 1.3 times). In 7% rate conditions, however, the 10-year bond is 2.7 times as price sensitive as the 3-year bond (up from 2.2 times) and the 30-year bond is 80% riskier than the 10-year issue (up from 30%). Therefore, the dramatic collapse in interest rates from the 14% level in 1984 to the 7% level in 1986 brought with it an increased risk of exposing portfolio holdings to progressively longer maturity sectors.

Observation: *Maturity extensions are increasingly risky in lower yield environments.*

Duration as a function of sinking fund and call features. Duration is impacted by the sinking fund and call features attached to a bond. *Sinking fund features shorten the effective maturity of a bond, as symbolized by the bond's WAM.* Higher percentage sinkers create shorter WAMs which, in turn, lead to commensurately shorter durations.[7] For example, a 10-year bond devoid of any sinking fund provisions carries a 7.36-year duration (recall Exhibit 6–2). A 10-year bond with an 80% sinker bears only a 6.22-year duration (recall Exhibit 6–1).

---

[7] The distribution of the sinking fund payments is also important. Earlier and more sizable sinking fund payments tend to drag down the bond's WAM and, as a result, the bond's duration.

Exhibit 6–19. Macaulay's durations (in years) for bonds of various maturities and various

Coupon Rate	Maturity (Years)										
	1	2	3	4	5	6	7	8	9	10	11
0%	1.00	2.00	3.00	4.00	5.00	6.00	7.00	8.00	9.00	10.00	11.00
1%	1.00	1.98	2.96	3.92	4.87	5.80	6.71	7.61	8.49	9.34	10.17
2%	1.00	1.97	2.92	3.85	4.75	5.62	6.47	7.29	8.07	8.83	9.55
3%	0.99	1.95	2.88	3.78	4.64	5.47	6.26	7.02	7.73	8.42	9.06
4%	0.99	1.94	2.85	3.72	4.55	5.33	6.08	6.78	7.45	8.08	8.67
5%	0.99	1.93	2.82	3.66	4.46	5.21	5.92	6.59	7.21	7.80	8.35
6%	0.99	1.91	2.79	3.61	4.38	5.10	5.78	6.41	7.01	7.56	8.08
7%	0.98	1.90	2.76	3.56	4.30	5.00	5.65	6.26	6.83	7.36	7.85
8%	0.98	1.89	2.73	3.51	4.24	4.91	5.54	6.12	6.67	7.18	7.65
9%	0.98	1.88	2.70	3.47	4.17	4.83	5.44	6.00	6.53	7.02	7.48
10%	0.98	1.87	2.68	3.43	4.12	4.75	5.35	5.89	6.41	6.89	7.33
11%	0.97	1.86	2.66	3.39	4.06	4.68	5.26	5.80	6.30	6.76	7.20
12%	0.97	1.84	2.63	3.35	4.01	4.62	5.18	5.71	6.20	6.65	7.08
13%	0.97	1.83	2.61	3.32	3.97	4.56	5.11	5.63	6.11	6.56	6.98
14%	0.97	1.82	2.59	3.29	3.92	4.51	5.05	5.55	6.03	6.47	6.88
15%	0.97	1.82	2.57	3.26	3.88	4.46	4.99	5.49	5.95	6.39	6.80
16%	0.96	1.81	2.55	3.23	3.84	4.41	4.93	5.42	5.88	6.31	6.72
17%	0.96	1.80	2.54	3.20	3.81	4.36	4.88	5.37	5.82	6.25	6.65
18%	0.96	1.79	2.52	3.17	3.77	4.32	4.83	5.31	5.76	6.18	6.58
19%	0.96	1.78	2.50	3.15	3.74	4.28	4.79	5.26	5.71	6.13	6.52
20%	0.96	1.77	2.49	3.13	3.71	4.25	4.75	5.22	5.66	6.07	6.47

Call features also reduce the effective maturity of a bond. An early call can radically change the date at which the principal of the bond is returned to the investor. A new-issue telephone utility bond with a 40-year term to maturity generally features only 5 years of refunding protection. If interest rates decline sufficiently, the issuer will call the bonds away from the holder as early as 5 years hence. The issuer's option to call the bond prematurely leads to several possible durations for the bond:

1. *Duration to maturity.* The duration of the bond to the final maturity date (the call option is not expected to be exercised).

2. *Duration to call.* The duration of the bond to the first call date (the call option is expected to be exercised).

3. *Effective duration* (call-adjusted duration, option-adjusted duration, adjusted duration). The duration of the bond given a level of interest rate volatility and a resulting probability of option exercise (not a discrete *yes* or *no*). The effective duration lies between the duration to first call and the duration to maturity.

coupon rates. The YTM of each bond is 7.00%.

					*Maturity (Years)*							
12	*13*	*14*	*15*	*16*	*17*	*18*	*19*	*20*	*30*	*40*	*50*
12.00	13.00	14.00	15.00	16.00	17.00	18.00	19.00	20.00	30.00	40.00	50.00
10.98	11.77	12.52	13.25	13.95	14.62	15.26	15.87	16.44	20.30	21.08	20.07
10.24	10.89	11.51	12.10	12.65	13.17	13.65	14.10	14.52	17.03	17.44	16.96
9.67	10.24	10.78	11.28	11.75	12.19	12.59	12.96	13.31	15.38	15.89	15.78
9.22	9.74	10.22	10.67	11.09	11.48	11.84	12.17	12.48	14.40	15.04	15.15
8.86	9.34	9.79	10.20	10.59	10.95	11.28	11.59	11.87	13.74	14.49	14.76
8.56	9.01	9.43	9.83	10.19	10.53	10.85	11.14	11.41	13.26	14.12	14.50
8.31	8.74	9.14	9.52	9.87	10.20	10.50	10.79	11.05	12.91	13.84	14.31
8.10	8.51	8.90	9.26	9.60	9.92	10.22	10.50	10.76	12.63	13.63	14.17
7.91	8.32	8.69	9.05	9.38	9.69	9.98	10.26	10.52	12.41	13.47	14.06
7.75	8.15	8.52	8.86	9.19	9.50	9.79	10.06	10.32	12.23	13.33	13.97
7.61	8.00	8.36	8.70	9.03	9.33	9.62	9.89	10.15	12.08	13.22	13.89
7.49	7.87	8.22	8.56	8.88	9.18	9.47	9.74	10.00	11.95	13.13	13.83
7.38	7.75	8.10	8.44	8.76	9.06	9.34	9.61	9.87	11.85	13.05	13.78
7.28	7.65	8.00	8.33	8.65	8.95	9.23	9.50	9.76	11.75	12.98	13.73
7.19	7.55	7.90	8.23	8.55	8.85	9.13	9.40	9.66	11.67	12.92	13.69
7.10	7.47	7.82	8.14	8.46	8.76	9.04	9.31	9.57	11.60	12.87	13.66
7.03	7.39	7.74	8.06	8.38	8.68	8.96	9.23	9.49	11.53	12.82	13.63
6.96	7.32	7.67	7.99	8.30	8.60	8.89	9.16	9.42	11.47	12.78	13.60
6.90	7.26	7.60	7.93	8.24	8.54	8.82	9.09	9.35	11.42	12.74	13.57
6.84	7.20	7.54	7.87	8.18	8.48	8.76	9.03	9.29	11.37	12.71	13.55

For example, a newly issued 7% coupon telephone utility bond has a final maturity of 40 years and a 5-year refunding call at 106.00. The bond's potential durations are given below.[8]

1. *Duration to maturity:* 13.84 years

2. *Duration to call:* 4.30 years

3. *Effective duration:* 8.50 years

The derivation of effective durations and an in-depth analysis of options are beyond the scope of this book. Suffice it to say that call features tend to dampen the observed volatility of a bond (recall Exhibit 4–42 from Chapter 4).

---

[8] In reality, the potential duration of the bond is any of the numerous durations lying between the duration to first call and the duration to maturity, inclusive. The duration to first call and duration to maturity represent the extreme values. The effective duration attempts to provide the single best representative duration for the bond, given the infinite number of individual durations comprising the range of potential durations. The 8.50 effective duration figure is used for illustrative purposes only. Depending on the assumptions underlying the effective duration calculation, the resulting figure may differ somewhat from the 8.50-year estimate.

Exhibit 6–20. Macaulay's durations (in years) for par bonds in a variety of yield environments

YTM	1	2	3	4	5	6	7	8	9	10	11
0.0%	1.00	2.00	3.00	4.00	5.00	6.00	7.00	8.00	9.00	10.00	11.00
0.5%	1.00	1.99	2.98	3.97	4.94	5.92	6.89	7.85	8.81	9.77	10.72
1.0%	1.00	1.99	2.96	3.93	4.89	5.84	6.78	7.71	8.63	9.54	10.44
1.5%	1.00	1.98	2.95	3.90	4.84	5.76	6.67	7.57	8.45	9.32	10.18
2.0%	1.00	1.97	2.93	3.86	4.78	5.68	6.57	7.43	8.28	9.11	9.93
2.5%	0.99	1.96	2.91	3.83	4.73	5.61	6.47	7.30	8.12	8.91	9.69
3.0%	0.99	1.96	2.89	3.80	4.68	5.54	6.37	7.17	7.95	8.71	9.45
3.5%	0.99	1.95	2.87	3.77	4.63	5.46	6.27	7.05	7.80	8.52	9.22
4.0%	0.99	1.94	2.86	3.74	4.58	5.39	6.17	6.93	7.65	8.34	9.01
4.5%	0.99	1.94	2.84	3.71	4.53	5.33	6.08	6.81	7.50	8.16	8.80
5.0%	0.99	1.93	2.82	3.68	4.49	5.26	5.99	6.69	7.36	7.99	8.59
5.5%	0.99	1.92	2.81	3.65	4.44	5.19	5.90	6.58	7.22	7.82	8.40
6.0%	0.99	1.91	2.79	3.62	4.39	5.13	5.82	6.47	7.08	7.66	8.21
6.5%	0.98	1.91	2.77	3.59	4.35	5.06	5.73	6.36	6.95	7.51	8.03
7.0%	0.98	1.90	2.76	3.56	4.30	5.00	5.65	6.26	6.83	7.36	7.85
7.5%	0.98	1.89	2.74	3.53	4.26	4.94	5.57	6.16	6.70	7.21	7.68
8.0%	0.98	1.89	2.73	3.50	4.22	4.88	5.49	6.06	6.58	7.07	7.52
8.5%	0.98	1.88	2.71	3.47	4.18	4.82	5.42	5.96	6.47	6.93	7.36
9.0%	0.98	1.87	2.70	3.45	4.13	4.76	5.34	5.87	6.35	6.80	7.20
9.5%	0.98	1.87	2.68	3.42	4.09	4.71	5.27	5.78	6.24	6.67	7.05
10.0%	0.98	1.86	2.67	3.39	4.05	4.65	5.20	5.69	6.14	6.54	6.91
10.5%	0.98	1.86	2.65	3.37	4.02	4.60	5.13	5.60	6.03	6.42	6.77
11.0%	0.97	1.85	2.64	3.34	3.98	4.55	5.06	5.52	5.93	6.30	6.64
11.5%	0.97	1.84	2.62	3.32	3.94	4.49	4.99	5.44	5.83	6.19	6.51
12.0%	0.97	1.84	2.61	3.29	3.90	4.44	4.93	5.36	5.74	6.08	6.38
12.5%	0.97	1.83	2.59	3.27	3.86	4.39	4.86	5.28	5.65	5.97	6.26
13.0%	0.97	1.82	2.58	3.24	3.83	4.35	4.80	5.20	5.56	5.87	6.14
13.5%	0.97	1.82	2.56	3.22	3.79	4.30	4.74	5.13	5.47	5.77	6.03
14.0%	0.97	1.81	2.55	3.20	3.76	4.25	4.68	5.05	5.38	5.67	5.92
14.5%	0.97	1.81	2.54	3.17	3.72	4.20	4.62	4.98	5.30	5.57	5.81
15.0%	0.97	1.80	2.52	3.15	3.69	4.16	4.56	4.91	5.22	5.48	5.71
15.5%	0.96	1.79	2.51	3.13	3.66	4.11	4.51	4.85	5.14	5.39	5.61
16.0%	0.96	1.79	2.50	3.10	3.62	4.07	4.45	4.78	5.06	5.30	5.51
16.5%	0.96	1.78	2.48	3.08	3.59	4.03	4.40	4.72	4.99	5.22	5.41
17.0%	0.96	1.78	2.47	3.06	3.56	3.98	4.35	4.65	4.91	5.13	5.32
17.5%	0.96	1.77	2.46	3.04	3.53	3.94	4.29	4.59	4.84	5.05	5.23
18.0%	0.96	1.77	2.45	3.02	3.50	3.90	4.24	4.53	4.77	4.98	5.15
18.5%	0.96	1.76	2.43	3.00	3.47	3.86	4.19	4.47	4.70	4.90	5.06
19.0%	0.96	1.75	2.42	2.98	3.44	3.82	4.15	4.41	4.64	4.83	4.98
19.5%	0.96	1.75	2.41	2.95	3.41	3.79	4.10	4.36	4.57	4.75	4.90
20.0%	0.96	1.74	2.40	2.93	3.38	3.75	4.05	4.30	4.51	4.68	4.82

Observation: *Sinking fund provisions and call features shorten the durations of the securities under consideration. The duration contraction is particularly acute for high-percentage sinkers and for long maturity bonds with short calls.*

and for a variety of maturities.

Maturity (Years)											
12	*13*	*14*	*15*	*16*	*17*	*18*	*19*	*20*	*30*	*40*	*50*
12.00	13.00	14.00	15.00	16.00	17.00	18.00	19.00	20.00	30.00	40.00	50.00
11.66	12.60	13.54	14.47	15.40	16.32	17.24	18.15	19.06	27.90	36.30	44.30
11.34	12.22	13.10	13.97	14.83	15.68	16.52	17.35	18.18	25.99	33.07	39.47
11.03	11.86	12.68	13.49	14.28	15.07	15.84	16.60	17.35	24.27	30.22	35.35
10.73	11.51	12.28	13.03	13.77	14.50	15.20	15.90	16.58	22.70	27.72	31.83
10.44	11.18	11.90	12.60	13.29	13.95	14.60	15.24	15.86	21.28	25.51	28.81
10.17	10.86	11.53	12.19	12.82	13.44	14.04	14.62	15.18	19.99	23.55	26.20
9.90	10.55	11.19	11.80	12.39	12.95	13.50	14.04	14.55	18.81	21.82	23.94
9.65	10.26	10.85	11.42	11.97	12.49	13.00	13.49	13.95	17.73	20.27	21.98
9.40	9.98	10.54	11.07	11.57	12.06	12.52	12.97	13.39	16.74	18.89	20.27
9.17	9.71	10.23	10.73	11.20	11.65	12.07	12.48	12.87	15.84	17.66	18.77
8.94	9.45	9.94	10.40	10.84	11.25	11.65	12.02	12.37	15.01	16.55	17.44
8.72	9.21	9.66	10.09	10.50	10.88	11.24	11.58	11.90	14.25	15.55	16.27
8.51	8.97	9.40	9.80	10.18	10.53	10.86	11.17	11.47	13.55	14.66	15.24
8.31	8.74	9.14	9.52	9.87	10.20	10.50	10.79	11.05	12.91	13.84	14.31
8.12	8.52	8.90	9.25	9.57	9.88	10.16	10.42	10.66	12.31	13.11	13.49
7.93	8.31	8.67	8.99	9.29	9.57	9.83	10.07	10.29	11.76	12.44	12.74
7.75	8.11	8.44	8.75	9.03	9.29	9.52	9.74	9.94	11.26	11.83	12.07
7.57	7.91	8.23	8.51	8.77	9.01	9.23	9.43	9.62	10.78	11.27	11.47
7.41	7.73	8.02	8.29	8.53	8.75	8.95	9.14	9.30	10.35	10.76	10.92
7.24	7.55	7.82	8.07	8.30	8.50	8.69	8.86	9.01	9.94	10.29	10.42
7.09	7.37	7.63	7.86	8.07	8.26	8.44	8.59	8.73	9.56	9.86	9.96
6.94	7.21	7.45	7.67	7.86	8.04	8.20	8.34	8.46	9.21	9.46	9.55
6.79	7.05	7.27	7.48	7.66	7.82	7.97	8.10	8.21	8.87	9.09	9.16
6.65	6.89	7.11	7.30	7.47	7.62	7.75	7.87	7.98	8.57	8.75	8.81
6.52	6.74	6.94	7.12	7.28	7.42	7.54	7.65	7.75	8.28	8.43	8.48
6.39	6.60	6.79	6.95	7.10	7.23	7.34	7.44	7.53	8.01	8.14	8.18
6.26	6.46	6.64	6.79	6.93	7.05	7.15	7.25	7.33	7.75	7.87	7.90
6.14	6.33	6.49	6.64	6.77	6.88	6.97	7.06	7.13	7.51	7.61	7.63
6.02	6.20	6.35	6.49	6.61	6.71	6.80	6.88	6.95	7.29	7.37	7.39
5.90	6.07	6.22	6.35	6.46	6.55	6.64	6.71	6.77	7.07	7.15	7.16
5.79	5.95	6.09	6.21	6.31	6.40	6.48	6.54	6.60	6.87	6.93	6.95
5.69	5.84	5.97	6.08	6.18	6.26	6.33	6.39	6.44	6.68	6.74	6.75
5.58	5.73	5.85	5.95	6.04	6.12	6.18	6.24	6.29	6.50	6.55	6.56
5.48	5.62	5.73	5.83	5.91	5.98	6.04	6.10	6.14	6.34	6.37	6.38
5.38	5.51	5.62	5.71	5.79	5.86	5.91	5.96	6.00	6.17	6.21	6.21
5.29	5.41	5.51	5.60	5.67	5.73	5.78	5.83	5.86	6.02	6.05	6.05
5.20	5.31	5.41	5.49	5.56	5.61	5.66	5.70	5.73	5.88	5.90	5.91
5.11	5.22	5.31	5.39	5.45	5.50	5.54	5.58	5.61	5.74	5.76	5.76
5.03	5.13	5.21	5.28	5.34	5.39	5.43	5.46	5.49	5.61	5.63	5.63
4.94	5.04	5.12	5.19	5.24	5.29	5.32	5.35	5.38	5.48	5.50	5.50

The influences on duration: Using duration tables to identify interrelationships

The impacts of a bond's term to maturity, coupon rate, and yield can be observed in a set of duration tables. Interrelationships between these factors are also identifiable in such a framework. Exhibits 6–19, 6–20, and 6–21 provide a total of over 2,000 durations organized in a

Exhibit 6–21. Macaulay's durations (in years) for a 30-year maturity bond in a variety of

					Coupon Rate (%)					
YTM	0	1	2	3	4	5	6	7	8	9
0.0%	30.00	26.60	24.47	23.00	21.96	21.15	20.52	20.00	19.59	19.24
0.5%	30.00	26.31	24.06	22.55	21.47	20.66	20.02	19.51	19.09	18.75
1.0%	30.00	25.99	23.63	22.08	20.97	20.15	19.51	19.01	18.59	18.25
1.5%	30.00	25.66	23.18	21.58	20.46	19.63	19.00	18.49	18.08	17.74
2.0%	30.00	25.29	22.70	21.06	19.93	19.10	18.47	17.97	17.57	17.24
2.5%	30.00	24.91	22.21	20.53	19.39	18.57	17.94	17.45	17.06	16.73
3.0%	30.00	24.49	21.69	19.99	18.84	18.03	17.41	16.93	16.54	16.23
3.5%	30.00	24.05	21.15	19.43	18.29	17.48	16.87	16.41	16.03	15.73
4.0%	30.00	23.59	20.60	18.86	17.73	16.93	16.34	15.88	15.52	15.23
4.5%	30.00	23.10	20.02	18.28	17.17	16.39	15.81	15.37	15.02	14.73
5.0%	30.00	22.58	19.44	17.70	16.60	15.84	15.28	14.86	14.52	14.25
5.5%	30.00	22.04	18.85	17.12	16.04	15.30	14.76	14.36	14.03	13.77
6.0%	30.00	21.48	18.24	16.54	15.49	14.77	14.25	13.86	13.56	13.31
6.5%	30.00	20.90	17.64	15.96	14.94	14.25	13.75	13.38	13.09	12.86
7.0%	30.00	20.30	17.03	15.38	14.40	13.74	13.26	12.91	12.63	12.41
7.5%	30.00	19.68	16.42	14.82	13.87	13.24	12.79	12.45	12.19	11.98
8.0%	30.00	19.05	15.81	14.26	13.35	12.75	12.32	12.01	11.76	11.57
8.5%	30.00	18.41	15.21	13.71	12.84	12.28	11.88	11.58	11.35	11.17
9.0%	30.00	17.76	14.62	13.18	12.36	11.82	11.45	11.17	10.95	10.78
9.5%	30.00	17.11	14.04	12.67	11.88	11.38	11.03	10.77	10.57	10.41
10.0%	30.00	16.46	13.48	12.17	11.43	10.96	10.63	10.39	10.20	10.06
10.5%	30.00	15.81	12.93	11.68	10.99	10.55	10.25	10.02	9.85	9.72
11.0%	30.00	15.17	12.39	11.22	10.57	10.16	9.88	9.67	9.51	9.39
11.5%	30.00	14.54	11.88	10.78	10.17	9.79	9.53	9.34	9.19	9.08
12.0%	30.00	13.93	11.39	10.35	9.79	9.44	9.20	9.02	8.89	8.78
12.5%	30.00	13.32	10.91	9.95	9.43	9.10	8.88	8.72	8.59	8.50
13.0%	30.00	12.74	10.46	9.56	9.08	8.78	8.58	8.43	8.32	8.23
13.5%	30.00	12.18	10.03	9.20	8.75	8.48	8.29	8.15	8.05	7.97
14.0%	30.00	11.63	9.62	8.85	8.44	8.19	8.02	7.89	7.80	7.73
14.5%	30.00	11.11	9.23	8.52	8.15	7.92	7.76	7.65	7.56	7.49
15.0%	30.00	10.61	8.87	8.21	7.87	7.66	7.51	7.41	7.33	7.27
15.5%	30.00	10.14	8.52	7.92	7.60	7.41	7.28	7.19	7.12	7.06
16.0%	30.00	9.69	8.19	7.64	7.35	7.18	7.06	6.98	6.91	6.86
16.5%	30.00	9.27	7.88	7.38	7.12	6.96	6.85	6.78	6.72	6.67
17.0%	30.00	8.87	7.59	7.13	6.90	6.75	6.66	6.59	6.53	6.49
17.5%	30.00	8.49	7.32	6.90	6.69	6.56	6.47	6.41	6.36	6.32
18.0%	30.00	8.13	7.06	6.68	6.49	6.37	6.29	6.23	6.19	6.16
18.5%	30.00	7.80	6.82	6.48	6.30	6.19	6.12	6.07	6.03	6.00
19.0%	30.00	7.49	6.60	6.28	6.13	6.03	5.96	5.92	5.88	5.85
19.5%	30.00	7.20	6.39	6.10	5.96	5.87	5.81	5.77	5.74	5.71
20.0%	30.00	6.92	6.19	5.93	5.80	5.72	5.67	5.63	5.60	5.58

manner designed to highlight the influences on a bond's duration as well as to provide the reader with a useful reference. The tables assume noncallable bullet bonds with no accrued interest.

Exhibit 6–19 tabulates the durations of bonds over a wide range of maturities (1 to 50 years) and coupon rates (1 to 20%). For this table, the YTM is held constant at 7.00%. Exhibit 6–20 looks at par bonds with a wide variety of maturities (1 to 50 years) for a range of yield environments and for a variety of assumed coupon rates.

					Coupon Rate (%)					
10	*11*	*12*	*13*	*14*	*15*	*16*	*17*	*18*	*19*	*20*
18.94	18.68	18.46	18.26	18.09	17.93	17.79	17.67	17.56	17.45	17.36
18.45	18.20	17.98	17.78	17.61	17.46	17.33	17.20	17.09	16.99	16.90
17.96	17.71	17.49	17.30	17.14	16.99	16.86	16.74	16.63	16.54	16.45
17.46	17.22	17.01	16.82	16.66	16.52	16.39	16.27	16.17	16.08	15.99
16.96	16.72	16.52	16.34	16.18	16.05	15.92	15.81	15.71	15.62	15.54
16.46	16.23	16.03	15.86	15.71	15.58	15.46	15.35	15.25	15.17	15.09
15.96	15.74	15.55	15.38	15.24	15.11	15.00	14.89	14.80	14.72	14.64
15.47	15.26	15.07	14.91	14.77	14.65	14.54	14.44	14.36	14.28	14.20
14.98	14.78	14.60	14.45	14.31	14.20	14.09	14.00	13.92	13.84	13.77
14.50	14.30	14.13	13.99	13.86	13.75	13.65	13.56	13.48	13.41	13.35
14.03	13.84	13.68	13.54	13.42	13.31	13.22	13.14	13.06	12.99	12.93
13.56	13.38	13.23	13.10	12.98	12.88	12.80	12.72	12.65	12.58	12.53
13.11	12.94	12.79	12.67	12.56	12.47	12.38	12.31	12.24	12.18	12.13
12.66	12.50	12.37	12.25	12.15	12.06	11.98	11.91	11.85	11.80	11.75
12.23	12.08	11.95	11.85	11.75	11.67	11.60	11.53	11.47	11.42	11.37
11.82	11.67	11.55	11.45	11.36	11.29	11.22	11.16	11.10	11.06	11.01
11.41	11.28	11.17	11.07	10.99	10.92	10.85	10.80	10.75	10.70	10.66
11.02	10.90	10.79	10.71	10.63	10.56	10.50	10.45	10.40	10.36	10.32
10.65	10.53	10.44	10.35	10.28	10.22	10.17	10.12	10.07	10.03	10.00
10.28	10.18	10.09	10.01	9.95	9.89	9.84	9.80	9.76	9.72	9.69
9.94	9.84	9.76	9.69	9.63	9.57	9.53	9.49	9.45	9.42	9.39
9.61	9.52	9.44	9.37	9.32	9.27	9.23	9.19	9.16	9.13	9.10
9.29	9.21	9.14	9.08	9.02	8.98	8.94	8.91	8.87	8.85	8.82
8.99	8.91	8.84	8.79	8.74	8.70	8.67	8.63	8.61	8.58	8.56
8.70	8.62	8.57	8.52	8.47	8.44	8.40	8.37	8.35	8.32	8.30
8.42	8.35	8.30	8.25	8.22	8.18	8.15	8.12	8.10	8.08	8.06
8.16	8.10	8.05	8.01	7.97	7.94	7.91	7.89	7.87	7.85	7.83
7.90	7.85	7.81	7.77	7.74	7.71	7.68	7.66	7.64	7.62	7.61
7.67	7.62	7.58	7.54	7.51	7.49	7.46	7.44	7.42	7.41	7.39
7.44	7.39	7.36	7.33	7.30	7.27	7.25	7.24	7.22	7.21	7.19
7.22	7.18	7.15	7.12	7.10	7.07	7.05	7.04	7.02	7.01	7.00
7.02	6.98	6.95	6.92	6.90	6.88	6.87	6.85	6.84	6.82	6.81
6.82	6.79	6.76	6.74	6.72	6.70	6.68	6.67	6.66	6.65	6.64
6.64	6.61	6.58	6.56	6.54	6.52	6.51	6.50	6.49	6.48	6.47
6.46	6.43	6.41	6.39	6.37	6.36	6.35	6.34	6.33	6.32	6.31
6.29	6.27	6.25	6.23	6.21	6.20	6.19	6.18	6.17	6.16	6.15
6.13	6.11	6.09	6.07	6.06	6.05	6.04	6.03	6.02	6.01	6.01
5.98	5.96	5.94	5.93	5.91	5.90	5.90	5.89	5.88	5.87	5.87
5.83	5.81	5.80	5.79	5.78	5.77	5.76	5.75	5.74	5.74	5.73
5.69	5.68	5.66	5.65	5.64	5.64	5.63	5.62	5.62	5.61	5.61
5.56	5.55	5.54	5.53	5.52	5.51	5.50	5.50	5.49	5.49	5.48

interest rates (0 to 20%). Exhibit 6–21 analyzes the duration behavior of a 30-year bond by varying its coupon rate (0 to 20%) and yield (0 to 20%). The triad of exhibits serves to confirm the following observations.

First, longer maturities create higher durations. For example, at a YTM of 7.00%, a 10% coupon bond bears a 0.98 duration as a 1-year issue, a 4.12 duration as a 5-year issue, a 6.89 duration as a 10-year issue, a 10.32 duration as a 20-year issue, and a 13.97 duration as a 50-year issue (Exhibit 6–19). *This effect is especially pronounced for low coupon bonds.* For example, a 4% coupon bond offers a 0.99 duration as a 1-year security. The same bond carries a 14.40 duration as a 30-year issue. A 20% coupon bond moves from a 0.96 duration to an 11.37 duration under the same conditions (Exhibit 6–19). Clearly, the lower coupon issue realizes a greater surge in duration than the higher coupon issue, given an identical extension in maturity.

Second, lower coupon rates create higher durations. For example, at a 7.00% YTM, a 20-year bond carries a 9.29 duration given a 20% coupon rate, a 9.66 duration given a 15% coupon rate, a 10.32 duration given a 10% coupon rate, an 11.87 duration given a 5% coupon rate, and a 20.00 duration given a 0% coupon rate (Exhibit 6–19). *This effect is exaggerated in long maturity issues.* For example, the duration of a 5-year bond moves from 3.71 to 5.00 as its coupon rate is lowered from 20 to 0%; the duration of a 30-year bond almost triples under the same conditions, surging from 11.37 to 30.00 (Exhibit 6–19).

Third, lower yield environments create higher durations. For example, a 10-year maturity par bond offers a 4.68 duration in a 20% yield environment, a 5.48 duration in a 15% yield environment, a 6.54 duration in a 10% yield environment, and a 7.99 duration in a 5% yield environment (Exhibit 6–20). *This effect is magnified in long maturity issues and low coupon issues.* For example, the duration of a 5-year par bond edges up from 3.38 to 4.49 as yields fall from 20 to 5%. The duration of a 50-year par bond races from 5.50 to 18.77 under the same conditions (Exhibit 6–20). A 20% coupon, 30-year bond's duration moves from 7.00 to 12.93 as yields decline from 15 to 5%. The duration of a 5% coupon bond of similar maturity surges from 7.66 to 15.84 under the same circumstances (Exhibit 6–21).

Exhibit 6–22. Summary of the factors influencing a bond's duration.

	Duration Behavior	
Factor	*Lower Duration*	*Higher Duration*
Term to maturity	shorter	longer
Coupon rate	higher	lower
Accrued interest	large	small
Market yield level	higher	lower
Sinking fund features	many	minimal
Call features	many	minimal

The variety of influences on a bond's duration are summarized in Exhibit 6–22. The reader can use the duration tables to estimate the impact of a selected change in one of the aforementioned factors. The broad range of maturities, coupon rates, and yield levels allows for a great degree of real-world applications.

The concept of modified duration

The usefulness of duration as a risk measure arises from an adjusted version of Macaulay's duration termed *modified duration* and calculated as follows:

$$\text{modified duration} = \frac{\text{Macaulay's duration}}{\left(1 + \dfrac{\text{IRR}}{m}\right)}$$

where

IRR = internal rate of return on the bond, expressed in decimal form

m = number of compounding periods per year

For a semiannual pay bond,

$$\text{modified duration} = \frac{\text{Macaulay's duration}}{\left(1 + \dfrac{\text{YTM}}{2}\right)}$$

The modification adjusts the duration for noncontinuous compounding of interest.[9]

The amount of duration adjustment is greater for longer maturity, higher duration issues and for higher yielding instruments. Exhibit 6–23 illustrates these effects for current-coupon U.S. Treasury bonds of 3- and 30-year maturities. For example, a 3-year bond in a 4% yield environment bears a modified duration of 2.80 years, slightly less than its unadjusted duration of 2.86 years. A 30-year bond has a 17.38-year modified duration in a 4% interest rate environment, ⅓ of a year less

---

[9] Macaulay's duration assumes continuous compounding of interest. Notice that if the m compounding periods is expanded to infinity (i.e., continuous compounding), IRR/m falls to zero, and the denominator becomes 1.0. Continuous compounding therefore requires no adjustment to the original Macaulay's duration figure.

Exhibit 6–23. Comparison of the durations and modified durations of a series of current-coupon U.S. Treasury bonds priced at par.

Issue	Duration (Years)		Modified Duration (Years)	
	YTM = 4%	*YTM = 10%*	*YTM = 4%*	*YTM = 10%*
3-year maturity bond	2.86	2.67	2.80	2.54
30-year maturity bond	17.73	9.94	17.38	9.47

Comments: *Modified duration adjustments are more severe: (1) the lower the general yield level and (2) the higher the duration of the bond under consideration.*

than its stated duration of 17.73 years. In higher yield (10%) conditions, the adjustment to the 30-year bond is approximately ½ year (9.94 − 9.47).

Observation: *Modified duration is simply an adjusted version of Macaulay's duration. Higher yield levels and longer duration instruments lead to more sizable differences between the two formulations.*

Using modified duration as a measure of a bond's price sensitivity. The modified duration figure allows one to estimate the price volatility of a bond with ease:

$$\text{percent change in bond price} = - \left(\text{modified duration} \right) \times \frac{\text{BP change in yield}}{100}$$

Chapter 2 introduced the inverse relationship between a bond's price and its yield. This relationship warrants the minus sign alongside the modified duration figure.

The modified duration is, in essence, a multiplier. A bond with a modified duration of 5.0, for example, experiences approximately a 5% change in price for every 100 basis point (i.e., 1%) change in yield:

Rates rise 100BP:

$$\text{percent change in bond price} = -5.0 \times \frac{100}{100}$$

$$= -5.0 \times 1$$

$$= -5.00\%$$

Rates fall 100BP:

$$\text{percent change in bond price} = -5.0 \times \frac{-100}{100}$$

$$= -5.0 \times (-1)$$

$$= +5.00\%$$

A higher duration bond is more sensitive to changes in market yield levels. For example, a bond with a modified duration of 20 years experiences approximately a 20% change in price for every 100BP shift in yield. A low duration bond exhibits a lesser degree of price volatility since its multiplier is a smaller figure. Modified duration is very handy in that it incorporates many of the factors impacting a bond's inherent volatility into a single representative number.[10]

> **Observation:** *A bond's modified duration is an estimate of the bond's price sensitivity to changes in yield. The modified duration figure acts as a multiplier.*

Modified duration and the price:yield function. Exhibit 6–24 summarizes the expected price behavior of a bond with a 5.0-year modified duration. The bond's price is projected to change at the same rate, 5% for every 100BP yield change, across a wide spectrum of absolute yield changes. Graphically speaking, the price:yield combinations of Exhibit 6–24 can be plotted as a straight line (see Exhibit 6–25). The slope of the line is the modified duration of the bond.[11]

Modified duration estimates the price:yield relationship as linear in nature. The actual price:yield relationship is curvilinear in nature (recall Exhibits 4–1 and 4–5 from Chapter 4). Plotting the modified duration line and the observed price:yield curve on the same graph reveals an interesting phenomenon. *The duration line is tangent to the*

---

[10] As illustrated throughout this chapter, a bond's duration reflects the bond's term to maturity, coupon rate, accrued interest, market yield level, and sinking fund features. For callable bonds, an *effective duration* can be used for comparative purposes.

[11] Modified durations are expressed as positive numbers (e.g., 1.57, 5.00). The fact that the slope of the line is negative is handled by the insertion of a minus sign alongside the modified duration figure in the price:yield equation shown earlier.

Exhibit 6–24. Expected price changes for a 5.0-year modified duration bond under a wide variety of yield shifts. The bond is initially priced at par (100.00).

(1) Yield Change (BP)	(2) = −5.0 × (1)/100 Percent Change in Bond Price	(3) = (2) × 100.00 Absolute Change in Bond Price
−400	+20.00	+20.00
−300	+15.00	+15.00
−200	+10.00	+10.00
−100	+ 5.00	+ 5.00
− 10	+ 0.50	+ 0.50
0	0	0
+ 10	− 0.50	− 0.50
+100	− 5.00	− 5.00
+200	−10.00	−10.00
+300	−15.00	−15.00
+400	−20.00	−20.00

bond's price:yield curve at the coordinates representing the current market price and current YTM of the bond in question (see Exhibit 6–26).[12] A numeric example explains the seeming inconsistency between modified duration (linear) and the actual bond price behavior observed in the marketplace (nonlinear).

A 7% coupon, 30-year U.S. Treasury bond is currently priced at par to yield 7.00%. Exhibit 6–27 follows the bond's price behavior over a wide range of interest rate scenarios (column 3). The observed prices are simply the result of recalculations of the bond's price today if yield levels shift by the designated amounts. The 30-year bond has a modified duration of 12.47 years; therefore, for every 100BP change in yield, the bond's price is expected to change by 12.47%. Column 5 of Exhibit 6–27 lists the individual price changes predicted by the modified duration measure. The last column in Exhibit 6–27 shows that modified duration does not completely capture all of the inherent price volatility of a bond. There is substantial error in the duration-predicted price changes if yields move sizably away from current levels.

Taken to the extreme, modified duration predicts a 187.29 price at a 0% yield, whereas the actual price at a 0% yield is 310.00, the

---

[12] Mathematically speaking, modified duration is the first derivative of the curvilinear price: yield function. Graphically, the first derivative is the slope of the price:yield curve at a specified point; a tangent line drawn through that point is used to calculate the slope.

Exhibit 6–25. Relationship between bond price and bond yield as expressed by modified duration (from Exhibit 6–24).

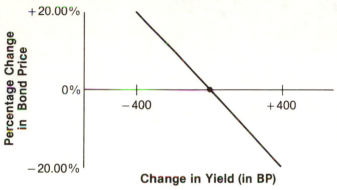

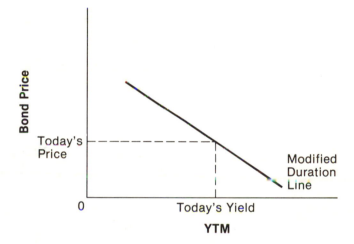

Exhibit 6–26. Relationship between bond prices and bond yields.

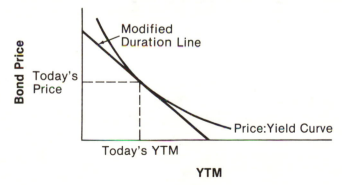

Exhibit 6–27. Price behavior of a 7% coupon, 30-year U.S. Treasury bond initially priced at par to yield 7.00% to maturity. The bond's modified duration is 12.47 years.

(1) Yield to Maturity (%)	(2) Yield Change (BP)	(3) Bond Price	$(4) = \dfrac{(3) - 100.00}{100.00}$ Actual Price Change (%)	$(5) = -12.47 \times \dfrac{(2)}{100}$ Duration-Suggested Price Change (%)	$(6) = (4) - (5)$ Unexplained Price Change (%)
0.00	−700	310.00	+210.00	+ 87.29	+122.71
1.00	−600	255.18	+155.18	+ 74.82	+ 80.36
2.00	−500	212.39	+112.39	+ 62.35	+ 50.04
3.00	−400	178.76	+ 78.76	+ 49.88	+ 28.88
4.00	−300	152.14	+ 52.14	+ 37.41	+ 14.73
5.00	−200	130.91	+ 30.91	+ 24.94	+ 5.97
6.00	−100	113.84	+ 13.84	+ 12.47	+ 1.37
6.90	− 10	101.26	+ 1.26	+ 1.25	+ 0.01
6.99	− 1	100.12	+ 0.12	+ 0.12	0
7.00	**0**	**100.00**	**0**	**0**	**0**
7.01	+ 1	99.88	− 0.12	− 0.12	0
7.10	+ 10	98.77	− 1.23	− 1.25	+ 0.02
8.00	+100	88.69	− 11.31	− 12.47	+ 1.16
9.00	+200	79.36	− 20.64	− 24.94	+ 4.30
10.00	+300	71.61	− 28.39	− 37.41	+ 9.02
11.00	+400	65.10	− 34.90	− 49.88	+ 14.78
12.00	+500	59.60	− 40.40	− 62.35	+ 21.95
13.00	+600	54.90	− 45.10	− 74.82	+ 29.72
14.00	+700	50.86	− 49.14	− 87.29	+ 38.15
15.02	+802	47.30	− 52.70	−100.00	+ 47.30

Exhibit 6–28. Relationship between bond price and bond yield for a 7% coupon, 30-year U.S. Treasury bond initially priced at par to yield 7.00% to maturity (data from Exhibit 6–27).

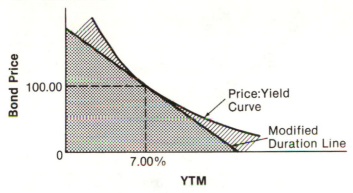

face value of all of the bond's future cash flows. At the other extreme, modified duration sees a zero price at a 15.02% yield (i.e., a 100.00% decline in price) rather than the actual price of 47.30 at that yield level. Indeed, duration suggests a negative bond price at yields exceeding a specific yield level (15.02% in this instance). In reality, bond prices cannot become negative.

Exhibit 6–28 graphs the data presented in Exhibit 6–27. The actual price:yield relationship is a cup-shaped curve. The duration-suggested prices lie on a straight line that is tangent to the price:yield curve at the point of the current market price and yield of the 30-year bond of interest. The extreme coordinates of the modified duration line appear as the *X*- and *Y*-intercepts.

Exhibit 6–28 vividly illustrates that modified duration explains less and less of the bond's price behavior as yields diverge further and further away from current levels. However, for small changes in yield (10BP or less), modified duration is an accurate predictor of bond price volatility. Graphically, the modified duration tangent line approximates the actual price:yield relationship for very small deviations from the current market yield level. For a 1BP yield change, the modified duration of 12.47 serves as an excellent indicator of the percentage price change. The price volatility associated with a 10BP yield change is forecasted within 1 to 2BP (recall Exhibit 6–27).

> **Observation:** *Modified duration reflects a bond's price:yield trade-off in a straight-line form. In actuality, the price:yield function is a curve. Consequently, error terms become large as prices and yields move away from current levels.*

Exhibit 6–29. Change in tangent duration lines on a 7% coupon, 30-year U.S. Treasury bond as yield levels shift (data from Exhibit 6–27).

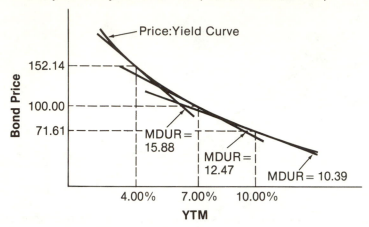

The assumptions underlying modified duration. The usefulness of modified duration as a bond risk proxy is predicated on three assumptions: a small change in yield (e.g., 10BP or less), a parallel shift in yield, and an instantaneous change in yield.[13] The assumption of a small yield change is precarious in today's volatile markets. Large changes in yield lead to greater degrees of error in using the modified duration line as an indicator of a bond's inherent price sensitivity. Indeed, the modified duration of a bond shifts as yield levels change; consequently, the modified duration based on today's yield level will differ from a modified duration at a newly established yield level.

Graphically speaking, a price:yield curve is made up of a series of individual points, each of which has associated with it a unique duration tangent line. As yields change, so does the slope of the line tangent to the price:yield curve at the newly established yield level. As yields fall, the appropriate tangent line becomes steeper and the slope of the line (i.e., the modified duration) increases. Conversely, as yields rise, tangent lines flatten out as their slopes (i.e., modified durations) fall. Exhibit 6–29 illustrates these realities for the 30-year U.S. Treasury bond of prior example. These results confirm the finding of an inverse relationship between duration and yield level earlier in this chapter.

The parallel yield shift assumption expects all bond yields to move

---

[13] In actuality, the duration tangent line assumes an infinitesimally small change in yield (i.e., a tiny fraction of a basis point). For practical purposes, however, the 10BP rule of thumb is adequate.

in an identical fashion. In reality, nonparallel yield shifts occur far more often than parallel ones, as sector spreads change (refer to Chapters 14 and 15). For example, history shows that over short-term periods, yields of short maturity instruments are more volatile than yields of long maturity instruments. The yield curve rarely shifts in a parallel manner. Consequently, price return differentials result, creating additional errors in the use of modified duration as a price volatility proxy.

The instantaneous yield change assumption is also critical to the usefulness of modified duration. As time passes, a bond's duration changes due to a shortening of the remaining term to maturity and due to the buildup and fall-off of accrued interest. Price: yield curves tend to flatten as a bond approaches maturity. Stated differently, the bond's modified duration falls, and its line of tangency flattens as the bond's inherent price volatility subsides (recall Exhibit 4–5 from Chapter 4).

> **Observation:** *The modified duration measure assumes small, instantaneous, parallel changes in yield. Under such conditions, modified duration serves as a reasonably accurate proxy for a bond's price sensitivity.*

Durations, durations, and more durations

The widespread use of duration as a bond risk measure has generated a proliferation of duration types: Macaulay's duration, modified duration, holding period duration, and relative duration. Analysis of callable bonds has introduced several additional measures of duration: duration to maturity, duration to call, effective (call-adjusted) duration, and observed duration. Exhibit 6–30 provides a brief definition of each of these duration interpretations. The table is valuable as a reference tool should duration semantics become confusing. This book focuses on Macaulay's duration and modified duration.

Given that duration changes over time, a *holding-period duration* attempts to provide a more accurate assessment of price sensitivity over a specified investment horizon. The concept of *relative duration* is outlined in Chapter 7. *Duration to maturity, duration to call,* and *effective duration* were described earlier in this chapter. *Effective duration* and *observed duration* are closely related.

Effective duration attempts to allow comparability between callable bonds and noncallable issues. Although the computations of effective duration are beyond the scope of this book, the concept is relatively simple: effective duration attempts to capture the inherent price volatility

Exhibit 6–30. Duration definitions.

Duration Type	Explanation
1. Macaulay's duration	The present value-weighted average maturity of a bond's total cash flow stream; the bond's IRR serves as the discount rate for all of the bond's cash flows. Macaulay's duration is simply referred to as *duration*.
2. Modified duration	A mathematically adjusted form of Macaulay's duration. Modified duration measures the sensitivity of a bond's price to small, instantaneous changes in yield.
3. Holding-period duration	The average duration of a bond over a pre-specified holding period. It attempts to provide a better measure of the average risk of the bond during the holding period. Alternatively, an end-of-period duration can be used. Each form can be expressed in either Macaulay's or modified Macaulay's terms.
4. Relative duration	The ratio of the duration of one investment vis-à-vis the duration of another investment. It attempts to provide a feel for the relative risk of two alternative bond investments (to be discussed in Chapter 7).
5. Duration to maturity	The duration to final maturity. This duration measure assumes no premature call on outstanding bonds. It can be calculated on a Macaulay's or a modified Macaulay's basis.
6. Duration to call	The duration to an assumed call date and call price. The duration to call can be expressed in a Macaulay's format or a modified Macaulay's format.
7. Effective duration	A duration that takes account of the option features attached to a bond. It attempts to better portray the price volatility of a callable issue without relying on a discrete *duration to call* or *duration to maturity* categorization. Effective duration is also termed *adjusted duration, call-adjusted duration,* and *option-adjusted duration*. Its strict definition is subject to a set of user-specified assumptions.
8. Observed duration	The price volatility of a bond as observed in real life. It is calculated as the actual percentage price change divided by the actual change in yield. Observed duration will fluctuate as a result of the magnitude and direction of the observed yield change.

of a bond that is subject to issuer options such as call and put features. An *observed duration* is similar in concept. For example, suppose that Bond A and Bond B behave in the following manner in up and down markets:

	Price Change (%) if:	
	Yields Fall 200BP	Yields Rise 200BP
Bond A	+25.00	−19.00
Bond B	+10.00	−10.00

Bond A experiences a 23.00% change in price (on average) given a 200BP yield shift, or an 11.50 observed duration. Bond B bears a 10.00% price alteration in up and down markets, or a 5.00 observed duration. In essence, Bond A is 2.3 times as risky as Bond B.

An effective duration measures the price volatility of a bond in much the same way, except that it projects the price return behavior across a wide range of yield changes and assigns a probability to the magnitude of yield shift. Larger changes in yield are, of course, less likely and, therefore, carry a lower weighting. Past or present levels of interest rate volatility often serve as the basis for the probability distribution of future yields.

> **Observation:** *Bond market participants are exposed to a myriad of duration measures. This book concentrates on the usage of Macaulay's duration and modified duration, the fundamental concepts underlying the more advanced price risk measures.*

Convexity

The concept of convexity

Given a small change in yield, a bond's modified duration acts as a good approximation of the bond's price volatility risk. Larger increments of yield change render the modified duration measure less meaningful, as the curvature of the price:yield function pulls away from the tangent line synonymous with the bond's modified duration. Exhibit 6–28 depicts the price:yield relationship as a cup-shaped curve facing away from the origin of the X- and Y-axes. The price:yield curve is convex to the origin, and the price returns above and beyond those explained by the

Exhibit 6–31. Price behavior of a 7% coupon, 3-year U.S. Treasury as attributable to duration and convexity. The bond is initially priced at par to yield 7.00% and bears a modified duration of 2.67 years.

		Price Change (%) Due to:		
(1)	*(2)*	$(3) = -2.67 \times \dfrac{(1)}{100}$	$(4) = (2) - (3)$	$(5) = \dfrac{(4)}{|(1)|/100}$
Yield Change (BP)	*Actual % Price Change*	*Modified Duration*	*Convexity*	*Convexity Factor*
−400	+11.39	+10.68	+0.71	0.18
−300	+ 8.40	+ 8.01	+0.39	0.13
−200	+ 5.51	+ 5.34	+0.17	0.09
−100	+ 2.71	+ 2.67	+0.04	0.04
0	0	0	0	0
+100	− 2.62	− 2.67	+0.05	0.05
+200	− 5.16	− 5.34	+0.18	0.09
+300	− 7.61	− 8.01	+0.40	0.13
+400	− 9.99	−10.68	+0.69	0.17

duration line are commonly called *convexity returns*.[14] Indeed, if there were no curvature in the price:yield relationship, convexity would not exist.

Higher duration bonds are inherently more convex than their lower duration counterparts. This convexity advantage is discernible when comparing short, intermediate, and long maturity issues. Exhibits 6–31, 6–32, and 6–33 analyze the price behavior of 3-, 10-, and 30-year U.S. Treasury bonds, respectively. Modified duration explains most of the price behavior of a 3-year bond over a wide variety of interest rate changes (Exhibit 6–31). Given a 400BP decline in rates, for example, duration accounts for almost 94% of the upward price move (10.68/11.39 = 0.938).

Subjecting a 10-year bond to an identical 400BP downward adjustment in yield creates a 34.34% price appreciation, only 83% of which is anticipated by the bond's 7.11-year modified duration (Exhibit 6–32). A 30-year bond's price return is substantially enhanced by its attractive convexity features. Assuming the same 400BP bond market rally, the 30-year issue garners a 78.76% price return, over one-third of which is contributed by the convexity component (Exhibit 6–33).

---

[14] Technically, convexity is the second derivative of the price:yield function. Higher order derivatives account for the small remainder of actual price change. For simplicity, this book includes these minor residual effects in the convexity return figures.

Exhibit 6–32. Price behavior of a 7% coupon, 10-year U.S. Treasury as attributable to duration and convexity. The bond is initially priced at par to yield 7.00% and bears a modified duration of 7.11 years.

(1)	(2)	Price Change (%) Due to:		
		$(3) = -7.11 \times \dfrac{(1)}{100}$	$(4) = (2) - (3)$	$(5) = \dfrac{(4)}{\lvert (1) \rvert / 100}$
Yield Change (BP)	Actual % Price Change	Modified Duration	Convexity	Convexity Factor
−400	+34.34	+28.44	+5.90	1.48
−300	+24.53	+21.33	+5.20	1.07
−200	+15.59	+14.22	+1.37	0.69
−100	+ 7.44	+ 7.11	+0.33	0.33
0	0	0	0	0
+100	− 6.80	− 7.11	+0.31	0.31
+200	−13.01	−14.22	+1.21	0.61
+300	−18.69	−21.33	+2.64	0.88
+400	−23.90	−28.44	+4.54	1.14

Exhibit 6–33. Price behavior of a 7% coupon, 30-year U.S. Treasury as attributable to duration and convexity. The bond is initially priced at par to yield 7.00% and bears a modified duration of 12.47 years.

(1)	(2)	Price Change (%) Due to:		
		$(3) = -12.47 \times \dfrac{(1)}{100}$	$(4) = (2) - (3)$	$(5) = \dfrac{(4)}{\lvert (1) \rvert / 100}$
Yield Change (BP)	Actual % Price Change	Modified Duration	Convexity	Convexity Factor
−400	+78.76	+49.88	+28.88	7.22
−300	+52.14	+37.41	+14.73	4.91
−200	+30.91	+24.94	+ 5.97	2.99
−100	+13.84	+12.47	+ 1.37	1.37
0	0	0	0	0
+100	−11.31	−12.47	+ 1.16	1.16
+200	−20.64	−24.94	+ 4.30	2.15
+300	−28.39	−37.41	+ 9.02	3.01
+400	−34.90	−49.88	+14.98	3.75

Convexity adds to a bond's return in both bull and bear markets. Convexity fuels returns in a market advance and cushion losses in a market decline. These *positive convexity* returns can be viewed numerically in the triad of aforementioned tables (in the *convexity* column) or observed graphically as the price:yield curve dominates the duration

Exhibit 6–34. Positive convexity of 3-, 10-, and 30-year 7% coupon U.S. Treasury bonds priced at par (data from Exhibits 6–31, 6–32, and 6–33).

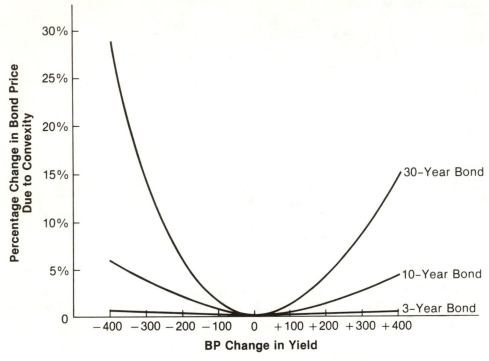

line in all yield scenarios (recall Exhibit 6–28). Although the convexity returns are not perfectly symmetrical, they do become a powerful influence on bond price volatility as (1) larger yield changes are encountered and (2) longer duration securities are studied. Exhibit 6–34 displays this fact by plotting the convexity returns of the 3-, 10-, and 30-year U.S. Treasuries of earlier example.

Long duration zero-coupon bonds offer impressive convexity attributes. A 30-year STRIPS, for example, experiences a 222.45% price appreciation if interest rates drop 400BP (see Exhibit 6–35). Almost half of this return is traceable to the convexity of this long duration instrument. With only a 200BP yield decline, the STRIPS' modified duration accounts for less than 75% of the bond's actual price surge. Graphically speaking, the price:yield curve for a 30-year STRIPS is significantly more cup-shaped than those of its lower duration cohorts.

> **Observation:** *Positive convexity or simply, convexity, arises from the curvature of the price:yield relationship of a noncallable bond. Convexity effects are magnified by large changes in yield and by high duration instruments.*

Exhibit 6–35. Price behavior of a 30-year STRIPS as attributable to duration and convexity. The bond is initially priced to yield 7.00% and bears a modified duration of 28.99 years.

		Price Change (%) Due to:		
(1)	*(2)*	$(3) = -28.99 \times \dfrac{(1)}{100}$	$(4) = (2) - (3)$	$(5) = \dfrac{(4)}{\|(1)\|/100}$
Yield Change (BP)	*Actual % Price Change*	*Modified Duration*	*Convexity*	*Convexity Factor*
−400	+222.45	+115.96	+106.49	26.62
−300	+140.11	+ 86.97	+ 53.14	17.71
−200	+ 79.06	+ 57.98	+ 21.08	10.54
−100	+ 33.72	+ 28.99	+ 4.73	4.73
0	0	0	0	0
+100	− 25.11	− 28.99	+ 3.88	3.88
+200	− 43.84	− 57.98	+ 14.14	7.07
+300	− 57.82	− 86.97	+ 29.15	9.72
+400	− 68.28	−115.96	+ 47.68	11.92

Comments: *Long STRIPS have awesome convexity characteristics.*

The use of convexity factors and price volatility multipliers

Convexity acts as a risk reducer. The benefits/(dangers) of duration are under/(over)stated due to convexity impacts. To quickly compare the convexities of a series of bonds, one can rely on *convexity factors*. Exhibits 6–31, 6–32, 6–33, and 6–35 calculate convexity factors as follows:

$$\text{convexity factor} = \frac{\text{convexity return (\%)}}{\dfrac{\text{BP change in yield}}{100}}$$

For example, a 7% coupon, 30-year U.S. Treasury bond sports a convexity factor of 2.99 given a 200BP decline in rates (Exhibit 6–33):

$$\text{convexity factor} = \frac{5.97}{\dfrac{200}{100}}$$

$$= \frac{5.97}{2}$$

$$= 2.99 \quad \text{(rounded to nearest two decimals)}$$

This factor suggests that if rates decline 200BP, this bond's price volatility will reflect the 12.47-year modified duration *plus* a 2.99-year convexity factor for a total price volatility multiplier of 15.46 years (12.47 + 2.99). In other words, a 200BP decline in yields should lead to a 30.92% surge in price [15.46 multiplier × (200BP yield change/100) = 30.92%]. Exhibit 6–33 verifies the accuracy (within 1BP). For rising interest rate conditions, convexity factors are subtracted from the modified durations to arrive at a price volatility multiplier:

$$\begin{array}{c} \text{price volatility} \\ \text{multiplier} \\ \text{(falling yields)} \end{array} = \dfrac{\text{modified}}{\text{duration}} + \dfrac{\text{convexity}}{\text{factor}}$$

$$\begin{array}{c} \text{price volatility} \\ \text{multiplier} \\ \text{(rising yields)} \end{array} = \dfrac{\text{modified}}{\text{duration}} - \dfrac{\text{convexity}}{\text{factor}}$$

A *price volatility multiplier* is simply a modified duration as adjusted for convexity impacts.

Unfortunately, convexity factors are not stable. These factors are influenced by (1) the magnitude of the yield change and (2) the direction of the yield change.[15] A commonly used convexity factor is an average based on the individual factors associated with a rise and fall in yields of 100BP.[16] Exhibit 6–36 lists the average convexity factors for 3-, 10-, and 30-year U.S. Treasury bonds given a 100BP change in yield. Longer maturity issues carry higher convexities. For example, the 10-year U.S. Treasury bond has a 0.320 average convexity factor, approximately 7 times as large as the 3-year bond's comparable factor. The 30-year issue offers almost 4 times the convexity of the 10-year bond (1.265 versus 0.320). These differentials are even more significant as the magnitude of the yield change is increased from the 100BP assumption.

Relating the average convexity factors to the durations of the underly-

---

[15] It is also clear that convexity factors assume a parallel shift in yield. A nonparallel yield shift introduces some degree of error in the convexity expectation. Callable bond convexities (to be discussed) are particularly unstable and are very much a function of the direction of market yield change.

[16] The user should gear the chosen magnitude around a forecast of expected future volatility in interest rates. The nonsymmetric nature of convexity factors introduces some degree of error in relying on an average figure, even if the volatility forecast is correct. If one has strong conviction about market direction, a single convexity factor can be used rather than an average representation.

Exhibit 6–36. Average convexity factors for various maturity U.S. Treasury bonds, assuming a 100BP yield change (data from Exhibits 6–31, 6–32, and 6–33).

Issue	*Average Convexity Factor*
3-year bond	0.045
10-year bond	0.320
30-year bond	1.265

Comments: *Longer maturity (i.e., longer duration) issues bear more positive convexity.*

Exhibit 6–37. Convexity as an increasing function of duration. Each security is priced to yield 7.00% to maturity (data from Exhibits 6–31, 6–32, 6–33, 6–35, and 6–36).

(1)	*(2)*	*(3)*	*(4) = (3)/(2)*
		Average	*Convexity*
	Modified	*Convexity*	*per Year*
Issue	*Duration*	*Factor*[*]	*of Duration*
3-year bond	2.67	0.045	0.017
10-year bond	7.11	0.320	0.045
30-year bond	12.47	1.265	0.101
3-year STRIPS	2.90	0.050	0.017
10-year STRIPS	9.66	0.490	0.051
30-year STRIPS	28.99	4.305	0.148

[*] Average convexity factors are based on a 100BP change in yields.

ing bonds reveals that convexity is an increasing function of duration. Exhibit 6–37 calculates the *convexity per year of duration* for 3-, 10-, and 30-year U.S. Treasuries and STRIPS. A 30-year U.S. Treasury bond offers 0.101 unit of convexity per year of modified duration purchased. A 3-year U.S. Treasury bond provides a 0.045 average convexity factor, or only 0.017 unit of convexity per year of duration. Long (30-year) STRIPS have an abundance of convexity, on both an absolute basis (4.305 average convexity factor) and a relative basis (0.148 convexity unit per duration-year).

The more sizable the amount of yield change, the more impressive these convexity advantages become (recall Exhibits 6–31, 6–32, 6–33, and 6–35). Exhibit 6–38 plots the duration:convexity relationship for current-coupon U.S. Treasury bonds of various durations. One conclusion which stems from the data collections referenced is that a dumbbell

Exhibit 6–38. Convexity as a function of duration. The convexity factors illustrated are from 7% coupon U.S. Treasury bonds initially priced at par to yield 7.00% to maturity. A 400BP change in yields is assumed (data from Exhibits 6–31, 6–32, and 6–33).

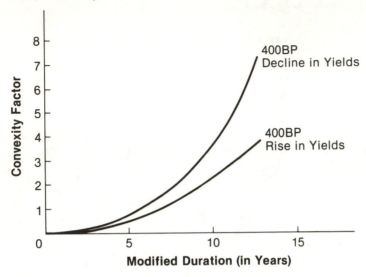

combination of short and long duration securities is more convex than a bullet (i.e., intermediate maturity issue) of similar average duration.

> **Observation:** *For noncallable bonds, the convex nature of the price:*
> *yield curve is responsible for price changes unanticipated by the modified*
> *duration measure alone. Convexity factors can be used in conjunction*
> *with modified durations to create price volatility multipliers, which*
> *serve as better predictors of a bond's price sensitivity. Long duration*
> *zero-coupon bonds are particularly blessed with positive convexity char-*
> *acteristics.*

Negative convexity

Up to this point, the convexity discussions have focused on noncallable bonds. These issues exhibit benefits from convexity as represented by incremental positive convexity returns or, simply, positive convexity. Callable or prepayable bonds suffer from *negative convexity*. Exhibit 6–39 plots the typical shape of a price:yield curve for a callable corporate bond. As market yields fall, the bond's price increases at a decreasing

Exhibit 6–39. Sample price:yield curve for a callable bond.

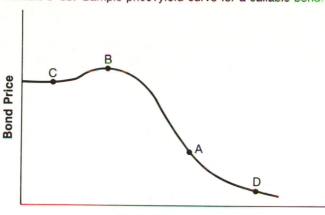

Market Yield Level

rate (Point A to Point B) until it peaks slightly above the call price (Point B). As rates continue to decline, the probability of early call becomes a virtual certainty and the bond's price declines to the stated call price. Further drops in rates have no impact on the bond's price.[17]

The shape of this price:yield curve is concave (i.e., cup-shaped toward the origin) from Points A to C. The terms *concavity* and *negative convexity* are synonymous. Indeed, if one draws a duration line tangent to a point on the curve along the A-to-C segment, the price:yield curve lies below the tangent line. In other words, the actual price of the bond will be lower than that predicted by the bond's modified duration. The returns attributable to convexity are negative. Notice that after yields rise to a certain level (Point A), the price:yield curve becomes convex in shape (Points A to D and beyond). These unusual twists and turns dictate that callable bonds be deemed special attention in the assessment of risk and return.

Observation: *Negative convexity plagues callable bonds. Over specific ranges of interest rates, the observed price volatility of a callable issue is less favorable than that suggested by the modified duration measure. Unexpected negative price impacts result.*

---

[17] The bond has a zero duration (i.e., no price volatility) at yields below Point C, a negative duration over the C → B arc (i.e., the bond price and bond yield move in the same direction), and a positive duration thereafter.

Portfolio duration and convexity

The duration of a portfolio of fixed-income securities is simply the weighted average of the durations of the individual issues comprising the portfolio. The formula for *portfolio duration* is as follows:

$$\text{portfolio duration} = \sum_{i=1}^{n} w_i D_i$$

where

w_i = market value weighting of security i

D_i = duration of security i

n = number of securities in the portfolio

Similarly, the *portfolio convexity* represents a weighted average of the convexities of the portfolio members:

$$\text{portfolio convexity} = \sum_{i=1}^{n} w_i C_i$$

where

w_i = market value weighting of security i

C_i = convexity factor for security i

n = number of securities in the portfolio

The individual convexity factors reflect price volatility projections for a chosen level of expected future interest rate volatility.[18] The convexity factor will be positive for a noncallable issue but may be negative for a callable security. It is conceivable that a portfolio convexity equal zero if the negative convexity influences exactly offset the positive convexity effects.

> **Observation:** *A portfolio duration is calculated as the weighted average of the component durations of the portfolio members. Portfolio convexity is calculated in a similar fashion, as a weighted average of the component convexities.*

---

[18] The investor may wish to use a subjectively determined weighted average of several magnitudes of volatility and their associated convexity factors rather than a single point estimate of future volatility and a single convexity input. Consistency in deriving the convexity factor for each individual security is critical to the credibility and subsequent interpretation and application of the portfolio convexity figure.

An application of portfolio duration and portfolio convexity

Exhibit 6–40 presents the duration and convexity characteristics of a bond portfolio made up of two issues: a 3-year U.S. Treasury bond and a 30-year U.S. Treasury bond. Approximately 55% of the portfolio is held in 3-year bonds, with the remaining 45% position in 30-year bonds. The portfolio's duration and convexity are calculated as follows:

$$\text{portfolio duration} = \sum_{i=1}^{2} w_i D_i$$

$$= w_1 D_1 + w_2 D_2$$

$$= 0.547\,(2.67) + 0.453\,(12.47)$$

$$= 1.4605 + 5.6489$$

$$= 7.11 \quad \text{(rounded to two decimals)}$$

$$\text{portfolio convexity} = \sum_{i=1}^{2} w_i C_i$$

$$= w_1 C_1 + w_2 C_2$$

$$= 0.547\,(0.09) + 0.453\,(2.57)$$

$$= 0.0492 + 1.1642$$

$$= 1.21 \quad \text{(rounded to two decimals)}$$

The price volatility multipliers, which incorporate both the duration and convexity impacts, are computed as follows:

$$\begin{array}{l}\text{price volatility} \\ \text{multiplier} \\ \text{(falling yields)} \end{array} = \begin{array}{l}\text{modified} \\ \text{duration} \end{array} + \begin{array}{l}\text{convexity} \\ \text{factor} \end{array}$$

$$= 7.11 + 1.21$$

$$= 8.32$$

$$\begin{array}{l}\text{price volatility} \\ \text{multiplier} \\ \text{(rising yields)} \end{array} = \begin{array}{l}\text{modified} \\ \text{duration} \end{array} - \begin{array}{l}\text{convexity} \\ \text{factor} \end{array}$$

$$= 7.11 - 1.21$$

$$= 5.90$$

Exhibit 6–40. Portfolio duration and convexity. An example using 7% coupon U.S. Treasury bonds priced at par to yield 7.00% to maturity.

Issue	*Modified Duration*	*Average Convexity Factor**	*Market Value Weighting (%)*
3-year bond	2.67	0.09	54.7
30-year bond	12.47	2.57	45.3
Portfolio average	**7.11**	**1.21**	**100.0**

* Average convexity factors are based on a 200BP change in yield (data from Exhibits 6–31 and 6–33).

Comments: *Portfolio duration and portfolio convexity are market-weighted averages of the component issue durations and convexities.*

The results for the simple 2-bond portfolio suggest that for every 100BP decline in interest rates, the portfolio value will rise by approximately 8.32%. Conversely, a 100BP increase in interest rates should lead to approximately a 5.90% decrease in portfolio value. The portfolio's positive convexity leads to enhanced upside results in a bull market and cushioned downside performance in a bear market.

The caveats of portfolio duration and portfolio convexity

Bond portfolios that appear of similar risk, as measured by portfolio duration, may exhibit noticeably different price volatilities as a result of the nonuniform nature of convexity. Exhibit 6–41 compares the convexities of the 2-bond portfolio of earlier example and a 10-year U.S. Treasury bond. Both the portfolio and the single security sport a modified duration of 7.11 years. However, the 3/30-year bond portfolio offers almost twice the convexity of the 10-year bond (1.21 versus 0.65). This convexity advantage is attributable to the fact that the 30-year bond component of the 3/30-year combination provides a disproportionately high amount of convexity relative to the 10-year issue. The introduction of nonparallel shifts in yield levels compounds the errancies. Comparisons of bond portfolios based solely on their average duration characteristics are, therefore, tenuous.

Equally dangerous is the use of a portfolio convexity factor that is based on the observed price volatility of a single bond bearing a duration similar to that of the portfolio. The law of averages does not apply to estimating portfolio convexity. Recall from Exhibit 6–37 that convexity does not increase uniformly as durations are lengthened. On

Exhibit 6–41. Comparing portfolio averages with individual securities. The portfolio is the 3/30-year U.S. Treasury combination from Exhibit 6–40. The individual issue is a 7% coupon, 10-year U.S. Treasury bond priced at par to yield 7.00% to maturity.

Investment	Modified Duration	Average Convexity Factor*
3/30-year U.S. Treasury portfolio	7.11	1.21
10-year U.S. Treasury bond	7.11	0.65

* Average convexity factors are based on a 200BP change in yield.

Comments: *Portfolio convexity often differs from the convexity of a single bond bearing the same modified duration as the portfolio.*

a per-year-of-duration basis, convexity increases as durations are extended. As a result, a portfolio of securities has inherently more convexity than a single bond bearing an identical duration. Only the meticulous consideration of each security's uniqueness lends validity to the overall portfolio average.

Observation: *Portfolio duration and portfolio convexity statistics should be treated carefully, as they are subject to the same limitations as singular duration and convexity factors.*

Yield value of a 32nd

The *yield value* (YV) *of a 32nd* is the average basis point change in yield that results from repricing a bond 1/32nd of a point higher and 1/32nd of a point lower than the bond's current market price. U.S. Treasury bonds are commonly quoted in dollars and fractions of a dollar as expressed in 32nds. As a result, the common convention is the yield value of the minimum price move, 1/32nd.[19]

The yield value of a 32nd is an accurate indicator of the price volatility of a bond for small changes in yield because it is based on the actual price volatility observed when small price moves occur. Using

[19] In reality, a U.S. Treasury bond price can be quoted in 64ths or 128ths, but the most common comparative base is the 32nd. For corporate bonds, one may choose to rely upon the basis point value of 1/8th point, since corporate bond prices are typically quoted in eighths rather than 32nds.

7% coupon U.S. Treasury bonds initially priced at par, the YV of a 32nd is calculated for a 1-, 5-, and 30-year bond as follows:

	Bond Price	YTM (%)	Absolute YTM Change (in BP)
	99–31	7.0329	3.29
1-year bond	100–00	7.0000	
	100–01	6.9671	3.29
	Average BP change in yield = 3.29BP		

	Bond Price	YTM (%)	Absolute YTM Change (in BP)
	99–31	7.0075	0.75
5-year bond	100–00	7.0000	
	100–01	6.9925	0.75
	Average BP change in yield = 0.75BP		

	Bond Price	YTM (%)	Absolute YTM Change (in BP)
	99–31	7.0025	0.25
30-year bond	100–00	7.0000	
	100–01	6.9975	0.25
	Average BP change in yield = 0.25BP		

For an individual issue, a small change in price leads to a symmetric change in yield (and vice versa) as observed in the three examples above. Across a spectrum of maturities, however, the impact of a 32nd on bond yields varies substantially. Exhibit 6–42 lists the YVs of a 32nd for a series of U.S. Treasury bonds ranging in maturity from 1 to 30 years. This table makes it clear that longer maturity bonds tend to carry lower YVs of a 32nd than shorter maturity issues. It takes a smaller change in yield to move a long bond's price by 1/32nd of a point than a short bond's price by the same amount. In other words, long bond prices are more sensitive to changes in yield than short bond prices (as demonstrated in many prior illustrations). Exhibit 6–43 diagrams the relationship between term to maturity and YV of a 32nd for the U.S. Treasury bonds of Exhibit 6–42.

The YV of a 32nd bond risk measure provides an easy-to-calculate

Exhibit 6–42. Yield value of a 32nd for a series of 7% coupon U.S. Treasury bonds of various maturities. Each bond is initially priced at par to yield 7.00% to maturity.

Issue	Yield Value of a 32nd (BP)
1-year bond	3.29
2-year bond	1.70
3-year bond	1.17
4-year bond	0.91
5-year bond	0.75
7-year bond	0.57
10-year bond	0.44
20-year bond	0.29
30-year bond	0.25

Comments: *The YV of a 32nd is inversely related to the maturity of a bond. Lower YVs of a 32nd imply more price sensitivity/risk.*

Exhibit 6–43. Yield value of a 32nd as a function of the bond's term to maturity. The issues illustrated are 7% coupon U.S. Treasury bonds initially priced at par to yield 7.00% to maturity (data from Exhibit 6–42).

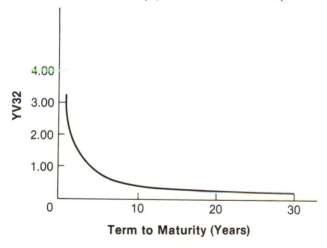

proxy of bond price volatility. Comparisons between individual bonds are useful in assessing relative risk. For example, a 5-year U.S. Treasury bond is approximately 4.4 times as risky as a 1-year issue (3.29BP/0.75BP = 4.4 times, per Exhibit 6–42). The 30-year U.S. Treasury, in turn, is 3 times as risky as the 5-year bond (0.75BP/0.25BP = 3 times). Keep in mind that *low BP values imply more, not less, risk.*

Exhibit 6–44. Summary of the advantages and disadvantages of three contemporary bond risk measures.

Risk Measure	Advantages	Disadvantages
1. Duration	Considers all cash flows Considers the time value of money Accurate assessment of price volatility with small yield changes	Time-consuming calculation Must be modified to be accurate Changes over time Changes as yields shift Assumes a parallel change in yield Fails to consider call risk (should use an option-adjusted duration)
2. Convexity	When combined with duration, provides a reasonably accurate price volatility predictor Forces the user to rigorously assess potential price behavior	Has a different value for different magnitudes of yield change Requires subjective price forecasts for callable bonds An *average* factor creates some prediction error
3. Yield value of a 32nd	Easy to calculate Same advantages as duration	Assumes small and instantaneous yield shifts Resulting number is more difficult to explain than duration (BPs versus *years*)

The YV of a 32nd bond risk measure suffers from the same limitations as modified duration. It assumes small and instantaneous shifts in prices and yields. Additionally, nonparallel shifts in yield are left unaccounted for. With large yield changes, positive convexity creates unexpected results. The YV of a 32nd, like its duration counterpart, changes with the passage of time. Although the YV of a 32nd is much easier to calculate than a bond's duration, it is more difficult to explain to investors.

Observation: *The yield value of a 32nd is a proxy for the marginal price sensitivity of a bond. It is easily derived, but is rendered inaccurate by violation of the rigid assumptions upon which it is based.*

This concludes the discussion of contemporary bond risk measures. Exhibit 6–44 summarizes the advantages and disadvantages of these measures. The next chapter assesses the future prospects for bond risk measurement.

Summary

The contemporary proxies for bond risk include duration, convexity, and the yield value of a 32nd. *Duration* is a WACF that relies on present value weights. It is the future point in time at which, on average, the investor has collected half of his original investment, in present value terms. Duration bears a positive relationship to the term to maturity but bears an inverse relationship to coupon rate, accrued interest, and market yield level. Sinking fund and call features reduce a bond's duration, as expressed in *effective duration* terms. A bond's *modified duration* makes the unadjusted estimate of price volatility (i.e., Macaulay's duration) more accurate. Duration figures are predicated on restrictive assumptions which render them faulty under sizable yield shifts, nonparallel yield changes, and modest passages of time.

Convexity arises from the cup-shaped nature of the price:yield relationship. A noncallable bond's price performance is better than that suggested by the (straight-line) modified duration concept. The unexpected excess return is termed *positive convexity*. A callable bond has a section of its price:yield curve that makes it susceptible to a *negative convexity* effect, which detracts from the duration-suggested price behavior. *Price volatility multipliers* incorporate the duration and convexity impacts into a single figure.

Portfolio duration and *portfolio convexity* are calculated as weighted averages of the individual security durations and convexities. Such composite representations should be treated with care, since durations and convexities change at different rates as yield levels shift and time passes. The *yield value of a 32nd* measures the average BP change in a bond's yield that results from a 1/32nd point (0.03125 in decimal terms) repricing of the bond. In many respects, the YV of a 32nd is similar to a bond's modified duration in terms of its strengths and weaknesses. The YV of a 32nd is easier to calculate, but more difficult to explain, than modified duration.

CHAPTER 7

Bond Risk Measures: The Future

The fast-changing pace of the fixed-income marketplace has brought with it a demand for better measures of bond risk. The evolution of bond risk measures appears to be heading toward a convergence with the types of risk proxies used across a broad range of capital assets. Studies of the risk and return attributes of multiple classes of assets rely on historically based mean returns and standard deviations in return.[1] For shorter term investment horizons, the alpha and beta concepts have been heavily employed, primarily in the equity markets. This chapter discusses the use of standard deviations, relative durations, relative standard deviations, and bond betas in the evaluation of the risk of fixed-income securities and portfolios.

Standard deviation of total return

The duration and convexity concepts outlined in Chapter 6 attempt to assess the instantaneous price risk of a bond or a portfolio of bonds. Returns occur over time, and therefore a measure that quantifies the

[1] See Siegel, Laurence B. and Katie B. Wiegel, *Stocks, Bonds, Bills, and Inflation* (*1987 Yearbook*): *Market Results for 1926–1986* (Chicago, IL: Ibbotson Associates, 1987).

variability in a bond's return over a specified holding period may be a more appropriate proxy for the bond's inherent riskiness. Asset allocation decisions are generally based on a historical review of the total returns registered by the various asset classes under consideration (e.g., T-bills, bonds, stocks, real estate, venture capital, metals, foreign bonds, foreign stocks) and the related risk (i.e., variability) in achieving those returns as quantified by the variance (VAR) and standard deviation (SD) concepts.[2]

> **Observation:** *The standard deviation concept is commonly used as a measure of the risk associated with an asset class return.*

Historical returns and standard deviations in the bond market

The U.S. taxable bond market, as represented by the Shearson Lehman Government/Corporate (SLGC) Bond Index, has generated annual returns averaging 9.87% over the past 14 years (1973–1986). The volatility associated with these returns has been sizable, particularly since 1979. Exhibit 7–1 provides the average annual total returns and standard deviations in return on the SLGC index for the 1973–1986 period and the 1973–1978 and 1979–1986 subperiods.

The 1973–1978 subperiod experienced low returns (5.75% average annual return) with a moderate level of volatility (5.94% standard deviation). Individual annual returns ranged from 0.17% (1974) to 15.59% (1976), as aggregated in Exhibit 7–2. The 1979–1986 period registered

---

[2] The standard deviation gives an indication of the dispersion of return results around the arithmetic mean return. For a normally distributed set of outcomes, approximately 68% of the data points lie within one standard deviation of the mean and approximately 95% of the observations lie within two standard deviations of the mean. Three standard deviations cover virtually all of the observations (99.7%). Throughout this chapter, the *average* returns are calculated as arithmetic mean returns:

$$\text{arithmetic mean } (\mu) = \frac{x_1 + x_2 + \cdots + x_N}{N}$$

The standard deviations are derived by the following formula:

$$\sigma = \sqrt{\frac{\sum_{i=1}^{N} (x_i - \mu)^2}{N}}$$

A sample standard deviation relies on a divisor of $(n - 1)$ rather than N, where n is the sample size. Since populations of data are used in the examples, sample standard deviations are not appropriate.

Exhibit 7–1. Return and risk in the U.S. taxable bond market, as measured by the annual returns and standard deviations of the Shearson Lehman Government/Corporate Index for the period 1973–1986 and the subperiods 1973–1978 and 1979–1986.

Period	Average Annual Total Return (%)	Standard Deviation of Total Return (%)
1973–1986	9.87	8.73
1973–1978	5.75	5.94
1979–1986	12.96	9.21

Comments: *Data courtesy of Shearson Lehman Brothers (supporting data provided in Exhibit 7–2). Average annual returns are arithmetic mean returns and figures are rounded to two decimal places.*

Exhibit 7–2. Annual total returns in the U.S. taxable bond market, as measured by the Shearson Lehman Government/Corporate Index for the period 1973–1986 (data courtesy of Shearson Lehman Brothers).

Year	Annual Total Return (%)
1973	2.28
1974	0.17
1975	12.30
1976	15.59
1977	2.98
1978	1.19
1979	2.30
1980	3.06
1981	7.26
1982	31.09
1983	8.00
1984	15.02
1985	21.30
1986	15.62

appreciably higher total returns (12.96% average annual return) and significantly higher volatility in returns (9.21% standard deviation). Returns ranged from a paltry 2.30% in 1979 to a whopping 31.09% in 1982. The rise and subsequent decline in interest rates caused the disparate returns.

Exhibit 7–3. Return and risk in the U.S. taxable bond market, as measured by the Shearson Lehman Government/Corporate Index (quarterly data, 1973–1986).

Year	*Average Quarterly Total Return (%)*	*Standard Deviation of Total Return (%)*
1973	0.57	1.13
1974	0.10	3.41
1975	2.98	2.69
1976	3.70	1.60
1977	0.75	1.43
1978	0.31	1.52
1979	0.61	2.78
1980	1.26	10.38
1981	1.89	5.09
1982	7.09	4.39
1983	1.95	0.70
1984	3.65	4.33
1985	4.99	2.93
1986	3.74	2.84
Average	2.40	3.23

Comments: *Data courtesy of Shearson Lehman Brothers. An average quarterly return is an arithmetic mean of the 4 quarterly returns experienced during the year, with variability in the quarterly returns represented by the standard deviation measure. Figures are rounded to two decimal places.*

Annual returns and standard deviations tend to smooth out the volatility inherent in fixed-income portfolios. For a long-term asset allocation, this smoothing is appropriate. However, for short-term tactical moves and for performance evaluation purposes, intrayear assessments of return volatility are important. Exhibit 7–3 compiles the quarterly returns and standard deviations for the SLGC index for each year in the 1973–1986 period. Exhibit 7–4 applies the same methodology to monthly returns over the past 14 years.

Both the quarterly and monthly data reveal the sizable surge in bond return volatility in the 1980–1982 period. Return volatility has stabilized over the past 5 years (1982–1986), with both monthly and quarterly return deviations for the most recent year (1986) running close to the average volatility for the 14-year period 1973–1986. Exhibit 7–5 reveals the quieting of extreme volatility by examining the monthly total

Exhibit 7–4. Return and risk in the U.S. taxable bond market, as measured by the Shearson Lehman Government/Corporate Index (monthly data, 1973–1986).

Year	Average Monthly Total Return (%)	Standard Deviation of Total Return (%)
1973	0.20	1.45
1974	0.03	1.86
1975	0.98	1.89
1976	1.22	0.81
1977	0.25	0.87
1978	0.10	0.80
1979	0.21	2.19
1980	0.33	4.15
1981	0.64	3.35
1982	2.30	1.91
1983	0.65	1.48
1984	1.19	1.91
1985	1.64	1.66
1986	1.23	1.77
Average	**0.78**	**1.86**

Comments: *Data courtesy of Shearson Lehman Brothers. An average monthly return is an arithmetic mean of the 12 monthly returns experienced during the year, with variability in the monthly returns represented by the standard deviation measure. Figures are rounded to two decimal places.*

returns on the SLGC bond index in the volatile 1981 year and the year just completed (1986).

Observation: *Volatility in bond market returns surged during the late 1970s and early 1980s. Return volatility has stabilized at a normal level in the mid-1980s.*

Return volatility over the long run

Bond portfolio risk can be assessed from both a long-run point of view (standard deviation of annual returns) and a short-run perspective (standard deviation of monthly or quarterly returns). For example, Exhibit 7–6 lists the annual returns for two hypothetical portfolios, A and B, over the 10-year period ending December 31, 1986. A quick glance at the raw numbers in Exhibit 7–6 suggests that Portfolio A has experienced

Exhibit 7–5. Monthly total returns for the Shearson Lehman Government/Corporate Index for the years 1981 and 1986 (data courtesy of Shearson Lehman Brothers).

	Return (%)	
Month	1981	1986
January	−0.03	0.59
February	−1.63	4.19
March	2.39	3.54
April	−3.22	0.45
May	3.19	−1.98
June	0.15	2.90
July	−1.78	0.65
August	−1.68	2.64
September	0.02	−1.25
October	5.45	1.45
November	8.04	1.22
December	−3.19	0.36

Exhibit 7–6. Annual total returns for two hypothetical bond portfolios (1977–1986 period).

	Return (%)	
Year	Portfolio A	Portfolio B
1977	4.00	2.50
1978	5.50	0.50
1979	7.50	1.00
1980	1.50	−2.30
1981	7.30	5.20
1982	22.00	38.50
1983	7.50	3.35
1984	12.30	18.70
1985	14.50	24.30
1986	11.25	21.50

less volatility in returns than Portfolio B. Exhibit 7–7 confirms this notion by calculating the standard deviations in each portfolio's total return figures. Portfolio B exhibits over twice the return volatility shown by Portfolio A, for both the 5-year (11.26% versus 4.81%, or 2.34 times) and 10-year investment periods (12.86% versus 5.61%, or 2.29

Exhibit 7–7. Return and risk on two hypothetical bond portfolios, as measured by the annual returns and related standard deviations (5- and 10-year periods ending December 31, 1986).

Period	Average Annual TR (%)		Standard Deviation (%)	
	A	B	A	B
1982–1986 (5 years)	13.51	21.27	4.81	11.26
1977–1986 (10 years)	9.34	11.33	5.61	12.86

Comments: *Supporting data in Exhibit 7–6. Figures are rounded to two decimal places.*

times). According to the standard deviation measure, Portfolio B is approximately 2.3 times as risky as Portfolio A.

Return volatility over the short run

To gain a better feel for the short-term volatility of each fund, one can analyze the monthly return history for the past 3 years (see Exhibit 7–8). Exhibit 7–9 computes the average monthly returns and standard deviations for the years 1984, 1985, and 1986. Several results emerge from the confluence of data. First, Portfolio B is riskier than Portfolio A. B's standard deviation in return consistently exceeds A's. Second, the relative risk of B versus A varies in different years. For example, in 1985, Portfolio B had over 4 times the risk of Portfolio A (4.50% SD versus 1.07% SD). In 1984 and 1986, however, the risk multiple was a lower, but still significant, 2½ to 2¾ times.

Third, the absolute risk of a given portfolio changes from year to year. Portfolio A had a sizable decline in volatility during 1985 (versus 1984) and a doubling of risk in 1986 (versus 1985). Portfolio B has recorded increasing amounts of volatility over the 1984–1986 period, with a standard deviation in monthly total return at 5.94% in 1986, versus 4.50% in 1985 and 4.04% in 1984 (see Exhibit 7–9). In sum, Portfolio B is quite a bit riskier than Portfolio A, but both the absolute and relative risk magnitudes vary from year to year.

Comparison of portfolio standard deviations to a similar quantification of the risk of a bond market benchmark (such as the SLGC index) is helpful. The standard deviations in monthly returns for the SLGC index during 1984, 1985, and 1986 are 1.91%, 1.66%, and 1.77%, respectively (see Exhibit 7–4). Portfolio A had a risk similar to that of

Exhibit 7–8. Monthly total returns for two hypothetical bond portfolios (1984–1986 period).

| | Return (%) | |
Month	Portfolio A	Portfolio B
1/84	0.80	0.75
2/84	−0.60	− 1.50
3/84	−0.75	− 3.40
4/84	−0.40	− 2.70
5/84	−1.30	− 5.65
6/84	0.60	3.20
7/84	2.70	8.25
8/84	1.80	4.60
9/84	0.90	3.05
10/84	4.30	7.15
11/84	1.30	2.50
12/84	2.45	1.98
1/85	1.10	3.75
2/85	0.65	− 7.45
3/85	2.10	6.30
4/85	1.25	4.75
5/85	2.35	7.40
6/85	1.10	3.70
7/85	0.60	− 4.60
8/85	1.20	6.20
9/85	0.85	− 3.60
10/85	0.05	2.00
11/85	1.10	2.50
12/85	1.01	2.23
1/86	0.40	0.85
2/86	0.80	6.65
3/86	4.85	12.60
4/86	0.20	− 4.65
5/86	−4.45	− 9.40
6/86	2.60	7.45
7/86	2.05	2.40
8/86	3.50	2.50
9/86	−0.50	− 5.85
10/86	0.60	6.30
11/86	1.10	2.88
12/86	−0.15	0.01

Exhibit 7–9. Return and risk on two hypothetical bond portfolios, as measured by the monthly returns and related standard deviations over the 1984–1986 period, by year.

Year	Average Monthly TR (%)		Standard Deviation (%)	
	A	B	A	B
1984	0.98	1.52	1.57	4.04
1985	1.11	1.93	1.07	4.50
1986	0.92	1.81	2.22	5.94

Comments: *Supporting data in Exhibit 7–8. Figures are rounded to two decimal places.*

the market benchmark during 1984–1986, with standard deviations of 1.57%, 1.07%, and 2.22%, respectively (see Exhibit 7–9). Based on the 1986 results, Portfolio A has evolved from a lower-than-market risk portfolio to one that is more risky than the market portfolio as represented by the SLGC index (in 1986, 2.22% SD versus 1.77% SD). Portfolio B has had significantly more risk than the market portfolio, exhibiting 2 to 3½ times more volatility in monthly returns over the 1984–1986 period.[3]

One must be concerned with the future volatility to which one will be exposed by owning an individual bond or set of bonds. History, particularly very recent experience, may serve as a reasonable guide to future behavior. If the general level of volatility in the bond market changes dramatically, as it did in the post-1978 period, or the management style of the specific fund is altered, historical standard deviations lose some degree of potency. The standard deviation of total return concept is a risk measure that allows for comparability across many asset classes and is likely to gain advocates in bond market circles.

Observation: *The standard deviation of total return is typically used to assess the risk of a given investment. Its application to bond portfolios is relatively simple. A short-term or long-term approach can be taken with regard to periodic fluctuations in returns. The current focus on instantaneous price risk (as assessed by a duration measure) seems rather shortsighted. The standard deviation concept allows for a more*

---

[3] The reader may have noticed that the returns on Portfolio B have generally exceeded those of the market benchmark and Portfolio A. The mathematics of bond return is outlined in Chapter 8 and the concept of risk-adjusted return is discussed in Chapter 11.

realistic assessment of bond portfolio risk in the context of an appropriate time frame for a specific investor. Comparability to the return deviations of alternative asset classes is an added feature.

Relative measures of bond risk

A relative measure of risk attempts to assess the risk of a bond portfolio in relation to a chosen benchmark. The degree to which the individual portfolio's risk differs from that of the benchmark can be estimated by a ratio of the nominal risk measures of the two funds. Relative measures of bond risk can be derived for the duration concept of Chapter 6 and for the standard deviation concept introduced in this chapter. The resulting constructs are termed *relative duration* and *relative standard deviation*, respectively. Finally, relative risk can be ascertained through the use of a regression-based *bond beta*.

Relative duration

A *relative duration* is simply the ratio of a portfolio's duration to the duration of a chosen bond market benchmark. The SLGC index currently has a duration of 5.29 years.[4] Bond portfolio X is a collection of long maturity U.S. Treasury bonds. Portfolio X carries a 9.00-year duration and, therefore, has a relative duration of 1.70:

$$\text{relative duration (RDUR)} = \frac{\text{portfolio duration}}{\text{benchmark duration}}$$

$$= \frac{9.00}{5.29}$$

$$= 1.70$$

The portfolio RDUR of 1.70 implies that Portfolio X is 1.7 times as volatile as the market index. In other words, if the bond market experiences a 10.00% appreciation, Portfolio X should rise in value by 17.00%

---

[4] Data is as of December 31, 1986, and is courtesy of Shearson Lehman Brothers. The 5.29-year figure is a Macaulay's duration to maturity. The comparable *effective* or *option-adjusted* duration on the SLGC index is approximately 4.75 years. A more accurate relative duration reflects the ratio of effective durations.

(10.00% × 1.70 RDUR = +17.00%). Conversely, a market decline on the order of 5.00% should translate into an 8.50% loss for Portfolio X (−5.00% × 1.70 RDUR = −8.50%).

A relative duration is subject to several caveats. First, duration numbers are only an indication of instantaneous price volatility.[5] As time passage is introduced, the duration ratio fails to account accurately for the volatility in bond returns. As a result, the standard deviation of total return becomes a more applicable risk measure. Second, duration figures lose their potency as yields and/or yield curves change and convexity impacts become appreciable. Call and sinking fund features render many of the traditional duration measures inaccurate as reflections of inherent price volatility. A relative comparison of effective or option-adjusted durations is often more appropriate.

Despite the inherent limitations, a relative duration is an initial indicator of the short-term price risk of a portfolio relative to an established benchmark. Cross-comparisons can also be made between individual portfolios. For example, Portfolio Y, with a RDUR of 0.75, has considerably less risk than the aforementioned Portfolio X, and has slightly less risk than the market portfolio.

It is not imperative that the benchmark index be a capitalization-weighted index such as the SLGC index. The benchmark of choice should reflect the client's investment objectives. For a client desiring incremental total return while controlling market risk, the SLGC index may be appropriate given its middle-of-the-market duration. Deviations from the market portfolio duration introduce incremental risk, justified only by enhanced returns.

A pension fund client may wish to minimize the periodic volatility in pension expense and bottom-line net income by targeting the pension fund liability duration as the benchmark portfolio duration.[6] Pension fund obligations tend to have long durations (10 to 15 years). A bond portfolio with a duration of 4 to 5 years creates a sizable duration (and relative volatility) mismatch between pension assets and pension liabilities. For example, a portfolio with a 5.0-year duration sports only a 0.40 relative duration compared to a benchmark liability stream with a duration of 12.50 years:

---

[5] Technically, modified durations should be used in the ratio calculation. However, the use of nonmodified durations generally has an insignificant impact on the result.

[6] In many cases, the recently enacted FASB Statements No. 87 and 88 lead to increased volatility in annual pension expense and bottom-line net income if the typical bond market index is used in structuring a company's pension fund assets.

$$\text{relative duration} = \frac{\text{portfolio duration}}{\text{benchmark duration}}$$

$$= \frac{5.00}{12.50}$$

$$= 0.40$$

The typical bond index fund is an extremely defensive instrument when viewed in this light.[7] An offensive or defensive bet implicitly made by a pension plan may be exposed by the calculation of a relative duration.

> **Observation:** *A relative duration is a quick and dirty method of assessing the relative risk of a bond portfolio. This measure is an indicator of the short-term price volatility of a portfolio vis-à-vis a designated benchmark. A relative duration is subject to the inherent limitations of the duration concept as a comprehensive bond risk proxy.*

Relative standard deviation of total return

The relative standard deviation concept. Insofar as a standard deviation of total return is a cleaner proxy for bond risk than a duration, a ratio of standard deviations serves as a better measure of relative risk. A *relative standard deviation* is derived as follows:

$$\frac{\text{relative standard}}{\text{deviation (RSD)}} = \frac{\text{standard deviation of portfolio return}}{\text{standard deviation of benchmark return}}$$

The benchmark, by definition, has an RSD of 1.0. The benchmark can be a bond index, such as the SLGC index, or any desired target benchmark such as a portfolio of future liabilities. In general, the historical standard deviation should be based on holding-period returns of a comparable length to the anticipated future holding period.

For example, a long-term pension fund should rely on a standard deviation based on annual return volatility over a long-term period (e.g., 10 to 20 years). A short-term performance-oriented account, on the other hand, might find a 1-year holding period appropriate and therefore rely on standard deviations in monthly returns for a series of recent 1-year

---

[7] Bond indexing is discussed at greater length in Chapter 15.

periods. The user should choose the historical standard deviation comparison that best reflects the return volatility expected in the future. One may decide to rely upon an average of several historical standard deviations or one may simply use the past as a guide to be modified by current expectations.

> **Observation:** *A relative standard deviation (RSD) is a method of assessing the volatility of a portfolio's returns relative to a chosen benchmark portfolio. The selection of an appropriate benchmark and the use of a representative historical time frame are critical to the effective application of RSDs.*

Applications of the relative standard deviation. The two hypothetical bond portfolios of earlier illustration can be analyzed in a relative standard deviation framework. Using the SLGC index as the benchmark portfolio, Exhibit 7–10 generates RSDs for Portfolio A based on a series of historical standard deviations. Exhibit 7–11 provides a similar analysis on the riskier Portfolio B. The results lead to several conclusions. First, RSDs tend to exhibit more stability over long time horizons.[8] Additionally, the magnitude of the long-term RSDs is less dramatic than RSDs derived over shorter measurement periods. For example, Portfolio B carries RSDs of 1.46 and 1.38, respectively, for the past 5 and 10 years of annual return data. Over long-run horizons, therefore, Portfolio B generates 38 to 46% more total return volatility than the SLGC index. Over short horizons (e.g., annual periods), Portfolio B is considerably more volatile, with RSDs in the range 2.12 to 3.36 over the past 3 years (1984–1986).

Second, Portfolio A is a defensive investment, with RSDs of 0.62 and 0.60 over the 5- and 10-year periods ending December 31, 1986. These figures suggest that Portfolio A creates only 60 to 62% of the return volatility displayed by the benchmark index. Short-run measurement periods find Portfolio A defensively structured as well, with RSDs less than 1.0. The year 1986 is an exception, with an RSD of 1.25 registered. The manager of Portfolio A should be monitored closely, as

---

[8] The reduced impact of price returns over long horizons and the dominance of coupon and reinvestment returns lead to such results (refer to Chapter 8). Of course, a major change in management style can shift the long-term RSD measure sizably, with even more dramatic impacts on short-term RSDs.

Exhibit 7–10. Relative standard deviations for hypothetical bond Portfolio A for various historical periods (1 year, 5 years, 10 years).

	Standard Deviation of TR (%)		
Period	*(1)* *Portfolio A*	*(2)* *SLGC Index*	*(3) = (1)/(2)* *RSD*
Annual return volatility during:			
(a) 1977–1986 (10 years)	5.61	9.32	0.60
(b) 1982–1986 (5 years)	4.81	7.70	0.62
Monthly return volatility during:			
(a) 1984	1.57	1.91	0.82
(b) 1985	1.07	1.66	0.64
(c) 1986	2.22	1.77	1.25

Comments: *Supporting data in Exhibits 7–1, 7–2, 7–4, 7–7, and 7–9. Figures are rounded to two decimal places.*

Exhibit 7–11. Relative standard deviations for hypothetical bond Portfolio B for various historical periods (1 year, 5 years, 10 years).

	Standard Deviation of TR (%)		
Period	*(1)* *Portfolio B*	*(2)* *SLGC Index*	*(3) = (1)/(2)* *RSD*
Annual return volatility during:			
(a) 1977–1986 (10 years)	12.86	9.32	1.38
(b) 1982–1986 (5 years)	11.26	7.70	1.46
Monthly return volatility during:			
(a) 1984	4.04	1.91	2.12
(b) 1985	4.50	1.66	2.71
(c) 1986	5.94	1.77	3.36

Comments: *Supporting data in Exhibits 7–1, 7–2, 7–4, 7–7, and 7–9. Figures are rounded to two decimal places.*

the 1986 RSD may foretell a shift toward a more aggressive investment stance.

> **Observation:** *A relative standard deviation is a measure of the relative risk of a bond portfolio in comparison to a chosen benchmark. Insofar as the standard deviation of total return is superior to portfolio duration in assessing bond portfolio risk, the relative standard deviation is a better measure of relative risk than a relative duration.*

Bond beta

The beta concept. The concept of beta spills over from the equity market usage of historical betas. The stock market portfolio, as represented by the Standard & Poor's 500, has a beta of 1.0 by definition. A stock, or portfolio of stocks, with a beta of less than 1.0 is deemed a less risky, defensive equity investment. A beta greater than 1.0 signifies more than market risk and a more aggressive, volatile investment.

A *beta* is derived by assessing the historical relationship between the total return of a security or portfolio and the total return of the market portfolio, as discerned by regression line analysis. A stock beta of 2.0, for example, suggests that an investment will rise/(fall) twice as much as the S&P 500 index. If the S&P 500 appreciates by 10%, the value of the investment is expected to increase by 20% (10% × 2.0 β = +20%). A 7% decline in the S&P 500 should correspond with a 14% drop in the worth of the investment (−7% × 2.0 β = −14%).

Similarly, a *regression-based bond beta* can be derived by analyzing the historical relationship between the returns of a bond or portfolio of bonds vis-à-vis the returns of a bond market portfolio such as the Shearson Lehman Government/Corporate Bond Index. The market index, by definition, carries a beta of 1.0.

The basics of regression line analysis. The betas commonly cited in equity research are based on historical regression analysis. A stock's return is regressed against the return of the market portfolio (e.g., the S&P 500 index). Graphically, the regression line is the linear relationship that best describes the observed pairings of a stock's return and the market portfolio's return over a specified historical period. This line is called the *least-squares regression line* since it is the line that minimizes the sum of the squared deviations between the observed points and the

Exhibit 7–12. Least-squares regression line.

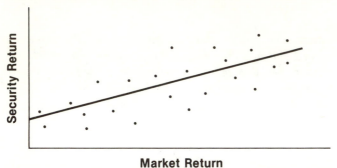

plotted line.[9] Exhibit 7–12 illustrates a regression line for a given set of data points.

The term *beta* arises from the expression of a linear relationship in formula terms:

$$R_i = \alpha + \beta\,(R_m) + e$$

where

R_i = return on security (or portfolio) i

R_m = return on the market portfolio

α = alpha (i.e., the Y-intercept)

β = beta (i.e., the slope of the regression line)

e = random error term (this term should, on average, equal zero)

Beta is simply the slope of the regression line. For a security (or a portfolio of securities) bearing a one-to-one relationship with the market returns (e.g., a stock index fund), the beta is 1.0. A security with a beta of 2.0 exhibits a steeper regression line, with excess returns in a positive environment and more severely negative returns in an unfavorable environment. A security with a flatter regression line carries a beta of less than 1.0 and portrays less volatility in returns than the market portfolio. A perfectly flat regression line implies no relationship between security returns and market returns ($\beta = 0.0$). A negatively sloped regression line suggests an inverse relationship between the returns of the individual security and the returns of the market ($\beta < 0.0$). Such *negative beta* instruments move in the opposite direction as market returns and serve

[9] See Brown, Steven J. and Mark P. Kritzman, *Quantitative Methods for Financial Analysis* (Homewood, IL: Dow Jones-Irwin, 1987).

Exhibit 7–13. Regression lines of securities with betas of −1.0, 0.0, 0.5, 1.0, and 2.0. The alpha intercept is assumed to be zero.

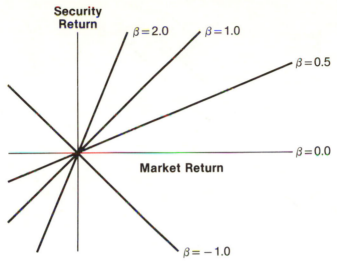

as major reducers of portfolio risk. Exhibit 7–13 plots the various types of regression lines cited: positive, flat, and negative.

The alpha term (α) is the security's return given a zero return by the market portfolio. In an efficient market, the alpha is expected to equal zero. In an inefficiently priced market, a skilled portfolio manager can generate *positive alphas* by adept security and sector selection. An inferior manager garners *negative alphas* by poor selection of individual securities and sectors. Exhibit 7–14 illustrates the alpha concept in a graphical form. A positive alpha shifts the regression line upward and a negative alpha pushes the regression line downward, each in a parallel fashion.

Regression analysis applied to fixed-income securities. The concept of regression line analysis applies to fixed-income securities (or portfolios) as well as to equity instruments:

$$R_i = \alpha + \beta(R_m) + e$$

where R_i and R_m are the returns on the fixed-income security (or portfolio) and the bond market portfolio, respectively. Graphically, the (x,y) coordinates reflect the best approximation of the actual return pairings based on a series of historical observations.

Exhibit 7–14. Regression lines of securities with positive, zero, and negative alphas. The beta of each security is assumed to equal 1.0.

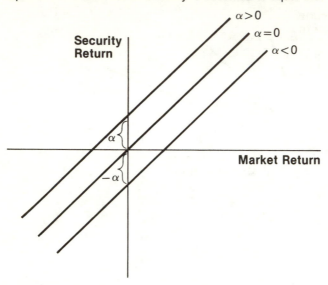

Exhibit 7–15. Annual total returns (%) for two hypothetical bond portfolios and for the Shearson Lehman Government/Corporate Bond Index over the 5-year period 1982–1986 (data per Exhibits 7–2 and 7–6).

	Return (%)		
Year	*Portfolio A*	*Portfolio B*	*SLGC Index*
1982	22.00	38.50	31.09
1983	7.50	3.35	8.00
1984	12.30	18.70	15.02
1985	14.50	24.30	21.30
1986	11.25	21.50	15.62

For example, Exhibit 7–15 contains the annual returns of the two sample portfolios of earlier illustration (Portfolios A and B) over the 5-year period 1982–1986 as compared to the market portfolio as represented by the Shearson Lehman Government/Corporate Bond Index. The least-squares regression lines solve to:

$$R_A = \alpha_A + \beta_A(R_{SLGC}) + e$$
$$= 2.25 + 0.62 R_{SLGC}$$
$$\alpha_A = 2.25$$
$$\beta_A = 0.62$$

$$R_B = \alpha_B + \beta_B(R_{\text{SLGC}}) + e$$
$$= -4.63 + 1.42R_{\text{SLGC}}$$
$$\alpha_B = -4.63$$
$$\beta_B = 1.42$$

In each instance, e is assumed to equal zero.

Portfolio A bears a 0.62 beta for the 5-year period under analysis. This portfolio offers lower-than-market risk and serves as a modestly defensive investment. If the market portfolio rises by 10.00%, Portfolio A increases by approximately 6.20% (10.00% $\times$ 0.62 β = 6.20%). Conversely, a downmarket leads to cushioned losses. For example, a 5.00% market decline corresponds with a 3.10% loss in the value of Portfolio A (-5.00% $\times$ 0.62 β = -3.10%).

Portfolio B, on the other hand, exhibits above-average volatility with a beta of 1.42. This portfolio rises 42% more than the market in a bull period and falls 42% more than the market in a bear period. For example, if the SLGC index posts a 20.00% return, Portfolio B registers approximately a 28.40% return (20.00% $\times$ 1.42 β = 28.40%). Conversely, a 10.00% market decline leads to approximately a 14.20% loss for Portfolio B (-10.00% $\times$ 1.42 β = -14.20%). Exhibit 7–16 plots the regression lines for Portfolios A and B.

The use of regression analysis is fraught with difficulties in application. These complicating factors are summarized below:

1. *Lack of an adequate number of historical observations.* A minimum of 5 years of data is necessary, with 10 to 15 years of data more preferable. An individual portfolio may lack a long history over which to gain a valid assessment of the portfolio's volatility versus the market benchmark. A projection of anticipated future return behavior may be the only viable alternative.

2. *Regression betas are unstable.* A regression beta is a function of the historical period under review. The historical period may not be reflective of the security's current behavior in the marketplace. Over time, for example, a bond beta is likely to decline relative to a dynamic market index as the bond's maturity and inherent price sensitivity diminish. A portfolio manager may have instituted a new style in the most recent period, warranting skepticism about the use of old-

Exhibit 7–16. The least-squares regression lines for Portfolio A and Portfolio B. The portfolios are regressed versus the Shearson Lehman Government/Corporate Bond Index (SLGC) (data per Exhibit 7–15).

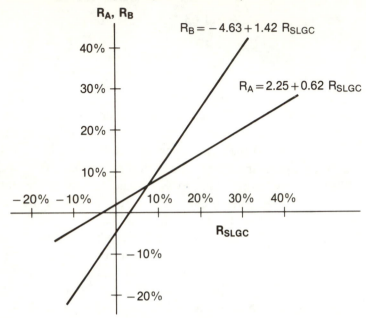

style results. Finally, a bull market period such as 1982–1986 may not adequately assess a bond's corresponding behavior in a bear market. A full market cycle analysis is probably more appropriate.

3. *A regression beta is a function of the periodicity of return comparisons.* Annual, quarterly, and monthly data may render sizably different beta terms. The relative risk assessment is therefore a function of the anticipated future holding period and the length of the performance measurement intervals.

4. *Projecting return results outside the confines of the historical observations is dangerous.* For example, a portfolio bearing a beta of 1.20 is expected to exhibit 1.2 times the return levels emanating from the market portfolio. If the market portfolio returns have ranged from −10 to +15% over the period studied, an assertion that the sample portfolio will experience a 36% return, given a 30% market return, is questionable.

5. *The alpha intercept may or may not appropriately reflect the risk-free rate of interest* (e.g., a T-bill return over the period).

6. *The least-squares regression line may not adequately describe the relationship between the return variables.* A curvilinear relationship may provide a better fit for the observed data. A multiple regression may offer a better solution.[10]

7. *The market portfolio must be an appropriate comparative base for the individual security (or portfolio) under consideration.* The client's needs, circumstances, objectives, and constraints must be taken into account. Accuracy in the pricing and return calculations of both the individual portfolio and the market portfolio is equally critical.

Despite the inherent limitations of regression analysis, the use of bond betas is likely to become more widespread as a focus on both the risk and return elements of a bond manager's style receive increased attention. In the past and present, too much reliance has been placed solely on the latter element, total return performance. Chapter 11 delves into the process of incorporating risk into the evaluation of manager returns.

> **Observation:** *A bond beta is predicated on a series of historical pairings of portfolio return and market return. The beta represents the slope of the least-squares regression line. This beta expresses the relative risk of a portfolio relative to the chosen market index as observed over the historical period analyzed.*

Summary

The contemporary measures of bond risk (duration, convexity, and the yield value of a 32nd) focus on the short-term price volatility of a bond portfolio. A *relative duration*, allows one to make a rough assessment of the short-term price sensitivity of a portfolio in comparison to a selected benchmark.

From an intermediate- to longer-term point of view (e.g., 1-year periods and longer), investment risk is traditionally ascertained by the use of a *standard deviation in total return*. The asset allocation decisions in multi-asset portfolios often rely on historical returns and standard

---

[10] Dr. Boyce Greer of the Ryan Financial Strategy Group has derived historical bond betas through the use of multiple regression analysis. The Ryan Treasury Index serves as the market benchmark for Dr. Greer's work [see "Beta: A Tool for Portfolio Risk Management" (New York, NY: Ryan Financial Strategy Group, 21 May 1987)].

deviations. The widely cited studies by Ibbotson and Sinquefield illustrate this methodology.

Given that many bond investors are longer term in their orientation (e.g., pension funds), the *standard deviation* is a more appropriate device by which to judge the risk of a bond portfolio. The preponderance of coupon and reinvestment cash flows over time renders the short-term, price-driven volatility measures (such as duration) inaccurate proxies for portfolio risk. This chapter argues that the standard deviation of return should gain wider acceptance by pension plan consultants and clients in the near future. The calculations behind the standard deviation were outlined and illustrated through a series of examples. A *relative standard deviation* provides a feel for the volatility of a portfolio's return as compared to that of a designated benchmark.

Finally, a *bond beta* is perhaps the most rigorous approach to assessing relative risk. The use of regression analysis to derive bond betas emanates from equity market usage. Subject to the inherent assumptions and limitations of historical regression analysis, the calculated bond beta can be used as a comprehensive measure of the risk of a bond (or a portfolio of bonds) relative to a selected benchmark of fixed-income securities. Comparison between individual portfolios is then made possible.

THE FUNDAMENTALS OF BOND RETURN

CHAPTER 8

Total Return and Realized Compound Yield

Influences on the RCY

Summary

Appendix A
Choosing an Appropriate Reinvestment Rate

Appendix B
A Case Study of Total Return Attribution

This chapter begins the discussion of the Fundamentals of Bond Return. The concepts of total return and realized compound yield are investigated through both exposition and illustration. Total return is dissected into three component parts: price return, coupon return, and reinvestment return. These component returns are influenced by factors including the holding-period length, the coupon rate of interest, the market rate of interest, and the assumed reinvestment rate. The relative importance of each component is articulated in this chapter.

Chapter 9 compares and contrasts the concepts of bond yield (Chapter 3) and bond return (this chapter). The interchangeability of yield and return, although naively accepted by many investors, is seriously questioned. Chapter 10 analyzes the concepts of bond gains and losses in the context of market-based, total return performance. The misleading nature of accounting-oriented measures is emphasized. Chapter 11 concludes this section by outlining the concept of risk-adjusted return. Risk-adjusted return scales the total return according to the risk undertaken to achieve the bottom-line performance. Through this type of analysis, a more comprehensive assessment of a portfolio manager's abilities can be made.

The concept of holding-period return

The most visible reflection of a portfolio manager's talent lies in the total return performance numbers reported to clients and other interested publics on a quarterly basis. Often this performance is compared to that of a benchmark such as a bond market index. While the portfolio manager must deal with a series of client-specific needs, performance evaluation services tend to focus on the periodic return figures as the basis for discerning management style and as a reasonably objective screening device for determining above-average and below-average results.

Performance is measured as the *holding-period return* (HPR) on the security or portfolio of interest:

$$\text{holding-period return} = \frac{\text{ending market value} + \text{income receipts}}{\text{beginning market value}} - 1$$

For example, if an investor purchases a bond at a price of $800.00 and sells the bond in one year for $975.00 after receiving $61.00 in interest payments during the year (including interest-on-interest), the investor records a holding-period return of 29.50%:

$$\text{holding-period return} = \frac{\$975.00 + \$61.00}{\$800.00} - 1$$

$$= \frac{\$1,036.00}{\$800.00} - 1$$

$$= 1.2950 - 1$$

$$= 0.2950$$

$$= 29.50\%$$

For fixed-income securities, the holding-period return is a measure of the investment's *total return* over a given time span. As such, the HPR is subject to several specifications:

1. A holding-period return is a *time-weighted rate of return.*[1]

2. Beginning and ending market values reflect the bond's *full price* (i.e., the price including accrued interest).

---

[1] A time-weighted rather than dollar-weighted rate of return is commonly accepted in practice. Changes in the investment base through additional contributions or early withdrawals create a divergence between the time-weighted and dollar-weighted approaches. This issue is discussed at greater length in Chapter 15.

3. *Income receipts* include coupon interest payments and any interest-on-interest earned. For sinking fund bonds and mortgage-backed securities, partial returns of principal must also be included.

One might call the holding-period return a *dollars-in, dollars-out* approach to assessing performance.

> **Observation:** *A bond's holding-period return is the total return generated by the bond over a specified period. The HPR represents the increase/(decrease) in the investor's wealth position for the period covered. Both income receipts and market value fluctuations influence the HPR, albeit to varying degrees.*

Holding-period returns on a 30-year U.S. Treasury bond

Stable rate scenario. Using a 30-year U.S. Treasury bond as an illustration, one can calculate holding-period returns for stable, rising, and falling interest rate environments. The bond bears a 7% coupon and is initially priced at par to yield 7.00%. Over a 1-year investment horizon, if yields remain at 7.00%, the bond generates a 7.12% total return:

$$\text{HPR (stable rates)} = \frac{\$1,000.00 + (\$35.00 + \$35.00 + \$1.23)^*}{\$1,000.00} - 1$$

$$= \frac{\$1,000.00 + \$71.23}{\$1,000.00} - 1$$

$$= \frac{\$1,071.23}{\$1,000.00} - 1$$

$$= 1.0712 - 1$$

$$= 0.0712$$

$$= 7.12\%^\dagger$$

---

[*] Income receipts determined as follows:
   a. Two semiannual coupons of $35.00 each ($1,000.00 par × 7% coupon rate × ½ year = $35.00).
   b. Interest-on-interest of $1.23 (a $35.00 coupon reinvested at a 7% annual rate for 6 months; $35.00 × 0.07 × ½ year = $1.23).

[†] Rounded to the nearest two decimal places.

Rising rate scenario. Assuming a 100 basis point rise in yields to 8.00%, the 30-year issue suffers a 4.08% loss over a 1-year investment period:

$$\text{HPR (rising rates)} = \frac{\$887.85^* + (\$35.00 + \$35.00 + \$1.31)^\dagger}{\$1,000.00} - 1$$

$$= \frac{\$887.85 + \$71.31}{\$1,000.00} - 1$$

$$= \frac{\$959.16}{\$1,000.00} - 1$$

$$= 0.9592 - 1$$

$$= -0.0408$$

$$= -4.08\%^\ddagger$$

* Bond's market value 1 year hence at an 8.00% YTM.
† Income receipts determined as follows:
    a. Two semiannual coupons of $35.00 each ($1,000.00 par × 7% coupon rate × ½ year = $35.00).
    b. Interest-on-interest of $1.31 (a $35.00 coupon reinvested at a 7.50% annual rate for 6 months; $35.00 × 0.075 × ½ year = $1.31).
‡ Rounded to the nearest two decimal places.

Falling rate scenario. A fall in interest rates from 7.00% to 6.00% creates a 20.78% return for the 30-year issue over the 1-year holding period:

$$\text{HPR (falling rates)} = \frac{\$1,136.66^{**} + (\$35.00 + \$35.00 + \$1.14)^{\dagger\dagger}}{\$1,000.00} - 1$$

$$= \frac{\$1,136.66 + \$71.14}{\$1,000.00} - 1$$

$$= \frac{\$1,207.80}{\$1,000.00} - 1$$

$$= 1.2078 - 1$$

$$= 0.2078$$

$$= 20.78\%^{\ddagger\ddagger}$$

** Bond's market value 1 year hence at a 6.00% YTM.
†† Income receipts determined as follows:
    a. Two semiannual coupons of $35.00 each ($1,000.00 par × 7% coupon rate × ½ year = $35.00).
    b. Interest-on-interest of $1.14 (a $35.00 coupon reinvested at a 6.50% annual rate for 6 months; $35.00 × 0.065 × ½ year = $1.14).
‡‡ Rounded to the nearest two decimal places.

In all three cases (stable rates, rising rates, and falling rates), the ending market value reflects the price of the bond 1 year hence as determined by the market yield level then prevailing. The change in market yield is assumed to occur at a uniform rate across the 1-year horizon. The reinvestment rate is therefore an average of the beginning and ending yield levels and rises/(falls) in a bear/(bull) market.

The components of total return

The total return (i.e., holding-period return) of a bond is attributable to three sources: price return, coupon return, and reinvestment return. Each return component is discussed in turn.

Price return

Price return is the price change or capital appreciation/(depreciation) occurring over the holding period. That is,

$$
\begin{array}{ccc}
\text{price return} & \text{ending bond} & \text{beginning bond} \\
\text{(dollars)} \quad = & \text{price (excluding} \quad - & \text{price (excluding} \\
& \text{accrued interest)} & \text{accrued interest)}
\end{array}
$$

The price return is traceable to two factors:

1. The *scientific amortization* of the bond's premium or discount. A bond's price changes over time despite a stable interest rate environment as the bond's value marches inexorably toward par value (i.e., $1,000.00) at the final maturity date.[2] This price component is a positive/(negative) figure for a discount/(premium) bond. A bond selling at par experiences no scientific amortization.

2. The price change resulting from changes in market yields. If yields decline, this price return component is positive. Rising yields drive this price return component into negative territory.

---

[2] For a callable bond trading in expectation of an early retirement, the bond's price gravitates toward the call price rather than toward the par value.

Coupon return

Coupon return is the dollars received in semiannual coupon payments over the specified holding period plus any incremental accrued interest earned but not yet paid. That is,

$$
\begin{array}{rcl}
\text{coupon return} & & \text{coupon payments} \qquad \text{net increase/} \\
\text{(dollars)} & = & \text{received during } + \text{ (decrease) in} \\
& & \text{the period} \qquad\quad \text{accrued interest}
\end{array}
$$

Note that coupon return includes accrued interest attached to the bond at the end of the holding period less accrued interest purchased at the beginning of the period. For simplicity, unless otherwise indicated, examples in this book purchase and sell bonds at issuance or on an interest payment date. The bonds have no accrued interest attached on those specific days; therefore, the coupon return equals the actual coupon payments made during the holding period.

Reinvestment return

Reinvestment return is the interest earned on the reinvestment of coupon payments.[3] That is,

$$
\begin{array}{rcl}
\text{reinvestment return} & & \text{interest earned on the} \\
\text{(dollars)} & = & \text{reinvestment of coupon} \\
& & \text{cash flows}
\end{array}
$$

For sinking fund bonds and mortgage-backed securities, reinvestment returns are earned on both coupon payments and partial principal repayments.

Total return

In sum, *total return* can be expressed either in dollars or percentages, with three components[4]:

---

[3] If reinvestments are made into a T-bill or other instrument with a stable principal value, the reinvestment return is the interest earned on that separate investment. However, if coupons are reinvested in bonds which, due to market volatility, experience fluctuations in value, the reinvestment return is the total return garnered from the bond holding, of which coupon payments are only a part. Consequently, an active manager can experience wide ranges of reinvestment rates. Appendix A elaborates on this subject.

[4] Appendix B provides an in-depth analysis of the components of total return on a sample U.S. Treasury bond for the 3-year period from June 30, 1984 to June 30, 1987.

total		price		coupon		reinvestment
return	=	return	+	return	+	return
(dollars)		(dollars)		(dollars)		(dollars)

total		price		coupon		reinvestment
return	=	return	+	return	+	return
(percent)		(percent)		(percent)		(percent)

Observation: *A bond's total return has three elements: price return, coupon return, and reinvestment return.*

Expressions of total return

A bond's total return can be shown in either a noncompounded form or a compounded form. A *noncompounded total return* is simply the holding-period return of the bond:

$$\text{noncompounded TR} = \frac{\text{total return (dollars)}}{\text{initial investment (dollars)}}$$

For example, if a bond is purchased at par (i.e., $1,000.00) and generates $350.00 in returns over a 2-year period, the bond records a 35.00% noncompounded total return:

$$\text{noncompounded TR} = \frac{\$350.00}{\$1,000.00}$$

$$= 35.00\%$$

The 35.00% compounded return is equivalent to a 16.19% annually compounded return, a 15.58% semiannually compounded return, a 15.29% quarterly compounded return, and a 15.10% monthly compounded return. A *compounded return* assumes a periodic compounding of previously accumulated returns. Total returns covering periods up to and including 1 year are typically reported in a noncompounded format. Multiyear returns are presented in an annually compounded equivalent form. Realized compound yields (to be discussed later in this chapter) are described in a semiannually compounded manner, similar to YTMs.

Observation: *A bond's total return can be expressed in either a compounded or noncompounded form. The selection is a function of the holding-period length and the intended use of the figure for comparative purposes.*

Exhibit 8–1. Components of total return for a 7% coupon, 30-year U.S. Treasury bond initially priced at par to yield 7.00% to maturity. One-year holding-period returns are calculated assuming (1) stable rates, (2) a 100BP rise in rates, and (3) a 100BP fall in rates. Results are expressed both in dollar terms and percentage terms for a $1,000.00 par bond.

Interest Rate Scenario	Return Component (Dollars)							
	Price	+	Coupon	+	Reinvestment	=	Total
1. Stable rates	0.00	+	70.00	+	1.23	=	71.23
2. Rising rates	−112.15	+	70.00	+	1.31	=	−40.84
3. Falling rates	136.66	+	70.00	+	1.14	=	207.80

Interest Rate Scenario	Return Component (Percentages)							
	Price	+	Coupon	+	Reinvestment	=	Total
1. Stable rates	0.00	+	7.00	+	0.12	=	7.12
2. Rising rates	−11.22	+	7.00	+	0.13	=	− 4.08
3. Falling rates	13.67	+	7.00	+	0.11	=	20.78

Comments: *The dollar price change reflects the market value of the bond 1 year hence at the designated yield level with a 29-year remaining term to maturity. The percentage returns are derived by dividing the respective dollar returns by the initial investment of $1,000.00.*

Component returns on a 30-year U.S. Treasury bond

Exhibit 8–1 organizes the component return data related to the 30-year U.S. Treasury bond of earlier illustration. The upper half of the table presents the results in a dollar price format. The bottom half of the table converts the dollar returns into percentage returns. This table reveals several interesting facts.

First, in a stable interest rate environment, a par bond experiences no price return.[5] Second, a modest change in yields creates a sizable price return effect for a 30-year bond. A 100BP rise in rates chops away 11.22% of the bond's value over a 1-year horizon. A decline in rates of similar magnitude (100BP) leads to a 13.67% appreciation in bond price. Third, the coupon component of return is a steady supplier of positive return in all yield scenarios ($70.00 or 7.00% per year). Finally, the reinvestment return over a 1-year horizon is negligible, adding

---

[5] Discount and premium bonds, however, are affected by price change in a stable rate environment as the result of discount and premium amortization. This effect is illustrated later in the chapter.

just over $1.00 in incremental wealth per $1,000.00 bond under the variety of interest rate environments presented.

The drudgery associated with hand calculations of holding-period returns is alleviated by computer software programs that provide the desired results expediently and effortlessly. However, an occasional walk through the mire of computations is instructive insofar as the tedium reminds the user of the forces behind the final tabulation. The illustration that follows is intended to incorporate all of the factors influencing a holding-period return, including the scientific amortization implicitly associated with discount and premium bonds.

Component returns on discount and premium bonds

Exhibit 8–2 is a compendium of the dollar returns on a 4% coupon U.S. Treasury bond and a 10% coupon U.S. Treasury bond. Each bond is a 5-year maturity issue currently priced to yield 7.00%. A 2-year investment horizon is assumed with three interest rate scenarios projected: (1) rates decline 100BP to 6.00%, (2) rates remain stable at 7.00%, and (3) rates rise 100BP to 8.00%. Exhibit 8–3 translates the data of Exhibit 8–2 into a percentage return-on-investment format. The computations supporting the total returns presented in these exhibits are now isolated component by component.

Exhibit 8–2. Dollar returns on 4% coupon and 10% coupon 5-year U.S. Treasury bonds initially priced to yield 7.00% to maturity. Two-year holding-period returns are calculated assuming (1) a 100BP decline in rates, (2) stable rates, and (3) a 100BP rise in rates.

		2-Year Component Returns ($) if Rates:		
Investment		*Fall 100BP*	*Unchanged*	*Rise 100BP*
4% bond	Price	70.58	44.82	19.91
($875.25 cost)	Coupon	80.00	80.00	80.00
	Reinvestment	3.98	4.29	4.62
		154.56	129.11	104.53
10% bond	Price	− 16.41	− 44.82	− 72.33
($1,124.75	Coupon	200.00	200.00	200.00
cost)	Reinvestment	9.97	10.75	11.54
		193.56	165.93	139.21

Comments: *Supporting calculations provided in Exhibits 8–4, 8–8, and 8–9.*

Exhibit 8–3. Percentage returns on 4% coupon and 10% coupon 5-year U.S. Treasury bonds initially priced to yield 7.00% to maturity. Two-year holding-period returns are calculated assuming (1) a 100BP decline in rates, (2) stable rates, and (3) a 100BP rise in rates. Realized compound yields (RCYs) are also calculated.

Investment		*2-Year Component Returns (%) if Rates:*		
		Fall 100BP	*Unchanged*	*Rise 100BP*
4% bond	Price	8.06	5.12	2.27
	Coupon	9.14	9.14	9.14
	Reinvestment	0.45	0.49	0.53
		17.66	14.75	11.94
	RCY→	**8.30**	**7.00**	**5.72**
10% bond	Price	− 1.46	− 3.98	− 6.43
	Coupon	17.78	17.78	17.78
	Reinvestment	0.89	0.96	1.03
		17.21	14.75	12.38
	RCY→	**8.10**	**7.00**	**5.92**

Comments: *The percentage returns are derived by dividing the corresponding dollar returns by the amount of the original investment (refer to Exhibit 8–2).*

The price component. The upper half of Exhibit 8–4 shows the ending bond prices for the 4% coupon and 10% coupon U.S. Treasury issues under falling, stable, and rising rate environments. In stable yield conditions at 7.00%, the discount bond rises in value from $875.25 to $920.07, a handsome $44.82 increase over the 2-year period. Using a similar status quo assumption, the premium bond falls to a $1,079.93 value, a sizable $44.82 drop from its current market value of $1,124.75. The culprit behind these mysterious price moves is scientific amortization.

Exhibit 8–5 computes the natural price accretion/(decretion) that occurs through time as a discount/(premium) bond approaches final maturity. Holding yield levels constant at 7.00%, the discount bond's value rises by varying amounts between $20 and $30 per year until, at the end of the fifth year, it reaches par ($1,000.00) and is retired. The premium bond falls in value by between $20 and $30 per year and, like the discount bond, rests at par value at maturity. The direction of the convergence differs, but the end result is the same: all bonds mature at par value. Scientific amortization is nonexistent on a current-coupon

Exhibit 8–4. Dollar prices and dollar price returns on 4% coupon and 10% coupon 5-year U.S. Treasury bonds initially priced to yield 7.00% to maturity. Two-year dollar price returns are calculated assuming (1) a 100BP decline in rates, (2) stable rates, and (3) a 100BP rise in rates.

Issue	Today's Price	Bond Price in 2 Years with Bond Yields at:		
		6.00%	7.00%	8.00%
4% bond	$ 875.25	$ 945.83	$ 920.07	$ 895.16
10% bond	1,124.75	1,108.34	1,079.93	1,052.42

Issue	2-Year Dollar Price Returns if Bond Yields:		
	Fall 100BP	Unchanged	Rise 100BP
4% bond	$70.58	$44.82	$19.91
10% bond	− 16.41	− 44.82	− 72.33

Comments: *The dollar prices reflect the market value of the bonds 2 years hence at the designated yield level with a 3-year remaining term to maturity. The dollar price return is calculated as the difference between the ending dollar price and the beginning dollar price (per $1,000.00 par bond).*

bond priced at par. Exhibit 8–6 presents the amortization process for premium, discount, and par bonds in a graphical context.

Referring back to Exhibit 8–4, one can now understand why all of the future prices on the 4% coupon bond are biased to lie above the current price of $875.25. The natural accretion pushes the price to $920.07 in 2 years (7.00% yield level). A 100BP fall in rates adds another $25.76 in price appreciation, for a $70.58 total price surge to the $945.83 level. A rise in yields to 8.00% erases $24.91 of the natural price increase, leaving a paltry $19.91 in price return (the lower half of Exhibit 8–4 summarizes the dollar price returns).

Conversely, the premium bond suffers from a natural tendency to generate negative price returns as maturity nears (see Exhibit 8–4). With no alteration in yield level, the 10% coupon bond trades at $1,079.93 in 2 years, $44.82 below its current market price of $1,124.75. Lower yields result in an ending price of $1,108.34, $28.41 above the natural price of $1,079.93, thereby reducing the price loss to $16.41. Rising rates accentuate the declining price trend in the premium bond. An 8.00% yield level abets a $72.33 fall-off in price, leaving only $52.42 between

Exhibit 8–5. Impact of scientific (or effective interest) amortization on discount, par, and premium U.S. Treasury bonds with a 5-year remaining term to maturity and a price to yield 7.00% to maturity.

Issue	Years Remaining to Maturity	Bond Price (YTM = 7.00%)	Annual Scientific Amortization
(a) 4% coupon U.S. Treasury	5	$ 875.25	+$21.64
	4	896.89	+ 23.18
	3	920.07	+ 24.83
	2	944.90	+ 26.60
	1	971.50	+ 28.50
	0	1,000.00	
(b) 7% coupon U.S. Treasury	5	$1,000.00	
	4	1,000.00	
	3	1,000.00	
	2	1,000.00	
	1	1,000.00	
	0	1,000.00	
(c) 10% coupon U.S. Treasury	5	$1,124.75	−$21.64
	4	1,103.11	− 23.18
	3	1,079.93	− 24.83
	2	1,055.10	− 26.60
	1	1,028.50	− 28.50
	0	1,000.00	

the premium bond's price and its par value. Exhibit 8–7 illustrates the price gyrations of premium, discount, and par bonds vis-à-vis the natural accreted price change that occurs over time.

> **Observation:** *Price return is composed of both natural price action [i.e., scientific amortization of a bond's premium/(discount)] and market-related price changes generated by yield shifts.*

The coupon component. The coupon return calculation is the least demanding of the three component return derivations. The 4% coupon bond generates $80.00 in coupon flow over the 2-year holding period ($20.00 semiannual coupon × 4 semiannual periods = $80.00). The 10% coupon bond provides $200.00 in coupon income over 2 years ($50.00 semiannual coupon × 4 semiannual periods = $200.00).

> **Observation:** *On an annual basis, coupon return is calculated as the principal amount of a bond times the coupon rate of interest.*

Exhibit 8–6. Typical price behavior of a premium, a discount, and a par bond attributable to scientific amortization. Yield levels remain stable.

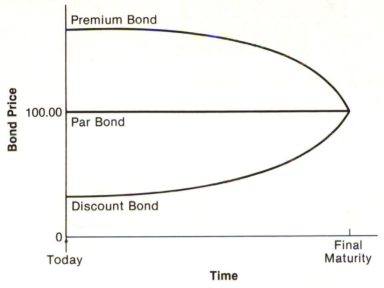

The reinvestment component. The most burdensome calculation is that of the reinvestment return because the reinvestment rate may change every 6 months. Exhibit 8–8 organizes the mathematics behind the reinvestment return computation for a 4% coupon, 5-year U.S. Treasury over a 2-year investment period. Exhibit 8–9 subjects a 10% coupon U.S. Treasury bond to an equally rigorous exercise. The amount of dollars available for reinvestment, called the *accumulated investment base* (AIB), is simply a collection of all of the coupon payments and interest-on-interest received to date. Every 6 months, the AIB is increased by (1) the interest-on-interest earned over the past 6 months, and (2) the next semiannual coupon payment. The reinvestment rate reflects the market yield environment at the time of reinvestment. Rising interest rate environments lead to higher reinvestment rates. The opposite is true for declining rate scenarios.

Exhibits 8–8 and 8–9 conjure up a few important insights with regard to reinvestment returns. First, the AIB grows rapidly over time. Interest earned on this reinvestment base expands quickly. Not surprisingly, reinvestment returns dominate total returns over long investment horizons, as will be demonstrated later in this chapter. Second, higher assumed reinvestment rates lead to higher reinvestment returns. For example, the 4% coupon bond generates $4.62 in reinvestment return over 2

Exhibit 8–7. Typical price behavior of a premium, a discount, and a par bond under the assumption of fluctuating interest rates.

a) Premium Bond.

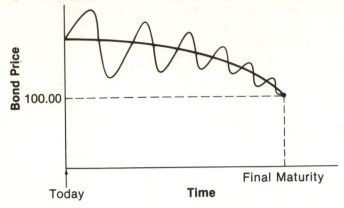

b) Par Bond.

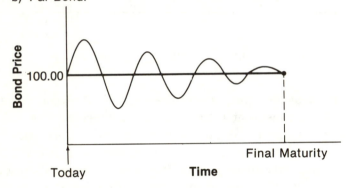

c) Discount Bond.

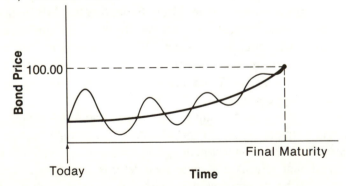

Comments: *Bond prices fluctuate around their natural accreted values; the price fluctuations dampen as maturity nears.*

Exhibit 8–8. Calculation of the coupon and reinvestment returns on a 4% coupon, 5-year U.S. Treasury bond over a 2-year investment horizon. The bond is initially priced to yield 7.00% to maturity. Three alternative interest rate scenarios are analyzed: (1) rates decline 100BP to 6.00%, (2) rates remain stable at 7.00%, and (3) rates rise 100BP to 8.00%.

(1) Rate Scenario	*(2)* t *(Years)*	*(3)* AIB at Beginning of Period	*(4)* Semi-annual Reinvestment Rate	*(5) = (3) × (4)* Reinvestment Return	*(6)* Coupon Payment	*(7) = (5) + (6)* Addition to AIB
Falling rates	0.5	$ 0.00	0.0325	$0.00	$20.00	$20.00
	1.0	20.00	0.0325	0.65	20.00	20.65
	1.5	40.65	0.0325	1.32	20.00	21.32
	2.0	61.97	0.0325	2.01	20.00	22.01
				$3.98	$80.00	
				↑ Total reinvestment return	↑ Total coupon return	
Stable rates	0.5	$ 0.00	0.0350	$0.00	$20.00	$20.00
	1.0	20.00	0.0350	0.70	20.00	20.70
	1.5	40.70	0.0350	1.42	20.00	21.42
	2.0	62.12	0.0350	2.17	20.00	22.17
				$4.29	$80.00	
				↑ Total reinvestment return	↑ Total coupon return	
Rising rates	0.5	$ 0.00	0.0375	$0.00	$20.00	$20.00
	1.0	20.00	0.0375	0.75	20.00	20.75
	1.5	40.75	0.0375	1.53	20.00	21.53
	2.0	62.28	0.0375	2.34	20.00	22.34
				$4.62	$80.00	
				↑ Total reinvestment return	↑ Total coupon return	

Comments: *The accumulated investment base (AIB) is the amount of dollars subject to reinvestment. Reinvestment return is also called interest-on-interest. The semiannual reinvestment rates are simply one-half of the assumed annual reinvestment rates. The annual rates of reinvestment are 6.50%, 7.00%, and 7.50%, respectively, for the falling, stable, and rising interest rate environments. These rates reflect an average reinvestment rate over the 2-year period.*

Exhibit 8–9. Calculation of the coupon and reinvestment returns on a 10% coupon, 5-year U.S. Treasury bond over a 2-year investment horizon. The bond is initially priced to yield 7.00% to maturity. Three alternative interest rate scenarios are analyzed: (1) rates decline 100BP to 6.00%, (2) rates remain stable at 7.00%, and (3) rates rise 100BP to 8.00%.

(1) Rate Scenario	(2) t (Years)	(3) AIB at Beginning of Period	(4) Semi-annual Reinvestment Rate	(5) = (3) × (4) Reinvestment Return	(6) Coupon Payment	(7) = (5) + (6) Addition to AIB
Falling rates	0.5	$ 0.00	0.0325	$ 0.00	$ 50.00	$50.00
	1.0	50.00	0.0325	1.63	50.00	51.63
	1.5	101.63	0.0325	3.30	50.00	53.30
	2.0	154.93	0.0325	5.04	50.00	55.04
				$ 9.97	$200.00	
				↑	↑	
				Total reinvestment return	Total coupon return	
Stable rates	0.5	$ 0.00	0.0350	$ 0.00	$ 50.00	$50.00
	1.0	50.00	0.0350	1.75	50.00	51.75
	1.5	101.75	0.0350	3.56	50.00	53.56
	2.0	155.31	0.0350	5.44	50.00	55.44
				$10.75	$200.00	
				↑	↑	
				Total reinvestment return	Total coupon return	
Rising rates	0.5	$ 0.00	0.0375	$ 0.00	$ 50.00	$50.00
	1.0	50.00	0.0375	1.88	50.00	51.88
	1.5	101.88	0.0375	3.82	50.00	53.82
	2.0	155.70	0.0375	5.84	50.00	55.84
				$11.54	$200.00	
				↑	↑	
				Total reinvestment return	Total coupon return	

Comments: *The accumulated investment base (AIB) is the amount of dollars subject to reinvestment. Reinvestment return is also called interest-on-interest. The semiannual reinvestment rates are simply one-half of the assumed annual reinvestment rates. The annual rates of reinvestment are 6.50%, 7.00%, and 7.50%, respectively, for the falling, stable, and rising interest rate environments. These rates reflect an average reinvestment rate over the 2-year period.*

years if interest rates rise 100BP and reinvestments are made at a 7.50% annual rate. A declining rate environment accompanied by a 6.50% annual reinvestment rate leads to only $3.98 reinvestment return over 2 years, 14% less than the $4.62 level. These differentials in return become more sizable the longer the investment horizon, the wider the differential in reinvestment rate, and the higher the coupon rate of the security involved. These issues are addressed in more detail later in this chapter.

Finally, high coupon bonds generate greater amounts of reinvestment return than do low coupon bonds as more dollars are available for reinvestment. Recall that the 4% coupon U.S. Treasury bond earned only $4.62 in reinvestment return over 2 years at a 7.50% rate. The (higher coupon) 10% issue, on the other hand, garnered $11.54 in reinvestment return over the same period, more than 2½ times the amount obtained by the 4% coupon security.

> **Observation:** *Reinvestment return is earned on the periodic coupon receipts generated by a bond. This interest-on-interest component of return is fueled by long investment horizons, high coupon rates, and high interest rate environments.*

Putting the pieces together. Exhibit 8–2 summarizes the return contributions of each component (price, coupon, reinvestment) in dollar terms. By expressing the same figures in a percentage return format, Exhibit 8–3 makes a few basic assertions. *First, the price component of total return can have a significant impact over short-term investment horizons, with or without a change in the market yield level.*

For example, the 4% coupon bond registers a 2-year holding-period return of 14.75% under a stable interest rate scenario. Approximately 35% of the bond's total return is contributed by the price appreciation of 5.12%. The 10% coupon bond posts an identical 14.75% total return over 2 years in a stable yield environment. The price component on this bond, however, detracts 3.98% from the total return, once again a significant proportion. It is clear that price returns from scientific amortization of a bond's premium or discount have important ramifications for the bond's total return. Combined with modest yield changes of 100BP, the price return covers a range of 2.27 to 8.06% for the discount bond and −1.46 to −6.43% for the premium bond. These ranges are sizable in relation to the magnitude of the total returns generated.

Second, the coupon component is a major contributor to total return. Not surprisingly, higher coupon bonds are disproportionately affected by coupon returns. The 4% coupon bond records a 9.14% return attributable to coupon, accounting for 50 to 75% of the bond's total return over the 2-year investment period. Coupon returns comprise virtually all of the 10% coupon bond's returns, with an offset due to principal loss.

Third, the reinvestment component is only a small proportion of total return over short-term investment horizons. Reinvestment return adds approximately 50BP and 100BP to the returns of the discount bond and the premium bond, respectively. Although relatively small, the reinvestment returns are not insignificant relative to the total returns of 12 to 17%.

Appendix B provides a case study of total return attribution for a U.S. Treasury bond purchased on June 30, 1984, and held for the 3-year period ending June 30, 1987. The three components of total return are segregated, with the price element traced to duration, convexity, yield curve, and issue specific effects. The reader is encouraged to review this appendix to gain a better feel for all of the real-world influences on a U.S. Treasury bond's return performance.

The relative importance of the components of total return differs across a variety of holding periods, coupon rates, market yield levels, and reinvestment rates. The impact of these factors on the price, coupon, and reinvestment contributions is the next topic to be discussed.

> **Observation:** *Over a short-term (2-year) holding period, the price return component is most influential if yields are subject to fluctuation. In such conditions, the coupon return component also has a major impact on the total return registered. Reinvestment return has a minimal impact. Given a 2-year holding period and a stable interest rate environment, the coupon return component prevails, with price return a modest influence and reinvestment return a quiet contributor.*

The influences on component returns

The impact of holding-period length

Over the short term, the price component has a powerful influence on total return (recall Exhibits 8–1 and 8–3). This strength is magnified by progressively shorter holding periods and by incrementally larger changes in market yield. Exhibit 8–10 analyzes the component return behavior of a 30-year U.S. Treasury bond initially priced at par to yield 7.00%. Interest rate levels are projected to fall 300BP to 4.00%, to remain stable at 7.00%, or to rise 300BP to 10.00%. The holding periods

Exhibit 8–10. Relative importance of the components of total return as yield levels change over various holding periods. The market yield level is initially at 7.00%. Three interest rate scenarios are employed: (1) interest rates decline to 4.00%, (2) interest rates remain stable at 7.00%, and (3) interest rates rise to 10.00%. The issues illustrated are 7% coupon, 30-year U.S. Treasury bonds initially priced at par to yield 7.00% to maturity.

Rate Scenario	Holding Period (Years)	Return Contribution (%)			
		Price	Coupon	Reinvestment	Total
	1	87.8	12.0	0.2	100.0
Rates fall	3	68.6	29.3	2.1	100.0
to 4%	10	30.9	52.7	16.3	100.0
	30	0	40.3	59.7	100.0
	1	0	98.3	1.7	100.0
Rates stable	3	0	91.6	8.4	100.0
at 7%	10	0	70.7	29.3	100.0
	30	0	30.5	69.5	100.0
	1	−$282.3	$ 70.0	$ 1.5	−$210.8
Rates rise	3	−$278.5	$210.0	$23.6	−$ 44.9
to 10%	10	− 31.7	86.2	45.5	100.0
	30	0	22.9	77.1	100.0

Comments: *Since each bond is originally purchased at par, the price return over 30 years (to maturity) is zero. Lower interest rates lead to strong price returns over short and intermediate investment horizons. Higher interest rates lead to sizable negative price returns over short and intermediate horizons (dollar price impacts shown for a $1,000.00 par bond under "rates rise to 10%" case because of the difficulty of interpreting the percentage contributions of the negative total returns over the 1- and 3-year periods). Reinvestment returns are stronger in higher interest rate scenarios than in lower interest rate scenarios. It is assumed that the reinvestment rates are 5.50% (bullish scenario), 7.00% (stable scenario), and 8.50% (bearish scenario).*

considered range from 1 to 30 years. The table contents reveal the following.

First, given a modest change in yield, the price component of total return dominates over short-term horizons. For example, price return accounts for 87.8% of the 1-year holding-period return if yields decline to the 4.00% level. A 300BP surge in yields generates a $282.30 drop in price over a 1-year investment period, resulting in a $210.80 net loss, which is cushioned by $70.00 in coupon and $1.50 in reinvestment return.

Second, a 10-year holding period allows the coupon and reinvestment components time to overpower the dominance of price return. A falling rate environment finds coupon return comprising 52.7% of the bond's total return over a 10-year period. The influence of price return declines from an 87.8% majority position (for the 1-year horizon) to a more modest 30.9% stance. Similar parallels can be drawn for the rising yield environment case.

Third, long-term holding periods are most influenced by reinvestment return to the extent of 60 to 75%, with coupon return accounting for the remaining 25 to 40%. Notice that for bonds purchased at par and held to maturity, price return is not a consideration.

A bond market composite such as the Shearson Lehman Government/ Corporate (SLGC) Bond Index similarly reflects the findings of Exhibit 8–10. Short-term holding periods (e.g., 1 month, 1 year) see the price component of the SLGC index accounting for a large proportion of total return (refer to Exhibit 8–11). An intermediate-term holding period such as the 4-year period January 1, 1973–December 31, 1976 finds the coupon component as the dominator, explaining 84.1% of the index's total return. The 14-year period January 1, 1973–December 31, 1986, a reasonably long horizon, allows the reinvestment return component

Exhibit 8–11. Total returns and component returns of the Shearson Lehman Government/Corporate Bond Index over a variety of holding periods (short, intermediate, long). Data courtesy of Shearson Lehman Brothers.

	Return Component (%)			
Holding Period	*Price*	*Coupon*	*Reinvestment*	*Total*
August 1982	4.06	1.08	NA	5.14
May 1984	−3.61	0.99	NA	−2.62
The year 1985	9.10	11.02	1.19	21.30
Percent of total return	**42.7**	**51.7**	**5.6**	**100.0**
The 4-year period				
1/1/73–12/31/76	−1.31	27.72	6.57	32.98
Percent of total return	**(4.0)**	**84.1**	**19.9**	**100.0**
The 14-year period				
1/1/73–12/31/86	−2.66	112.68	147.84	257.86
Percent of total return	**(1.0)**	**43.7**	**57.3**	**100.0**

Comments: *Price returns tend to dominate over short-term periods. Intermediate-term horizons find coupon cash flows of utmost influence. Reinvestment returns capture the spotlight over long-term holding periods.*

Exhibit 8–12. Relative contributions of the components of total return as a function of the length of the holding period. Issues illustrated are 30-year U.S. Treasury bonds priced to yield 7.00%. Market yield levels remain stable at 7.00%.

Issue	*Holding Period (Years)*	*Return Contribution (%)*			
		Price	*Coupon*	*Reinvestment*	*Total*
4% coupon bond	1	8.7	89.7	1.6	100.0
	3	8.7	83.6	7.7	100.0
	10	8.7	64.6	26.7	100.0
	30	8.7	27.9	63.4	100.0
7% coupon bond	1	0	98.3	1.7	100.0
	3	0	91.6	8.4	100.0
	10	0	70.7	29.3	100.0
	30	0	30.5	69.5	100.0
10% coupon bond	1	−4.0	102.1	1.7	100.0
	3	−4.0	95.2	8.7	100.0
	10	−4.0	73.5	30.4	100.0
	30	−4.0	31.7	72.2	100.0

Comments: *Notice that in flat yield environments, coupon return tends to dominate the short and intermediate holding periods while reinvestment powers the long-term horizon. This effect is particularly pronounced for higher coupon issues. The price returns on the discount and premium bonds reflect scientific amortization. Notice that the rate of amortization remains constant throughout the bond's life, although the absolute dollar amount of amortization per year does change (recall Exhibit 8–5).*

to gain relative strength and to capture 57.3% of the SLGC index's total return.

Holding yield levels constant, coupon return is the driving force in the short-to-intermediate run while reinvestment return dominates over the long run. For example, Exhibit 8–12 shows that coupon accounts for 90 to 100% of 1-year horizon returns for par, discount, and premium bonds. Ten-year holding periods find that the coupon component gives ground to reinvestment accumulation. In the case of 30-year investments, returns are attributable primarily to the reinvestment contribution (65 to 75%). Coupon returns provide the bulk of the remaining 25 to 35% of long-term returns, with price returns from scientific amortization having a negligible impact.

Observation: *Generally speaking, total returns are most influenced by the price return component over short holding periods (e.g., 1*

Exhibit 8–13. Relative importance of the total return components as a function of holding-period length, given a modest change in yield over the period.

Length of Holding Period	*Relative Importance of:*		
	Price	*Coupon*	*Reinvestment*
Short	High	Moderate	Low
Intermediate	Moderate	High	Moderate
Long	Low	Moderate	High

year), with coupon return a modest influence and reinvestment return a negligible force. Intermediate-term horizons (e.g., 10 years) find coupons as the primary source of return, while price and reinvestment returns provide only modest impacts. Long-run holding periods (e.g., 30 years) have return structures comprised principally of reinvestment cash flows, with coupon return a moderate impact and price return of little consequence. Exhibit 8–13 summarizes these observations and Exhibit 8–14 illustrates the findings in a pictorial manner.

The impact of coupon rate

As one would expect, the higher the coupon rate of interest, the more influential are the coupon and reinvestment contributions to a bond's

Exhibit 8–14. Relative importance of price, coupon, and reinvestment returns over short-, intermediate-, and long-term investment horizons (a typical breakdown).

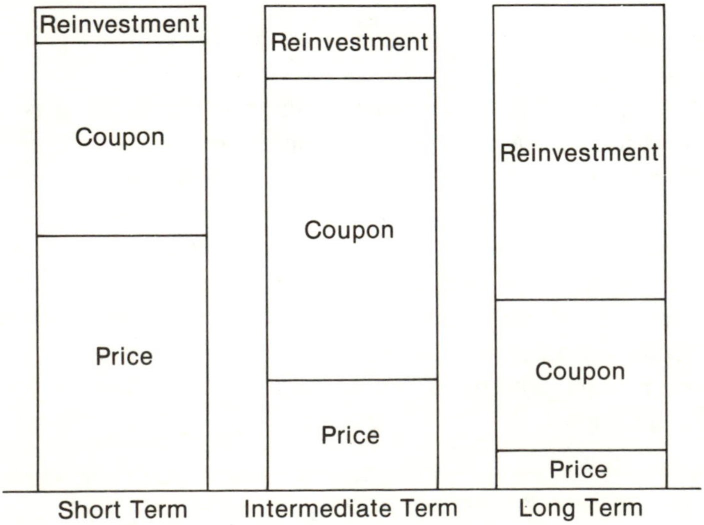

total return. Exhibit 8–12 illustrates that, over a short-term holding period of 1 year, coupon return accounts for 89.7% of a 4% discount bond's total return. The 1-year returns on the higher coupon 7% and 10% issues are almost entirely due to coupon payments (98.3 to 102.1%). Over long-term horizons (e.g., 30 years), coupon return contributes only 31.7% of the premium bond's total return and 27.9% of the discount bond's return, as reinvestment becomes paramount. Over a 30-year investment period, fully 72.2% of the return on the 10% coupon bond is the result of reinvestment return, whereas the 4% coupon bond can assign only 63.4% of its return to the reinvestment source.

> **Observation:** *Higher coupon bonds experience greater relative contributions of coupon and reinvestment return than those of their lower coupon counterparts.*

The impact of market yield level

Higher yield environments lead to a greater proportion of total return generated by reinvestment return. Exhibit 8–15 summarizes the component return behavior for 30-year maturity U.S. Treasuries priced at par in a variety of yield environments (4%, 7%, 10%, and 14%). Over short-term horizons, coupon return dominates total return on all of the four U.S. Treasury issues presented. However, in high yield surroundings, a greater proportion of a bond's return is attributable to the reinvestment component.

For example, a 1-year horizon in a 14% yield environment creates a 3.4% relative return contribution from reinvestment, almost 3½ times the paltry 1.0% reinvestment proportion in a 4% yield environment. Over a 10-year period, the reinvestment component surges to over 50% of return in a 14% rate scenario, while increasing to only 17.7% under 4% interest rate conditions. As the accumulated investment base (AIB) rapidly grows in a high yield environment, the relative contribution of reinvestment cash flow explodes to 92.6% of the 30-year horizon return in the 14% rate environment. Lower rate surroundings (4%) allow the reinvested cash flows to account for only a 47.4% proportion of total return given the same 30-year period.

> **Observation:** *In periods of high interest rates, reinvestment return is magnified, allowing it to become a larger and larger percentage of total return. In low interest rate environments, reinvestment return is of less importance.*

Exhibit 8–15. Relative contributions of the components of total return as a function of the market yield level. Issues illustrated are 30-year U.S. Treasury bonds priced at par. Market yields remain stable at 4%, 7%, 10%, and 14%, respectively.

Issue	Holding Period (Years)	Return Contribution (%) Price	Coupon	Reinvestment	Total
4% coupon bond	1	0	99.0	1.0	100.0
	3	0	95.1	4.9	100.0
	10	0	82.3	17.7	100.0
	30	0	52.6	47.4	100.0
7% coupon bond	1	0	98.3	1.7	100.0
	3	0	91.6	8.4	100.0
	10	0	70.7	29.3	100.0
	30	0	30.5	69.5	100.0
10% coupon bond	1	0	97.6	2.4	100.0
	3	0	88.2	11.8	100.0
	10	0	60.5	39.5	100.0
	30	0	17.0	83.0	100.0
14% coupon bond	1	0	96.6	3.4	100.0
	3	0	83.9	16.1	100.0
	10	0	48.8	51.2	100.0
	30	0	7.4	92.6	100.0

Comments: *In stable yield environments, coupon return dominates short- and intermediate-term holding-period returns and reinvestment return dominates long-term holding-period returns. The power of reinvestment returns is magnified by higher yield environments over all holding periods, particularly long investment horizons.*

The impact of the reinvestment rate

Logic dictates that the higher the assumed reinvestment rate, the more influential is the reinvestment component of total return. Exhibit 8–16 illustrates this notion by using three different reinvestment rates (5%, 7%, 9%) on 7% coupon U.S. Treasury bonds of various maturities. Over a 1-year investment horizon, the incremental amount of reinvestment return contribution is 1.0% as the rate is raised from 5 to 9% (2.2% − 1.2% = 1.0%). Over a 10-year horizon, this differential surges to 14.5% (36.2% versus 21.7%).

Over 30 years, the contrast is striking. A 5% reinvestment rate leads to a 55.9% contribution to total return by the reinvested cash flows. Using a 9% reinvestment rate and holding all other factors constant,

Exhibit 8–16. Relative contribution of the components of total return as a function of the reinvestment rate employed. Issues illustrated are 7% coupon U.S. Treasury bonds maturing at the end of the holding period. Each bond is initially priced at par.

Reinvestment Rate	Holding Period (Years)	Return Contribution (%)			
		Price	Coupon	Reinvestment	Total
	1	0	98.8	1.2	100.0
5%	3	0	93.9	6.1	100.0
	10	0	78.3	21.7	100.0
	30	0	44.1	55.9	100.0
	1	0	98.3	1.7	100.0
7%	3	0	91.6	8.4	100.0
	10	0	70.7	29.3	100.0
	30	0	30.5	69.5	100.0
	1	0	97.8	2.2	100.0
9%	3	0	89.3	10.7	100.0
	10	0	63.8	36.2	100.0
	30	0	20.7	79.3	100.0

Comments: *Progressively higher reinvestment rates lead to increasing dominance of the reinvestment return component of total return, particularly over long horizon periods.*

the reinvestment return jumps to 79.3% of the total return registered, a 23.4 percentage-point leap in relative importance. Given that the bonds in Exhibit 8–16 are purchased at par and held to maturity, the coupon contribution to total return declines in relative importance at the expense of the increasing dominance of the reinvestment component.

Observation: *The relative importance of the reinvestment component of total return is positively related to the size of the reinvestment rate assumed. This relationship is magnified over long investment horizons.*

Realized compound yield

The concept of a realized compound yield

Total returns can be expressed in absolute dollars (Exhibits 8–1 and 8–2) or in percentages (Exhibits 8–1 and 8–3). An alternative way of reporting percentage returns is in a semiannually compounded form commonly termed a realized compound yield (RCY).[6] The realized compound yield is the discount rate that equates the future value of a bond investment to its current market price. Mathematically, it is the same basic present value formula, $PV = FV/(1 + i)^n$, restated as:

$$\text{bond price} = \frac{FV_T}{\left(1 + \dfrac{RCY}{2}\right)^T}$$

where

bond price = bond's current market value

FV_T = total future value of the bond investment (including principal, coupons, and reinvestment) at the end of the investment holding period

T = number of semiannual compounding periods to the end of the investment holding period

RCY = realized compound yield

The realized compound yield might be more appropriately termed the *realized compound return* or *compounded total return* of a bond since it is intricately tied to the bond's total return, not to the bond's beginning or ending yield level.[7] This book uses the original terminology rather than repackaging the old concept and creating confusion.

> **Observation:** *The realized compound yield (RCY) of a bond is the total return of the bond as expressed in an annualized form with semiannual compounding.*

Applications of the RCY

As an example of the RCY application, Exhibit 8–17 summarizes the 2-year holding-period returns for the 5-year U.S. Treasury bonds of earlier illustration (recall Exhibits 8–2 and 8–3). The table also provides

---

[6] The realized compound yield concept was introduced by Homer and Leibowitz in *Inside the Yield Book* (Englewood Cliffs, NJ: Prentice-Hall, 1972). The RCY concept was outlined in Chapter 3. The reader is encouraged to review the earlier discussion before proceeding further.

[7] The differences between *yield* and *return* are outlined in Chapter 9.

Exhibit 8–17. Total returns and realized compound yields for 4% and 10% coupon, 5-year U.S. Treasury bonds each initially priced to yield 7.00% to maturity. A 2-year holding period is analyzed under three alternative interest rate scenarios: (1) a 100BP decline in yields, (2) stable yields, and (3) a 100BP rise in yields. Reinvestments made at the average of the beginning and ending yields.

Issue	Rate Scenario	2-Year Total Return		
		Dollars	*Percent*	*RCY*
4% coupon	Falling rates	154.56	17.66	8.30
bond	Stable rates	129.11	14.75	7.00
	Rising rates	104.53	11.94	5.72
10% coupon	Falling rates	193.56	17.21	8.10
bond	Stable rates	165.93	14.75	7.00
	Rising rates	139.21	12.38	5.92

Comments: *Changes in interest rate levels can sizably alter the RCY of an investment away from either its beginning or ending YTM rate.*

a realized compound yield for each bond under falling, stable, and rising yield scenarios. The 4% coupon issue offers an 8.30% RCY in a falling interest rate environment:

$$FV_T = \begin{array}{c}\text{market value of the} \\ \text{bond at the end of} \\ \text{the holding period}\end{array} + \begin{array}{c}\text{coupons} \\ \text{received}\end{array} + \begin{array}{c}\text{reinvestment} \\ \text{returns}\end{array}$$

$$= \$945.83 + \$80.00 + \$3.98 \quad \text{(data from Exhibits 8–4 and 8–8)}$$

$$= \$1,029.81$$

$$\text{bond price} = \frac{FV_T}{\left(1 + \dfrac{RCY}{2}\right)^T}$$

$$\$875.25 = \frac{\$1,029.81}{\left(1 + \dfrac{RCY}{2}\right)^4}$$

The RCY solves to 0.0830 or 8.30%. The 10% coupon issue generates a 5.92% RCY in a rising interest rate environment:

$$FV_T = \begin{array}{c} \text{market value of the} \\ \text{bond at the end of} \\ \text{the holding period} \end{array} + \begin{array}{c} \text{coupons} \\ \text{received} \end{array} + \begin{array}{c} \text{reinvestment} \\ \text{returns} \end{array}$$

$$= \$1,052.42 + \$200.00 + \$11.54 \qquad \begin{array}{l}\text{(data from} \\ \text{Exhibits} \\ \text{8–4 and} \\ \text{8–9)} \end{array}$$

$$= \$1,263.96$$

$$\text{bond price} = \frac{FV_T}{\left(1 + \dfrac{RCY}{2}\right)^T}$$

$$\$1,124.75 = \frac{\$1,263.96}{\left(1 + \dfrac{RCY}{2}\right)^4}$$

The RCY solves to 0.0592 or 5.92%. The remaining RCYs in Exhibit 8–17 are derived similarly.

The usefulness of the RCY

An RCY is handy in that it boils down to a single number the annual return earned by a bond over a specified holding period.[8] Dollar returns must be considered in light of the dollar amount originally invested. For example, in a falling rate environment, the 4% coupon U.S. Treasury records $154.56 in total return over the 2-year investment period (Exhibit 8–17). The 10% coupon issue registers a hefty $193.56 return under the same conditions, outpacing the 4% issue by $39.00. However, when one considers the size of the original investment in each issue, the 4% bond comes out ahead with a 17.66% return on investment, an attractive 45BP better than the 17.21% return earned by the higher coupon security over 2 years. On an annual basis, the excess return is only 20BP (8.30% RCY versus 8.10% RCY).

The RCY explicitly incorporates all of the factors affecting a bond's total return and serves as an excellent proxy for comparing the total

---

[8] Since the RCY assumes semiannual compounding of the return, the actual 1-year total return will be a few basis points higher. The RCY is subject to the validity of the assumptions made regarding interest rate change, the reinvestment rate realized, and the length of the holding period.

return prospects of a series of potential bond investments. A *scenario-weighted RCY* can be created by a subjectively determined probability assignment to a range of possible future outcomes. A *portfolio RCY* is simply the market value-weighted average of the RCYs of the individual issues comprising the portfolio.

RCYs, like total returns, are influenced by the same factors: the length of the holding period, the bond's coupon rate, the market yield level (and changes in the yield level), and the reinvestment rate assumed. The impact of these variables is the next topic of discussion. A series of illustrations assesses the sensitivity of the RCY to these factors.

Influences on the RCY

The impact of holding-period length

Longer holding periods lead to higher total returns, in both a dollar and a percentage sense. Exhibit 8–18 confirms this fact by examining the returns of 30-year U.S. Treasury bonds over a variety of holding periods. A 7% coupon bond, for example, creates $71.20 in return (7.12%) over a 1-year holding period. A 30-year horizon accumulates $6,878.10 in total return, or a 687.81% return on the original investment of $1,000.00.

The 4% discount bond and the 10% premium bond generate lower and higher dollar returns, respectively, compared to the 7% current-coupon issue. However, on a percentage return on investment basis, all three issues register identical returns and, consequently, identical RCYs. The RCYs are stable at 7.00% because the market yield level is projected to remain constant at 7.00% and all reinvestments are made at the same 7.00% rate. Indeed, the RCY of a bond coincides with the bond's YTM when (1) yields remain steady (or the bond is held to maturity), and (2) reinvestments are made at the YTM rate. Tax consider-ations aside, an investor is indifferent between the 4%, 7%, and 10% bond issues presented in Exhibit 8–18 given the underlying assumptions. A 7.00% annual return is all one can hope to receive.[9]

---

[9] As alluded to earlier, the annual return actually exceeds the RCY by a few basis points due to the effect of semiannual compounding. In this instance, the annual return is 7.12% (as shown for the 1-year holding-period return in percent, Exhibit 8–18), with the extra 12BP arising from intrayear coupon reinvestment.

Exhibit 8–18. Total returns and realized compound yields as a function of holding period and coupon rate. Issues illustrated are 30-year U.S. Treasury bonds priced to yield 7.00% to maturity. Market yield levels remain stable at 7.00%.

Issue	Holding Period (Years)	Total Return Dollars	Total Return Percent	RCY
4% coupon bond	1	44.60	7.12	7.00
	3	143.50	22.93	7.00
	10	619.40	98.98	7.00
	30	4,304.50	687.81	7.00
7% coupon bond	1	71.20	7.12	7.00
	3	229.30	22.93	7.00
	10	989.80	98.98	7.00
	30	6,878.10	687.81	7.00
10% coupon bond	1	97.90	7.12	7.00
	3	315.00	22.93	7.00
	10	1,360.10	98.98	7.00
	30	9,451.70	687.81	7.00

Comments: *Notice that the percentage returns are identical between bonds purchased at the same yield with reinvestments made at the YTM rate. The dollar returns differ because of the variance in initial dollar investment between the 4% discount bond, the 7% par bond, and the 10% premium bond. Exhibit 8–12 presents the relative contributions to total return by its price, coupon, and reinvestment components for this illustration.*

Changes in market yield lead to volatile behavior in total returns and RCYs, particularly in the short run. Exhibit 8–19 displays both the total returns and RCYs for a 7% coupon, 30-year U.S. Treasury bond in bullish, stable, and bearish interest rate scenarios. The holding period is varied from 1 to 30 years. Over a 1-year period, total returns range from +58.31% (bullish case) to −21.08% (bearish case), with a moderate posture (+7.12%) in the stable rate environment.

The severity of these total return differences dampens over time. For example, the 10-year period finds a range of RCYs from 6.04% (bearish case) to 8.63% (bullish case). There are two basic causes of this return smoothing. First, a bond's inherent price volatility declines as time passes (e.g., its duration falls over time). Second, the price return is spread over a larger number of years.

At first glance, the long-term (30-year) horizon results appear contradictory. How can the bullish scenario lead to a lower total return (520.83%)

Exhibit 8–19. Total returns and realized compound yields as a function of changes in market yield level. The market yield level is initially at 7.00%. Three interest rate scenarios are employed: (1) interest rates decline to 4.00%, (2) interest rates remain stable at 7.00%, and (3) interest rates rise to 10.00%. The issues illustrated are 7% coupon, 30-year U.S. Treasury bonds initially priced at par to yield 7.00% to maturity.

Rate Scenario	Holding Period (Years)	Total Return		
		Dollars	Percent	RCY
Rates fall to 4%	1	583.10	58.31	51.65
	3	717.60	71.76	18.87
	10	1,327.20	132.72	8.63
	30	5,208.30	520.83	6.18
Rates stable at 7%	1	71.20	7.12	7.00
	3	229.30	22.93	7.00
	10	989.80	98.98	7.00
	30	6,878.10	687.81	7.00
Rates rise to 10%	1	− 210.80	− 21.08	−22.33
	3	− 44.90	− 4.49	− 1.52
	10	812.30	81.23	6.04
	30	9,182.10	918.21	7.89

Comments: *Exhibit 8–10 presents the relative contributions to total return by its price, coupon, and reinvestment components for this illustration.*

and RCY (6.18%) than the bearish scenario (918.21% and 7.89%, respectively)? Because the bond is retired at par at final maturity in 30 years, the prevailing market yield level becomes completely irrelevant and has no effect on the bond's ending price, which is always par. Recall from Exhibit 8–10 that the price contribution to total return is zero for a bond purchased at par and held to maturity.

The higher yield (bearish) surroundings lead to a higher reinvestment rate (8.50%), which, in turn, pulls the RCY up to 7.89% for the entire 30-year period. The lower yield (bullish) conditions allow only a 5.50% return on reinvestment, dragging the RCY down to 6.18% for the 30-year time span (see Exhibit 8–19). Exhibit 8–10 provides a reminder of how important the reinvestment component of total return is over long horizons. The RCY results serve to confirm this.

Observation: *Longer holding periods create larger nominal total returns, but not necessarily higher RCYs. Short-term holding-period returns and RCYs can fluctuate wildly, given sizable moves in market* *yield. Long-term investment periods tend to smooth out market fluctuations, with reinvestment returns assuming a more prominent role.*

The impact of coupon rate

A higher coupon rate does not, in itself, lead to superior total returns and RCYs. A bond's realized return is strongly influenced by the price at which the bond is purchased and the rate at which reinvestments are made. For example, Exhibit 8–18 illustrates that 4% coupon, 7% coupon, and 10% coupon bonds render identical percentage returns and RCYs to an investor if each bond is purchased at a price to yield 7.00% and reinvestments are made at the YTM rate of 7.00%.

> **Observation:** *The coupon rate on a bond bears no direct relationship to the bond's total return or RCY. The purchase price and the assumed reinvestment rate are critical to the determination of a bond's total return and RCY prospects.*

The impact of market yield level

The level of market yields and the magnitude of total return and RCY are, of course, positively related.[10] There are two primary reasons for this phenomenon. First, higher yield environments allow an investor to purchase bonds at lower prices, which enhances total return prospects. Viewed another way, a higher yield environment gives the investor the ability to purchase par bonds with higher coupon rates. For example, in a 7% yield environment, an investor can purchase a $1,000.00 bond priced at par and receive $70.00 per annum in coupons. In a 14% interest rate environment, that same $1,000.00 investment can buy a bond bearing a 14% coupon rate and generating $140.00 in annual coupon cash flow.

Second, the reinvestment rates available in a higher yield environment allow for an enhancement of total returns from the interest-on-interest component of return. Each of these two effects leads to a positive relationship between the market yield level and the total return and RCY recorded.

As an illustration, Exhibit 8–20 compiles the total returns and RCYs of a series of 30-year U.S. Treasury bonds purchased at par in four different interest rate environments (4%, 7%, 10%, and 14%). Assuming

---

[10] This presumes the bond is held to maturity. An early sale of the bond in a rising yield environment creates a capital loss.

Exhibit 8–20. Total returns and realized compound yields as a function of market yield level. The issues illustrated are 30-year U.S. Treasury bonds initially priced at par. Market yield levels remain stable at 4%, 7%, 10%, and 14%, respectively.

		Total Return		
Issue	*Holding Period (Years)*	*Dollars*	*Percent*	*RCY*
4% coupon par bond	1	40.40	4.04	4.00
	3	126.20	12.62	4.00
	10	485.90	48.59	4.00
	30	2,281.00	228.10	4.00
7% coupon par bond	1	71.20	7.12	7.00
	3	229.30	22.93	7.00
	10	989.80	98.98	7.00
	30	6,878.10	687.81	7.00
10% coupon par bond	1	102.50	10.25	10.00
	3	340.10	34.01	10.00
	10	1,653.30	165.33	10.00
	30	17,679.20	1,767.92	10.00
14% coupon par bond	1	144.90	14.49	14.00
	3	500.70	50.07	14.00
	10	2,869.70	286.97	14.00
	30	56,946.40	5,694.64	14.00

Comments: *It is clear that higher yield environments create the propensity for greater investment gains, particularly over long periods. Notice that the 1-year holding-period returns exceed the RCY by the annual BP add-on for reinvestment of coupons received during the year. Exhibit 8–15 presents the relative contributions to total return by its price, coupon, and reinvestment components for this illustration.*

no change from the yield level at purchase date, the high coupon 14% issue outreturns the 4% coupon issue by a modest amount over a 1-year horizon (14.49% versus 4.04%). Over a long-term horizon of 30 years, the 14% issue accumulates $56,946.40 in return, 25 times the wealth generated by the 4% issue ($2,281.00). The higher coupon cash flow and higher assumed reinvestment rate (14%) contribute to the 14% coupon bond's impressive return statistics. On an annualized basis, the high coupon bond provides 3½ times the return of the low coupon issue (14.00% RCY versus 4.00% RCY).

A less dramatic shift from a 7% yield environment to a 10% yield environment still portends sizable differences in return. A par bond in

10% interest rate surroundings offers 44%, 48%, 67%, and 157% more total return over 1-, 3-, 10-, and 30-year holding periods, respectively, than a par bond in 7% interest rate surroundings (per Exhibit 8–20). On an annualized basis, the 10% bond outperforms the 7% bond by 3 percentage points in return (10.00% RCY versus 7.00% RCY), or approximately 43%.

> **Observation:** *Higher market yield levels lead to greater total returns, both on an absolute and a percentage basis. The higher percentage returns translate into higher RCYs.*

The impact of the reinvestment rate

Total returns and RCYs are positively related to the assumed rate of reinvestment. Exhibit 8–21 shows this relationship vividly by calculat-

Exhibit 8–21. Total returns and realized compound yields for a 14% coupon, 30-year U.S. Treasury bond initially priced at par and held to maturity. The sensitivity to changes in reinvestment rate is illustrated across a wide range of potential choices.

Reinvestment Rate (%)	30-Year Total Return	
	Dollars	*RCY*
0	4,200.00	5.57
1	4,883.90	6.00
2	5,716.90	6.45
3	6,735.00	6.94
4	7,983.60	7.45
5	9,519.40	8.00
6	11,413.70	8.58
7	13,756.20	9.18
8	16,659.30	9.80
9	20,264.90	10.45
10	24,750.90	11.13
11	30,341.50	11.82
12	37,319.00	12.53
13	46,038.30	13.26
14	56,946.40	14.00
15	70,606.00	14.76
16	87,724.90	15.53
17	109,194.40	16.31
18	136,135.40	17.10
19	169,958.50	17.89
20	212,437.10	18.70

Exhibit 8–22. Relationship between the RCY and the assumed reinvestment rate for a 14% coupon, 30-year U.S. Treasury bond purchased at par and held to maturity (data from Exhibit 8–21).

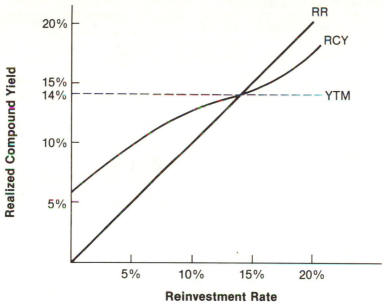

ing the total returns and RCYs for a 14% coupon, 30-year U.S. Treasury bond purchased at par and held to maturity, with reinvestments made at rates ranging from 0 to 20%. Exhibit 8–22 plots the reinvestment rate:RCY pairings to illustrate how the reinvestment rate tugs the RCY toward it.

At a 0% reinvestment rate (RR), the investor earns only a 5.57% RCY over 30 years. A 5% RR creates an 8.00% RCY while a 10% RR pushes the RCY over 11.00%. At a 14% RR, the RCY exactly equals the YTM at which the bond is purchased, 14.00%. A 20% RR allows the investor to record an 18.70% rate of return, as reported by the RCY. In general, the following relationship exists for bonds purchased and held to maturity:

1. If RR < YTM, then RCY < YTM.
2. If RR = YTM, then RCY = YTM.
3. If RR > YTM, then RCY > YTM.

The tugging effect of the reinvestment rate is less dramatic over shorter holding periods. Exhibit 8–23 examines the influence of the RR on 7% coupon U.S. Treasury bonds over various investment horizons

Exhibit 8–23. Total returns and realized compound yields as a function of the reinvestment rate employed. The issues illustrated are 7% coupon U.S. Treasury bonds maturing at the end of the holding period. Each issue is initially priced at par to yield 7.00% to maturity.

Reinvestment Rate	Holding Period (Years)	Total Return		
		Dollars	Percent	RCY
4%	1	70.70	7.07	6.95
	3	220.80	22.08	6.76
	10	850.40	85.04	6.25
	30	3,991.80	399.18	5.43
7%	1	71.20	7.12	7.00
	3	229.30	22.93	7.00
	10	989.80	98.98	7.00
	30	6,878.10	687.81	7.00
10%	1	71.80	7.18	7.05
	3	238.10	23.81	7.25
	10	1,157.30	115.73	7.84
	30	12,375.40	1,237.54	8.83

Comments: *It is clear that higher assumed reinvestment rates lead to greater total returns, particularly over longer investment horizons. The dollar returns, percentage returns, and RCYs all reflect this phenomenon. Notice that the 1-year holding-period returns exceed the RCY by the annual BP add-on for reinvestment of coupons received during the year.*

using three alternative RRs (4%, 7%, 10%). Over a 1-year horizon, the RCYs range from 6.95 to 7.05% for the three choices of RR. The 3-year cycle sees this range widen to 49BP. The 10-year period expands the range between high and low RCY to 159BP (7.84% RCY versus 6.25% RCY). The 4% RR pulls the 30-year RCY down to only 5.43%, while the 10% RR pushes the 30-year RCY up 340BP to 8.83%. The 30-year figures differ substantially from the 7.00% RCY experienced in a stable 7.00% rate environment.

The impact of differential reinvestment rates is even more noticeable with the dollar total return figures. A 7% coupon bond with reinvestments made at 7% generates $6,878.10 in total return over its 30-year life span. The same bond with coupons reinvested at a 4% rate provides only a $3,991.80 appreciation in wealth over 30 years. A 10% RR leads to a handsome ending wealth increment of $12,375.40 for the long investment horizon.

Observation: *Higher reinvestment rates create more substantial total returns and larger RCYs.*

Summary

The *total return* concept is intended to reflect the wealth enhancement provided by an investment over a specified period. A bond's total return is comprised of price return, coupon return, and reinvestment return. The *price component* arises from both scientific amortization of bond premium/(discount) and from shifts in market yields. The *coupon component* is a slow but steady contributor to return. The *reinvestment component* is especially critical over long horizons, where higher market yield levels accelerate reinvestment returns. The relative importance of the individual return components is a function of the holding-period length, the coupon rate, the beginning and ending market yield levels, and the reinvestment rate.

The *realized compound yield* (RCY) concept is simply a compounded version of the total return figure. Rather than expressing the total return in dollar form or in a nonannualized percentage form, the RCY standardizes the presentation by utilizing an annual percentage return format with semiannual compounding. In this way, an RCY is a YTM adjusted for the realities of the marketplace.

Choosing an Appropriate Reinvestment Rate

The body of this chapter illustrates the importance of the assumed reinvestment rate (RR) in the derivation of a bond's total return. Long investment horizons and high coupon issues reinforce the influence of the reinvestment rate. This appendix questions the typically casual treatment of the reinvestment rate assumption and suggests that even over short-term holding periods, the appropriate selection of a RR has important implications for total return results.

The YTM assumption

The YTM rate, when used as an indicator of a bond's total return potential, implicitly assumes that all reinvestments are made at the YTM rate.[1] Exhibits 8–21 and 8–23 showed that if the actual RR differs from

[1] Chapter 9 provides an in-depth discussion of the implications of the assumptions underlying the YTM rate.

the YTM rate, the bond's total return gravitates toward the RR. Indeed, over long-term holding periods, the RR may be better proxy for the bond's RCY than the YTM.

Reinvestment rates and zero-coupon bonds

Zero-coupon bonds (e.g., STRIPS) bear no reinvestment rate risk. The appropriate RR assumption is simply the YTM at which the bonds are purchased. STRIPS are completely oblivious to changes in RRs since there is no interim cash flow to be reinvested. On a hold-to-maturity assumption, STRIPS have perfect predictability: the total return, as expressed in RCY form, is exactly equal to the purchased YTM. If liquidated prior to final maturity, STRIPS are subject to unexpected changes in yields, raising or lowering the compounded total return (recall Exhibits 8–17, 8–19, and 8–20).

Long-term holding periods

Investors generally rely on the yields currently available in the marketplace as an estimate of the reinvestment rate for a bond holding. Long-term investment horizons demand the use of a RR assumption that reflects the returns available over extended periods of time. The current period may or may not be representative of the long-term average bond yield. During any single year, the total return registered by a broad market index can vary widely. For example, the SLGC index experienced annual returns ranging from 0.17 to 31.09% over the 1973–1986 time span (recall Exhibit 7–2 from Chapter 7). However, from a longer-term perspective, bond market returns typically plot in the 4 to 7% area.

Short-term holding periods

As noted in this chapter, short-term horizons warrant a lesser degree of concern about reinvestment rate risk. However, the volatility in short-term reinvestment rates can be severe. Consequently, the impact of reinvestment rate fluctuations must be considered. For example, if one reinvests coupon cash flows in the bond market portfolio as represented by the SLGC index, the semiannual returns earned by such reinvestments may be negative, zero, or significantly positive.[2]

---

[2] Given the availability of bond index funds that mirror the return behavior of the broad market indexes, reinvesting in *the bond market* is very feasible.

Exhibit 8A–1 organizes the semiannual returns on the SLGC index for the period January 1, 1973–June 30, 1987. The table compares the actual return realized on a coupon reinvested over the designated half-year with the beginning-of-period YTM on the SLGC index. The reinvestment rate commonly assumed by investors is the YTM rate available on the bond(s) selected as the vehicle for reinvestment of coupon proceeds. If interest rates remain stable, the YTM rate serves as a reasonably accurate proxy for the return garnered on reinvested coupons. However, changes in market yield levels are responsible for sizable discrepancies between the returns *expected* and the returns *realized* on the reinvestment proceeds. Column 3 of Exhibit 8A–1 calculates these differentials for each semiannual period in the January 1, 1973–June 30, 1987 interval.[3]

In general, rising interest rates lead to disappointments in actual reinvestment returns vis-à-vis yield-predicted returns.[4] For example, coupons reinvested on June 30, 1979 earned a -8.10% return (annualized) over the last half of 1979 as market yields rose 190BP, to 11.08% from 9.18%. The error in the reinvestment rate assumption is a solid 17.28% [9.18% $-$ (8.10%) = 17.28%]. Conversely, falling yields lead to pleasant surprises in actual reinvestment returns. As an illustration, the second half of 1984 saw yields decline approximately 250BP (13.64% $-$ 11.16% = 2.48%), allowing for a 32.84% annualized return on coupons reinvested at midyear, far in excess of the 13.64% suggested by the YTM measure.

The aforementioned effects are exaggerated by long maturity bond holdings. For example, Exhibit 8A–2 summarizes the semiannual yields and returns of the Shearson Lehman Long Treasury (SLLT) Index for the January 1, 1973–June 30, 1987 period. This index is particularly sensitive to market yield variations. The returns earned on the SLLT index over a given 6-month period have ranged from 66.32% in the last half of 1982 to -16.95% in the last half of 1980, on an annualized basis. These figures differ markedly from the yield-based return projections, which were 13.84% and 10.11% for the same periods. Exhibits 8A–1 and 8A–2 reveal a few remarkable statistics.

First, the actual reinvestment rate earned by an investor over a short-term holding period is often negative. The SLGC index has experi-

---

[3] The table uses January 1–July 1 and July 1–January 1 as the semiannual periods. One might also look at the semiannual returns for alternative breakdowns (e.g., February 15–August 15: August 15–February 15). The results will be similar in concept: short-term reinvestment returns are quite volatile.

[4] The phrases *reinvestment rate* and *reinvestment return* are used interchangeably since the reinvestment rate is essentially a rate of return.

Exhibit 8A–1. Semiannual yields and returns on the Shearson Lehman Government/Corporate Bond Index over the January 1, 1973–June 30, 1987 period. (Data courtesy of Shearson Lehman Brothers.)

Semiannual Period	(1) YTM (%)	(2) Actual Return (Annualized %)	(3) = (2) − (1) Difference (%)
1973 I	6.99	− 0.30	− 7.29
II	7.50	4.86	− 2.64
1974 I	7.67	−10.40	−18.07
II	9.22	11.32	2.10
1975 I	8.65	13.30	4.65
II	8.30	10.60	2.30
1976 I	8.10	10.10	2.00
II	8.03	20.08	12.05
1977 I	6.90	4.40	− 2.50
II	7.27	1.56	− 5.71
1978 I	7.95	0.38	− 7.57
II	8.81	1.98	− 6.83
1979 I	9.78	13.24	3.46
II	9.18	− 8.10	−17.28
1980 I	11.08	16.42	5.34
II	10.09	− 9.54	−19.63
1981 I	12.95	1.40	−11.55
II	14.48	13.02	− 1.46
1982 I	14.53	12.82	− 1.71
II	14.92	46.38	31.46
1983 I	10.75	9.64	− 1.11
II	11.03	6.06	− 4.97
1984 I	11.61	− 2.40	−14.01
II	13.64	32.84	19.20
1985 I	11.16	21.12	9.96
II	9.95	19.44	9.49
1986 I	9.11	19.92	10.81
II	8.02	10.30	2.28
1987 I	7.60	− 0.88	− 8.48
II	8.47	NA	NA
Mean absolute difference[*] →			**8.48**

[*]Represents the average error in using the YTM rate as an indication of the reinvestment return to be earned.

Comments: *The YTM reflects the average YTM on the SLGC index at the beginning of the period; the actual return represents the annualized total return earned over the period by reinvesting in the SLGC index. Reinvestment rates are commonly stated in an annualized format; the actual dollar returns are calculated on a 6-month holding period and reflect one-half of the annual figures.*

Exhibit 8A–2. Semiannual yields and returns on the Shearson Lehman Long Treasury Index over the January 1, 1973–June 30, 1987 period. (Data courtesy of Shearson Lehman Brothers.)

Semiannual Period	(1) YTM (%)	(2) Actual Return (Annualized %)	(3) = (2) − (1) Difference (%)
1973 I	6.65	−1.40	− 8.05
II	7.06	3.70	− 3.36
1974 I	7.26	− 4.02	−11.28
II	7.93	14.33	6.40
1975 I	7.85	6.76	− 1.09
II	8.01	9.60	1.59
1976 I	7.99	7.94	− 0.05
II	7.99	25.26	17.27
1977 I	7.21	0.95	− 6.26
II	7.55	− 1.05	− 8.60
1978 I	7.97	− 4.69	−12.66
II	8.65	1.86	− 6.79
1979 I	9.01	13.27	4.26
II	8.79	−13.45	−22.24
1980 I	10.14	12.10	1.96
II	10.11	−16.95	−27.06
1981 I	11.97	− 6.51	−18.48
II	13.31	7.50	− 5.81
1982 I	13.79	12.92	− 0.87
II	13.84	66.32	52.48
1983 I	10.66	7.50	− 3.16
II	11.12	1.24	− 9.88
1984 I	11.85	−13.88	−25.73
II	13.75	46.95	33.20
1985 I	11.64	28.06	16.42
II	10.65	30.75	20.10
1986 I	9.54	39.50	29.96
II	7.98	7.26	− 0.72
1987 I	7.96	− 7.48	−15.44
II	8.78	NA	NA
Mean absolute difference* →			**12.80**

*Represents the average error in using the YTM rate as an indication of the reinvestment return to be earned.

Comments: *The YTM reflects the average YTM on the SLLT index at the beginning of the period; the actual return represents the annualized total return earned over the period by reinvesting in the SLLT index. Reinvestment rates are commonly stated in an annualized format; the actual dollar returns are calculated on a 6-month holding period and reflect one-half of the annual figures.*

enced negative total returns in 6 of the 29 semiannual periods studied, or approximately 20% of the observations. The SLLT index registered negative returns 30% of the time (9 out of the 29 observations). Many investors fail to incorporate the possibility of a negative reinvestment rate in their total return projections.

Second, the actual reinvestment rate earned over short-term holding periods falls short of the YTM rate over 50% of the time. For the SLGC index, 55% of the periods studied (16 out of 29) generated negative surprises. The SLLT index finds a 66% *disappointment rate* (19 out of 29). Investors who rely on the YTM rate as a short-term proxy for the RR should beware.

Finally, contrary to popular wisdom, reinvestment returns are often experienced in exactly the opposite direction as the movement in market yields, which typically serve as the benchmark for reinvestment rate assumptions. The general consensus is that declines in interest rates lead to lower reinvestment rates and increases in interest rates lead to higher reinvestment rates. While this holds true for the long-term investor, the short-term investor registers an opposing phenomenon: lower yields create bond price appreciations which, in turn, lead to higher returns on coupons that are reinvested in bond investments. Conversely, higher yields create bond price depreciations which, in turn, create lower returns on reinvested coupons than either the beginning YTM or the ending YTM rate suggests. Bull market periods create high reinvestment returns and bear markets portend low (or negative) reinvestment returns. The magnitude of the differences in actual reinvestment return earned in these contrasting market periods is dramatic. Twenty to 30 point divergences in reinvestment returns are not unusual.

> **Observation:** *When reinvestments are made in the bond market, the actual reinvestment returns may differ sizably from the returns implied by the YTM construct. Fluctuations in market yield levels are responsible for these divergences. Negative reinvestment rates are not uncommon, particularly during bear market periods.*

The impact of varying reinvestment rates on short-term performance

The wide variations in potential short-term reinvestment rates pose a threat to bond investors. Exhibit 8A–3 illustrates the impact of a range of reinvestment rates on the 1-year returns of a series of U.S. Treasuries priced at par. A 4% coupon bond finds a 20BP alteration in total return

Exhibit 8A–3. Impact of a wide range of reinvestment rates on the 1-year total returns of par bonds with 4%, 7%, and 10% coupons. The general level of yields is held constant in order to isolate the reinvestment rate impact.

	1-Year Total Return (%) on a Par Bond with a:		
Reinvestment Rate (%)	*4% Coupon*	*7% Coupon*	*10% Coupon*
−30	3.40	5.95	8.50
−20	3.60	6.30	9.00
−10	3.80	6.65	9.50
0	4.00	7.00	10.00
10	4.20	7.35	10.50
20	4.40	7.70	11.00
30	4.60	8.05	11.50

Comments: *Sizable fluctuations in reinvestment rates can have material impacts on coupon-bearing bonds, particularly higher coupon issues. Over short-term holding periods (e.g., 1 year), these influences cannot be ignored.*

as a result of a 10 percentage-point change in the RR. For example, a 20% RR earns the 4% coupon bond a 4.40% return, 20BP more than the 4.20% return assuming a 10% RR. The higher coupon 10% bond is more sensitive to shifts in the RR. A 10 percentage-point change in the RR translates into a 50BP move in total return. For example, a −20% RR leads to a 9.00% return rather than the 10.00% return earned in a 0% RR environment (100BP return change for a 20 percentage-point change in RR or, on average, 50BP per 10 percentage-point change in RR). Recall from earlier illustrations that 20 percentage-point changes in the realized RR are not uncommon.

Observation: *Market volatility leads to fluctuations in potential reinvestment returns. These variations can have material impacts on short-term total return performance (e.g., 40 to 100BP).*

Short-term holding-period returns: A final illustration

Reinvestment rate assumptions are commonly applied in an inconsistent manner in short-term return projections. For example, assume that interest rates are currently at a 7.00% level. Over the forthcoming year, rates are expected to either rise 200BP or fall 200BP. The typical application of RRs uses an average of the beginning and ending yields as the proxy for the RR. In this case, the assumed RR is 8.00% in the rising rate environment [(7.00% + 9.00%)/2 = 8.00%] and 6.00% in the falling rate environment [(7.00% + 5.00%)/2 = 6.00%]. Indeed, given the following conditions, these RRs are accurate:

1. Reinvestments made in cash instruments (e.g., T-bills).
2. A flat yield curve.
3. A uniform rate of change in yield levels.
4. Coupons received at midyear.

In reality, however, coupon cash flows are not generally reinvested in Treasury bills.[5] The coupon proceeds typically flow back into the portfolio through additional bond purchases. Second, the yield curve is rarely found in a flat shape (refer to Chapter 12). Third, interest rates often change in a nonuniform manner. Finally, coupons are reinvested at various points during the year, not necessarily at midyear.

Exhibit 8A–4 analyzes the 1-year total return behavior of short-term (3-year), intermediate-term (10-year), and long-term (30-year) bonds in the traditional framework (RR = average YTM) and in a more consistent manner (RR = the total return on a coupon reinvested in the same bond issue). Each bond pays coupons on June 30 and December 31 and, therefore, one coupon is received at midyear and is subject to reinvestment. The second coupon is received at year-end and is not reinvested since the holding period terminates at that time.

The *actual RRs* reflect the annualized total returns garnered by reinvesting in the identical bond from which the coupon originated. In a rising interest rate environment (+200BP), the actual RRs fall below the average YTMs and become increasingly negative as longer maturity instruments serve as the reinvestment device. The *expected TRs*, based on the RR=YTM assumption, differ from the *actual TRs* by 6 to 37BP. Not surprisingly, the actuals fall short of the expecteds. A falling interest rate environment finds the actual returns exceeding the expected returns by 6 to 52BP since the realized RRs are larger than their average YTM counterparts.

Observation: *Reinvesting coupon cash flows in a bond instrument opens up the potential for sizably positive/(negative) returns on reinvestment over short-term horizons. Contrary to popular convention, rising*

---

[5] For simplicity, most of the illustrations in this book assume reinvestment in a T-bill at the average yield over the specified period.

Exhibit 8A–4. One-year total returns of short (5-year), intermediate (10-year), and long (30-year) maturity, 7% coupon U.S. Treasury bonds initially priced at par to yield 7.00%. Interest rates are projected to (1) rise 200BP or (2) fall 200BP.

(1)	(2)	(3)	(4)	(5)	(6) = (5) − (4)
Issue	Average YTM (%)	Actual RR (%)	Expected TR (%)	Actual TR (%)	Difference (BP)
(a) Rates rise 200BP					
3-year bond	8.00	4.38	3.55	3.49	(6)
10-year bond	8.00	− 4.48	− 5.02	− 5.24	(22)
30-year bond	8.00	−12.91	−13.35	−13.72	(37)
(b) Rates fall 200BP					
3-year bond	6.00	− 9.72	10.87	10.93	6
10-year bond	6.00	19.95	21.46	21.70	24
30-year bond	6.00	35.51	37.55	38.07	52

Comments: *Interest rates shift at a uniform rate during the year. Coupons are paid on a June 30:December 31 cycle. Reinvestments are made in a cash instrument providing the same yield as the underlying bond investment (i.e., the yield curve is flat) for expected total return calculations; reinvestments are made in the underlying bond investment for actual total return calculations. Reinvestment rates are stated on an annualized basis.*

Exhibit 8A–5. Critique of the typical reinvestment rate assumptions made for various holding periods.

Holding Period	Typical Reinvestment Rate	Comment
1. Long-term (hold to maturity)	YTM rate	A long-term average rate of return on bonds is more appropriate; for STRIPS, the YTM rate *is* the proper RR.
2. Short-term (active investor)	T-bill rate	Only appropriate if coupons are actually reinvested in T-bills; must estimate future T-bill rates.
	YTM rate	Interest rate fluctuations render this approximation faulty; a projected total return on a bond or a series of bonds (e.g., a bond market index) may be more appropriate.

yield environments do not lead to higher levels of reinvestment return, but exactly the opposite. Falling yield environments enhance reinvestment returns. An active bond manager operating on a short-to-intermediate-term holding-period basis should keep these return behaviors in mind.

Summing it up

A zero-coupon bond bears no reinvestment rate uncertainty if its maturity coincides with the end of the holding period. Coupon-bearing issues, however, carry the risk that reinvestment rates change from current levels. On a long-term basis, the actual RR is likely to lie in the 4 to 7% range. The actual RR tugs the RCY of the bond in its direction. On a short-term basis, cash flows are likely to find their way back into a bond investment rather than a cash instrument. Bull and bear markets can dramatically alter the reinvestment returns realized, and can therefore influence short-term total return performance. Exhibit 8A–5 critiques the traditionally accepted norms for reinvestment rate usage. The choice of an appropriate reinvestment rate is a more critical decision than is commonly perceived, even for the active bond manager.

A Case Study of Total Return Attribution

An overview

As noted in this chapter, a bond's total return can be dissected into three basic components: price return, coupon return, and reinvestment return. The price return element is attributable to several factors[1]:

1. Duration
2. Convexity
3. Yield curve rolls (as a result of the passage of time)
4. Change in yield curve shape (steepening, flattening)
5. Individual issue behavior

---

[1] This appendix focuses on the U.S. Treasury bond sector. In non-Treasury issues, price returns may also be influenced by: call features, credit concerns, quality sector yield shifts, issuer sector yield shifts, and supply/demand imbalances in specific issues and sectors.

Exhibit 8B–1. Actual issue data for U.S. Treasury 13⅛% due May 15, 1994. The bond moves from a 10-year maturity status to a 7-year maturity status over the 3-year period June 30, 1984–June 30, 1987.

Date	Maturity Sector (Year)	Bond Price	Accrued Interest	Full Price	YTM (%)	Modified Duration
June 30, 1984	10	96.16	1.64	97.80	13.84	5.27
June 30, 1987	7	124.81	1.64	126.45	8.31	4.72

Comments: *The full price is simply the bond's price including accrued interest.*

Duration and convexity impacts were discussed in Chapter 6. Recall that these two factors assume an instantaneous and parallel shift in yield. Nonparallel yield curve shapes introduce yield curve roll effects as time passes and bonds move into shorter maturity sections of the curve. Nonparallel yield curve shifts (i.e., changes in yield curve shape) further compound the price impact in either a positive or negative fashion. Yield curve shapes and shifts are outlined in detail in Chapter 12. Individual issues add one more level of complexity in that their unique features (e.g., coupon rate, quality, liquidity, call provisions) affect their price returns. Chapter 14 elaborates on individual issue characteristics.

Coupon returns are easily derived as the sum of all coupon payments made during the investment period plus any net change in accrued interest. Reinvestment returns were discussed at length in this chapter as well as in Appendix A. The illustration that follows is intended to demonstrate the real-world impacts of the factors influencing U.S. Treasury bond returns. The reader can follow the example without the need for a review of the forthcoming chapters cited above. The total return on the U.S. Treasury 13⅛% due May 15, 1994 for the 3-year period June 30, 1984–June 30, 1987 is the subject of interest.

The case study

Exhibit 8B–1 lists the issue data for the U.S. Treasury 13⅛% due May 15, 1994 as of the beginning and end of the performance period (June 30, 1984–June 30, 1987). In mid-1984, the bond was the current-coupon 10-year U.S. Treasury issue and traded a few points below par. By mid-1987, the bond had moved into a 7-year off-the-run U.S. Treasury status. The 13⅛'s yield declined from 13.84 to 8.31%

Exhibit 8B–2. Total return and component returns on the U.S. Treasury 13⅛% due May 15, 1994 for the 3-year period June 30, 1984–June 30, 1987.

Format	(1) Price Return	(2) Coupon Return	(3) Reinvestment Return	(4) = (1) + (2) + (3) Total Return
Dollars	28.65	39.38	5.60	73.63
Percent	29.29	40.27	5.73	75.29
Percent contribution to total return	38.91	53.48	7.61	100.00

Comments: *The price return reflects the dollar price change (using full prices) over the period (124.81 − 96.16 = 28.65, per Exhibit 8A–1). The coupon return incorporates 3 years of coupon cash flow (6 semiannual coupons) at a 13⅛% annual rate and no net change in accrued interest. Reinvestments are made in the SLGC bond index and reflect the total returns garnered from such investments (Shearson Lehman data per Exhibit 8A–1). The total return is simply the sum of the component returns. The percentage returns are based on an original cost of 97.80 (full price per Exhibit 8B–1). The percentage contributions are simply the relative contributions of each return component. All figures are rounded to the nearest two decimal places.*

Exhibit 8B–3. Total return and component price returns for the U.S. Treasury 13⅛% due May 15, 1994 for the 3-year period June 30, 1984–June 30, 1987.

Price Return Component	Price Impact	Contribution (%)
Attributable to scientific amortization of bond discount (no yield change)	0.68	2.37
Parallel yield shift:		
Attributable to duration	23.27	81.22
Attributable to convexity	4.34	15.18
Nonparallel yield shift:		
Attributable to maturity sector shift (and corresponding yield curve rolldown) of 5BP	0.30	1.05
Attributable to yield curve steepening of 8BP	0.48	1.68
Attributable to individual issue behavior (a 7BP rise in yield as the 13⅛s moved from an on-the-run status to an off-the-run status)	(0.42)	(1.47)
Total price return[*]	28.65	100.00

[*]Ending full price (126.45) less beginning full price (97.80) per Exhibit 8B–1. Totals are subject to rounding error.

Exhibit 8B–4. Issue data on June 30, 1987 assuming no change in YTM over the 3-year period ending on June 30, 1987.

Issue	YTM (%)	Bond Price	Accrued Interest	Full Price	Modified Duration
U.S. Treasury 13⅛% due May 15, 1994	13.84	96.84	1.64	98.48	4.32

Comments: *If yields had remained stable over the 3-year period, the 13⅛'s price would have appreciated from 97.80 to 98.48 (in full price terms) as a result of scientific amortization of the bond's discount (recall Exhibit 8B–1 for June 30, 1984 issue data).*

over the 3-year period for a 553BP downward shift. The bond's modified duration slipped by approximately one-half year, from 5.27 to 4.72.

As a result of the dramatic fall-off in market yields over the June 30, 1984–June 30, 1987 holding period, the 13⅛s recorded a total return of 75.29% (see Exhibit 8B–2). In dollar terms, the bond notched a 73.63-point return on the original investment of 97.80. Exhibit 8B–2 shows the price return accounting for almost 40% of the bond's total return. The coupon cash flows provided approximately 53% of the total return and the reinvestment of coupons contributed approximately 7% of the aggregate return.

The price return of 28.65 is subdivided into six component parts in Exhibit 8B–3. Scientific amortization forced the bond price upward by 0.68 point. Recall that the bond was purchased at a 13.84% YTM on June 30, 1984 (96.16 price excluding accrued interest). Holding yield levels constant at 13.84%, the bond's price appreciates to 96.84 on June 30, 1987 (see Exhibit 8B–4). The ⅔-point increase is attributable to the natural tendency of a bond's price to approach par as its final maturity date nears.

Duration contributes the bulk of the price return (23.27 of the 28.65 total, per Exhibit 8B–3). An end-of-holding-period modified duration is used to assess the price return attributable to this factor.[2] The bond's modified duration at the end of the holding period (on June 30, 1987), assuming stable yields, is 4.32 years (see Exhibit 8B–4). For total return calculation purposes, the bond is repriced to the lower yield

---

[2] In reality, the end-of-holding-period duration is the best proxy for the bond's price sensitivity since the repricing, for performance calculation purposes, takes place on that date. Durations at earlier points in time become irrelevant.

Exhibit 8B–5. Actual yield spread data for June 30, 1984 and June 30, 1987. The U.S. Treasury 13⅛% due May 15, 1994 moves from an on-the-run 10-year status to an off-the-run 7-year status over the 3-year period.

	June 30, 1984	*June 30, 1987*
Current-coupon 7-to-10-year spread	+ 5BP	+13BP
U.S. Treasury 13⅛% '94 versus the current-coupon Treasury issue maturing in 1994	0BP	+ 6BP
10-year current-coupon U.S. Treasury yield	13.84%	8.37%

level on that day, and therefore the modified duration on June 30, 1987 is the most applicable duration figure. To isolate the impacts of yield curve shapes, rolls, shifts, etc., the yield shift is assumed to be parallel in nature. Exhibit 8B–5 shows that 10-year current-coupon U.S. Treasuries recorded a 547BP yield decline over the June 30, 1984–June 30, 1987 period. The 13⅛ issue is assumed to experience an identical 547BP yield shift, and therefore expects a 23.63% price change attributable to duration:

$$\frac{\text{percent change in}}{\text{bond price}} = -\left(\frac{\text{modified}}{\text{duration}}\right) \times \frac{\text{BP change in yield}}{100}$$

$$= -4.32 \times \frac{-547}{100}$$

$$= -4.32 \times (-5.47)$$

$$= 23.63\%$$

In dollar terms, this translates into 23.27 points:

$$\begin{array}{c}\text{dollar price change} \\ \text{attributable to} \\ \text{duration}\end{array} = \begin{array}{c}\text{percentage} \\ \text{change in} \\ \text{bond price}\end{array} \times \begin{array}{c}\text{full price on June 30, 1987} \\ \text{(before the shift} \\ \text{in yield)}\end{array}$$

$$= 23.63\% \times 98.48$$

$$= 23.27$$

Convexity assumes the same parallel yield shift as under the derivation of the duration contribution. Consequently, the price return attributable to convexity is 4.41%, or 4.35 points:

	(1)	$(2) = -(1) \times \left(\dfrac{-547}{100}\right)$	(3)	$(4) = (3) - (2)$
Issue	*Modified Duration*	*Duration- Suggested Price Change*	*Actual Price Change*[*]	*Return Attributable to Convexity*
13⅛% due May 15, 1994	4.32	23.63%	28.04%	4.41%

[*] Given a 547BP decline in yields.

$$\begin{array}{l}\text{dollar price change}\\\text{attributable to} \quad = 4.41\% \times 98.48\\\text{convexity}\end{array}$$

$$= 4.34$$

The 13⅛ issue, however, did not experience a parallel shift in yield relative to the 10-year current-coupon U.S. Treasuries. The 13⅛ bond recorded a 553BP yield decline (per Exhibit 8B–1) rather than the 547BP drop noted by the 10-year Treasuries (Exhibit 8B–5). The extra 6BP yield decline is traceable to three nonparallel yield shift factors (refer to Exhibits 8B–3 and 8B–5):

BP Yield Impact (BP)	*Explanation*
−5	1. The 13⅛ issue moved from a 10-year maturity to a 7-year maturity over the 3-year period. Given the yield curve shape on June 30, 1984 between current-coupon Treasuries, the 13⅛s should have rolled down the yield curve by 5BP (i.e., the 7-to-10-year spread was +5BP).
−8	2. The yield curve (7-to-10-year section) steepened by 8BP over the 3-year period to a +13BP spread between current-coupon 7s and 10s. The 13⅛s should have garnered this additional 8BP in yield curve rolldown.
+7	3. The 13⅛ issue experienced a 7BP increase in yield relative to current-coupon U.S. Treasuries as a result of its move to off-the-run status (on June 30, 1984, the 13⅛ was the current-coupon issue; as of June 30, 1987, the bond traded 7BP cheaper than the current-coupon 7-year Treasury issue).
−6	Net effect (a 6BP additional decline in yield)

These three nonparallel yield shift factors accounted for 0.30 point, 0.48 point, and (0.42) point impacts on the price return of the 13⅛ issue (see Exhibit 8B–3).

In terms of relative influence on price return, the duration and convexity elements loom large in this example, explaining over 96% of the price return (Exhibit 8B–3). Scientific amortization and nonparallel yield shifts exhibited much smaller effects. However, beware that these less influential components can exert sizable pressures on bond price returns if:

1. The bond is originally purchased at a large premium or a large discount (scientific amortization factor).

2. Nonparallel yield shifts are more pronounced (e.g., 40 to 50BP changes rather than 5 to 10BP alterations); some sections of the yield curve experience more volatility in yield spread changes than the 7-to-10-year area of illustration. Corporate bonds and esoteric instruments are particularly susceptible to nonparallel yield shifts.

3. Longer maturity (e.g., 20-to-30-year) issues are involved. Recall that small basis point changes in yield can have sizable effects on long maturity bond returns.

CHAPTER 9
Yields Versus Returns

Chapter 3 analyzed the various yield measures used by bond market participants: current yield, yield to maturity, yield to call, yield to average life, cash flow yield, call-adjusted yield, and realized compound yield. Chapter 8 focused on the concept of total return. This chapter both compares and contrasts the notions of yield and total return by analyzing the yield-to-maturity and current yield concepts in the context of total return results. The dangers of relying on yield measures as proxies for a bond's total return prospects are clearly expounded through illustration.

Yield to maturity versus total return

The YTM concept: A recap

Recall that a bond's *yield to maturity* (YTM) is simply the discount rate that equates the present value of all of the bond's future cash flows with the bond's current market price:

$$\text{bond price} = \sum_{t=1}^{n} \frac{\text{CF}_t}{\left(1 + \dfrac{\text{YTM}}{2}\right)^t}$$

As such, the YTM is the internal rate of return (IRR) for the bond. By definition, the YTM is an alternative way of expressing the bond's price. For example, all other factors held equal, a bond with a higher yield sells at a lower price.[1] Conversely, an identical bond carrying a lower yield sells at a higher price. The YTM serves a useful purpose as a relative *price* indicator. Unfortunately, the YTM is often implemented as a relative *return* indicator, a most tenuous application.

The YTM as a total return estimate

Subject to certain restrictive assumptions, the YTM can fill the role as a total return proxy. These assumptions are, in turn, a function of the investment horizon:

1. Long-term investment horizon (buy and hold to maturity)
   a. All reinvestments are made at the YTM rate.
   b. For semiannual-pay bonds, an annual BP add-on is required to determine the equivalent annual return.[2]
2. Short-term investment horizon (bond is sold prior to maturity)
   a. The bond is sold at a price that reflects the same YTM rate as that on the date of purchase (i.e., interest rates are stable and the yield curve is perfectly flat).
   b. All reinvestments are made at the YTM rate.
   c. For semiannual-pay bonds, an annual BP add-on is required to determine the equivalent annual return.

The precarious nature of these assumptions is now discussed.

Observation: *The YTM measure is a reflection of a bond's price. Only under a series of restrictive assumptions can the YTM serve as a total return proxy for a bond.*

For the buy-and-hold investor (long-term horizon). The buy-and-hold investor purchases a bond as a long-term investment. The investor holds the bond until final maturity, at which time the bond is retired at par

---

[1] The terms *yield to maturity* and *yield* are used interchangeably in this book for the sake of brevity.

[2] For that matter, any bond bearing coupons more frequently than annually (e.g., monthly, quarterly, semiannually) will require a specific upward adjustment to arrive at an annual equivalent. The BP add-on is noted because total returns are generally reported in an annualized format.

value. The YTM rate is often perceived as the return that this type of conservative investor earns over the life span of the issue. Although it is true that the volatile price return component attributable to market yield fluctuations is eliminated under a hold-to-maturity assumption, there are two remaining considerations that can create a return on investment differing from the YTM-suggested result.[3] These two factors are described in turn.

Assumption 1: All reinvestments are made at the YTM rate.

Caveat to Assumption 1: In reality, each coupon cash flow is reinvested at the prevailing market yield on the date of cash receipt. Insofar as the actual reinvestment rates differ from the YTM rate, the total return earned by the investor varies from the YTM rate.

The buy-and-hold investor's greatest threat to future potential return is represented by *reinvestment risk*. Exhibit 9–1 shows the total returns on a 7% coupon, 30-year U.S. Treasury bond purchased at par and held to maturity. A variety of reinvestment rates are employed to illustrate the sensitivity of the bottom-line total return to alterations in the available return on reinvested coupons. As noted in Chapter 8, reinvestment return is the largest component of total return over long horizons. Therefore, the actual reinvestment rate realized is a critical determinant of the total return earned.[4]

For example, reinvesting at a 4% rate drags the total return down to only 5.43%, a 22% reduction from the 7.00% return projected by the YTM measure. Conversely, a 10% reinvestment rate leads to a 26% surge in total return to an 8.83% compounded rate. The buy-and-hold investor prefers a subsequently higher yield environment because it enhances reinvestment returns while leaving the price and coupon returns intact.[5]

---

[3] The market-sensitive component of price return is that portion of price return *not* attributable to the scientific amortization of the bond's premium or discount.

[4] In reality, each coupon cash flow will probably be reinvested at a different rate reflecting the market yield level at the time the cash flow is received. For simplicity, a single *average* reinvestment rate is utilized.

[5] The bond is redeemed at par value at maturity, and therefore the price return is not adversely affected by the higher yield surroundings. For callable bonds, higher yield environments reduce the potential for early call as well as provide incremental reinvestment returns. Purchasing a bond in a low yield environment and subsequently experiencing a surge in interest rates does, however, create an *opportunity loss*, a subject beyond the scope of this book.

Exhibit 9–1. Total returns of a 7% coupon, 30-year U.S. Treasury bond assuming a variety of reinvestment rates. The bond is initially priced at par to yield 7.00% and is held to maturity.

Bond's YTM (%)	Reinvestment Rate (%)	Total Return (%)
7.00	0	3.81
7.00	4	5.43
7.00	5	5.92
7.00	6	6.45
7.00	7	7.00
7.00	8	7.58
7.00	9	8.20
7.00	10	8.83
7.00	14	11.60

Comments: *In general, higher reinvestment rates lead to higher total returns. At reinvestment rates below the YTM rate, the total return ends up somewhat less than the YTM level. At reinvestments above the YTM rate, the total return registers a figure somewhat above the YTM level. At a reinvestment rate exactly equal to the YTM rate, the total return matches the YTM rate. The total returns are expressed as realized compound yields.*

The impact of reinvestment rate risk is dulled over shorter holding periods. Exhibit 9–2 calculates the total returns for 1-, 3-, 10-, and 30-year U.S. Treasury bonds bought and held to maturity. The same selection of reinvestment rates as in Exhibit 9–1 is illustrated. Exhibit 9–3 presents the data of Exhibit 9–2 in a *BP impact* format. A 1-year bond has a negligible amount of reinvestment risk. A 300BP change in reinvestment rate (from 7.00%) generates only a 5BP change in total return. In the case of a 3-year bond, this range expands to ±25BP in return while a 10-year issue sees a sizable 75 to 85BP fluctuation in return as reinvestment rates are jostled up and down 300BP from the initial 7.00% level. As illustrated earlier, the 30-year bond is subject to a dramatic shift in total return (160 to 180BP) under the same degree of reinvestment rate variability.

Reinvestment rate risk is particularly pronounced with high coupon bonds. Exhibit 9–4 illustrates that a 7% coupon U.S. Treasury bond and a 14% coupon U.S. Treasury bond generate different levels of return despite the fact that each bond is purchased at a price to yield 7.00%

Exhibit 9–2. Total returns of 7% coupon U.S. Treasury bonds assuming a variety of reinvestment rates and holding periods. Each bond is initially priced at par and matures at the end of the specified holding period.

Bond's YTM (%)	Reinvestment Rate (%)	Total Return (%) Over:			
		1 Year	3 Years	10 Years	30 Years
7.00	0	6.88	6.46	5.38	3.81
7.00	4	6.95	6.76	6.25	5.43
7.00	5	6.97	6.84	6.49	5.92
7.00	6	6.98	6.92	6.74	6.45
7.00	7	7.00	7.00	7.00	7.00
7.00	8	7.02	7.08	7.27	7.58
7.00	9	7.03	7.16	7.55	8.20
7.00	10	7.05	7.25	7.84	8.83
7.00	14	7.12	7.59	9.10	11.60

Comments: *In general, higher reinvestment rates lead to higher total returns. The longer the investment period, the more influential is the reinvestment rate employed. Thirty-year investment horizons tend to find the reinvestment rate, rather than the YTM, as the best predictor of the bond's total return. The total returns are expressed as realized compound yields.*

to maturity. If reinvestment rates (RR) fall below the YTM rate, the high coupon issue suffers to a greater degree. For example, a 4% RR forces a 5.30% compounded total return on the 14% coupon issue, 13BP below the 5.43% return realized by the 7% coupon issue under identical conditions. Higher-than-expected RRs benefit the higher coupon issue. For example, the 14% bond outperforms the 7% bond by 10BP if RRs rise to 10% (8.93% versus 8.83%).

Observation: *For the buy-and-hold investor, the horizon total return is subject to reinvestment rate risk. This risk is amplified by long investment horizons and high coupon securities. The realized return may differ substantially from that inferred by the YTM.*

Assumption 2: For semiannual-pay bonds, an annual BP add-on is required to determine the equivalent annual return. This conversion is necessary due to the reporting of total returns on an annualized basis. The amount of the BP add-on is directly related to the magnitude of total return figures. Exhibit 9–5 provides the BP add-ons for a variety of semiannually compounded return levels. The basic

Exhibit 9–3. BP impact of alternative reinvestment rates on the expected returns of U.S. Treasury bonds priced to yield 7.00% to maturity (data derived from Exhibit 9–2). The bonds are assumed to be held to maturity.

Reinvestment Rate (%)	*BP Impact on Total Return Over:*			
	1 Year	*3 Years*	*10 Years*	*30 Years*
0	−12	−54	−162	−319
4	− 5	−24	− 75	−157
5	− 3	−16	− 51	−108
6	− 2	− 8	− 26	− 55
7	0	0	0	0
8	+ 2	+ 8	+ 27	+ 58
9	+ 3	+16	+ 55	+120
10	+ 5	+25	+ 84	+183
14	+12	+59	+210	+460

Comments: *The table figures represent the basis point difference between the actual total return and the bond's YTM of 7.00%. Notice that when reinvestments are made at 7.00% (the YTM rate), there are no surprises. Higher/(lower) reinvestment rates lead to positive/(negative) impacts on total return. Reinvestment rate risk is directly related to the length of the holding period.*

formula for calculating the add-on is as follows (assuming semiannual compounding):

$$BP\ add\text{-}on = [(1 + semiannual\ return)^2$$
$$- [1 + (2 \times semiannual\ return)]] \times 10,000$$

For example, at a 10% yield level (i.e., 5% semiannually), a 25BP add-on applies[6]:

$$BP\ add\text{-}on = [(1 + 0.05)^2 - [1 + (2 \times 0.05)]] \times 10,000$$
$$= (1.1025 - 1.10) \times 10,000$$
$$= 0.0025 \times 10,000$$
$$= 25$$

---

[6] As in Chapter 8, the terms *reinvestment rate* and *reinvestment return* are used interchangeably.

Exhibit 9–4. Total returns on a 7% coupon U.S. Treasury bond and a 14% coupon U.S. Treasury bond under a variety of reinvestment rates. Each bond is initially priced to yield 7.00% to maturity and is held to maturity in 30 years.

Bond's YTM (%)	Reinvestment Rate (%)	Total Return (%) 7% Coupon Bond	Total Return (%) 14% Coupon Bond
7.00	0	3.81	3.43
7.00	4	5.43	5.30
7.00	5	5.92	5.84
7.00	6	6.45	6.40
7.00	7	7.00	7.00
7.00	8	7.58	7.62
7.00	9	8.20	8.26
7.00	10	8.83	8.93
7.00	14	11.60	11.77

Comments: *Higher reinvestment rates lead to higher total returns. This effect is particularly true for higher coupon bonds. The total returns are expressed as realized compound yields.*

The BP add-on simply reflects the reinvestment return earned on one coupon payment for 6 months at the designated yield level. At high interest rate levels, the BP add-ons can become significant. For example, at a 14% annual rate, the BP add-on is a sizable 49BP. Generally speaking,

Exhibit 9–5. Basis point (BP) add-ons necessary to translate semiannually compounded returns into annual returns. A variety of return environments are illustrated.

(1) Semiannually Compounded Return (%)	(2) Annual Return Equivalent (%)	(3) = (2) − (1) BP Add-On
4.00	4.04	+ 4
5.00	5.06	+ 6
6.00	6.09	+ 9
7.00	7.12	+12
8.00	8.16	+16
9.00	9.20	+20
10.00	10.25	+25
11.00	11.30	+30
12.00	12.36	+36
13.00	13.42	+42
14.00	14.49	+49

however, the BP add-on effect is relatively insensitive to modest changes in yield (e.g., 100BP). The reinvestment rate impacts are far more significant.

> **Observation:** *The BP add-on necessary to arrive at an annual return figure is easily estimable based on the current market yield level and is relatively insensitive to modest changes in yield.*

In sum, on a buy-and-hold basis, the YTM measure views the total return of a bond in the following manner:

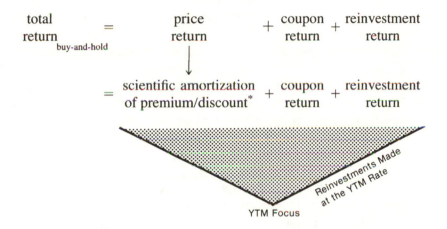

$$\text{total return}_{\text{buy-and-hold}} = \text{price return} + \text{coupon return} + \text{reinvestment return}$$

$$= \text{scientific amortization of premium/discount}^* + \text{coupon return} + \text{reinvestment return}$$

Reinvestments Made at the YTM Rate

YTM Focus

The YTM effectively encompasses all of the return components in a buy-and-hold scheme. The reinvestment rate assumption (RR = YTM) is subject to error, especially over long horizons. A modest BP add-on must be made to attain an annualized status.

For the active investor (short-term horizon). The active bond manager is concerned about short-term total return performance. This investor rarely holds a bond to maturity and therefore is subject to fluctuations in market yield and the related impacts on bond values. To this investor, the influence of price gains and losses is more pertinent than reinvestment return considerations. Under these circumstances, there are three assumptions that render the YTM measure faulty as a proxy for a bond's total return prospects. These assumptions are discussed in the same order as before.

---

*There is no price gain or loss attributable to yield change in a buy-and-hold framework.

Assumption 1: Interest rates are stable, and the bond is sold at a yield level exactly equal to the YTM on the date of purchase.

Caveat to Assumption 1: Over short-term investment horizons, interest rates can be quite volatile and the related price returns sizable in magnitude. Nonparallel yield curves can be responsible for additional unexpected price impacts. The resulting total returns may bear little resemblance to the YTM figure.

As illustrated for the buy-and-hold investor, a bond's return is sensitive to reinvestment rate fluctuations over long-term horizons. The same measure is ultrasensitive to yield (and price) fluctuations over short-term holding periods.

For example, Exhibit 9–6 computes 1-year total returns on a 7% coupon, 30-year U.S. Treasury bond across a variety of potential yield scenarios. The results clearly demonstrate that neither the beginning YTM nor ending YTM of the bond comes close to representing the bond's total return prospects. A negligible 10BP yield change leads to either a 5.90% return (if yields rise) or an 8.37% return (if yields decline), each figure sizably different from the bond's initial 7.00% YTM. A modest 100BP yield change creates a much wider range in return, from −4.08% (bearish case) to 20.78% (bullish case). The total return results bear little resemblance to the YTM figures cited.

The YTM requires a perfectly stable yield environment and a flat yield curve to serve a useful role as a total return indicator.[7] In today's world of volatile interest rates and an orientation toward short-term performance, the YTM fails miserably as a total return proxy.

Observation: *For the active investor, modest fluctuations in market yield levels create large swings in total return behavior. These unexpected price returns render the YTM measure a poor indicator of a bond's total return potential.*

[7] Reinvesting coupon cash flows in a similar, but progressively shorter maturity, bond of identical yield is a critical underlying assumption. A flat and stable yield curve satisfies this requirement. In actuality, however, a leftward-shifting yield curve may best describe the yield curve assumption underlying the YTM rate. In other words, every bond bears its original YTM (on purchase date) through time, which allows for the aforementioned reinvestments. For pedagogical purposes, however, a flat yield curve assumption is more easily understood. Additionally, in the spot and forward rate discussions of Chapter 12, the assumption of a flat yield curve is imperative in supporting the YTM rate.

Exhibit 9–6. One-year total returns on a 7% coupon, 30-year U.S. Treasury bond initially priced at par to yield 7.00% to maturity. A variety of interest rate scenarios are illustrated.

Initial YTM (%)	Yield Change (BP)	Ending YTM (%)	1-Year Total Return (%)
7.00	−300	4.00	58.31
7.00	−100	6.00	20.78
7.00	− 25	6.75	10.29
7.00	− 10	6.90	8.37
7.00	0	7.00	7.12
7.00	+ 10	7.10	5.90
7.00	+ 25	7.25	4.11
7.00	+100	8.00	− 4.08
7.00	+300	10.00	−21.08

Comments: *Reinvestments are made at the average of the beginning and ending yield levels (for simplicity, a 7.00% reinvestment rate is used for the 6.75 to 7.25% ending yield cases).*

Assumption 2: All reinvestments are made at the YTM rate.

Caveat to Assumption 2: The actual reinvestment rate(s) will probably differ from the YTM rate. Over short-term horizons, however, the impact of this variance is minor.[8] The price impacts associated with a change in market yield level far outweigh the reinvestment return implications.

The relative sensitivity of the price and reinvestment return components is a function of the length of the holding period. Short horizons tend to be severely affected by price changes but are relatively insensitive to reinvestment rate fluctuations. Conversely, long investment horizons display strong susceptibility to changes in reinvestment rates while exhibiting little concern over interim price volatility. Exhibits 9–7 and 9–8 isolate these unique differences by examining the return behavior of a 7% coupon, 30-year bond. Four alternative holding periods are presented, with price and reinvestment return sensitivities shown across a wide range of yield levels (4.00 to 10.00%).

---

[8] This is true if reinvestments are made in cash instruments. The illustrations in Appendix 8A show that reinvestments made back into the bond market, rather than the cash market, subject the active investor to return surprises.

Exhibit 9–7. Impact of changing yield levels on a 30-year U.S. Treasury bond's total return components over 1- and 3-year time horizons. The bond bears a 7% coupon and is initially priced at par to yield 7.00%.

Yield Change (BP)	Ending YTM (%)	BP Impact on TR Component Over			
		1 Year		3 Years	
		Price	Reinvestment	Price	Reinvestment
−300	4.00	5,122	−5	1,196	−12
−100	6.00	1,367	−2	357	− 4
− 50	6.50	649	−1	174	− 2
− 10	6.90	125	0	34	0
0	7.00	0	0	0	0
+ 10	7.10	− 122	0	− 34	0
+ 50	7.50	− 588	+1	−165	+ 2
+100	8.00	−1,121	+2	−321	+ 4
+300	10.00	−2,823	+5	−868	+12

Comments: *Reinvestments are made at the average of the beginning and ending yield levels. The total return impacts are the impacts on the realized compound yield of the bond. It is clear that changing yield levels have a dramatic impact on price returns, with no impact on coupon returns, and a very small impact on reinvestment returns (over short-term horizons of 1 to 3 years).*

To reiterate, short-term holding periods find price impacts substantial and reinvestment influences immaterial.[9] For example, a 50BP yield decline allows the price component to add 649 and 174BP to total return over 1- and 3-year horizons, respectively. The reinvestment return decreases by only 1 or 2BP under the same conditions (see Exhibit 9–7). Longer holding periods tend to nullify some of the price impact while aggravating the reinvestment rate influence. A 10-year period return, for example, is favorably affected by a 50BP decline in interest rates, with the price advance adding 29BP to the compound total return. The lower reinvestment rate subtracts 7BP from the compound total return (see Exhibit 9–8).

Over a 30-year horizon, the influence of a change in market yield levels is concentrated entirely on the reinvestment component of total return. A 50BP decline in rates portends a 14BP decrement in reinvestment return and hence in total return. The bond earns a 6.86% compounded

---

[9] Reinvestment rate impacts are immaterial *relative to* the price impacts. Recall from Appendix 8A, however, that 10-to-20 point fluctuations in the reinvestment rate can have a material influence on total return. Of course, the related percentage changes in price would also be sizable.

Exhibit 9–8. Impact of changing yield levels on a 30-year U.S. Treasury bond's total return components over 10- and 30-year time horizons. The bond bears a 7% coupon and is initially priced at par to yield 7.00%.

		BP Impact on TR Component Over			
		10 Years		*30 Years*	
Yield Change (BP)	*Ending YTM (%)*	*Price*	*Reinvestment*	*Price*	*Reinvestment*
−300	4.00	195	−39	0	−82
−100	6.00	59	−13	0	−28
− 50	6.50	29	− 7	0	−14
− 10	6.90	6	− 1	0	− 3
0	7.00	0	0	0	0
+ 10	7.10	− 6	+ 1	0	+ 3
+ 50	7.50	− 27	+ 7	0	+14
+100	8.00	− 53	+13	0	+29
+300	10.00	−143	+41	0	+89

Comments: *Reinvestments are made at the average of the beginning and ending yield levels. The total return impacts are the impacts on the realized compound yield of the bond. It is clear that changing yield levels have a modest impact on price returns over intermediate-term horizons (e.g., 10 years) and a small impact on reinvestment returns. Over long-term horizons (e.g., 30 years), changing yield levels have a minimal effect on price returns (and no impact on price returns if the bond is held to maturity) and a sizable influence on reinvestment returns.*

total return rather than a 7.00% return as a result of the lower reinvestment rate. The bond is retired at par, and therefore the ending market yield levels are ignored in the total return derivation.

Observation: *For the active investor, reinvestment rate risk is a minor problem since short-term horizon returns are impacted negligibly by changes in the reinvestment rate assumption.*

Assumption 3: For semiannual-pay bonds, an annual BP add-on is required to determine the equivalent annual return.

The nature of this add-on was discussed earlier in this chapter and requires no further elaboration. The modest impact is the same for the short-term investor as it is for the long-term investor.

In sum, for the active investor, the YTM measure views the total return prospects of a bond in the following way:

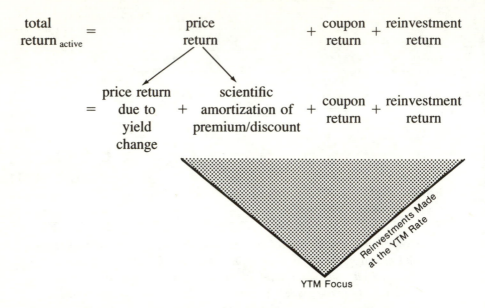

The YTM ignores the most important component of short-term total return: price gains/(losses) attributable to market yield fluctuations. In so doing, the YTM becomes a misleading proxy for a bond's short-term total return potential.

Other issues to consider in the YTM versus total return controversy

Higher yields and higher returns (long-term horizon). Higher yielding bonds are biased to outperform lower yielding bonds over long-term horizons. This phenomenon arises from the fact that a bond purchased at a higher yield provides a greater amount of future cash flows per dollar invested than a lower yielding issue.[10] As an illustration, Exhibit 9–9 compares the returns of a 7% coupon U.S. Treasury bond and a 14% coupon U.S. Treasury bond. The 7% issue is purchased at a price

---

[10] For bonds with identical coupon rates, the higher yield bond will sell at a lower price. For bonds with different coupon rates, the actual dollar prices paid are less indicative of the inherent values of the bonds than their YTMs. Otherwise, discount bonds would always be favored because of their low dollar prices. The return per dollar invested should be the focus of investors wishing to maximize their future wealth positions.

Exhibit 9–9. Total returns of (1) a 7% coupon U.S. Treasury bond priced to yield 7.00%, and (2) a 14% coupon U.S. Treasury bond priced to yield 7.50%. Each bond is held to maturity in 30 years and reinvestments are made at a 7.00% rate.

Yield to Maturity (%)			Total Return (%)	
7% Bond	*14% Bond*		*7% Bond*	*14% Bond*
7.00	7.50		7.00	7.19*

* If reinvestments are made at 7.50%, this figure is exactly 7.50%.

Comments: *Total returns expressed in terms of realized compound yields.*

to yield 7.00% to maturity; the 14% issue is priced at a 7.50% yield. If one can reinvest the coupons of the individual bonds at their respective YTM rates, the 14% coupon bond will outperform the 7% coupon bond by approximately 50BP in compound total return, 7.50% versus 7.00%.

In all likelihood, however, the coupons will be reinvested at the same rate (in this case, 7.00%). The high coupon bond creates a 19BP incremental annual return advantage over the low coupon issue, assuming a 7.00% RR. There is a lot of credence to the adage that *over the long run, it's hard to beat yield!* A yield differential reflects a relative price advantage that, if significant enough, instills a superior return potential in the higher yielding issue.

Observation: *Higher yielding bonds have a bias to outperform lower yielding bonds over long investment horizons.*[11] *The lower relative price paid and the commensurately greater level of future cash flows per dollar invested give the higher yielding vehicle a total return advantage.*

Higher yields and higher returns (short-term horizon). The positive relationship between higher yields and higher total returns over long-run investment periods is not as clear over short-run horizons. Market-induced changes in yield (and price) overwhelm the influence of an incremental yield advantage/disadvantage. Exhibit 9–10 analyzes two 30-year U.S. Treasury bonds initially priced to yield 7.00%. Under generally stable yield conditions, the yield spread between the two issues

[11] The focus here is on noncallable U.S. Treasury bonds. When credit/default risk and call risk are introduced, this assertion is not as easily generalized. Adjustments must be made for defaulted issues and for issues called away prior to maturity.

Exhibit 9–10. One-year total returns on a 7% coupon U.S. Treasury bond and a 14% coupon U.S. Treasury bond. Each bond bears a 30-year maturity and is initially priced to yield 7.00%. General yield levels are held stable, but the yield spread between the two bonds is altered to determine the effect of yield spread changes on relative performance.

Ending YTM (%)		*Yield Spread (BP)*		*1-Year Total Return (%)*	
7% Bond	*14% Bond*	*Initial*	*Ending*	*7% Bond*	*14% Bond*
7.00	6.75	0	−25	7.12	9.97
7.00	6.90	0	−10	7.12	8.25
7.00	7.00	0	0	7.12	7.12
7.00	7.10	0	+10	7.12	6.02
7.00	7.25	0	+25	7.12	4.40

Comments: *The yield spread is the difference between the yield of the 14% coupon bond and the yield of the 7% coupon bond. Changes in relative yields can create sizable divergences in return results.*

is varied from −25BP to +25BP over a 1-year investment horizon. The total return differences are sizable, despite the only modest alterations in yield spread. The starting yield levels of 7.00% on each bond suggest that the future total returns experienced by the two issues should be similar. In fact, however, the 1-year returns vary from each other by 100 to 300BP for yield spread changes of only 10 to 25BP. Once again, unexpected price returns dominate short-term performance results.

Exhibit 9–11 gives the 14% coupon issue a 50BP initial yield advantage. Under the same changes in yield spread, the 14% issue does exhibit a bias to outperform the 7% issue over a 1-year horizon. However, if the 14% coupon issue increases in yield relative to the lower coupon issue, the yield advantage is quickly and decisively overwhelmed by the disproportionate price suffrage of the 14% coupon issue. A small 10BP spread widening (to +60BP) reduces the high coupon bond's 1-year return to 6.57%, 55BP below the 7.12% return of the 7% coupon issue. A 25BP spread widening damages the 14% coupon bond to the extent that its return lags that of its counterpart by 212BP (5.00% versus 7.12%). It is clear that over short-term horizons, relative price impacts can offset relative yield advantages. If yield spreads remain stable, the higher yielding bond generates a 1-year excess return approximately equal to its yield advantage. Bond swaps and yield spread impacts are discussed at greater length in Chapter 14.

Exhibit 9–11. Short-term total returns on (1) a 7% coupon, 30-year U.S. Treasury bond initially priced to yield 7.00%, and (2) a 14% coupon, 30-year U.S. Treasury bond initially priced to yield 7.50%. General yield levels remain stable, but the yield of the 14% coupon issue changes over the period. Reinvestments are made at a 7.00% rate.

Ending YTM (%)		Ending Yield Spread (BP)	Total Return (%) Over:			
			1 Month		1 Year	
7% Bond	14% Bond		7% Bond	14% Bond	7% Bond	14% Bond
7.00	7.25	+25	0.59	3.42	7.12	10.39
7.00	7.40	+40	0.59	1.73	7.12	8.72
7.00	7.50	+50	0.59	0.62	7.12	7.63
7.00	7.60	+60	0.59	−0.46	7.12	6.57
7.00	7.75	+75	0.59	−2.05	7.12	5.00

> **Comments:** *The ending yield spread is the difference between the ending YTM on the 14% coupon bond and the ending YTM on the 7% coupon bond. A yield advantage creates an excess return bias for the higher yielding issue. However, an adverse yield spread change can quickly dissolve this inherently superior stance.*

> **Observation:** *Over short-term holding periods, the yield advantage of a given bond can easily be offset by adverse yield spread changes.*

Current yield versus total return

The current yield concept: A recap

Recall from Chapter 3 that a bond's *current yield* (CY) is its annual coupon return per dollar invested. The current yield is calculated as follows:

$$\text{current yield (percent)} = \left(\frac{\text{annual coupon cash flow (dollars)}}{\text{bond price (dollars)}} \right) \times 100$$

Since the annual coupon cash flow is fixed ($1,000.00 par × coupon rate), the bond's current yield varies inversely with the bond's price. As the bond's price rises, its current yield naturally falls since its coupon return is now a lesser amount per dollar of bond value. The opposite case is true for scenarios of declining bond prices. Stable bond prices portend stable current yields.

Observation: *Current yield is a measure of the coupon income generated by a bond.*

Current yield as a total return estimate

Does a higher current yield lead to a higher total return? Not necessarily. The current yield measure focuses solely on the coupon return component. Pictorially, one can view the current yield:total return relationship as

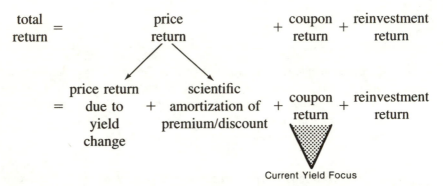

Current Yield Focus

This presentation explains why premium bonds appear attractive and discount bonds look unattractive from a current yield perspective. By ignoring the natural amortization of the bond's premium, the total return of a premium bond is overestimated by the CY measure. Conversely, scientific amortization adds principal value to a discount bond as its price converges with par at maturity. This inherent principal appreciation is completely disregarded in the CY computation. The scientific amortization process occurs hand in hand with coupon accrual, on a daily basis, and cannot be ignored.[12] It is therefore puzzling to find investors who fail to incorporate the equally certain effect of scientific amortization into their evaluation of a bond's short-term return potential.

Exhibit 9–12 provides a summary of the price, yield, and total return behavior of a 4% coupon, 10-year U.S. Treasury bond over its life span assuming that market yields remain stable at 7.00%. The bond is currently priced at $786.81. Its price gradually rises to par value ($1,000.00) at the end of 10 years. Consequently, the bond's CY falls over time, from its current level of 5.08% to 4.00% at maturity. Given a stable rate environment with reinvestments made at the YTM rate of

---

[12] The mechanics of scientific amortization are explained in greater detail in Chapter 10.

Exhibit 9–12. Price, yield, and return behavior of a 4% coupon, 10-year U.S. Treasury bond initially priced to yield 7.00% to maturity. Yields remain stable throughout the bond's life.

(1)	(2)	(3)	(4) = $40.00/(3)	(5)	(6) = (4) − (5)
				1-Year	
			Current	Total	CY versus
Time	YTM	Bond	Yield	Return	TR
Period	(%)	Price	(%)	(%)	(%)
Year 1	7.00	$ 786.81	5.08	7.12	−2.04
Year 2	7.00	802.15	4.99	7.12	−2.13
Year 3	7.00	818.59	4.89	7.12	−2.23
Year 4	7.00	836.19	4.78	7.12	−2.34
Year 5	7.00	855.05	4.68	7.12	−2.44
Year 6	7.00	875.25	4.57	7.12	−2.55
Year 7	7.00	896.89	4.46	7.12	−2.66
Year 8	7.00	920.07	4.35	7.12	−2.77
Year 9	7.00	944.90	4.23	7.12	−2.89
Year 10	7.00	971.50	4.12	7.12	−3.00
Maturity		1,000.00	4.00		

> **Comments:** *Bond prices are as of the beginning of the period and reflect scientific amortization of the discount. Reinvestments are made at a 7.00% rate. It is clear that current yield tends to understate the implicit total return bias of a discount bond.*

7.00%, the bond's YTM (7.00%) provides a good estimate of the bond's total return (7.12%). The CY measure, by ignoring the natural accretion of the bond's price, grossly underestimates the 1-year returns by 200 to 300BP (column 6).

Exhibit 9–13 analyzes the price, yield, and total return behavior of a 10% coupon, 10-year U.S. Treasury under identical circumstances. The premium bond is currently priced at $1,213.19. The bond progressively loses its $213.19 premium as maturity nears. Given the stable interest rate scenario, the bond's 7.00% YTM serves as a reasonably accurate indicator of the bond's annual return. By ignoring the natural price depreciation experienced by the premium issue, the bond's CY overestimates the bond's annual return by 100 to 260BP (column 6).

A final illustration of the misleading nature of the current yield measure is given in Exhibit 9–14. This table compares the YTMs, CYs, and 1-year total returns of three 2-year maturity U.S. Treasury bonds of varying coupon rate. The discount bond bears a 4% coupon and

Exhibit 9–13. Price, yield, and return behavior of a 10% coupon, 10-year U.S. Treasury bond initially priced to yield 7.00% to maturity. Yields remain stable throughout the bond's life.

(1)	*(2)*	*(3)*	*(4) = $100.00/(3)*	*(5)*	*(6) = (4) − (5)*
				1-Year	
			Current	*Total*	*CY versus*
Time	*YTM*	*Bond*	*Yield*	*Return*	*TR*
Period	*(%)*	*Price*	*(%)*	*(%)*	*(%)*
Year 1	7.00	$1,213.19	8.24	7.12	+1.12
Year 2	7.00	1,197.85	8.35	7.12	+1.23
Year 3	7.00	1,181.41	8.46	7.12	+1.34
Year 4	7.00	1,163.81	8.59	7.12	+1.47
Year 5	7.00	1,144.95	8.73	7.12	+1.61
Year 6	7.00	1,124.75	8.89	7.12	+1.77
Year 7	7.00	1,103.11	9.07	7.12	+1.95
Year 8	7.00	1,079.93	9.26	7.12	+2.14
Year 9	7.00	1,055.10	9.48	7.12	+2.36
Year 10	7.00	1,028.50	9.72	7.12	+2.60
Maturity		1,000.00	10.00		

Comments: *Bond prices are as of the beginning of the period and reflect scientific amortization of the discount. Reinvestments are made at a 7.00% rate. It is clear that current yield tends to overstate the implicit total return bias of a premium bond.*

Exhibit 9–14. Deceiving nature of current yield. Issues illustrated are 2-year maturity U.S. Treasury bonds with 4%, 7%, and 14% coupon rates, priced to yield 7.10%, 7.00%, and 6.90% to maturity, respectively. Assumes a stable interest rate environment with reinvestments made at a 7.00% rate.

Issue	*YTM (%)*	*Bond Price*	*Current Yield (%)*	*1-Year Total Return (%)*
4% coupon bond	7.10	$ 943.13	4.24	7.22
7% coupon bond	7.00	1,000.00	7.00	7.12
14% coupon bond	6.90	1,130.55	12.38	7.02

Comments: *On short maturity issues, current yield differentials tend to be far wider than YTM differences. Premium bonds sport excessively high current yields, and discount bonds carry paltry levels of current yield.*

yields 7.10% to maturity. The current-coupon bond carries a 7% coupon and is priced at par to yield 7.00%. The 14% coupon premium issue is priced to yield 6.90% to maturity. A stable interest rate environment is assumed for the 1-year holding period. As a result, the 1-year returns vary from 7.02 to 7.22%, a 20BP range similar to that separating the YTMs (6.90 to 7.10%). The current yields, however, vary wildly. The premium bond offers *538BP more CY* than the par bond but generates *10BP less return* than the par bond (7.02% versus 7.12%). The lowly discount bond, with *276 BP less CY* than the par bond (4.24% versus 7.00%) *outperforms* the par bond in total return terms (7.22% TR versus 7.12% TR).

Dissecting the total return of a bond reveals the bias of the current yield measure to concentrate on coupon return. For example, the 14% coupon bond of Exhibit 9–14 records a 1-year total return of 7.02%, categorized as follows:

$$\text{total return} = \underset{\diagdown}{\underset{\diagup}{\text{price return}}} + \text{coupon return} + \text{reinvestment return}$$

$$= \begin{array}{c}\text{price return}\\ \text{due to}\\ \text{yield change}\end{array} + \begin{array}{c}\text{scientific}\\ \text{amortization of}\\ \text{premium/}\\ \text{discount}\end{array} + \begin{array}{c}\text{coupon}\\ \text{return}\end{array} + \begin{array}{c}\text{reinvestment}\\ \text{return}\end{array}$$

$$\$79.39 = \underset{\text{(no yield change)}}{\$0.00} + (\$63.06) + \$140.00 + \$2.45$$

In percentage terms,

$$7.02\% = 0\% + (5.58\%) + 12.38\% + 0.22\%$$

Current Yield Focus

The current yield of 12.38% is derived solely from the $140.00 in coupon cash flows. The remaining influences on the bond's total return are of little concern to the current yield measure. The sizable 5.58% negative return contribution attributable to premium amortization is conveniently overlooked. Yields are assumed to remain stable in this particular example.

Over short-term investment horizons, a modest change in yield can significantly impact the total return of a bond, particularly a longer maturity issue. Longer investment periods find the reinvestment rate a critical variable. Neither of these factors is incorporated into the current yield calculation, rendering the measure faulty as an estimator of a bond's total return prospects. The shortfalls of the CY measure glaringly reveal the danger of focusing on any single component of total return in making an assessment of a bond's relative attractiveness.

Observation: *The current yield measure is a seriously questionable indicator of a bond's total return potential. By considering only one component of total return (i.e., coupon), the CY leaves sizable gaps in its predictive ability. A rigorous assessment of all of a bond's return components is necessary to arrive at a reasonable projection of the bond's expected future return.*

The abuse of the current yield measure is perhaps best demonstrated by the advertisements of bond mutual funds. Rather than relying on a YTM or historical total return figure, these funds have traditionally reported the current yield of the fund as the representative measure. The sizable decline in interest rates over the 1982–1986 period forced many bonds into a premium status. As noted in several examples, premium bonds tend to bear high current yields when, in fact, the YTMs and total return potentials are significantly lower. This gross overstatement of return potential is particularly concentrated in short maturity issues (e.g., 1-to-2-year maturity bonds). Naive investors may interpret a bond fund's CY as analogous to a bank CD yield or a money market investment fund's yield. While the latter provide a stable principal base on which interest is earned, the former suffers from principal loss as bond premiums quickly amortize away. The bottom-line dollar return the investor receives is less than an expectation predicated on the reported CY figure.

Summary

Yield measures tend to serve as inaccurate indicators of a bond's total return potential. This chapter discussed the two most popular yield proxies, *yield to maturity* and *current yield,* in the context of a bond's *total return* prospects. The YTM falls short as a total return indicator when, over long-term horizons, the actual reinvestment rate(s) differs from the yield-to-maturity rate and when, over short-term horizons, market yields fluctuate and/or the yield curve is positively or negatively sloped. In addition, an annual total return figure exceeds the semiannually compounded rate by a specified *BP add-on.*

The current yield measure is even less useful than the yield to maturity as a total return proxy. Current yield focuses solely on a bond's coupon return per dollar invested, ignoring (the important) total return impacts from market yield fluctuations, scientific amortization of bond premium/(discount), and reinvestment rate variations. Bond yield measures are not intended to act as total return mirrors.[13] Unfortunately, investors often misuse yield formulations by applying them as total return projections.

---

[13] Realized compound yield (RCY) is not a measure of a bond's yield (recall the Chapter 3 discussion). The RCY is a semiannually compounded expression of the total return experienced (or expected to be realized) by a bond. The RCY incorporates all of the factors affecting a bond's return into its derivation. The RCY is more appropriately termed the realized compound *return* of a bond. As such, the RCY is an excellent reflection of the total return potential offered by a bond.

CHAPTER 10

Gains, Losses, and Returns

Chapter 8 discussed the concept of total return and its component parts. Chapter 9 analyzed the similarities and differences between the total return concept and the most commonly used bond yield measures. This chapter looks at performance results from both a gain/(loss) perspective and a total return viewpoint. The misleading nature of gains and losses contrasts with the more accurate assessment of true performance as represented by the total return concept. The focal point of this chapter is the nontaxable investor, such as the typical private or public pension plan.[1]

Gains and losses

The book value concept

Gains and losses are predicated on the concept of book value:

Book value of an asset: The amortized cost, or cost basis, of the asset.

---

[1] Tax considerations can significantly alter the findings of this chapter. Book gains and losses can have a sizable impact on after-tax total return; the timing of asset sales becomes a critical issue.

Exhibit 10–1. Calculation of scientific amortization and book value for a discount bond over its 10-year life. The 4% coupon U.S. Treasury bond is purchased at a price of $786.81 to yield 7.00% to maturity.

Time Period	Book Value at Beginning of Period	Annual Amortization
Year 1	$ 786.81	$15.34
Year 2	802.15	16.44
Year 3	818.59	17.60
Year 4	836.19	18.86
Year 5	855.05	20.20
Year 6	875.25	21.64
Year 7	896.89	23.18
Year 8	920.07	24.83
Year 9	944.90	26.60
Year 10	971.50	28.50
Maturity	1,000.00	

Comments: *Book values represent the bond's price at a constant 7.00% yield to maturity. The annual amortization is the change in book value during the year.*

For a bond investment, the book value is calculated as follows. On the date of purchase, the book value equals the purchase price net of accrued interest.[2] At subsequent points in time, the book value is the purchase price as adjusted for scientific amortization of the bond's premium or discount.[3] For bonds purchased at par, the book value is always the par amount since there is no scientific amortization to record.

Exhibits 10–1 and 10–2 calculate the book values for a 10-year discount bond and a 10-year premium bond, respectively, across their life spans on an annual basis. The 4% coupon bond is purchased at $786.81. Its book value increases by $15 to $30 annually until, at final maturity in 10 years, the book value rests at $1,000.00 (par value). The 10% coupon bond costs $1,213.19 at a YTM of 7.00%. The book

---

[2] The accrued interest portion of a bond's full purchase price acts as an offset to the income recorded on the bond's first coupon payment date. For simplicity, the illustrations in this chapter utilize bonds purchased on issue date or coupon payment date, with no attendant accrued interest.

[3] Alternatively, the investor may use straight-line amortization rather than scientific amortization. This decision is generally predicated on tax considerations. The general concepts and illustrations presented in this chapter are not materially changed by a straight-line amortization assumption. The reader is encouraged to consult tax accounting texts for elaboration on the applications and impacts of straight-line amortization versus scientific, or effective interest, amortization.

Exhibit 10–2. Calculation of scientific amortization and book value for a premium bond over its 10-year life. The 10% coupon U.S. Treasury bond is purchased at a price of $1,213.19 to yield 7.00% to maturity.

Time Period	Book Value at Beginning of Period	Annual Amortization
Year 1	$1,213.19	−$15.34
Year 2	1,197.85	− 16.44
Year 3	1,181.41	− 17.60
Year 4	1,163.81	− 18.86
Year 5	1,144.95	− 20.20
Year 6	1,124.75	− 21.64
Year 7	1,103.11	− 23.18
Year 8	1,079.93	− 24.83
Year 9	1,055.10	− 26.60
Year 10	1,028.50	− 28.50
Maturity	1,000.00	

Comments: *Book values represent the bond's price at a constant 7.00% yield to maturity. The annual amortization is the change in book value during the year.*

value of this bond falls over time, as scientific amortization eats away the $213.19 premium at $15 to $30 annually. Similar to the discount bond, the premium bond sees its book value converge with its par value at final maturity.

Book gains and losses

A book gain or loss is based on the book value concept:

Book gain/(loss): An accounting gain/(loss) reflecting the change in book value during the year. Additionally, for an asset sold during the year, the book gain/(loss) includes the difference between the sale price of the asset and the book value of the asset on the date of sale [i.e., the *realized gain/(loss)*].[4]

Book gains arise from two sources: the amortization of a bond's discount and/or the sale of a bond at a price exceeding its book value as of the sale date.

---

[4] An *unrealized gain or loss* is calculated as the difference between an asset's current market value and the asset's current book value. A sale transaction translates an unrealized gain/(loss) into a realized gain/(loss) status and creates a potential tax consequence. Book gains/(losses) fail to take account of unrealized gains or losses.

As an illustration, Exhibit 10–1 computes the annual amortization on a 4% discount bond with 10 years remaining to maturity. In Year 1, the bond records a book gain of $15.34 as its book value increases from $786.81 to $802.15. In Year 2, the bond generates an additional $16.44 in book gains. Notice that the annual amortization is calculated with no reference to changes in market yield level. If interest rates fall over the first 2 years such that the 4% bond trades at a $900.00 value at the beginning of Year 3, and the bond is sold at that time, the book gain/(loss) for the third year is an $81.41 gain ($900.00 sale price − $818.59 book value on date of sale). Once a bond is sold, it is taken off the books, and future book gains/(losses) stem from the book value and amortization schedule of the newly purchased issue.

Book losses stem from the amortization of a bond's premium and the sale of a bond at a price below its current book value. As an example, Exhibit 10–2 presents the annual amortization on a 10% premium bond with a 10-year remaining life. In its first year, the bond incurs a book loss of $15.31 as its book value falls from $1,213.19 to $1,197.85. In Year 2, the bond creates an additional $16.44 in book losses as its premium erodes further. Once again, annual amortization is oblivious to market yield changes. If, however, the bond is sold at a price of $1,100.00 at the beginning of Year 3 (reflecting a rise in market yield levels), the bond incurs a book loss of $81.41 during Year 3 ($1,100.00 sale price − $1,181.41 book value on sale date). The replacement bond establishes a new cost basis and a new amortization schedule.

These two examples show that discount bonds create book gains over time, premium bonds generate book losses as time passes, and par bonds provide neither book gains nor book losses. If a bond is sold prior to final maturity, the bond is responsible for an additional book gain/(loss) depending upon whether market yield levels have risen (creating a book loss) or fallen (creating a book gain) since the date of original purchase. This incremental book gain/(loss) reflects only the difference between the sale price and the book value on the sale date, not the cumulative difference between the sale price and the original cost.

Total returns

The total return concept: A recap

Chapter 8 described the concept of total return in great detail. The total return on an asset can be defined as follows:

Total return: The increase or decrease in the total market value of an asset, including income receipts and accruals, over a specified period of time. The total return can be positive, negative, or zero.

For example, a bond is purchased for $1,000.00 at the beginning of the year. During the year, the bond generates $85.00 in income receipts, including reinvestment income. If the bond is valued at $1,065.00 at year-end, the bond is credited with a $150.00 total return for the year ($65.00 market value increase + $85.00 income receipts = $150.00 total return), or a 15% return on the $1,000.00 investment. An alternative definition of a bond's total return expresses the concept as a function of three components:

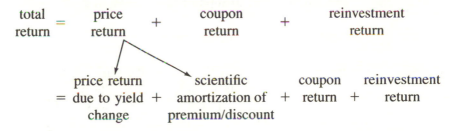

$$
\begin{aligned}
\text{total} \\ \text{return}
\end{aligned}
=
\begin{aligned}
\text{price} \\ \text{return}
\end{aligned}
+
\begin{aligned}
\text{coupon} \\ \text{return}
\end{aligned}
+
\begin{aligned}
\text{reinvestment} \\ \text{return}
\end{aligned}
$$

$$
=
\begin{aligned}
\text{price return} \\ \text{due to yield} \\ \text{change}
\end{aligned}
+
\begin{aligned}
\text{scientific} \\ \text{amortization of} \\ \text{premium/discount}
\end{aligned}
+
\begin{aligned}
\text{coupon} \\ \text{return}
\end{aligned}
+
\begin{aligned}
\text{reinvestment} \\ \text{return}
\end{aligned}
$$

Because these component returns have been discussed at length in earlier passages, they deserve no further elaboration.

Gains, losses, and total returns

Book gains and losses focus on only one component of a bond's total return until the bond is sold: scientific amortization. On the date of sale, a second component of return is incorporated into the book gain/(loss) calculation: price return due to yield change.

The total return concept incorporates all price returns (realized and unrealized) into its derivation, as well as coupon cash flows, reinvestment returns, and changes in the cost basis resulting from scientific amortization.[5] The narrow focus of book gain/(loss) renders it faulty as an indi-

[5] The *book values* reflect an *amortization rate based on an original YTM on purchase date* of 10.00%. The market values (stable yield environment) incorporate scientific amortization of the bonds' discounts for a YTM of 7.00% (i.e., the YTM at the beginning of the current year). Therefore, the higher yield (and lower price) basis for the book value computation generates more discount amortization than the current market yield level assumes. In general, *total return* computations implicitly include scientific *amortization at a rate utilizing the YTM rate at the beginning of the measurement period* (e.g., at the beginning of the year).

Exhibit 10–3. Issue data for Portfolio A as of 1/1/19X1. Each issue was originally purchased at a 10.00% YTM. The issues are currently trading at prices to yield 7.00% to maturity.

Par Amount Held (Thousands)	Issue Description	Maturity (Years)	Amortization Cost (Book Value) per Bond	Market Value per Bond
$1,000	U.S. Treasury 4% coupon	3	$847.73	$920.07
$1,000	U.S. Treasury 4% coupon	10	626.13	786.81
$1,000	U.S. Treasury 4% coupon	30	432.12	625.83

cator of the performance of a bond or a portfolio of bonds. The examples that follow serve to support this assertion.

Illustration 1: Stable interest rates

Perhaps the easiest way to observe the differentials between gain/(loss) and total return is in a stable interest rate environment using a buy-and-hold bond portfolio. Exhibit 10–3 lists the issue data for Portfolio A, a composite of three U.S. Treasury bonds trading at a discount. The 4% coupon bonds were originally purchased to yield 10.00%, a figure reflected in the January 1, 19X1 book values of $847.73, $626.13, and $432.12 for the 3-, 10-, and 30-year bonds, respectively. By the end of 19X1, their book values accrete toward par, particularly for the 3-year issue (see Exhibit 10–4). The December 31, 19X1 market values of the bonds also increase somewhat in a stable rate environment, albeit at a different rate of amortization (per Exhibit 10–4).

Exhibit 10–5 calculates the 19X1 book gain/(loss) and total return

Exhibit 10–4. Calculation of book values and market values for Portfolio A at 12/31/19X1 under two interest rate scenarios: (1) rates remain stable at 7.00%, and (2) rates rise to 9.00% (issue data in Exhibit 10–3).

Issue Description	Maturity (Years)	12/31/X1 Book Value per Bond	12/31/X1 Market Value per Bond Assuming:	
			YTM = 7.00%	YTM = 9.00%
U.S. Treasury 4% coupon	3	$893.62	$944.90	$910.31
U.S. Treasury 4% coupon	10	649.31	802.15	696.00
U.S. Treasury 4% coupon	30	435.41	629.70	487.69

Exhibit 10–5. Calculation of book gains/(losses) and total returns for Portfolio A for the year 19X1 under two interest rate scenarios: (1) rates remain stable at 7.00%, and (2) rates rise to 9.00% (supporting data in Exhibits 10–3 and 10–4).

| | | 19X1 Total Return Assuming: | |
| | | --- | --- |
Issue	*19X1 Book Gain/(Loss)*	*Rates Stable at 7.00%*	*Rates Rise to 9.00%*
3-year bond	$45,890	$ 65,510	$ 31,000
10-year bond	23,180	56,020	(49,960)
30-year bond	3,290	44,560	(97,320)
Total portfolio	$72,360	$166,090	$(116,280)

Comments: *Reinvestments made at 7.00% and 8.00%, respectively, under stable and rising interest rate scenarios.*

for Portfolio A, assuming yields remain stable.[6] Portfolio A registers a $72,360 book gain during 19X1, attributable to the scientific amortization of the component bonds' discounts. Portfolio A's total return for 19X1, however, is $166,090, substantially higher than the book gain recorded during the same year. The coupon and reinvestment components of total return account for the bulk of the $93,730 difference.[7]

A premium-coupon bond portfolio of similar structure behaves quite differently under equally stable conditions, when viewed from a book gain/(loss) perspective. Assume that at the end of 19X0, an investor sells Portfolio A to buy Portfolio B (issues listed in Exhibit 10–6). By moving up in coupon and up in dollar price, the investor owns a lesser par amount of the new securities. Assuming a stable interest rate environment during 19X1 (at 7.0%), the new portfolio incurs a sizable $58,541 book loss during 19X1 (see Exhibits 10–7 and 10–8).

The total return for 19X1, however, is identical to the $166,090 earned by the original portfolio (Portfolio A). This result reveals the danger of focusing on book gains/(losses) as an indicator of a bond's true performance. Premium bond portfolios have a natural tendency to generate book losses; however, their superior coupon and reinvestment returns can more than offset the price loss stemming from scientific amortization. In considering only one component of return, the book

[6] The rising yield environment data in Exhibits 10–4 and 10–5 are the subject of an upcoming illustration.

[7] Some of the variance is due to a difference in the rate of scientific amortization of the discounts (YTM = 10.00% for book gain purposes; YTM = 7.00% for total return purposes).

Exhibit 10–6. Issue data for Portfolio B as of 1/1/19X1. Each issue was originally purchased at a 7.00% YTM. The issues are currently trading at prices to yield 7.00% to maturity.

Par Amount Held (Thousands)	Issue Description	Maturity (Years)	Amortization Cost (Book Value) per Bond	Market Value per Bond
$775	U.S. Treasury 14% coupon	3	$1,186.50	$1,186.50
525	U.S. Treasury 14% coupon	10	1,497.43	1,497.43
335	U.S. Treasury 14% coupon	30	1,873.07	1,873.07

gain/(loss) measure understates the 19X1 performance of Portfolio B by $224,631 ($58,541 book loss versus $166,090 positive total return).

> **Observation:** *A stable interest rate environment portends differences between book gains/(losses) and total returns. Coupon and reinvestment returns contribute to a portfolio's total return, but have no impact on the portfolio's book gain/(loss) outcome. Holdings of discount bonds and premium bonds further widen the gain/(loss):return differential as amortization amounts diverge.*

Illustration 2: Unstable interest rates

Building on the data underlying the first illustration, the impact of a rising interest rate environment is incorporated in Exhibits 10–3 through 10–5 for Portfolio A and in Exhibits 10–6 through 10–8 for Portfolio B. Assume that, during 19X1, interest rates rise to the 9.00% level. The discount bond Portfolio A incurs a $116,280 negative return for 19X1 under these conditions (Exhibit 10–5). The premium bond

Exhibit 10–7. Calculation of book values and market values for Portfolio B at 12/31/19X1 under two interest rate scenarios: (1) rates remain stable at 7.00%, and (2) rates rise to 9.00% (issue data in Exhibit 10–6).

Issue Description	Maturity (Years)	12/31/X1 Book Value per Bond	12/31/X1 Market Value per Bond Assuming: YTM = 7.00%	YTM = 9.00%
U.S. Treasury 14% coupon	3	$1,128.56	$1,128.56	$1,089.69
U.S. Treasury 14% coupon	10	1,461.64	1,461.64	1,304.00
U.S. Treasury 14% coupon	30	1,864.02	1,864.02	1,512.31

Exhibit 10–8. Calculation of book gains/(losses) and total returns for Portfolio B for the year 19X1 under two interest rate scenarios: (1) rates remain stable at 7.00%, and (2) rates rise to 9.00% (supporting data in Exhibits 10–6 and 10–7).

| | | *19X1 Total Return Assuming:* | |
| | | | |
Issue	*19X1 Book Gain/(Loss)*	*Rates Stable at 7.00%*	*Rates Rise to 9.00%*
3-year bond	$(41,427)	$ 65,510	$ 35,700
10-year bond	(15,032)	56,020	(26,600)
30-year bond	(2,082)	44,560	(72,850)
Total portfolio	$(58,541)	$166,090	$(63,750)

Portfolio B suffers only a $63,750 loss for the year (Exhibit 10–8). The 19X1 book gains/(losses) of each portfolio are unaffected by the yield change since the bonds are held for the entire year. Consequently, the book gains/(losses) of $72,360 and ($58,541) substantially misrepresent the total return performances of ($116,280) and ($63,750) for Portfolios A and B, respectively.

Of particular interest is the fact that Portfolio A outperformed Portfolio B on a book basis by $130,901 ($72,360 book gain versus $58,541 book loss) while underperforming on a total return basis by $52,530 ($116,280 TR loss versus $63,750 TR loss). An investor should be more concerned with changes in wealth position than with book gains and losses. By effectively capturing all of the realities affecting a portfolio of securities, the total return result is more pertinent than an accounting-based outcome.

> **Observation:** *The price returns created in an unstable interest rate environment lead to sizable differences between book gains/(losses) and total returns.*

Illustration 3: Over an interest rate cycle

Exhibit 10–9 contains the issue data for a 3-bond portfolio (Portfolio C) as of January 1, 19X1. It is interesting to observe the behavior of this portfolio over a 3-year interest rate cycle. Assume that market yields are currently at 7.00%. During 19X1, yields rise to 8.00%. In 19X2, yields surge to 10.00% before falling back to 7.00% at the end of 19X3. Exhibit 10–10 calculates the book values and annual book gains/(losses)

Exhibit 10–9. Issue data for Portfolio C, which is established on 1/1/19X1. Each bond is priced to yield 7.00% to maturity.

Par Amount Held (Thousands)	*Issue Description*	*Maturity (Years)*	*Cost and Market Value per Bond on 1/1/19X1*
$1,000	U.S. Treasury 4% coupon	3	$ 920.07
$1,000	U.S. Treasury 7% coupon	10	1,000.00
$1,000	U.S. Treasury 10% coupon	30	1,374.17

for the portfolio over the 3-year period. Exhibit 10–11 provides a similar analysis based on market values and annual total returns. On a book basis, the 4% discount bond posts sizable gains year after year (Exhibit 10–10). The 10% premium bond incurs modest book losses each year, and the 7% coupon issue experiences neither book gains nor book losses. The portfolio as a whole records annual gains of $21,000 to $24,000 on a book basis.

From a total return perspective, however, a completely different picture arises. During 19X1, Portfolio C eeks out a positive return of only $8,160 (per Exhibit 10–11) as the rise in interest rates creates price depreciations that offset almost all of the coupon and reinvestment returns. The 2% surge in yields during 19X2 perpetrates a $101,705 loss on Portfolio C for the year. The sizable 300BP drop in rates during

Exhibit 10–10. Calculation of the book values and annual book gains/(losses) for Portfolio C. Each bond is originally purchased to yield 7.00% to maturity (issue data in Exhibit 10–9).

Issue	*Book Value per Bond at:*			
	1/1/19X1	*12/31/19X1*	*12/31/19X2*	*12/31/19X3*
4% bond	$ 920.07	$ 944.90	$ 971.50	$1,000.00
7% bond	1,000.00	1,000.00	1,000.00	1,000.00
10% bond	1,374.17	1,370.30	1,366.15	1,361.70

Issue	*Annual Book Gain/(Loss) During:*		
	19X1	*19X2*	*19X3*
4% bond	$24,830	$26,600	$28,500
7% bond	0	0	0
10% bond	(3,870)	(4,150)	(4,450)
Total portfolio	$20,960	$22,450	$24,050

Exhibit 10–11. Calculation of the market values and annual total returns for Portfolio C. Each bond is originally purchased to yield 7.00% to maturity (issue data in Exhibit 10–9).

	Market Value per Bond at:			
Issue	*1/1/19X1*	*12/31/19X1*	*12/31/19X2*	*12/31/19X3*
4% bond	$ 920.07	$ 927.40	$ 944.22	$1,000.00
7% bond	1,000.00	936.70	837.43	1,000.00
10% bond	1,374.17	1,224.30	1,000.00	1,361.70
	Annual Total Return During:			
Issue	*19X1*		*19X2*	*19X3*
4% bond	$ 48,120		$ 60,220	$105,205
7% bond	8,000		(29,835)	273,495
10% bond	(47,960)		(132,090)	553,835
Total portfolio	$ 8,160		$(101,705)	$932,535

Comments: *Market yield levels are 7.00% at the beginning of 19X1, rise to 8.00% by year-end 19X1, rise further to 10.00% by year-end 19X2, and fall to 7.00% by year-end 19X3.*

19X3, from 10.00% to 7.00%, is largely responsible for the stellar $932,535 total return posted by the portfolio. The significant price appreciations created by the yield decline are further enhanced by the steady flow of coupon and reinvestment returns.

Once again, the differentials between annual book gains/(losses) and total returns are vast. The surrounding market conditions should not be ignored when making a performance appraisal. Therefore, the total return measure provides a clearer assessment of the actual value added or taken away over a specified time frame.

Observation: *Over an interest rate cycle, a myriad of market influences affect a bond portfolio's total return results. These same factors are, for the most part, ignored by the book gain/(loss) measure.*

Book gains/(losses) versus reality: A final appraisal

Several generalizations can be made with regard to book gains and losses. Although an accounting and reporting reality, book gains and losses in themselves are not inherently *good* or *bad*. They must be considered in light of the total returns generated by the investment and the resulting net increase or decrease in the wealth position of the investor.

First, a high interest rate environment has a high propensity to create book losses on assets sold, as the original cost is undoubtedly based on a lower yield level (i.e., market value < book value). The same environment, however, blesses newly purchased bonds with a bias to generate future book gains either through capital appreciation as yields subsequently decline and bonds are sold (i.e., market value > book value) or through scientific amortization of the bond's discount over time.[8] The converse of the foregoing statements holds true in a low yield scenario.

Second, book gains and losses can be created through the actual sale of the asset. Amortization losses from premium bonds can be offset by the sale of bonds with a low-cost basis. The timing of asset sales can be used to manipulate the reported book gain/(loss) figure. Of course, the economic reality of the investor's wealth position is unaffected by such maneuvers.[9]

Third, propitious purchases of zero-coupon bonds can add significant returns, both on a book basis and a total return basis. A zero-coupon bond is the ultimate discount security, with no periodic coupon or reinvestment cash flows. The accretion of a zero-coupon bond's price is reflected daily, both on a book and a total return basis. Of course, yield fluctuations will affect only the total return results.

In sum, the focus of an investor should be on wealth enhancement rather than avoidance of book losses. Bond swaps that add to the investor's ending wealth position should be undertaken, regardless of the book gain or loss ramifications of the trade.

> **Observation:** *The total return prospects of an investment should prevail over gain and loss considerations. A holding-period return assesses the true change in an investor's wealth position.*

Summary

Gains and losses are not necessarily synonymous with positive and negative returns. *Gains and losses* are generally associated with *book values,* whereas *total returns* are intricately related to *market values.* Book gains

---

[8] High interest rate environments leave few bonds in a par or premium status. The majority of available bonds trade at a discount, with some at substantial discounts.

[9] The wealth position of a taxable investor is affected by the timing of asset sales, sometimes to a significant degree. Once again, however, the focus of this book remains on the nontaxable entity.

are fueled by deep discount bonds and low-cost bases; positive total returns are created by price, coupon, and reinvestment cash flows. The total return figure reports wealth enhancement. Gains and losses are more of an accounting phenomenon than a market reality, particularly with discount and premium bonds. Insofar as gains and losses focus on one or two of the components of total return, they are inadequate representations of a portfolio's true performance over a given period.

CHAPTER 11

Risk-Adjusted Return

Investments are assessed in two dimensions: risk and return. The *Fundamentals of Bond Risk* section of this book (Chapters 4–7) delineated the potential measures of bond risk. Chapters 8 through 10 discussed the various aspects of a bond's return, with the focus on the total return concept. This chapter concludes the *Fundamentals of Bond Return* section by considering an investment's return in light of the risk associated with the investment. A narrow focus on total return results fails to address the other critical element in the investment equation: risk. Enhancing return while controlling risk is the notion behind efficient portfolios, a major underlying theme of this chapter.

This chapter begins with a discourse on the rationale behind risk-adjusting returns. The risk-averse nature of investors is emphasized. The task of risk-adjusting returns is illustrated in three methodologies: capital market line analysis, security market line analysis, and risk : return quadrant analysis. This chapter includes commentary on the caveats in usage of these techniques. Its appendix outlines the use of security market line analysis in enhancing the total returns of a bond portfolio.

Exhibit 11–1. The risk-averse nature of investors dictates a positive relationship between risk and return. Riskier investments (e.g., stocks) must offer incremental returns in order to entice investors to purchase them.

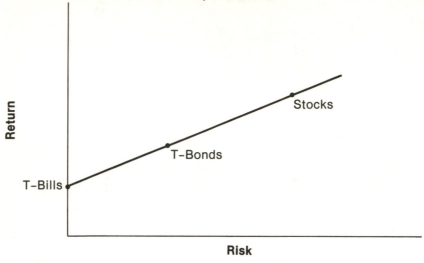

The basics of risk-adjusting returns

The rationale behind risk-adjusting returns

Investors can be classified according to their risk preferences. *Risk-averse investors* demand a higher rate of return as compensation for additional risk undertaken. *Risk-neutral investors* are indifferent with regard to investment risk, neither seeking it nor avoiding it. *Risk-seeking investors* enjoy risk and accept a lower rate of return in exchange for a higher level of investment risk. In general, investors behave in a risk-averse fashion and are willing to take on additional risk only if incremental returns are expected (see Exhibit 11–1). The degree of risk aversion varies across investors, with conservative investors feeling comfortable with only a modest degree of investment risk and aggressive investors able to deal with a high level of investment risk.

Consequently, over long-term investment periods, U.S. Treasury bills offer a low rate of return, U.S. Treasury bonds provide a modest rate of return, and common stocks generate a high rate of return.[1] As an illustration, for the 1920–1986 period, the Frank Russell Company

[1] See Siegel, Laurence B. and Katie B. Weigel, *Stocks, Bonds, Bills, and Inflation 1987 Yearbook: Market Results for 1926–1986* (Chicago, IL: Ibbotson Associates, 1987).

Exhibit 11-2. Historical risk premium evidence annual rates of return, 1920–1986 (Source: Frank Russell Company).

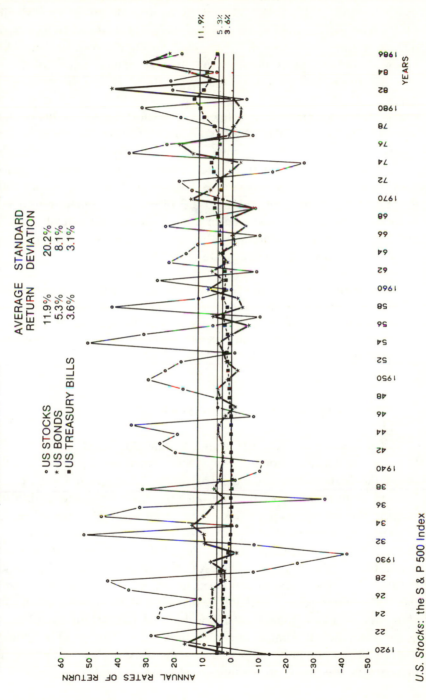

U.S. Stocks: the S & P 500 Index

U.S. Bonds: a composite index—the S & P High-Grade Corporate Bond Index (1920–1972); the Shearson Lehman Long–Term High Quality Government/Corporate Bond Index (1973–1986).

U.S. Treasury Bills: 3–month Treasury Certificates (1920–1931); 13–week U.S. Treasury Bills (1932–1986).

(FRC) plots the annual returns of these asset classes and calculates average annual returns and standard deviations in annual returns (see Exhibit 11–2). The FRC compilations confirm the traditional risk:return trade-off—over time, more return is obtained through investment in riskier assets. Common stocks provided an average annual return of 11.9% over the 1920–1986 period, with annual returns ranging from approximately −40.00 to 50.00%. Notice the sizable fluctuations in year-to-year performance on stock investments. The substantial volatility of stock returns is reflected in the 20.2% standard deviation in annual returns. United States bonds offered annual returns of only 5.3% (on average), but subjected the investor to a much lesser degree of return volatility than stocks (standard deviation = 8.1%). United States Treasury bills, the least risky investment, garnered a 3.6% average annual return with (a low) 3.1% standard deviation in annual returns. Graphically, the T-bill returns plot a relatively smooth line, bond returns show some ups and downs, and stock returns gyrate significantly.

> **Observation:** *Investors are risk-averse by nature. Riskier investments typically provide investors with incremental returns in order to induce investors to allocate funds to these more volatile alternatives. T-bills are a low-risk instrument and common stocks are a higher-risk investment. Bond investments offer a modest degree of risk.*

The concepts of efficient portfolios and an efficient frontier

The concept of risk aversion underlies the notions of efficient portfolios and the efficient frontier. An *efficient portfolio* is a portfolio that offers the highest level of expected return for a given level of risk. Viewed from another perspective, an efficient portfolio is a portfolio offering the lowest level of risk for a given level of expected return. Graphically, a series of efficient portfolios (one at each level of risk) forms the *efficient frontier* (see Exhibit 11–3). Investors, by their risk-averse nature, always prefer to invest in portfolios that lie on the efficient frontier. The risk:return tradeoffs on this frontier represent the optimal risk:return combinations available to investors. Risk:return combinations above the efficient frontier are infeasible and risk:return combinations below the efficient frontier are suboptimal or inefficient. The efficient portfolio concept can be addressed in a multi-asset class context or, for purposes of this book, in a single-asset class context (e.g., bonds). In

Exhibit 11–3. Bond portfolios, efficient bond portfolios, and the efficient frontier.

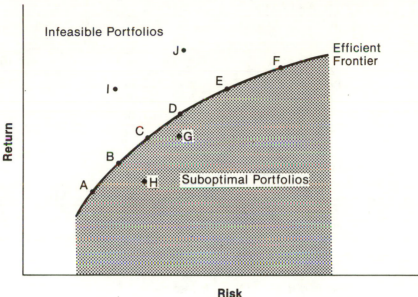

each instance, a maximization of return for a given level of risk is the underlying objective.

As an example, Exhibit 11–3 plots a hypothetical efficient frontier for bond portfolios. Portfolios A through F rest on the efficient frontier and are desirable investments. Portfolios G and H are suboptimal investments since they lie below the efficient frontier. For example, Portfolio C, which lies on the efficient frontier, is preferred over Portfolio H (less return, same risk) and Portfolio G (same return, more risk). Portfolios I and J represent infeasible risk:return combinations. The choice of an appropriate investment portfolio is a function of an investor's tolerance for risk. A conservative, low-risk investor may select Portfolio A or B (low risk:low return combination). An aggressive, long-term investor may choose Portfolio F since it is expected to offer superior returns. The high level of interim return volatility (i.e., risk) of Portfolio F is manageable to this investor.

Observation: *An efficient portfolio offers an investor the highest level of return for a given level of risk. Investors prefer efficient portfolios. The risk:return tradeoffs of these portfolios are the optimal combinations available in the marketplace. The efficient frontier is the sequence of*

Exhibit 11–4. Annual returns of two hypothetical bond portfolio managers over a recent 5-year period.

Year	*Annual Percentage Return for:*	
	Manager A	*Manager B*
1982	+25.70	+14.50
1983	−34.60	+17.40
1984	+62.10	+15.50
1985	− 4.80	+16.40
1986	+58.55	+11.30
5-year compounded annual return (1982–1986)	15.00	15.00

efficient portfolios arranged according to the degree of risk undertaken (low risk → high risk).

Risk and return in bond investments

A bond investment is subject to the same degree of scrutiny as alternative investments such as stocks, real estate, metals, and U.S. Treasury bills. Bond investors behave in a risk-averse fashion: they demand additional return for additional investment risk. As a hypothetical illustration, Exhibit 11−4 presents the annual returns for Bond Portfolio Managers A and B for the most recent 5-year period. Each manager provided a 15.00% compounded annual return over the 5-year period. Manager A experienced sizable fluctuations in annual return (−34.60 to 62.10%), whereas Manager B provided a consistent, stable stream of annual returns (11.30 to 17.40%).

Given an identical total return for the entire 5-year timespan (15.00% compounded annually), an investor prefers Manager B due to the lower-risk profile with which the returns were obtained. The higher-risk Manager A failed to provide the investor with incremental returns for the incremental risk undertaken. Investors are concerned about both risk *and* return. Unfortunately, too much emphasis is often placed on the bottom-line performance (i.e., return) with lack of appropriate consideration of the risk (i.e., volatility of return) undertaken to achieve the return.

Observation: *Bond investors consider both the risk and return attributes of a specific issue or portfolio of issues. For a given level of return,*

Exhibit 11–5. A capital market line for bond investments.

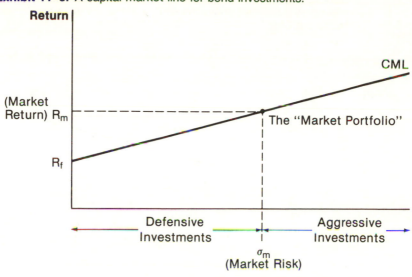

investors prefer a lower degree of risk. For a given level of risk, investors seek the highest level of return.

The techniques of risk-adjusting returns

Capital market line analysis

A *capital market line* (*CML*) plots risk: return combinations in a straight-line form (see Exhibit 11–5). The risk-free rate of return R_f (e.g., a T-bill rate) serves as the Y-intercept and the *market portfolio* (e.g., the Shearson Lehman Government/Corporate bond index) is shown at the coordinates (σ_m, R_m). The line connecting the two points is, by definition, the capital market line for the bond market. In an efficient market, all potential investments lie on the CML, with riskier investments located at points progressively to the right. For bond investments, issues or portfolios with less-than-market risk appear to the left of the market portfolio coordinates. Greater-than-market risk is found in issues or portfolios positioned on the CML to the right of the market portfolio coordinates.[2]

[2] One can plot individual issues, portfolios, or portfolio managers in risk: return space. The concept remains the same: identification of superior investments.

Exhibit 11–6. A capital market line for bond investments, with superior managers positioned above the CML and inferior managers positioned below the CML.

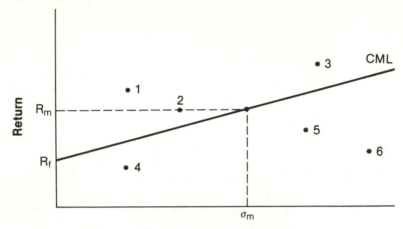

Standard Deviation of Return

In reality, the bond market is probably inefficient in nature. That is, superior investments can consistently outperform the return level suggested by the CML for a specified level of risk. Conversely, inferior investments fail to attain the returns inferred by the CML for a specified amount of risk undertaken. Exhibit 11–6 illustrates this phenomenon. Portfolio Managers #1, #2, and #3 provide greater-than-expected returns at their respective risk levels. Portfolio Managers #4, #5, and #6 generate less-than-expected returns for the risks they undertake. An investor can use CML analysis in two ways:

1. The CML highlights the investments (or managers) that are superior and inferior.

2. For a given level (or range) of risk, an investor seeks a manager who provides a superior level of return. If there are no superior managers in that risk range, the investor can purchase a market index portfolio to achieve the return indicated by the CML.[3]

> **Observation:** *Capital market line analysis attempts to identify superior investments by plotting market portfolio risk:return combinations on a straight line. Investments (or managers) lying above the CML are judged superior; those lying below the CML are judged inferior.*

---

[3] The amount of an investor's funds to be placed in the market index portfolio is a function of the risk posture desired (see the appendix to this chapter for more detail).

Exhibit 11–7. A security market line for bond investments.

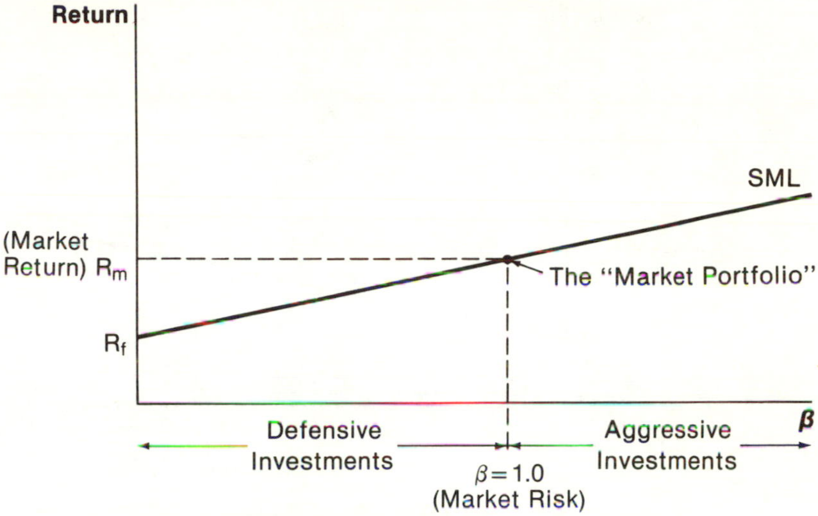

Security market line analysis

The concept of a bond beta was discussed in Chapter 7. A *security market line* (*SML*) is similar in concept to the capital market line just introduced. A security market line plots the risk:return tradeoffs in a straight-line form by using beta as the risk measure (see Exhibit 11–7). Recall that a beta is an expression of the covariance between security (or portfolio) return and market return. As such, a beta serves as an indicator of return variation relative to a market benchmark. Whereas the standard deviation of CML analysis is an *absolute* measure of risk, the beta of SML analysis is a *relative* measure of risk.

The identification of superior and inferior investments is identical to the approach used in CML analysis: investments plotted above the SML are judged superior and investments positioned below the SML are deemed inferior. Exhibit 11–8 presents this screening process in graphical form. Investments #14, #15, and #16 are superior relative to market expectations and investments #17, #18, and #19 are unattractive relative to market alternatives.

Observation: *Security market line analysis utilizes the beta concept as the measure of risk. Investments positioned above the SML are deemed superior; investments falling below the SML are judged inferior.*

Exhibit 11–8. Screening for superior and inferior investments using SML analysis.

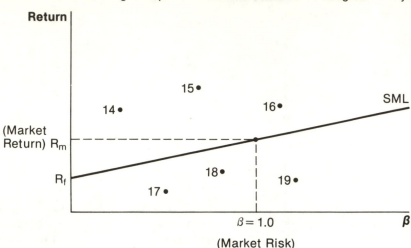

(Market Risk)

Comments: *Investments (or portfolios) positioned above the SML are deemed superior; those below the SML are judged inferior.*

CML and SML analyses: An application. Exhibit 11–9 summarizes the risk and return data for a series of hypothetical bond portfolios for the 10-year period January 1, 1977–December 31, 1986. For comparative purposes and for beta calculations, the market portfolio is the Shearson Lehman Government/Corporate (SLGC) bond index. In total return terms, Portfolio U records the highest returns at 17.50% on an annually com-

Exhibit 11–9. Compounded annual returns, standard deviations, and betas for a series of hypothetical portfolios over the 10-year period January 1, 1977–December 31, 1986.

Portfolio	*Compounded Annual Return (1977–1986) (%)*	*Standard Deviation in Annual Returns (%)*	*Portfolio Beta*
Q	7.00	3.00	0.45
R	9.50	12.40	1.30
S	10.40	4.50	1.00
T	12.80	9.30	0.80
U	17.50	12.00	2.00
SLGC index	10.41	9.32	1.00

Comments: *The market portfolio is the Shearson Lehman Government/Corporate (SLGC) bond index. The risk-free rate of return over the period was 9.30% as measured by the average 91-day U.S. Treasury bill rate (Source: Salomon Brothers Inc.).*

Exhibit 11–10. A capital market line for the U.S. domestic taxable fixed-income market over the 10-year period January 1, 1977–December 31, 1986. Bond Portfolios Q, R, S, T, and U are plotted in relation to the CML (data from Exhibit 11–9).

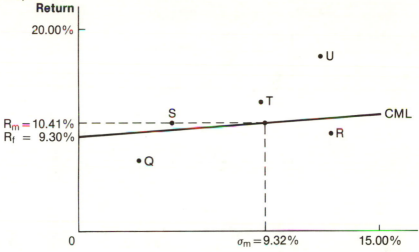

pounded basis. In risk terms, Portfolio Q is the least risky investment, with a standard deviation of only 3.00% and a portfolio beta of only 0.45.

On a risk-adjusted return basis, the risk:return combinations can be compared to a capital market line (Exhibit 11–10) or a security market line (Exhibit 11–11). The CML analysis highlights Portfolios S, T, and U as superior investments and suggests that Portfolios Q and R are inferior investments. The SML analysis finds Portfolios T and U attractive, Portfolio S neutral, and Portfolios Q and R inferior. The ultimate choice of an investment is a function of the investor's tolerance for risk. For example, Portfolio U looks attractive on both a total return basis and a risk-adjusted return basis; however, this portfolio's greater-than-market risk may be inappropriate for the conservative investor.

The caveats of CML and SML analyses. The usefulness of CML and SML analyses in assessing the risk:return combinations offered by various investments is subject to myriad assumptions. *First, the relationship between risk and return is linear.*[4] In reality, the risk:return tradeoff

[4] If the assumptions underlying the SML are met, an investor can create a linear risk: return tradeoff by using combinations of the risk-free asset and the market portfolio. Leveraged portfolios can be constructed by borrowing at the risk-free rate and investing in the market portfolio. These aggressive portfolios provide incremental returns in a linear fashion (i.e., points to the right of the market portfolio coordinates on a SML graph).

Exhibit 11–11. A security market line for the U.S. domestic taxable fixed-income market over the 10-year period January 1, 1977–December 31, 1986. Bond Portfolios Q, R, S, T, and U are plotted in relation to the SML (data from Exhibit 11–9).

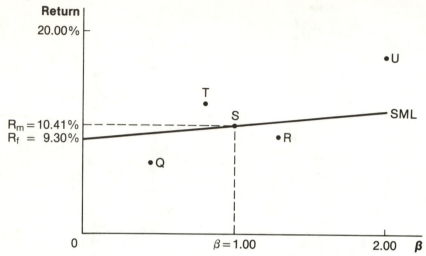

is probably nonlinear for bond investments. The dominance of coupon returns and reinvestment returns (recall Chapter 8) negates much of the ability of highly volatile instruments to substantially outperform their less-volatile counterparts, particularly over intermediate-to-long investment horizons.

Second, the risk-free rate of return R_f is well defined. Typically, a 91-day U.S. Treasury bill serves as the risk-free investment proxy. In reality, a variety of risk-free rates exist, depending upon the maturity and the liquidity of the instrument involved. *Third, the market portfolio is well defined.* In actuality, there is no universally accepted proxy for the bond market. The appropriate market portfolio (and related CML and SML) should reflect the risk preferences of the investor. Given the wide range of maturities available on bond investments, a series of market portfolios can be developed, each for a different point on the maturity/risk spectrum.

Fourth, the market portfolio is an efficient portfolio. In reality, the bond market may be inefficient in nature, and market proxies reflect the underlying component security behaviors. *Fifth, the market portfolio is very liquid and can easily be purchased on margin or shorted.* The

Exhibit 11–12. An SML for the bond market for 1980. The SLGC bond index serves as the market portfolio (data courtesy of Shearson Lehman Brothers); the average 91-day T-bill rate serves as the risk-free rate (data courtesy of Salomon Brothers Inc.).

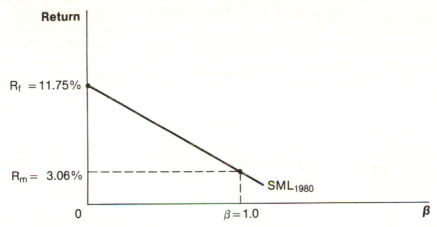

Comments: *Periods of rising interest rates, such as the year 1980, find the SML in a downward-sloping form.*

bond market lacks such features in its broad-based proxies. *Sixth, the investor can borrow at the risk-free rate of interest.* In actuality, a (higher) broker loan rate is probably more applicable. *Finally, the investor incurs no transaction costs.*

In addition to the more academically inclined caveats just presented, there are several practical limitations to CML and SML analyses. *First, the slopes of the CML and SML change over time.* Over short-term measurement periods, these lines are particularly volatile in both shape and level. During periods of rising interest rates, the CML and SML are negatively sloped (see Exhibit 11–12). Periods of falling interest rates find the CML and SML steeply upward-sloping (see Exhibit 11–13). As a result, a portfolio's risk:return coordinates relative to the CML or SML are subject to change. A superior portfolio in a bull market environment may assume an inferior stance in a bear market environment. The investment horizon of the client is critical in determining the appropriate historical period over which to review a specific portfolio's risk:return features relative to the CML or SML. A short-term oriented investor is concerned with periodic fluctuations in a portfolio's return relative to a market benchmark. A long-term oriented investor focuses

Exhibit 11–13. An SML for the bond market for 1986. The SLGC bond index serves as the market portfolio (data courtesy of Shearson Lehman Brothers); the average 91-day T-bill rate serves as the risk-free rate (data courtesy of Salomon Brothers Inc.).

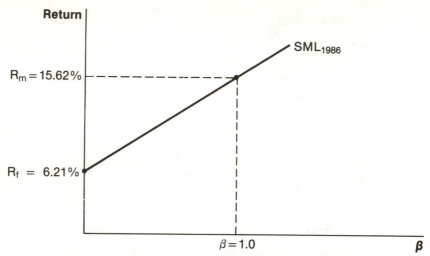

Comments: *Periods of falling interest rates, such as the year 1986, find the SML in an upward-sloping form.*

on a full market cycle (or longer) approach to finding superior risk: return combinations.

Second, a portfolio manager may change the management style of a given portfolio as time passes. Consequently, the historical behavior of the fund relative to the CML or SML may not be representative of the recent or of the future risk:return practices of the fund. A careful assessment of management style is a prerequisite to prudent investment selection. *Third, a reasonably long performance record (e.g., 10 years) is a prerequisite to an adequate assessment of the risk:return behavior of a particular fund.* Unfortunately, many managers in the fixed-income arena lack a track record of more than a few years. *Fourth, total return measures and, therefore, standard deviations and betas, are subject to inaccuracy.* The lack of an organized bond exchange and commonly agreed-upon security prices leads to error terms in periodic returns that should not be glossed over casually. Consistent performance measurement between the market portfolio and individual portfolios does not currently exist.

Fifth, the risk measures of CML and SML analyses (standard devia-

tion, beta) are inadequate. These measures fail to fully account for risks such as liquidity risk, credit risk, and call/prepayment risk. A portfolio that is less than fully diversified may run a disproportionately high exposure to these risks. In addition, risk postures change over time as a result of repositionings of portfolio holdings, gradual shifts in the composition of the market portfolio, alterations in management style, and shifts in the general level of interest rates.

Finally, there are management fees and incremental transaction costs associated with various bond investments and bond portfolio managers. These differential costs may or may not be reflected in the total return figures tallied.[5] In general, a bond index fund which replicates the market portfolio can be administered at a low management fee and with minimal transaction costs. Adjustments should be made to the reported return figures of active bond managers for any significant fee differentials.

> **Observation:** *CML and SML analyses are subject to a series of assumptions that warrant caution in the application of these techniques. Assumptions regarding linearity, a well-defined risk-free rate of return, an efficient bond market, and a liquid and well-defined market portfolio lead to tenuous results. Practicalities of shifting CMLs and SMLs, management style changes, inadequate performance records, faulty risk and return measures, management fees, and transaction costs muddy the interpretation of the data as well.*

Risk:return quadrant analysis

The methodology of risk:return quadrant analysis. A composite review of risk:return pairings can be accomplished through the use of *risk:return quadrants*. Quadrant analysis entails plotting the risk:return coordinates for a series of potential investments on a graph similar to those presented earlier in this chapter under the CML and SML analyses. Total return is plotted vertically and risk (e.g., standard deviation, beta) is plotted horizontally.

Exhibit 11–14 portrays a typical quadrant analysis. The graph is sliced into four quadrants: superior portfolios (Quadrant I: upper left),

---

[5] Typically, transaction costs are incorporated in the total return performance number. Management fees, however, are not usually deducted to arrive at the total return figure. Consequently, to allow for comparability of results, an adjustment should be made for the specific management fees incurred. For a typical pension account ($50 million), management fees average 30–40BP for active bond managers and 10BP for bond index fund managers.

Exhibit 11–14. A typical presentation of the four risk:return quadrants—superior, aggressive, inferior, and defensive portfolios.

Total Return	Quadrant I: Superior Portfolios (low risk, high return)	Quadrant II: Aggressive Portfolios (high risk, high return)
Median Total Return	Quadrant IV: Defensive Portfolios (low risk, low return)	Quadrant III: Inferior Portfolios (high risk, low return)
	Median Risk	**Risk (SD, Beta)**

aggressive portfolios (Quadrant II: upper right), inferior portfolios (Quadrant III: lower right), and defensive portfolios (Quadrant IV: lower left). The quadrants are dictated by the median return (horizontal line) and the median risk (vertical line) of the universe of portfolios under scrutiny.

Superior portfolios offer the investor a combination of low risk and high return. Given the risk-averse nature of investors, these portfolios are the most attractive candidates for purchase. *Aggressive portfolios* provide the investor with a high level of return but at a high level of risk. *Inferior portfolios* are the least desired by investors since they offer a low rate of return and a high degree of risk. Finally, *defensive portfolios* are conservative in style and subject the investor to a low level of risk while providing a low rate of return.

Exhibit 11–15 presents a risk:return quadrant analysis used by the Frank Russell Company. A universe of 134 fixed-income accounts is plotted in risk:return space, with the median return and the median risk forming the cross hairs within the graph. Four accounts are highlighted (data per Exhibit 11–16). *Account A* is a superior portfolio, achieving a higher-than-average return (10.5%) at a much lower-than-average level of risk (6.9%) over the 10-year period. *Account B* is an aggressive portfolio with a higher-than-average return (10.6%) and a higher-than-average risk posture (12.5%). *Account C* is an inferior portfolio, providing a lower-than-average return (8.7%) and a higher-than-average risk (11.6%). *Account D* is a defensive portfolio with lower-than-average return (8.6%) and lower-than-average risk (6.9%). The portfolios in the upper-left

Exhibit 11–15. A risk:return quadrant analysis using 134 portfolios from the Frank Russell Company universe of fixed-income accounts for the 10-year period ending June 30, 1987. For comparative purposes, the Shearson Lehman Government/Corporate index (SHLM G/C) is plotted on the graph (courtesy of the Frank Russell Company).

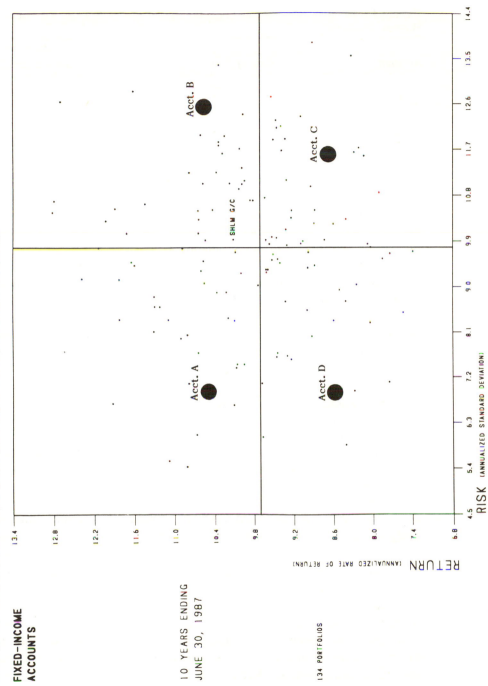

FIXED–INCOME
ACCOUNTS

10 YEARS ENDING
JUNE 30, 1987

134 PORTFOLIOS

Risk:return quadrant analysis plots the risk:return coordinates of a selected universe of investments or portfolios and calculates median return and median risk levels. The resulting graph is divided into four sections or quadrants. These quadrants contain superior portfolios (low risk, high return), aggressive portfolios (high risk, high return), inferior portfolios (high risk, low return), and defensive portfolios (low risk, low return). Reflecting their risk-averse nature, investors seek portfolios of the superior type (Quadrant I). Subject to some limitations, risk: return quadrant analysis is an attractive method of screening for superior portfolios and/or portfolio managers.

CHAPTER 11 APPENDIX

Security Market Line Analysis and Enhancing Total Returns

The security market line as an efficient frontier

Chapter 11 discussed the basics of security market line (SML) analysis. This appendix describes more of the intricacies of SML analysis and applies them in a total return enhancement framework. Recall that a SML plots the risk:return tradeoffs available in the marketplace across a variety of potential risk preferences (recall Exhibit 11–7). The SML and the efficient frontier of potential investments are closely related. The efficient frontier plots the curve that represents the set of efficient portfolios encompassing the risk spectrum (recall Exhibit 11–3). By definition, the market portfolio is an efficient portfolio and, as such, rests on the efficient frontier at the risk level for the market ($\beta = 1.00$). The SML is the line tangent to the efficient frontier curve at that point (see Exhibit 11A–1). The SML appears to be an infeasible set of portfolios

Exhibit 11A–1. The SML and the efficient frontier.

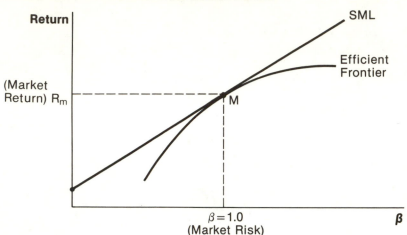

Comments: *The security market line (SML) dominates the efficient frontier and represents an even more efficient set of portfolios.*

since it lies above the efficient frontier curve, except at the point representing the market portfolio (Point M) which is attainable. However, when the assumptions underlying the SML are met, the SML becomes the efficient frontier since it dominates the old curvature as shown in Exhibit 11A–1. The necessary assumptions underlying the SML are summarized as follows.

1. The risk-free rate (R_f) equals the Y-intercept for the line drawn tangent to the efficient frontier at the point representing the market portfolio's risk:return coordinates.
2. The bond market is an efficient market.
3. The market portfolio is well defined and is an efficient portfolio.
4. The market portfolio is highly liquid and is easily purchased on margin or sold short.
5. The investor can borrow at the risk-free rate.
6. There are no transaction costs.

Consequently, the SML is a straight-line expression of a risk:return relationship that is both desirable and attainable. Investors prefer a combi-

Exhibit 11A–2. Defensive, neutral, and aggressive portfolios in a SML framework.

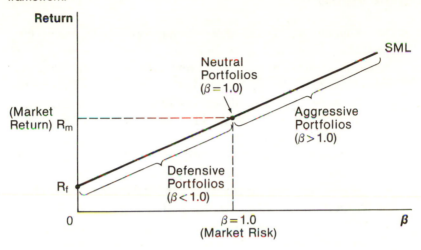

Comments: *Defensive portfolios have betas of less than 1.0; aggressive portfolios have betas in excess of 1.0. A neutral portfolio bears market risk and carries a beta of 1.0.*

nation of the risk-free asset and the market portfolio that satisfies their risk preference:

Risk Preference	Portfolio Beta	Optimal Portfolio
Less-than-market risk (defensive portfolios)	β < 1.00	<100% invested in the market portfolio; the balance is invested in the risk-free asset (a long position in cash)
Market risk (neutral portfolios)	β = 1.00	100% invested in the market portfolio
Greater-than-market risk (aggressive portfolios)	β > 1.00	>100% invested in the market portfolio; the balance is borrowed at the risk-free rate (a short position in cash)

Exhibit 11A–2 illustrates the concepts of defensive, neutral, and aggressive portfolios in a graphical context. Seeking the highest attainable level of return at a given level of risk, investors always choose to invest in a combination of the market portfolio and the risk-free asset.

Active strategies to enhance returns
using SML analysis

In an inefficient market, active bond portfolio managers can enhance portfolio returns in two primary ways: (1) by concentrating portfolio holdings in inefficiently priced, undervalued securities/sectors, and (2) by propitiously altering the market risk exposure of the portfolio. The former strategy of careful security/sector selection creates an upward shift in the SML (see Exhibit 11A–3). This excess return is commonly called *alpha* (α) and represents the incremental layer of return on top of the market-dictated SML return. In an efficient market, alpha returns are unobtainable.

The second strategy involves altering the *beta* (i.e., market exposure) of the portfolio at advantageous points in time. Recall that the SML shifts in both level and slope as bear market periods and bull market periods come and go. As noted in the chapter, bear markets portend downward-sloping SMLs and bull markets create upward-sloping SMLs. If a portfolio manager can successfully forecast the direction of future interest rates and, therefore, the shape of the SML, the manager can position the portfolio to take advantage of the expected shifts. In anticipation of rising interest rates (i.e., a bear market period), the manager reduces market exposure and secures a high return position on the leftward

Exhibit 11A–3. Adding alpha to portfolio returns.

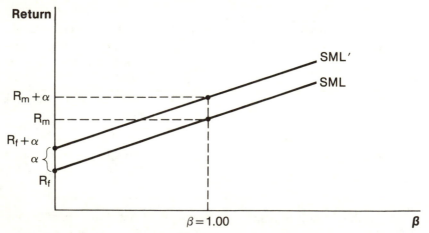

Comments: *In an inefficient market, an investor can generate excess returns by adept selection of undervalued securities or sectors. An upward shift in the SML (to SML') results.*

Exhibit 11A–4. Changing beta (i.e., market risk exposure) to enhance portfolio returns.

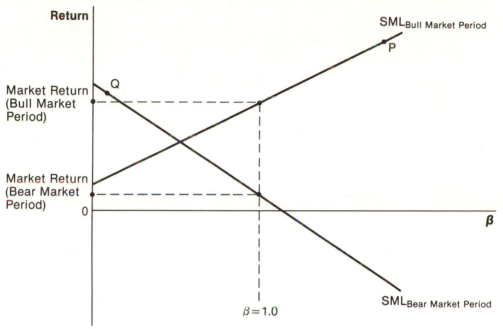

Comments: *Investors who are successful at interest rate forecasting maintain a high level of market risk exposure in bull market periods (Point P) and a low level of market risk exposure in bear market periods (Point Q). Over short-term periods, the shifting shape and level of the SML allows astute investors to enhance portfolio returns in this manner.*

portion of the downward-sloping SML. Conversely, a period of falling interest rates (i.e., a bull market period) warrants a high level of exposure to the market and a high return position on the rightward portion of the upward-sloping SML. Exhibit 11A–4 summarizes the objectives of this strategy in a graphical context. Unfortunately, *beta-changers* or *market-timers* have not proved to be terribly successful at their craft. Forecasting future interest rates is a very tenuous and frustrating exercise.

Observation: *Using SML analysis, investors can enhance total returns by (1) moving to a higher efficient frontier (i.e., the SML); (2) creating a higher SML through adept security and sector selection; and (3) propitiously anticipating the future moves in interest rates and changing the market exposure of the portfolio to benefit from such shifts (altering the portfolio's position on the SML).*

APPLICATIONS
OF THE FUNDAMENTALS

CHAPTER 12

Yield Curve Analysis

The final section of this text focuses on applications of the fundamentals presented in Chapters 1 through 11. The fundamentals provide the building blocks for the analysis of yield curves (Chapter 12), the development of total return curves (Chapter 13), the evaluation of bond swaps (Chapter 14), and the assessment of portfolio risk and return (Chapter 15).

The yield curve

The yield curve concept

The *term structure of interest rates* or, the *yield curve,* depicts the yields to maturity of a series of bonds versus their respective terms to maturity. The U.S. Treasury yield curve is a graphical presentation of the yields of U.S. Treasury bonds across a broad spectrum of maturities. Exhibit 12–1 plots the U.S. Treasury yield curve as of June 30, 1987. The issues used in creating a yield curve should differ only with respect to the term to maturity. The liquidity risk, credit risk, call risk, and degree of premium/discount should be reasonably equivalent between

Exhibit 12–1. U.S. Treasury yield curve as of June 30, 1987.

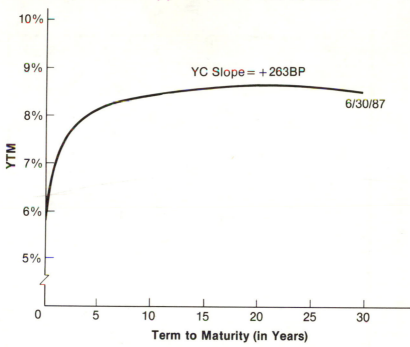

the issues in order for an effective yield comparison to be made.[1] The yield curve serves as a crude representation of the risk:return tradeoff of bond investment alternatives.[2]

To provide a historical perspective of the path of interest rates, Exhibit 12–2 shows the yield level of the 10-year U.S. Treasury bond since 1950. Exhibits 12–3 through 12–9 provide a sampling of the levels and shapes of the U.S. Treasury yield curve over the past four decades. Exhibit 12–10 shows the yield level of the Ryan Treasury Index during the 1980s (January 1, 1980–June 30, 1987). The Ryan Treasury Index is an equally-weighted composite of the current auction U.S. Treasuries in the 2- to 30-year maturity range. The 1980s have proved to be a

---

[1] Consequently, distinctly different yield curves should be drawn for liquid versus illiquid issues, high grade (e.g., U.S. Treasuries, AAA-rated corporates) versus low grade bonds (e.g., BBB-rated corporates), high coupon versus low coupon bonds, and callable versus noncallable issues.

[2] Recall Chapter 5's discussion of the limitations of term to maturity as an adequate risk measure and Chapter 9's exposition on the drawbacks of yield as a total return proxy.

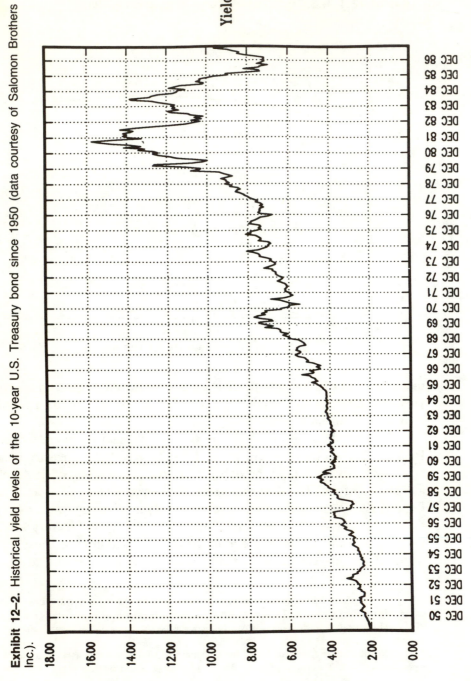

Exhibit 12–2. Historical yield levels of the 10-year U.S. Treasury bond since 1950 (data courtesy of Salomon Brothers Inc.).

Exhibit 12–3. U.S. Treasury yield curve as of June 15, 1950 (data courtesy of Salomon Brothers Inc.).

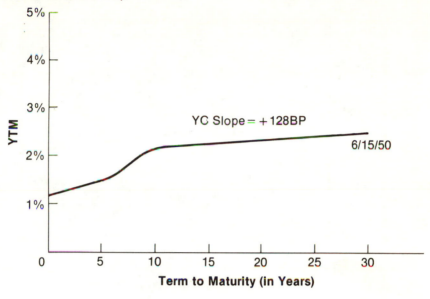

Exhibit 12–4. U.S. Treasury yield curve as of June 30, 1960 (data courtesy of Salomon Brothers Inc.).

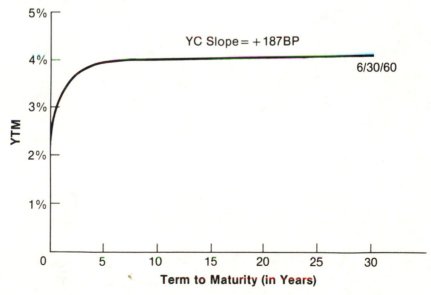

Exhibit 12–5. U.S. Treasury yield curve as of June 30, 1970 (data courtesy of Salomon Brothers Inc.).

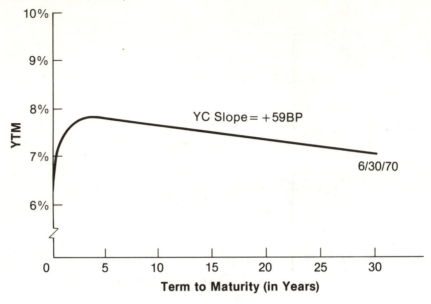

Exhibit 12–6. U.S. Treasury yield curve as of March 31, 1980 (data courtesy of Salomon Brothers Inc.).

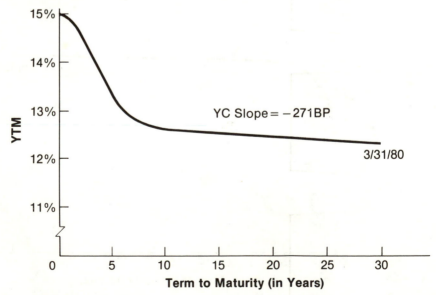

Exhibit 12–7. U.S. Treasury yield curve as of May 31, 1980 (data courtesy of Salomon Brothers Inc.).

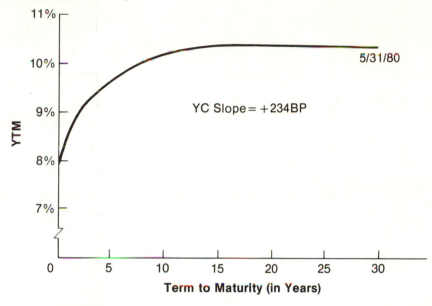

Exhibit 12–8. U.S. Treasury yield curve as of August 31, 1981 (data courtesy of Salomon Brothers Inc.).

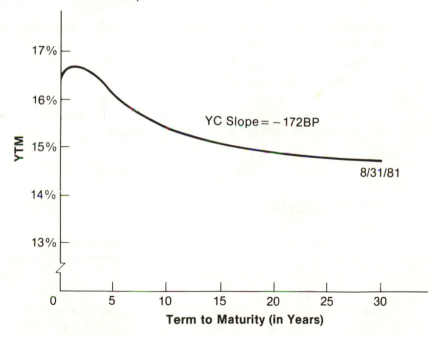

Exhibit 12–9. U.S. Treasury yield curve as of December 31, 1986.

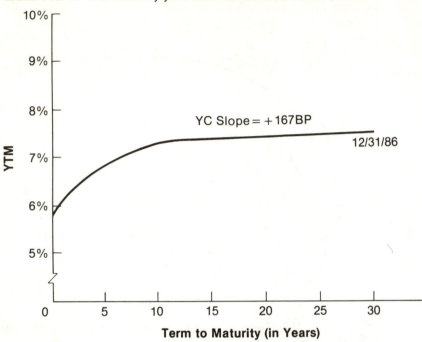

violent historical period for financial instruments, with long-term U.S. Treasuries ranging from 16% levels in 1981 to 7% levels in 1986. Currently (as of June 30, 1987), long-term yields are parked in the lower end of that range, at approximately an 8.50% level.

> **Observation:** *A yield curve plots the yields to maturity of a series of bonds against their respective terms to maturity.*

Determinants of the absolute level of the yield curve

A *nominal interest rate* can be dissected into three basic components:

$$\text{nominal interest rate} = \text{real interest rate} + \text{inflation premium} + \text{risk premium}$$

The *real interest rate* is the compensation to the investor for deferring consumption to a future period. Even if inflation is stable at 0%, a riskless investment such as a U.S. Treasury bill must offer a positive

Exhibit 12–10. The historical yield level of the Ryan Treasury Index over the January 1, 1980–June 30, 1987 period (Source: Ryan Financial Strategy Group).

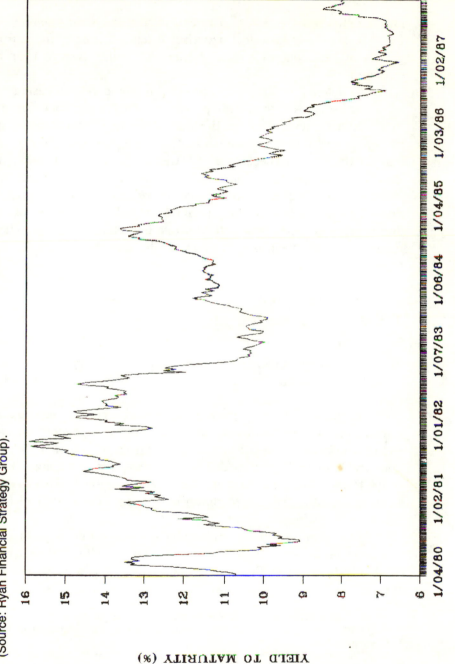

rate of return to an investor.[3] The real interest rate component averages 2 to 3% over long historical periods.[4] It tends to mimic the real GNP growth in the economy, which exhibits a similar average over long-term horizons.

The *inflation premium* is intended to preserve the purchasing power of the investor over time. This premium reflects an expectation of the future inflation level over the lifespan of the investment. Expectations of higher levels of future inflation lead to higher interest rate levels today. Conversely, expectations of lower levels of future inflation allow for lower nominal interest rates today. Inflation expectations are subject to a sizable degree of error, as investors over/(under)estimate the ramifications of economic and monetary policies and fail to incorporate all future events impacting the actual inflation rate into their prognoses. The *risk premium* protects the investor against all other potential negatives, including:

1. Credit or default risk
2. Call or early redemption risk
3. Liquidity or marketability risk
4. Risk of unexpected changes in inflation (i.e., the degree of unpredictability in assessing future inflation)

The yield levels of all fixed-income securities reflect the real interest rate, the inflation premium, and the risk premium component for volatility in future inflation. Non-U.S. Treasury securities offer higher yields than comparable U.S. Treasuries due to the credit, call, and liquidity risks of the former. The yield increment ascribed to non-U.S. Treasury issues is incorporated in the risk premium component of the nominal interest rate of such issues.

Consequently, different issuer sectors plot different yield curves. Lower quality sectors trade at progressively higher yield levels (see Exhibit 12–11). For example, the BBB corporate bond yield curve lies above the AAA corporate bond yield curve. Callable bonds trade at higher

---

[3] Need satisfaction places a premium on current consumption. The investor may accept a 0% return on a U.S. Treasury bill if he values the safekeeping of his investment funds by the U.S. government.

[4] Leuthold in "Interest Rates and Inflation" [see Fabozzi, Frank J. and Irving M. Pollack, *The Handbook of Fixed Income Securities* (Homewood, IL: Dow Jones-Irwin, 1983)] notes the 3% real return over long-term periods but questions its validity over short-term horizons.

Exhibit 12–11. Typical yield curves for a variety of quality sectors (U.S. Treasury, federal agency, AAA, AA, A, BBB, BB, B).

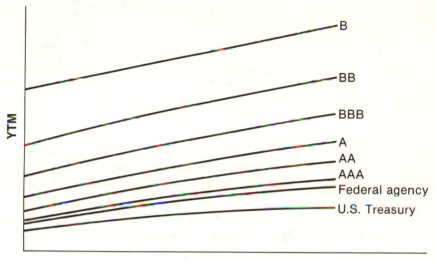

Term to Maturity (in Years)

yields than similar quality noncallable issues (see Exhibit 12–12). Less liquid issues trade at a concession to the current-coupon, on-the-run issues (see Exhibit 12–13).

> **Observation:** *A stated, or nominal, interest rate is comprised of a real rate plus a compensation for inflation and other risks.*

Exhibit 12–12. Typical yield curves for callable bonds and noncallable bonds.

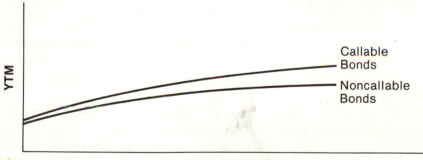

Term to Maturity (in Years)

Exhibit 12–13. Typical yield curves for liquid and less liquid issues.

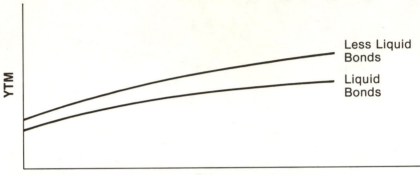

Term to Maturity (in Years)

Determinants of the shape of the yield curve

A yield curve can exhibit four basic shapes: positively sloped, negatively (inversely) sloped, flat, and humped. Exhibit 12–14 draws these four configurations for illustrative purposes. Recent history has provided all four patterns: positive (at June 30, 1985 per Exhibit 12–15), negative (at March 31, 1980, recall Exhibit 12–6), reasonably flat (at March 31, 1982 per Exhibit 12–16), and humped (at June 30, 1982 per Exhibit 12–17).

The principal factor affecting the short maturity section of the yield curve is monetary policy as executed by the Federal Reserve Board, primarily through its open market operations. A restrictive monetary policy drives short-term interest rates higher, creating a flat or inverted yield curve shape. An accommodative monetary policy forces short-term interest rates to lower levels, steepening the yield curve.

The long maturity segment of the yield curve is most sensitive to inflationary expectations. If inflation fears infiltrate the financial markets, the yield curve is likely to display a positive slope, as investors require a higher inflation premium for longer term investments. Conversely, as inflation concerns subside and investors expect declining interest rates, the yield curve flattens or inverts as the demand for long maturity issues surges, driving up prices and pushing down yields relative to short maturity issues.

Non-U.S. Treasury yield curves (e.g., corporate bond yield curves) reflect not only macroeconomic influences (Fed policy, inflationary expectations) but also micro factors such as liquidity risk, credit risk, and call risk. These risks are more acute for long maturity bonds than for short maturity issues. As a consequence, non-U.S. Treasury yield curves are generally more positively sloped than their U.S. Treasury counterparts.

Exhibit 12–14. Four basic yield curve shapes.

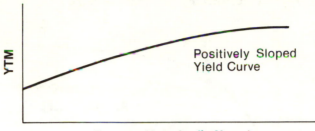

(a) Positive.

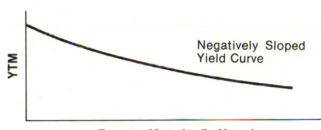

(b) Negative.

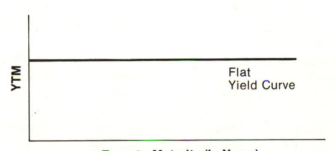

(c) Flat.

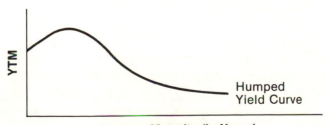

(d) Humped.

Exhibit 12–15. Example of a positively sloped U.S. Treasury yield curve at June 30, 1985 (data courtesy of Salomon Brothers Inc.).

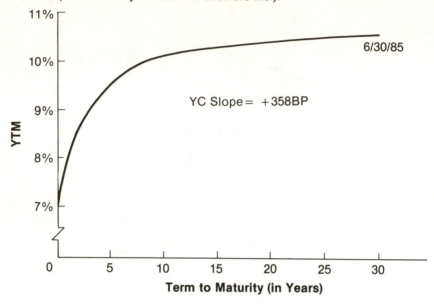

Exhibit 12–16. Example of a flat (or reasonably flat) U.S. Treasury yield curve at March 31, 1982 (data courtesy of Salomon Brothers Inc.).

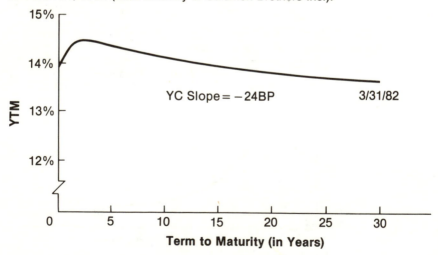

Exhibit 12–17. Example of a humped U.S. Treasury yield curve at June 30, 1982 (data courtesy of Salomon Brothers Inc.).

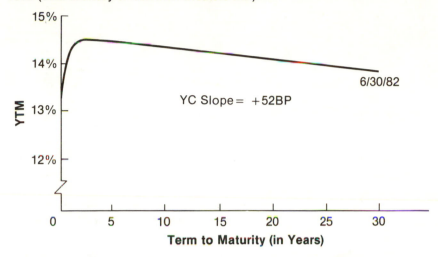

Term to Maturity (in Years)

Observation: *The shape of the U.S. Treasury yield curve is influenced primarily by monetary policy and inflationary expectations. Non-U.S. Treasury yield curves are also affected by perceptions of liquidity risk, credit risk, and call risk.*

Theories explaining the yield curve shape

Liquidity preference theory. There are three primary theories postulating the shape of the yield curve: liquidity preference, market segmentation, and expectations theory. The *liquidity preference theory* asserts that the yield curve will be upward sloping because of the preference by investors for liquidity. Long-term securities are less liquid than short-term securities, and, as a result, longer issues should trade at a yield concession to shorter issues. *Liquidity,* in this sense, is defined as the ability to recover the principal of a bond in a reasonably short period of time.[5] Adverse market moves can drive down bond prices and force the investor to wait until maturity to fully recover the principal amount. By implication, highly (price) volatile issues are commensurately less liquid. Exhibit 12–18 plots a typical yield curve as explained by the liquidity preference theory.

---

[5] *Liquidity,* by this definition, does not represent the magnitude of the bid-offer spread (or marketability) of the security. Other references in this book treat liquidity in the more traditional sense as *the ability to buy/sell a security at a price reasonably close to the most recent purchase/ sale price.*

Exhibit 12–18. Typical yield curve as suggested by the liquidity preference theory (modestly upward sloping).

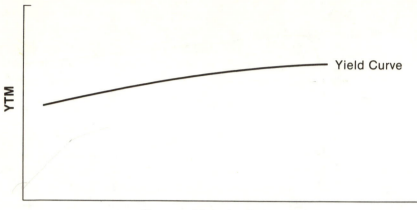

Term to Maturity (in Years)

Observation: *The liquidity preference theory deems a higher yield for longer maturity issues due to their lesser degree of liquidity. The yield curve should therefore be positively sloped.*

Market segmentation theory. The *market segmentation theory* views the fixed-income market as a series of distinct markets, segregated by maturity strata. Individual investors and issuers are restricted to specific maturity sectors. In other words, individual investors and issuers do not have complete maturity flexibility. Within a given maturity range, the relative supply and demand for funds determines the appropriate interest rate. Money is a commodity, the price of which is called the *interest rate:*

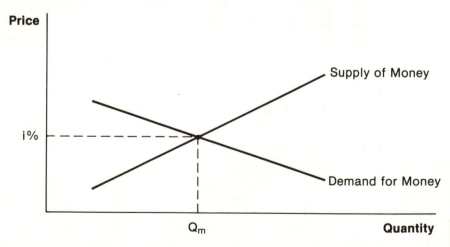

The supply of, and demand for, money differ in various maturity sectors due to the size of the respective constituents involved. For example, if the demand for long-term investments surges relative to the new supply of bond issues, bond prices rise and yields fall in the long maturity sector. Conversely, if the demand for long-term assets dries up while the new supply (i.e., new issuance) continues unabated, the long-term segment of the marketplace falls in price and rises in yield terms. In each instance, a new market-clearing price is established for the issues in a particular maturity sector.

According to the market segmentation theory, the yield curve portrays a series of supply/demand conditions which create a sequence of market-clearing prices (i.e., interest rates) for funds. The market segmentation theory can explain each of the four basic yield curve shapes as follows:

1. *Positively sloped yield curve*. The short-term segment of the market is dominated by investors (buyers) rather than by issuers (sellers); the relative lack of supply pushes bond prices up and yields down. The long-term sector, however, suffers from a relative imbalance of sellers versus buyers. The relative oversupply forces bond prices down and yields up. The magnitude of the slope of the yield curve is a function of the severity of the supply/demand imbalances.

2. *Negatively sloped yield curve*. This curve reflects the reverse of the conditions laid out in the positive yield curve scenario. Excessive borrowing in short maturities drives up yields and excessive buying in long maturities forces bond yields downward.

3. *Flat yield curve*. Both the short-term and long-term segments of the marketplace are experiencing similar supply/demand conditions such that the relative balances or imbalances create like yield levels and a flat yield curve.

4. *Humped yield curve*. A humped yield curve is positively sloped from the short maturity sector to the intermediate sector, but assumes a negative slope from intermediates to longs. In this case, the relative supply of intermediate bonds far outweighs the normal demand for the issues, forcing prices lower and yields higher than those observed in either the short maturities or the long maturities.

Observation: *The market segmentation theory finds an investor's lack of complete maturity flexibility creating submarkets for funds. As a* *result, the supply and demand characteristics of these individual maturity sectors connect to create the overall composite yield curve.*

Expectations theory. The *expectations theory* contends that the shape of the yield curve reflects the market consensus forecast of future interest rate levels. A positively sloped yield curve implies that interest rates are expected to rise in the future, and a downward-sloping yield curve suggests a prognosis for lower interest rates. A flat yield curve represents a market consensus for stable yields. A humped yield curve shows that market participants expect a rising rate environment over the intermediate term followed by a longer term decline in yield levels.

The expectations theory is predicated on several critical assumptions:

1. Investors are risk-neutral and have no liquidity preference. Risk neutrality states that investors are indifferent with regard to risk, neither desiring it (risk-seeking) nor avoiding it (risk-averse). In reality, investors behave in a risk-averse manner, demanding to be compensated with incremental return for additional risk undertaken.

2. Investors and issuers have complete maturity flexibility. In reality, some degree of market segmentation exists.

3. The market consensus forecast of interest rates is unbiased. In reality, there are periods of overreaction to economic events, causing an emotional bias in the consensus expectation.

4. There are no transaction costs. In reality, all bonds carry some degree of transaction cost, with long maturity bonds trading at wider bid-offer spreads than short maturity issues.[6]

Observation: *The expectations theory postulates that the yield curve shape is a function of investors' forecasts of future interest rate levels. Investors have complete flexibility with regard to the choice of maturity sectors.*

Summing it up

The shape of the yield curve is best explained by a combination of the three aforementioned theories. Yield curves tend to exhibit a modestly positive slope over long periods of time, reflecting the market participants' desire for liquidity (*liquidity preference*). *Market segmenta-*

---

[6] See Chapters 14 and 15 for discussions of transaction costs and liquidity.

Exhibit 12–19. Steeply positive yield curve (at June 30, 1984), reflecting a market consensus forecast for significantly higher yield levels. The forecast could not have been more incorrect (data courtesy of Salomon Brothers Inc.).

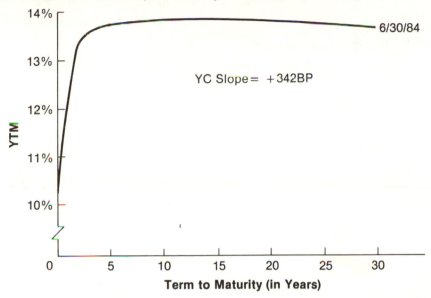

tion shows up as an influence on yield curve shape, particularly over short-term horizons (e.g., U.S. Treasury auction periods) and within specific issuer sectors (e.g., mortgage-backed issues, industrial bond issues, telephone utility issues). Imbalances of supply and demand create bumps on the yield curve at various maturity points for specific periods of time. Finally, there are an adequate number of investors with maturity flexibility (e.g., mutual funds, pension plans) to validate a degree of *expectations* reflected in the yield curve's shape. Inflation fears tend to steepen the slope of the yield curve while disinflation expectations act to flatten or invert the yield curve. Of course, the eventual outcome of future interest rates is often substantially different from that implied or expected by investors.

The market consensus forecast of interest rates is often wrong. Forecasting the direction of interest rates has proved difficult. For example, the yield curve on June 30, 1984 (see Exhibit 12–19) was steeply positive and yet interest rates at that time were at an intermediate peak for the 1981–1986 period. Rates subsequently declined to the 7.00% level (recall Exhibit 12–9). Forecasting the direction *and* the magnitude of interest rate change is an even more precarious endeavor.

Observation: *Three theories attempt to explain the shape of the yield curve: liquidity preference, market segmentation, and expectations. Each theory contributes to a thorough analysis of the yield curve.*

Spot rates and forward rates

The concept

The concept of spot rates and forward rates stems from the expectations theory. Keeping in mind the assumptions underlying the expectations theory, the definitions of spot and forward rates are as follows:

Spot rate: the interest rate on a single cash flow received at a future time period. It is, theoretically, the interest rate on a pure discount (i.e., zero-coupon) bond of a specified maturity. A series of spot rates arranged by maturity comprises the spot rate curve.

Forward rate: the future interest rate implied by the shape of the spot rate curve. A forward rate is a marginal yield, that is, a yield on the margin between two successive spot rates:

$$1 + FR_t = \frac{(1 + SR_{t+1})^{t+1}}{(1 + SR_t)^t}$$

Exhibit 12–20. Hypothetical spot rate curve (1- to 3-year maturity sector).

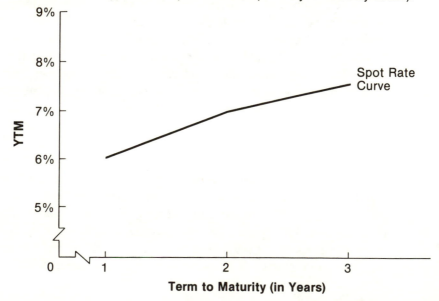

where

SR$_t$ = spot rate for a pure discount bond maturing at time period t

SR$_{t+1}$ = spot rate for a pure discount bond maturing at time period $t + 1$

FR$_t$ = forward rate for a single-period, pure discount bond at time period t

Observation: *A spot rate is the interest rate on a pure discount security; a forward rate is the marginal yield between two successive spot rates.*

An illustration of spot rate and forward rate calculations

As an example, assume that the spot rate curve in the 1- to 3-year maturity sector has a positive slope as shown in Exhibit 12–20 with spot and forward rates as follows:

t	Maturity (Years)	Spot Rate, SR$_t$ (%)	1-Year Forward Rate, FR$_t$ (%)
1	1	6.00	
2	2	7.00	8.00 (beginning of year)
3	3	7.50	8.50 (beginning of year)

The forward rates force an equalization of the expected returns of all investors. The 1-year forward rates at the end of the first and second years can be quickly derived by using two consecutive spot rates (per earlier illustration). In general,

$$1 + FR_t = \frac{(1 + SR_{t+1})^{t+1}}{(1 + SR_t)^t}$$

Specifically,

$$1 + FR_2 = \frac{(1 + SR_2)^2}{(1 + SR_1)^1}$$
$$= \frac{(1 + 0.07)^2}{(1 + 0.06)^1}$$
$$= \frac{(1.07)^2}{1.06}$$

$$= \frac{1.1449}{1.0600}$$
$$= 1.0800$$

$$FR_2 = 1.0800 - 1$$
$$= 0.0800$$
$$= 8.00\%$$

$$1 + FR_3 = \frac{(1 + SR_3)^3}{(1 + SR_2)^2}$$
$$= \frac{(1 + 0.075)^3}{(1 + 0.07)^2}$$
$$= \frac{(1.075)^3}{(1.07)^2}$$
$$= \frac{1.2423}{1.1449}$$
$$= 1.0850$$

$$FR_3 = 1.0850 - 1$$
$$= 0.0850$$
$$= 8.50\%$$

By definition, one can think of a spot rate as a geometric average of consecutive forward rates.[7]

[7] In general:

$$(1 + SR_t)^t = (1 + SR_1) \times (1 + FR_2) \times \cdots \times (1 + FR_t)$$

For the example cited earlier,

$$(1 + SR_2)^2 = (1 + SR_1) \times (1 + FR_2)$$
$$= (1 + 0.06) \times (1 + 0.08)$$
$$= 1.06 \times 1.08$$
$$= 1.1448$$

The SR_2 solves to 0.0700, or a 7.00% spot rate for year 2.

$$(1 + SR_3)^3 = (1 + SR_1) \times (1 + FR_2) \times (1 + FR_3)$$
$$= (1 + 0.06) \times (1 + 0.08) \times (1 + 0.085)$$
$$= 1.06 \times 1.08 \times 1.085$$
$$= 1.2421$$

The SR_3 solves to 0.0750, or a 7.50% spot rate for year 3. Spot rates can therefore be calculated by linking together the forward rates leading up to that spot rate maturity. The initial period establishes the spot rate upon which subsequent forward rates are applied.

The interpretation of spot rates and forward rates

The expectations theory implicitly assumes that, for a specified holding period, all investors experience an equivalent change in wealth position. Utilizing the three zero-coupon bonds of earlier illustration (1-year, 2-year, 3-year), an investor expects to accumulate wealth over three alternative horizons (1 year, 2 years, 3 years) as follows:

1 year: $\$1,000.00 \times (1 + 0.06)^1 = \$1,060.00$ ⎫ these are the fu-

2 years: $\$1,000.00 \times (1 + 0.07)^2 = \$1,144.90$ ⎬ ture values of $\$1,000.00$ in-

3 years: $\$1,000.00 \times (1 + 0.075)^3 = \$1,242.30$ ⎭ vested today at current rates

For simplicity, annual compounding is assumed.

The expectations theory asserts that every investor will obtain an identical ending wealth position given the same initial outlay (in this example, $\$1,000.00$), regardless of the maturity originally purchased. In a positive yield curve environment, there are three alternative ways to invest:

1. Buy a discount bond that matures at the end of the investment period and hold it to maturity.
2. Buy a short-term maturity bond and reinvest the proceeds at higher yields.
3. Buy a long-term bond and sell it at a loss prior to maturity.

The forward rates for years 2 and 3 are calculated as the ratio of the end-of-year wealth position to the beginning-of-year wealth position:

$$
\begin{aligned}
FR_{\text{year 2}} &= \frac{\text{wealth position (end of year 2)}}{\text{wealth position (end of year 1)}} - 1 \\
&= \frac{\$1,144.90}{\$1,060.00} - 1 \\
&= 1.0800 - 1 \\
&= 0.0800 \\
&= 8.00\%
\end{aligned}
$$

$$FR_{year\ 3} = \frac{\text{wealth position (end of year 3)}}{\text{wealth position (end of year 2)}} - 1$$

$$= \frac{\$1,242.30}{\$1,144.90} - 1$$

$$= 1.0850 - 1$$

$$= 0.0850$$

$$= 8.50\%$$

In this way, all investors reach similar wealth positions as time progresses. Investors who purchase short maturity, lower yielding instruments catch up to longer maturity issue holders by reinvesting at progressively higher yields. Long maturity investors, who gained an initial yield advantage, give back excess returns by the price depreciations associated with the higher yield environments of the future.

As an illustration, for a 2-year investment horizon and a $1,000.00 initial outlay, Investors A, B, and C follow three different strategies:

1. *Investor A* purchases 2-year discount bonds at a 7.00% yield and holds them to maturity:

   $$\$1,000.00(1.07)(1.07) = \$1,144.90 \quad \text{(end of year 2)}$$

2. *Investor B* purchases 1-year discount bonds at a 6.00% yield and rolls the proceeds into new 1-year discount bonds at the end of the first year:

   $$\$1,000.00(1.06) = \$1,060.00 \quad \text{(end of year 1)}$$

   $$\$1,060.00(1.08) = \$1,144.90 \quad \text{(end of year 2)}$$

3. *Investor C* purchases 3-year discount bonds at a 7.50% yield and sells them at the end of 2 years at the prevailing market rate of interest (8.50%):

   $$\$1,000.00(1.075)(1.075)(1.075) = \$1,242.30 \quad \text{(end of year 3)}$$

   $$\frac{\text{market value at}}{\text{end of year 2}} = \frac{\text{value at end of year 3}}{1 + \text{annual spot rate at the end of year 2}}$$

   $$= \frac{\$1,242.30}{1 + 0.085}$$

   $$= \$1,144.90$$

Notice that each investor garners a $144.90 return over the 2-year period, irrespective of the original strategy undertaken.

> **Observation:** *The concepts of spot and forward rates are an outgrowth of the expectations hypothesis. Spot and forward rates ensure an equalization in investor returns given an accurate implied market forecast of future interest rates.*

The limitations of spot rate curves

The spot rate curve is not directly observable. The curve is derived from the market prices of both coupon-bearing and pure discount (e.g., T-bills, zero-coupon STRIPS) securities. In other words, the actual prices of traded securities determine where a pure discount security of a specified maturity *should* trade. As a result, the spot rate curve is a theoretical construct. Although the earlier example utilized annual intervals for spot rates and forward rates, sophisticated models generate spot rate curves on daily time intervals, creating overnight forward rates for any single day in the future.

The zero-coupon (STRIPS) curve does not represent the spot rate curve for U.S. Treasuries, although theoretically it should. Insufficient liquidity and inefficient pricing due to supply/demand imbalances create deviations from theoretically accurate valuations. These discrepancies are disappearing as the liquidity of the STRIPS market increases and as stripping and reconstituting of U.S. Treasury bonds allows arbitrageurs to profit from inefficient pricings. The assumption of risk neutrality (expectations theory) precludes the attainment of a theoretical spot rate curve as rational investors continue to behave in a risk-averse fashion; duration differences between individual issues are noticed by market participants. A 10-year STRIPS, for example, is perceived as a more risky investment than a 10-year coupon-bearing U.S. Treasury bond due to the greater inherent price volatility of the STRIPS (recall Chapter 4). The expectations theory suggests that interim fluctuations in portfolio value are ignored by investors, an assumption that does not have credence in real-life investing.

> **Observation:** *Spot rates do not accurately reflect investor preferences. The derived nature of spot and forward rates and the inefficient pricing of STRIPS limit the applicability of these concepts.*

Using spot rates to calculate theoretical bond prices

The concept of spot rates as discount rates of interest. Spot rate curve analysis shows that in a positively sloped yield curve environment, cash flows received at earlier points in time are discounted at lower yields than cash flows received farther into the future. In a negative yield curve environment, the opposite case is true. Since a coupon-bearing bond is a series of future cash flows, an appropriate price for the bond should be calculated with consideration to the timing of all the cash flows. The YTM measure treats all cash flows indiscriminantly, discounting each at the YTM rate.

In environments of nonflat yield curves, the traditional YTM calculation does not properly assess the true value of a coupon-bearing bond.[8] The bond may be over- or undervalued relative to the value of the sum of the bond's cash flows as discounted according to spot rates at their respective positions on the yield curve. This leads to several generalizations:

1. In a positively sloped yield curve environment, coupon-bearing bonds have a tendency to be worth more than their traditional YTM-calculated price suggests, because the coupon payments are discounted at the lower discount rates leading up to the final maturity payment date.[9] In a positive yield curve environment, high coupon bonds should trade at lower YTMs than lower coupon bonds of similar maturity.

2. In a negatively sloped yield curve environment, coupon-bearing bonds have a tendency to be worth less than their traditional YTM-calculated price suggests, because the coupon payments are discounted at the higher discount rates leading up to the final maturity payment date.[10] In a negative yield curve environment, high coupon bonds should trade at higher yields than lower coupon bonds of similar maturity.

3. The actual richness or cheapness of a security depends on the shape of the spot rate curve, liquidity characteristics of the bond, tax features

---

[8] The YTM implicitly assumes a flat yield curve, with correspondingly flat spot rate and forward rate curves. It is rare to find a prolonged period of flat yield curve shape.

[9] The theoretical value is also influenced by the spot rate applied to the final maturity cash flow (principal payment + final coupon payment). If the spot rate for the final maturity date lies *above* the YTM of the bond, the enhanced value created by the coupons is at least partially (and is perhaps fully) offset by the lesser value of the principal cash flow.

[10] If the spot rate for the final maturity date lies *below* the YTM of the bond, the value losses created by the coupons at least partially (and perhaps fully) offset the greater value of the lump sum payment at maturity.

of the bond, reinvestment rate considerations, supply/demand forces in the bond and/or the bond's maturity sector, and so on.

Theoretical bond prices: An application. In order to validly compare coupon-bearing bond issues, each respective cash flow should be discounted at a yield that is appropriate for that cash flow, given the point in time at which it is received in the future. A spot rate curve is derived from the actual observed prices of U.S. Treasuries traded in the marketplace. This spot rate curve is then used to discount each singular cash flow attached to a bond. As a result, consistent comparisons can be made between individual securities. In formula terms:

$$\text{bond value} = \sum_{t=1}^{N} \frac{CF_t}{(1 + SR_t)^t}$$

where

CF_t = cash flow received at the end of period t

SR_t = spot rate for period t

N = number of periods to final maturity

For semiannual-pay bonds, the SR_t is expressed in a semiannual form and t represents the number of semiannual periods. For example, an investor can purchase a 5-year, 10% coupon U.S. Treasury bond at 110.70 to yield 7.40% to maturity. Given the spot rate curve in Exhibit 12–21, Exhibit 12–22 calculates the theoretical value of the bond at

Exhibit 12–21. Hypothetical spot rate curve.

Maturity (Years)	Spot Rate (%)
0.5	4.50
1.0	4.75
1.5	5.00
2.0	5.50
2.5	5.75
3.0	6.00
3.5	6.50
4.0	7.00
4.5	7.25
5.0	7.50

Exhibit 12–22. Calculation of the theoretical value of a 5-year, 10% coupon U.S. Treasury bond, given the spot rate curve presented in Exhibit 12–21.

(1) Time Period t	(2) Cash Flow (CF_t)	(3) PV Factor	(4) = (2) × (3) $PV(CF_t)$
1	$ 50.00	0.9780	$ 48.90
2	50.00	0.9541	47.71
3	50.00	0.9286	46.43
4	50.00	0.8972	44.86
5	50.00	0.8679	43.40
6	50.00	0.8375	41.88
7	50.00	0.7994	39.97
8	50.00	0.7594	37.97
9	50.00	0.7258	36.29
10	50.00	0.6920	34.60
10	1,000.00	0.6920	692.00
		Theoretical bond value →	$1,114.00

111.40. The bond appears to be undervalued in the marketplace by $7/10$ of a point. Bonds trading at prices cheaper than their theoretical values should be purchased. Bonds selling at prices that are expensive vis-à-vis their theoretical values should be sold or shorted. The assumption is that, over time, bond prices are biased to return to, or at least approach, their theoretical values.

The justification for theoretical values. Theoretical bond valuation provides a consistent method of analyzing securities with cash flows occurring at various points in time.[11] Any cash flow received in a given period is discounted at a consistent, specified rate. For example, a 2-year cash flow is discounted at the 2-year spot rate, despite whether the cash flow is a coupon flow or a return of principal. It is inappropriate to discount a principal cash flow at a rate that is different from the rate

[11] A theoretical duration can be used in comparing securities valued on a spot rate curve basis. Recall that Macaulay's duration is predicated on YTM-based discount factors. A *theoretical duration* is derived by using spot rate discount factors, which may differ for each cash flow. The theoretical duration will therefore differ somewhat from the Macaulay's duration commonly cited.

For example, the 5-year, 10% coupon U.S. Treasury bond of Exhibit 12–22 bears a Macaulay's duration of 4.11 years at a YTM of 7.40%. Using the spot rate curve of Exhibit 12–21, the theoretical duration solves to 4.09 years. This divergence is more sizable (1) the steeper (in either a positive or inverted manner) the shape of the spot rate curve and (2) the longer the maturity of the bond under review.

applied to a coupon cash flow. The YTM measure, in a nonflat yield curve environment, bears this fault.

Theoretical bond valuations are particularly appropriate for buy-and-hold strategies. If a bond is held to maturity and the expectations on future interest rates implied in the spot rate curve prove to be correct, the investor has added value to the portfolio by buying securities that are currently underpriced on a theoretical basis. Theoretical values and actual values converge to the bond's par value at maturity. There is no potential for misvaluation at that point in time.

Four caveats should be kept in mind when utilizing theoretical bond valuations. *First, the results are subject to the same rigid assumptions discussed under the expectations theory (risk-neutral investors, no liquidity preference, complete maturity flexibility, no transaction costs, an unbiased consensus forecast of future interest rates). Second, generating spot rate curves using issues that are alike in every respect except for their terms to maturity is, in the real world, very difficult.* Compromises are made in order to obtain reasonably representative spot rate curves.[12]

Third, the bond in question may appear attractive from a theoretical perspective, but from a trading point of view may be expensive relative to previous history. In other words, the bond may be theoretically cheap (e.g., ¼ point), but the bond is not as theoretically valuable as in recent history (e.g., ¾ point). In the short run, performance can be adversely impacted. Active investors are not judged by the usage of theoretical market prices![13] *Finally, the bond of interest may have characteristics (e.g., liquidity, credit, call) that warrant that it trade cheaper than other similar securities.*

> **Observation:** *Theoretical bond values are predicated on derived spot and forward rate curves. The discounting of individual cash flows at unique spot rates allows for a consistent valuation of a wide variety of fixed-income securities and cash flow structures. The other factors influencing a bond's value (e.g., liquidity, call risk, credit risk) should not be ignored and the restrictive assumptions underlying spot rate curves should not be treated casually.*

---

[12] Note that a unique spot rate curve must be constructed for each traditional yield curve employed. In other words, a spot rate curve derived from U.S. Treasury prices is applicable only to U.S. Treasury securities. Spot rate curves are predicated on securities that are alike in all respects except for maturity date.

[13] Performance evaluation is discussed in Chapter 15.

Summary

Yield curve analysis addresses phenomena such as the absolute level of the yield curve, the shape of the yield curve, and the derivation of bond values. A *yield curve* or *term structure of interest rates* portrays the YTMs and maturities of a series of bonds of similar type (e.g., U.S. Treasury current-coupon issues). The yield, or *nominal interest rate,* associated with a specific security is comprised of a *real interest rate,* an *inflation premium,* and a *risk premium.* These three factors determine the general level of the yield curve. The shape of the yield curve is a function of Federal Reserve policy, inflation concerns, liquidity desires, and supply/demand conditions. The yield curve can be positively sloped, negatively sloped, humped, or flat. Three theories attempt to explain the yield curve shape: *liquidity preference, market segmentation,* and *expectations.* In reality, a combination of the three theories serves as the best explanatory device.

Spot rates and forward rates can be used to assess relative values among alternative bond investments. A *spot rate* is the (implied) yield on a pure discount bond of a specified maturity. A *spot rate curve* displays the spot rates for a variety of maturities. A *forward rate* is the marginal yield between two successive spot rates. *Theoretical bond values* are calculated through the use of spot rate curves and the cash flow discounting process. The results are subject to the restrictive assumptions underlying the derivation of spot rate curves. Real-world considerations and judgments must also be incorporated into the final conclusion on the relative attractiveness of alternative investments.

Total Return Curve Analysis

The yield curve concept was discussed at length in Chapter 12. Recall that the yield curve plots the yields to maturity of a series of bonds versus their respective terms to maturity, holding all other factors equal. The traditional yield curve is a primitive expression of the risk:return tradeoff of various fixed-income securities. Chapter 5 showed that the term to maturity serves as a poor proxy for bond risk. Chapter 9 demonstrated that the yield to maturity falls short as an indication of bond return. Consequently, the fundamentals of bonds suggest that a more representative matrix of the true underlying risk:return tradeoff of bonds is found in using a better measure of risk (e.g., duration, standard deviation of total return, beta) and a better measure of return (i.e., total return). These improvements underlie the construction of total return curves, the subject of this chapter.

The rationale for a total return curve

The drawbacks of a traditional yield curve

Exhibit 13–1 draws a typical yield curve by using term to maturity as the risk measure (on the x axis) and yield to maturity as the return measure (on the y axis). Three basic problems arise from the usage of

Exhibit 13–1. Typical yield curve using the term to maturity on the *x* axis and the yield to maturity on the *y* axis.

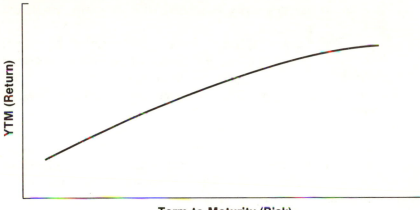

Term to Maturity (Risk)

traditional yield curves. *First, maturity by itself is a poor indicator of bond price volatility.* A better measure of bond risk is a duration construct (e.g., Macaulay's duration, modified duration, or effective duration). Bond swaps are risk-controlled by duration weightings (see Chapter 14). In assessing relative value, a duration comparison is a more effective screening device than a maturity comparison. By incorporating the maturity, sinking fund/prepayment schedule, coupon rate, yield level, and call features (effective duration only) of a bond, the duration concept acts as a superior proxy for bond risk.[1]

 Second, the yield to maturity (YTM) is simply another way of expressing a bond price. The traditional yield curve is, in reality, a form of price curve rather than a total return configuration. The YTM is not a clear reflection of the return potential offered by a bond because:

1. For the passive, buy-and-hold investor, the YTM assumes that all cash flows received prior to maturity are reinvested at the YTM rate. In addition, the YTM rate requires an annual basis point add-on.
2. For the active investor, the YTM assumes that the bond, if sold prior to maturity, is sold at a yield equal to that of the bond's YTM on date of purchase. Rarely is one able to sell a bond at exactly the same yield as on purchase date; unexpected capital gains and losses

[1]The focus of this chapter is on the risk of individual bonds. In a total portfolio context, a standard deviation or beta risk measure may be more appropriate than a duration construct.

result. Also, the YTM assumes reinvestments made at the YTM rate, ignores the need for an annual basis point add-on, and fails to incorporate transaction costs associated with the early sale of the security.

Performance evaluation services assess ability by comparing portfolio return (not portfolio yield) to that of a specified benchmark. Consequently, the energies of a portfolio manager must be focused on the total return potential offered by a bond, not on the bond's yield characteristics.

Third, the most commonly observed yield curve is composed of fewer than 10 U.S. Treasury issues. This *current-coupon yield curve* does not adequately encompass the yield: maturity tradeoffs of a myriad of other market sectors (e.g., off-the-run U.S. Treasuries, agencies, corporate bonds, mortgage-backed securities). A multiple series of yield curves is necessary in order to assess the realm of opportunities available to a bond investor at any given point in time.

> **Observation:** *The traditional yield curve serves as a poor schematic for risk:return tradeoffs—the maturity figure inadequately describes risk and the YTM is an inaccurate return proxy. In addition, a single yield curve, such as the U.S. Treasury bond yield curve, fails to portray the myriad of other yield curves that exist.*

The total return curve concept

A *total return (TR) curve* attempts to overcome the inherent deficiencies of a yield curve by plotting total return (expected or historical) on the *y* axis and situating a duration measure on the *x* axis.[2] To assist the reader in the transition from yield curves to total return curves, the term to maturity is used on the *x* axis in the initial series of illustrations. Exhibit 13–2 provides a sample configuration of a TR curve for U.S. Treasuries. The TR curve strives to better portray the risk: return tradeoffs provided by alternative fixed-income investments. A composite of TR curves for various market sectors can help the investor discern relative values more readily than by the use of yield curves alone.

Two basic types of TR curves can be constructed: historical and

---

[2] In this chapter, Macaulay's duration is used as the better risk measure. Alternatively, one may use a standard deviation of return or a bond beta on the *x* axis. A total return curve can be drawn with the term to maturity on the *x* axis in order to allow for comparability between similar maturity assets.

Exhibit 13–2. Sample configuration of a total return curve for U.S. Treasuries.

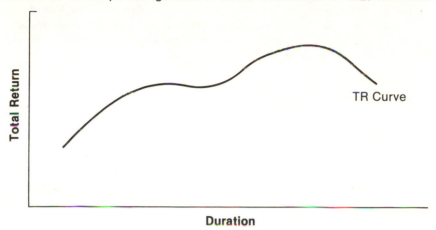

projected. A *historical TR curve* displays the actual total return earned over a specified historical period versus the average duration over that period. A *projected TR curve* portrays the expected future total return against the current duration of the security involved.[3] Investments are made to garner future returns; therefore, projected TR curves are the ultimate tool for making investment decisions. Insofar as history is a teacher of many lessons, historical TR curves can and should be used as an input into the creation of projected TR curves.

Several assumptions form the basis for the total return projections. *First, the length of the holding period is specified (e.g., 3 months, 1 year, 5 years). Second, the general level of interest rates is forecast. Third, sector spreads (maturity, quality, coupon, issuer) are estimated. Fourth, a reinvestment rate assumption is made. Finally, transaction costs are incorporated into the analysis.*[4] It is clear that there is some degree of subjectivity and judgment involved in the task of constructing total return curves.

---

[3] One might more appropriately use the average duration expected over the future holding period; however, investors tend to assess portfolio risk based on today's duration and, therefore, the current duration (Macaulay's, modified, or effective) is used in the illustrations in this chapter. The actual price return impact, of course, is based solely on the end-of-holding-period duration.

[4] The total return curves illustrated in this chapter ignore transaction costs. Since the bond market is a negotiated market and transaction costs are not fixed, the reader can apply an appropriate adjustment to the gross return figures. This transaction cost adjustment can be viewed as a downward shift in the total return curve, with a disproportionately larger shift in the long maturity and non-U.S. Treasury sectors, where transaction costs are generally higher.

Observation: *A total return curve plots total returns, rather than yields, against a selected bond risk measure. Typically, duration is the risk measure of choice. Total return curves can be either historical or projected in nature. The latter type requires a series of assumptions to be made about future conditions.*

Baseline total return curves

Perhaps the least subjective type of total return curve is a baseline total return curve, which assumes absolutely no change in the general level of yields, no change in the shape of the yield curve, and no change in sector spreads.[5] Additional simplifying assumptions include:

1. A 1-year investment horizon
2. All reinvestments made in the middle of the yield curve
3. No transaction costs

One would expect to find few surprises in a baseline TR curve. In actuality, the *no change* total returns can differ sizably from yield-based expectations of return.

Observation: *A baseline total return curve is predicated on a status quo (i.e., unchanged) environment.*

An illustration of a baseline total return curve

For example, the U.S. Treasury yield curve for January 30, 1987 is reviewed in Exhibit 13–3 and plotted in Exhibit 13–4. The yield curve is positively sloped, with yield pickups captured on each progressive extension along the maturity spectrum. One would think that in a *no change,* stable yield environment, the total return pickups associated with maturity extensions would mimic the aforementioned yield increments. In reality, however, half (3 out of 6) of the extension trades incur incremental losses in total return in a baseline scenario (see Exhibit 13–5).

---

[5] A limited degree of subjectivity is involved in estimating the *roll factor* for any single maturity sector simply because there might not be a comparable issue trading at a 1-year shorter maturity slot. An estimation must be made as to where such an issue would trade, given the price data on other issues concentrated in that sector. For example, a 7-year current-coupon AA corporate bond may not have a comparable counterpart in the 6-year maturity sector. In this case, an approximation must be made of where a 6-year bond of similar characteristics would trade vis-à-vis 6-year maturity U.S. Treasuries or other corporate bond issues in the 6-year sector.

Exhibit 13–3. Yields and Macaulay's durations on current-coupon U.S. Treasury bonds as of January 30, 1987.

Maturity (Years)	Macaulay's Duration	YTM (%)	YTM Pickup on Extension (BP)
2	1.91	6.29	+13
3	2.56	6.42	+20
4	3.49	6.62	+ 6
5	4.23	6.68	+30
7	5.60	6.98	+18
10	7.07	7.16	+31
30	12.12	7.47	

Exhibit 13–4. U.S. Treasury yield curve on January 30, 1987 (current-coupon issues only; data per Exhibit 13–3).

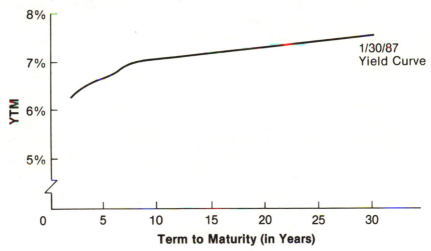

Exhibit 13–5. One-year baseline total returns on the current-coupon U.S. Treasury bonds as of January 30, 1987. The yield curve is unchanged in both shape and level one year hence. Reinvestments are made at a 7.00% rate.

Maturity (Years)	1-Year Total Return (%)	Total Return Pickup on Extension (BP)
2	6.72	
3	6.81	+ 9
4	7.10	+29
5	6.91	−19
7	7.48	+57
10	6.96	−52
30	6.67	−29

The subtle changes creating yield:total return differentials. The discrepancies between yield pickups and total return pickups arise from the fact that, even in a status quo environment, there are changes going on. As time passes, bonds age and carry progressively shorter remaining terms to maturity. In addition, a bond's liquidity characteristics can change over time (e.g., a move from on-the-run status to off-the-run status).[6] Given a positive yield curve configuration, a bond *rolls down* to a newer and lower yield. Negative yield curves find bonds *rolling up* to higher yields. This quiet and often overlooked change in yield creates price appreciations and depreciations unexpected by the YTM measure, which assumes no change in yield as time passes.

A *yield curve roll factor* is the BP change in yield that results from the passage of time as a bond ages and moves to a shorter maturity position on the yield curve. The impact of the yield curve roll is a function of two variables: the absolute size of the yield change (in BP), and the price sensitivity (e.g., modified duration) of the security involved. The total return alteration attributable to a yield curve roll is positively related to each of these factors. The larger the BP change in yield, the larger the resulting impact on the bond's total return. Long duration bonds are particularly sensitive to roll factors because of the multiplier

[6] The move from on-the-run status to off-the-run status is damaging to the current auction issues. The related dropoff in liquidity warrants a higher yield for the bond as it becomes an *old* issue. This transition occurs quarterly with most U.S. Treasury auction issues (monthly with the 2-year note). Additionally, the move into an off-the-run maturity sector (e.g., a 30-year bond moving to a 29-year status, a 10-year bond moving to a 9-year status, a 7-year bond moving to a 6-year status) compounds the downfall.

effect of duration on a bond's price for a given change in yield. Recall from Chapter 6:

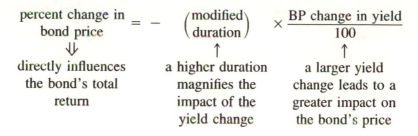

$$\begin{array}{ccc} \underset{\text{bond price}}{\text{percent change in}} = - & \left(\begin{array}{c}\text{modified}\\ \text{duration}\end{array}\right) & \times \dfrac{\text{BP change in yield}}{100} \\ \Downarrow & \uparrow & \uparrow \\ \text{directly influences} & \text{a higher duration} & \text{a larger yield} \\ \text{the bond's total} & \text{magnifies the} & \text{change leads to a} \\ \text{return} & \text{impact of the} & \text{greater impact on} \\ & \text{yield change} & \text{the bond's price} \end{array}$$

For example, if a bond with a modified duration of 1 year rolls down the yield curve by 10BP, the bond's price appreciates by approximately 10BP ($-1.0 \times -10/100 = 0.10\%$ or 10BP).[7] As a result, the bond's total return is increased by a like amount (10BP). A long maturity U.S. Treasury bond sporting a modified duration of 12 years experiences a 120BP surge in price return given the same 10BP rolldown ($-12.0 \times -10/100 = 1.20\%$ or 120BP). As another illustration, a 50BP rolldown adds approximately 50BP to a 1.0-year duration bond's return ($-1.0 \times -50/100 = 0.50\%$ or 50BP) and approximately 350BP to a 7.0-year duration security's return ($-7.0 \times -50/100 = 3.50\%$ or 350BP). Small changes in yield can significantly affect longer maturity bond prices and returns.

> **Observation:** *The impact on a bond's total return is positively related to both the absolute size of the yield change and the modified duration of the security under consideration. Positively sloped or negatively sloped yield curves create underlying return biases that should not be overlooked. A baseline total return curve helps to highlight these biases.*

An illustration of yield curve rolls and total return impacts. The current-coupon U.S. Treasuries noted in Exhibit 13–3 are subject to the yield curve roll factors listed in Exhibit 13–6. The resulting 1-year total returns were referred to earlier (see Exhibit 13–5). A quick glance at the current-coupon U.S. Treasury yield curve (Exhibit 13–4) fails to reveal the underlying tendencies of the Treasury issues to behave quite differently from their yield-suggested relationships. Exhibit 13–7 plots

---

[7] The price and total return impact occurs on the terminal date of the holding period. Therefore, the bond's modified duration at that point in time is the pertinent volatility figure, not the bond's duration today (unless an instantaneous roll is assumed, as in this case).

Exhibit 13–6. Yield curve roll factors for the current-coupon U.S. Treasury bonds as of January 30, 1987.

Maturity (Years)	Yield Curve Roll Factor (BP)
2	−34
3	−17
4	−14
5	− 3
7	− 8
10	+ 5
30	+ 8

Comments: *The yield curve roll factors estimate the 1-year change in yield resulting from a 1-year decline in the remaining term to maturity and a move to off-the-run status.*

the baseline total return curve for the same seven U.S. Treasury auction issues using the data derived in Exhibit 13–5.

Exhibit 13–8 overlays the total return curve on the yield curve to illustrate the vast difference between initial perception (yield) and reality (return). On a yield basis, the 30-year issue appears to be the most attractive issue, offering a 7.47% yield, 31BP in excess of its nearest competitor (the 10-year issue). However, on a total return basis, the

Exhibit 13–7. Baseline total return curve for the current-coupon U.S. Treasury bonds on January 30, 1987 (data per Exhibit 13–5).

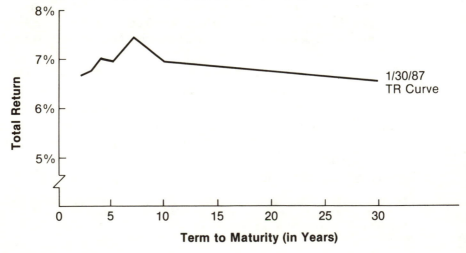

Exhibit 13–8. Comparison of the yield curve and the 1-year baseline total return curve for current-coupon U.S. Treasury bonds as of January 30, 1987 (data per Exhibits 13–3 and 13–5).

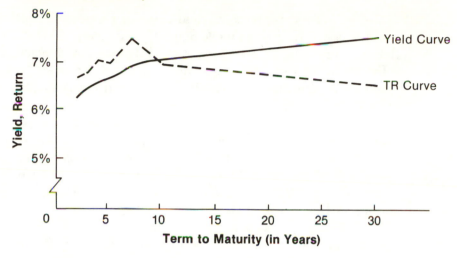

Comments: *The appearance of a yield curve can be very deceiving.*

same 30-year bond is the least attractive of the seven auction issues, providing only a 6.67% return versus the 6.72 to 7.48% range of offerings by its six counterparts. Indeed, the 7-year U.S. Treasury stands out as the winning issue in a *no change* scenario, registering a 7.48% 1-year total return, a full 38BP in front of the runner-up, 4-year maturity issue.

Statistically speaking, a baseline scenario is unlikely to actually occur. However, the usefulness of a baseline TR curve lies in the fact that this curve lays out the initial return biases held by the issues under focus. In other words, changes from the baseline scenario have an impact on the baseline TR projections. A bond's YTM is an inappropriate starting point because the YTM itself makes a series of rather heroic assumptions (flat yield curve, no change in yield levels, reinvest at the YTM rate) that do not represent the purest case of a *no change* scenario.

Observation: *Yield curve roll factors can create sizable discrepancies between the perceived return (i.e., the yield) and the actual return (i.e., the total return).*

Using a more comprehensive U.S. Treasury yield curve and total
return curve

The U.S. Treasury bond yield curve of previous example reveals
the danger of relying on a sample of the approximately 160 U.S. Treasury
bonds available in the 2- to 30-year maturity range. A complete plotting
of every traded issue shows the small rollups in certain sections of the
yield curve and the rolldowns in other maturity sectors (see Exhibit
13–9). The yield curve is hardly the smooth curve typically visualized.
Investors clearly indicate a preference for liquidity (on-the-run auction
issues) and specific maturities (2, 3, 4, 5, 7, 10, and 30 years). Off-
the-run bonds tend to trade at higher yields than their on-the-run counterparts, and off-the-run maturities (e.g., 2½, 6, 8, and 20 years) tend to
offer higher yields than a straight-line interpolation between the popular
maturities would suggest (see Exhibit 13–10).

Exhibit 13–11 summarizes the yields available on a selection of
off-the-run U.S. Treasury issues as of January 30, 1987. The comparable
baseline total returns are calculated in Exhibit 13–12. Exhibit 13–13
plots the yield curve and total return curve for the off-the-run issues.
Once again, the yield figures can be very misleading. The total return

Exhibit 13–9. Typical plotting of a comprehensive U.S. Treasury yield curve.

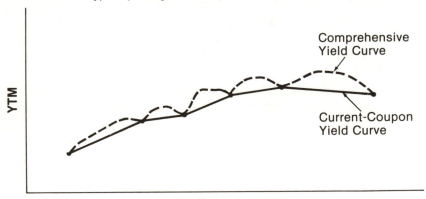

Term to Maturity (in Years)

Comments: *Caveat—the yield curve presented above includes bonds
with dissimilar characteristics (coupon rate, liquidity) and caution
should be taken in utilizing the individual issues comprising the curve.
The point here is simply that the yield curve provides more of a disjointed
roller-coaster ride than is commonly perceived.*

Exhibit 13–10. Typical segment of the U.S. Treasury yield curve. Off-the-run maturity sectors tend to trade more cheaply than a simple linear interpolation would suggest (using solely off-the-run U.S. Treasuries as an illustration).

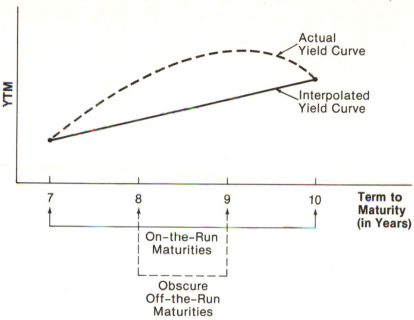

Comments: *Neglected maturity sectors tend to offer better relative value for the long-term investor. Off-the-run maturities trade at higher yields than an interpolated line would suggest.*

curve highlights the inherent inefficiencies in the marketplace. Significant twists and turns in the TR curve present swap opportunities for the value-minded investor. The issues that stand out as attractive risk:return combinations are the 6-year bond (7.70% TR), the 8-year bond (7.73% TR), and the 15-year bond (8.66% TR). In addition to all of the current-coupon issues, the 5-year, 7-year, and 29-year off-the-runs represent overvalued market sectors in a risk:return sense. One should seek alternative investments that offer more return and less risk.

Exhibit 13–14 compares the baseline TR curves of the on-the-run U.S. Treasuries and the off-the-run U.S. Treasuries on a duration, rather than a term-to-maturity, basis. This representation clearly illustrates that the market does not appraise risk in a consistent fashion. On a relative basis, the off-the-run paper with 4 to 5 years and 8 to 9 years in duration appears attractive. The issues with durations in the 5- to 7-year and 9-

Exhibit 13–11. Yields and Macaulay's durations on representative off-the-run U.S. Treasury bonds as of January 30, 1987.

Maturity (Years)	Macaulay's Duration	YTM (%)	YTM Pickup on Extension (BP)
1	0.97	5.95	+36
2	1.80	6.29	+22
3	2.57	6.51	+18
4	3.36	6.69	+13
5	3.98	6.82	+16
6	4.52	6.98	+ 5
7	5.26	7.03	+10
8	5.55	7.13	+ 8
9	6.31	7.21	+40
14	7.82	7.61	+15
15	8.49	7.76	+ 1
16	8.76	7.77	− 9
20	9.55	7.68	+ 2
29	11.33	7.70	

Comments: *The maturity breakdown utilizes a representative off-the-run issue in the particular sector. Due to the lack of a 15-year issue, a 15½-year issue is used as a reasonable proxy.*

Exhibit 13–12. One-year baseline total returns on representative off-the-run U.S. Treasury bonds as of January 30, 1987. The yield curve is unchanged in both shape and level 1 year hence. Reinvestments are made at a 7.00% rate.

Maturity (Years)	1-Year Total Return (%)	Total Return Pickup on Extension (BP)
1	6.11	+65
2	6.76	+26
3	7.02	+25
4	7.27	+ 8
5	7.35	+35
6	7.70	−32
7	7.38	+35
8	7.73	+ 5
9	7.78	+66
14	8.44	+22
15	8.66	−37
16	8.29	−50
20	7.79	+ 2
29	7.81	

Exhibit 13–13. Yield curve and baseline total return curve for representative off-the-run U.S. Treasury bonds as of January 30, 1987 (data from Exhibits 13–11 and 13–12).

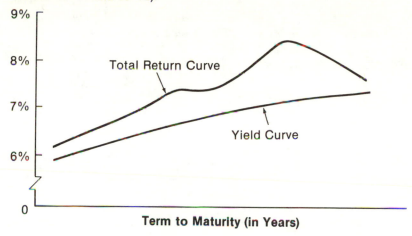

Exhibit 13–14. Baseline total return curves for on-the-run and off-the-run U.S. Treasury bonds as of January 30, 1987 (data from Exhibits 13–5 and 13–12).

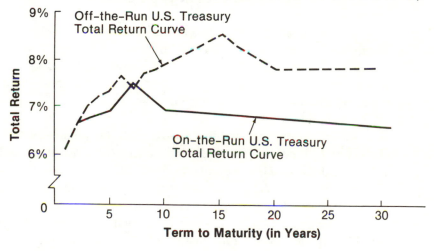

to 12-year ranges seem overpriced, given their neighbors' ability to outreturn them while assuming the same or less duration risk. The on-the-runs provide lower returns and are unappealing in a risk : return framework; however, the enhanced liquidity of these issues must be considered in light of the investor's needs and circumstances.

Exhibit 13–15. Yields and 1-year baseline total returns on representative off-the-run Federal Farm Credit Bank (FFCB) bonds on January 30, 1987.

Maturity (Years)	Macaulay's Duration	YTM (%)	YTM Pickup on Extension (BP)	1-Year Total Return (%)	Total Return Pickup on Extension (BP)
1	0.98	6.04		6.15	
			+41		+79
2	1.85	6.45		6.94	
			+44		+84
3	2.65	6.89		7.78	
			+15		−20
4	3.65	7.04		7.58	
			+26		+67
5	4.03	7.30		8.25	
			+16		− 4
6	4.69	7.46		8.21	
			+16		+21
7	5.05	7.62		8.42	

Observation: *A comprehensive baseline total return curve attempts to provide a more realistic starting point for assessing relative value across the maturity or duration spectrum. This curve highlights the perennial areas of inefficiency in bond valuation.*

Baseline total return curves by issuer sector

The total return curve concept applies to all issuer sectors, not simply U.S. Treasuries. Indeed, a series of total return curves can be created and overlayed as a method of screening the marketplace for undervalued sectors. With callable bond issues, an option-adjusted or effective duration is a more appropriate comparative base than is a Macaulay's duration.[8]

As an illustration, Exhibit 13–16 plots the Federal Farm Credit Bank (FFCB) baseline TR curve using January 30, 1987 data (see Exhibit 13–15). Exhibit 13–16 also compares the FFCB returns to U.S. Treasuries of similar maturity and similar duration. Once again, the TR curve offers many surprises. Relative to U.S. Treasuries, the 3-year, 5-year, and 7-year FFCBs stand out as superior investments. Numerically speaking, the FFCB spreads over similar maturity U.S. Treasuries (in a total return format) are far from uniform. Exhibit 13–17 lists the 1-year TRs expected on the FFCBs and U.S. Treasuries under a *no change* environment. The *total return spreads* are plotted in Exhibit 13–18. It becomes clear that, relative to U.S. Treasuries, 3-year, 5-year, and 7-year FFCBs at

---

[8] Refer to Chapter 6 for a thorough discussion of duration concepts.

Exhibit 13–16. Baseline total return curves for off-the-run U.S. Treasury bonds and FFCB bonds in the 1- to 7-year maturity sector (data from Exhibits 13–11, 13–12, and 13–15).

(a) Using term to maturity as the risk proxy.

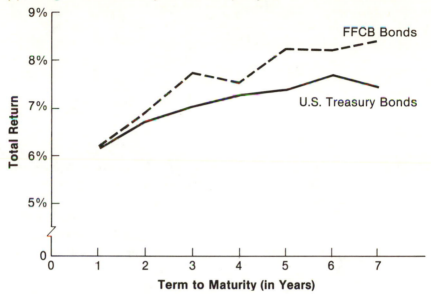

(b) Using duration as the risk proxy.

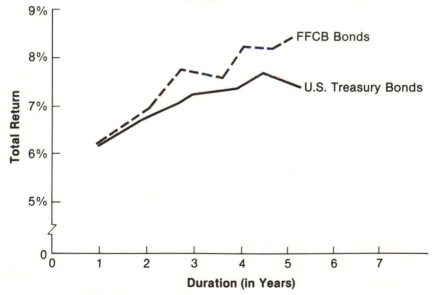

Exhibit 13–17. One-year baseline total returns on representative off-the-run FFCB bonds and comparable maturity off-the-run U.S. Treasury bonds (data from Exhibits 13–12 and 13–15).

| *Maturity* | *1-Year Total Return (%)* | | *Total Return* |
(Years)	*U.S. Treasury*	*FFCB*	*Spread (BP)*
1	6.11	6.15	+ 4
2	6.76	6.94	+ 18
3	7.02	7.78	+ 76
4	7.27	7.58	+ 31
5	7.35	8.25	+ 90
6	7.70	8.21	+ 51
7	7.38	8.42	+104

Comments: *The total return spread is the basis point difference between the FFCB return and the comparable U.S. Treasury return.*

+76BP, +90BP, and +104BP, respectively, are the attractive issues. Traditional yield spread analysis (see Exhibit 13–19) fails to capture the jagged increments in return, portraying the FFCB issues as modestly more attractive than comparable U.S. Treasuries. The 3-year FFCBs at +38BP in YTM hide the true bias of these bonds to outperform the

Exhibit 13–18. Return advantage of various maturity FFCBs over their U.S. Treasury counterparts (data from Exhibit 13–17).

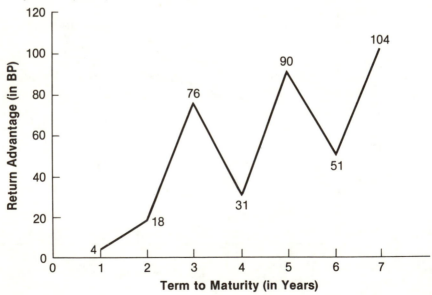

Exhibit 13–19. Traditional yield spread analysis of representative off-the-run FFCB bonds versus comparable maturity off-the-run U.S. Treasury bonds (data from Exhibits 13–11 and 13–15).

Maturity (Years)	Yield to Maturity (%)		Yield Spread (BP)
	U.S. Treasury	FFCB	
1	5.95	6.04	+ 9
2	6.29	6.45	+16
3	6.51	6.89	+38
4	6.69	7.04	+35
5	6.82	7.30	+48
6	6.98	7.46	+48
7	7.03	7.62	+59

Comments: *The yield spread is the basis point difference between the FFCB yield and the comparable U.S. Treasury yield.*

3-year U.S. Treasuries by 76BP in total return. Five-year FFCBs are another sleeper, with a modest 48BP yield spread guising the inherent tendency toward a 90BP TR enhancement.

Baseline TR curves, therefore, act as helpful flares that highlight the potentially under/(over)valued sectors of the market. A similar analysis can be performed on FNMAs, FHLBs, STRIPS, corporate bonds, and mortgage-backed securities. Caution must be taken with option-impacted securities to evaluate them on an option-free basis in order to allow comparability to a noncallable, risk-free U.S. Treasury benchmark issue.

Observation: *Baseline TR curves can be created by issuer sector. The resulting configurations often reveal total return biases that the YTM measure tends to overlook. Appropriate sector over/(under)weightings can then be initiated.*

Total return curves under changing market conditions

Baseline total return curves are a helpful supplement to the traditional yield curve in screening the marketplace for undervalued and overvalued issues or sectors. A portfolio manager may anticipate a general change in market yield levels, a change in maturity spreads (i.e., yield curve shape), and/or a change in sector spreads (e.g., quality, coupon, issuer).

Exhibit 13–20. Yields and 1-year baseline total returns for a hypothetical set of U.S. Treasury bonds each priced at par. Reinvestments are made at 6.50%.

Maturity (Years)	Macaulay's Duration	YTM (%)	1-Year Roll (BP)	1-Year Total Return (%)
1	0.99	5.00	NA*	5.08
2	1.91	6.00	−100	7.06
3	2.78	6.25	− 25	6.82
4	3.59	6.40	− 15	6.91
5	4.35	6.50	− 10	6.95
7	5.68	6.80	− 15	7.64
10	7.36	7.00	5	7.44
30	12.61	7.25	0	7.37

* Not applicable since the bond matures 1 year hence.

By incorporating these expectations into the total return simulation process, the manager can revise the initial baseline findings accordingly.

Parallel shifts in yield

For example, Exhibit 13–20 calculates baseline total returns for a series of U.S. Treasury bonds over a 1-year investment horizon. The

Exhibit 13–21. One-year total returns for a hypothetical set of U.S. Treasury bonds under a 100BP parallel shift in yields. Reinvestments are made at 6.00% and 7.00% under the +100BP and −100BP yield change scenarios, respectively (issues per Exhibit 13–20).

Maturity (Years)	1-Year Total Return (%) if Yields:	
	+100BP	−100BP
1	5.09	5.07
2	6.10	8.03
3	4.98	8.69
4	4.26	9.65
5	3.55	10.51
7	2.89	12.69
10	1.10	14.34
30	−3.58	20.67

2-year (7.06% TR) and 7-year (7.64% TR) issues appear to be the most attractive on a relative return basis. Assuming a 100BP parallel shift in yield, the relative values of individual issues change sizably. Exhibit 13–21 shows, for example, that the 1- and 2-year issues offer the most appealing risk:return tradeoffs in a 100BP rising yield environment. With falling rates, however, the 10- and 30-year issues provide sizable return advantages over their shorter maturity counterparts.[9] Exhibit 13–22 plots the three TR curves (baseline, +100BP, −100BP) for the selected U.S. Treasury bonds. The appropriate selection of issues is a function of the interest rate forecast.

Alternatively, a portfolio manager may decide to make the investment decision based on a *scenario-weighted return analysis*. For example, if the manager assigns a 50% probability to the baseline *no change* case, a 40% probability to the + *100BP* scenario, and a 10% probability to the − *100BP* outcome, the resulting probability-weighted TR composites are calculated in Exhibit 13–23 and diagrammed in Exhibit 13–24. The composite figures highlight the 2-year bond as the issue of choice in the short maturity area with a 6.77% TR (versus 5.08% for the 1-year, 6.27% for the 3-year, and 6.12% for the 4-year). The intermediate and long maturity sectors find the 7-year bond as the preferred issue with a 6.25% TR (versus 5.95% for the 5-year, 5.59% for the 10-year, and 4.32% for the 30-year).

Nonparallel shifts in yield

A nonparallel change in yield levels can have a significant impact on the relative returns registered by various maturity sectors. Continuing the U.S. Treasury bond example (data from Exhibit 13–20), a portfolio manager expects a general flattening of the yield curve over the forthcoming year. The magnitude of the flattening process is noted in Exhibit 13–25 along with the resulting 1-year TRs for the individual U.S. Treasury issues. The general level of yields is held constant in order to isolate the impact of the nonparallel shift.[10]

The projected flattening of the yield curve enhances the returns of the longer maturity issues vis-à-vis the baseline TRs of Exhibit 13–20.

---

[9] Keep in mind that the total returns are influenced by yield curve roll factors that arise from the natural aging of bond issues and the related shortening of their remaining terms to maturity and durations.

[10] As in the parallel yield shift example, total returns incorporate appropriate yield curve roll factors.

Exhibit 13–22. One-year total return curves for a series of U.S. Treasury bonds under rising rates, falling rates, and stable rates (data from Exhibit 13–23).

(a) Using term to maturity as the risk proxy.

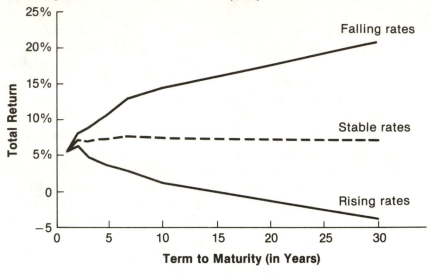

(b) Using duration as the risk proxy.

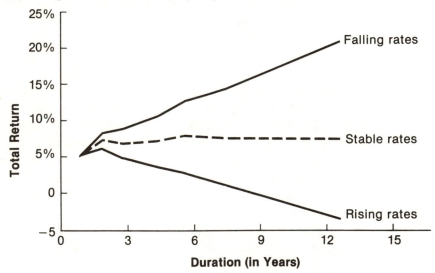

Exhibit 13–23. One-year scenario-weighted total returns for a hypothetical set of U.S. Treasury bonds (data from Exhibits 13–20 and 13–21).

Maturity (Years)	Total Return (%) if Yields: No Change	Total Return (%) if Yields: +100BP	Total Return (%) if Yields: −100BP	Scenario-Weighted 1-Year Total Return (%)
1	5.08	5.09	5.07	5.08
2	7.06	6.10	8.03	6.77
3	6.82	4.98	8.69	6.27
4	6.91	4.26	9.65	6.12
5	6.95	3.55	10.51	5.95
7	7.64	2.89	12.69	6.25
10	7.44	1.10	14.34	5.59
30	7.37	−3.58	20.67	4.32

Comments: *Scenario-weighted returns reflect a 50% probability of no change, a 40% probability of +100BP change, and a 10% probability of −100BP change.*

For example, the 7-year issue adds 149BP to its annual TR thanks to the nonparallel yield shift of −35BP. With the help of a 45BP drop in yield, the 10-year issue registers a sizable 304BP jump in expected return, giving it a 10.48% TR figure for the year. The dramatic yield curve flattening in the long maturity 30-year area (−70BP yield change) leads to a staggering 904BP of added return, for a total return of 16.41% over the 1-year period. It is abundantly clear that the 7-, 10-, and (especially) 30-year issues are the preferred alternatives in this total return simulation. The shorter maturity bonds either participate to a lesser degree (e.g., 3-year, 4-year, 5-year) or to no degree (e.g., 1-year, 2-year). Exhibit 13–26 draws the *nonparallel shift TR curve* alongside the baseline TR curve to graphically display this numeric finding. A steepening of the yield curve renders opposing results, with short maturity issues shining in relative value terms.

Sector spread changes

A manager may expect both the level and shape of the yield curve to remain stable while anticipating a shift in sector spreads. For example, a selection of AA-rated corporate bonds is described in Exhibit 13–27.

Exhibit 13–24. Scenario-weighted total return curve for a series of U.S. Treasury bonds (data from Exhibit 13–23).

(a) Using term to maturity as the risk proxy.

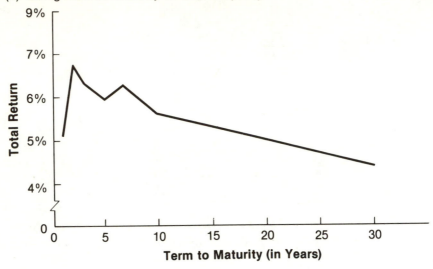

(b) Using duration as the risk proxy.

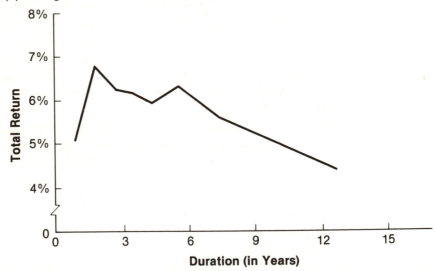

Exhibit 13–25. One-year total returns for a hypothetical set of U.S. Treasury bonds under a nonparallel shift in yield levels (in this case, a flattening yield curve). Reinvestments are made at a 6.50% rate.

Maturity (Years)	Today's YTM (%)	Expected Yield Change (BP)	Expected Ending YTM (%)	1-Year Total Return (%)	Excess Total Return versus Baseline Case (BP)
1	5.00	Unchanged	5.00	5.08	0
2	6.00	−25	5.75	7.06	0
3	6.25	−25	6.00	7.28	+ 46
4	6.40	−25	6.15	7.59	+ 68
5	6.50	−25	6.25	7.83	+ 88
7	6.80	−35	6.45	9.13	+149
10	7.00	−45	6.55	10.48	+304
30	7.25	−70	6.55	16.41	+904

Comments: *Each issue rolls down into the immediately preceding maturity over the next year. For the 7-, 10-, and 30-year issues, the roll factors are assumed to be 45, 50, and 70BP, respectively, as they roll into the 6-, 9-, and 29-year sectors.*

The table computes the yield spreads over comparable maturity U.S. Treasuries in addition to the 1-year baseline TRs and TR spreads versus similar U.S. Treasury bonds. The results indicate that the yield advantage of AA corporate bonds tends to bias these issues to outperform their U.S. Treasury counterparts. The degree of excess return varies widely, from 13BP (2-year maturity) to 161BP (3-year maturity). The differences in 1-year roll factors create a good deal of this variation; the initial yield spread advantage accounts for the remainder. Based on a *no change* environment, the investor is best compensated for the additional credit risk of owning AA bonds by concentrating the holdings in 3-year (+161BP incremental TR) and 30-year (+129BP incremental TR) issues.

Assuming a 20BP yield spread narrowing between AA corporate bonds and similar maturity U.S. Treasuries over the next year, Exhibit 13–28 presents the 1-year TRs and excess TRs of the aforementioned corporate issues. The sector spread narrowing enhances the relative attractiveness of the AA issues vis-à-vis the U.S. Treasuries, particularly in the long maturity sector, where a 20BP change in yield has a more sizable price and return impact than in the short maturity sector (recall Chapter 4). For example, the 30-year AA issue outperforms the 30-

Exhibit 13–26. One-year total return curves for a series of U.S. Treasury bonds under a baseline scenario and a nonparallel yield curve shift—flattening scenario (data from Exhibits 13–23 and 13–25).

(a) Using term to maturity as the risk proxy.

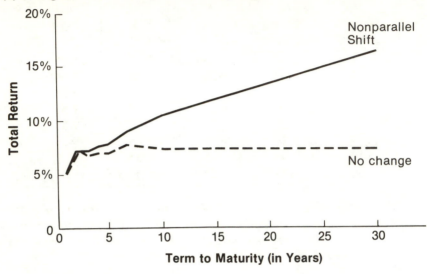

(b) Using duration as the risk proxy.

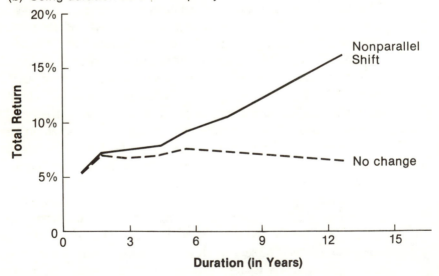

Exhibit 13–27. Yields, spreads, and 1-year baseline total returns of a hypothetical set of AA-rated corporate bonds, each priced at par. Reinvestments are made at a 7.50% rate (U.S. Treasury data per Exhibit 13–20).

Maturity (Years)	Macaulay's Duration	YTM (%)	Yield Spread versus Treasuries (BP)	1-Year Total Return (%)	1-Year Total Return Spread versus Treasuries (BP)
1	0.99	5.50	+ 50	5.60	+ 52
2	1.91	6.30	+ 30	7.19	+ 13
3	2.76	7.00	+ 75	8.43	+161
4	3.55	7.15	+ 75	7.68	+ 77
5	4.28	7.30	+ 80	7.95	+100
7	5.54	7.70	+ 90	8.32	+ 68
10	7.07	8.00	+100	8.47	+103
30	11.26	8.50	+125	8.66	+129

Comments: *The yield spread represents the difference between the corporate bond's yield and the yield of a comparable maturity U.S. Treasury bond. The 1-year total return spread represents the difference between the corporate bond's 1-year baseline total return and the 1-year baseline total return of a comparable maturity U.S. Treasury bond.*

Exhibit 13–28. One-year total returns for a hypothetical set of AA-rated corporate bonds under an assumption of a 20BP spread narrowing to comparable maturity U.S. Treasury bonds. Reinvestments are made at a 7.50% rate (U.S. Treasury data per Exhibit 13–20).

Maturity (Years)	1-Year Total Return (%)	1-Year Total Return Advantage over U.S. Treasuries (BP)
1	5.60	+ 52
2	7.38	+ 32
3	8.80	+198
4	8.35	+144
5	8.64	+169
7	9.28	+164
10	9.75	+231
30	10.84	+347

Comments: *The 1-year total return advantage is the excess return (BP) earned by the corporate bond versus its similar maturity U.S. Treasury bond given a 20BP narrowing in corporate bond yield spreads and no change in U.S. Treasury yields. Yield curve roll factors are incorporated into the results.*

Exhibit 13–29. One-year total return curves for AA-rated corporate bonds under a baseline scenario and a 20BP sector spread narrowing scenario. A comparable U.S. Treasury bond baseline total return curve is provided for perspective (data from Exhibits 13–20, 13–27, and 13–28).

(a) Using term to maturity as the risk proxy.

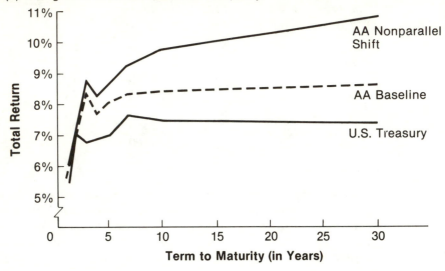

(b) Using duration as the risk proxy.

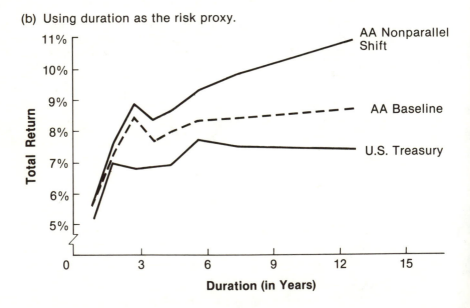

year U.S. Treasury by 347BP, 218BP of which is due to the 20BP
spread narrowing. The 3-year AA bond, on the other hand, outdoes its
Treasury equivalent by 198BP, only 37BP of which is attributable to
the 20BP shift in *AA versus Treasury* yields. Exhibit 13–29 plots the
TR curves for the AA corporates under both the baseline case and the
sector spread narrowing case, providing for comparative purposes the
U.S. Treasury baseline results. The 10- and 30-year AA corporate bonds
set the pace in the spread narrowing environment and appear to be the
issues of choice if one has such a predilection on future spread change.

> **Observation:** *Total return curves can encompass the expectation of
> changing market conditions rather than a simple baseline scenario.
> Parallel yield curve shifts, nonparallel yield curve shifts, and sector
> spread changes contribute to wide variations from the baseline case.
> The highlighted issue of choice is likely to differ.*

A baseline total return curve tends to highlight the areas of the
maturity (or duration) spectrum that appear rich or cheap. By incorporating
expectations about future changes in general yield levels, yield curve
shape, and sector spreads, a total return curve can be tailored to one's
specifications. If the prognostications prove correct, incremental return
is added to the bond portfolio by concentrating the portfolio holdings
in sectors deemed cheap according to the TR analysis.

Summary

A *total return curve* is a modified version of the traditional yield curve.
In an attempt to better portray the true risk:return tradeoffs available
in the marketplace, the total return curve plots expected total returns
(rather than yields) and durations (rather than terms to maturity). The
resulting configuration is a clearer screening device for finding under-
and overvalued bond market sectors than the traditional yield curve alone.
A *baseline total return curve* displays the inherent biases in market
sector return performance. A series of total return curves can be generated
for various issuer sectors, quality sectors, coupon sectors, and so on.
A portfolio manager's expectations regarding the general interest rate
level, the yield curve shape, and sector spreads form the basis for the
total return scenario analysis. The intent in all of these analyses is to
identify attractive and unattractive issues/sectors, with total return enhancement as the ultimate goal.

CHAPTER 14

Bond Swaps

This chapter applies the fundamentals of bond mathematics, bond risk, and bond return to individual bond swaps. Bond swaps can be classified into five basic types: YTM enhancement swaps, current yield enhancement swaps, quality enhancement swaps, liquidity enhancement swaps, and total return enhancement swaps. Total return enhancement swaps, the broadest category of bond swaps, can be subdivided into risk-neutral and risk-altering swaps.

Each of these swap types is discussed and illustrated in the order presented. The final section of the chapter provides a simple methodology for assessing the impact of a bond swap on a portfolio's risk and return characteristics. The impact of transaction costs is an important subject that is also addressed in the concluding section.

Before delving into the intricacies of individual bond swaps, a general distinction must be made between a proceeds trade and a par-for-par trade. In a *proceeds trade or swap*, an investor sells Bond A to purchase an equivalent dollar amount of Bond B. That is, the full proceeds of the sale of Bond A are reinvested in Bond B. In a *par-for-par (PFP) trade or swap*, the investor trades a specified par amount of Bond A for an equivalent par amount of Bond B. In other words, for every A bond sold there is a B bond purchased. Both the proceeds trade and the PFP trade may involve a dollar payup or dollar takeout.

A *dollar payup* signifies that the price of the purchased bond exceeds the price of the bond sold, requiring an additional outlay for the PFP swapper and establishing a higher cost basis per bond for both types of swappers. A *dollar takeout* finds the price of the sale candidate surpassing the cost of the newly purchased issue, thus entitling the PFP swapper to a net cash inflow and establishing a lower cost basis per bond for both the proceeds and PFP traders. Notice that dollar payups and dollar takeouts do not affect the net cash position of the proceeds swapper. The investor merely buys a lesser and greater par amount, respectively, of the new bond in order to remain fully invested. For bonds trading at similar dollar prices, the difference between a proceeds swap and a PFP swap is minor.

Generally speaking, bond swaps are analyzed on a proceeds, not a par-for-par, basis. The pool of dollars invested is typically held constant. Total returns are calculated as a percentage return per dollar invested, not per par amount held. Durations are based on market values rather than par amounts. For these reasons, the illustrations in this chapter focus on proceeds trades.[1] The concepts of dollar payups and dollar takeouts are important to the proceeds swapper because, although immune from a net inflow/(outflow) on the trade date, the investor is concerned about altering the dollar price of the securities held.[2] With this basic groundwork laid, it is now time to describe the various types of bond swaps that a portfolio manager commonly encounters.

Yield-to-maturity enhancement swap

A *yield-to-maturity (YTM) enhancement or yield-pickup swap* is simply a swap from a lower yielding bond to a higher yielding issue. Using June 30, 1987 data, an investor sells a 30-year U.S. Treasury bond (8¾% due 5/15/2017) at an 8.50% YTM (102–22 price), purchases a Bell Telephone of Pennsylvania (BLIP) 40-year bond (8¾% due

---

[1] The reader should keep in mind that a duration-weighted trade (to be illustrated) qualifies as a proceeds trade insofar as it uses cash equivalents to maintain equality between the sale proceeds and the purchase outlay. In a duration-weighted trade, the cash investment is treated as a bond, albeit one of very short maturity.

Trades based on the use of the *yield value of a 32nd* risk measure (to be discussed in the Appendix to this chapter) are weighted according to par amounts. The proceeds invested are likely to change, an exception to the chapter illustrations.

[2] Recall the discussion of book gains/(losses) in Chapter 10. Reinvestment rate risk and call/convexity risk have additional implications for bonds of different price levels.

4/1/2026) at a 9.58% YTM (91.50 price), and picks up 108BP in YTM (9.58% versus 8.50%). Alternatively, the investor can enhance yield by moving up in coupon. For example, a move from BLIP 8¾% due 4/1/2026 to BLIP 9⅝% due 7/15/2014 renders the investor a 23BP increase in yield (9.81% versus 9.58%).

A repositioning along the yield curve can enhance yield. For example, swap from a 2-year U.S. Treasury (6⅝% due 8/15/1989) into a 30-year U.S. Treasury (8¾% due 5/15/2017) garners an additional 97BP in yield (8.50% versus 7.53%). As another example, one can shorten maturity by 10 years and pick up 16BP by trading a 30-year U.S. Treasury (10⅝% due 8/15/2015) for a 20-year U.S. Treasury (10¾% due 8/15/2005). The 20-year maturity hump in the yield curve allows this yield enhancement (8.76% versus 8.60%). Finally, one can add yield by moving into lower quality corporate bonds. For example, an investor swapping from Florida Power and Light (FP&L) 9% due 10/1/2016 (rated Aa3/AA−) into Philadelphia Electric (PE) 10¼% due 11/1/2016 (rated Baa3/BBB−) enhances yield by 73BP (10.58% versus 9.85%).[3] The five YTM-enhancing swaps are summarized in Exhibit 14–1.

The attractiveness of the YTM enhancement swap stems from the fact that higher yielding bonds tend to outperform lower yielding bonds over long investment horizons.[4] If one reinvests at the YTM rate, the differences in ending wealth position can be substantial. Exhibit 14–2 looks at the impact of initial yield level on a $1,000.00 bond investment over 2-year, 10-year, and 30-year horizons. Using the 7.00% yield level as a benchmark, the investor sees his $1,000.00 contribution grow to $1,147.50 at the end of 2 years, to $1,989.80 at the end of 10 years, and to $7,878.10 at the end of 30 years. A swap into a bond yielding 7.10% (a 10BP yield enhancement) adds only $2.20 to the ending wealth position over a 2-year investment horizon ($1,149.70 − $1,147.50). However, over a 30-year period, the investor earns an additional $231.60 ($8,109.70 − $7,878.10) on the capital base, or an incremental 23.16% return on the original $1,000.00 investment.

A 100BP yield pickup leads to more sizable changes in the terminal wealth position. For example, a swap from a 7.00% YTM bond to an 8.00% YTM bond creates a modest $22.40 in added value over a 2-year period ($1,169.90 versus $1,147.50). The identical 100BP yield

---

[3] This type of yield enhancement positions the investor on a new, higher level yield curve. Recall from Chapter 12 that lower quality issues appear on progressively higher yield curves.

[4] The reader may wish to review Chapter 9's comment on this subject before proceeding.

Exhibit 14–1. Sample YTM enhancement swaps (6/30/87 data).

Issue Data	Rating	Price	YTM (%)
(a) S: U.S. Treasury 8¾% due 5/15/17	Aaa/AAA	102-22	8.50
B: BLIP 8¾% due 4/1/26	Aa1/AA+	91.50	9.58
YTM enhancement ⟶			108BP
(b) S: BLIP 8¾% due 4/1/26	Aa1/AA+	91.50	9.58
B: BLIP 9⅝% due 7/15/14	Aa1/AA+	98.25	9.81
YTM enhancement ⟶			23BP
(c) S: U.S. Treasury 6⅝% due 8/15/89	Aaa/AAA	98-08	7.53
B: U.S. Treasury 8¾% due 5/15/17	Aaa/AAA	102-22	8.50
YTM enhancement ⟶			97BP
(d) S: U.S. Treasury 10⅝% due 8/15/15	Aaa/AAA	121-09	8.60
B: U.S. Treasury 10¾% due 8/15/05	Aaa/AAA	117-30	8.76
YTM enhancement ⟶			16BP
(e) S: FP&L 9% due 10/1/16	Aa3/AA−	91.86	9.85
B: PE 10¼% due 11/1/16	Baa3/BBB−	97.00	10.58
YTM enhancement ⟶			73BP

enhancement leads to $201.30 in incremental return over 10 years ($2,191.10 versus $1,989.80) and a $2,641.50 surge in ending wealth over a 30-year horizon ($10,519.60 versus $7,878.10). The 30-year figure represents an added 264.15% return on the original investment and a 33.53% increase in ending wealth position over the 7% baseline bond. Yield-giveup swaps reduce the terminal wealth position commensurately and therefore conjure up investor resistance.[5]

A static focus on YTM changes can be dangerous. Additional risks

[5] YTM pickup swaps are comforting to most investors because of the relationships displayed in Exhibit 14–2. Yield giveup swaps are, not surprisingly, annoying to the same investors. Yield pickup trades are generally regarded as *good* trades and yield giveup trades as *bad* trades. However, for a total return manager judged on a short-term performance basis (e.g., quarterly, annually), a myriad of other factors differentiate yield enhancements from total return enhancements (refer to Chapter 9). Call risk, reinvestment rate risk, and credit/default risk must be considered by the buy-and-hold investor in making the yield pickup decision. Often the higher yielding bond carries incremental exposure to these factors.

Exhibit 14–2. Growth of a $1,000.00 investment in bonds of various yields to maturity. Each issue is initially purchased at par and is held to maturity, with all reinvestments made at the YTM rate.

Bond's YTM (%)	Ending Wealth Position in:		
	2 Years	*10 Years*	*30 Years*
4.00	$1,082.40	$1,485.90	$ 3,281.00
5.00	1,103.80	1,638.60	4,399.80
6.00	1,125.50	1,806.10	5,891.60
6.50	1,136.50	1,895.80	6,814.00
6.75	1,142.00	1,942.30	7,327.10
6.90	1,145.30	1,970.70	7,653.00
7.00	1,147.50	1,989.80	7,878.10
7.10	1,149.70	2,009.10	8,109.70
7.25	1,153.10	2,038.40	8,469.80
7.50	1,158.70	2,088.20	9,105.10
8.00	1,169.90	2,191.10	10,519.60
9.00	1,192.50	2,411.70	14,027.40
10.00	1,215.50	2,653.30	18,679.20

Comments: *Wealth positions are enhanced by yield pickups, particularly over longer horizons. Seemingly modest yield changes (e.g., 50BP) have substantial impacts on wealth positions over long investment horizons. Conversely, yield giveups detract from the terminal wealth stance. The wealth enhancements illustrated above assume no default or premature call.*

such as call risk, reinvestment rate risk, credit risk, general interest rate risk, yield curve risk, and liquidity risk can mitigate the yield advantage offered by a particular bond.[6] The incremental risks associated with the yield-pickup trades of earlier illustration are as follows:

---

[6] *Call risk* stems from a higher probability that the issue will be prematurely taken from the investor. A lower yield environment exacerbates this risk. *Reinvestment rate risk* arises from the danger that a bond's coupons may be reinvested at a rate somewhat below the assumed YTM rate of reinvestment. Incremental yield advantages are thereby reduced and, in some cases, eliminated. *Credit/default risk* is created by a lower quality issuer. *General interest rate risk* is attributable to an extension of the duration of the bond investment. A rise in interest rates drives down the value of the newly purchased bond vis-à-vis the bond sold. *Yield curve risk* is generated by nonparallel shifts in yields along the maturity spectrum. A maturity alteration leads to this type of incremental risk. *Liquidity risk* stems from a move to a less liquid investment (e.g., a corporate bond versus a U.S. Treasury issue).

1. Tsy 8¾% due 5/15/2017 to BLIP 8¾% due 4/1/2026

   Yield enhancement: 108BP
   Incremental risk(s):   Call risk, credit risk, reinvestment rate risk, general interest rate risk, and yield curve risk

2. BLIP 8¾% due 4/1/2026 to BLIP 9⅝% due 7/15/2014

   Yield enhancement: 23BP
   Incremental risk(s):   Call risk, reinvestment rate risk, and yield curve risk

3. Tsy 6⅝% due 8/15/1989 to Tsy 8¾% due 5/15/2017

   Yield enhancement: 97BP
   Incremental risk(s):   Reinvestment rate risk, general interest rate risk, and yield curve risk

4. Tsy 10⅝% due 8/15/2015 to Tsy 10¾% due 8/15/2005

   Yield enhancement: 16BP
   Incremental risk(s):   Reinvestment rate risk and yield curve risk

5. FP&L 9% due 10/1/2016 to PE 10¼% due 11/1/2016

   Yield enhancement: 73BP
   Incremental risk(s):   Call risk, credit risk, and reinvestment rate risk

A YTM enhancement is simply that—an increase in YTM. It may or may not lead to enhanced total returns.

> **Observation:** *A YTM enhancement swap entails a trade into a higher yielding bond. The yield enhancement tends to create an upward bias in returns, particularly over long-term investment horizons. However, the attendant risks associated with the higher yielding bond should not be ignored.*

Current yield enhancement swap

A *current yield enhancement swap,* as its name implies, is designed to increase the current yield of a bond holding. Recall from Chapter 3 that current yield is the annual coupon return generated by a bond,

Exhibit 14–3. Sample current yield enhancement swaps (6/30/87 data).

Issue Data	*Price*	*YTM (%)*	*CY (%)*
(a) S: U.S. Treasury 6⅝% due 7/31/88	99-15	7.14	6.66
B: U.S. Treasury 14% due 7/15/88	106-30	6.95	13.09
Current yield enhancement ⟶			643BP
(b) S: U.S. Treasury 6⅝% due 8/15/89	98-07	7.54	6.75
B: U.S. Treasury 14½% due 7/15/89	113-02	7.47	12.82
Current yield enhancement ⟶			607BP
(c) S: U.S. Treasury 6⅝% due 5/15/92	94-13	8.03	7.02
B: U.S. Treasury 13¾% due 5/15/92	122-10	8.11	11.24
Current yield enhancement ⟶			422BP
(d) S: U.S. Treasury 8% due 8/15/01	95-15	8.56	8.38
B: U.S. Treasury 15¾% due 11/15/01	157-05	8.70	10.02
Current yield enhancement ⟶			164BP
(e) S: U.S. Treasury 7¼% due 5/15/16	85-19	8.61	8.47
B: U.S. Treasury 11¼% due 2/15/15	127-00	8.66	8.86
Current yield enhancement ⟶			39BP

Comments: *Current yield buyers focus on shorter maturity issues, driving their prices up and their YTMs down. For example, the 14% coupon bond of 7/15/88 trades at an appreciably lower YTM than a similar maturity 6⅝% coupon issue (6.95% versus 7.14%).*

expressed as a percentage of the bond's current market price. Exhibit 14–3 analyzes five swaps that enhance current yield. The illustrations employ U.S. Treasury bonds in the 1-year, 2-year, 5-year, 15-year, and 30-year maturity sectors.

The results clearly show that for bonds of similar maturity and yield, higher coupon issues provide incremental current yield over their lower coupon counterparts. This effect is particularly pronounced in the short maturity sectors. For example, in the 1-year maturity sector, an investor swaps from a 6⅝% bond to a 14% bond and picks up 643BP in current yield (13.09% versus 6.66%). Similar trades in the 2-, 5-, 15-, and 30-year sectors offer 607BP, 422BP, 164BP, and 39BP enhancements in current yield, respectively. For reasons cited in Chapter 9, short maturity issues with widely divergent coupon rates tend to offer the greatest potential for current yield enhancement.

Exhibit 14–4 calculates the current yields of a series of discount, par, and premium bonds of various maturities (1 year, 5 years, 30 years), each priced to yield 7.00%. One can see that, holding YTM constant, premium bonds provide a great deal more current (coupon) return than do discount issues of like maturity. Once again, short maturity premium bonds, having lower dollar prices than their longer maturity counterparts, offer an overabundance of current yield.

For an investor requiring a specified level of annual coupon income, current yield increments can be beneficial. However, for the total return investor or for the investor who wishes to control losses in principal value, additions of current yield may or may not be appropriate. The sizable discrepancies between total return and current yield were noted in Chapter 9.[7] The scientific amortization of a bond's premium and corresponding reductions in principal value were likewise analyzed.

> **Observation:** *A current yield enhancement swap involves a trade into a bond offering a higher current yield. This type of swap provides incremental coupon returns to a bond portfolio, often at the expense of principal positions. Current yield enhancements are most dramatic in short maturity, high coupon issues.*

Quality enhancement swap

A *quality enhancement swap* entails an upward move in the credit quality of the issues held. One may sell a BBB-rated corporate bond and replace it with an AA-rated issue. Alternatively, one may decide to increase holdings in U.S. Treasuries at the expense of federal agency bond

---

[7] Indeed, Exhibit 14–3 illustrates that investors seeking high current yields concentrate their purchases in high coupon, short maturity issues. Bond mutual funds and money market funds report their fund status in terms of current yield. These buyers have driven premium bond prices up to the point where the bonds yield less than current-coupon issues (on a YTM basis). For example, the U.S. Treasury 14% due 7/15/1988 trades at a price to yield 6.95%, a solid 19BP less than the yield of the similar maturity 6⅝% coupon issue. The 2-year maturity area finds the 14½% coupon security selling at a price to yield 7BP less than a 6⅝% coupon bond of similar maturity. The incremental current yield of 600+ basis points offered by these two high coupon issues is irresistible to bond mutual fund managers. The 1-year maturity bond is particularly appealing since it requires only a 7½ point payup in price (106–30 versus 99–15). A long maturity current yield play requires the establishment of a significantly higher average dollar price. For example, in the 15-year maturity area, a swap from an 8% coupon to a 15¾% coupon requires over a 60-point payup in price (157–05 versus 95–15), and the trade nets only 164BP in additional current yield. Hence the focus of current yield buyers is in the shorter maturities.

Exhibit 14–4. Current yields of discount (4.00%), current-coupon (7.00%), and premium (14.00%) bonds priced to yield 7.00% to maturity.

Maturity Sector	Issue	YTM (%)	Price	Current Yield (%)
1-year	4.00% coupon	7.00	97.15	4.12
	7.00% coupon	7.00	100.00	7.00
	14.00% coupon	7.00	106.65	13.13
5-year	4.00% coupon	7.00	87.53	4.57
	7.00% coupon	7.00	100.00	7.00
	14.00% coupon	7.00	129.11	10.84
30-year	4.00% coupon	7.00	62.58	6.39
	7.00% coupon	7.00	100.00	7.00
	14.00% coupon	7.00	187.31	7.47

Comments: *High coupon issues of similar maturity and yield display current yield advantages over their low coupon counterparts. This effect is especially noticeable in short maturity sectors.*

holdings.[8] Any of a wide variety of quality enhancements can be undertaken (e.g., A to AAA, A− to A+, BBB to A). The common theme is an upgrade in quality, the magnitude of which is at the discretion of the investor. A derivative form of quality enhancement is a swap into a similarly rated issue with the anticipation that the newly purchased bond is an improving credit and will be upgraded in the near future. In the same vein, a move from a deteriorating credit to a stable credit of similar quality can be viewed as a quality enhancement swap since it is an attempt to avoid a future downgrading into a lower quality class.

Exhibit 14–5 provides three examples of quality enhancement swaps. In the first case, an Aa1/AA+ telephone utility bond is sold to purchase U.S. Treasury bonds. The second example swaps out of a 10-year federal agency bond into a similar maturity U.S. Treasury. The final illustration upgrades an electric utility holding from Baa3/BBB− quality to an Aa3/AA− distinction.

Investors often have minimum quality requirements (e.g., A or higher quality) and restrictions on the percentage amount of a portfolio that can be invested in a specific quality sector (e.g., a maximum of

---

[8] The securities of federal agencies are not directly guaranteed by the U.S. government. The government:agency relationship is more of an implicit tie or a moral obligation. As such, agency paper is deemed a quality between that of a U.S. Treasury bond and a AAA-rated corporate issue.

Exhibit 14–5. Sample quality enhancement swaps (6/30/87 data).

	Issue Data	Rating	Price	YTM (%)
(a)	S: BLIP 8¾% due 4/1/26	Aa1/AA+	91.50	9.58
	B: U.S. Treasury 8¾% due 5/15/17	Aaa/AAA	102-22	8.50
	Quality enhancement ⟶ Strong AA to AAA (Treasury)			
(b)	S: FNMA 7.60% due 1/10/97	Agency	91-26	8.89
	B: U.S. Treasury 7¼% due 11/15/96	Aaa/AAA	92-14	8.43
	Quality enhancement ⟶ Agency to AAA (Treasury)			
(c)	S: PE 10¼% due 11/1/16	Baa3/BBB−	97.00	10.58
	B: FP&L 9% due 10/1/16	Aa3/AA−	91.86	9.85
	Quality enhancement ⟶ Weak BBB to weak AA			

10% in the A-rated sector) or issuer quality sector (e.g., a maximum of 20% in corporate bonds, a minimum of 50% in U.S. Treasury bonds). Quality enhancement swaps can help maintain those required levels. Unfortunately, quality enhancement swaps tend to render lower yields to the newly purchased issues.[9] Quality enhancements are not explicitly intended to create incremental total returns.

> **Observation:** *A quality enhancement swap moves into a higher quality bond issue. U.S. Treasury bonds offer the highest degree of credit quality.*

Liquidity enhancement swap

A *liquidity enhancement swap* is designed to increase the liquidity, or tradeability, of the portfolio holdings. *Liquidity* is defined as the ease with which a bond can be purchased or sold at a fair market price in a timely manner. Liquidity can be observed by the size of the bond's bid-offer spread and by the level of daily trading activity in the issue.

The outstanding issue size reflects, to some degree, the relative liquidity of a particular bond. Exhibit 14–6 provides a sampling of the outstanding amounts of a variety of issues and issuer types. In general, larger issue sizes correlate with superior liquidity characteristics. Several rules of thumb apply to degrees of liquidity:

1. U.S. Treasury bonds offer the highest degree of liquidity, with the current auction issues providing more liquidity than the off-the-run issues.

---

[9] A quality enhancement swap moves the investor onto a new, lower level yield curve on which the higher quality issues are priced. Recall from Chapter 12 that higher quality issues appear on progressively lower yield curves.

2. Federal agency bonds and mortgage-backed securities are the next most liquid items, with recently issued or current-coupon bonds providing the best liquidity.

3. Corporate bonds have liquidity characteristics that are slightly less attractive than federal agency credits. Once again, recently issued bonds tend to trade at narrower bid-offer spreads than older, more seasoned issues. Large issue sizes and shorter maturities find enhanced liquidity as well.

4. Esoteric issues (e.g., private placements, structured mortgage-backed products) have the least liquidity in the universe of fixed-income investments. It is not unusual to wait days before a transaction can be consummated. These items are appropriately termed *illiquid*.

Exhibit 14–7 presents four illustrative liquidity enhancement swaps. The first example swaps an off-the-run, less frequently traded, U.S. Treasury 30-year bond for the current auction issue U.S. Treasury in the 30-year sector. The second swap proposal moves from an agency

Exhibit 14–6. Sampling of U.S. Treasury, federal agency, and corporate bonds and their par amounts outstanding as of June 30, 1987.

Issuer Sector Type	Amount Outstanding (Millions)
U.S. Treasury bonds	
U.S. Treasury 7½% due 11/15/16	18,500
U.S. Treasury 8¾% due 5/15/17	9,250
U.S. Treasury 10⅝% due 8/15/15	6,500[*]
U.S. Treasury 13⅛% due 5/15/01	1,800
Federal agency bonds	
FFCB 11½% due 10/20/88	1,075
FFCB 11.80% due 10/20/93	440
FHLB 8¼% due 6/25/96	1,000
FHLB 7.70% due 8/26/96	450
FNMA 7⅜% due 10/10/91	1,000
FNMA 7.80% due 10/10/91	400
Corporate bonds	
Bell Tel PA 8¾% due 4/1/26	275
General Motors 8⅛% due 4/15/16	500
Honeywell 9⅞% due 6/1/17	100
Kansas P&L 8⅝% due 3/1/17	50
GTEL-South 9½% due 5/1/27	50

[*] Of this amount, a large portion has been stripped and sold as zero-coupon bonds, making the available supply of intact issues even more restricted.

Comments: *Issues with large amounts outstanding tend to offer better liquidity than smaller issues.*

Exhibit 14–7. Sample liquidity enhancement swaps (6/30/87 data).

Issue Data	*Price*	*YTM (%)*
(a) S: U.S. Treasury 10⅝% due 8/15/15	121-09	8.60
B: U.S. Treasury 8¾% due 5/15/17	102-22	8.50
Liquidity enhancement ————→	Off-the-run issue to on-the-run issue	
(b) S: FFCB 13¾% due 7/20/92	120-18	8.64
B: U.S. Treasury 13¾% due 5/15/92	122-10	8.11
Liquidity enhancement ————→	Agency issue to U.S. Treasury issue	
(c) S: BLIP 8¾% due 4/1/26	91.50	9.58
B: U.S. Treasury 8¾% due 5/15/17	102-22	8.50
Liquidity enhancement ————→	Corporate issue to U.S. Treasury issue	
(d) S: GM 9% due 10/1/05 (private)*	92.50	9.89
B: GM 8⅛% due 4/15/16	86.00	9.56
Liquidity enhancement ————→	Private placement to publicly traded issue	

* A hypothetical issue.

bond (Federal Farm Credit Bank) to a U.S. Treasury bond of similar characteristics. The third trade enhances liquidity by shifting from a corporate bond into a U.S. Treasury issue. The final illustration sells a private placement and replaces it with a (more liquid) publicly traded issue of the same name.

Liquidity needs are a function of both the investor's objectives/ desires and the management style used in the investment process. An investor requirement of reasonable stability in portfolio returns necessitates a liquid portfolio that can easily be dismantled should market conditions deteriorate rapidly. An investor using the portfolio in an asset allocation context must maintain a high degree of liquidity in the portfolio as asset reallocations may deem an expedient reduction in the bond portfolio component of the multi-asset schematic. An active bond management style involving yield curve swapping and interest rate anticipation strategies warrants a high degree of portfolio liquidity, with actively traded issues comprising the bulk of the portfolio assets. A buy-and-hold-to-maturity portfolio requires a lesser degree of liquidity, with incremental yield assuming a more prominent investment role.

> **Observation:** *A liquidity enhancement swap entails a trade into a more liquid security. This type of swap is intended to add flexibility to a portfolio by allowing for timely, low-cost transactions. U.S. Treasury bonds provide the greatest degree of market liquidity. Recently issued, actively traded bonds of large issue size offer more liquidity than off-the-run, seasoned issues of smaller size. Private placements and other esoteric securities are relatively illiquid.*

Total return enhancement swap

The final category of swaps, those of the total return enhancing variety, are the most pertinent type in today's performance-oriented environment. Good performance is differentiated from bad performance in total return terms. Benchmark bond indexes are followed with utmost concern for the bottom-line monthly, quarterly, and annual total return figures. Active bond managers are under increasing pressure to outperform prescribed benchmarks with the indexation of bond portfolios a ready alternative for dissatisfied clients.[10]

Total return enhancement swaps can be classified into two broad types: *risk-neutral swaps* and *risk-altering swaps*. The former are designed to nullify the effect of any general move in interest rates, while the latter attempt to profit from an expected shift in yields by altering the portfolio's market risk exposure appropriately. Risk-neutral swaps come in four basic varieties: substitution swaps, convexity enhancement swaps, reinvestment rate protection swaps, and sector swaps. Risk-altering swaps are of two general forms: *interest rate anticipation swaps* and *riding-the-yield-curve swaps*.

Risk-neutral swaps

Substitution swap. A *substitution swap* is the quintessential risk-neutral swap. This swap entails trading one bond for another bond with

---

[10] Performance measurement and bond indexation are discussed at length in Chapter 15.

identical characteristics (coupon rate, maturity, call/sinking fund features, credit quality, issuer, liquidity) that is selling at a lower price. Recall that the bond market is an over-the-counter dealer network, not an organized exchange.[11] A riskless arbitrage is performed by selling a bond to Dealer A at price X and buying the same bond from Dealer B at a price less than X. In a liquid, efficiently priced market, riskless arbitrages such as the one described are difficult to execute and usually create negligible incremental returns. However, in less liquid securities (e.g., seasoned corporate bonds, off-the-run federal agency bonds, esoteric products), riskless substitution swaps can be carried out.

A generic issuer sector allows for swaps between very similar, but not identical, securities. Although these swaps fail to fit the purest definition of a substitution swap, they can often be used to generate similar results as market inefficiencies are worked out. *Generic,* or *plain vanilla,* sectors include U.S. Treasuries, FNMAs, FFCBs, FHLBs, and telephone utilities.[12]

Exhibit 14–8 proposes four substitution swaps between nearly identical securities. The first illustration trades from one U.S. Treasury to another of an identical coupon in the same maturity area (15 years). The final three examples are conducted between telephone utility issues of similar quality, coupon, and maturity. In each case, the lower yielding bond is sold and the highest yielding substitute bond is purchased.[13]

> **Observation:** *A substitution swap attempts to replace a bond holding with an identical (or nearly identical) bond trading at a higher yield and, therefore, at a lower relative price.*

Convexity enhancement swap. The *convexity enhancement swap* intends to add positive convexity, or reduce negative convexity, while

---

[11] The focus of this book is on the institutional investor market, not the odd-lot, retail bond market. A series of some 1,500 U.S. corporate bonds are listed and traded on the New York Stock Exchange. The liquidity and pricing efficiency of bonds traded on this organized exchange market are poor. An organized trading locale for institutional round lots is not currently in place.

[12] The telephone utility sector is becoming less generic as the Bell operating subsidiaries are progressively deregulated and individual companies pursue different ventures and encounter varying degrees of business risk. The impact of individual state public utility commissions is an additional differentiating factor.

[13] For issues with identical coupon rates and maturities, the higher yielding bond sells at a lower dollar price, allowing a dollar *takeout* on the substitution trade.

Exhibit 14–8. Sample substitution swaps (6/30/87 data).

Issue Data	Rating	Price	YTM (%)
(a) S: U.S. Treasury 10¾% due 2/15/05	Aaa/AAA	116-26	8.75
B: U.S. Treasury 10¾% due 5/15/03	Aaa/AAA	116-26	8.77
(b) S: NYT 8⅝% due 5/15/24	Aa3/AA+	89.50	9.67
B: NYT 8¾% due 4/1/23	Aa3/AA+	90.50	9.70
(c) S: IBT 8½% due 4/22/26	Aa1/AAA	89.50	9.53
B: ChesPot Va. 8½% due 9/1/26	Aaa/AA+	89.00	9.58
(d) S: PacNW Bell 8⅝% due 4/1/26	Aa1/AA	90.25	9.58
S: SNET 8⅝% due 8/15/26	Aa1/AA+	89.75	9.64
B: SoBell 8⅝% due 9/1/26	Aa1/AA+	89.50	9.66

Comments: *A pure substitution swap is a riskless arbitrage in the same issue. The swaps above are substitution swaps between nearly identical securities. The higher yielding issue is always the preferential choice.*

Exhibit 14–9. Issue data on 7.00% coupon U.S. Treasury bonds priced at par to yield 7.00% to maturity.

Issue	Price	YTM (%)	Modified Duration
2-year 7.00% coupon Treasury	100.00	7.00	1.84
7-year 7.00% coupon Treasury	100.00	7.00	5.46
30-year 7.00% coupon Treasury	100.00	7.00	12.47

holding the average duration constant.[14] Extending duration naturally enhances convexity, but it does so at an increased level of general market risk.[15] Risk-neutral swaps attempt to control the overall market risk exposure while adding incremental returns. Convexity is a concept predicated on instantaneous yield changes; therefore, the examples that follow operate under an instantaneous return assumption.

Exhibit 14–9 presents issue data for three U.S. Treasury bonds in a 7% yield environment. Exhibit 14–10 shows that a dumbbell combination of short maturity and long maturity bonds (2s and 30s) offers enhanced convexity characteristics while maintaining an average duration identical

---

[14] The reader is encouraged to review Chapter 6 for an explanation of the convexity concept.

[15] A convexity enhancement through duration extension is implicitly incorporated in the total return enhancements of an interest rate anticipation swap, a type of *risk-altering* swap discussed later in this chapter.

Exhibit 14–10. Instantaneous price returns for individual U.S. Treasury bonds and a dumbbell portfolio of 2- and 30-year issues (supporting issue data in Exhibit 14–9).

Change in Yield (BP)	Price Return (%):				Return Advantage (2/30 versus 7) (%)
	2-Year	7-Year	30-Year	2/30-Year Portfolio	
−300	+5.71	+18.16	+52.14	+21.54	+3.38
−200	+3.76	+11.69	+30.91	+13.02	+1.33
−100	+1.86	+ 5.65	+13.84	+ 5.95	+0.30
− 50	+0.92	+ 2.78	+ 6.56	+ 2.84	+0.06
− 10	+0.18	+ 0.55	+ 1.26	+ 0.55	0
0	0	0	0	0	0
+ 10	−0.18	− 0.54	− 1.23	− 0.54	0
+ 50	−0.91	− 2.68	− 5.93	− 2.62	+0.06
+100	−1.81	− 5.28	−11.31	− 5.05	+0.23
+200	−3.59	−10.22	−20.64	− 9.40	+0.82
+300	−5.32	−14.85	−28.39	−13.19	+1.66

Comments: *The 2/30-year portfolio is a combination of 2-year bonds (65.90% market value weighting) and 30-year bonds (34.10% market value weighting). The weighted average modified duration of the 2/30-year portfolio is 5.46 years, equivalent to that of the 7-year bond.*

to that of a single intermediate maturity bullet bond (a 7-year issue). Chapter 6 illustrated this phenomenon in fuller detail. Exhibit 14–11 displays the convexity advantage of the dumbbell combination in a curvilinear format.

Exhibit 14–12 analyzes the instantaneous price return behavior of a dumbbell combination with even greater duration disparity: a cash/30-year zero portfolio. This portfolio offers 2 to 3 times the convexity of the 2-year/30-year Treasury bond combination of Exhibit 14–10 (compare the return advantages). The heightened concentration of positive convexity inherent in long zeros accounts for this effect. Vis-à-vis the 7-year Treasury, the cash/30-year zero portfolio outperforms by 55–822BP given parallel yield shifts in the 100–300BP range.[16] Indeed, an investor

[16] The assumptions of parallel, instantaneous, and sizable yield shifts are precarious. A small, nonparallel yield change can completely negate the anticipated benefits of a positive convexity advantage. The spread risk between the coupon-bearing U.S. Treasuries and the STRIPS should not be ignored.

Exhibit 14–11. Incremental convexity of a 2-year/30-year dumbbell combination versus a bullet bond of similar duration (data from Exhibit 14–10).

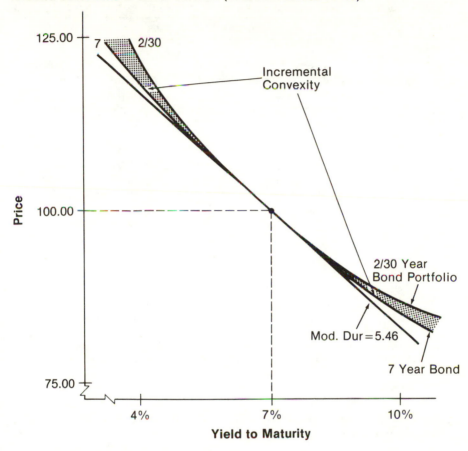

Comments: *Dumbbell combinations of bonds offer a convexity advantage over a bullet bond of similar duration.*

desiring to maximize convexity is always biased toward holding severely dumbbelled portfolios.

Exhibit 14–13 summarizes two illustrative convexity enhancement swaps. The first example, a bullet dumbbell swap, was outlined above. The second illustration entails a move from a callable corporate bond (an electric utility issue) into a U.S. Treasury bond of similar call-adjusted, or effective, duration. The convexity enhancement is evidenced by the increase from a convexity factor of 1.76 to a convexity factor of 2.21. Convexity enhancement swaps serve to increase total return potential

Exhibit 14–12. Comparison of the instantaneous price returns of a dumbbell portfolio of cash and 30-year zeros versus a portfolio of 7-year U.S. Treasury bonds. Each portfolio bears a modified duration of 5.46 years.

		Instantaneous Price Return			
Change in Yield (BP)	*Cash*	*7-Year Treasury (%)*	*30-Year Zero (%)*	*Cash/30-Year Zero Portfolio* (%)*	*Return Advantage† (%)*
−300	0	+18.16	+140.11	+26.38	+8.22
−200	0	+11.69	+ 79.06	+14.89	+3.20
−100	0	+ 5.65	+ 33.72	+ 6.35	+0.70
− 50	0	+ 2.78	+ 15.62	+ 2.94	+0.16
− 10	0	+ 0.55	+ 2.94	+ 0.55	0
0	0	0	0	0	0
+ 10	0	− 0.54	− 2.86	− 0.54	0
+ 50	0	− 2.68	− 13.48	− 2.54	+0.14
+100	0	− 5.28	− 25.11	− 4.73	+0.55
+200	0	−10.22	− 43.84	− 8.26	+1.96
+300	0	−14.85	− 57.82	−10.89	+3.96

* The portfolio combination holds 81.17% in cash and 18.83% in 30-year zeros on a market value weighted basis. The resulting portfolio duration is 5.46 years on a modified basis, exactly equal to that of the 7-year Treasury bond portfolio. The above table makes it clear that dumbbell combinations have superior convexity characteristics vis-à-vis bullet portfolios of identical duration. The wider the duration disparity of the dumbbell portfolio components, the greater the convexity advantage.

† Attributable to more positive convexity.

by creating a mathematical bias for excess returns, particularly in highly volatile interest rate environments.[17]

> **Observation:** *A convexity enhancement swap involves a trade into a bond offering a greater degree of positive convexity. Total return potential is enhanced by benefiting from interest rate changes in both bull and bear market scenarios. The average duration of a bond portfolio is neither extended nor contracted by a convexity enhancement swap.[18] Noncallable bonds and dumbbell combinations of bonds offer the greatest possibilities for convexity enhancement.*

[17] In stable yield environments, convexity enhancement swaps tend to reduce total return prospects since securities with more convexity generally trade at lower yields.

[18] This is true because of this book's classification of a convexity enhancement swap as a risk-neutral trade. One can sizably increase the convexity of a bond portfolio by swapping into long duration securities; however, a commensurate increase in market risk accompanies such a move and qualifies the swap in the interest rate anticipation variety.

Exhibit 14–13. Sample convexity enhancement swaps.

Swap Proposal (7% Yield Environment)	Price	YTM (%)	Modified Duration
S: 7-year U.S. Treasury	100.00	7.00	5.46
B: 2-year U.S. Treasury (65.90%)	100.00	7.00	1.84
B: 30-year U.S. Treasury (34.10%)	100.00	7.00	12.47

Convexity enhancement: The dumbbell 2/30 combination offers more positive convexity than a bullet 7-year bond of similar average duration (recall Exhibit 14–10).

Swap Proposal (6/30/87 Data)	Price	YTM (%)	Effective Duration	Convexity Factor
S: CWE 10½% due 2/15/16	101.25	10.36	8.73	−1.76
B: U.S. Treasury 10¾% due 8/15/05	117-16	8.80	8.73	2.21

Convexity enhancement: A noncallable U.S. Treasury bond offers more convexity than a callable electric utility (*Commonwealth Edison*) bond of similar effective duration. The convexity factors reflect a ±200BP change in yield levels.

Reinvestment rate protection swap

Definition and purpose. The *reinvestment rate protection (RRP) swap* enhances total returns by ensuring excess performance in an environment of lower interest rates.[19] The need for reinvestment rate protection is particularly acute over long-term investment periods. An unexpected decline in reinvestment rates can substantially reduce realized compound yields (recall Chapter 8).

In general, a swap from a high coupon bond into a lower coupon issue qualifies as a reinvestment rate protection swap.[20] The ultimate reinvestment rate protection is offered by a zero-coupon bond since the

[19] The focus of this section is on noncallable U.S. Treasury bonds. The addition of call features and default potential in corporate bonds stresses the need for reinvestment rate protection. Changes in call features are handled in the *convexity enhancement swap* section; alterations in credit quality are addressed in the *quality enhancement swap* section.

[20] If, however, the high coupon bond provides a significant yield advantage over its lower coupon counterpart, the higher coupon bond should be held. In these instances, the lower relative cost of the high coupon issue allows it to experience an abnormally low reinvestment rate and still outperform the more (relatively) expensive, low coupon issue. This point is illustrated in a forthcoming example in this chapter.

reinvestment returns are internally compounded and are not externally reliant on prevailing market interest rates. Three additional axioms should be kept in mind:

1. The longer the investment holding period, the more sensitive is a bond's total return to changes in the rate of reinvestment.

2. The narrower the yield spread between the high coupon and low coupon issues, the greater the reinvestment rate risk assumed by the higher coupon bond. Conversely, a high coupon issue trading at a sizable yield concession vis-à-vis a low coupon (or zero-coupon) bond allows for a greater degree of reinvestment rate protection.

3. The higher the initial yield environment, the greater the reinvestment rate risk of the higher coupon bond given the greater probability of a subsequent decline in interest rates and therefore potential reinvestment rates.

A buy-and-hold assumption is often made in these analyses.[21] For two bonds of similar maturity, the horizon period is the maturity of the shorter bond.

> **Observation:** *A reinvestment rate protection swap attempts to provide a greater degree of total return maintenance in a future period of lower interest rates. Lower coupon bonds offer better insurance against the adverse effects of lower reinvestment rates. Zero-coupon bonds have no reinvestment rate risk if they are held to maturity.*

Using breakeven reinvestment rates to assess reinvestment rate protection. A *breakeven reinvestment rate* (BERR) is useful in assessing reinvestment rate risk. The BERR can be defined as the rate of reinvestment that equalizes the total returns of the two bonds under consideration over the assumed investment period. If the actual reinvestment rate (RR) falls short of the BERR, the lower coupon issue outperforms the higher coupon issue. If the actual RR exceeds the BERR, the higher coupon bond records the superior return. If the actual RR exactly matches the

---

[21] For an active investor who plans to sell the bonds prior to final maturity, a BERR can be calculated for the expected holding period. Of course, the shorter the holding period, the less important is reinvestment return (recall Chapter 8). Changes in market yield level over the shorter horizon can dramatically alter the total returns earned by the investor, primarily due to price appreciation/(depreciation). BERR analyses generally assume stable principal values in order to isolate the reinvestment rate effect. Hence hold-to-maturity assumptions are often made.

BERR, the investor is equally well off in either the high coupon or the low coupon issue. Three general rules apply to BERRs:

1. If the YTM of the high coupon bond exceeds the YTM of the low coupon alternative, the BERR lies somewhere below the YTM of the low coupon issue. The greater the yield advantage of the high coupon bond, the lower the BERR.

2. If the YTM of the high coupon issue is exactly equal to the YTM of the lower coupon replacement, the BERR is exactly equal to the YTM at which the bonds currently trade. If future interest rates decline to any degree, the higher coupon bond underperforms the lower coupon issue.

3. If the high coupon security trades at a YTM less than the YTM of the low coupon substitute, the BERR lies somewhere above the YTM of the low coupon issue. In this case, interest rates must rise in order for the high coupon issue to match or exceed the returns generated by the low coupon bond.

These three basic relationships are diagrammed in Exhibit 14–14.

> **Observation:** *A breakeven reinvestment rate is the threshold reinvestment rate below which the higher coupon bond underperforms the lower coupon bond over the specified holding period. Higher BERRs imply greater degrees of reinvestment risk.*

Breakeven reinvestment rates: An illustration. Exhibit 14–15 uses currently available U.S. Treasury issues to illustrate the BERR concept. A pair of bonds from each of the 2-year, 10-year, and 30-year maturity sectors are the focus of discussion. In the 2-year maturity sector, the high coupon 14½% issue trades at a price to yield 7.47% to maturity, 7BP less than the 7.54% yield offered by the low coupon 6⅝% bond. It is not surprising, therefore, that the BERR of 8.25% lies above the yield of the low coupon bond. The 14½% coupon issue requires a RR of at least 8.26% in order to outperform the 6⅝% coupon bond over the 2-year investment horizon. Given T-bill yields in the range 5.50 to 6.00%, the 14½% coupon bond necessitates a 250BP surge in interest rates (to the 8.00 to 8.50% level) to catch up to the 6⅝% coupon bond in terms of 2-year total returns. This dramatic yield increase must occur quickly in order to allow all of the coupons on the 2-year high coupon bond to be reinvested at the more attractive

Exhibit 14–14. Relationship between the breakeven reinvestment rate (BERR) and the YTMs of high coupon and low coupon bonds.

(a) High coupon bond outyields the low coupon bond.

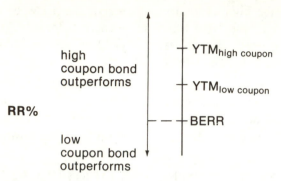

(b) High coupon bond and low coupon bond bear equivalent yields.

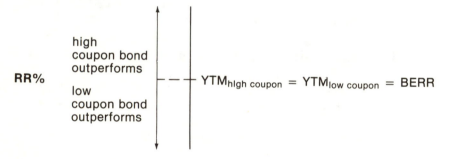

(c) High coupon bond offers less yield than the low coupon bond.

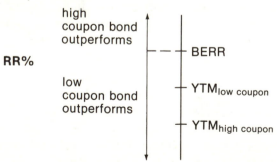

Comments: *The high coupon bond outperforms the low coupon bond at reinvestment rates exceeding the BERR.*

Exhibit 14–15. Breakeven reinvestment rates for three sets of U.S. Treasury bonds (6/30/87 data).

Maturity Sector	Issue Data	Price	YTM (%)
2-year	U.S. Treasury 14½% due 7/15/89	113-02	7.47
	U.S. Treasury 6⅝% due 8/15/89	98-07	7.54
	BERR = 8.25%		
10-year	U.S. Treasury 12⅝% due 5/15/95	124-04	8.37
	U.S. Treasury 7⅜% due 5/15/96	93-13	8.44
	BERR = 9.10%		
30-year	U.S. Treasury 11¼% due 2/15/15	127-00	8.66
	U.S. Treasury 7¼% due 5/15/16	85-19	8.61
	BERR = 8.00%		

Comments: *The breakeven reinvestment rate (BERR) is the rate at which the periodic coupons on the higher coupon issue must be reinvested in order to provide a return equal to that of the lower coupon issue. At a reinvestment rate below the BERR, the higher coupon issue underperforms the lower coupon issue. At a reinvestment rate above the BERR, the higher coupon bond outperforms the lower coupon bond.*

interest rate level. On a total return basis, the 14½% coupon issue appears unattractive relative to current-coupon bonds in its maturity class.[22]

In the 10-year maturity sector, the higher coupon 12⅝% issue requires that reinvestments of coupon cash flow be made at a 9.10% rate in order to match the returns of the lower coupon 7⅜% bond. The lower yield of the 12⅝% issue vis-à-vis the 7⅜% issue and the long investment horizon (8 years) lead to the necessity of a higher BERR. The 30-year sector finds the high coupon 11¼% issue outyielding the low coupon 7¼% bond by 5BP. This paltry differential allows for a BERR of 8.00%, a yield somewhat below that of the 8.61% YTM rate on the low coupon issue. Should interest rates subsequently decline, the approximate 60BP reinvestment rate cushion may not be enough

[22] However, on a current yield basis, the 14½% coupon bond appears very attractive vis-à-vis the 6⅝% coupon issue. The 14½s offer 607BP in incremental current yield (12.82% versus 6.75%). Current yield buyers are not as concerned with the total return implications of the high coupon issue.

to satisfy investors with 30-year horizons. Recall that the 7¼% issue outperforms the 11¼% bond at any reinvestment rate below 8.00%. Exhibit 14–16 plots the BERRs of the three illustrated pairings and shows that high coupon issues do not currently appear attractive on a reinvestment rate protection basis. Swaps from high coupon bonds to low coupon bonds of similar maturity enhance the total return potential of the bond portfolio on a hold-to-maturity basis by providing much better protection against the threat of stable to lower reinvestment rates.

Reinvestment rate protection between high coupon bonds and low coupon bonds: A comprehensive illustration. The relative attractiveness of high coupon bonds is predominantly influenced by three factors: the incremental yield offered by the high coupon bond, the length of the investment horizon, and the initial yield level. Exhibit 14–17 calculates the BERRs between a high coupon 14.00% bond and a current-coupon 7.00% bond in a 7.00% yield environment. A variety of yield spreads between the high coupon bond and the low coupon bond are tested, over both 2-year and 30-year holding periods.

The results lead to the general conclusion that the greater the yield advantage of the high coupon bond, the more substantial the reinvestment rate protection. Over short-term horizons, the yield advantage induces a total return bias that the reinvestment rate influence finds difficult to overcome given the short time span over which the reinvestment returns accumulate. For example, a 2-year 14.00% coupon bond yielding 25BP more than a similar maturity 7.00% coupon issue (7.25% versus 7.00% in this instance) allows reinvestment rates to fall to 1.00% before the high coupon issue begins to underperform its current-coupon counterpart. Even a modest 10BP yield advantage biases the 14.00% issue to outreturn the 7.00% issue at reinvestment rates above the 4.65% level. As an earlier example portrayed, a negative yield spread (i.e., high coupon bond's YTM < low coupon bond's YTM) forces the higher coupon issue to obtain substantially higher reinvestment rates in order simply to match the lower coupon bond's return. Over the 2-year horizon, for example, the 14.00% bond requires a 235BP surge in yields to the 9.35% level to attain the 7.00% bond's return if the higher coupon issue sells at a price to yield 10BP less than the lower coupon issue (6.90% versus 7.00% in this case).

Longer investment horizons allow a higher yielding issue a greater degree of reinvestment rate protection at progressively wider yield spread advantages. In the yield enhancement swap discussion earlier in this

Exhibit 14–16. Breakeven reinvestment rates (BERRs) and YTMs of a series of U.S. Treasury bonds (data from Exhibit 14–15).

(a) 2–year maturity issues.

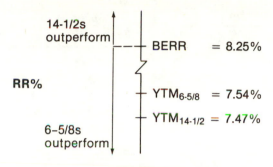

(b) 10–year maturity issues.

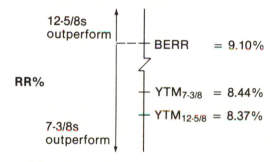

(c) 30–year maturity issues.

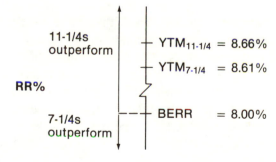

Exhibit 14–17. Calculation of the breakeven reinvestment rates (BERRs) between high coupon 14.00% bonds and 7.00% current-coupon bonds in a 7.00% yield environment. A variety of yield spreads between the premium bonds and the current-coupon bonds is illustrated. Each bond is held to maturity.

Yield to Maturity (%)		*Yield*	
14.00% Coupon	*7.00% Coupon*	*Spread (BP)*	*BERR (%)*
A. 2-year bonds			
7.50	7.00	+50	0*
7.25	7.00	+25	1.00
7.10	7.00	+10	4.65
7.05	7.00	+ 5	5.80
7.00	7.00	0	7.00
6.95	7.00	5	8.20
6.90	7.00	−10	9.35
6.75	7.00	−25	12.90
B. 30-year bonds			
7.50	7.00	+50	3.01
7.25	7.00	+25	4.80
7.10	7.00	+10	6.05
7.05	7.00	+ 5	6.51
7.00	7.00	0	7.00
6.95	7.00	− 5	7.53
6.90	7.00	−10	8.09
6.75	7.00	−25	10.15

*At a 50BP yield spread advantage, there is no positive rate of interest at which the high coupon issue underperforms the low coupon issue over a 2-year time horizon.

chapter, it was noted that "over the long run, it's hard to beat yield." Exhibit 14–17 analyzes 30-year maturity bonds in addition to 2-year maturity issues. For a high coupon 14.00% bond yielding 50BP more than a 7.00% coupon security, the BERR is a (low) 3.01% over the 30-year time span, historically good protection. A 25BP yield advantage raises the BERR to 4.80% and a small 10BP positive yield differential allows interest rates to decline 95BP to 6.05% before the 14.00% coupon bond begins to underperform the 7.00% coupon bond on a total return basis.

The range of BERRs is narrower in the 30-year example than in the 2-year case. The yield advantage of the higher coupon issue can be overcome by progressively lower assumed RRs over a 30-year investment

Exhibit 14–18. Calculation of the breakeven reinvestment rates (BERRs) between a 14.00% coupon bond and a 7.00% coupon bond in a 14.00% yield environment. A variety of yield spreads between the bonds is illustrated. Each bond is held to maturity in 30 years.

Yield to Maturity (%)		Yield	
14.00% Coupon	7.00% Coupon	Spread (BP)	BERR (%)
15.00	14.00	+100	5.40
14.50	14.00	+ 50	8.35
14.25	14.00	+ 25	10.50
14.10	14.00	+ 10	12.33
14.05	14.00	+ 5	13.10
14.00	14.00	0	14.00
13.95	14.00	− 5	15.10
13.90	14.00	− 10	16.50

period. The 2-year horizon does not allow the power of reinvestment returns to offset the return bias implied by the relative YTMs. For example, a 25BP yield advantage aids the higher coupon 14.00% issue in achieving superior returns in reinvestment rate conditions as adverse as a 1.00% available yield. The identical 25BP yield advantage requires a 4.80% threshold to ensure superior total return performance over 30 years (Exhibit 14–17).

A high yield environment carries with it a greater degree of reinvestment risk. For example, Exhibit 14–18 computes the BERRs between 14.00% coupon bonds and 7.00% coupon bonds of similar maturity assuming a 14.00% interest rate environment. The BERRs over the 30-year investment horizon are a function of the relative yields at which the bonds are purchased. It is clear that more positive yield spreads provide the premium bond with greater reinvestment rate protection. For example, a 25BP yield advantage renders the 14.00% coupon bond a 350BP cushion should rates subsequently decline (10.50% BERR). However, the absolute level of the BERR is substantially higher than under the 7.00% yield environment of earlier illustration. For example, if a 30-year high coupon issue offers 25BP in incremental yield over a 7.00% coupon issue of similar maturity, the BERR between the two issues is 4.80% given an initial yield environment of 7.00% (see Exhibit 14–17). Yield conditions of 14.00% raise the BERR to 10.50%, a historically high interest rate level (see Exhibit 14–18). There is more danger that over the 30-year investment horizon, the actual reinvestment rate falls below the BERR given a current market environment of high interest rates. In times of surging inflation and high yields, premium bonds should, all other factors held equal, sell at more sizable yield concessions to low coupon bonds than during periods of stable, low interest rates. Indeed, the dramatic decline in interest rates over the past 5 years (1982–1986) has witnessed a significant narrowing in such yield spreads.

> **Observation:** *Higher coupon bonds offer greater degrees of reinvestment rate protection the greater the incremental yield provided vis-à-vis a lower coupon issue, the shorter the investment horizon, and the lower the initial yield level.*

Using breakeven yield spreads to assess reinvestment rate risk. An alternative approach to assessing reinvestment rate risk is through the use of a *breakeven yield spread* between two bonds for a conservatively assumed rate of reinvestment and a specified holding period. For example, Exhibit 14–19 calculates the breakeven yield spread between 14.00% coupon bonds and 7.00% coupon bonds assuming a current market environment of 7.00% interest rates and a 5.00% rate of reinvestment on the coupon cash flows received over the life of the investments. The results indicate that a 2-year premium bond must offer at least 8BP in incremental yield in order to appear unattractive vis-à-vis the lower coupon issue. At a yield concession of less than 8BP, the premium bond underperforms the current-coupon issue on a total return basis over the 2-year holding period. Assuming a 10-year investment horizon, the conservative 5.00% RR demands a 27BP yield premium in order for the high coupon bond to appear equally attractive versus the current-coupon issue. Premium bonds offering more/(less) than 27BP in additional yield generate more/(less) total return over the 10-year investment period than their current-coupon counterparts, assuming a 5.00% rate of reinvestment on interim coupon payments. A 30-year horizon warrants at least a 22BP yield concession for high coupon bonds.[23]

> **Observation:** *A reinvestment rate protection swap attempts to provide a greater degree of certainty that returns do not fall short of a prescribed level. The use of breakeven reinvestment rates and breakeven yield spreads helps in quantifying the notions of reinvestment rate protection. High coupon bonds, long investment horizons, and high initial yield environments exacerbate the danger of lower-than-expected returns.*

---

[23] The power of yield over long-term investment horizons (e.g., 30 years) allows the yield premium to shrink slightly from the 27BP required over a 10-year investment horizon. The breakeven yield spread is, however, still in excess of the 8BP experienced over a 2-year time span.

Exhibit 14–19. Calculation of the breakeven yield spreads between 14.00% high coupon bonds and 7.00% current-coupon bonds of similar maturity, assuming a 5.00% rate of reinvestment. Market yields are currently at a 7.00% level. Each bond is held to maturity.

Investment Horizon (Years)	Breakeven Yield Spread (BP)
2	+ 8
10	+27
30	+22

Comments: *The breakeven yield spread is the yield concession at which the high coupon bond must trade vis-à-vis the low coupon bond in order to make it as attractive as the low coupon issue in terms of total return, given the specified reinvestment rate and holding period.*

Sector swaps. The final category of risk-neutral total return enhancements is *sector swaps*. These swaps move within and between various market sectors based on relative value assessments. Sector swaps come in six forms: maturity sector swaps, coupon sector swaps, quality sector swaps, issuer sector swaps, intra-issuer sector swaps, and issue-specific swaps. Each of these sector swaps is discussed and illustrated in turn. To ensure risk neutrality, these swaps are duration-weighted.[24] That is, the bond trades are weighted such that the market value weighted average duration of the bond(s) bought is equal to that of the bond(s) sold. In the weighting process, modified durations are preferred over Macaulay's durations, although the weighting differences are minimal between the two approaches. In general,

$$\text{duration}_S = \text{duration}_B$$

where

duration_S = duration of the *sell* bond(s)
duration_B = duration of the *buy* bond(s)

In general, an abnormally narrow yield spread between two sectors justifies a swap into the lower yielding sector. Conversely, an abnormally wide

---

[24] Alternatively, one can risk-neutralize swaps based on a risk measure such as the expected standard deviation of total return, the yield value of a 32nd, or the bond beta. Duration-weighted trades are most commonly used and are therefore the focus of discussion. The concept is one of adding incremental return while holding market risk constant.

Exhibit 14–20. Sector swaps attempt to exploit anomalies in spread relationships within and between various market sectors. Total return is enhanced when yield spreads change in the anticipated direction.

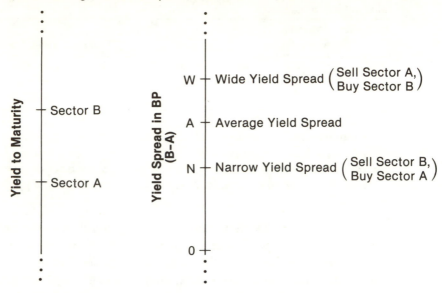

yield spread between two markets warrants a move into the higher yielding sector. Exhibit 14–20 graphically portrays these basic rules of thumb.

Maturity sector swap. A *maturity sector swap* sells a relatively expensive maturity sector and buys an attractively priced maturity sector. These swaps are of three types: duration-weighted extension swaps, duration-weighted contraction swaps, and dumbbell/bullet swaps.

Duration-weighted extension swap. A *duration-weighted extension swap* sells a shorter maturity issue and buys a longer maturity issue with the expectation that the yield spread between the two issues will narrow (i.e., the yield curve will flatten).[25] In order to maintain a similar overall duration, the sale proceeds from the short maturity bond cannot be fully invested in the longer maturity bond. The (riskier) long maturity bond investment must be combined with a specified amount of cash instruments, as follows:

---

[25] This assumes a positive yield curve environment. Given a negatively sloped yield curve, a duration-weighted extension is performed in expectation of a steeper inversion. In such a case the yield spread between the issues is projected to widen.

$$\text{duration}_{ST} = \text{duration}_{LT}(x) + \text{duration}_C(1 - x)$$
$$= \text{duration}_{LT}(x) + 0(1 - x)$$
$$= \text{duration}_{LT}(x)$$

where

C = cash equivalent investments

ST = short maturity bond

LT = long maturity bond

Solving for the appropriate weightings finds

$$x = \frac{\text{duration}_{ST}}{\text{duration}_{LT}}$$
$$= \text{long maturity bond allocation}$$

$$1 - x = \text{cash allocation}$$

As an example, if a 5.00-year duration bond is sold to finance the purchase of an 8.00-year duration bond, only 62.50% of the sale proceeds are invested in the long bond, with the remaining 37.50% stored in a cash asset:

$$x = \frac{5.00}{8.00}$$
$$= 0.6250$$
$$= 62.50\%$$

$$1 - x = 1 - 0.625$$
$$= 0.3750$$
$$= 37.50\%$$

Using June 30, 1987 data per Exhibit 14–21, an investor can swap from a 10-year U.S. Treasury bond (7⅜% due 5/15/1996) into a 30-year U.S. Treasury bond (7¼% due 5/15/2016) for a yield pickup of 17BP (8.61% − 8.44%). A duration-weighted extension swap from 10s to 30s is detailed in Exhibit 14–22. If the investor anticipates a 10BP narrowing of the 10- to 30-year spread to 7BP over the next month, the incremental total return garnered from the duration-weighted extension is approximately 60BP. This excess return is achieved regardless of the absolute level of interest rates 1 month hence. Indeed, Exhibit 14–22

Exhibit 14–21. U.S. Treasury issue data as of June 30, 1987.

Issue Data	Maturity (Years)	Price	YTM (%)	Modified Duration
U.S. Treasury bills	NA	NA	5.75	0.0*
U.S. Treasury 7⅜% 5/15/96	10	93-13	8.44	6.26
U.S. Treasury 7¼% 5/15/16	30	85-19	8.61	10.77

*Invested in a cash instrument with a stable principal value and therefore a duration of zero.

Exhibit 14–22. Example of a duration-weighted maturity extension swap. An investor sells 10-year U.S. Treasury bonds and buys a duration-weighted amount of 30-year U.S. Treasury bonds (issue data per Exhibit 14–21). Over a 1-month investment horizon, the yield spread between the 10s and 30s narrows by 10BP. The general level of yields changes only modestly.

Percent Weighting	Swap Proposal	Modified Duration	1-Month Total Return (%) if Rates:		
			−50BP	Unchanged	+50BP
S: 100.0	10-year Treasury	6.52	3.87	0.70	−2.35
B: 58.0	30-year Treasury	11.23	7.54	1.80	−3.44
B: 42.0	Cash	0.00	0.48	0.48	0.48
Weighted average B ⟶		6.52	4.57	1.25	−1.79
Total return enhancement, B−S ⟶			0.70	0.55	0.56

illustrates that higher, lower, and stable yield environments all render approximately the same amount of enhanced return to the maturity swapper who makes moves on a duration-weighted basis.

Observation: *A duration-weighted extension swap is executed with the expectation that longer maturity issues will outperform shorter maturity issues on a risk-adjusted basis. In other words, the yield curve is projected to flatten to some degree.*

Duration-weighted contraction swap. A *duration-weighted contraction swap* is a bet that the yield curve will steepen.[26] Longer maturity

[26] In an inverted yield curve environment, a duration-weighted contraction reflects the anticipation of a flattening yield curve or, perhaps, a shift to a positively sloped configuration. In this instance, the yield spread between the issues is expected to become less negative and, possibly, assume a positive status.

Exhibit 14–23. Example of a duration-weighted maturity contraction swap. An investor sells 30-year U.S. Treasury bonds and buys a duration-weighted amount of 10-year U.S. Treasury bonds (issue data per Exhibit 14–21). Over a 1-month investment horizon, the yield spread between the 10s and 30s widens by 10BP. The general level of yields changes only modestly.

Percent Weighting	Swap Proposal	Modified Duration	1-Month Total Return (%) if Rates:		
			−50BP	Unchanged	+50BP
S: 58.0	30-year Treasury	11.23	5.18	−0.35	−5.40
S: 42.0	Cash	0.00	0.48	0.48	0.48
Weighted average S $\longrightarrow$		6.52	3.21	0.00	−2.94
B: 100.0	10-year Treasury	6.52	3.87	0.70	−2.35
Total return enhancement, B−S $\longrightarrow$			0.66	0.70	0.59

issues are replaced with shorter maturity issues at narrow yield giveups. The trade is later reversed at a wider yield spread. Exhibit 14–23 calculates 1-month total returns for an investor who sells 30-year U.S. Treasuries and buys 10-year U.S. Treasuries at a 17BP yield giveup. The 10- to 30-year yield spread widens to +27BP by the end of the month and the investor gains an average of 65BP in incremental return in up, down, and flat markets. Notice that a duration-weighted shortening trade requires an additional cash investment in the shorter duration instrument in order to maintain a similar overall duration. A proceeds-to-proceeds trade is a bearish move, shortening the duration of the bond portfolio. A greater amount of the shorter bonds must be purchased in order to mimic the duration of the long bonds sold. In formula terminology,

$$\text{duration}_S = \text{duration}_B$$

$$\text{duration}_{LT} = \text{duration}_{ST} (x)$$

$$x = \frac{\text{duration}_{LT}}{\text{duration}_{ST}}$$

$x > 1$ which means that additional cash must be invested in order to finance the short bond purchase

For example, if an 8.00-year duration bond is swapped for a 5.00-year duration issue, a 60% additional investment must be made in the shorter bond to maintain duration equivalence:

$$x = \frac{\text{duration}_{LT}}{\text{duration}_{ST}}$$
$$= \frac{8.00}{5.00}$$
$$= 1.60$$
$$= 160\%$$

Viewing the short bond as the full investment, the long bond funds 62.50% of the purchase (100%/160% = 0.625), with the remaining 37.50% financed with cash instruments (60%/160% = 0.375). Exhibits 14–24 and 14–25 summarize the notions of duration-weighted extensions and contractions, respectively, in a graphical context.

Observation: *A duration-weighted contraction swap is executed with the expectation that shorter maturity issues will outperform longer maturity issues on a risk-adjusted basis. In other words, the yield curve is expected to steepen to some degree.*

Exhibit 14–24. Duration-weighted extension swap reflects the expectation of a flatter yield curve.

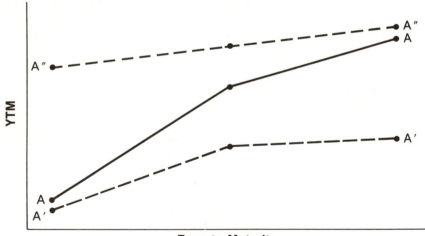

Comments: *The investor is betting on a flattening of the yield curve, independent of the general movement of interest rates. This flattening may occur as the yield curve shifts from AA to A'A' or from AA to A"A".*

Exhibit 14–25. Duration-weighted contraction swap reflects the expectation of a steeper yield curve.

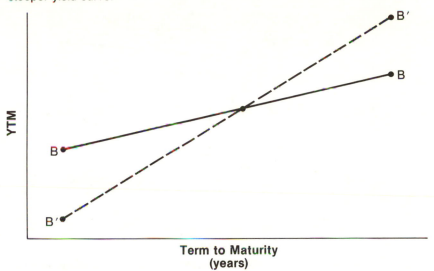

Comments: *A shift from BB to B'B' indicates a steepening of the yield curve.*

Dumbell/bullet swaps. Dumbbell/bullet (DB) swaps involve combinations of assets, rather than a single *sell bond* and a single *purchase bond.* In general, three types of bonds are considered in DB trades: a short maturity bond, an intermediate maturity bond, and a long maturity bond. The maturity coverage of a DB swap can be narrow (e.g., 1-year/2-year/3-year) or wide (e.g., 2-year/7-year/30-year). The terms *short, intermediate,* and *long* are used in a broader sense than the typical interpretation. The combination of short and long bonds is typically called the *dumbbell* and the intermediate maturity bond is referred to as the *bullet.*

Two basic types of dumbbell/bullet swaps exist. A *dumbbell-to-bullet swap* sells a duration-weighted combination of short-term and long-term securities to purchase an intermediate-term security, with the expectation that the middle bond will experience declines in yield relative to the short and long bonds. Exhibit 14–26 illustrates the concept of a dumbell/bullet swap graphically. A *bullet-to-dumbbell swap,* on the other hand, moves from an intermediate maturity bond to a duration-weighted combination of short-term and long-term securities in anticipation of a cheapening of the intermediate sector vis-à-vis the short maturity

Exhibit 14–26. Dumbbell-to-bullet swap reflects an expectation of a flattening of the intermediate maturity yields relative to short maturity and long maturity yields.

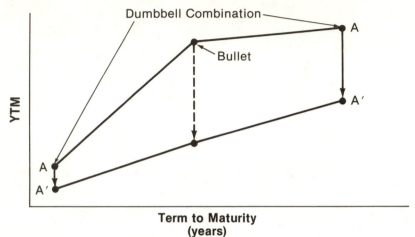

Comments: *The bullet bond outperforms the short/long combination if the yield curve shifts from AA to A'A'.*

Exhibit 14–27. Bullet-to-dumbbell swap reflects an expectation of a steepening of the intermediate maturity yields relative to short maturity and long maturity yields.

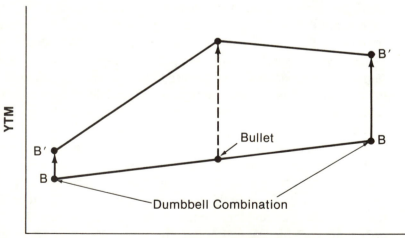

Comments: *The short/long combination outperforms the bullet bond if the yield curve shifts from BB to B'B'.*

and long maturity sectors. Exhibits 14–26 and 14–27 display the dumbbell/bullet strategies in a graphical context.

As an example of a dumbbell-to-bullet swap, Exhibit 14–28 presents the yield spreads between 2-year, 7-year, and 30-year U.S. Treasuries as of December 31, 1984. The U.S. Treasury yield curve is steeply positive between 2s and 7s but exhibits flatness between 7s and 30s. This was a golden opportunity to execute a dumbbell-to-bullet swap from 2s/30s into 7s. Exhibit 14–29 summarizes the issue data for a representative U.S. Treasury in each of the aforementioned maturity sectors. During 1985, the U.S. Treasury yield curve flattened in the 2–7-year area and steepened from 7s to 30s (see Exhibit 14–30) as yield levels in general fell by 200–250BP (see Exhibit 14–31). The bullet 7-year bond outperformed its duration-weighted 2/30-year combination

Exhibit 14–28. U.S. Treasury yield spreads as of December 31, 1984 (using current auction issues).

Maturity Sector Swap	*BP Spread*	*Expectation of Future Spread*
2-year bond to 7-year bond	+143	Narrower
7-year bond to 30-year bond	+ 5	Wider

Exhibit 14–29. U.S. Treasury issue data for a dumbbell-to-bullet swap (as of December 31, 1984).

Maturity (Years)	*Issue*	*Price*	*YTM (%)*
2	12¾% due 2/15/87	104-26	10.15
7	14⅝% due 2/15/92	114-24	11.53
30	12½% due 8/15/14	107-22	11.57

Exhibit 14–30. U.S. Treasury yield spreads and yield spread changes during 1985 (current auction issues).

	Yield Spread (BP)		*Change in Yield Spread*
Maturity Sector Swap	*12/31/84*	*12/31/85*	*During 1985 (BP)*
2-year bond to 7-year bond	+143	+89	−54
7-year bond to 30-year bond	+ 5	+43	+38

Comments: *The U.S. Treasury yield curve flattened in the intermediate maturity sector and steepened sizably in the long maturity sector during 1985.*

Exhibit 14–31. Yield changes on three representative U.S. Treasury bonds during 1985.

Maturity	U.S. Treasury Issue	Change in Yield During 1985 (BP)
2	12¾% due 2/15/87	−229
7	14⅝% due 2/15/92	−262
30	12½% due 8/15/14	−188

Comments: *It is clear that the 7-year sector experienced superior yield declines during 1985 vis-à-vis the 2-year and 30-year maturities. The outcomes incorporate rolls down the yield curve from the 1-year aging of the securities.*

by an impressive 320BP (see Exhibit 14–32). Exhibit 14–33 shows the general change in yield curve shape during 1985. Exhibit 14–34 plots the 1985 total returns in risk:return space.

A bullet-to-dumbbell swap is undertaken in the opposite direction, with the sale of the intermediate bond financing the purchase of the two opposing ends of the maturity spectrum. A subsequent steepening of the yield curve in the intermediate maturity sector vis-à-vis the short and long maturities renders this swap a profitable one.

Exhibit 14–32. One-year total return performance of a dumbbell-to-bullet swap executed on December 31, 1984 (issue data per Exhibit 14–29).

Percent Weighting	Swap Details	Modified Duration	1984 Total Return (%)
S: 57.9	2-year U.S. Treasury	1.76	12.77
S: 42.1	30-year U.S. Treasury	7.94	29.12
Weighted average S ⟶		4.36	19.65
B: 100.0	7-year U.S. Treasury	4.36	22.85
Total return enhancement, B−S ⟶			3.20

Comments: *Modified duration as of December 31, 1984. An 11.50% reinvestment rate is assumed for coupon cash flows received during the year.*

Exhibit 14–33. Superior performance of bullets versus dumbbells during 1985 was attributable to a flattening of intermediate maturity bond yields vis-à-vis short bond yields and long bond yields (U.S. Treasury auction issue data).

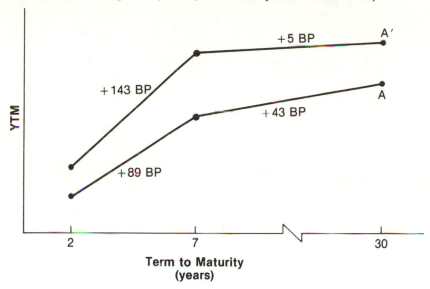

Exhibit 14–34. Total return curve for 1985, using three representative U.S. Treasury issues (data per Exhibits 14–29, 14–31, and 14–32).

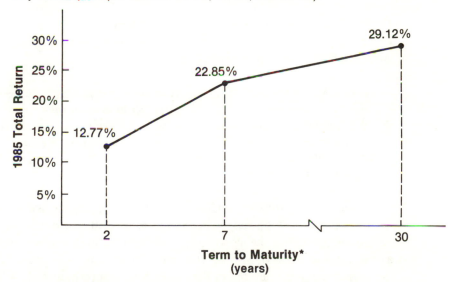

*As of the beginning of 1985.

Exhibit 14–35. Risks inherent in duration-weighted swaps (extensions, contractions, and dumbbell/bullets).

1. The yield spread fails to change in the expected direction (e.g., the yield curve steepens rather than flattens).
2. Dramatic swings in interest rates force the duration weighting to fall out of balance, creating unexpected price gains and losses.
3. As time passes, the duration weighting falls out of balance due to duration drift and accrued interest buildup and dropoff. The related change in market risk exposure causes unanticipated alterations in total return results.
4. The passage of time allows yield differentials and yield curve roll factors to impact the realized total returns in either a favorable or unfavorable manner. For example, a duration-weighted extension swap in a positive yield curve environment can make the workout time a critical factor because of the low yielding cash position held in combination with the longer maturity asset. The generally lower average yield of the purchased assets (cash + long bond) works against the investor over time. Differences in yield curve roll factors create even more sizable divergences in expected return due to the leveraging effect of duration.

> **Observation:** *Dumbbell/bullet swaps take advantage of situations in which intermediate maturity issues are inexpensive vis-à-vis short maturity and long maturity issues (dumbbell-to-bullet swap) and vice versa (bullet-to-dumbbell swap) on a risk-adjusted basis.*

Duration-weighted swaps are subject to several risks, as summarized in Exhibit 14–35. A careful assessment of these dangers is critical to the success of the duration-weighted trade.

> **Observation:** *Maturity sector swaps attempt to capitalize on inexpensively priced segments of the yield curve. Risks are controlled by duration-weighting the swaps, which can be of the extension type, the contraction type, or the dumbbell/bullet form. Total returns are enhanced by the fulfillment of the expected yield spread changes between the various maturity sectors.*

Coupon sector swap. *Coupon sector swaps* concentrate portfolio holdings in the coupon ranges perceived to offer the best relative value. A *coupon spread* is the yield spread between a high coupon issue and a low coupon issue of similar maturity. If the coupon spread is wide, the higher coupon issue offers the better total return potential. A narrow

Exhibit 14–36. Issue data for coupon sector swaps (as of June 30, 1987).

Maturity Sector (Years)	U.S. Treasury Issue	Price	YTM (%)	Modified Duration
7	7% due 4/15/94	93-19	8.25	5.18
	13⅛% due 5/15/94	124-27	8.30	4.71
30	7¼% due 5/15/16	85-19	8.61	10.77
	11¼% due 2/15/15	127-00	8.66	9.76

Comments: *Coupon spreads are unusually narrow, with only 5BP yield pickups available for sizable increases in coupon rate. Not surprisingly, the lower coupon issues bear higher durations.*

coupon spread warrants a move down in coupon.[27] In the current market (June 30, 1987), coupon spreads are extremely narrow in the U.S. Treasury bond sector. Exhibit 14–36 compares the yields of a pair of representative intermediate U.S. Treasuries of similar maturity and a pair of long U.S. Treasury bonds. In each grouping, only 5BP in yield separates the high coupon bond from the low coupon bond. If coupon spreads widen to average levels, the high coupon issues will suffer a disproportionate share of price loss versus their low coupon counterparts. Keep in mind the fact that a yield spread reflects the relative price differential between two bonds. Insofar as the relative prices change (as indicated by a yield spread shift), price returns and total returns are affected.

Exhibit 14–37 proposes trading down in coupon with the expectation that the future holds a 15BP widening in coupon spreads for both the intermediate and long maturity sectors. A 1-month investment horizon is employed, with stable to modestly changing interest rates in general. The results clearly show that sizable total return enhancements are possible both in the intermediate maturity sector (65 to 70BP) and in the long maturity sector (140 to 160BP). The coupon swaps are duration-weighted such that general moves in yields do not negate the return enhancements to any significant degree. Conversely, the anticipation of narrower coupon

---

[27] The focus here is on noncallable U.S. Treasury coupon spreads. Coupon spreads between callable bonds are more tenuous to interpret given that market sentiment, market volatility, and the call price:market price relationship are important factors to consider. The use of effective duration comparisons and convexity analyses can assist in making judgments on relative value in callable bond alternatives. The purpose of this section is to isolate the impact from a change in the general spreads between coupon strata.

Exhibit 14–37. Sample coupon sector swaps (issue data per Exhibit 14–36). Coupon spreads widen by 15BP in both the intermediate and long maturity sectors over a 1-month horizon.

		1-Month Total Return (%) if Yields:		
Swap Proposal	*Modified Duration*	*−50BP*	*Unchanged*	*+50BP*
S: 13⅛% due 5/15/94	4.71	2.34	−0.01	−2.29
B: 7% due 4/15/94	5.18	3.29	0.69	−1.83
Total return enhancement* ⟶		0.70	0.68	0.67
S: 11¼% due 2/15/15	9.76	4.24	−0.72	−5.27
B: 7¼% due 5/15/16	10.77	6.35	0.71	−4.43
Total return enhancement* ⟶		1.56	1.41	1.30

*The swaps are duration-weighted; therefore, the total return enhancements reflect a small proportion in cash equivalents that earn 5.75% annually.

spreads warrants trading into higher coupon issues. The subsequent tightening of coupon spreads creates superior total return performance.

> **Observation:** *Coupon sector swaps trade up in coupon if coupon spreads appear wide and trade down in coupon in the event of narrow coupon spreads. Correctly anticipated spread changes lead to incremental price appreciation and commensurately enhanced total returns.*

Quality sector swap. A *quality sector swap* moves from one quality sector to another with the expectation that quality spreads will change in a manner that enhances total return. A *quality spread* is the yield spread between a high quality issue and a low quality issue of similar maturity. If quality spreads are narrow, a move up in quality is desirable. Abnormally wide quality spreads warrant a move down in quality. In each case, the return to a normal spread relationship is anticipated.

Exhibit 14–38 provides the issue data for a series of quality sector swaps outlined in Exhibit 14–39. In the first example, an investor sells U.S. Treasury quality paper to buy an agency quality issue (FNMA), with the expectation that quality spreads between U.S. Treasuries and federal agencies will narrow by 10BP. Over a 1-month time horizon, total return is enhanced by 69BP if the spread contraction occurs. In the second case, a move into higher quality utilities is warranted by the anticipation of a widening of quality spreads. The 20BP expansion in *AA versus BBB* utility yield spread renders the investor a 1.66% total return enhancement over a 1-month period.

Exhibit 14–38. Issue data for quality sector swaps (as of June 30, 1987).

Issue Description	Rating	Price	YTM (%)	Modified Duration
U.S. Treasury 7¼% due 11/15/96	Aaa/AAA	92-14	8.43	6.52
FNMA 7.60% due 1/10/97	Agency	91-26	8.89	6.28
FP&L 9% due 10/1/16	Aa3/AA−	91.86	9.85	9.43
PE 10¼% due 11/1/16	Baa3/BBB−	97.00	10.58	8.87

Exhibit 14–39. Sample quality sector swaps (issue data per Exhibit 14–38). The investor expects quality spreads to narrow 10BP between FNMAs and U.S. Treasuries. Quality spreads between low-grade utilities and high-grade utilities are expected to widen by 20BP. A 1-month horizon is assumed with stability in the general level of rates, and reinvestments made at 8.50%.

Swap Proposal	Modified Duration	1-Month Total Return (%)
S: 10-year U.S. Treasury	6.52	0.70
B: 10-year FNMA	6.28	1.38
Total return enhancement* ⟶		0.69
S: 30-year Philadelphia Electric	8.87	−0.85
B: 30-year Florida P&L	9.43	0.83
Total return enhancement* ⟶		1.66

*The swaps are duration-weighted; therefore, the total return enhancements reflect a small proportion in cash equivalents that earn 5.75% annually.

Note that quality sector swaps differ from the quality enhancement swaps of earlier discussion in two important respects. First, quality sector swaps attempt to exploit relative value regardless of the direction of the quality move. Second, quality sector swaps are predicated on a spread change anticipation, with the intent of adding incremental return. Quality enhancement swaps always involve an upward move in quality, with no consideration for relative value or total return potential.

Observation: *Quality sector swaps attempt to enhance total returns by moving into low quality issues when quality spreads are wide and by trading into high quality issues in times of narrow quality spreads.*

Exhibit 14–40. Issue data for issuer sector swaps (as of June 30, 1987).

Issue Description	Issuer Sector	Price	YTM (%)	Modified Duration
U.S. Treasury 8¾% due 5/15/17	Treasury	102-22	8.50	10.64
BLIP 8¾% due 4/1/26	Utility	91.50	9.58	9.99
Amoco 8⅝% due 12/15/16	Industrial	91.38	9.50	9.93
FP&L 9% due 10/1/16	Utility	91.86	9.85	9.43

Issuer sector swap. In the U.S. domestic taxable fixed-income market, there are seven primary issuer sectors: U.S. Treasury, federal agency, mortgage-backed, industrial, utility, bank and finance, and yankee.[28] Swaps between overvalued issuer sectors and undervalued issuer sectors can lead to attractive total return enhancements. Exhibit 14–40 contains the issue data supporting the issuer sector swap illustrations presented in Exhibit 14–41. The first example sells long telephone utility bonds and buys long U.S. Treasury bonds in anticipation of a 10BP spread widening between the U.S. Treasury and utility sectors. An 87BP return enhancement is garnered over a 1-month horizon if the expectations prove correct. The second example shows the result of moving from the industrial sector into the utility sector with the assessment that industrials are currently overvalued. The return enhancement from a modest 20BP yield spread change is a sizable 190BP over a 1-month investment period.

Observation: *Issuer sector swaps move between general issuer categories as relative values change. Total return enhancements are captured by timely trades out of relatively expensive issuer sectors and into relatively inexpensive issuer sectors.*

Intra-issuer sector swap. Within a given issuer sector, swap opportunities arise from shifts in the relative attractiveness of the various issuer sector components. For example, in the utility sector, telephone utilities may become attractively priced vis-à-vis electric utilities, warranting an overweighting in the phones. Intra-issuer sector swaps operate within the domain of an issuer sector, exploiting yield spread anomalies in an attempt to enhance total return.

Exhibit 14–43 provides two sample intra-issuer sector swaps (supporting issue data in Exhibit 14–42). The first swap moves from an

---

[28] An in-depth discussion of market sector components is provided in Chapter 15.

Exhibit 14–41. Sample issuer sector swaps (issue data per Exhibit 14–40). The investor expects long telephone utility bond yields to widen by 10BP vis-à-vis long U.S. Treasury bond yields. Sector spreads between industrials and electric utilities are expected to narrow by 20BP, with industrial bonds experiencing increases in yield vis-à-vis similar maturity utility issues. A 1-month horizon is assumed, with the general level of market yields remaining stable.

Swap Proposal	Modified Duration	1-Month Total Return (%)
S: BLIP 8¾% due 4/1/26	9.99	−0.18
B: U.S. Treasury 8¾% due 5/15/17	10.64	0.71
Total return enhancement* ⟶		0.87
S: Amoco 8⅝% due 12/15/16	9.93	−1.15
B: FP&L 9% due 10/1/16	9.43	0.83
Total return enhancement* ⟶		1.90

* The swaps are duration-weighted; therefore, the total return enhancements reflect a small proportion in cash equivalents that earn 5.75% annually.

FFCB bond to a similar maturity FNMA bond (within the federal agency sector) at an 8BP yield giveup. Over a 1-month horizon, if the spread widens to (a more normal) 30BP, the swap enhances total return by a handsome 75BP. The second trade takes place in the industrial sector. In anticipation of higher oil prices and commensurately lower automobile and truck sales, an investor swaps from an auto industry bond (GM) into an oil industry bond (Amoco) and gains 191BP in incremental return in the event of a general rise in auto bond yields vis-à-vis oil bond yields.

Observation: *Intra-issuer sector swaps take advantage of opportunities within general issuer sector categories. Subgroupings are bought and sold on the basis of expected changes in yield spreads. Total return potential is the focus of trading activity.*

Exhibit 14–42. Issue data for intra-issuer sector swaps (as of June 30, 1987).

Issue Description	Issuer Sector	Subsector	Price	YTM (%)	Modified Duration
FFCB 13¾% due 7/20/92	Agency	FFCB	120-18	8.64	3.59
FNMA 10⅛% due 6/10/92	Agency	FNMA	106-06	8.56	3.86
GM 8⅛% due 4/15/16	Industrial	Auto	86.00	9.56	9.77
Amoco 8⅝% due 12/15/16	Industrial	Oil	91.38	9.50	9.93

Exhibit 14–43. Sample intra-issuer sector swaps (issue data per Exhibit 14–42). In the agency sector, the investor swaps from an FFCB issue to an FNMA issue in anticipation of a spread widening of 22BP (to the 30BP level). In the industrial sector, autos are expected to cheapen vis-à-vis oils in a 20BP spread widening. A 1-month horizon is assumed, with the general level of market yields stable and reinvestments made at an 8.50% rate.

Swap Proposal	Modified Duration	1-Month Total Return (%)
S: FFCB 13¾% due 7/20/92	3.59	−0.04
B: FNMA 10⅛% due 6/10/92	3.86	0.73
Total return enhancement* ⟶		0.75
S: GM 8⅛% due 4/15/16	9.77	−1.11
B: Amoco 8⅝% due 12/15/16	9.93	0.80
Total return enhancement* ⟶		1.93

*The swaps are duration-weighted; therefore, the total return enhancements reflect a small proportion in cash equivalents that earn 5.75% annually.

Issue-specific swap. The *issue-specific swap* carries the intra-issuer concept one step further. In this case, swaps are concentrated between issuers of the same industry type. Additionally, swaps are made between individual issues backed by the same issuer to take advantage of structural characteristics and inefficient pricings. For example, an investor moves from a subordinated debt issue to a senior debt issue guaranteed by the same company. A trade from a private placement to a publicly traded issue of the same firm qualifies as an issue-specific swap. Swaps into issues with superior call protection and/or stronger sinking funds are also applicable. Each of these swaps is undertaken with the intent of enhancing total returns of a bond portfolio through the richening of the price of the purchased bond vis-à-vis the value of the bond sold.

Exhibit 14–44 summarizes the issue data supporting the total return calculations in Exhibit 14–45. The latter table shows two examples of issue-specific swaps, one between automobile industry firms (GM and Ford) and one between telephone industry companies (Southwestern Bell Telephone and Bell Telephone of Pennsylvania). Total returns are enhanced by 57 to 96BP over a 1-month horizon given a 10BP spread change between the respective issues.

Observation: *Issue-specific swaps capture incremental total returns by trading between issues that differ with respect to only one or two factors. Supply/demand imbalances create anomalies between individual issuers (e.g., Ford versus GM) and/or individual issues (senior versus subordinated debt, large new issue versus small seasoned issue).*

Summing it up

The total return enhancement swap illustrations reveal the importance of relative value assessments in long maturity bonds. The impact of a 10BP yield spread widening or narrowing has a more pronounced

Exhibit 14–44. Issue data for issuer-sector swaps (as of June 30, 1987).

Issue Description	Subsector	Price	YTM (%)	Modified Duration
GMAC 8⅞% due 3/1/96	Auto finance	97.50	9.30	5.74
FMC 8⅞% due 3/1/96	Auto finance	97.50	9.30	5.74
SWBT 8¾% due 11/1/24	Telephone utility	89.50	9.81	9.89
BLIP 8¾% due 4/1/26	Telephone utility	91.50	9.58	9.99

Exhibit 14–45. Sample issue-specific swaps (issue data from Exhibit 14–44). In the first case, the investor expects Ford Motor Credit (FMC) paper to richen to 10BP through GMAC paper (they currently trade at equivalent yields). In the second example, Southwestern Bell Telephone (SWBT) paper is projected to cheapen by 10BP vis-à-vis Bell Telephone of Pennsylvania (BLIP) paper. A 1-month investment horizon is assumed, with the general level of market yields stable.

Swap Proposal	Modified Duration	1-Month Total Return (%)
S: GMAC 8⅞% due 3/1/96	5.74	0.79
B: FMC 8⅞% due 3/1/96	5.74	1.36
Total return enhancement* ⟶		0.57
S: SWBT 8¾% due 11/1/24	9.89	−0.15
B: BLIP 8¾% due 4/1/26	9.99	0.81
Total return enhancement* ⟶		0.96

*The swaps are duration-weighted; therefore, the total return enhancements reflect a small proportion in cash equivalents that earn 5.75% annually.

effect on long bond returns than on short bond returns, as a result of the duration multiple. In general, the BP impact on total return can be estimated as:

$$\frac{\text{BP impact on}}{\text{total return}} = \frac{\text{modified}}{\text{duration}} \times \frac{\text{yield spread}}{\text{change (BP)}}$$

For example, a risk-neutral swap is performed between two bonds with an identical modified duration of 2.50 years. The yield spread separating the bonds changes by 10BP. The resulting impact on total return is approximately 25BP:

$$\begin{aligned} \text{BP impact on total return} &= 2.50 \times 10\text{BP} \\ &= 25\text{BP} \end{aligned}$$

A 10BP yield spread change leads to a more sizable 120BP return alteration when trading in the 12.00-year duration sector (12.0 × 10BP = 120BP). Whether the return impact is favorable or unfavorable depends on the direction of the yield spread change (versus expectations). Relaxing the instantaneous yield spread change assumption requires two modifications to the formulation:

$$\frac{\text{BP impact on}}{\text{total return}} = \left(\begin{array}{c} \text{modified duration} \\ \text{at the end of the} \\ \text{holding period} \end{array} \times \begin{array}{c} \text{yield} \\ \text{spread} \\ \text{change} \\ \text{(BP)} \end{array} \right) + \begin{array}{c} \text{average} \\ \text{yield} \\ \text{impact} \\ \text{(BP)} \end{array}$$

where

$$\frac{\text{average yield}}{\text{impact (BP)}} = \left(\begin{array}{c} \text{average YTM} \\ \text{of bonds} \\ \text{purchased} \end{array} - \begin{array}{c} \text{average YTM} \\ \text{of bonds} \\ \text{sold} \end{array} \right) \times \begin{array}{c} \text{holding} \\ \text{period} \\ \text{(years)} \end{array} \times 100$$

For example, a risk-neutral swap between bonds with 8.00-year modified durations involves a 100BP YTM pickup. The modified duration of the bonds slips to 7.70 years over the next 6 months. If the yield spread changes favorably by 20BP over the forthcoming 6 months, the return enhancement is approximately 204BP:

$$\begin{aligned}
\text{BP impact on} \atop \text{total return} \quad &= \quad {\text{incremental return} \atop \text{from the yield} \atop \text{spread change}} \quad + \quad {\text{incremental} \atop \text{return from the} \atop \text{yield pickup}} \\
&= \quad (7.70 \times 20\text{BP}) \quad + \quad (100\text{BP} \times \tfrac{1}{2}) \\
&= \quad 154\text{BP} + 50\text{BP} \\
&= \quad 204\text{BP}
\end{aligned}$$

It is clear that yield-pickup trades provide an additional reward to the investor over the holding period. Yield-giveup trades detract from the return attributable to the anticipated spread change and force a shorter workout time.

Risk-altering swaps

Risk-altering swaps change the market risk exposure of a bond portfolio. The alteration is predicated on the portfolio manager's expectations regarding future yield levels: rising, stable, or falling. Risk-altering swaps come in two varieties: the *interest rate anticipation swap* and the *riding-the-yield-curve swap*. The former is implemented in anticipation of rising or falling yields, whereas the latter is useful when a stable interest rate environment is expected.

Interest rate anticipation swap. An *interest rate anticipation swap,* as its name implies, is predicated on an expected movement in the general level of interest rates. When interest rates are expected to fall, durations are lengthened by swapping into long maturity, low coupon, call-protected issues. Conversely, bearish expectations warrant a reduction in duration positions, with short maturity, high coupon issues assuming an important role.

Recall from Chapter 4 that long maturity bonds exhibit substantially more price volatility than do short maturity issues. Chapter 6 presented the duration concept and illustrated that long duration securities offer more upside and downside volatility than do short duration securities. Properly deploying this leveraging and deleveraging of price returns can lead to enhanced total returns.

Exhibit 14–46 aggregates the basic issue data on three U.S. Treasury bonds: a short maturity (2-year) issue, an intermediate maturity (7-year) issue, and a long maturity (30-year) issue. Exhibit 14–47 shows the results of four successfully placed interest rate anticipation swaps. The

Exhibit 14–46. Issue data on short maturity (2-year), intermediate maturity (7-year), and long maturity (30-year) U.S. Treasury bonds as of June 30, 1987.

Issue Data	*Maturity (Years)*	*Price*	*YTM (%)*	*Modified Duration*
U.S. Treasury 7⅜% due 6/30/89	2	99-26	7.48	1.83
U.S. Treasury 7% due 4/15/94	7	93-19	8.25	5.18
U.S. Treasury 8¾% due 5/15/17	30	102-22	8.50	10.64

Exhibit 14–47. Sample interest rate anticipation swaps (using issue data from Exhibit 14–46). Reinvestments are made at an 8.00% rate.

	6-Month Total Return (%) if Rates Fall by:	
Swap Proposal (Bullish)	*100BP*	*200BP*
S: 2-year U.S. Treasuries	5.15	6.58
B: 30-year U.S. Treasuries	15.89	29.94
Total return enhancement ⟶	10.74	23.36
S: 7-year U.S. Treasuries	9.25	14.70
B: 30-year U.S. Treasuries	15.89	29.94
Total return enhancement ⟶	6.64	15.24

	6-Month Total Return (%) if Rates Rise by:	
Swap Proposal (Bearish)	*100BP*	*200BP*
S: 30-year U.S. Treasuries	−5.43	−13.60
B: 2-year U.S. Treasuries	2.35	1.00
Total return enhancement ⟶	7.78	14.60
S: 30-year U.S. Treasuries	−5.43	−13.60
B: 7-year U.S. Treasuries	−0.71	− 5.23
Total return enhancement ⟶	4.72	8.37

Comments: *A bullish expectation warrants a move into longer duration securities; a bearish expectation demands a shortening of duration. The total return enhancement from properly timed rate anticipation moves can be significant. Conversely, incorrectly placed timing moves can be very costly.*

Exhibit 14–48. Six-month total returns for short, intermediate, and long maturity, 7.00% coupon U.S. Treasury bonds initially priced at par to yield 7.00% to maturity. A variety of interest rate scenarios are illustrated.

	Modified	*6-Month Total Return (%) if Yields:*			
Issue Data	*Duration*	*−200BP*	*−100BP*	*+100BP*	*+200BP*
2-year U.S. Treasury	1.84	6.36	4.91	2.11	0.75
7-year U.S. Treasury	5.46	14.48	8.82	−1.49	− 6.18
30-year U.S. Treasury	12.47	34.18	17.25	−7.76	−17.07

first two examples are bullish swaps that extend duration in a falling interest rate environment. The 2-year to 30-year swap adds 10.74% and 23.36% in incremental total return over the assumed 6-month horizon, given parallel 100BP and 200BP yield declines, respectively. A move from intermediate maturity bonds to long maturity bonds creates enhanced returns of 6.64% and 15.24% under the same conditions. In both cases the incremental returns are impressive relative to the excess returns attainable through issuer sector selection.[29] The final two swap illustrations of Exhibit 14–47 assume bearish interest rate scenarios of a 100BP and a 200BP rise in yields. The proposed duration shortening trades add 4.72%–14.60% to the total return of the issue purchased versus that of the issue sold. The more dramatic the reduction in duration, the more sizable the return enhancement and principal protection.

Exhibit 14–48 provides a generic analysis of U.S. Treasury issues under rising and falling interest rate scenarios. A 7.00% initial yield environment is assumed with current-coupon bonds employed. The general notions of enhanced leverage in long maturity bonds (returns range from −17.07% to 34.18% on the 30-year issue) and reduced leverage in short maturity bonds (returns range from 0.75% to 6.36% on the 2-year issue) are vividly portrayed. These effects are stronger/(weaker) in lower/(higher) yield environments. Exhibit 14–49 plots the price:yield curve for an interest rate anticipator. Using the principles of leverage in a successful interest rate anticipation approach can lead to greatly enhanced total returns. Unsuccessful moves, however, carry a commensurately severe penalty.

> **Observation:** *An interest rate anticipation swap is designed to benefit from an expected future movement in interest rate levels. An anticipation*

---

[29] Sector returns and relative performance are discussed in detail in Chapter 15.

*of higher yields warrants a shortening of duration by selling long
maturity bonds and buying short maturity bonds. An expectation of a
decline in yields calls for a lengthening of duration through the swapping
of short maturity bonds for long maturity bonds. The impact of the
trade is a function of the magnitude of the shortening/lengthening undertaken. Total returns are enhanced insofar as interest rates move in
the anticipated direction.*

Riding-the-yield-curve swap. Given an expectation of stable to modestly changing interest rates, a more docile method of enhancing total
returns is by *riding-the-yield-curve*. In a positively sloped yield curve
environment, an investor swaps out of a short maturity bond into a
slightly longer maturity issue and sells the longer maturity issue at the
end of the investment horizon. Assuming no major change in the shape
or level of the yield curve, the investor earns an excess return over
buying and holding the shorter maturity, lower yielding instrument. The
return enhancement arises from two general sources:

1. A higher yield on the longer maturity issue (more coupon return).
2. Capital appreciation from *riding* or *rolling* down the yield curve to
   a lower yield and a higher price (incremental price return).

As an example, Exhibit 14–50 displays the basic data for three
U.S. Treasury bonds: a 1-year issue, a 2-year issue, and a 3-year issue.
If an investor has a 1-year horizon and expects stability in market yields,
what returns can the investor expect to garner from each of these bonds?
The YTM figures suggest an additional 45BP can be captured by holding
2-year maturities rather than 1-year issues (7.48% versus 7.03%). In
this case, the baseline 1-year total returns calculate to 7.16% for the
1-year bond, 8.05% for the 2-year bond, and 8.46% for the 3-year bond
(see Exhibit 14–51). Riding-the-yield-curve leads to a total return enhancement of 89BP by holding 2-year issues in lieu of 1-year bonds, and an
additional 41BP in return from holding 3-year bonds as opposed to
2-year bonds (Exhibit 14–51). Exhibit 14–52 presents the general concept
of riding-the-yield-curve in a graphical form.

The riding-the-yield-curve strategy is threatened by two events:
(1) a general rise in interest rates, and (2) a flattening or inversion of
the yield curve. The expected yield curve rolls fail to materialize under
these conditions, and total return enhancements are of a smaller magnitude. Higher yield levels create some unexpected price depreciation in

Exhibit 14–49. Optimal price: yield curve for an interest rate anticipator. The investor desires to hold long duration securities in a declining interest rate environment and short duration securities in a rising interest rate environment. Par bonds are illustrated and are initially priced to yield 7.00%.

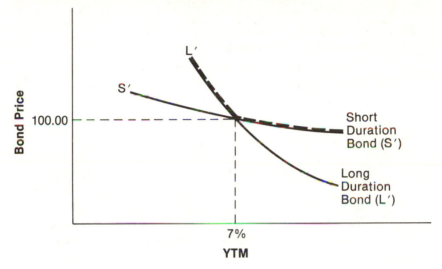

Comments: *The interest rate anticipator attempts to capture the upside potential of a long duration bond in a bull market and to secure the principal protection of a short duration bond in a bear market.*

the longer maturity issues and are responsible for a reduction or elimination of excess returns. One can assess the risk of higher yields by calculating a *breakeven yield level* for the longer maturity bond(s).

Exhibit 14–53 calculates the breakeven yields for the 2- and 3-year maturity bonds given a 1-year investment horizon. One year hence, if the current 2-year bond (at that point in time having 1 year remaining to maturity) trades at higher than a 7.96% yield, the use of the 2-year issue as a riding substitute for the 1-year buy-and-hold bond fails to enhance total return. At an ending yield lower than 7.96%, the swap

Exhibit 14–50. Issue data on 1-year, 2-year, and 3-year maturity U.S. Treasury bonds as of June 30, 1987.

Issue Data	Maturity (Years)	Price	YTM (%)	Modified Duration
U.S. Treasury 7% due 6/30/88	1	99-31	7.03	0.95
U.S. Treasury 7⅜% due 6/30/89	2	99-26	7.48	1.83
U.S. Treasury 7¼% due 6/30/90	3	98-20	7.76	2.65

Exhibit 14–51. Sample swaps using a riding-the-yield-curve strategy (using issue data from Exhibit 14–50). A baseline (no change) environment is assumed, with reinvestments made at a 7.50% rate.

Swap Proposal	YTM (%)	1-Year Roll (BP)	1-Year Total Return (%)
(a) S: 1-year U.S. Treasury	7.03	NA*	7.16
B: 2-year U.S. Treasury	7.48	−45	8.05
Total return enhancement ⟶			89BP
(b) S: 2-year U.S. Treasury	7.48	−45	8.05
B: 3-year U.S. Treasury	7.77	−29	8.46
Total return enhancement ⟶			41BP

*Not applicable since the bond matures in 1 year.

Comments: *The 2-year bond appreciates to a 100.33 price 1 year hence as a result of rolling down the yield curve to a 7.03% yield; the 3-year bond appreciates to 99.58 over the forthcoming year as its yield falls to 7.48% from 7.77%. A portion of these price appreciations is attributable to scientific amortization of the bonds' discounts.*

Exhibit 14–52. Riding-the-yield-curve in a stable environment. Baseline 1-year total returns are illustrated in general terms.

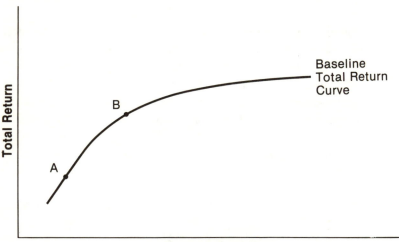

Comments: *Riding-the-yield-curve attempts to garner incremental returns in a stable rate environment. In this instance, the investor swaps from Bond A to Bond B to enhance total return.*

Exhibit 14–53. Calculation of breakeven yields for two riding-the-yield-curve swaps (supporting data in Exhibits 14–50 and 14–51).

Issue	YTM (%)	Baseline 1-Year Total Return (%)	Breakeven YTM 1 Year Hence (%)
1-year bond	7.03	7.16	NA*
2-year bond	7.48	8.05	7.96
3-year bond	7.77	8.46	7.68

*Not applicable since the bond matures in 1 year.

Comments: *The 2-year bond can rise in yield to 7.96% over the next year before it begins to underperform the 1-year issue. Phrased another way, 1-year bonds can experience a 93BP rise in yield (from 7.03% to 7.96%) before the 1- to 2-year swap becomes a return giveup trade. Stable rates or a modest rise of up to 93BP in 1-year yields allows the 2-year issue to outperform the 1-year buy-and-hold bond. The 3-year bond must fall to a 7.68% yield in order to keep pace with the 2-year bond. In other words, yields on 2-year issues 1 year hence can rise from the 7.48% level of today to the 7.68% level before the 2- to 3-year swap fails to add incremental return, not much margin for error.*

adds total return. At exactly a 7.96% terminal yield, the trade breaks even, neither enhancing nor detracting total returns. The corresponding breakeven yield for the 3-year bond is 7.68%, allowing little margin for error if general yield levels rise or the yield curve flattens or inverts. The higher the breakeven yield, the more probable the enhanced profitability of the riding strategy.

Flat yield curves offer no roll or ride; therefore, longer maturity issues provide no return enhancements in a stable yield environment. A negatively sloped yield curve forces the investor to seek portions of the curve with minimal *rollup*, given an assumption of a stable interest rate environment. The optimal environment for a riding-the-yield-curve swap is one in which the yield curve is currently very steep and the investor expects interest rates to remain stable or decline modestly.[30] A constrained rise in rates is bearable, but it detracts from the baseline total return enhancement in a stable yield environment.

[30] The anticipation of a sizable decline in rates warrants a more aggressive duration extension than that associated with the typical riding swap.

Observation: *A riding-the-yield-curve swap involves a modest extension of maturity with the expectation of a stable yield environment. The capture of incremental yield (and yield curve roll) in a positively sloped yield curve environment and the avoidance of yield curve rollup and related price depreciation in an inverted yield curve environment provide the incentive for the riding swap. Enhanced total returns are generated as a result.*

Exhibit 14–54. Summary of total return enhancement swaps.

Type of Swap	Example	Expectation
	A. Risk-Neutral Swaps	
Maturity sector swap	1. Swap up in coupon	Narrower coupon spreads
	2. Swap down in coupon	Wider coupon spreads
Coupon sector swap	1. Duration-weighted extension	Flatter yield curve
	2. Duration-weighted contraction	Steeper yield curve
	3. Dumbbell-to-bullet	Flattening of intermediate maturity bond yields versus short maturity and long maturity bond yields
	4. Bullet-to-dumbbell	Steepening of intermediate maturity bond yields versus short maturity and long maturity bond yields
Quality sector swap	1. Swap up in quality	Wider quality spreads
	2. Swap down in quality	Narrower quality spreads
Issuer sector, intra-issuer sector, and issue-specific swaps	1. Swap up in yield	Narrower yield spreads
	2. Swap down in yield	Wider yield spreads
	B. Risk-Altering Swaps	
Interest rate anticipation swap	1. Lengthen duration	Declining yields
	2. Shorten duration	Rising yields
Riding-the-yield-curve swap	A modest extension in maturity	Relatively stable market conditions

Exhibit 14–55. Summary of the basic types of swaps and their primary objectives.

Type of Swap	Primary Objective
I. YTM enhancement swap	To increase the average yield of the portfolio holdings
II. Current yield enhancement swap	To increase the annual coupon cash flow generated by the portfolio holdings
III. Quality enhancement swap	To increase the average quality of the portfolio holdings
IV. Liquidity enhancement swap	To increase the flexibility and tradeability of the portfolio
V. Total return enhancement swap	To increase the probability of superior total return performance by the portfolio holdings

In sum, total return enhancement swaps come in a wide variety of forms, ranging from the low risk substitution swap to the risky interest rate anticipation swap. A review of the total return enhancement swaps is provided in Exhibit 14–54. Exhibit 14–55 is a capsule summary of the general types of swaps outlined and illustrated in this chapter.[31]

Other considerations in bond swapping

Transaction costs

The illustrations in this chapter assume no transaction costs.[32] In reality, bond swaps are subject to an upfront load which is characterized by the bid-offer spread. As such, transaction costs reduce the attractiveness of a swap proposal. For example, an investor swaps from Bond A to Bond B and expects to add 120BP in incremental return over a 1-year horizon. However, a bid-offer spread of ½ point decreases the total return enhancement to approximately 70BP:

[31] The reader is encouraged to review the bond swap presentations of Homer and Leibowitz [*Inside the Yield Book* (Englewood Cliffs, NJ: Prentice-Hall, 1972)] and Seix [Chapter 29 (pp. 646–653) in Fabozzi and Pollack's *The Handbook of Fixed Income Securities* (Homewood, IL: Dow Jones-Irwin, 1987)].

[32] All of the illustrations employ bid side market quotes. The *no transaction cost assumption* allows the investor to apply the appropriate bid-offer spread to the results obtained. For a given security or swap, the bid-offer spread is negotiated between the dealer and the institutional investor. Large investors can generally deal on more favorable terms and narrow the quoted bid-offer spread to some degree. Smaller investors have less latitude in reducing transaction costs.

Issue	*Expected 1-Year Total Return (%)*	*Impact of Transaction Cost (½ Point)*	*Net Return Enhancement*
Bond A	9.00		
Bond B	10.20		
Total Return enhancement	+120BP	(50BP)*	+70BP

*Assumes that the bonds are trading close to par value.

A ½-point transaction cost translates into a 50BP total return impact on par bonds (0.50/100.00 = 0.0050 or 50BP). The impact of the ½-point spread is greater/(less) for discount/(premium) bonds. Exhibit 14–56 calculates the BP impact of a variety of transaction costs on the total returns of par, discount, and premium bonds. In general:

$$\frac{\text{TR impact of}}{\text{transaction cost (\%)}} = \frac{\text{bid-offer spread}}{\text{bond price}} \times 100$$

For example, a ½-point bid-offer spread on a bond priced at 85.00 is equivalent to approximately 59BP in total return:

$$
\begin{aligned}
\text{TR impact (\%)} &= \frac{0.50}{85.00} \times 100 \\
&= 0.00588 \times 100 \\
&= 0.588\% \\
&= 59\,\text{BP}
\end{aligned}
$$

The 59BP impact, of course, detracts from the total return of the purchased bond devoid of transaction costs. Transaction costs range from ⅟32 point to several points, depending on the issue type and maturity sector. Exhibit 14–57 provides a sampling of typical bid-offer spreads in a variety of bond categories.

A longer holding period deflects the impact of the transaction cost by spreading the upfront load over a longer investment period. Short time horizons and high turnover ratios generate substantial loads and commensurately more sizable negative impacts on total return performance. Due to transaction costs, bond swaps create total return patterns that commence in negative territory. Exhibit 14–58 shows this phenomenon graphically, on a quarter-by-quarter basis. This can create stress on portfolio managers who operate on a very short-term performance

Exhibit 14–56. Impact of transaction costs on nonannualized bond returns. A variety of bid-offer spreads and bond price levels are examined.

Bid-Offer Spread (Points)	*Negative Impact (BP) of the Bid-Offer Spread on the Total Return of a Bond Priced at:*							
	20	*40*	*60*	*80*	*100*	*120*	*140*	*160*
⅟₃₂	15	8	5	4	3	3	2	2
²⁄₃₂	31	16	10	8	6	5	5	4
⅛	63	31	21	16	13	10	9	8
¼	125	63	42	31	25	21	18	16
⅜	188	94	63	47	38	31	27	23
½	250	125	83	63	50	42	36	31
¾	375	188	123	94	75	63	54	47
1	500	250	167	125	100	83	71	63
2	1,000	500	333	250	200	167	143	125

Comments: *For a given bid-offer spread, a lower dollar price bond suffers a more sizable negative impact from the transaction cost. For a given dollar price bond, the wider the bid-offer spread, the more damaging the total return impact. Table figures are rounded to the nearest basis point.*

measurement basis. Even the best of trades begins in the minus column (recall Exhibit 14–56). Patience over a reasonable workout period (e.g., 1 year) is essential to investment success.

The impact of transaction costs on a portfolio's return can be found in multiplying the average annual turnover rate by the average transaction cost (in %):

$$\frac{\text{portfolio TR}}{\text{impact}} = \frac{\frac{\text{portfolio turnover percent per annum}}{100}}{} \times \frac{\text{average transaction cost}}{(\%)}$$

For example, a portfolio with 400% annual turnover and an average transaction cost of ⅜ point (or 37.5BP on a portfolio with bonds priced, on average, at par) incurs a 150BP reduction in total return as a result of swapping activity:

$$\text{portfolio TR impact} = \frac{400\%}{100} \times 0.375\%$$
$$= 4 \times 0.375\%$$
$$= 1.50\%$$
$$= 150\text{BP}$$

Exhibit 14–57. Ranges of typical bid-offer spreads on a variety of issuer sectors and maturities. Table figures are expressed in points.

| | Maturity Sector: | | |
Issuer Sector	*Short*	*Intermediate*	*Long*
U.S. Treasury	$\frac{1}{32}$–$\frac{2}{32}$	$\frac{2}{32}$–$\frac{4}{32}$	$\frac{2}{32}$–$\frac{8}{32}$
Federal agency	$\frac{2}{32}$–$\frac{8}{32}$	$\frac{4}{32}$–$\frac{16}{32}$	$\frac{12}{32}$–$\frac{32}{32}$
Corporate	$\frac{1}{4}$	$\frac{3}{8}$–$\frac{1}{2}$	$\frac{1}{2}$–1
Mortgage pass-through	$\frac{2}{32}$–$\frac{4}{32}$	$\frac{4}{32}$–$\frac{8}{32}$	NA
Esoteric products[*]	$\frac{1}{2}$	1–2	2–5

[*] Esoteric products include investments such as private placements and structured mortgage-backed securities.

Comments: *U.S. Treasuries generate the least transaction cost. Non-U.S. Treasury sectors offer lesser degrees of liquidity and esoteric products trade at the widest bid-offer spreads.*

Exhibit 14–58. Typical quarter-by-quarter return pattern (using unannualized return impacts) of a successful bond swap, a neutral bond swap, and an unsuccessful bond swap. A normal transaction cost is incorporated into the results.

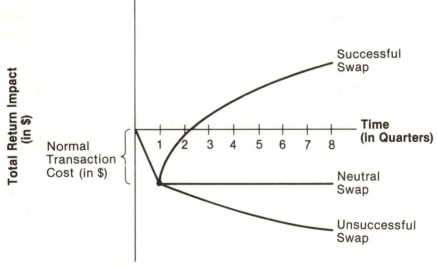

Comments: *Unless transaction costs can be eliminated, all trades incur an upfront load and an initial negative return. As time passes, the success of the trade determines eventual future outcomes. Neutral trades churn the portfolio and generate return losses equal to the transaction cost.*

If the manager is adding incremental returns of 400BP, the portfolio nets a 250BP gain. However, if the portfolio manager is executing neutral (no effect) trades, the portfolio suffers a 150BP return loss vis-à-vis the *0% turnover,* or buy-and-hold, case.[33] The negative impact of transaction costs does not suggest that bond swapping is *bad*. It merely emphasizes that careful consideration must be made of the upfront load incurred in carrying out any bond trade.[34] The total return projections must be assessed *net* of related transaction costs. If possible, spreading transactions over several periods of time alleviates the pain of negative upfront impacts. Giving the trade adequate time to work out is critical.

> **Observation:** *Transaction costs chip away at the total return offered by a bond swap; a portfolio's total return is likewise affected. The upfront load can be sizable with less liquid issues. A bond swap evaluation should take account of the reality of transaction costs.*

The impact of individual bond swaps on portfolio risk and return

A complete explanation of bond portfolio risk and return comprises the final chapter of this book (Chapter 15). A smooth transition from the current chapter to that concluding chapter is effected by applying the concepts of bond swapping in a portfolio context. In general, the impact of a bond swap on an entire portfolio is a function of two factors:

1. *The size of the bond swap relative to the portfolio size* (in market value weighted terms). The larger the swap, the greater the potential impact on the portfolio.

2. *The magnitude of the risk:return alteration resulting from the bond swap*. The larger the change in risk:return, the greater the potential impact on the bond portfolio's risk:return structure.

A bond portfolio's risk structure is affected by bond swaps that create either more or less market risk. A risk-neutral swap, by definition, has no impact on portfolio risk.[35] A risk-altering swap changes the duration

---

[33] In an efficient market, therefore, portfolio managers are destined to underperform an index of the market holdings.

[34] Since portfolio evaluations are made by using bid side market quotes, the return recorded in the month in which the bond is purchased suffers to the extent of the transaction cost.

[35] The focus here is on changes in general market risk exposure. A series of additional risks (credit, call, liquidity, etc.) may also be affected by a bond swap. These types of risk are discussed at length in Chapter 15.

of the bond holdings; consequently, the bond portfolio experiences a derivative shift in average duration:

$$\text{impact on portfolio average duration} = \text{percent of portfolio (MV terms)} \times \text{change in duration}$$

For example, an interest rate anticipation trade swaps 2-year duration bonds for 10-year duration bonds. The 8-year increase in duration is applied to only 20% of the portfolio. The overall portfolio duration, therefore, rises by 1.60 years:

$$\text{impact on portfolio duration} = 20\% \times (+8.0 \text{ years})$$
$$= +1.60 \text{ years}$$

A modest 1.00-year duration extension on 20% of the portfolio (e.g., through a riding-the-yield-curve swap) generates a 0.20-year increase in portfolio duration (20% × 1.00 = 0.20). A bond portfolio's return is similarly affected. In general:

$$\text{impact on portfolio total return} = \text{percent of portfolio (MV)} \times \text{change in total return}$$

For example, a bond swap involving 25% of the portfolio's assets creates an incremental 100BP in total return over a 1-year time horizon. The swap increases the total portfolio return by 25BP:

$$\text{impact on portfolio TR} = 25\% \times (+100\text{BP})$$
$$= +25\text{BP}$$

If only 5% of the portfolio is used in the aforementioned trade, the portfolio's return is enhanced by only 5BP (5% × 100BP = 5BP). The return projections should be stated net of related transaction costs in order to properly reflect the corresponding portfolio impact.

Observation: *A bond swap has more influence on the overall portfolio's risk and return characteristics (1) the larger the swap, and (2) the more dramatic the risk:return implications of the swap.*

Summary

Bond swaps can be categorized into YTM enhancement swaps, current yield enhancement swaps, quality enhancement swaps, liquidity enhancement swaps, and total return enhancement swaps. Total return enhancements come in two varieties: risk-neutral and risk-altering.

A *YTM enhancement swap* is designed to increase the average YTM of a bond portfolio. A *current yield enhancement swap* raises the coupon cash flow generated annually by the portfolio. A *quality enhancement swap* moves into higher quality issues in order to create an overall upgrade in average portfolio quality. A *liquidity enhancement swap* increases the liquidity, or tradeability, of the portfolio. A *total return enhancement swap* attempts to create an upward bias in the future total returns generated by the portfolio. A *risk-neutral swap* holds the portfolio risk constant while enhancing total return prospects. A *risk-altering swap* purposely shifts the portfolio duration in anticipation of a move in interest rates.

Bond swaps impact portfolio risk and return, and transaction costs are an important consideration.

CHAPTER 14 APPENDIX

Weighting Swaps by Using Duration and the Yield Value of a 32nd

Duration-weighted swaps

Risk-neutral trades mandate that weightings be placed on bonds purchased and sold in order to ensure a nullification of inherent risk differentials. In general, the objective can be stated in equation form:

$$\text{duration}_S = \text{duration}_B$$

where the duration of the *sell* bond(s) equals the duration of the *buy* bond(s).[a]

In the remainder of this Appendix, the following abbreviations are used in the various formulas:

duration = selected duration measure (in this case, modified duration)

S = *sell* bond(s)

B = *buy* bond(s)

---

[a] If a combination of bonds and/or cash is sold, a weighted average duration serves as the representative *sell bond* duration. In the same vein, a composite of bonds and/or cash purchased is summarized in a weighted average duration figure. In both cases, market values are used in the weighting process.

ST = short maturity bond

IT = intermediate maturity bond

LT = long maturity bond

C = cash investments

The mechanics behind duration-weighted extension swaps

For a *duration-weighted extension swap,* the weightings are calculated as follows:

$$\text{duration}_S = \text{duration}_B$$

$$\text{duration}_{ST} = \text{duration}_{LT}\,(x) + \text{duration}_C\,(1 - x)$$

$$= \text{duration}_{LT}\,(x) + 0(1 - x)$$

$$= \text{duration}_{LT}\,(x)$$

$$x = \frac{\text{duration}_{ST}}{\text{duration}_{LT}} = \text{long maturity bond allocation (\%)}$$

$$1 - x = \text{cash allocation (\%)}$$

For example, if a short maturity bond with a duration of 3.00 years is swapped for a long maturity bond bearing an 8.00-year duration, the sale proceeds are allocated 37.50% to the long maturity bond and 62.50% to cash equivalents:

$$3.00 = 8.00(x) + 0(1 - x)$$

$$= 8.00(x)$$

$$x = \frac{3.00}{8.00}$$

$$= 0.375$$

$$= 37.50\% \quad \text{(long maturity bond allocation)}$$

$$1 - x = 1 - 0.375$$

$$= 0.625$$

$$= 62.50\% \quad \text{(cash allocation)}$$

Verification of the weightings is straightforward:

$$\text{duration}_S = \text{duration}_B$$

$$3.00 = 8.00(0.375) + 0(0.625)$$

$$= 3.00 + 0$$

$$= 3.00 \quad \text{(verified)}$$

In market value terms, the amount of long maturity bonds to be purchased is calculated as follows:

$$
\begin{array}{c}\text{market value of}\\ \text{long bonds}\\ \text{(to be purchased)}\end{array} = \begin{array}{c}\text{market value of}\\ \text{short bonds}\\ \text{(to be sold)}\end{array} \times \begin{array}{c}\text{long bond}\\ \text{allocation (\%)}\end{array}
$$

Recalling that the long maturity bond allocation is simply the ratio of the short maturity bond duration to the long maturity bond duration, it follows that:

$$
\begin{array}{c}\text{market value of}\\ \text{long bonds}\\ \text{(to be purchased)}\end{array} = \begin{array}{c}\text{market value of}\\ \text{short bonds}\\ \text{(to be sold)}\end{array} \times \frac{\text{duration of short maturity bond}}{\text{duration of long maturity bond}}
$$

For example, a $10 million position (market value) of 3.00-year duration bonds can be swapped into a $3.75 million position (market value) of 8.00-year duration bonds.

$$
\begin{array}{c}\text{market value of}\\ \text{long maturity bonds}\\ \text{(to be purchased)}\end{array} = \$10 \text{ million} \times \frac{3.00}{8.00}
$$
$$
= \$10 \text{ million} \times 0.375
$$
$$
= \$3.75 \text{ million}
$$

with the $6.25 million balance invested in cash instruments. The wider the disparity between the duration of the short maturity bond sold and the duration of the long maturity bond purchased, the smaller the percentage of long maturity bonds that can be purchased in order to maintain duration equivalence.

Verification of the duration neutrality can be made by calculating a weighted average duration as follows:

$$
\text{duration}_S = \text{duration}_B
$$

$$
\sum_{i=1}^{N_S} \left(\frac{\text{market value of sell bond}_i}{\text{total sale proceeds}} \times \text{duration of sell bond}_i \right)
$$
$$
= \sum_{i=1}^{N_B} \left(\frac{\text{market value of buy bond}_i}{\text{total purchase outlay}} \times \text{duration of buy bond}_i \right)
$$

where

N_S = number of securities sold

N_B = number of securities bought

In this case,

$$\left(\frac{\$10 \text{ million}}{\$10 \text{ million}} \times 3.00\right) = \left(\frac{\$3.75 \text{ million}}{\$10.00 \text{ million}} \times 8.00\right)$$

$$+ \left(\frac{\$6.25 \text{ million}}{\$10.00 \text{ million}} \times 0.00\right)$$

$$3.00 = (0.375 \times 8.00) + (0.625 \times 0.00)$$
$$= 3.00 + 0$$
$$= 3.00 \quad \text{(verified)}$$

Using the duration-dollar concept in risk-neutralizing trades

An alternative approach to maintaining risk neutrality in bond swaps involves the concept of duration-dollars. *Duration-dollars* are simply the product of the duration of a bond and its current market value:

$$\text{duration-dollars} = \text{duration} \times \text{market value (dollars)}$$

For a portfolio of bonds, the duration-dollar position is a summation of the component durations as weighted by their respective market values:

$$\begin{matrix} \text{duration-dollars} \\ \text{(for a portfolio)} \end{matrix} = \sum_{i=1}^{N} (\text{duration}_i \times \text{market value}_i)$$

where

i = ith security in the portfolio

N = total number of securities comprising the portfolio

Continuing the earlier example, assume that the $10 million position (market value of short maturity bonds) accounts for the entire bond portfolio holdings of the manager under scrutiny. The portfolio has a 30 million duration-dollar position:

$$\begin{matrix} \text{duration-dollars} \\ \text{(before swap)} \end{matrix} = 3.00 \times \$10 \text{ million}$$
$$= \$30 \text{ million}$$

Upon completion of a duration-weighted swap, the portfolio's duration-dollar position remains unchanged:

$$\begin{array}{l} \text{duration-dollars} \\ \text{(before swap)} \end{array} = \$30 \text{ million}$$

$$\begin{array}{l} \text{duration-dollars} \\ \text{(after swap)} \end{array} = \underbrace{\frac{(8.00 \times \$3.75 \text{ million})}{\text{long maturity bond holdings}}}_{} + \underbrace{\frac{(0.00 \times \$6.25 \text{ million})}{\text{cash holdings}}}_{}$$

$$= \$30 \text{ million} + \$0$$
$$= \$30 \text{ million}$$

No net change in duration-dollars indicates a risk-neutral trade on a duration-weighted basis.

The duration-dollar concept is most helpful when dealing with multi-bond swaps (e.g., sell four bond positions to purchase seven bond positions). The market value weighted duration calculations can become arduous; the mathematics of duration-dollars is less tedious. As an illustration, a portfolio manager sells a basket of securities having durations ranging from 1.00 to 4.00 years (see Exhibit 14A–1). A total sale of 50 million duration-dollars is made. A myriad of combinations of replacement bonds can be made while maintaining a 50 million duration-dollar position (see Exhibit 14A–2).

The duration-dollar concept has another useful feature: it can be used to derive a market value *weighted average duration* for a collection of bonds. The general formula is as follows:

$$\text{weighted average duration} = \frac{\text{duration-dollars}}{\text{market value (dollars)}}$$

Exhibit 14A–1. Sample portfolio of securities have durations ranging from 1 to 4 years and a duration-dollar position of $50 million.

	(1)	*(2)*	*(3) = (1) × (2)*
			Duration-
	Modified	*Market Value*	*Dollars*
Security	*Duration*	*(Millions)*	*(Millions)*
Bond 1	1.00	$30.00	$30.00
Bond 2	1.40	5.00	7.00
Bond 3	2.30	4.00	9.20
Bond 4	3.80	1.00	3.80
		$40.00	$50.00

Exhibit 14A–2. Sample replacement portfolios with $40 million market values and $50 million duration-dollar positions.

	(1)	(2)	(3) = (1) × (2)
			Duration-
	Modified	*Market Value*	*Dollars*
	Duration	*(Millions)*	*(Millions)*
Portfolio A			
Cash	0.00	$36.00	$ 0.00
Bond 5	12.50	4.00	50.00
		$40.00	$50.00
Portfolio B			
Cash	0.00	$11.60	$ 0.00
Bond 5	12.50	1.00	12.50
Bond 6	0.80	24.40	19.50
Bond 7	6.00	3.00	18.00
		$40.00	$50.00
Portfolio C			
Bond 6	0.80	$29.40	$23.50
Bond 8	2.50	10.60	26.50
		$40.00	$50.00

For example, a set of seven bonds supports a combined duration-dollar figure of $100 million:

	(1)	(2)	(3) = (1) × (2)
	Modified	*Market Value*	*Duration-*
Security	*Duration*	*(Millions)*	*Dollars (Millions)*
Bond A	1.00	$ 0.50	$ 0.50
Bond B	2.80	1.00	2.80
Bond C	3.50	2.00	7.00
Bond D	4.60	0.50	2.30
Bond E	7.10	2.00	14.20
Bond F	9.30	4.00	37.20
Bond G	12.00	3.00	36.00
		$13.00	$100.00

The weighted average duration of the 7-bond portfolio is 7.69 years:

$$\text{weighted average duration} = \frac{\text{total duration-dollars}}{\text{total market value}}$$

$$= \frac{\$100.00 \text{ million}}{\$13.00 \text{ million}}$$

$$= 7.69 \text{ years}$$

Duration-weighted swaps: A practical application

Exhibit 14A–3 summarizes the durations of a series of current-coupon U.S. Treasury bonds in a 7% yield environment. An investor who owns a portfolio of 5-year maturity bonds can swap into a combination of 10-year maturity issues (58.40%) and cash equivalents (41.60%) to risk-neutralize the trade:

$$x = \frac{4.15 \text{ (duration of the 5-year bond)}}{7.11 \text{ (duration of the 10-year bond)}}$$

$$= 0.5837$$

$$= 58.37\% \quad \text{(long maturity bond allocation)}$$

$$1 - x = 1 - 0.5837$$

$$= 0.4163$$

$$= 41.63\% \quad \text{(cash allocation)}$$

If the investor owns $100 million (market value) of the 5-year bonds, the investor can purchase $58.37 million (market value) of the 10-year

Exhibit 14A–3. Durations and yield values of a 32nd for a series of 7.00% coupon U.S. Treasury bonds priced at par in a 7.00% yield environment.

Issue	Modified Duration	Yield Value of 1/32nd (BP)
1-year bond	0.95	3.29
2-year bond	1.84	1.70
3-year bond	2.67	1.17
4-year bond	3.44	0.91
5-year bond	4.15	0.75
7-year bond	5.46	0.57
10-year bond	7.11	0.44
20-year bond	10.68	0.29
30-year bond	12.47	0.25

bonds. In this case, since both bonds are trading at par value, the investor sells $100 million (par) 5-year issues and buys $58.37 million (par) 10-year issues and invests $41.63 million in cash equivalents.

Using June 30, 1987 data, Exhibit 14A–4 calculates the durations of a series of U.S. Treasury issues of various maturities. An investor who owns a portfolio of 4-year bonds (U.S. Treasury 7⅞% due 6/30/91) executes a duration-weighted extension swap into 30-year bonds (U.S. Treasury 8¾% due 5/15/17) by investing only 31.67% of the proceeds in the long maturity bond (3.37/10.64 = 0.3167 or 31.67%), with the balance funding cash instrument purchases. If the investor currently owns $100 million (par amount) of the 4-year bonds, selling the bonds at 99–25 renders $99,802,766.40 in proceeds (July 1, 1987 settlement date):

$$
\begin{array}{ll}
\$99,781,250.00 & \text{principal} \\
+\ \underline{\quad 21,516.40} & \text{interest} \\
\$99,802,766.40 & \text{total proceeds}
\end{array}
$$

The long maturity bond investment constitutes a $31,607,536.12 outlay:

$$
\begin{array}{ccc}
\$99,802,766.40 & 31.67\% & \$31,607,536.12 \\
& \times \text{ long maturity bond} = \text{long maturity bond} \\
\text{sale proceeds} & \text{allocation (\%)} & \text{allocation (\$)}
\end{array}
$$

Exhibit 14A–4. Durations and yield values of a 32nd for a series of U.S. Treasury bonds (June 30, 1987 data).

Maturity (Years)	Issue	Price	YTM (%)	Modified Duration	YV of a 32nd (BP)
1	7% due 6/30/88	99-31	7.03	0.95	3.33
2	7⅜% due 6/30/89	99-26	7.48	1.83	1.72
3	7¼% due 6/30/90	98-20	7.77	2.65	1.20
4	7⅞% due 6/30/91	99-25	7.94	3.37	0.93
5	6⅝% due 5/15/92	94-13	8.02	3.98	0.81
7	7% due 4/15/94	93-19	8.25	5.16	0.64
10	8½% due 5/15/97	100-26	8.38	6.55	0.47
20	9⅜% due 2/15/06	106-03	8.71	8.73	0.33
30	8¾% due 5/15/17	102-22	8.50	10.64	0.28

The long maturity bond allocation translates into a par amount of approximately $30,450,000.00:

$$\text{par amount} = \frac{\text{market value allocation (\$)}}{\text{cost per \$1 par}}$$

$$= \frac{\$31,607,536.12}{\$1.03805 \text{ (including accrued)}}$$

$$= \$30,448,953.00$$

$$\approx \$30,450,000.00$$

Keep in mind that duration-weighted swaps are predicated on market value weights.[b] These weights must then be converted into par value amounts as illustrated above.

The contrast between market value proportions and par value amounts is magnified by bonds selling at dramatically different dollar prices. For example, Exhibit 14A–5 presents U.S. Treasury issue data on a set of bonds trading at sizably divergent prices. If an investor owns $10 million par amount of the U.S. Treasury 8¾% due 8/15/94, how much par value of the long U.S. Treasury 11¼% bond can the investor swap into, given a desire to maintain similar market risk? Alternatively, how much of the long U.S. Treasury 7¼% bond can the investor bear, in par value terms? Exhibit 14A–6 provides the answers to these questions: $4,220,000 par of the U.S. Treasury 11¼% bond and $5,800,000 par of the U.S. Treasury 7¼% bond. This table makes it clear that the market value allocations to the long bonds (52.25% and 47.35%, respectively) carry significant discrepancies from the relative par amounts purchased (42.20% and 58.00%, respectively). An error in applying the calculated weightings can easily mitigate the intended effect of the swap. This danger is highlighted because trades using the yield value of a 32nd as the risk measure (to be explained shortly) rely on par value weightings, not market value weights. Only when the bonds involved are trading at par do the results of market value weighting and par value weighting converge.

---

[b] Since duration is an estimate of the percentage change in *market value* of a bond given a specified change in yield, the weightings must be market value based. This stands in contrast to the par value weights used under the yield value of a 32nd schematic.

Exhibit 14A–5. Durations and yield values of a 32nd for a sample of five U.S. Treasury bonds (June 30, 1987 data).

Maturity (Years)	Issue	Price	YTM (%)	Modified Duration	YV of a 32nd (BP)
2	7⅜% due 6/30/89	99-26	7.48	1.83	1.72
7	13⅛% due 5/15/94	124-27	8.30	4.71	0.52
7	8¾% due 8/15/94	102-22	8.24	5.10	0.58
30	11¼% due 2/15/15	127-00	8.66	9.76	0.24
30	7¼% due 5/15/16	85-19	8.61	10.77	0.34

Exhibit 14A–6. Duration-weighted extension swaps into long maturity U.S. Treasuries. The investor sells a portfolio of $10 million par amount U.S. Treasury 8¾% due 8/15/94 (modified duration = 5.10 years) to buy a combination of cash equivalents and either (1) U.S. Treasury 11¼% due 2/15/15 or (2) U.S. Treasury 7¼% due 5/15/16 (issue data per Exhibit 14A–5).

Swap Proposal	MV Allocation (%) Long Maturity Bond	Cash	Long Maturity Bond Cost per $1 Par	Par Amount of Long Maturity Bond Purchased
Buy 11¼% bond + cash equivalents	52.25	47.75	1.31227	4,220,000
Buy 7¼% bond + cash equivalents	47.35	52.65	0.86520	5,800,000

Comments: *The market value allocations maintain a weighted average duration of 5.10 years. The MV allocations (%) are multiplied by the sale proceeds of $10,597,479.28 to arrive at dollar allocations to the long maturity bond of $5,537,182.92 for the 11¼s and $5,017,906.44 for the 7¼s. The par amount of long maturity bond purchased is simply the dollar allocation to the long maturity bond divided by the cost per $1 par (par amounts are rounded to the nearest 5,000 bonds in this example). The long maturity bond cost per $1 par includes accrued interest.*

The mechanics behind duration-weighted contraction swaps

The Appendix illustrations to this point have focused on duration-weighted extension swaps. The two alternative swaps, duration-weighted contractions and dumbbell/bullets, warrant similar analyses. A *duration-weighted contraction swap* requires bond weightings as follows:

$$\text{duration}_S = \text{duration}_B$$

$$\text{duration}_{LT} = \text{duration}_{ST}\ (x)$$

$$x = \frac{\text{duration}_{LT}}{\text{duration}_{ST}}$$

$$= \text{short maturity bond allocation (\%)}$$

It is clear that in this case, $x > 100.00\%$.

If an investor sells an 8.00-year duration bond and buys a 3.00-year duration security, the investor must purchase 267.00% short maturity bonds ($x = 8.00/3.00 = 2.67$ or 267.00%) in order to maintain duration equivalence. In other words, additional cash must be invested in the short maturity bond. Expressed as a percentage of the total purchase of short maturity bonds, 37.50% of the funding arises from long maturity bond sales ($100.00\%/267.00\% = 0.3750$ or 37.50%) and the remaining 62.50% comes from cash balances ($167.00\%/267.00\% = 0.6250$ or 62.50%). An alternative way of viewing a duration-weighted contraction swap is:

$$\text{duration}_S = \text{duration}_B$$

$$\text{duration}_{LT}\ (x) + \text{duration}_C\ (1 - x) = \text{duration}_{ST}$$

$$\text{duration}_{LT}\ (x) + 0(1 - x) = \text{duration}_{ST}$$

$$\text{duration}_{LT}\ (x) = \text{duration}_{ST}$$

$$x = \frac{\text{duration}_{ST}}{\text{duration}_{LT}} = \frac{\text{long maturity bond}}{\text{allocation (\%)}}$$

$$1 - x = \text{cash allocation (\%)}$$

In this instance,

$$x = \frac{3.00}{8.00}$$

$$= 0.375$$

$$= 37.50\% \quad \text{[long bond allocation (sale)]}$$

$$1 - x = 1 - 0.375$$

$$= 0.625$$

$$= 62.50\% \quad \text{[cash allocation (sale)]}$$

In market value terms, the amount of short maturity bonds to be purchased is as follows:

$$\begin{matrix} \text{market value of} \\ \text{short maturity} \\ \text{bonds} \\ \text{(to be purchased)} \end{matrix} = \begin{matrix} \text{market value of} \\ \text{long maturity} \\ \text{bonds (to be sold)} \end{matrix} \times \frac{\text{duration of long maturity bond}}{\text{duration of short maturity bond}}$$

The funding for the purchase is derived from two sources:

$$\begin{matrix} \text{market value of} \\ \text{short maturity} \\ \text{bonds} \\ \text{(to be purchased)} \end{matrix} = \begin{matrix} \text{market value of} \\ \text{long maturity bonds} \\ \text{(to be sold)} \end{matrix} + \begin{matrix} \text{market value of} \\ \text{cash allocation} \\ \text{(to be sold)} \end{matrix}$$

$$100.00\% \quad = \quad 37.50\% \quad + \quad 62.50\%$$

Verification of the duration neutrality of the swap follows similar procedures to those earlier diagrammed, and the use of the duration-dollar concept applies equally to duration-weighted contractions as to extensions. In each case, maintaining a similar amount of duration-dollar holdings ensures a risk-neutral stance.

The mechanics behind duration-weighted dumbbell/bullet swaps

A *duration-weighted dumbbell/bullet swap* is predicated on the notion of duration equality:

$$\text{duration}_S = \text{duration}_B$$

For a *dumbbell-to-bullet swap:*

$$\underset{\text{(sell)}}{\text{duration}_{ST}(x)} + \underset{\text{(sell)}}{\text{duration}_{LT}(1-x)} = \underset{\text{(buy)}}{\text{duration}_{IT}}$$

where

$x =$ short maturity bond allocation (%)

$1 - x =$ long maturity bond allocation (%)

For a *bullet-to-dumbbell swap:*

$$\underset{\text{(sell)}}{\text{duration}_{IT}} = \underset{\text{(buy)}}{\text{duration}_{ST}(x)} + \underset{\text{(buy)}}{\text{duration}_{LT}(1-x)}$$

where

x = short maturity bond allocation (%)

$1 - x$ = long maturity bond allocation (%)

For example, in a 7.00% yield environment, an investor selling a 2-year/30-year combination to buy a 10-year bullet calculates the appropriate weightings as follows (data per Exhibit 14A–3):

$$\underset{\text{(sell)}}{\text{duration}_{\text{2-year bond}} (x)} + \underset{\text{(sell)}}{\text{duration}_{\text{30-year bond}} (1 - x)} = \underset{\text{(buy)}}{\text{duration}_{\text{10-year bond}}}$$

$$1.84x + 12.47(1 - x) = 7.11$$

$$1.84x + 12.47 - 12.47x = 7.11$$

$$-10.63x + 12.47 = 7.11$$

$$-10.63x = 7.11 - 12.47$$
$$= -5.36$$

$$x = \frac{-5.36}{-10.63}$$
$$= 0.5042$$
$$= 50.42\% \quad \text{(2-year}$$
$$\text{bond allocation)}$$

$$1 - x = 1 - 0.5042$$
$$= 0.4958$$
$$= 49.58\% \quad \text{(30-year}$$
$$\text{bond allocation)}$$

In this instance, approximately 50% of the 10-year bond purchase is furnished by long maturity bond sales and 50% stems from short maturity bond redemptions. The accuracy of the proposed weightings is quickly assessed:

$$\text{duration}_S = \text{duration}_B$$

$$1.84(50.42\%) + 12.47(49.58\%) = 7.11$$

$$0.92773 + 6.18263 = 7.11$$

$$7.11 \quad \text{(rounded to two decimals)} = 7.11 \quad \text{(verified)}$$

In market value terms, the funding of intermediate maturity bond purchases is as follows:

$$
\begin{array}{ccc}
\text{market value of} & \text{market value of} & \text{market value of} \\
\text{10-year bonds} = & \text{2-year bonds} + & \text{30-year bonds} \\
\text{(to be purchased)} & \text{(to be sold)} & \text{(to be sold)} \\
100.00\% \quad = & 50.42\% \quad + & 49.58\%
\end{array}
$$

A duration-weighted *bullet-to-dumbbell swap* operates on the same precepts, but moves in the opposite direction. For example, using June 30, 1987 data (per Exhibit 14A–4), an investor swaps out of 7-year U.S. Treasuries (7% due 4/14/94) into a combination of 1-year (7% due 6/30/88) and 10-year bonds (8½% due 5/15/97). What is the appropriate proportion of 1s and 10s to purchase?

$$
\begin{array}{c}
\text{duration}_{\text{7-year bond}} = \text{duration}_{\text{1-year bond}}(x) + \text{duration}_{\text{10-year bond}}(1-x) \\
\text{(sell)} \qquad\qquad \text{(buy)} \qquad\qquad\qquad \text{(buy)}
\end{array}
$$

$$
\begin{aligned}
5.16 &= 0.95x + 6.55(1-x) \\
&= 0.95x + 6.55 - 6.55x \\
&= -5.60x + 6.55 \\
5.60x &= 6.55 - 5.16 \\
&= 1.39
\end{aligned}
$$

$$
\begin{aligned}
x &= \frac{1.39}{5.60} \\
&= 0.2482 \\
&= 24.82\% \quad \text{(1-year bond allocation)}
\end{aligned}
$$

$$
\begin{aligned}
1 - x &= 1 - 0.2482 \\
&= 0.7518 \\
&= 75.18\% \quad \text{(10-year bond allocation)}
\end{aligned}
$$

The sale of 7-year bonds is invested in approximately 25.00% short bonds and 75.00% long bonds. The validity of the weightings can be easily verified:

$$
\begin{aligned}
\text{duration}_S &= \text{duration}_B \\
5.16 &= 0.95(24.82\%) + 6.55(75.18\%) \\
&= 0.23579 + 4.92429 \\
&= 5.16 \quad \text{(rounded to two decimals)}
\end{aligned}
$$

In market value terms, the sale of 7-year bonds funds the purchase of 1s and 10s as follows:

market value of 1-year bonds (to be purchased)		market value of 10-year bonds (to be purchased)		market value of 7-year bonds (to be sold)
24.82%	+	75.18%	=	100.00%

Once again, the duration-dollar concept can be applied in order to maintain a desired level of risk.

Weighting swaps by using the yield value of a 32nd[c]

Sample calculations

Chapter 6 introduced the yield value of a 32nd (YV32) as a contemporary measure of bond risk. As such, the YV32 serves as an instrument to control risk exposure in individual bond swaps. Recall that the YV32 reports the average absolute basis point (BP) change in yield that occurs from repricing a bond 1/32nd of a point higher and 1/32nd of a point lower than its current market price.

Exhibit 14A–3 calculates the YV32 for a series of current-coupon U.S. Treasury bonds in a 7.00% yield environment. YV32s decline as the maturity of the bond lengthens. In other words, it takes a smaller change in yield to effect the same 1/32-point move in bond price (i.e., long maturity bonds are more price volatile than short maturity bonds). The relative price volatility between two bonds can be estimated by the ratio of the YV32s:

$$\frac{\text{relative price volatility}}{\text{of Bond B versus Bond A}} = \frac{\text{YV32 of Bond A}}{\text{YV32 of Bond B}}$$

For example, a 30-year bond is three times as volatile as a 5-year bond (data per Exhibit 14A–3):

---

[c] Alternatively, one can employ the yield value of a 1/8th (i.e., 0.125 point). Recall that a 32nd (0.03125 point) is the minimum price move in U.S. Treasury and federal agency bonds. Corporate bond prices are typically quoted in eighths.

$$\frac{\text{relative price volatility}}{\text{of 30-year versus 5-year bond}} = \frac{\text{YV32 of the 5-year bond}}{\text{YV32 of the 30-year bond}}$$

$$= \frac{0.75}{0.25}$$

$$= 3.00$$

Using June 30, 1987 data (per Exhibit 14A–4), the 7-year U.S. Treasury (7% due 4/15/94) is approximately five times as volatile as a 1-year U.S. Treasury (7% due 6/30/88):

$$\frac{\text{relative price volatility}}{\text{of 7-year versus 1-year bond}} = \frac{\text{YV32 of the 1-year bond}}{\text{YV32 of the 7-year bond}}$$

$$= \frac{3.33}{0.64}$$

$$= 5.20$$

YV32-weighted extension swaps

The YV32 formulation is applicable to the risk-neutralization process of weighted extension swaps, weighted contraction swaps, and dumbbell/bullet swaps. Conceptually, duration and the YV32 are quite similar. In usage, however, the constructs differ in that duration relies on market value weightings, whereas the YV32 is par value based.[d] In a *YV32-weighted extension swap:*

$$\frac{\text{par amount of}}{\text{long maturity bond}} = \frac{\text{par amount of}}{\text{short maturity bond}} \times \frac{\text{YV32 of long maturity bond}}{\text{YV32 of short maturity bond}}$$
$$\text{(to be purchased)} \quad \text{(to be sold)}$$

For example, a move from $10 million (par amount) 2-year bonds into 20-year bonds allows the investor to purchase only $1.7 million (par amount) of the long maturity issue if the investor wishes to maintain a similar risk posture (data from Exhibit 14A–3):

$$\frac{\text{par amount of}}{\text{20-year bond}} = \$10 \text{ million} \times \frac{0.29}{1.70}$$
$$\text{(to be purchased)}$$

$$= \$10 \text{ million} \times 0.1706$$

$$= \$1.706 \text{ million}$$

[d] Par value weightings arise from the fact that the YV32 concept assesses the BP yield change resulting from a $\frac{1}{32}$-point change *per bond* (i.e., per par amount), *not* per dollar invested (i.e., market value).

YV32-weighted contraction swaps

A *YV32-weighted contraction swap* operates from the following base:

$$
\begin{array}{c}
\text{par amount of} \\
\text{short maturity bond} \\
\text{(to be purchased)}
\end{array}
=
\begin{array}{c}
\text{par amount of} \\
\text{long maturity bond} \\
\text{(to be sold)}
\end{array}
\times
\frac{\text{YV32 of short maturity bond}}{\text{YV32 of long maturity bond}}
$$

As an illustration, an investor swapping from 30-year U.S. Treasuries into 20-year U.S. Treasuries must purchase approximately 18% more par amount of the shorter issue to maintain an equivalent market risk stance. Using data from Exhibit 14A–4, if an investor sells $100 million (par amount) 30s, the investor is obligated to buy $117.9 million 20s:

$$
\begin{array}{c}
\text{par amount of} \\
\text{20-year bond} \\
\text{(to be purchased)}
\end{array}
\begin{aligned}
&= \$100 \text{ million} \times \frac{0.33}{0.28} \\
&= \$100 \text{ million} \times 1.1786 \\
&= \$117.86 \text{ million}
\end{aligned}
$$

YV32-weighted dumbbell/bullet swaps

A dumbbell/bullet swap behaves according to the same methodology. The general formulation is as follows:

$$
\begin{array}{c}
\text{par amount of} \\
\text{intermediate} \\
\text{maturity bond}
\end{array}
=
\left(
\begin{array}{c}
\text{par amount of} \\
\text{short maturity} \\
\text{bond}
\end{array}
\times
\frac{\text{YV32 of intermediate maturity bond}}{\text{YV32 of short maturity bond}}
\right)
$$

$$
+
\left(
\begin{array}{c}
\text{par amount of} \\
\text{long maturity bond}
\end{array}
\times
\frac{\text{YV32 of intermediate maturity bond}}{\text{YV32 of long maturity bond}}
\right)
$$

The dumbbell-to-bullet swap acts as a combination extension (from short maturity to intermediate maturity) and contraction (from long maturity to intermediate maturity). The bullet-to-dumbbell swap is part extension (from intermediate maturity to long maturity) and part contraction (from intermediate maturity to short maturity). As such, bullet/dumbbell swaps utilize the concepts presented under both the extension and contraction analyses.

CHAPTER 15
Bond Portfolio Analysis

Bond portfolio return
    The dollar-weighted rate of return versus the time-weighted rate of return
    The arithmetic mean return versus the geometric mean return
    Performance measurement and comparison
    Portfolio returns versus benchmark returns
    Historical market and sector returns
    Portfolio return as influenced by sector holdings

Bond portfolio risk
    Bond portfolio risk as explained by total return variability
    Bond portfolio risk as explained by a portfolio beta
    Systematic and unsystematic risk
    The components of bond portfolio risk
        Duration risk
        Yield curve risk
        Call/convexity risk
        Quality/credit risk
            Using a quality distribution
            Using an average quality measure
        Issuer sector risk
        Intra-issuer sector risk
        Issue-specific risk
        Liquidity risk
        Product risk

Summary

Appendix A
The Structure of the Major Bond Market Indexes

Appendix B
The Danger of Portfolio Averages

The first three sections of this text reviewed the fundamentals of bond mathematics, the fundamentals of bond risk, and the fundamentals of bond return, respectively. These basics have been applied to yield curve analysis (Chapter 12), total return curve analysis (Chapter 13), and bond swapping (Chapter 14). This chapter integrates the fundamental concepts and their applications in a portfolio context. Portfolio risk and return is assessed in light of the realities of performance evaluation and benchmark comparison. Appendix A describes the most commonly used bond market indexes, which form a basis for ascertaining the relative risk and return of a specific portfolio. Appendix B warns of the dangers of portfolio averages and provides a comprehensive analysis of a bond portfolio by using the computer software of Capital Management Sciences, a Los Angeles-based consulting firm.

Bond portfolio return

A bond portfolio's return is typically expressed as a *holding-period return*. Recall from Chapter 8 that a holding-period return is defined as the change in market value of the asset over the period plus any income received during the period, expressed as a percentage of the initial investment:

$$\text{holding-period}\atop\text{return } (\%) = \frac{\text{ending market value} + \text{income receipts}}{\text{beginning market value}} - 1$$

Holding-period return or, simply, *total return,* can be decomposed as follows:

$$\text{total return}\atop(\$) = \frac{\text{price return}}{(\$)} + \frac{\text{coupon return}}{(\$)} + \frac{\text{reinvestment return}}{(\$)}$$

$$\text{total return}\atop(\%) = \frac{\frac{\text{price return}}{(\$)} + \frac{\text{coupon return}}{(\$)} + \frac{\text{reinvestment return}}{(\$)}}{\text{initial investment } (\$)}$$

For reporting purposes, total returns are calculated on an annual basis with quarterly updates.[1]

Portfolio return can be derived from the aggregate returns attributable to price change, coupon receipts, and reinvestment cash flows. Alternatively, portfolio return is the weighted average of the total returns of the individual securities comprising the portfolio, where the beginning-of-period market values of the component issues serve as the weights:

$$R_p = \sum_{i=1}^{N} (w_i \times R_i)$$

where

R_p = portfolio total return (%)
R_i = total return on security i (%)
w_i = market value weighting of the ith security
N = number of securities comprising the portfolio

> **Observation:** *Portfolio return is calculated as a weighted average of the returns of the component issues. Portfolio return stems from price return, coupon return, and reinvestment return.*

The dollar-weighted rate of return versus the time-weighted rate of return

A *dollar-weighted rate of return* (DWROR) is the internal rate of return for the portfolio. As such, the DWROR is heavily influenced by

---

[1] Monthly, weekly, or in some cases daily total returns are computed for internal purposes in the portfolio monitoring and review process.

additions to, or withdrawals from, the portfolio. For example, the ABC bond mutual fund is established on January 1, 19X1 with $100 million. During 19X1, the fund posts a 50% return. This dramatic success attracts $150 million in new contributions to the fund at the beginning of 19X2. Unfortunately, during 19X2, the ABC bond fund suffers a 30% setback, leading to a DWROR of −11.83% for the 2-year period:

$$\frac{\text{initial}}{\text{investment}} = \sum_{t=1}^{n} \frac{CF_t}{(1 + DWROR)^t}$$

where

n = number of compounding periods in the investment horizon

In this case,

$$\$100 \text{ million} = \sum_{t=1}^{2} \frac{CF_t}{(1 + DWROR)^t}$$

$$= \frac{-\$150 \text{ million}^*}{(1 + DWROR)^1} + \frac{\$210 \text{ million}^\dagger}{(1 + DWROR)^2}$$

The DWROR solves to −0.1183 or −11.83%.

The cash flows are presented in a timeline format in Exhibit 15–1. The dollar-weighted rate of return is the average annual return on the fund for the 2-year period, and is influenced by the additional contribution received at the beginning of 19X2. Therefore, the −11.83% reported return, as an internal rate of return, understates the true return over the 2-year period since the DWROR weights the second-year (the losing year) results more heavily than the first-year outcome.

---

[*] Notice that additional contributions are designated as negative cash flows; returns of those cash flows at the end of the holding period are, of course, shown in a positive cash flow form.

[†] The $210 million cash flow is the market value of the fund (including any coupon and reinvestment) at the end of the holding period (2 years). This figure is calculated as follows:

$100 million	market value at 1/1/X1
× (1 + 0.50)	50% total return during 19X1
$150 million	market value at 12/31/X1, original investment
+ 150 million	additional contribution on 1/1/X2
$300 million	market value at 1/1/X2
× (1 − 0.30)	30% negative return during 19X2
$210 million	market value at 12/31/X2

Exhibit 15–1. Timeline of the cash flows for the ABC bond mutual fund over a 2-year period.

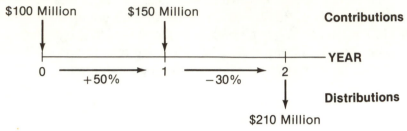

As another illustration, Exhibit 15–2 plots the cash flow contributions to the DEF bond mutual fund during the years 19X1 and 19X2. Like the ABC bond fund, the DEF fund is set up on January 1, 19X1 with $100 million and receives an additional $150 million in contributions on January 1, 19X2. The return pattern on the DEF fund, however, is strikingly different from that of the ABC fund. This fund experiences a 50% loss during 19X1 and a 100% gain in 19X2. The DEF fund is valued at $400 million on December 31, 19X2:

$100 million	market value at 1/1/X1
× (1 − 0.50)	50% negative return during 19X1
$ 50 million	market value at 12/31/X1, original investment
+ 150 million	additional contribution on 1/1/X2
$200 million	market value at 1/1/X2
× (1 + 1.00)	100% total return during 19X2
$400 million	market value at 12/31/X2

Consequently, the 2-year dollar-weighted rate of return is an impressive 38.60%:

$$\frac{\text{initial}}{\text{investment}} = \sum_{t=1}^{n} \frac{CF_t}{(1 + DWROR)^t}$$

In this case,

$$\$100 \text{ million} = \sum_{t=1}^{2} \frac{CF_t}{(1 + DWROR)^t}$$

$$= \frac{-\$150 \text{ million}}{(1 + DWROR)^1} + \frac{\$400 \text{ million}}{(1 + DWROR)^2}$$

Exhibit 15–2. Timeline of the cash flows for the DEF bond mutual fund over a 2-year period.

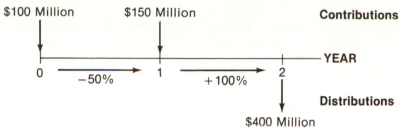

The DWROR solves to 0.3860 or 38.60%.

Once again, the DWROR is the internal rate of return for the fund's cash flows over the 2-year period. The 38.60% figure is strongly influenced by the sizable contribution received at the beginning of the second year and invested for a whopping 100% return during 19X2. In reality, however, an investor who purchased shares in the fund on January 1, 19X1 and held them for 2 years garnered a 0% net increase in wealth. For example, a $1,000.00 investment in the DEF fund falls to a $500.00 value at the end of 19X1 (−50% total return) and recovers to the original $1,000.00 value by the end of 19X2 (+100% total return).

It is clear that the dollar-weighted rate of return distorts the true results by implicitly rendering a disproportionate weighting to the *high dollar contribution periods*. In the ABC fund, the poor performance during the *heavy dollar* 19X2 year dragged the 2-year DWROR down to −11.83%, understating the true return of approximately 2.50% annually for the individual who bought and held the fund for the 2-year time span ($1,000.00 original investment + 50% 19X1 return = $1,500.00 at December 31, 19X1; $1,500.00 − 30% 19X2 loss = $1,050.00 at December 31, 19X2; $1,050.00/$1,000.00 − 1 = 1.05 − 1 = 0.05 or 5.00% over 2 years or, approximately, 2.50% per annum).

The DWROR essentially leverages the returns recorded during periods in which the assets under management are large. This process distorts the true performance of a single investment in the fund. The manager of the fund should be judged by the returns accorded the investor who owned a constant number of fund shares throughout the measurement period.

> **Observation:** *The dollar-weighted rate of return (DWROR) is an internal rate of return. Consequently, the DWROR is influenced by portfolio contributions and/or withdrawals. Returns garnered during periods*

of high contributions are deemed more weight than returns achieved during periods of low contributions or net withdrawals.

The time-weighted rate of return (TWROR) provides a more accurate assessment of the fund manager's abilities. A time-weighted rate of return is simply a geometric average of a series of linked subperiod returns:

$$(1 + TWROR)^n = (1 + R_1) \times (1 + R_2) \times \cdots \times (1 + R_n)$$

where

$R_1, R_2, \ldots, R_n$ = holding-period returns in periods $1, 2, \ldots, n$

n = total number of compounding periods in the investment horizon

More simply, the TWROR is the discount rate connecting the future value of the investment with the present (i.e., beginning of measurement period) value of the investment:

$$PV = \frac{FV}{(1 + TWROR)^n}$$

where n is the number of compounding periods.

For example, the ABC bond mutual fund (recall Exhibit 15–1) experiences a 50% return during 19X1 and a -30% return for the year 19X2. The future value (FV) of a $1,000.00 investment in the fund is $1,050.00, and the TWROR is 2.47%:

$$PV = \frac{FV}{(1 + TWROR)^2} \quad \text{two annual compounding periods}^*$$

$$\$1,000.00 = \frac{\$1,000.00(1 + 0.50)(1 - 0.30)}{(1 + TWROR)^2}$$

$$= \frac{\$1,500.00(0.30)}{(1 + TWROR)^2}$$

$$= \frac{\$1,050.00}{(1 + TWROR)^2}$$

---

*In performance evaluations, multiyear returns are reported on an annually compounded basis. Intrayear returns (e.g., monthly, quarterly, semiannually) are reported as holding-period returns with no compounding.

Exhibit 15–3. Timeline of the cash flows for the XYZ bond mutual fund over a 2-year period.

The TWROR solves to 0.0247 or 2.47%.

In the DEF bond mutual fund case (recall Exhibit 15–2), the investor suffers a 50% decline in value during 19X1 and experiences a 100% resurgence during 19X2. The future value (FV) of a $1,000.00 investment in the fund is (an unchanged) $1,000.00 and, not surprisingly, the TWROR is 0.00%:

$$PV = \frac{FV}{(1 + TWROR)^2} \quad \text{two annual compounding periods}$$

$$\$1,000.00 = \frac{\$1,000.00(1 - 0.50)(1 + 1.00)}{(1 + TWROR)^2}$$

$$= \frac{\$500.00(2.00)}{(1 + TWROR)^2} = \frac{\$1,000.00}{(1 + TWROR)^2}$$

The TWROR solves to 0.0000 or 0.00%. The 2-year TWRORs of 2.47% (ABC fund) and 0.00% (DEF fund) are the most realistic appraisals of the funds' performances over the 2-year period.

It is worth noting that the time-weighted rate of return and the dollar-weighted rate of return are identical if no additional contributions or withdrawals take place during the measurement period. For example, Exhibit 15–3 displays in a timeline format the cash flows and returns associated with the XYZ bond mutual fund for the years 19X1 and 19X2. The fund's 15.00% return earned during 19X1 is followed by a modest 10.00% return during 19X2. With no additional contributions, the fund reports a 12.47% annually compounded return for the 2-year period, on both a time-weighted and dollar-weighted basis:

(*a*) *time-weighted rate of return calculation:*

$$(1 + \text{TWROR})^2 = (1 + R_1)(1 + R_2)$$
$$= (1 + 0.15)(1 + 0.10)$$
$$= (1.15)(1.10)$$
$$= 1.265$$

$$1 + \text{TWROR} = \sqrt{1.265}$$

$$\text{TWROR} = 1.1247 - 1$$
$$= 0.1247 \text{ or } 12.47\%$$

(*b*) *dollar-weighted rate of return calculation:*

$$\text{initial investment} = \sum_{t=1}^{2} \frac{\text{CF}_t}{(1 + \text{DWROR})^t}$$

$$\$100 \text{ million} = \frac{0}{(1 + \text{DWROR})^1} + \frac{\$126.5 \text{ million}}{(1 + \text{DWROR})^2}$$
$$= \frac{\$126.5 \text{ million}}{(1 + \text{DWROR})^2}$$

The DWROR solves to 0.1247 or 12.47%.

Due to its superior ability to discern true performance results despite shifts from contributions and withdrawals, the time-weighted rate of return is the total return measure employed by performance evaluation services in both the fixed-income and equity markets. Given a time-weighted orientation, the differences between arithmetic mean returns and geometric mean returns are now assessed.

> **Observation:** *The time-weighted rate of return (TWROR) is the return earned on a single investment made at the beginning of the performance period. For multiyear periods, the TWROR is typically expressed on an annually compounded basis. Additional contributions or withdrawals have no impact on the TWROR. Consequently, the TWROR is a better measure of the true performance of a bond fund than the DWROR. The TWROR is the commonly accepted measure of manager/fund total return performance.*

The arithmetic mean return versus the geometric mean return

An *arithmetic mean return* is the simple average of a series of individual component returns:

$$\bar{R} = \frac{R_1 + R_2 + \cdots + R_N}{N}$$

where

$$\bar{R} = \text{arithmetic mean return}$$
$$R_1, R_2, \ldots, R_N = \text{holding-period returns in periods } 1, 2, \ldots, N$$
$$N = \text{number of periods under consideration}$$

In the ABC bond fund illustrated earlier, the annual returns registered by the fund were 50% and (30%), respectively, for the years 19X1 and 19X2. The arithmetic mean annual return for the 2-year period is 10.00%:

$$
\begin{aligned}
\bar{R}_{\text{ABC}} &= \frac{50\% + (30\%)}{2} \\
&= \frac{20\%}{2} \\
&= 10.00\%
\end{aligned}
$$

For the DEF and XYZ funds, the corresponding arithmetic mean returns over the identical period are 25.00% and 12.50%, respectively:

$$
\begin{aligned}
\bar{R}_{\text{DEF}} &= \frac{(50\%) + 100\%}{2} \\
&= \frac{50\%}{2} \\
&= 25.00\%
\end{aligned}
$$

$$
\begin{aligned}
\bar{R}_{\text{XYZ}} &= \frac{15\% + 10\%}{2} \\
&= \frac{25\%}{2} \\
&= 12.50\%
\end{aligned}
$$

Arithmetic mean returns can dramatically misrepresent the true financial impacts. In the DEF fund example, the 2-year arithmetic mean works out to 25.00%, a far cry from the unchanged wealth position of the investor who rode the roller coaster of severely negative first-year returns (−50%) and strongly positive second-year results (+100%). The arithmetic mean return provides an inaccurate assessment of the returns garnered by the investor. It is biased to overstate the actual returns earned by the investor vis-à-vis the more accurate geometric mean return measure, particularly during periods of volatile returns.

> **Observation:** *The arithmetic mean return is a simple average of a series of component returns. By nature, the arithmetic mean return fails to accurately reflect the returns garnered by an investor, particularly under conditions of highly volatile returns. An overstatement of the actual returns is typically the result.*

The *geometric mean return* is simply the compounded return that connects the present value of an investment to its future value. As such, the geometric mean return is an internal rate of return. Generally speaking, annual compounding is assumed.[2] The time-weighted rate of return (of earlier illustration) is an example of a geometric mean return. The geometric mean return smooths out the year-to-year fluctuations in returns by looking at only the beginning and ending wealth positions and solving for the annual rate of return, which, on a consistent year-to-year basis, builds the initial position into the (known) ending status. The geometric mean return (GMR) provides an excellent reflection of the true *average* annual increase in wealth that occurred over the specified measurement period. As a corollary, of course, an investor may also desire to know the interim volatility in annual returns endured en route to the final position. A risk measure such as the standard deviation of annual returns can assist in accomplishing this assessment (recall Chapter 7).

In sum, the geometric mean is preferred to the arithmetic mean because of the inherent flaws of the latter, particularly during volatile environments such as experienced during the 1980s. The time-weighted rate of return provides a clearer picture of manager performance than does the dollar-weighted rate of return. Consequently, the current standard for portfolio return assessment is the time-weighted rate of return, which is expressed as a holding-period return over intrayear measurement horizons and as a geometric mean annual return for multiyear performance appraisals.

> **Observation:** *The geometric mean return is the compounded total return on an investment. This measure is the internal rate of return that connects the present value of an investment to its (ending) future value.*

---

[2] The reader should note, however, that the geometric mean return can accommodate any specified compounding period (e.g., monthly, quarterly, semiannually, annually).

The geometric mean return is a better measure of the true return garnered by an investor than the arithmetic mean return, since it smooths out the periodic fluctuations in return by focusing solely on the beginning and ending investment values.

Performance measurement and comparison

The total return performance of a broad universe of fixed-income portfolio managers is tabulated quarterly by consulting firms including PIPER, Frank Russell, SEI, and Wilshire Associates. In addition to providing a detailed breakdown of a portfolio composition (e.g., by issuer sector, by maturity, by coupon), these firms plot portfolio returns vis-à-vis the returns on the universe of portfolios under scrutiny on a quarterly, annual, and multiyear basis.[3] In addition, comparisons to widely used bond market indexes are employed. Exhibit 15–4 presents the annual returns of the Shearson Lehman Government/Corporate (SLGC) Bond Index in the typical SEI layout for each of the last 10 years (1977–1986). Geometric average annual returns for multiyear periods (2 years, 3 years, . . . , 10 years) are tabulated in Exhibit 15–5.

In addition to assessing the nominal returns, SEI reports the relative returns of the individual portfolio (e.g., the SLGC index) versus the universe of portfolios analyzed. The *percentile ranking* assesses the performance of a specific portfolio (or portfolio manager) relative to the composite of portfolios included in the analysis. For example, during 1986 the SLGC index registered a 15.6% total return, earning it a percentile ranking of 41 (Exhibit 15–4). The 41st percentile ranking states that approximately 41% of the portfolios in the selected universe outperformed the SLGC index while 59% underperformed the widely used benchmark. The median portfolio (50th percentile ranking) captured a 14.9% return for the year 1986.

The percentile rankings of Exhibits 15–4 and 15–5 are commonly discussed in terms of *quartile performance* rankings. Four quartiles describe the spread of reported returns: the 1st quartile (1st–25th percentile range), the 2nd quartile (26th–50th percentile range), the 3rd quartile (51st–75th percentile range), and the 4th quartile (76th–100th percentile range). On an annual basis, the SLGC index tends to perform in the

---

[3] The quarterly and annual figures are time-weighted total returns with no intraperiod compounding; the multiyear returns are geometric average annual returns calculated on a time-weighted basis assuming annual compounding.

Exhibit 15–4. Annual returns on the Shearson Lehman Government/Corporate Bond Index as compared to the SEI universe of bond portfolios for the years 1977–1986 (Source: SEI Funds Evaluation Inc.).

Bonds: Rates of Return
(For Years Ending December 31)

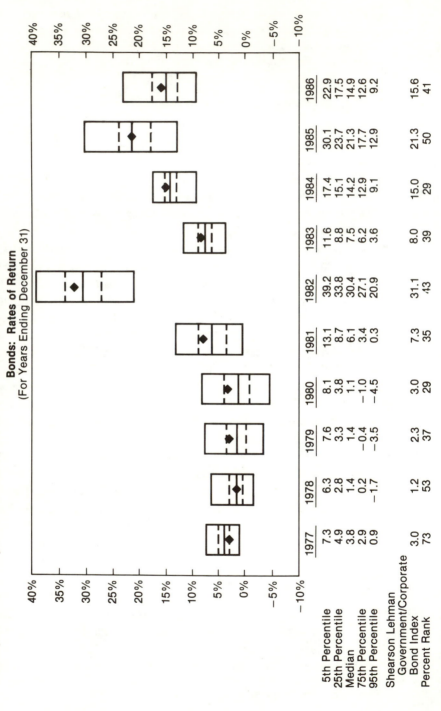

	1977	1978	1979	1980	1981	1982	1983	1984	1985	1986
5th Percentile	7.3	6.3	7.6	8.1	13.1	39.2	11.6	17.4	30.1	22.9
25th Percentile	4.9	2.8	3.3	3.8	8.7	33.8	8.8	15.1	23.7	17.5
Median	3.8	1.4	1.4	1.1	6.1	30.4	7.5	14.2	21.3	14.9
75th Percentile	2.9	0.2	−0.4	−1.0	3.4	27.1	6.2	12.9	17.7	12.6
95th Percentile	0.9	−1.7	−3.5	−4.5	0.3	20.9	3.6	9.1	12.9	9.2
Shearson Lehman Government/Corporate										
Bond Index	3.0	1.2	2.3	3.0	7.3	31.1	8.0	15.0	21.3	15.6
Percent Rank	73	53	37	29	35	43	39	29	50	41

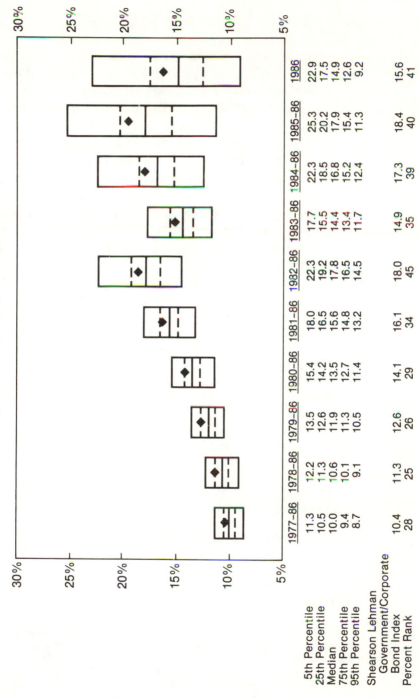

Bonds: Annualized Rates of Return
(For Periods Ending December 31, 1986)

	1977-86	1978-86	1979-86	1980-86	1981-86	1982-86	1983-86	1984-86	1985-86	1986
5th Percentile	11.3	12.2	13.5	15.4	18.0	22.3	17.7	22.3	25.3	22.9
25th Percentile	10.5	11.3	12.6	14.2	16.5	19.2	15.5	18.5	20.2	17.5
Median	10.0	10.6	11.9	13.5	15.6	17.8	14.4	16.8	17.9	14.9
75th Percentile	9.4	10.1	11.3	12.7	14.8	16.5	13.4	15.2	15.4	12.6
95th Percentile	8.7	9.1	10.5	11.4	13.2	14.5	11.7	12.4	11.3	9.2
Shearson Lehman Government/Corporate Bond Index	10.4	11.3	12.6	14.1	16.1	18.0	14.9	17.3	18.4	15.6
Percent Rank	28	25	26	29	34	45	35	39	40	41

507

middle of the second quartile, rarely underperforming the median manager. SEI delineates the quartile breaks by dashes and solid lines, with supporting figures below the graphical display.[4]

Exhibit 15–5 illustrates that over longer measurement periods, the divergence between manager performance tends to narrow. The bar graphs encompassing the 5th–95th percentile rankings become more compact over long horizons (e.g., 10 years). The margin between 1st quartile and 3rd quartile performance narrows to approximately 100BP on a 10-year investment period such as 1977–1986 (10.5% − 9.4% = 1.1%). This same ranking differential measures almost 500BP during the 1-year period 1986 (17.5% − 12.6% = 4.9%). The results indicate that consistent, sizable excess returns are very difficult to achieve. On the other hand, a modest excess return of 50BP per year versus the median manager earns a manager a top quartile ranking over the 10-year period 1977–1986 (per Exhibit 15–5, 10.5% versus 10.0% compounded annual return), while never placing the manager in the top quartile of performance during any single year over the period (per Exhibit 15–4). A 100BP excess return earned consistently on an annual basis never deems the manager a top quartile performer for any individual year, but the same 100BP premium performance propels the manager into the top decile (i.e., the 10th percentile and higher) for the 10-year period 1977–1986.

> **Observation:** *Pension fund consultants such as SEI Funds Evaluation Inc. tabulate the total return performance of fixed-income portfolio managers and bond funds. Relative assessments of performance are made by comparisons to bond market index returns and median manager returns. Percentile ranking in a universe of bond portfolio managers allows for a more refined grading of total return performance.*

Portfolio returns versus benchmark returns

The total return performance of a bond portfolio can be compared to the returns generated by three basic types of benchmarks:

1. *Median manager performance.* Several consulting firms tabulate the total returns registered by a broad composite of fixed-income portfolio

---

[4] Although SEI tabulates the performance of individual portfolios, common parlance fails to distinguish between portfolio performance and manager performance. For purposes of illustration and comparison, these differences are not important; therefore, the author uses the terms interchangeably with respect to SEI data. Note that the upper and lower bounds of the rectangular bar plotting represent the 5th percentile performance and the 95th percentile performance, respectively. The outliers (top 5%, bottom 5%) appear outside the bounds of the rectangular bar configuration.

managers. The median (i.e., 50th percentile) performance is reported for comparative purposes.

2. *Bond index performance.* The total return garnered by a bond index is often used as a comparative base for relative performance assessment. The index of choice may be a broad-based, market capitalization-weighted index (e.g., Shearson Lehman Government/Corporate Bond Index, Shearson Lehman Aggregate Bond Index, Salomon Brothers Broad Investment Grade Bond Index, Merrill Lynch Domestic Master, Merrill Lynch Corporate and Government Master) or a specialized index (e.g., Shearson Lehman Long Treasury Index, Shearson Lehman Yankee Bond Index).

3. *Client objectives.* The total return objective of the client may prescribe a nominal target (e.g., an 8% annual return minimum), a relative target (e.g., a real return—that is, a nominal return in excess of the rate of inflation), an income target (e.g., a 6% income cash flow per year), or a liability target (e.g., funding a future stream of pension liabilities or minimizing the annual pension expense volatility introduced by FASB Statements Nos. 87 and 88). The total return performance objective must be considered in light of other client factors (e.g., liquidity needs, income needs, degree of risk aversion, length of investment horizon, tax considerations, regulatory and legal constraints).

Median manager performance is a useful benchmark only if the universe of managers under purview is of a similar management style. Unfortunately, in the fixed-income evaluation process of today, inadequate attention is given to the segregation of bond managers by style (e.g., indexers, immunizers, dedicators, market timers, sector rotators, value-added managers). A composite of a myriad of managers of varying style is commonly used as the comparative universe.

An appropriate classification of fixed-income managers into categories of management style is a desirable and necessary objective for independent evaluation services to adopt in order to ensure valid performance comparisons. The Frank Russell Company is attempting to address this issue by categorizing fixed-income managers according to their investment style(s). Managers of similar style are compared to each other as well as to appropriate index benchmarks. Exhibits 15–6 through 15–10 look at five management styles, respectively: short-intermediate, long-term, active duration, active sector rotation, and high yield. This differentiation allows for a better assessment of good performance and bad performance.

Exhibit 15–6. Total return performance of fixed-income accounts of a short-intermediate maturity management style (Source: The Frank Russell Company).

Universe Criteria: Short-Intermediate Accounts

Accounts investing in securities with maturities of 0 to 5 years (instruments with longer maturities may be included if they have floating coupons or are hedged with futures). Primarily bank pooled funds but also nonbank investment advisors accounts, several of which are primarily invested in Eurodollar floating rate notes. Results are total returns. Maximum duration is 3 years.

Indexes

ML1–2.99—Merrill Lynch – US Treasury 1–2.99 Years

PR 2YR—Payden & Rygel 2-year Treasury Notes

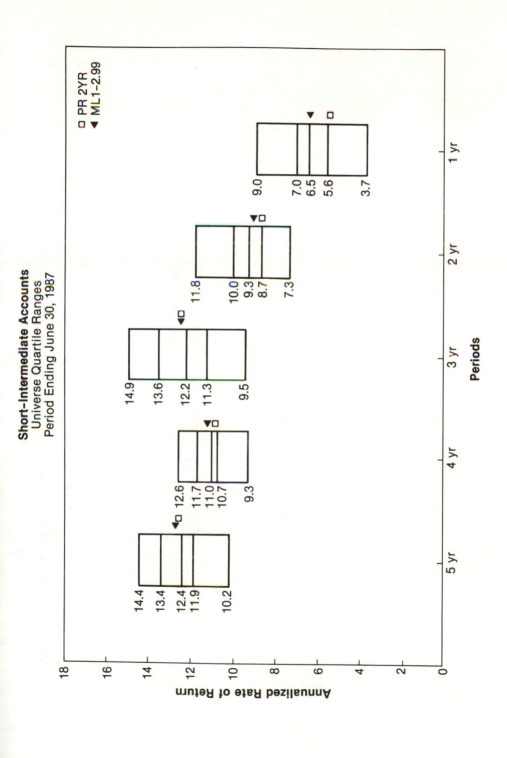

Short-Intermediate Accounts
Universe Quartile Ranges
Period Ending June 30, 1987

☐ PR 2YR
▼ ML1–2.99

Annualized Rate of Return

Periods

Exhibit 15-7. Total return performance of fixed-income accounts of a long-term maturity management style (Source: The Frank Russell Company).

Universe Criteria: Long-Term Bond Accounts

Accounts invested primarily in securities with maturities over 10 years or having no maturity restrictions and managed with an orientation toward remaining fully invested in longer term securities. Includes bank pooled funds and investment advisors' results. Minimum duration is 4 years.

Indexes

SHLM LG—Shearson Lehman Government/Corporate Bond Index – Long–Term

SB CORP—Salomon Brothers Inc. Corporate Bond Index

Long-Term Bond Accounts
Universe Quartile Ranges
Period Ending June 30, 1987

□ SB CORP
▼ SHLM LG

Annualized Rate of Return

Periods

Period	Values
1 yr	13.0 / 6.6 / 4.9 / 3.7 / −1.1
2 yr	19.1 / 15.2 / 14.0 / 12.3 / 9.3
3 yr	26.7 / 21.7 / 19.1 / 17.4 / 14.7
4 yr	17.4 / 15.6 / 13.7 / 13.1 / 10.8
5 yr	21.7 / 19.2 / 17.9 / 16.5 / 14.8

Exhibit 15–8. Total return performance of fixed-income accounts of an active duration management style (Source: The Frank Russell Company).

Universe Criteria: Active Duration Accounts

Accounts which reflect active maturity management as a primary strategy, frequently in combination with other strategies. Duration strategies may be hedged through using a combination of maturities or financial futures. Includes bank and insurance company pooled funds and investment advisor separate accounts. Duration range is 0 to 10 years.

Indexes

SHLM G/C—Shearson Lehman Government/Corporate Bond Index

SHLM AGG—Shearson Lehman Aggregate Bond Index

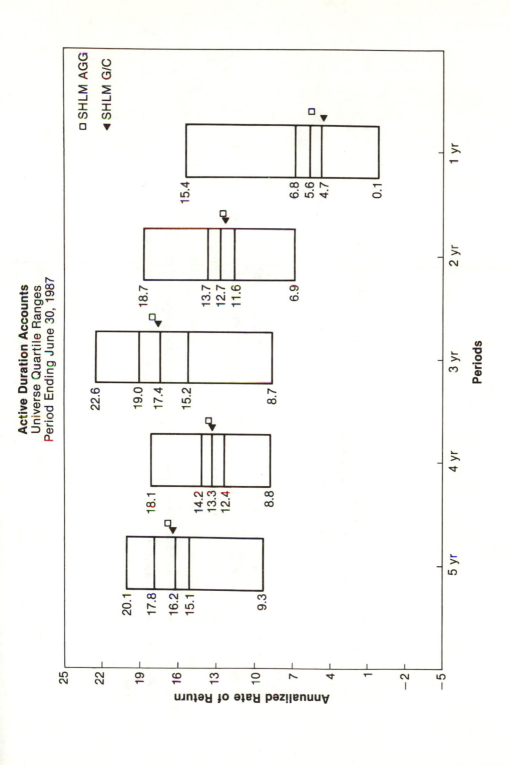

Active Duration Accounts
Universe Quartile Ranges
Period Ending June 30, 1987

□ SHLM AGG
▼ SHLM G/C

Annualized Rate of Return

Periods

5 yr: 20.1, 17.8, 16.2, 15.1, 9.3
4 yr: 18.1, 14.2, 13.3, 12.4, 8.8
3 yr: 22.6, 19.0, 17.4, 15.2, 8.7
2 yr: 18.7, 13.7, 12.7, 11.6, 6.9
1 yr: 15.4, 6.8, 5.6, 4.7, 0.1

515

Exhibit 15–9. Total return performance of fixed-income accounts of an active sector rotation management style (Source: The Frank Russell Company).

Universe Criteria: Active Sector Rotation Accounts

Accounts which change interest rate exposure relative to the Shearson Lehman Government/Corporate Bond Index (SHLM G/C) to a lesser degree than active duration accounts. Changes in portfolio interest rate sensitivity are limited to approximately ±20% of the duration of the index. Emphasis is placed on the selection of undervalued sectors or issues. Includes bank and insurance company pooled funds and investment advisor separate accounts. Durations have historically been 3.5 to 6 years.

Indexes

SHLM G/C—Shearson Lehman Government/Corporate Bond Index

SHLM AGG—Shearson Lehman Aggregate Bond Index

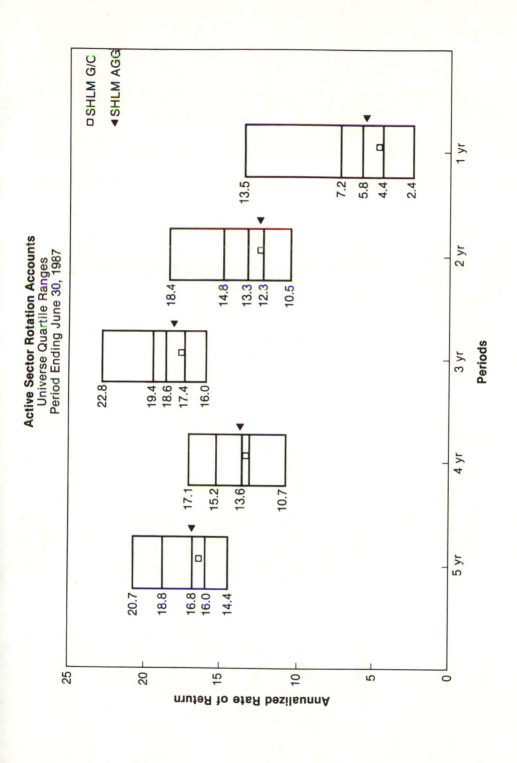

Active Sector Rotation Accounts
Universe Quartile Ranges
Period Ending June 30, 1987

□ SHLM G/C
▼ SHLM AGG

Annualized Rate of Return

Periods

517

Exhibit 15–10. Total return performance of fixed-income accounts of a high yield management style (Source: The Frank Russell Company).

Universe Criteria: High Yield Bond Accounts

Accounts invested primarily in lower rated bonds. Includes mutual funds, commingled funds, and separate accounts. Some accounts may include lower quality convertible securities.

Indexes

SHLM G/C—Shearson Lehman Government/Corporate Bond Index

SB HIYLD—Salomon Brothers Inc. High-Yield All Securities Index

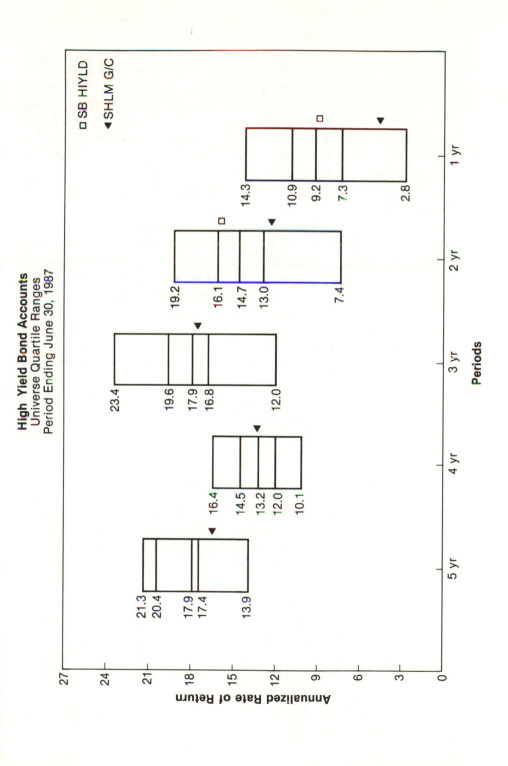

High Yield Bond Accounts
Universe Quartile Ranges
Period Ending June 30, 1987

□ SB HIYLD
▼ SHLM G/C

Annualized Rate of Return

Periods

Due to the lack of widely available manager subuniverse comparisons, many fixed-income portfolio managers and pension plan consultants rely on various bond indexes as representative benchmarks for assessing style differences. For active managers attempting to add excess returns over the bond market, a broad-based bond index is probably an appropriate comparative benchmark. Indexes such as the Shearson Lehman Government/Corporate Bond Index, the Shearson Lehman Aggregate Bond Index, the Salomon Brothers Broad Investment Grade Index, the Merrill Lynch Domestic Master, and the Merrill Lynch Corporate and Government Master Index are designed to serve these constituents.

For more specialized management approaches or client needs, subindexes can be designed and tailored to the specific style/need. Three major brokerage firms (Shearson Lehman Brothers, Salomon Brothers Inc., Merrill Lynch) provide the ability to slice the bond market into desired segments and create an appropriate universe of issues weighted in a manner to reflect the characteristics and performance of the specified subsector. Merrill Lynch, for example, tracks over 150 indexes and subindexes on a daily basis. A long-term oriented manager, for example, may be compared to the U.S. Treasuries 15+ Years Index. A client attempting to meet a future stream of liabilities may select a specialized index with a duration targeted to match that of the projected liability stream.[5] With regard to specific client needs (e.g., nominal return, real return, income return), portfolio performance is easily judged (e.g., 10% income return versus 8% objective).

> **Observation:** *Portfolio return is often gauged in relation to benchmarks including median bond manager performance, bond index performance, and client objectives. The median bond manager comparison should reflect a similar management style. An appropriate bond index benchmark should be carefully selected; a specialized or customized bond index may emerge as a superior comparative base.*

Historical market and sector returns

Appendix A reviews the concept and rationale of bond indexing and describes the major bond market indexes in usage today. The annual returns on four of the most popular bond indexes for the 1980–1986 time period are compared in Exhibit 15–11. Although differing to some

---

[5] Alternatively, the returns on the liability stream itself can serve as the comparative base. [See Leibowitz, Martin L., "Liability Returns: A New Perspective on Asset Allocation," Salomon Brothers Inc. (May 1986)].

Exhibit 15–11. Comparison of the annual total returns for several of the popular bond market indexes over the 1980–1986 period. A geometric average return for the most recent 5-year period is also provided. The indexes employed are the Ryan Treasury Index, the Salomon Brothers Broad Investment Grade Bond Index, the Shearson Lehman Aggregate Bond Index, and the Shearson Lehman Government/Corporate Bond Index. (Data courtesy of the Ryan Financial Strategy Group, Salomon Brothers Inc., and Shearson Lehman Brothers.)

Index	*1980*	*1981*	*1982*	*1983*	*1984*	*1985*	*1986*	*1982– 1986*
Ryan	2.65	6.93	32.50	5.27	15.11	24.24	17.19	18.51
SB Broad	2.90	6.53	31.51	8.26	14.93	22.31	15.44	18.23
SL Agg	2.70	6.25	32.62	8.35	15.15	22.11	15.27	18.42
SLGC	3.06	7.26	31.09	8.00	15.02	21.30	15.62	17.96
7-year U.S. Treasury[*]	3.09	6.62	33.71	4.66	14.92	25.22	17.15	18.73
Rank[†]								
5th percentile	8.1	13.1	39.2	11.6	17.4	30.1	22.9	22.3
25th percentile	3.8	8.7	33.8	8.8	15.1	23.7	17.5	19.2
50th percentile (median)	1.1	6.1	30.4	7.5	14.2	21.3	14.9	17.8

[*] Data represents the Ryan 7-year Treasury Index.

[†] Data courtesy of SEI Funds Evaluation Inc.

Comments: *Index performances tend to converge over time as the common influences of the general interest rate level and the shape of the yield curve determine the primary behavior of returns. The 7-year U.S. Treasury is a surprisingly good proxy for the entire bond market. The SB Broad index and the SL Agg index both tend to outperform the SLGC index because they include the higher yielding mortgage-backed securities sector. Notice the narrow difference between 1st quartile and median performance. The indexes tend to outperform the median, and often place themselves near the 25th percentile.*

degree on an annual basis, the index returns are strikingly similar over longer time spans. For example, the 5-year period 1982–1986 finds the index returns clustered in a 50BP range from 18.0 to 18.5%. The dominance of the influence of general yield levels and the yield curve shape on bond market returns leads to strong correlations between the returns of the bond market indexes, as illustrated in a recent study by Reilly, Wong, and Wright.[6]

Over short-term horizons (e.g., 1 year), index returns diverge as a result of sizable shifts in general yield levels, changes in yield curve shapes, and changes in sector spreads. Differences in average duration, maturity distribution, and sector weightings are responsible for these return discrepancies.

Intermediate-term holding periods (e.g., 5 years) find index returns converging as the impacts of general shifts in yield level, change in yield curve shape, and alternations in sector spreads are smoothed over a longer measurement horizon. It is remarkable that a simple 7-bond index, such as the Ryan Treasury Index, captures approximately 95 to 98% of the return variability of the 4,000 to 5,000 bond agglomerations. The Ryan Treasury Index tracks the return behavior of the U.S. Treasury yield curve. All sectors, Treasury and non-Treasury, are priced and valued vis-à-vis the current shape and level of the U.S. Treasury yield curve. Consequently, the Ryan Treasury Index mimics the total return performance of the broader-based indexes quite well.

Over intermediate holding periods, the return behavior of the bond market can be estimated by the middle-of-the-road 7-year U.S. Treasury bond. This single issue bears a strong resemblance to the Ryan Treasury Index returns as well as to the complex, multi-thousand-bond indexes of widespread use (recall Exhibit 15–11). Major nonparallel shifts in the yield curve tend to distort this close relationship, but over intermediate-term periods, the yield curve normally experiences only modest changes in overall shape. Over the past 5 years (1982–1986), this single-bond bogey has been a difficult benchmark to beat, with a 5-year average return of 18.73% placing it in the upper portion of the 2nd quartile of manager performance.

Long-term investment horizons (e.g., 10 years and longer) favor the higher yielding indexes over the lower yielding, higher quality benchmarks. The 100 to 150BP yield advantage of mortgage-backed securities (MBS) over their similar-duration U.S. Treasuries renders the MBSs an excess return bias over long periods of time. The 100 to 150BP of additional yield traditionally offered by BBB-rated corporate bonds versus their higher quality AAA-rated counterparts creates a return advantage for the lower quality issues. The following analysis of market sector returns tends to validate these assertions.

---

[6] See Reilly, Frank K., Wenchi Wong, and David J. Wright, "An Analysis of Alternative Bond Market Indicator Series" (South Bend, IN: University of Notre Dame, January 1987).

> **Observation:** *Historical reviews of bond market sector returns reveal a tendency for individual sector returns to deviate over short-term periods and to converge over longer horizons, with higher yielding sectors exhibiting a bias to outperform other sectors. The returns of the 7-year U.S. Treasury bond provide a strikingly good indication of overall bond market returns.*

Portfolio return as influenced by sector holdings

Exhibit 15–12 summarizes the sector returns for the equity market and the bond market for the final quarter of 1986 as well as for the full year 1986. During 1986, the best performing sector in the equity market was the health sector with a 31.6% annual return. The worst performing equity sector for 1986 was technology with a −2.3% annual return. The spread between best performing and worst performing equity sectors was a staggering 33.9% [31.6% − (2.3%)].[7] Bond market sectors generated divergent returns, although not as dramatic as the equity market figures. During 1986, for example, the long maturity sector outperformed the intermediate maturity sector by 8.30% (21.80% − 13.50% = 8.30%). The sector return variations between issuer sectors, quality sectors, and corporate bond sectors were in the range 2.0 to 4.0%. It is clear that bond market sector returns do not behave as dissimilarly as do equity market components.

In the bond market, the *maturity or duration decision* reigns paramount with respect to short-term returns. Exhibit 15–13 compares the 1986 returns of bond market subsectors broken down by maturity sector. It quickly becomes evident that bull market years such as 1986 render superior returns to long maturity sectors (e.g., 25 to 30 years) as opposed to short maturity sectors (e.g., 1 to 5 years). The long U.S. Treasury sector (25 to 30 years), for example, recorded a 24.47% return during 1986, surpassing the short maturity (1 to 5 years) U.S. Treasuries by 13.21% (24.47% − 11.26% = 13.21%).

The *issuer sector decision* had a more modest impact on 1986 bond portfolio returns. The *best versus worst* sector returns ranged from an 80BP differential in the 1–5-year maturity sector [12.06% (utilities) − 11.26% (Treasuries) = 0.80%] to an impressive 1,019BP in the 25-

---

[7] For simplicity, the SEI-denoted sectors are the focus of discussion. In all likelihood, other specialized subsectors of the equity market may have experienced even more widely divergent returns.

to 30-year maturity sector [24.47% (Treasuries) − 14.28% (industrials) = 10.19%]. Well-placed issuer sector weightings have a more beneficial effect on long duration securities than on short duration issues.

The *quality sector decision* led to divergences in 1986 returns of 100 to 200BP. Unlike their longer-term average tendencies, higher quality issues outperformed lower quality issues in many instances during the year. Exhibit 15–14 shows the 1986 returns on the AAA-, AA-, A-, and BBB-rated corporate bond market sectors. The AAA bonds generated a total return of 17.63% during 1986, an attractive 150BP better than the 16.13% return tallied by the BBB bonds. The AA and A sectors recorded returns in the middle ground, at 16.50 to 16.60%. The divergence in quality sector returns is magnified in the long-term maturity area, with AAAs outperforming BBBs by almost 200BP (20.13% versus 18.37%). Exhibit 15–15 plots the downward-sloping quality sector return curve for 1986 on both a composite basis and a long-term maturity basis.

Over long-term holding periods, however, lower quality sectors tend to outperform higher quality sectors due to the yield advantage of the lower quality issues. Exhibit 15–16 calculates the 10-year average returns on the quality sectors comprising the Shearson Lehman Corporate Bond Index for the period ending December 31, 1986. This presentation

Exhibit 15–12. Performance summary of the equity and bond market sector returns for periods ending December 31, 1986 (Source: SEI Funds Evaluation Inc.).

	Equity Industry Sectors	
	Rates of Return	
	*Current Quarter**	*One Year*
Producer durables	10.9	18.1
Health	10.2	31.6
Consumer staples	7.5	30.1
Consumer discretionary	6.9	22.9
Energy	5.2	19.8
Materials & processing	4.6	20.4
Utilities	4.4	30.3
Transportation	2.2	5.0
Building	2.1	24.8
Finance	1.1	7.2
Technology	0.7	−2.3

Returns are capitalization-weighted for S&P 500 stocks.

Exhibit 15–12 (con't)

	*Current Quarter**	*One Year*
Issuer Type		
Government/agencies	2.8	15.5
Mortgages	3.8	13.4
Corporates		
Finance	3.5	15.1
Industrials	4.0	15.7
Utilities	5.3	19.3
Quality		
AAA-AA†	3.2	15.3
A	4.4	17.1
BBB	4.2	16.1
Maturity		
Intermediate	3.0	13.5
(Average maturity: 4.6 years)		
(Average duration: 3.5 years)		
Long-term	4.4	21.8
(Average maturity: 23.1 years)		
(Average duration: 9.7 years)		

Bond Market Sectors

Salomon Broad Bond Index information courtesy of Salomon Brothers Inc.

* Three-month returns are unannualized.

† AAA-AA rates of return include corporate and government issues.

Comments: *Equity sector performance diverges more widely than bond sector performance, on both a quarterly and an annual basis.*

Exhibit 15–13. Returns for 1986 on bond market issuer sectors, by maturity classification. (Data courtesy of Shearson Lehman Brothers.)

Maturity Classification (Years)	*Issuer Sector Return (%)*				
	Treasury	*Corporate*	*Industrial*	*Utility*	*Finance*
1–5	11.26	11.79	11.54	12.06	11.80
5–10	17.38	14.99	14.35	14.23	16.47
10–15	22.36	18.79	16.96	21.31	18.33
15–20	23.68	19.56	17.49	21.41	19.24
20–25	24.11	19.68	16.54	21.13	19.38
25–30	24.47	17.21	14.28	18.49	22.72

Comments: *Sector returns tend to diverge more in long maturities than in short maturities.*

Exhibit 15–14. Total returns for 1986 on the quality sectors comprising the U.S. corporate bond market, on both a composite basis as well as on an intermediate maturity component and a long maturity component basis. (Data courtesy of Shearson Lehman Brothers.)

Quality Sector	Maturity Sector Return (%)		
	Intermediate	*Long*	*Composite*
AAA	13.41	20.13	17.63
AA	13.11	18.95	16.60
A	13.74	18.42	16.51
BBB	13.60	18.37	16.13

Comments: *During any single investment year, lower quality does not necessarily lead to higher returns. During 1986, exactly the opposite occurred to the composite and long maturity corporate bond sectors. The intermediate maturity sector had mixed results, with AAAs outperforming AAs and As outperforming BBBs, while As and BBBs outreturned their higher quality counterpart AAAs and AAs.*

illuminates the fact that BBB issues have a bias to outperform their higher quality AAA, AA, and A comrades. Over the 1977–1986 period, the BBBs garnered a 160BP total return advantage over AAAs (11.41% − 9.81%), 141BP excess over AAs (11.41% − 10.00%), and a 96BP increment over As (11.41% − 10.45%). Exhibit 15–17 plots the 10-year quality sector returns as an upward-sloping configuration.

In sum, bond market sector returns (maturity, issuer, quality) diverge over short-term measurement periods, but tend to converge over longer-term horizons with higher yielding sectors (e.g., long maturity issues, non-Treasury issuers, lower quality corporate bonds) biased to outperform the lower yielding sectors by a modest margin. Annual returns on individual sectors show that the timely sector decisions can lead to superior total return performance. Exhibit 15–18 reviews the annual returns of the sector components of the Shearson Lehman Government/Corporate Bond Index since inception on January 1, 1973 and the Shearson Lehman Aggregate Bond Index since January 1, 1976. The maturity and issuer sector decisions are clearly the most critical judgments to be made. The maturity, and issuer, and quality sector structure of the chosen benchmark index provides a baseline from which to make sector bets.

Observation: *Sector holdings can have a sizable influence on portfolio return. The maturity sector or duration decision is most critical, with issuer and quality sector weightings assuming a lesser, but still important, role.*

Exhibit 15–15. Quality sector returns in the U.S. corporate bond market for 1986, distributed by rating (AAA, AA, A, and BBB). (Data per Exhibit 15–14 and courtesy of Shearson Lehman Brothers.)

(a) On a composite basis.

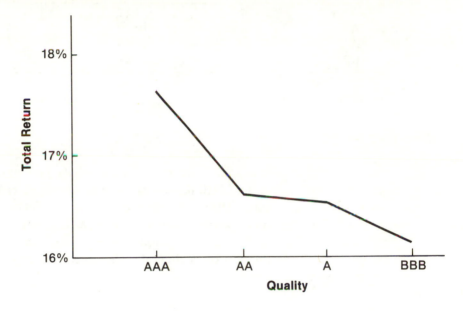

(b) On long–term issues only.

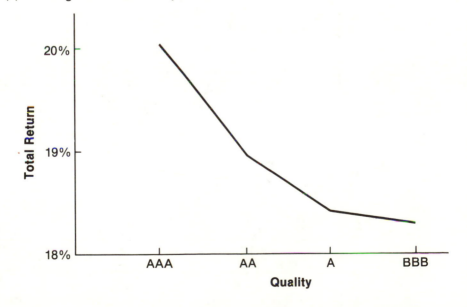

Exhibit 15–16. Average annual returns on the quality components of the Shearson Lehman Corporate Bond Index for the 10-year period 1977–1986. (Data courtesy of Shearson Lehman Brothers.)

Quality Sector	Average Annual Return, 1977–1986 (%)
AAA	9.81
AA	10.00
A	10.45
BBB	11.41

Comments: *The average annual return is a geometric mean return.*

Bond portfolio risk

Analysis of bond portfolio risk is far more challenging than the straightforward calculation of bond portfolio return. The definition of risk is, in itself, an elusive exercise. The mathematics of standard deviations, correlation coefficients, and covariances complicate the task of bond portfolio risk analysis. Finally, the lack of rigorous application of capital market theory to fixed-income portfolios finds the theoretical underpinnings in a half-dressed state of affairs.

Exhibit 15–17. Quality sector returns in the U.S. corporate bond market for the 10-year period 1977–1986. (Data per Exhibit 15–16 and courtesy of Shearson Lehman Brothers.)

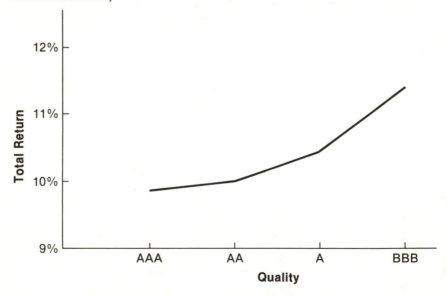

This book addresses the bond portfolio risk dilemma through three presentations. First, the concept of bond portfolio risk is expressed through the use of standard deviations and portfolio betas. These instruments were discussed at length in Chapter 7 and are briefly reviewed here. Second, bond portfolio risk is outlined in the general framework of systematic and nonsystematic components. Finally, and most comprehensively, a pragmatic analysis of the nine primary contributors to bond portfolio risk is provided. An application of these specific risk factors to a real-world portfolio is given in Appendix B. In this way, both the general concepts and the specific realities of bond portfolio risk are explained in a detailed and concise manner.

Bond portfolio risk as explained by total return variability

As discussed in Chapter 7, the risk associated with a specific asset type is often summarized by the *standard deviation* statistic. Historical returns are tabulated and the variability in those returns is expressed by a return variance, the square root of which is called the standard deviation[8]:

$$\text{variance} \; (\sigma^2) = \sum_{i=1}^{N} \frac{(R_i - \mu)^2}{N}$$

$$\text{standard deviation} \; (\sigma) = \sqrt{\sigma^2}$$

$$= \sqrt{\sum_{i=1}^{N} \frac{(R_i - \mu)^2}{N}}$$

where

R_i = total return in the ith period

μ = arithmetic mean return of the N period returns

N = total number of periods

With a portfolio of bonds, the standard deviation of the portfolio's returns over time serves as a measure of portfolio risk. Return variability

---

[8] A sample standard deviation requires division by $(n - 1)$ rather than N, where n is the sample size.

Exhibit 15–18. Annual total returns on the Shearson Lehman bond indexes and their components for the period 1973–1986. (Data courtesy of Shearson Lehman Brothers.)

	1973	1974	1975	1976	1977	1978	1979	1980	1981	1982	1983	1984	1985	1986
Government/Corporate	**2.28**	**0.17**	**12.30**	**15.59**	**2.98**	**1.19**	**2.30**	**3.06**	**7.26**	**31.09**	**8.00**	**15.02**	**21.30**	**15.62**
Government	3.08	6.57	8.39	12.35	2.81	1.80	5.40	5.19	9.36	27.74	7.39	14.50	20.43	15.31
Corporate	1.51	-5.86	16.70	19.34	3.16	0.35	-2.11	-0.29	2.95	39.21	9.27	16.63	24.06	16.53
Mortgage Backed	-	-	-	16.31	1.90	2.41	0.13	0.65	0.07	43.04	10.13	15.79	25.21	13.45
Yankee	-	-	-	15.08	5.23	2.91	-0.43	1.91	3.48	35.82	9.43	16.38	25.99	16.27
Aggregate	-	-	-	15.60	3.03	1.40	1.93	2.70	6.25	32.62	8.35	15.15	22.11	15.27
Government/Corporate	**2.28**	**0.17**	**12.30**	**15.59**	**2.98**	**1.19**	**2.30**	**3.06**	**7.26**	**31.09**	**8.00**	**15.02**	**21.30**	**15.62**
Intermediate	3.34	5.87	9.49	12.32	3.32	2.13	5.99	6.42	10.51	26.11	8.60	14.37	18.06	13.14
Long Term	1.06	-6.30	16.42	20.53	2.46	-0.27	-3.30	-2.69	0.08	43.70	6.11	16.44	29.77	21.44
Government Bond Index	**3.08**	**6.57**	**8.39**	**12.35**	**2.81**	**1.80**	**5.40**	**5.19**	**9.36**	**27.74**	**7.39**	**14.50**	**20.43**	**15.31**
Intermediate	3.36	7.03	8.33	11.73	3.01	2.22	6.59	6.65	10.78	25.42	8.22	14.29	18.00	13.06
Long Term	0.88	3.36	9.08	17.44	1.30	-1.11	-0.86	-2.96	0.48	42.08	2.23	14.81	31.54	24.08
Treasury	3.51	7.05	8.07	11.81	2.68	2.06	5.73	5.61	9.24	27.84	7.05	14.47	20.91	15.61
Intermediate	3.61	7.18	8.03	11.39	2.90	2.44	6.92	7.12	10.95	24.98	8.03	14.23	18.15	13.03
Long Term	1.14	5.02	8.34	17.10	-0.05	-1.44	-0.53	-2.94	0.37	41.76	1.99	14.79	31.56	24.10
Agency				13.00	3.06	1.25	5.20	5.14	9.73	26.71	8.32	14.52	18.13	13.76
Intermediate				12.20	3.26	1.68	6.08	5.93	10.32	25.99	8.62	14.50	17.45	13.22
Long Term				17.76	2.14	-1.25	-1.57	-2.50	1.75	42.72	2.62	14.03	28.96	22.94
Corporate	**1.51**	**-5.86**	**16.70**	**19.34**	**3.16**	**0.35**	**-2.11**	**-0.29**	**2.95**	**39.21**	**9.27**	**16.63**	**24.06**	**16.53**
Intermediate	3.19	1.06	14.16	14.63	4.60	1.65	3.35	5.34	8.98	30.02	10.66	14.87	18.46	13.48
Long Term	1.09	-7.61	17.56	21.03	2.67	-0.10	-4.08	-2.60	-0.15	44.52	8.32	17.66	27.99	18.71
Industrial	1.97	-3.35	15.27	17.45	3.11	1.12	-1.57	-0.72	1.90	37.53	9.72	15.36	24.85	15.02
Intermediate	3.13	3.30	12.73	14.09	3.73	1.32	4.16	4.86	8.73	28.13	10.79	14.73	20.34	13.33
Long Term	1.79	-4.52	15.93	18.47	2.92	1.05	-3.35	-2.81	-1.38	42.76	8.97	15.68	27.90	16.27
Utility	1.09	-7.35	17.84	20.74	2.94	-0.15	-3.21	-0.33	2.29	40.65	8.08	17.86	25.93	18.50
Intermediate	3.21	0.37	15.49	14.71	4.81	2.23	2.61	7.86	8.83	30.71	9.51	15.18	17.45	13.50
Long Term	0.68	-8.82	18.45	22.32	2.49	-0.71	-4.51	-2.31	0.21	44.14	7.54	18.75	28.78	20.12
Finance	2.70	-3.68	14.68	17.97	4.11	0.61	0.35	0.37	6.20	37.64	11.42	15.56	20.05	15.06
Intermediate	3.23	0.80	13.03	14.99	5.10	1.23	3.51	3.23	9.29	30.77	11.54	14.66	17.88	13.60
Long Term	2.21	-7.84	16.63	21.70	2.99	-0.07	-3.81	-3.79	1.02	50.68	10.92	16.91	24.95	18.51

	1974	1975	1976	1977	1978	1979	1980	1981	1982	1983	1984	1985	1986
AAA	1.34	-1.76	17.49	1.57	0.01	-1.83	-0.97	1.38	39.31	6.75	16.17	25.33	17.63
Intermediate	3.22	2.93	13.56	3.19	1.48	3.98	4.26	9.17	28.16	9.19	14.47	17.91	13.41
Long Term	0.88	-2.96	18.66	1.10	-0.41	-3.62	-2.96	-1.64	43.02	4.95	16.71	29.95	20.13
AA	1.45	-4.08	18.23	2.41	0.35	-1.96	-0.52	2.95	38.51	7.88	16.22	24.15	16.60
Intermediate	3.12	2.79	14.15	3.63	1.27	3.27	4.62	9.28	29.09	9.73	14.58	18.04	13.11
Long Term	1.04	-5.08	19.71	1.98	0.01	-4.21	-3.03	-0.70	45.44	6.57	16.84	28.24	18.95
A	1.66	-8.34	19.60	3.78	0.62	-2.19	-0.04	3.51	38.67	9.89	16.44	23.67	16.51
Intermediate	3.19	-0.67	14.63	5.32	1.79	3.27	5.98	8.59	30.13	11.06	14.68	18.10	13.74
Long Term	1.26	-10.19	21.47	3.22	0.22	-4.03	-2.34	0.70	43.55	9.23	17.60	27.52	18.42
Baa	1.75	-14.44	25.48	6.56	0.27	-2.98	1.08	4.09	41.25	12.24	17.89	24.50	16.13
Intermediate	3.37	-3.45	17.43	6.95	2.40	2.51	7.37	8.90	32.70	12.41	15.84	20.06	13.60
Long Term	1.30	-17.51	29.10	6.41	-0.62	-5.24	-1.79	1.39	47.21	11.96	19.69	28.16	18.37
Mortgage	-	-	16.31	1.90	2.41	0.13	0.65	0.07	43.04	10.13	15.79	25.21	13.43
GNMA	-	-	16.31	1.90	2.15	0.16	0.75	0.47	42.40	9.47	15.19	25.23	12.51
SF	-	-	16.31	1.90	2.15	0.16	0.75	0.41	42.25	9.40	15.21	25.49	12.77
Mobile										8.47	14.48	19.18	5.52
Jockeys											13.32	22.15	4.81
Graduated									44.37	10.16	15.55	23.84	13.63
FHLMC					4.03	0.02	0.32	-2.35	46.04	11.64	17.26	25.82	15.29
15 year													6.17
30 year					4.03	0.02	0.32	-2.35	46.04	11.64	17.26	25.82	16.17
FNMA											16.86	24.26	14.11
15 year													6.79
30 year										15.26	16.86	24.26	14.86
Yankee	-	-	15.08	5.23	2.91	-0.43	1.91	3.48	35.82	9.43	16.38	25.99	16.27
Intermediate			13.53	4.78	2.72	4.12	6.53	9.05	28.94	10.80	15.08	20.76	14.82
Long Term			15.90	5.48	3.06	-3.26	-0.89	-0.39	42.65	8.04	17.72	31.23	17.55
Canadian			15.11	5.91	3.37	-1.84	0.19	1.35	37.84	9.39	17.05	28.10	16.63
Intermediate			11.79	5.54	2.89	3.83	7.31	8.28	29.10	12.04	15.52	21.80	14.84
Long Term			15.64	5.97	3.47	-2.91	-1.18	-0.74	42.46	7.98	17.94	31.80	17.67
Sovereign			12.67	6.22	3.91	1.39	5.53	7.55	30.53	10.03	15.83	23.14	15.23
Intermediate			12.91	6.06	3.24	4.13	6.99	9.72	26.81	10.38	14.99	19.65	13.97
Long Term			6.36	7.57	5.95	-5.53	1.91	2.60	39.06	9.14	17.57	28.61	16.74
Supranational			15.41	3.59	1.53	0.70	1.96	4.32	35.24	9.20	15.27	23.27	16.28
Intermediate			14.43	3.65	2.12	4.23	5.13	8.76	30.43	9.87	14.64	20.24	15.37
Long Term			16.64	3.36	0.70	-3.33	-1.42	-1.06	46.10	7.64	16.72	30.76	18.24

Comments: *The maturity decision (intermediate versus long term) is most critical. The issuer sector decision (U.S. Treasuries, federal agencies, industrials, utilities, finance, mortgage-backed, yankee) is another major factor impacting portfolio returns. The quality decision (AAA versus AA versus A versus BBB) has less relative importance.*

presents a risk to the investor. Consequently, a higher standard deviation of return implies a riskier portfolio; a lower standard deviation of return suggests a less risky portfolio. The standard deviations of the returns of individual portfolios and benchmark portfolios can then be compared to assess relative riskiness (recall Chapter 7 illustrations).

A portfolio's return is simply a weighted average of the returns of the individual issues comprising the portfolio. A portfolio's risk, as represented by the standard deviation of return, is *not* a simple weighted average of the standard deviations of the individual issues filling the portfolio. Due to less-than-perfect positive correlation of individual bond returns, the portfolio's standard deviation is somewhat lower than a weighted average risk measure[9]:

$$\text{portfolio risk} = \text{standard deviation in portfolio returns}$$

$$\text{risk}_P < \sum_{i=1}^{N} (w_i \times \text{risk}_i)$$

where

risk_P = portfolio risk (i.e., the standard deviation in the returns of the portfolio)

risk_i = risk of security i (i.e., the standard deviation in the returns of security i)

w_i = market value weight of security i

N = number of securities comprising the portfolio

Only if all of the portfolio component returns move in exactly the same direction and magnitude will the components be perfectly positively correlated, allowing no risk reduction from diversification.

In virtually all practical cases, however, securities are less than perfectly correlated. For example, AA-rated corporate bond returns do not move in lock-step with U.S. Treasury bond returns. Mortgage-backed security returns form a different pattern from agency bond returns. AAA-rated corporate bond returns deviate from BBB-rated corporate bond returns as quality sector spreads expand and contract at various points in the economic cycle. Recall, however, that over longer periods of time, bond returns are highly correlated and a sizable reduction in portfolio risk should not be expected from diversification across sectors.

---

[9] For a review of the statistics underlying portfolio risk and return analysis, the reader is encouraged to consult Brown, Steven J. and Mark P. Kritzman, *Quantitative Methods for Financial Analysis* (Homewood, IL: Dow Jones–Irwin, 1987).

> **Observation:** *Bond portfolio risk can be described by the variability in periodic total returns. Such variability is typically captured by the standard deviation and variance measures. In portfolios of bonds, risk reduction is accomplished through the less-than-perfectly correlated return behavior of the individual securities comprising the portfolio.*

Bond portfolio risk as explained by a portfolio beta

Chapter 7 introduced the concept of a bond beta and illustrated its use with bond portfolios. The *beta* concept emanates from equity market research. A regression line is calculated for a series of total return pairings. The line that best describes the relationship between a portfolio's return and the market portfolio's return is called the *least-squares regression line*, the slope of which is termed the beta:

$$R_P = \alpha + \beta (R_m) + \epsilon$$

where

R_P = return on the portfolio

R_m = return on the market portfolio

α = y-intercept (alpha)

β = slope of the line (beta)

ϵ = random error term

The *market portfolio,* by definition, carries a beta of 1.0. Individual portfolios can be classified into three basic types, according to the beta value found by historical regression analysis:

Portfolio Beta	Portfolio Risk Description
$\beta < 1.0$	below-average risk; defensive posture
$\beta = 1.0$	market risk; neutral posture
$\beta > 1.0$	above-average risk; aggressive posture

More specifically, a bond portfolio with a beta of 1.40, for example, experiences 40% more volatility in periodic returns than the market portfolio (e.g., the SLGC bond index). A 10.00% return on the market portfolio suggests a 14.00% return for the individual portfolio (10.00% × 1.40 beta = 14.00%). A −5.00% market return corresponds with a −7.00%

portfolio return ($-5.00\% \times 1.40$ beta $= -7.00\%$). Bond portfolio betas are not yet in widespread use. The reader is encouraged to review Chapter 7 for additional applications of bond betas.

> **Observation:** *Bond portfolio risk can be represented by a portfolio beta. A portfolio beta measures the relationship between the portfolio return and the market return. Bond portfolios with betas equal to 1.0 are deemed neutral; bond portfolios with betas less than 1.0 are viewed as defensive; bond portfolios with betas greater than 1.0 are judged as aggressive.*

Systematic and unsystematic risk

Bond portfolio risk can be segmented into two general types: systematic risk and unsystematic risk. *Systematic or market risk* is the risk stemming from general market forces, such as general changes in market yield level, shifts in the general shape of the yield curve, and general changes in sector spreads. The phrase *systematic* arises from the concept of system-wide influences that cannot be diversified away. The market portfolio, a fully diversified portfolio by definition, is exposed only to systematic risk.

Unsystematic or diversifiable risk is that component of portfolio risk attributable to the lack of complete diversification. A nondiversified bond portfolio is subject to additional risks that arise from several sources:

1. Having a portfolio duration differing from that of the market portfolio (duration risk).

2. Having a maturity (or duration) distribution contrasting to that of the market portfolio (yield curve risk).

3. Having an issuer sector, quality sector, or coupon sector distribution differing from that of the market portfolio (call risk, quality risk, issuer sector risk, intra-issuer sector risk).

4. Being unable to purchase an appropriate weighting of each issue comprising the market portfolio; the sampling process undertaken to create a portfolio that replicates the market always instills some degree of unsystematic risk in the portfolio (issue-specific risk, liquidity risk).

5. Utilizing fixed-income products or designing synthetic securities that are not included in the market portfolio (product risk).

The market portfolio is immune to such *extra-market* risks. The general concepts of systematic and unsystematic bond portfolio risk are analogous to the same references in equity market research. Application to fixed-income securities and portfolios is constrained by the lack of a commonly accepted *bond market portfolio* to which individual bonds and/or bond portfolios would be compared in the derivation of *bond alphas* and *bond betas*. Capital market research is still in its infancy in the world of fixed-income portfolio management.

A pragmatic analysis of the basic components of bond portfolio risk is fruitful. It begins with a look at the portfolio risk measures commonly used, and ends with an assessment of the portfolio risks that these measures tend to overlook.

> **Observation:** *Bond portfolio risk can be divided into two general types: systematic and unsystematic. Systematic or market risk emanates from general market conditions. This risk component cannot be eliminated through diversification. Unsystematic or extra-market risk stems from the unique risks associated with individual issues and/or sectors. This risk component can be diversified away through a large array of portfolio holdings that mimic the composition of the market portfolio.*

The components of bond portfolio risk

Bond portfolio risk can be dissected into nine component parts: duration risk, yield curve (maturity or duration distribution) risk, call/convexity risk, quality/credit risk, issuer sector risk, intra-issuer sector risk, issue-specific risk, liquidity risk, and product risk.

Each of these risk components is discussed in terms of current applications as well as proposed future applications. Bond portfolio risk can be analyzed in absolute terms (e.g., average Macaulay's duration, average convexity) or in relative terms versus a benchmark index (e.g., issuer sector distribution comparison, quality distribution comparison). Some aspects of portfolio risk must be handled with qualitative concerns in addition to quantitative factors (e.g., intra-issuer sector risk, issue-specific risk, liquidity risk, product risk). Each of these elements is incorporated into the following component-by-component discussion of bond portfolio risk.

Duration risk. Chapter 6 showed that Macaulay's duration (in modified form) is a reasonably accurate measure of bond price volatility given a small, instantaneous, parallel change in yields. A *portfolio duration* is simply a weighted average of the durations of the individual issues comprising the portfolio:

$$D_P = \sum_{i=1}^{N} (w_i \times D_i)$$

where

D_P = duration of the portfolio

D_i = duration of security i

w_i = market value weight of security i

N = number of securities comprising the portfolio

For example, Exhibit 15–19 contains the issue data for the holdings of four portfolios (A, B, C, D). The Macaulay's duration and modified duration are calculated for each issue. Exhibit 15–20 lists the market value weighted holdings in each of the four portfolios. Using the data from Exhibits 15–19 and 15–20, Exhibit 15–21 computes the portfolio durations on both a Macaulay's and a modified Macaulay's basis. Using

Exhibit 15–19. Issue data (as of June 30, 1987).

Issue Description	Price	YTM (%)	Macaulay's Duration (Years)	Modified Duration (Years)	Convexity Factor
U.S. Treasury 6⅝% due 8/15/89	98-07	7.54	1.97	1.90	0.09
U.S. Treasury 7⅜% due 5/15/96	93-13	8.44	6.52	6.26	1.02
U.S. Treasury 7¼% due 5/15/16	85-19	8.61	11.23	10.77	4.03
BLIP 9⅝% due 7/15/14	98.25	9.81	9.49	9.05	−3.37
BLIP 8¾% due 4/1/26	91.50	9.58	10.47	9.99	1.86

Comments: *The convexity factor is an average convexity factor based on a ±200BP change in interest rates. The BLIP 9⅝% issue is expected to rise to the current refunding price (105.89) in the bull market scenario; the bear market is expected to allow its yield spread to narrow 20BP vis-à-vis U.S. Treasury bonds. The BLIP 8¾% issue is expected to rise to a 110.00 price under bull market conditions; the bear market scenario sees its yield spread narrow by 10BP vis-à-vis U.S. Treasury bonds.*

Exhibit 15–20. Portfolio holdings for hypothetical bond Portfolios A, B, C, and D (issue data per Exhibit 15–19).

	Market Value Weighting (%) in Portfolio:			
Issue Description	*A*	*B*	*C*	*D*
U.S. Treasury 6⅝% due 8/15/89	0	10	51	39
U.S. Treasury 7⅜% due 5/15/96	100	40	0	0
U.S. Treasury 7¼% due 5/15/16	0	35	49	0
BLIP 9⅝% due 7/15/14	0	5	0	61
BLIP 8¾% due 4/1/26	0	10	0	0
	100	100	100	100

Exhibit 15–21. Portfolio durations and convexities for hypothetical bond Portfolios A, B, C, and D. (Data per Exhibits 15–19 and 15–20.)

	Portfolio			
Risk Measure	*A*	*B*	*C*	*D*
Portfolio duration (Macaulay's)	6.52	8.26	6.52	6.56
Portfolio duration (modified)	6.26	7.92	6.26	6.26
Portfolio convexity	1.02	1.85	2.02	−2.02

Comments: *Portfolio durations and convexities are market value-weighted averages of the durations and convexities of the individual issues comprising the respective portfolios.*

the formula for deriving a portfolio duration, the figures in Exhibit 15–21 are verified as follows:

$$D_P = \sum_{i=1}^{N} (w_i \times D_i) \qquad \text{GENERAL FORMULA}$$

$$D_A(\text{Macaulay's}) = (1.00)(6.52)$$
$$= 6.52 \qquad \textit{Portfolio A}$$

$$D_A(\text{modified}) = (1.00)(6.26)$$
$$= 6.26$$

$$D_B(\text{Macaulay's}) = (0.10)(1.97) + (0.40)(6.52) + (0.35)(11.23)$$
$$+ (0.05)(9.49) + (0.10)(10.47)$$
$$= 8.26 \qquad \textit{Portfolio B}$$

$$D_B(\text{modified}) = (0.10)(1.90) + (0.40)(6.26) + (0.35)(10.77)$$
$$+ (0.05)(9.05) + (0.10)(9.99)$$
$$= 7.92$$

$$D_C(\text{Macaulay's}) = (0.51)(1.97) + (0.49)(11.23)$$
$$= 6.52 \qquad \textit{Portfolio C}$$

$$D_C(\text{modified}) = (0.51)(1.90) + (0.49)(10.77)$$
$$= 6.26$$

$$D_D(\text{Macaulay's}) = (0.39)(1.97) + (0.61)(9.49)$$
$$= 6.56 \qquad \textit{Portfolio D}$$

$$D_D(\text{modified}) = (0.39)(1.90) + (0.61)(9.05)$$
$$= 6.26$$

A 1-security portfolio (e.g., Portfolio A) bears a portfolio duration equal to that of the single issue comprising the portfolio. A multisecurity portfolio (Portfolio B, C, or D) carries a portfolio duration equal to a market value weighted composite of the individual security durations making up the character of the portfolio.

Generally speaking, portfolio durations are reported in a Macaulay's, not a modified Macaulay's, form. A more accurate assessment of a portfolio duration risk utilizes the modified measure.[10] As a relative risk proxy, however, a portfolio duration based on Macaulay's derivation is reasonably accurate. For example, if Portfolio X sports a Macaulay's duration of 5.50 years (5.29 years in modified form, given an 8.00% average YTM) and the market benchmark index carries an average Macaulay's duration of 5.00 years (4.81 years in modified form, given an 8.00% average YTM), Portfolio X bears 10% more duration risk than the market index, both in Macaulay's (5.50/5.00 = 1.10) and modified Macaulay's (5.29/4.81 = 1.10) terms.

Recall from Chapter 6 the relationship between a bond's modified duration and the bond's price sensitivity:

$$\text{percentage change in bond} \atop \text{(or portfolio) price} = - \left(\text{modified} \atop \text{duration} \right) \times \frac{\text{BP change in yield}}{100}$$

---

[10] A better measure of portfolio duration risk is the portfolio's *effective* (*option-adjusted*) *duration*. The broad-based bond market indexes are now reported in terms of both Macaulay's duration and effective duration. Rather than commingling them in an effective duration figure, the effects of general market risk and call/convexity are discussed separately for purposes of clarity.

For a given change in yield, a portfolio's modified duration has a multiplier effect on the portfolio's market value. A portfolio with a 7.50-year modified duration, for example, suffers approximately a 7.50% decline in value for every 100BP rise in yields. Conversely, the same portfolio reaps approximately a 7.50% appreciation in value for every 100BP fall in yields.

Duration risk is in the eye of the beholder. A bond portfolio bearing a 7.50-year modified duration is 50% riskier than a benchmark with a 5.00-year modified duration. The identical portfolio carries 25% less risk than a benchmark with a modified duration of 10.00 years (e.g., a liability stream). In addition to being a nominal concept, duration is a relative measure of portfolio risk. The yardstick against which the portfolio's performance is compared serves as the benchmark for assessing relative duration risk.

> **Observation:** *A portfolio's duration risk is its general exposure to market or interest rate risk. A portfolio's duration is simply the weighted average duration of the portfolio's component issues. The portfolio's modified duration is a measure of the price volatility of the portfolio: for every 100BP change in interest rates, the portfolio's market value changes in the opposite direction by a multiple amount dictated by the modified duration figure.*

Yield curve risk. Portfolio duration fails to capture all of the price sensitivity of a bond portfolio. Over short to intermediate holding periods, nonparallel yield curve shifts often occur. These nonparallel shifts are completely unexpected by the portfolio duration measure. The resulting impacts on portfolio returns can be significant. For example, using the bond data from Exhibit 15–19, if the U.S. Treasury yield curve steepens by 10BP such that the U.S. Treasury 7⅜% due May 15, 1996 rises to an 8.54% YTM with the remaining maturity sectors unaffected, Portfolio A incurs losses versus Portfolios C and D, despite identical modified durations (recall Exhibits 15–20 and 15–21). Portfolio A's concentration in the 9-year maturity sector makes it very susceptible to nonparallel yield curve shifts. In this case, Portfolio A loses approximately 63BP in value (6.26 modified duration × 10BP change in yield = 62.6BP) versus Portfolios C and D, which are dumbbelled away from the middle of the yield curve. This simplistic example serves to illustrate that minor shifts in the yield curve shape can have substantial impacts on portfolio return, impacts concealed by the portfolio duration measure.

A portfolio's yield curve risk can be assessed by a single measure such as the *nonparallel duration* developed by Capital Management Sciences (Los Angeles, California) or by a comparison of the maturity or duration distribution of the portfolio vis-à-vis the benchmark portfolio. Using the Shearson Lehman Government/Corporate (SLGC) Bond Index as the benchmark portfolio, the nonparallel duration of the SLGC index was 0.67 as of June 30, 1987 (Source: Capital Management Sciences). The maturity and duration distributions of the SLGC index holdings as of June 30, 1987 are given in Exhibit 15–22. Deviations from either the average measure (nonparallel duration) or the maturity/duration distribution introduce yield curve risk into a portfolio.[11] The magnitude of the deviations dictates the degree of yield curve risk to which the portfolio is exposed.

Observation: *A portfolio's yield curve risk is its sensitivity to nonparallel shifts in yield levels across the maturity spectrum. A portfolio's average duration is important, but the distribution of that duration along the yield curve is also critical to maintaining a portfolio risk similar to that of an identified benchmark.*

Call/convexity risk. Noncallable bonds, by nature, offer an investor some degree of *positive convexity*. Recall from Chapter 6 that positive convexity arises from the curvature of the price:yield relationship. Positive convexity is particularly concentrated in long duration securities. Callable bonds, however, subject the investor to an element of *negative convexity*. Call features do not allow the price:yield function to assume its normal, convex shape.

A *portfolio convexity* is simply the weighted average convexity of the individual securities comprising the portfolio:

$$C_P = \sum_{i=1}^{N} (w_i \times C_i)$$

where

C_P = convexity of the portfolio

C_i = convexity of security i

---

[11] A *nonparallel duration* greater than 0.67 implies a concentration in the middle of the yield curve (vis-à-vis the SLGC index); a nonparallel duration smaller than 0.67 infers a concentration on the short and long ends of the maturity spectrum (a dumbbell portfolio) vis-à-vis the SLGC index. The reader is encouraged to contact Capital Management Sciences in Los Angeles, California, for an explanation of the derivation of nonparallel duration.

Exhibit 15–22. Maturity and duration distributions of the Shearson Lehman Government/Corporate Bond Index as of June 30, 1987. (Data courtesy of Shearson Lehman Brothers.)

Maturity Distribution		Duration Distribution	
Years*	Market Value Weight (%)	Duration† (Years)	Market Value Weight (%)
0–1	0.0	0–1	1.9
1–2	18.5	1–2	19.6
2–3	10.8	2–3	13.4
3–4	9.2	3–4	11.3
4–5	7.9	4–5	10.4
5–6	5.1	5–6	8.1
6–7	5.4	6–7	6.7
7–8	3.9	7–8	4.1
8–9	5.1	8–9	8.4
9–10	4.0	9–10	11.2
10–15	4.5	10–11	4.8
15–20	7.7	11–12	0.0
20–30	16.9	12+	0.0
30+	1.2		

* Years to final maturity.
† Adjusted (effective) duration.

Comments: *A detailed breakdown of the distribution of maturities and/or durations is helpful in controlling yield curve risk. Market values (%) are rounded to the nearest tenth of a percent.*

w_i = market value weight of security i

N = number of securities comprising the portfolio

Due to the fact that convexity is an increasing function of duration, a portfolio convexity is not represented by the convexity of a single bond bearing a modified duration identical to that of the portfolio. The convexity factors (C_i) are a function of the magnitude of the yield change assumed (e.g., ±100BP, ±200BP) and represent an average of the convexity effects in an upmarket and a downmarket.

As an illustration, Exhibit 15–19 calculates the average convexity factors for several bond issues as of June 30, 1987. Building on an earlier example, convexities for Portfolios A, B, C, and D are summarized in Exhibit 15–21. Three basic conclusions emerge from the results.

First, longer duration (noncallable) U.S. Treasury bond portfolios carry larger positive convexities. Portfolio B, for example, has a 7.92-year modified duration, rendering it a 1.85 portfolio convexity factor. Portfolio A carries only a 6.26-year modified duration and a convexity factor of only 1.02. Indeed, a portfolio consisting solely of long U.S. Treasury bonds (U.S. Treasury 7¼% due 5/15/16) bears a modified duration of 10.77 years and a convexity of 4.03 (see Exhibit 15–19).

Second, dumbbell U.S. Treasury portfolios (i.e., a mix of short maturity and long maturity issues) offer more positive convexity than bullet (i.e., intermediate maturity) U.S. Treasury portfolios of similar duration. For example, Portfolios A and C have identical modified durations (6.26 years) but dumbbell Portfolio C contains twice as much convexity as Portfolio A.

Third, portfolios appearing identical on a duration basis may subject the investor to considerably different convexity risk. For example, Portfolio D is largely comprised of a long callable corporate bond (Bell Telephone of Pennsylvania 9⅝% due 7/15/14), giving the portfolio a sizable negative convexity of -2.02. Its similar duration counterpart portfolios (A and C) offer positive convexities of 1.02 to 2.02. Callable corporate bonds introduce some degree of negative convexity into a portfolio's structure.

The convexity of the benchmark (e.g., the SLGC index) can be used as a relative measure of portfolio convexity.[12] It is generally desirable to construct a portfolio with similar convexity features if the benchmark is to be mimicked. A bias to outperform the benchmark is usually accomplished by maintaining a portfolio with more positive convexity than the benchmark portfolio.[13]

A less precise method of controlling the call/convexity risk of a portfolio is by the use of a coupon distribution. Exhibit 15–23 is a matrix of the coupon distribution of the SLGC index as of December 31, 1986. The issues most subject to call risk (or negative convexity) are the high coupon issues (10% and higher) in the nongovernment/agency issuer sectors. If one matches the coupon : issuer sector matrix on a market value weighted basis, a sizable reduction of the portfolio's

---

[12] It is critical to apply the same volatility and spread change assumptions to the benchmark index as to the individual portfolio in order to allow comparability of results. Capital Management Sciences calculates portfolio convexities for many of the popular bond indexes as well as for specialized indexes and individual portfolios.

[13] There are occasions, however, when convexity is priced too expensively in the marketplace and a lower-than-benchmark convexity is desirable.

Exhibit 15–23. Coupon distribution of the Shearson Lehman Government/Corporate Bond Index, by issuer sector as of December 31, 1986. (Data courtesy of Shearson Lehman Brothers).

Coupon Rate (%)	*Distribution (%) for Issuer Sector:*				
	U.S. Treasury	*Agency*	*Industrial*	*Utility*	*Finance*
0–4.99	0.00	0.17	0.14	0.66	0.25
5–5.99	0.00	0.01	0.05	0.27	0.06
6–6.99	7.30	0.26	0.35	0.35	0.43
7–7.99	9.58	2.35	0.72	1.24	0.73
8–8.99	6.61	1.39	1.54	2.58	1.58
9–9.99	6.55	1.03	1.48	2.03	0.94
10–10.99	9.10	2.26	0.96	0.71	0.82
11–11.99	12.11	2.04	0.93	0.66	0.93
12–12.99	5.17	0.71	0.75	0.74	0.72
13–13.99	4.60	0.36	0.47	0.34	0.26
14–14.99	2.43	0.31	0.33	0.15	0.15
15–15.99	0.41	0.09	0.04	0.31	0.11
16–16.99	0.00	0.03	0.02	0.23	0.03
17+	0.00	0.00	0.00	0.04	0.02
	63.86	11.01	7.78	10.31	7.03

call/convexity risk relative to the SLGC benchmark can be achieved. Of course, a *maturity or duration distribution* similar to that of the benchmark is also necessary to ensure a reasonable level of control over the convexity differentials introduced by alternative patterns of bond holdings.

A portfolio manager desiring enhanced call protection and more positive convexity can purposely skew the portfolio holdings to lower coupon sectors and to noncallable issuer sectors (i.e., U.S. Treasuries, federal agencies). A manager expecting a low level of future volatility and/or a bias toward higher future yields may wish to utilize high coupon, callable issues at the expense of lower yielding, lower coupon bonds. In either case, the benchmark index establishes the starting point for deciding how much market value weighting in a given coupon sector is a *neutral or normal position*. Deviations from the norm introduce varying degrees of portfolio call/convexity risk relative to the benchmark.

Observation: *A portfolio's call or convexity risk can be assessed by the use of either a portfolio convexity factor or a coupon: issuer sector distribution matrix. If one can calculate the convexities of each of the*

Exhibit 15–24. Quality rating distributions for the Shearson Lehman Government/Corporate Bond Index and four hypothetical bond portfolios. (Shearson Lehman data as of July 1, 1987 and courtesy of Shearson Lehman Brothers.)

Quality Rating	SLGC Index (%)	Rating (%) for Portfolio: E	F	G	H
U.S. Treasury	64.3	30	65	65	50
Federal agency	10.8	10	10	10	32
AAA	2.2	10	0	0	0
AA	8.3	5	15	0	7
A	9.4	5	0	25	7
BBB	5.1	40	10	0	4

Comments: *The rating category includes all gradations within the specific category (e.g., the AA category includes AA+, AA, and AA− bonds). Market values determine the weightings.*

issues comprising the portfolio, the portfolio convexity is simply the weighted average of these figures. An average portfolio convexity as supplemented by a convexity distribution schedule provides a comprehensive method of assessing a portfolio's convexity stance.

Quality/credit risk

Using a quality distribution. A portfolio's quality or credit risk can be summarized by (1) an analysis of the portfolio's quality distribution, or (2) an average portfolio quality measure. A quality distribution simply breaks out the portfolio holdings by issuer quality: U.S. Treasury, federal agency, AAA, AA, A, and BBB.[14] The two most prominent rating agencies are Moody's Investors Service and Standard and Poor's (S&P's). Benchmark indexes typically use Moody's and/or S&P's in their quality differentiation process. These firms' credibility is widely accepted and therefore the rating distribution is predicated on their judgments.

Exhibit 15–24 provides the quality distributions of the SLGC index and four hypothetical bond portfolios (E, F, G, H). A casual glance shows that Portfolio E is a lower quality portfolio vis-à-vis the benchmark SLGC index. Portfolio E contains only 30% U.S. Treasuries (versus 64.3% for the SLGC index) but maintains a sizable 40% position in BBB credits (versus 5.1% for the SLGC index). Portfolios F and G

---

[14] Junk bond indexes cover the less than investment grade ratings of BB, B, CCC, CC, C, and D. The focus of this book is on the investment grade bond market.

provide a similar quality risk stance versus the SLGC benchmark, each with 65% U.S. Treasuries, 10% federal agencies, and 25% corporates. In the corporate bond sector, the SLGC index has approximately 9% in both the AA- and A-rated categories, with smaller percentages in the quality tails (AAA, BBB). Portfolio G concentrates all of its corporate holdings in the A-rated sector, while Portfolio F straddles the A rating with 15% of its issues in AA status and 10% of its issues in the BBB category. Portfolio H is a high quality portfolio, with 82% of its holdings in the U.S. Treasury and federal agency ranks and only 18% in the corporate bond classification. Portfolio H represents the typical quality distribution of an *aggregate bond index* portfolio which includes mortgage-backed securities in its agency classification.

A superior method of analyzing a portfolio's quality distribution is on a duration-weighted basis. Exhibit 15–25 looks at the quality distribution of the SLGC bond index using this enhanced methodology. The top panel of the table uses Macaulay's durations and the bottom panel weights the results based on option-adjusted Macaulay's durations. A comparison of the Macaulay's and adjusted durations reveals that:

1. The average durations of the U.S. Treasury and federal agency sectors are significantly shorter than the average durations of the corporate sectors, on both an unadjusted and an adjusted basis. The 3.65 to 4.81 duration range covers the U.S. Treasury and federal agency sectors, whereas the corporate bond market plots durations in the 6.45 to 7.01 range (Macaulay's basis) and in the 5.25 to 5.85 range (adjusted basis).

2. The average durations between the corporate bond quality sectors (AAA, AA, A, BBB), on both an unadjusted and adjusted basis, remain within a fairly narrow range of approximately ½ year.

3. The option adjustment has virtually no impact on the U.S. Treasury and federal agency quality sector durations (0.04- to 0.06-year contractions), but the same adjustment forces a sizable reduction in the durations of the corporate quality sectors.[15]

---

[15] The U.S. Treasury and federal agency sectors contain a low proportion of callable issues. There are a series of old (seasoned) 30-year U.S. Treasuries that are callable at par 5 years prior to final maturity. The market value weightings of these callable issues are relatively small, and the 5-year shortening in potential maturity has only a modest impact on the bonds' adjusted durations. The federal agency sector is even less subject to call features. Consequently, duration adjustments stemming from option provisions are negligible. The prevalence of call features on corporate bonds, however, leads to a sizable difference between a Macaulay's duration (to maturity date) and an option-adjusted duration. Corporate issues are often subject to significant reductions in maturity in the event of early call.

Exhibit 15–25. Quality distribution of the Shearson Lehman Government/Corporate Bond Index as of July 1, 1987, on a duration-weighted basis. (Data courtesy of Shearson Lehman Brothers.)

	(a) Macaulay's Duration Basis			
	(1)	*(2)*	*(3) = (1) × (2)*	*(4) = (3)/5.18*
Quality Sector	*Market Value (%)*	*Duration (Years)*	*Duration Contribution (Years)*	*Duration Weight (%)*
U.S. Treasury	64.30	4.81	3.09	59.65
Federal agency	10.77	3.69	0.40	7.72
AAA	2.20	6.45	0.14	2.70
AA	8.32	7.01	0.58	11.20
A	9.35	6.83	0.64	12.36
BBB	5.06	6.48	0.33	6.37
	100.00		5.18	100.00

↑
Total portfolio
duration

	(b) Adjusted Duration Basis			
	(1)	*(2)*	*(3) = (1) × (2)*	*(4) = (3)/4.86*
Quality Sector	*Market Value (%)*	*Adjusted Duration (Years)*	*Duration Contribution (Years)*	*Duration Weight (%)*
U.S. Treasury	64.30	4.75	3.05	62.76
Federal agency	10.77	3.65	0.40	8.23
AAA	2.20	5.71	0.13	2.67
AA	8.32	5.86	0.49	10.08
A	9.35	5.66	0.53	10.91
BBB	5.06	5.28	0.27	5.56
	100.00		4.86	100.00

↑
Total portfolio
duration

The overall portfolio (i.e., the SLGC index portfolio) experiences a noticeable 0.32-year decline in average duration as a result of the option adjustment (5.18 − 4.86 = 0.32). The duration contributions of Exhibit 15–25 give the user an idea of the amount of portfolio price volatility attributable to each respective sector. The duration contribution is calculated as the product of the sector's weighting (based on market values) and the sector's average duration:

$$\frac{\text{duration}}{\text{contribution}} = \frac{\text{market value}}{\text{weighting}} \times \frac{\text{average}}{\text{duration}}$$

For example, the AA-rated corporate bond sector contributes 0.58 years of Macaulay's duration (0.49 years on an adjusted basis) to the overall portfolio duration:

$$\frac{\text{Macaulay's}}{\text{duration}}_{\text{contribution}_{AA}} = \frac{\text{market value}}{\text{weighting}_{AA}} \times \frac{\text{average}}{\text{Macaulay's}}_{\text{duration}_{AA}}$$
$$= 0.0832 \times 7.01 \text{ years}$$
$$= 0.58 \text{ years}$$

$$\frac{\text{adjusted}}{\text{duration}}_{\text{contribution}_{AA}} = \frac{\text{market value}}{\text{weighting}_{AA}} \times \frac{\text{average}}{\text{adjusted}}_{\text{duration}_{AA}}$$
$$= 0.0832 \times 5.86 \text{ years}$$
$$= 0.49 \text{ years}$$

Recall that a portfolio duration is simply a weighted average of the durations of the individual component issues or, in this case, the individual component sectors.

The final column of Exhibit 15–25 calculates the duration weights of each quality sector. A *duration weight* is simply the duration contribution expressed in a percentage form:

$$\text{duration weight} = \frac{\text{duration contribution}}{\text{total portfolio duration}}$$

For example, the A-rated corporate bond sector holds a 9.35% market value weighting in the SLGC index. On a Macaulay's duration basis, this sector contributes 0.64 years, or 12.36%, of the SLGC index's total duration of 5.18 years:

$$\text{duration weight}_A = \frac{\text{duration contribution}_A}{\text{total portfolio duration}_{SLGC}}$$
$$= \frac{0.64}{5.18}$$
$$= 12.36\%$$

Exhibit 15–26. Comparison of the quality sector weightings of the Shearson Lehman Government/Corporate Bond Index as of July 1, 1987, on an option-adjusted basis. (Supporting data per Exhibit 15–25.)

Quality Sector	*(1)* Market Value Weight (%)	*(2)* Duration Weight (%)	*(3) = (2) − (1)* Difference (%)
U.S. Treasury	64.30	62.76	−1.54
Federal agency	10.77	8.23	−2.54
AAA	2.20	2.67	0.47
AA	8.32	10.08	1.76
A	9.35	10.91	1.56
BBB	5.06	5.56	0.50
	100.00	100.00	

Comments: *Market value weightings can provide an inaccurate picture of the true contribution of each sector. On individual portfolios, the differences between market value weights and duration weights are often sizable.*

On an option-adjusted duration basis, this percentage works out to 10.91% (Exhibit 15–25). The duration contributions and duration weightings go one step beyond a simple market value weighting. The former attempt to provide a clearer picture of the absolute (i.e., years) and relative (i.e., percentage) volatility attributable to each respective market sector.

Observation: *A duration contribution measures the absolute amount of duration contributed to the overall portfolio duration by a specified portfolio component (e.g., sector, issue). A duration weight shows the percentage of a portfolio's total duration that is traceable to a specified portfolio component. The concepts of market value weight, duration contribution, and duration weight can be applied to any sector or subsector classification.*

A *market value weight* simply assesses the relative amount of the total portfolio value that is attributable to a specified portfolio member or group of members (e.g., a sector). For the SLGC index, the market value weightings are compared to the duration weightings on a quality sector segregation in Exhibit 15–26. This table makes it clear that the corporate bond sectors wield a greater influence on the market portfolio than their market value weightings imply.

Exhibit 15–27. Quality distributions of two hypothetical bond portfolios (J and K), on a market value
weighted basis.

	Market Value Weighting (%) in Portfolio:	
Quality Category	J	K
U.S. Treasury	70	60
Federal agency	10	10
AAA	0	0
AA	20	30
A	0	0
BBB	0	0

Market value weighted quality distributions can, in themselves, be misleading. Exhibit 15–27 presents the market value weightings of the quality categories for two hypothetical bond portfolios (J and K). It appears as though Portfolio J is a better quality portfolio than Portfolio K, with 70%/10%/20% weightings in the Treasury/agency/AA sectors versus Portfolio K's 60%/10%/30% weightings for the same categories. However, the AA holdings in Portfolio J are concentrated in the long maturity/duration sector and carry an average adjusted duration of 9.00 years (Exhibit 15–28). Portfolio K's corporate bond issues are short-term in nature, sporting only a 2.00-year average adjusted duration (see Exhibit 15–28). Consequently, the duration contribution of the AA-rated bonds is 1.80 years for Portfolio J, three times the exposure of Portfolio K, whose duration contribution from the AA quality sector is 0.60 years. The 50% *higher* market value weightings of AAs in Portfolio J (30.0% versus 20.0%) masks the true, volatility-weighted influence of the AA sector as 67% *lower* (0.60 versus 1.80). This example shows that it is important to know not only what the portfolio holds, but where the component issues are positioned along the maturity (or duration) spectrum.

In comparison to the SLGC benchmark index, Portfolios J and K have identical portfolio durations (4.86 on an adjusted basis). In terms of relative quality, Portfolio J has a higher average quality than the benchmark on a market value weighted basis. Conversely, Portfolio K offers a lower average quality than the SLGC index. On a duration contribution basis, however, the positions are reversed, with Portfolio K providing a higher-than-benchmark quality and Portfolio J a lower-

Exhibit 15–28. Quality distributions of hypothetical bond Portfolios J and K, on an adjusted duration-weighted basis.

Quality Category	Portfolio J			Portfolio K		
	(1) Market Value (%)	(2) Adjusted Duration (Years)	(3) = (1) × (2) Duration Contribution (Years)	(1) Market Value (%)	(2) Adjusted Duration (Years)	(3) = (1) × (2) Duration Contribution (Years)
U.S. Treasury	70.00	3.87	2.71	60.00	6.43	3.86
Federal agency	10.00	3.50	0.35	10.00	4.00	0.40
AAA	0.00	—	—	0.00	—	—
AA	20.00	9.00	1.80	30.00	2.00	0.60
A	0.00	—	—	0.00	—	—
BBB	0.00	—	—	0.00	—	—
	100.00		4.86 ← Total portfolio duration	100.00		4.86 ← Total portfolio duration

than-benchmark quality. Portfolio K reports a 4.26 duration contribution from the high quality U.S. Treasury and federal agency sectors (versus 3.45 for the SLGC index, per Exhibit 15–25) and only a 0.60 duration contribution from the (lower quality) AA sector versus a 1.42 contribution from the combination of the AAA/AA/A/BBB sectors in the SLGC index. Portfolio J, on the other hand, carries only a 3.06 duration contribution in the U.S. Treasury and federal agency quality sectors and a sizable 1.80-year duration contribution in the AA quality sector.

Using an average quality measure. An average portfolio quality can be used either to replace or supplement a quality distribution analysis. Once again, an average portfolio quality measure can be based on (1) market value weightings or (2) duration-weighted contributions, with a preference for the latter. An arbitrary numeric assignment must first be made to the rating categories. For example:

Quality Category	Numeric Value
U.S. Treasury	1.0
Federal agency	1.5
AAA	2.0
AA	3.0
A	4.0
BBB	5.0

The SLGC bond index, for example, bears an average quality of AAA (to be shown in a forthcoming illustration).

Alternatively, one can target the average quality of the corporate bond sector while viewing the U.S. Treasury and federal agency sectors as distinct from the corporate sector:

Corporate Bond Quality Category	Numeric Value
AAA	1.0
AA	2.0
A	3.0
BBB	4.0

The corporate bond sector of the SLGC bond index, for example, has a weighted average quality of $A+$ (recall Exhibit 15–25). The gradations above can be further subdivided into ratings within an overall quality category:

Corporate Bond Quality Category	Numeric Value
AAA	1.00
AA+	1.67
AA	2.00
AA−	2.33
A+	2.67
A	3.00
A−	3.33
BBB+	3.67
BBB	4.00
BBB−	4.33

A weighted average portfolio quality can be calculated by using the numeric quality assignments as follows:

$$\text{average portfolio quality} = \sum_{i=1}^{N} (w_i \times quality_i)$$

where

$quality_i$ = numeric quality (e.g., 1, 2, 3, 4) of the ith security (or sector)

w_i = market value (or duration) weight of security (or sector) i

N = total number of securities (or sectors) comprising the portfolio

As an illustration, the quality rating distributions of the SLGC bond index and four hypothetical bond portfolios were given in Exhibit 15–24. The market value weighted average portfolio qualities are calculated in Exhibit 15–29. A sample calculation follows:

$$
\begin{aligned}
\text{average portfolio quality}_{\text{SLGC Index}} &= (0.643)(1.0) + (0.108)(1.5) \\
&\quad + (0.022)(2.0) + (0.083)(3.0) \\
&\quad + (0.094)(4.0) + (0.051)(5.0) \\
&= 1.73 \text{ (between an agency quality of} \\
&\quad 1.50 \text{ and a AAA quality of 2.00)}
\end{aligned}
$$

Exhibit 15–29. Weighted average portfolio quality of the SLGC bond index and a series of four hypothetical bond portfolios (data from Exhibit 15–24). A market value weighting is assumed, with quality assignments as follows: U.S. Treasury = 1.0, federal agency = 1.5, AAA = 2.0, AA = 3.0, A = 4.0, BBB = 5.0. The portfolios have average qualities in the middle of the respective rating categories so that no further gradations are required.

Portfolio	Average Quality
SLGC index	1.73 (AAA quality)
Portfolio E	3.00 (AA quality)
Portfolio F	1.75 (AAA quality)
Portfolio G	1.80 (AAA quality)
Portfolio H	1.67 (agency quality)

Comments: *The SLGC index is typically reported as a AAA average quality and an aggregate bond index portfolio (such as Portfolio H) is generally regarded as of agency quality. The distinction is somewhat arbitrary given that each lie between agency quality and AAA quality.*

When the average portfolio quality falls between two rating categories, an arbitrary assignment to the higher or lower quality distinction must be made (or a gradation of + or − attached). The numeric quality value can be used as a fine-tuning device for comparing individual portfolios.

An average portfolio quality based on duration weights is a more accurate reflection of the quality risk inherent in a portfolio. Exhibit 15–30 summarizes the duration contributions and duration weights of the quality sector components of the SLGC index and the two hypothetical portfolios of earlier illustration (Portfolios J and K, per Exhibits 15–27 and 15–28). Exhibit 15–31 calculates the average portfolio qualities for the three portfolios using the data compiled in Exhibit 15–30. It becomes clear that Portfolio K, despite its (lower) 60% U.S. Treasury weighting, is the highest quality portfolio, with an average portfolio quality of 1.29. The 1.29 placement gives the portfolio an average quality approximately halfway between that of an all-U.S. Treasury portfolio (1.00) and an all-federal agency portfolio (1.50). Both the SLGC index portfolio and Portfolio J rank closer to AAA (2.00) in average quality, with 1.82 and 1.78 average portfolio qualities, respectively (per Exhibit 15–31).

Observation: *Portfolio quality risk can be assessed by the use of either a weighted average portfolio quality measure or a quality distribution. In both cases, a duration-weighted approach more clearly indicates the quality risk to which the portfolio is exposed.*

Exhibit 15–30. Duration contributions and duration weights for the Shearson Lehman Government/Corporate Bond Index and two hypothetical bond portfolios. (Supporting data per Exhibits 15–25, 15–27, and 15–28.)

Quality Sector	Duration Contribution			Duration Weight (%)		
	SLGC Index	Portfolio J	Portfolio K	SLGC Index	Portfolio J	Portfolio K
U.S. Treasury	3.05	2.71	3.86	62.76	55.76	79.42
Federal agency	0.40	0.35	0.40	8.23	7.20	8.23
AAA	0.13	0	0	2.67	0	0
AA	0.49	1.80	0.60	10.08	37.04	12.35
A	0.53	0	0	10.91	0	0
BBB	0.27	0	0	5.56	0	0
	4.86	4.86	4.86	100.00	100.00	100.00

Comments: *The duration weights reflect the percentages of portfolio duration attributable to the individual quality sectors. Adjusted durations are the basis for the results.*

Exhibit 15–31. Calculation of weighted average portfolio qualities for the SLGC index and two hypothetical bond portfolios (supporting data per Exhibit 15–30). A duration contribution weighting is assumed, with quality assignments as follows: U.S. Treasury = 1.0, federal agency = 1.5, AAA = 2.0, AA = 3.0, A = 4.0, BBB = 5.0.

Portfolio	Average Quality
SLGC index	1.82 (AAA quality)
Portfolio J	1.78 (AAA quality)
Portfolio K	1.29 (agency quality)

The portfolio risks discussed up to this point (duration risk, yield curve risk, call/convexity risk, and quality/credit risk) are reasonably quantifiable. The remaining five portfolio risks (issuer sector risk, intra-issuer sector risk, issue-specific risk, liquidity risk, and product risk) are less easily quantified and often require a great deal of subjective judgment.

Issuer sector risk. Issuer sector risk arises from an over/(under)-concentration in a given issuer sector(s). Versus an all-U.S. Treasury

Exhibit 15–32. Issuer sector distribution of the SLGC bond index on a market value weighted basis and a duration contribution basis as of July 1, 1987. (Data courtesy of Shearson Lehman Brothers.)

	(a) Macaulay's Duration Basis			
Issuer Sector	*(1)* *Market Value* *(%)*	*(2)* *Macaulay's* *Duration*	*(3) = (1) × (2)* *Duration* *Contribution*	*(4) = (3)/5.18* *Duration Weight* *(%)*
U.S. Treasury	64.30	4.81	3.09	59.65
Federal agency	10.77	3.69	0.40	7.72
Industrial	7.46	6.87	0.51	9.85
Utility	9.81	7.94	0.78	15.06
Bank and finance	7.66	5.22	0.40	7.72
	100.00		5.18	100.00

	(b) Adjusted Duration Basis			
Issuer Sector	*(1)* *Market Value* *(%)*	*(2)* *Adjusted* *Duration*	*(3) = (1) × (2)* *Duration* *Contribution*	*(4) = (3)/4.86* *Duration Weight* *(%)*
U.S. Treasury	64.30	4.75	3.05	62.76
Federal agency	10.77	3.65	0.40	8.23
Industrial	7.46	5.77	0.43	8.85
Utility	9.81	6.46	0.63	12.96
Bank and finance	7.66	4.52	0.35	7.20
	100.00		4.86	100.00

benchmark such as the Ryan Treasury Index, any non-U.S. Treasury holdings (e.g., federal agencies, industrials, utilities, bank and finance securities, mortgage-backed securities, junk bonds) pose an additional risk to the portfolio. A specified benchmark portfolio (or a specific absolute guideline) dictates the normal weighting of a given issuer sector. For example, Exhibit 15–32 analyzes the issuer sector distribution of the SLGC index on a market value weighted, a duration contribution, and a duration-weighted basis. A similar analysis can be conducted on an individual portfolio with the resulting market value weightings, duration contributions, and duration weightings compared to those of the benchmark index.

For example, Exhibit 15–33 describes the issuer sector breakdown for hypothetical bond Portfolio L by both market value and duration criteria. Portfolio L maintains an adjusted duration equal to that of the

Exhibit 15–33. Issuer sector distribution of hypothetical bond Portfolio L, on a market value weighted basis and an adjusted duration contribution basis.

Issuer Sector	*(1)* Market Value (%)	*(2)* Adjusted Duration	*(3) = (1) × (2)* Duration Contribution	*(4) = (3)/4.86* Duration Weight (%)
U.S. Treasury	61.50	5.54	3.41	70.16
Federal agency	5.00	2.40	0.12	2.47
Industrial	7.50	9.33	0.70	14.40
Utility	12.00	4.00	0.48	9.88
Bank and finance	5.00	3.00	0.15	3.09
	100.00		4.86	100.00

SLGC benchmark index (4.86 years). On a market value weighted basis vis-à-vis the SLGC index, the portfolio is underexposed in U.S. Treasuries (61.50% versus 64.30%), federal agencies (5.00% versus 10.77%), and bank and finance paper (5.00% versus 7.66%). The portfolio is equally weighted in the industrial sector (7.50% versus 7.46%) and maintains an overexposure to the utility sector (12.00% versus 9.81%). Using the more-telling duration contribution statistics, Portfolio L is underweighted in federal agencies (0.12 versus 0.39), utilities (0.48 versus 0.63), and bank and finance (0.15 versus 0.35). On the same basis, the portfolio is overweighted in U.S. Treasuries (3.41 versus 3.06) and industrials (0.70 versus 0.43). The duration weights provided in the final column of the table confirm the *true* issuer sector risk. Once again, the market value sector weightings in themselves can be misleading.

Exhibit 15–34 illustrates a matrix of issuer sector and quality sector duration contributions vis-à-vis the Shearson Lehman Government/Corporate Bond Index, as reconstructed by Wilshire Associates (Santa Monica, California). This breakdown is handy in that it quickly reveals the implicit bets of a portfolio not only on an issuer sector basis but on a quality segregation within each issuer sector. For example, the sample portfolio bears an overall duration similar to that of the index benchmark (0.029 years longer). The U.S. Treasury and federal agency sectors are underweighted versus the index (notice the negative figures in the right-hand column) and the industrial, financial, and utility sectors are overweighted versus the index (notice the positive figures in the right-hand column). The bottom row, labeled *grand total*, reveals a sizable position in AA quality issues with offsetting underweightings in the AAA, A, and BBB quality ranks.

Exhibit 15–34. Duration contributions of a sample portfolio LDLOTS versus an index benchmark (the Shearson Lehman Government/Corporate Bond Index) as of June 30, 1987. (Data courtesy of Wilshire Associates.)

Issuer Sector	Quality Sector				Total
	AAA	*AA*	*A*	*BBB*	
U.S. Treasury	−0.165	NA	NA	NA	−0.165
Federal agency	−0.056	NA	NA	NA	−0.056
Industrial	0.062	0.027	0.079	−0.090	0.078
Financial	0.153	−0.109	0.113	−0.037	0.120
Utility	−0.053	0.285	−0.220	0.039	0.051
Grand total	−0.059	0.203	−0.027	−0.088	0.029

Comments: *Positive figures reflect an overweighting in market exposure vis-à-vis the benchmark; conversely, negative figures indicate an underweighting in market exposure vis-à-vis the benchmark. The column and row totals provide an overall view of the sector exposure versus the benchmark; the individual cells provide a snapshot of the contributions to that overall sector effect. This portfolio has the largest overweightings in AA utilities (0.285) and AAA financials (0.153) and the largest underweightings in A utilities (−0.220) and U.S. Treasuries (−0.165).*

Within the corporate issuer sectors (industrial, financial, utility), the industrials are overweighted in AAAs and As, with a slight bias toward AAs and a bias away from BBBs. The financial issues are heavily overweighted in the AAA and A qualities, with the AAs substantially underweighted and the BBBs modestly underweighted. The utility sector holdings are heavily skewed toward AA securities with offsetting light positions in the AAA and A qualities. This matrix layout clarifies the overall issuer sector bets vis-à-vis the index (right-hand column) and the distributional bets within a given issuer sector based on an additional characterization (in this case, quality).[16]

The degree to which one decides to over/(under)weight a specific issuer sector is a judgment based on a macroeconomic and microeconomic analysis of the industries involved. There is no simple way to boil down

---

[16] Wilshire Associates provides these types of analyses on a broad array of benchmark portfolios. The user can specify the type of cross-sectional comparison to be made (e.g., issuer versus quality, coupon rate versus issuer, maturity versus coupon rate, etc.). The author would like to thank Bob Kuberek for his assistance in developing this illustration.

the issuer sector risk into a single representative figure for the portfolio. A 5% overweighting in one sector (e.g., U.S. Treasuries) is not equivalent to a 5% overweighting in an alternative issuer sector (e.g., industrials). When used in combination with a thorough fundamental analysis of economic and industry conditions, duration contributions and duration weights serve as useful methods for assessing a portfolio's issuer sector risk. A more detailed breakdown of the issuer sector holdings is an additional tool that serves as the focal point of the next discussion.

> **Observation:** *A portfolio's issuer sector risk can be assessed by an analysis of the distribution of issuer sector holdings on both a market value weighted and a duration-weighted basis versus a specified benchmark index. Issuer sector risk stems from over/(under)weightings of an issuer sector included in the benchmark composition and positions in an issuer sector outside the benchmark domain. Duration contributions and duration weights can employ Macaulay's durations, modified durations, or (preferably) option-adjusted durations.*

Intra-issuer sector risk. Within a given issuer sector, subclassifications of issuer types exist. For example, the federal agency sector encompasses holdings in Federal Farm Credit Bank (FFCB), Federal Home Loan Bank (FHLB), Federal National Mortgage Association (FNMA), and a series of smaller, government-guaranteed issuers. Within the industrial issuer sector, one can find subcategories for oil companies, auto manufacturers, airlines, high technology firms, and so on. The utility sector has two major subclassifications: electric utility issuers and telephone utility issuers. Electric utility issuers may, in turn, be segregated according to nuclear power involvement. The bank and finance sector finds subsectors for money center banks, regional banks, consumer finance companies, auto finance companies, and equipment finance companies.

Intra-issuer sector portfolio risk arises from an over/(under)weighting of a given subsector vis-à-vis a specified benchmark. By failing to fully delineate the subsector structure of the issuer sectors under consideration, one can match the issuer sector weightings of a chosen benchmark on a market value weighted or duration-weighted basis while leaving the portfolio subject to intra-issuer sector risk. Details on the subsector breakdowns can be difficult to retrieve, but a full understanding of sector components is critical to a comprehensive assessment of portfolio risk.

> **Observation:** *A portfolio's intra-issuer sector risk can be assessed by a comparison to the subsectors of the benchmark index on a market*

value weighted or duration-weighted basis. Judgment must be used in evaluating macroeconomic and microeconomic industry factors to determine the appropriate intra-issuer sector weightings at any given point in time. An awareness of the implicit bets made by the current portfolio structure is critical.

Issue-specific risk. A portfolio's *issue-specific risk* stems from an over/(under)exposure to single issues or issuers. It is the most extreme example of a subsector breakdown, detailed to the extent of the market value weighted or duration-weighted holdings of individual issues and issuers. For example, one might overweight General Motors bonds versus Ford Motor Company bonds, or vice versa. Alternatively, one might utilize long maturity AT&T issues at the expense of short maturity AT&T bonds. With small portfolios of bonds, these issue/issuer-specific risks became particularly troublesome during the merger/acquisition and leveraged buyout craze of the mid-1980s. Lack of complete issuer diversification led to unpleasant surprises for many bond portfolio managers. Unique call or refunding features, coupon rates, sinking fund schedules, and so on, of an individual bond also contribute to a portfolio's issue-specific risk. The only way to eliminate this risk from the portfolio is to purchase every issue in the benchmark index in exactly the same proportions as those maintained by the benchmark.

Observation: *A portfolio's issue-specific risk arises from the inability to fully diversify the portfolio by purchasing an appropriate proportion of every single issue comprising the benchmark portfolio. The popularly used, multi-thousand-bond indexes of today subject a portfolio manager to some degree of issue-specific risk.*

Liquidity risk. *Liquidity* can be defined as *the ability to buy/sell an asset in a timely manner and at a price reasonably close to the last purchase/sale price of the asset.*[17] The concept of liquidity requires a fair market value, not a distressed sale price. Lacking an organized exchange, the bond market is an over-the-counter network of brokers and dealers. The liquidity of any particular issue or issuer sector is a function of (1) the amount of trading activity transpiring in the issue,

---

[17] For a bond that has not traded in several days or weeks, the purchase/sale price should reflect current market conditions (general market yield level, yield curve shape, sector spreads). The last purchase/sale price of a similar security is the relevant comparative base for establishing a fair market value.

and (2) the size of the average transaction. All other factors held equal, the greater the amount of trading activity and the larger the average transaction size, the more liquidity the security offers and the narrower the security's bid-offer spread. A $1 million par amount is regarded as a *round lot* for bond market transactions. An *odd lot* is defined as a bond transaction involving less than a $1 million par amount. Odd lots are less liquid than round lots and, consequently, trade at wider bid-offer spreads. The round lot market is the focus of discussion.

The degree of liquidity in the bond market is a function of several factors: issue size, maturity/volatility, hedging capability, and security type (generic versus unique). Larger issue sizes tend to offer more liquidity. For example, a multi-billion-dollar U.S. Treasury issue (e.g., U.S. Treasury 7¼% due 5/15/16 with $18 billion par amount outstanding) is more liquid than an older $1 to $3 billion issue (e.g., U.S. Treasury 13⅛% due 5/15/01 with $1.8 billion par amount outstanding). Not surprisingly, the 7¼% issue trades at a ⅛ point bid-offer spread and the 13⅛% issue is commonly quoted at a ¼ to ½ point spread. Short maturity issues (e.g., 2-year bonds) trade at narrower bid-offer spreads than long maturity issues (e.g., 30-year bonds). The price volatility, and therefore dealer position risk, of short maturity issues is substantially less than that of long maturity issues.

Liquidity is positively related to hedging capability. Issues that are easily hedged, either through the use of short cash positions or short positions in futures contracts, trade at narrower bid-offer spreads and offer enhanced liquidity versus issues that are difficult to hedge. Generic (i.e., standard structure) securities provide greater liquidity than esoteric (i.e., unique feature) securities. For example, mortgage passthroughs trade with superior ease in comparison to their packaged counterparts (e.g., CMOs, IOs, POs, stripped MBS). A passthrough issue may trade at a ¹⁄₁₆ to ⅛ point spread versus its partner's ½ to 1 point spread. Private placement issues bear unique provisions and trade so infrequently that a liquid market is a virtual impossibility. Consequently, esoteric products and private placements are generally viewed as longer-term investments and are often held to maturity.

Portfolio liquidity risk is a measure of the relative ease with which the portfolio's issues can be traded. A highly liquid portfolio consists of U.S. Treasury bonds, with concentrations in the current auction on-the-run issues. A benchmark index such as the Ryan Treasury Index offers a superior level of liquidity unparalleled by other bond market indexes. Portfolios with federal agency holdings, corporate bond holdings,

Exhibit 15–35. Liquidity continuum for the U.S. domestic taxable fixed-income market.

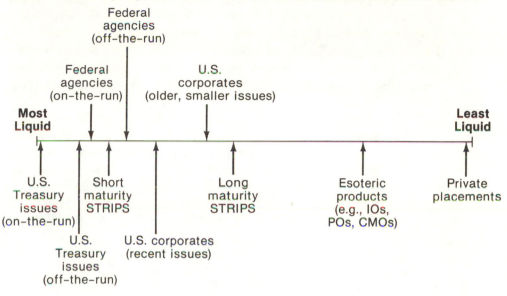

and mortgage-backed security holdings subject the investor to added degrees of portfolio liquidity risk. Esoteric products introduce high levels of illiquidity and commensurately more liquidity risk to the portfolio. A liquidity continuum is presented in Exhibit 15–35 to summarize the relative liquidity of the major issuer sectors.

> **Observation:** *A portfolio's liquidity risk is an assessment of the degree to which the portfolio's assets can be turned over at a fair market value in a timely fashion. Issuer sectors such as U.S. Treasuries and federal agencies offer superior liquidity to corporate bond and esoteric product sectors. Relative liquidity is deduced by a comparison to the liquidity of the chosen benchmark index.*

Product risk. A portfolio's *product risk* is created by holding issue types that are not included in the benchmark index. For example, zero-coupon bonds are not included in the U.S. Treasury component of the popular bond market indexes. The unique cash flow structure of a zero-coupon bond, a single cash flow at final maturity, renders it an element of product risk versus its U.S. Treasury coupon-bearing counterparts. As another example, structured mortgage-backed products (e.g., CMOs, IOs, POs, stripped MBS) offer specialized cash flow patterns to investors. These esoteric products present an incremental risk to bond portfolio managers.[18] Their less desirable liquidity characteristics have been previously discussed. As a final illustration, floating rate notes (FRNs) are not included in the commonly accepted bond market benchmarks. Their unusual cash flow characteristics vis-à-vis the fixed-rate oriented indexes introduce a degree of product risk to bond portfolios containing FRNs.

> **Observation:** *Purchasing fixed-income securities with unusual cash flow structures subjects a bond portfolio to a degree of product risk. A careful analysis of the unique features, a willingness to hold the issues for an extended period of time, and a self-imposed limitation on the percentage of a portfolio concentrated in such esoteric securities (e.g., 10%) can control the degree of product risk to which a portfolio is exposed.*

Summing up the portfolio risk elements

The risks associated with a bond portfolio have been segregated into nine categories: duration risk, yield curve risk, call/convexity risk, quality/credit risk, issuer sector risk, intra-issuer sector risk, issue-specific risk, liquidity risk, and product risk. The purpose of the detailed description of each risk is to make the reader aware of the range of forces that can beneficially or adversely impact a bond portfolio. Careful analysis of the component risks and deliberate over/(under)exposure to a given risk allow for a comprehensive control of portfolio risk and an enhancement of portfolio return. The common reliance on one or two average measures of a portfolio's risk (e.g., average duration, average quality) is inadequate. The danger of portfolio averages is explicitly addressed in Appendix B to this chapter.

Summary

The fundamentals and applications illustrated in the first 14 chapters of this book culminate in the analysis of portfolio risk and return. A thorough understanding of the two basic descriptive characteristics of an investment,

---

[18] To analytically oriented bond managers, the added complexity represents a challenge and, perhaps, an investment opportunity.

risk and *return*, is critical to successful bond portfolio management. A *portfolio's return* is calculated as a *time-weighted geometric return*. Portfolio return is a market value weighted composite of individual security returns. Bottom-line performance is often compared to median manager returns, bond index returns, and client return objectives in order to assess a portfolio manager's skill.

Bond portfolio risk has a series of component risks, including *duration risk, yield curve risk, call/convexity risk, quality/credit risk, issuer sector risk, intra-issuer sector risk, issue-specific risk, liquidity risk,* and *product risk*. Many of the component risks can be expressed in a market value weighted average form; a distribution of the contributing members is a valuable supplement. Some of the component risks are qualitative in nature and require a greater degree of subjective judgment. Duration-weighted assessments, rather than market value based judgments, provide a clearer picture of the true degree of price risk associated with a given bond or sector holding. In a broader sense, portfolio risk can be viewed in a *systematic*:*nonsystematic* framework or in a *total return variability* schematic. As noted in Chapter 11, the returns of a portfolio must be considered in light of the risk undertaken to achieve those returns.

The Structure of the Major Bond Market Indexes

A *bond index* is a composite of bond issues designed to replicate the structure and performance behavior of a specific segment of the bond market. The index may be domestic or international, dollar or nondollar, short or long in maturity terms, and broad or narrow in market coverage. A basic description of the major bond market indexes is given on a firm-by-firm basis:

1. Shearson Lehman Bond Indexes (Exhibit 15A–1)
2. Salomon Brothers Broad Investment Grade (BIG) Bond Index (Exhibit 15A–2)
3. Merrill Lynch Corporate and Government Master Index (Exhibit 15A–3)
4. Ryan Treasury Index (Exhibit 15A–4)

A comparison of the structure and mechanics of four of the most popular bond indexes in the U.S. domestic taxable fixed-income market is given

Exhibit 15A–1. Definitions of the Shearson Lehman Bond Indexes (courtesy of Shearson Lehman Brothers).

The Shearson Lehman Brothers Bond Market Report:

A monthly evaluation of the investment grade, taxable fixed income market. All major sectors of the fixed income market are analyzed, with price, coupon and total return reported on a month-end to month-end basis. Only notes and bonds with a minimum outstanding principal of $1 million and a minimum maturity of one year are included in the Corporate, Treasury, Agency, and Yankee indices. Issues with at least $15 million outstanding are included in the Mortgage Index.

With the exception of the Mortgage Backed Securities Index, each of the following Indices has an intermediate component consisting of issues with maturities between one and ten years and a long term component consisting of issues with maturities of ten years or greater. All returns are market-value weighted inclusive of accrued interest.

The Treasury Bond Index:

All public obligations of the U.S. Treasury. Flower bonds and foreign targeted issues are excluded.

The Agency Bond Index:

All publicly issued debt of agencies of the U.S. Government, quasi-federal corporations, and corporate debt guaranteed by the U.S. government. Mortgage backed securities are not included in the Government Index.

The Treasury Bond Index and the Agency Bond Index combine to form the Government Bond Index.

The Corporate Bond Index:

All public, fixed rate, non-convertible investment grade domestic corporate debt. Issues included in this index are rated at least Baa by Moody's Investors Service or BBB by Standard and Poor's Corporation, or, in the case of nonrated bonds, BBB by Fitch Investors Service. Collateralized Mortgage Obligations are not included in the Corporate Bond Index.

The Government Bond Index and the Corporate Bond Index combine to form the Government/Corporate Bond Index.

The Mortgage Backed Securities Index:

All fixed rate, securitized issues backed by mortgage pools of the Government National Mortgage Association, the Federal Home Loan Mortgage Corporation, and the Federal National Mortgage Association. Graduated Equity Mortgages are not included in the Mortgage Index; however, Graduated Payment Mortgages are included.

The Yankee Bond Index:

All U.S. dollar denominated, SEC registered, public, non-convertible debt issued or guaranteed by foreign sovereign governments, foreign municipalities, foreign governmental agencies or international agencies.

The Government/Corporate Bond Index, Mortgage Backed Securities Index and the Yankee Bond Index combine to form the Aggregate Bond Index.

in Exhibit 15A–5. The summary statistics on the same four indexes as of June 30, 1987 are displayed in Exhibit 15A–6. A breakdown of the market value weighted issuer sector distributions of the Shearson Lehman Government/Corporate Bond Index and the Salomon Brothers Broad

Exhibit 15A–2. Definition of the Salomon Brothers Broad Investment Grade Bond Index (courtesy of Salomon Brothers Inc.).

The Salomon Brothers Broad Investment Grade Bond Index measures the monthly total rate-of-return performance of all Treasury/agency, corporate and mortgage securities with a stated maturity of one year or longer and with at least $25 million outstanding. We do not believe that bonds with less than $25 million outstanding are reasonably "available" for institutional transactions, nor do we feel that they can be reliably priced on an individual basis—or by any other means.

Subject to these availability limitations, the bond universe is screened each month to determine the eligibility of particular securities. The overall composition of the Salomon Brothers Broad Investment Grade Bond Index is as follows:

● **Treasury/Agency** (except flower bonds)

● **Corporate** (BBB or better)
  ○ Utilities
  ○ Industrials
  ○ Financials
  ○ World Banks
  ○ U.S. Pay Canadians

● **Mortgage**
  ○ GNMAs
  ○ FHLMCs
  ○ FNMAs
  ○ Conventional Pass-Throughs
  ○ FHA Projects

Pricing. Every issue is individually trader priced on the bid side at the end of each month.

Computation. The Broad Index return is the market-weighted total return of all securities included in the index. Total returns are made up of the following components: price change, principal payments, coupon payments, accrued interest, and reinvestment income on intramonth cash flows. Principal payments for mortgage securities are computed on a pool-by-pool basis each month, covering more than 100,000 pools for September 1985.

Reweightings. The index is reweighted each month to reflect new issues, rating changes, scheduled and early repayment of principal, outstanding volume declining to below $25 million, and maturities rolling under one year.

Reinvestment. All intramonth cash flows are invested as received at the daily average one-month Treasury bill rate for that month. At month-end, the accumulated value of all the components of return are reinvested into a unit of the new month's revised portfolio.

Historical Data. Historical total returns and cumulative index values are available from January 1980 for the Broad Index and its subsectors—Treasury/agency, corporates and mortgages.

Exhibit 15A–3. Definition of the Merrill Lynch Corporate and Government Master Index (courtesy of Merrill Lynch Capital Markets).

Corporate and Government Master Index

General Criteria:

- Issues must be in the form of publicly placed, nonconvertible coupon-bearing domestic debt.

- Issues must carry a term to maturity of at least one year.

- Par amounts outstanding must be no less than $10 million at the start and at the close of the performance measurement period.

- Corporate instruments must be rated by Standard & Poor's Corporation or by Moody's Investors Service as investment grade issues (i.e., BBB/Baa or better).

- **The index excludes** Agency pass-throughs (which are included in the mortgage universe), collateralized mortgage obligations, flower bonds, floating rate debt, equipment trust certificates and Title 11 Securities.

Exhibit 15A–4. Definition of the Ryan Treasury Index (courtesy of the Ryan Financial Strategy Group).

The **Ryan Index** is the first daily total return index for bonds, created March 1983, measuring the total return of the Treasury yield curve from 1979. Its key features probably make it the most suitable bond index on which any prudent **Bond Index Fund** can be based.

Composition. Current coupon Treasuries.
- Allows for the most liquid fund.
- Allows for the only default-free fund.
- Allows for a defined maturity ladder to counter the effects of both inflation and deflation: the maintenance of such a maturity ladder is only feasible through the Treasury market.
- Allows for exact duplication of Index into an Index Fund: replicating the features of an index is less desirable since one can no longer guarantee the returns of that index.

Frequency. Daily.
- Allows for complete flexibility in withdrawals and contributions to the fund at any time.

Weighting. Equal weighting of issues in index.
- Prevents biases towards any sector of the market which could hinder accomplishing index fund objectives.

Pricing. All issues in the Ryan Index universe are priced by traders.
- Signifies verifiable and obtainable prices in the market: the alternative computer matrix pricing does not reflect prices that are readily available or verifiable.

Rebalancing. At Treasury Auctions.
- Allows for a very systematic rebalancing procedure.

Exhibit 15A–5. Basic structure and mechanics of four popular bond market indexes. (Data courtesy of Shearson Lehman Brothers, Salomon Brothers Inc., Merrill Lynch Capital Markets, and the Ryan Financial Strategy Group).

Structural Factor	Shearson Lehman Govt./Corp.	Salomon Broad	Merrill Lynch Govt./Corp.	Ryan
Issuer sectors	Treasury, agency, corporates	Treasury, agency, mortgage-backed, corporates, yankees	Treasury, agency, corporates, yankees	U.S. Treasuries (current auction issues)
Weighting	Market value	Market value	Market value	Equally weighted
Minimum issue size outstanding	$1 million	$25 million	$10 million	No minimum
Minimum remaining term to maturity	1 year	1 year	1 year	2 years
Maximum remaining term to maturity	None	None	None	30 years
Minimum quality	Baa3 by Moody's and BBB− by S&P's	BBB− by S&P's	At least a weak BBB credit as an average of Moody's and S&P's ratings	All Treasury

Quality category	If split-rated and meeting the minimum quality requirement, half of the MV goes into the Moody's category and half of the MV goes into the S&P's rating category. If NR by one agency, the single agency rating serves as the quality proxy.	Must be rated by S&P's	If split-rated, all of the MV goes into the weighted average category. If NR by one agency, the single agency rating serves as the quality proxy.	All Treasury
Index frequency	Monthly	Monthly	Daily	Daily
Pricing method	Trader pricing plus proprietary algorithm	All trader priced	All trader priced	Multiple trader pricing
Intramonth reinvestment	None	At the average 1-month T-bill rate	Yes—daily into the bond index	Yes—daily into the bond index
Data available from	December 31, 1972	December 31, 1979	December 31, 1972	December 31, 1979

Exhibit 15A–6. Summary statistics on four popular bond market indexes as of June 30, 1987. (Data courtesy of Shearson Lehman Brothers, Merrill Lynch Capital Markets, Salomon Brothers Inc., and the Ryan Financial Strategy Group.)

Summary Statistics	*SLGC*	*MLGC*	*Salomon* *Broad*	*Ryan*
Number of issues	5,410	4,752	4,413	7
Total market value (billions)	$1,605	$1,632	$2,096	$ 60
Average YTM (%)	8.46	8.45	8.77	8.05
Average maturity (years)	9.59	9.74	9.36	8.68
Average duration (Macaulay's)	5.10	5.12	4.97	5.06
Average effective duration (Macaulay's option-adjusted)	4.78	4.94	4.45	5.06
Average quality	AAA	Agency	Agency	U.S. Treasury

Comments: *Data reflect the characteristics of the Shearson Lehman Government/Corporate Bond Index, the Merrill Lynch Corporate and Government Master Index, the Salomon Brothers Broad Investment Grade Bond Index, and the Ryan Treasury Index. The averages are market value weighted based on June 30, 1987 pricings. For the Ryan Treasury Index, the averages represent equal (not market value) weightings.*

Investment Grade Bond Index is presented in Exhibit 15A–7. U.S. Treasury issues comprise the bulk of the bonds outstanding in the marketplace today. With U.S. government budget deficits remaining stubbornly high ($150 to $200 billion annually), the U.S. Treasury component of the major bond market indexes is likely to continue to grow.

The changing composition of the Shearson Lehman Government/Corporate Bond Index over the past 10 years (1977–1986) is telling. Exhibit 15A–8 gives the reader a feel for the degree of overall growth in the U.S. domestic taxable fixed-income market over the 1977– 1986 period. Exhibit 15A–9 shows that the U.S. Treasury sector has almost doubled its market share in the past 10 years, from a 35.2% weighting at the end of 1976 to a commanding 63.9% share as of the end of 1986. The agency, industrial, and utility sectors have lost substantial chunks of market share, while the finance sector has kept pace and maintained a 7% weighting in the SLGC index.

The mortgage-backed sector has experienced explosive growth during the 1980s, rising from an 11.6% weighting in the Salomon Brothers

Exhibit 15A–7. Issuer sector breakdown of the Shearson Lehman Government/Corporate Bond Index and the Salomon Brothers Broad Investment Grade Bond Index as of July 1, 1987. (Data courtesy of Shearson Lehman Brothers and Salomon Brothers Inc.)

Sector Distribution	Shearson Lehman Govt./Corp. (%)	Salomon Broad (%)
U.S. Treasury	64.3	48.7
Agency	10.8	8.3
Mortgage-backed	0.0	24.4
Industrial	7.5	5.6
Utility	9.8	6.6
Bank and finance	7.7	4.6
Yankee	0.0	1.6

Comments: *The figures above are market value weightings based on June 30, 1987 valuations.*

Exhibit 15A–8. Growth in the U.S. domestic taxable fixed-income market over the 1977–1986 period, as measured by the Shearson Lehman Government/Corporate Bond Index. (Data courtesy of Shearson Lehman Brothers.)

Year-end	Number of Issues	Market Value (Billions)	Average YTM (%)	Average Duration (Years)
1976	4,450	413.1	6.90	6.38
1977	4,569	433.7	7.95	6.11
1978	4,606	443.8	9.78	5.67
1979	4,651	461.7	11.08	5.23
1980	4,738	497.1	12.95	4.66
1981	4,823	564.9	14.53	4.14
1982	5,024	781.7	10.75	4.57
1983	5,045	885.9	11.61	4.36
1984	5,108	1,038.4	11.16	4.43
1985	5,311	1,305.7	9.11	4.81
1986	5,474	1,564.5	7.60	5.29

Comments: *Notice that the average duration varies inversely with the average yield level.*

BIG Index to a 24.4% weighting as of July 1, 1987 (see Exhibit 15A–10 and recall Exhibit 15A–7). In dollar terms, the mortgage component has surged from $50 billion to $500 billion over the past 7½ years. The strong emergence of mortgage-backed securities has compelled the

Exhibit 15A–9. Relative market shares of various issuer sectors over the 1977–1986 period, as measured by the components of the Shearson Lehman Government/Corporate Bond Index. (Data courtesy of Shearson Lehman Brothers.)

			Sector Weightings (%)			
Year-end	*U.S. Treasury*	*Federal Agency*	*Industrial*	*Utility*	*Finance*	*Other*
1976	35.2	16.7	14.3	25.4	6.4	2.0
1977	36.4	16.8	13.6	23.9	7.1	2.2
1978	39.3	16.8	12.4	22.4	7.1	2.0
1979	41.9	18.1	11.5	20.4	6.7	1.4
1980	44.1	19.3	10.7	18.4	6.6	0.9
1981	49.3	18.9	9.1	15.7	6.0	1.0
1982	51.5	17.4	8.8	15.0	6.1	1.2
1983	57.3	15.2	8.0	13.1	5.5	0.9
1984	60.8	14.7	7.0	11.6	6.0	0.0
1985	62.7	13.1	7.4	10.6	6.2	0.0
1986	63.9	11.0	7.8	10.3	7.0	0.0

Comments: *The U.S. Treasury sector has gained dominance in the marketplace; the finance sector has maintained its market share. The remaining sectors have lost preeminence, particularly the utility sector.*

Exhibit 15A–10. Growth of the mortgage-backed securities sector during the 1980s, using the mortgage component of the Salomon Brothers Broad Investment Grade Bond Index as a representative indicator. (Data courtesy of Salomon Brothers Inc.)

Year-end	*Broad Index Market Value (Billions)*	*Broad Index Average Duration (Years)*	*Mortgage Component (%)*
1979	520.7	5.30	11.6
1980	585.4	4.81	13.0
1981	631.9	4.38	12.9
1982	904.4	4.59	15.8
1983	1,063.2	4.50	18.4
1984	1,276.0	4.48	18.2
1985	1,609.5	4.65	20.5
1986	2,060.7	4.96	22.8

Comments: *The Salomon Broad Index recently crossed the $2 trillion mark. The growth in the mortgage component of the Index has been staggering in the past 7 years. Mortgage-backed products now comprise almost 25% of the Index. In dollar terms, the mortgage index now totals approximately $500 billion.*

Exhibit 15A–11. Components of the mortgage-backed securities component of the Salomon Brothers Broad Investment Grade Bond Index as of July 1, 1987. (Data courtesy of Salomon Brothers Inc.)

Issuer Sector	Market Value Weighting (%)
GNMA (30-year)	45.64
FHLMC (30-year)	27.97
FNMA (30-year)	15.47
15-year passthroughs (GNMA, FHLMC, FNMA)	10.59
FHA project loans	0.33
Total	100.00

major indexers to include this sector in their broad-based market composites (e.g., the Shearson Lehman Aggregate Bond Index, the Salomon Brothers Broad Investment Grade Bond Index, the Merrill Lynch Domestic Master). The mortgage-backed sector itself is composed of GNMA 30-year passthroughs (45.64%), FHLMC 30-year passthroughs (27.97%), FNMA 30-year passthroughs (15.47%), 15-year passthroughs (10.59%), and FHA project loans (0.33%)—see Exhibit 15A–11.

The management of bond portfolios to match a specified index's structure and performance is gaining popularity. The advent of bond indexation is a recent phenomenon, following on the heels of equity indexation which caught on in the mid-1970s. Over the past 5 years (1982–1986), assets under bond index management have risen from approximately $2 billion to $40 billion. The trend is clearly in place for continued growth in bond indexing. The reasons for a major shift to a bond indexing approach are compelling:

1. Superior total return performance versus median bond manager performance (recall Exhibits 15–4 and 15–5).
2. Controlled portfolio risk (at the market level).
3. Superior risk-adjusted returns.
4. Lower management fees (5 to 10BP versus 20 to 30BP).
5. Lower turnover/transaction costs.
6. Full diversification (little or no unsystematic risk).
7. Fewer surprises in performance (more predictability); remains fully invested, never missing a market turn.
8. Fewer reporting requirements and less frequent meetings.

The use of specialized indexes is growing. A *specialized or customized bond index* is designed according to a client's investment objectives and constraints. The broad-based indexes of earlier illustration bear durations in the 5.00-year area. Bearish investors or investors desiring reasonable stability in principal value may choose a short duration index such as the Shearson Lehman 1- to 5-year Government/Corporate Bond Index (average duration = 2.29 years as of June 30, 1987) or the Shearson Lehman Intermediate Government/Corporate Bond Index (average duration = 3.33 years as of June 30, 1987). Bullish investors or investors with long duration liability streams may desire a long duration index such as the Shearson Lehman Long Treasury Index (average duration = 9.61 years as of June 30, 1987), the Ryan 30-year Treasury Index (average duration = 11.09 years as of June 30, 1987), or a composite of long STRIPS (durations up to 30 years). The trend is currently in place for substantial growth in bond index products.

The Danger of Portfolio Averages

To simplify the mountains of descriptive characteristics available, bond market participants attempt to identify a single number that communicates the inherent risk of a bond portfolio. The weighted average maturity (WAM) fit the bill until Macaulay's duration came into vogue. Perhaps in the future, the magic number will be a portfolio standard deviation or a portfolio beta. For the time being, two portfolio risk measures stand on center stage: *average duration risk* and *average quality risk*.[a] Two supplemental presentations, *average yield curve risk* and *average convexity,* are gaining advocates and deserve attention here as well. This Appendix analyzes these average risk measures and concludes with a comprehensive assessment of portfolio risk through the use of the COMPARE software package of Capital Management Sciences (CMS).

---

[a] Other portfolio averages exist, including average price, average coupon, average yield to maturity, average current yield, and average maturity. The purpose of this Appendix is to focus on the popularized average portfolio risk measures and to illustrate the misleading nature of average risk statistics.

Exhibit 15B–1. Average portfolio durations fail to tell the whole story. Two portfolios (R and S) of identical duration perform quite differently in a parallel yield shift scenario. The portfolio holdings are currently priced at par to yield 7.00% to maturity. (Supporting data per Exhibits 14–9 and 14–10.)

Portfolio Description	Macaulay's Duration (Years)	Instantaneous Total Return (%) if Yields:	
		+200BP	−200BP
Portfolio R: 2-year/30-year U.S. Treasury combination	5.65	− 9.40	+13.02
Portfolio S: 7-year U.S. Treasury	5.65	−10.22	+11.69
Return differential, R − S		82BP	133BP

Comments: *Convexity differentials contribute to the divergent performance between similar duration bond portfolios.*

Average portfolio duration

Portfolio durations are commonly reported on a market value weighted Macaulay's basis. Even under the simplified case of a parallel (and instantaneous) shift in yield, Macaulay's duration fails to fully capture the price return differentials of portfolios of bonds. As an example, Exhibit 15B–1 calculates the instantaneous total return of two portfolios with an identical average Macaulay's duration of 5.65 years: a 1-bond portfolio (7-year U.S. Treasury) and a 2-bond portfolio (a combination of 2-year U.S. Treasury bonds and 30-year U.S. Treasury bonds). Given a 200BP shift in yields, the return differentials amount to 133BP and 82BP in bull and bear markets, respectively. These return differences are sizable, given the slim margin between 1st quartile and median manager performance (recall SEI Funds Evaluation figures presented in this chapter).

Three of the four portfolios of an earlier illustration (A, C, D) carry identical modified durations of 6.26 years (recall Exhibit 15–21). The same portfolios, however, differ sizably in convexity terms (1.02, 2.02, and −2.02, respectively), portending differentials in price return and total return between the portfolios. Exhibit 15B–2 shows the return variations between a noncallable U.S. Treasury bond and a callable utility bond of similar effective duration. In both bull and bear markets, the actual results differ by 24–69BP.

A nonparallel yield curve shift renders the average Macaulay's duration figure even more dubious. For example, Exhibit 15B–3 summa-

Exhibit 15B–2. Bonds with similar durations can exhibit appreciably different price returns (June 30, 1987 data).

	*Effective Duration** *(Years)*	*Price Change (%) if Yields:*	
Issue Data		+ *100BP*	−*100BP*
A: U.S. Treasury 13⅛% due 5/15/01	7.50	−6.90	7.68
B: BLIP 9⅝% due 7/15/14	7.50	−7.59	7.44
Return differential, A − B		69BP	24BP

* Depending on the model and assumptions utilized, the effective durations may differ somewhat from those presented.

Comments: *Equivalent durations, even on an effective basis, fail to capture all of the inherent return biases of different securities.*

rizes the instantaneous total returns on the same 1-bond and 2-bond portfolios of earlier example, but now assumes a 100BP yield decline for the 2-year bond, a 50BP yield drop for the 7-year issue, and a 75BP fall-off in yield for the 30-year security. The portfolio returns differ by a significant 189BP.

The equivalence of the portfolio durations hides many potential return biases. Average portfolio durations fail to discern differential call

Exhibit 15B–3. Nonparallel shift in yields creates sizable divergences in return between similar duration portfolios. The 2-year bond, 7-year bond, and 30-year bond experience 100BP, 50BP, and 75BP yield declines, respectively.

Portfolio Description	*Macaulay's Duration (Years)*	*Instantaneous Total Return (%)*
Portfolio R		
Weighting		
65.9% 2-year U.S. Treasury	1.90	1.86
34.1% 30-year U.S. Treasury	12.91	10.11
Portfolio averages	5.65	4.67
Portfolio S		
Weighting		
100.0% 7-year U.S. Treasury	5.65	2.78
Return differential, R − S		189BP

Exhibit 15B–4. Quality spread data for U.S. Treasuries and investment grade corporate bonds in the 30-year maturity sector. All issues are currently priced at par.

Issue	*YTM (%)*	*Yield Spread to U.S. Treasury (BP)*	*Expected Yield Spread Change (BP)*	*Expected Yield Spread (BP)*
U.S. Treasury	7.00	—	—	—
AAA corporate	7.50	+ 50	+10	+ 60
AA corporate	7.75	+ 75	+10	+ 85
A corporate	8.00	+100	+25	+125
BBB corporate	8.75	+175	+10	+185

features and sector exposure risks.[b] Additionally, as time passes, portfolio durations decline at different rates.

Average portfolio quality

A portfolio's quality is generally derived as a market value weighted average. Numeric assignments similar to those detailed in this chapter are useful devices for constructing an average quality figure. Such a numeric scheme is subject to judgment. For example, what value should be applied to U.S. Treasury holdings vis-à-vis federal agencies and corporate bonds? Additionally, the degree of quality grading must be decided. For example, does a AA− bond receive a lower score than a AA or a AA+ bond, or are all AAs lumped into a single numeric category? Quality classifications mask the issuer sector behind the particular grouping. Should AA finance companies, AA banks, AA industrials, and AA utilities be treated equally as AA quality, or should sector weightings also be considered? Are some AA industries declining in quality while others are improving their credit stance?

Perhaps the most troublesome aspect of the average portfolio quality concept is the occurrence of quality sector spread shifts. As an illustration, Exhibit 15B–4 lists the quality spreads between U.S. Treasuries and investment grade corporate bonds (AAA, AA, A, and BBB). Exhibit 15B–5 calculates the total returns for two corporate bond portfolios, each of single-A average quality, given a general rise in yields and a widening in quality spreads. It is clear that a nonparallel shift in quality

---

[b] Average effective (i.e., call-adjusted) durations adjust for differences in call features so that the portfolio durations are comparable. Sector spread risks (maturity, issuer, quality) remain unaddressed.

Exhibit 15B–5. Total returns on two corporate bond portfolios (M and N) of an average A quality. A nonparallel quality spread shift is assumed, with single-As cheapening vis-à-vis AAs and BBBs (data per Exhibit 15B–4). Interest rate levels in general remain stable.

Portfolio Description	Quality	Instantaneous Total Return (%)
Portfolio M		
Weighting		
50.0% 30-year corporate	AA	−1.18
50.0% 30-year corporate	BBB	−1.05
Portfolio averages	A	−1.12
Portfolio N		
Weighting		
100.0% 30-year corporate	A	−2.77
Return differential, M − N		165BP

sector spreads can lead to sizably different total returns between portfolios of similar average quality. The pure single-A bond portfolio underperforms the dumbbell AA/BBB portfolio by 165BP (−2.77% versus −1.12%).

Two final considerations should be made. First, a duration-weighted derivation of average quality is superior to the commonly used market value weighted measure. Capital Management Sciences has developed such a measure. Second, a maturity or, preferably, a duration distribution of quality sector holdings is an attractive supplement to an average measure. Shearson Lehman Brothers, for example, provides both distributions in a matrix format.

Average yield curve risk

Two of the less widely used portfolio average measures address yield curve risk and convexity risk, respectively. Recall that the portfolio duration construct is designed to deal with small, parallel shifts in yield. Nonparallel yield changes render the duration measure faulty, even assuming an instantaneous shift. Capital Management Sciences has developed and implemented a *nonparallel (NP) duration* concept that quantifies the yield curve risk of a bond portfolio. The NP duration assesses the sensitivity of a bond or a portfolio of bonds to nonparallel yield curve shifts. U.S. Treasury data for the cumulative period since 1971 form the basis for the calculated results. History shows that short maturity bond yields are more volatile than long maturity bond yields. Additionally, the bulk of the yield curve steepening or flattening occurs in the intermediate maturities. In yield terms, the short-to-intermediate segment of the yield curve is more subject to nonparallel shifts than the intermediate-to-long segment of the curve. Recall that a bond's price is affected by both the magnitude of yield shift and the price sensitivity of the bond, as reflected by the modified duration measure:

$$\begin{matrix}\text{percentage of change} \\ \text{in bond price}\end{matrix} = -\begin{pmatrix}\text{modified} \\ \text{duration}\end{pmatrix} \times \frac{\text{BP change in yield}}{100}$$

The nonparallel yield curve risk can be analyzed in three maturity classes:

1. Short maturity (0 to 2 years):

| low durations (low price sensitivity) | greatest degree of yield volatility | $\Rightarrow$ | modest degree of yield curve risk |

2. Intermediate maturity (3 to 5 years):

| modest durations (medium price sensitivity) | high degree of yield volatility | $\Rightarrow$ | highest degree of yield curve risk |

3. Long maturity (10 to 30 years):

| high durations (high price sensitivity) | lowest degree of yield volatility | $\Rightarrow$ | low degree of yield curve risk |

It is not surprising, therefore, that CMS found the NP duration to be greatest in the 3- to 4-year maturity sector. In other words, the bonds in this yield curve segment expose the investor to the highest relative degree of nonparallel yield curve risk.

Any single issue bears some degree of yield curve risk. The market value weighted average of all of the component NP durations forms a portfolio's NP duration. Exhibit 15B–10 (at the end of this Appendix) contains a sample portfolio with a NP duration of 0.80 as compared to the SLGC bond index's NP duration of 0.67, as calculated by CMS. In this instance, the bond portfolio manager has undertaken a greater-than-market exposure to a nonparallel yield shift in anticipation of a general steepening of the yield curve. A less-than-market exposure (e.g., a NP duration of 0.40) is a bet that the yield curve will flatten.[c] In sum, the CMS measure of NP duration can be used as an assessment of the degree to which a portfolio's duration distribution differs from that of a designated benchmark index. The NP duration boils down to a single number the price sensitivity of the portfolio to such nonparallel shifts in interest rates.

As a supplement to the average NP duration figure, a maturity distribution or, preferably, a duration distribution is helpful. Significant deviations from the prescribed benchmark weightings should be carefully monitored. The implicit bets made in the portfolio structure should be highlighted by both the aggregate representation and the component distribution. CMS provides its clients with both distributions as well as a comparison to a chosen benchmark bond index.

Of course, in the short run, the nonparallel YC shifts and issue-specific behaviors may or may not comply with the longer run historical averages upon which the CMS formulation is based. Manager judgment is critical in positioning the portfolio holdings in areas of the yield curve offering the best risk:reward prospects at a given point in time. Supply and demand conditions and issue-specific behaviors are simply impossible to capture in a broadly based quantitative technique such as a yield curve risk measure. A mathematical model is an aid to, not a replacement of, a professional bond portfolio manager.

Average convexity

A *portfolio convexity* is simply the market value weighted average convexity of the portfolio members. As such, a portfolio convexity is subject to the same influences as its component bond convexities. For example, convexity requires a judgment on the magnitude of expected yield change. Larger shifts in yield raise the average portfolio convexity, assuming a preponderance of noncallable holdings. Exhibit 15B–6 shows that convexity factors at 300BP yield shifts are 3 to 4 times the magnitude of the factors for a 100BP yield change. Additionally, convexity is a function of the direction of interest rate change. With noncallable bonds, lower yield levels are associated with higher convexity factors (see Exhibit 15B–7). For example, a par bond in a 3% yield environment bears twice the convexity of a par bond in a 7% yield environment (2.55

---

[c] The reader is encouraged to contact either Jim Kaplan or Brig Belvin at Capital Management Sciences for a further elaboration on the nonparallel duration concept.

Exhibit 15B–6. Convexities of a 30-year, 7% coupon U.S. Treasury bond priced at par to yield 7.00% to maturity. A variety of yield changes are analyzed, ranging from −400BP to +400BP. (Data per Exhibit 6–33.)

BP Change in Yield	Convexity*	Convexity Factor†
−400	+28.88	7.22
−300	+14.73	4.91
−200	+ 5.97	2.99
−100	+ 1.37	1.37
0	0	0
+100	+ 1.16	1.16
+200	+ 4.30	2.15
+300	+ 9.02	3.01
+400	+14.98	3.75

* Convexity is defined as the percentage change in bond price not attributable to modified duration. This particular bond carries a modified duration of 12.47 years.

† The convexity factor is the average amount of convexity per 100BP of yield change. For example, a 300BP fall in yield renders the bond an incremental 14.73% in convexity returns or, on average, 4.91% per 100BP of yield change (14.73%/3 = 4.91%). The convexity factors allow for better comparability.

Comments: *A given security bears a multiplicity of convexities. The bond's convexity is influenced by both the magnitude and the direction of the anticipated yield change.*

versus 1.27). Nine percent yield conditions portend a 30% reduction in convexity levels from the 7% baseline yield (0.93 versus 1.27). With callable bonds, the opposite occurs. These bonds suffer from negative convexity as yields decline. A portfolio composed of a mixture of callables and noncallables bears an average convexity figure that can be difficult to interpret and dangerous to compare.

For example, Exhibit 15B–8 presents two bonds with identical convexities. The supporting calculations are provided in Exhibit 15B–9. The latter table reveals vividly that the average convexity representation can be very misleading. Although the 3-year U.S. Treasury and the 40-year utility bond share an average convexity factor of 0.05, the variability in individual convexities in up- and downmarkets is sizable. As an illustration, the price behavior of the 3-year bond is well predicted by its modified duration of 2.66 years. Convexity adds 4 to 5BP of return in both bull and bear markets. The 40-year utility bond, however, exhibits a positive convexity in a bear market (1.88) and a negative convexity in a bull market (−1.78), for an average convexity of 0.05 [(1.88 −

Exhibit 15B–7. Convexity as a function of the general level of yields. The issues illustrated are 30-year, current-coupon U.S. Treasury bonds priced at par in a variety of yield environments. A 100BP change in yield is assumed for the convexity calculation.

Yield Level (%)	Modified Duration (Years)	Convexity[*]
3.00	19.69	2.55
4.00	17.38	2.12
5.00	15.45	1.77
6.00	13.84	1.49
7.00	12.47	1.27
8.00	11.31	1.08
9.00	10.32	0.93
10.00	9.47	0.80
11.00	8.73	0.69

[*] An average convexity for ±100BP change in yield. The convexity figure represents the incremental percentage change in bond price not attributable to modified duration. For example, at a 7.00% yield level, a current-coupon, 30-year U.S. Treasury can expect, on average, 1.27% more price appreciation than that predicted by its modified duration, given a 100BP change in yield.

Comments: *Convexity is inversely related to the general yield environment. As yields decline, convexities become progressively larger.*

1.78)/2 = 0.05]. The differences in return (attributable to convexity) between the identically convex bonds average 184BP in both bull and bear markets, significant unexpected discrepancies. It is clear that the average convexity fails to tell the whole tale.

Exhibit 15B–8. Two bonds with identical average convexities.

Issue Data	Bond Price	YTM (%)	Macaulay's Duration (Years)	Average Convexity Factor
3-year, 7% coupon U.S. Treasury bond	100.00	7.00	2.76	0.05
40-year, 9% coupon utility bond	100.00	9.00	11.27	0.05

Comments: *The average convexity factor assumes a 100BP change in yield level. Supporting data in Exhibit 15B–9.*

Exhibit 15B–9. Calculation of the average convexity factors for a U.S. Treasury bond and a utility bond (listed in Exhibit 15B–8).

Issue Data	(1) Change in Price (%)	(2) Duration Suggested Price Change (%)	(3) = (1) − (2) Return Attributed to Convexity (%)	Convexity Factor[*]
	Yields Rise 100BP			
3-year U.S. Treasury bond	−2.62	− 2.66	0.04	0.04
40-year utility bond	−8.90[†]	−10.78	1.88	1.88
	Yields Fall 100BP			
3-year U.S. Treasury bond	2.71	2.66	0.05	0.05
40-year utility bond	9.00	10.78	−1.78	−1.78

Average convexity factor (±100BP):

3-year U.S. Treasury bond: $(0.04 + 0.05)/2 = 0.045$ (rounded to 0.05)

40-year utility bond: $\dfrac{[1.88 + (-1.78)]}{2} = \dfrac{0.10}{2} = 0.05$

[*] As defined in Chapter 6: per 100BP change in yield.

[†] Assumes that the utility issue narrows by 10BP in yield vis-à-vis U.S. Treasuries in a rising (+100BP) yield environment and appreciates to 109.00 in a falling (−100BP) yield environment. The utility bond underperforms comparable duration U.S. Treasuries in an upmarket due to its call features.

Comments: *The bonds carry modified durations of 2.66 and 10.78, respectively.*

Dealing with the dangers of portfolio averages

This discourse on the dangers of portfolio averages is not intended to belittle the use of such averages. It merely attempts to reveal the inherent limitations of portfolio averages and proposes methods of alleviating the errancies (e.g., by the use of supplementary distribution schedules). The type of portfolio analysis conducted by Capital Management Sciences focuses on four portfolio average measures:

1. Average call-adjusted Macaulay's duration (*parallel duration*)
2. Average yield curve risk (*nonparallel duration*)

3. Average quality risk (*quality spread risk*)
4. Average convexity risk (*convexity*)

Supplemental presentations are provided by CMS to circumvent the dangers of sole reliance on average figures:

Average Measure	Supplemental Schedule
1. Parallel duration	Duration-weighted sector distribution
2. Nonparallel duration	Duration distribution along the yield curve
3. Quality	Quality distribution
4. Convexity	Total return scenario analysis for a wide range of interest rate shifts

Consistent comparisons to a chosen benchmark on both an average and a distribution basis are also included in the CMS analytical package.[d] Each of the factors impacting a portfolio's return is incorporated into a total return scenario analysis. A similar output can be obtained for the benchmark against which the portfolio is being compared for performance purposes. The total return figures reveal the individual behaviors lying behind the average portfolio representations. CMS clients have successfully utilized the aforementioned analytics to enhance portfolio returns versus a benchmark such as the Shearson Lehman Government/Corporate Bond Index. For the year 1986, excess returns averaged 40BP (Source: Capital Management Sciences). Exhibit 15B–10 provides a complete sample package of the CMS portfolio analysis product, with a comparison to the SLGC bond index as of June 30, 1987.

---

[d] It cannot be emphasized strongly enough that consistency in comparison is critical. Effective durations, yield curve risk assessments, quality risk exposure, and convexity features are subject to model assumptions. A comparison of effective durations, for example, is incorrect if the volatility assumption made for the portfolio issues differs from that made for the benchmark components. Such apple-to-orange comparisons lead to faulty conclusions.

Overview of Exhibit 15B–10

This exhibit contains a sample output of the COMPARE software package developed and utilized by Capital Management Sciences (CMS) of Los Angeles, California. A $100 million (market value) portfolio is compared to the benchmark which is, in this case, the Shearson Lehman Government/Corporate (SLGC) Bond Index as reconstructed by CMS. The sample portfolio, called *Multi-duration,* is composed of 33 bond issues. All data reflect June 30, 1987 valuations. The page-by-page highlights of the extensive report are summarized below:

Page 1: Portfolio listing. Each individual portfolio issue is described in traditional mannerisms (par amount, cusip number, etc.) as well as in CMS' innovative risk terms:

1. *Parallel duration:* The Macaulay's duration of the bond, incorporating accrued interest and adjusted for call features. The average volatility of T-bonds over the 1971–1986 period is assumed.

2. *Nonparallel duration:* The yield curve risk of the bond as created by nonparallel yield curve shifts.

3. *Quality spread duration:* A duration-weighted measure of the quality risk of the bond.

4. *Passthrough spread duration:* Only applicable to mortgage-backed securities (not elaborated in this text); bears no influence on either the portfolio *Multi-duration* or the SLGC index since neither contain mortgage-backed securities.

5. *Convexity:* The average convexity of the bond given a 100BP change in yield.

The asterisks denote bonds trading on a yield-to-call basis.

Page 2: The market value weighted average characteristics of the portfolio, as derived from the portfolio component figures on page 1.

Page 3: A comparison of the portfolio and the benchmark index on a distributional basis. The distributions cover duration, maturity, issuer sector, quality, coupon rate, and call provisions. These distribution schedules serve as good support for the average figures of page 2. The distributions are based on market value weightings.

Page 4: A comparison of the duration contributions, by issuer sector, of the portfolio vis-à-vis the SLGC index.

Page 5: A comparison of the traditional portfolio characteristics (YTM, CY, quality coupon, maturity) vis-à-vis the benchmark index [in CMS' usage, LBKL represents Lehman Brothers Kuhn Loeb (now Shearson Lehman Brothers) and LBGC stands for Lehman Brothers Government/Corporate—i.e., the SLGC index.]

Page 6: A comparison of the duration and convexity characteristics of the portfolio vis-à-vis the SLGC index.

Page 7: A calculation of 1-month portfolio returns, by component, for a broad range of changes in yields and spreads. Note that the income effect includes coupon accrual and scientific amortization of premiums/(discounts). The remaining factors reflect price return impacts. The total return impacts reflect a repricing of each component security in the portfolio; it is *not* based on an estimation through the use of the aforementioned portfolio averages.

Page 8: A comparison of the 1-month portfolio returns, by component, vis-à-vis the benchmark index. A broad range of yield and spread changes is illustrated.

Page 9: A projection of portfolio returns vis-à-vis the benchmark index for 3-, 6-, 9-, and 12-month horizons. A mean return difference is calculated in addition to 10%, 25%, 75%, and 90% confidence levels.

Exhibit 15B–10. A portfolio analysis of the 33-issue, $100 million bond portfolio called *Multi-duration*.

Risk measure:

   1. *Duration risk:* The portfolio's parallel duration is matched to the SLGC benchmark (4.63 years versus 4.62 years, per page 6). However, the portfolio's duration is highly concentrated in the 3- to 5-year duration sector vis-à-vis the index (see page 3). The maturity distribution is similarly lumped in the 4- to 7-year sector.

   2. *Yield curve risk:* The portfolio's nonparallel duration exceeds that of the benchmark (0.80 versus 0.67, per page 6). The overweighting in intermediate maturity issues creates this incremental risk. The duration and maturity distributions of page 3 further confirm this portfolio risk.

   3. *Quality risk:* The portfolio is more risky than the benchmark, in terms of average quality. The 1.50 quality spread figure exceeds the benchmark quality of 0.97 (see page 6); recall that higher figures portray greater degrees of quality risk. The average quality of the portfolio is AA, whereas the index bears a AAA average quality (see page 5). The quality distribution on page 3 is also revealing:

- The portfolio holds only 45% U.S. Treasury issues (versus 65% for the index).
- The federal agency holdings are approximately equivalent to those of the index (10% versus 11%).
- The portfolio holds far more AAAs (10% versus 2%), AAs (20% versus 9%), and BBBs (15% versus 5%) than the index, but the portfolio contains no A-rated issues (versus 8% for the index).

Not only is the portfolio positioned for a general narrowing of quality spreads, but it reflects a bias for AAAs, AAs, and BBBs (*not* agencies and As) to outperform in the anticipated narrowing move.

   4. *Call/convexity risk:* In average convexity terms, the portfolio is matched to the benchmark (0.10 versus 0.10, per page 6). The call provision distribution (page 3) is a mixed bag. The total return simulations on page 8 reflect a positive convexity bias in a bear market and a negative convexity tendency in a bull market (under the *parallel effect* column) relative to the SLGC benchmark. This return simulation is very effective in bringing out these subliminal tendencies in the portfolio's behavior vis-à-vis that of the benchmark. The average convexity figure, in itself, fails to reveal these critical characteristics.

   5. *Issuer sector risk:* Page 3 compares the issuer sector distribution of the portfolio to the benchmark index on a market value weighted basis. The portfolio is sizably underweighted in U.S. Treasuries (45% versus 65%), marginally underweighted in electric/gas bonds (4% versus 6%), approximately equally weighted in agency and finance bonds, and substantially overweighted in industrials (15% versus 7%), telephones (14% versus 3%), and internationals (5% versus 0%). The duration contribution (DC) scheme of page 4 is even more telling. It reveals that the portfolio is:

- Sizably underexposed to the U.S. Treasury (*government*) sector both in terms of MV held (45% versus 64%) and average duration of the issues held (3.97 versus 4.61). Consequently, the duration contribution of the U.S. Treasury sector is only 1.80 years, compared to 2.96 years for the index benchmark.
- Slightly overexposed to the federal agency sector (0.38 DC versus 0.36 DC) despite a marginal underweighting in MV terms.

- Heavily overexposed to the corporate bond sector, with a 45% MV weight (versus 25% for the index) combining with a 5.49 average duration (versus 5.14 for the index) to create a 2.44-year DC, almost twice that of the index (1.30). Within the corporate sector, the portfolio is overexposed to industrials (0.61 DC versus 0.41 DC), telephones (1.15 DC versus 0.23 DC), and internationals/yankees (0.31 DC versus 0.00 DC). The portfolio is underexposed to the electric/gas sector (0.14 DC versus 0.38 DC) and the finance sector (0.24 DC versus 0.28 DC).

6. *Intra-issuer sector risk, issue-specific risk, product risk, and liquidity risk:* The investor must assess the portfolio holdings in light of these risks on an issue-by-issue basis. With many of the non-Treasury positions comprising 3% of the portfolio (i.e., $3 million), care must be taken to monitor the credit and intra-issuer sector bets made versus the benchmark.

```
                                    COMPARE SYSTEM
PORTFOLIO: MULTI DURATION           PORTFOLIO APPRAISAL REPORT                        RUN DATE: 11/ 5/87
PRICING DATE:  6/30/87              --------------------------                        PAGE:        ( 1)
ENDING DATE:   7/30/87
```

| | | | | ($000) | (%) | YIELD TO | | -----DURATION YEARS---- | | PASS | |
| ($000) | | | QUALITY | COUPON | | PRICE | MARKET | TOTAL | MATURITY | | NON- | QUAL | THRU | |
PAR	CUSIP	ISSUER		(%)	MATURITY	6/30/87	VALUE	PORT.	(%)	PARA	PARA	SPRD	SPRD	CONVEX
3000	171205AP	CHRYSLER FIN	BAA	13.250	12/15/88	104.871	3163	3.1	9.583	1.37	0.90	1.37	0.00	0.01
3000	812387AH	SEARS ROEBUCK	AA	14.125	11/15/89	111.726	3405	3.4	8.552	2.08	1.06	1.04	0.00	0.02
2250	912827SZ	UNITED STATES TREAS NTS	GOV	9.125	2/15/91	103.610	2408	2.4	7.954	3.08	1.09	0.00	0.00	0.05
5000	912827US	UNITED STATES TREAS NTS	GOV	6.750	3/31/91	96.205	4895	4.9	7.934	3.31	1.13	0.00	0.00	0.06
3000	313311FT	FEDERAL FARM CR BANKS	AGY	14.100	4/22/91	117.418	3602	3.6	8.629	3.07	1.03	1.14	0.00	0.05
5000	912827TS	UNITED STATES TREAS NTS	GOV	7.500	8/15/91	98.296	5055	5.0	7.989	3.52	1.08	0.00	0.00	0.07
1000	122781AN	BURROUGHS CORP	BAA	8.000	9/15/91	95.442	978	1.0	9.328	3.45	1.05	3.45	0.00	0.00
1000	459056DC	INTERNATIONAL BK FOR RECON&D	AAA	16.625	11/ 1/91	128.748	1315	1.3	8.542	3.33	0.96	0.83	0.00	0.06
1500	616880AJ	J P MORGAN	AAA	7.100	11/15/91	95.501	1446	1.4	8.345	3.79	1.09	0.95	0.00	0.08
5000	912827RT	UNITED STATES TREAS NTS	GOV	11.625	1/15/92	113.171	5925	5.9	8.099	3.55	0.97	0.00	0.00	0.07
5000	912827SB	UNITED STATES TREAS NTS	GOV	11.750	4/15/92	114.177	5831	5.8	8.113	3.79	0.96	0.00	0.00	0.08
5000	912827NE	UNITED STATES TREAS NTS	GOV	13.750	5/15/92	122.296	6201	6.2	8.115	3.78	0.94	0.00	0.00	0.08
3000	880370AV	TENNECO INC	BAA	13.700	9/ 1/92	114.245	3563	3.5	10.087	3.81	0.87	3.81	0.00	0.09
3500	912827SV	UNITED STATES TREAS NTS	GOV	9.750	10/15/92	106.771	3808	3.8	8.144	4.22	0.93	0.00	0.00	0.10
3000	313388KR	FEDERAL HOME LN BKS	AGY	11.100	11/25/92	109.236	3309	3.3	8.905	4.22	0.90	1.56	0.00	0.10
2750	313311LF	FEDERAL FARM CR BANKS	AGY	10.650	1/20/93	107.797	3095	3.1	8.841	4.20	0.86	1.55	0.00	0.10
3000	912827TM	UNITED STATES TREAS NTS	GOV	7.375	4/15/93	96.336	2936	2.9	8.178	4.72	0.90	0.00	0.00	0.12
3500	912810BQ	UNITED STATES TREAS BONDS	GOV	7.500	8/15/93	96.426	3473	3.5	8.252	4.20	0.96	0.00	0.00	-0.31
3000	912827PV	UNITED STATES TREAS NTS	GOV	11.875	8/15/93	117.080	3646	3.6	8.261	4.49	0.78	0.00	0.00	0.12
3000	370424EK	GMAC	AA	8.000	10/15/93	96.371	2941	2.9	8.758	4.95	0.82	2.48	0.00	0.14
3000	538021AD	LITTON INDS INC *	BAA	11.500	7/ 1/95	106.033	3353	3.3	9.943	4.24	0.86	4.24	0.00	-0.00
3000	345370AL	FORD MTR CO DEL *	AA	10.750	7/ 1/95	107.018	3371	3.4	8.982	4.29	0.89	2.14	0.00	-0.00
3000	171196AJ	CHRYSLER CORP *	BAA	13.000	3/ 1/97	111.561	3476	3.5	10.738	5.29	0.55	5.29	0.00	0.14
1750	459056CA	INTERNATIONAL BK FOR RECO	AAA	9.350	12/15/00	101.906	1790	1.8	9.101	4.81	0.79	1.20	0.00	-0.84
500	837208AC	SO CENT BELL TEL	AAA	8.250	12/ 1/04	90.492	456	0.5	9.366	9.07	0.03	2.27	0.00	0.66
1000	912810CS	UNITED STATES TREAS BOND *	GOV	12.750	11/15/10	134.989	1366	1.4	8.859	8.70	0.06	0.00	0.00	0.56
500	674599AW	OCCIDENTAL PETE *	BAA	11.750	3/15/11	108.626	560	0.6	10.554	7.30	0.12	7.30	0.00	0.10
1750	650094AU	NY TELEPHONE	AA	8.300	8/15/12	87.903	1593	1.6	9.579	9.77	0.00	4.89	0.00	0.91
3000	845335AS	SOUTHWESTERN BELL TEL CO	AA	8.250	3/ 1/14	87.120	2695	2.7	9.594	9.94	0.00	4.97	0.00	0.96
3000	624284AU	MT STS TEL&TEL	AA	8.000	9/15/17	84.342	2600	2.6	9.594	10.23	0.00	5.12	0.00	1.09
3000	842332BE	SOUTHRN BELL TEL	AA	10.750	12/18/25	108.433	3264	3.3	9.894	6.06	0.43	3.03	0.00	-0.66
3000	837208AT	SO CENT BELL TELL	AAA	10.375	12/30/25	106.057	3182	3.2	9.768	7.15	0.21	1.79	0.00	-0.28
1750	459056JQ	INTERNATIONAL BK FOR RECON&D	AAA	8.875	3/ 1/26	95.037	1714	1.7	9.351	10.59	0.00	2.65	0.00	1.03

PORTFOLIO: MULTI DURATION   PORTFOLIO SUMMARY REPORT   RUN DATE: 11/ 5/87
PRICING DATE: 6/30/87   ------------------------   PAGE: (2)
ENDING DATE: 7/30/87

| | | | | | | | | ----DURATION IN YEARS---- | | | | |
| ----------($000)---------- | | ANNUAL | AVERAGE | AVERAGE COUPON | AVERAGE MATURITY | YIELD TO MATURITY | | NON- | QUAL | PASS THRU | |
PAR VALUE	MKT VALUE	INCOME	QUALITY	(%)	YEARS	(%)	PARA	PARA	SPRD	SPRD	CONVEXITY
92750	100415	9700	AA	10.661	9.937	8.806	4.63	0.80	1.50	0.00	0.10

COMPARE SYSTEM
PORTFOLIO DISTRIBUTION

PORTFOLIO: MULTI DURATION
PRICING DATE: 6/30/87
ENDING DATE: 7/30/87

RUN DATE: 11/ 5/87
PAGE: (3)

DURATION YEARS	PORTFOLIO % HELD	INDEX % HELD		MATURITY YEARS	PORTFOLIO % HELD	INDEX % HELD
CASH	0	0		CASH	0	0
0 - 1	0	2		0 - 1	0	0
1 - 2	3	16		1 - 2	3	12
2 - 3	3	17		2 - 3	3	11
3 - 4	41	15		3 - 4	11	11
4 - 5	32	13		4 - 5	27	10
5 - 6	3	9		5 - 7	27	12
6 - 7	3	4		7 - 10	10	12
7 - 8	4	6		10 - 15	2	7
8 - 9	1	8		15 - 20	0	10
9 - 10	5	5		20 - 25	2	6
10 +	4	5		25+	15	9

ISSUING SECTOR	PORTFOLIO % HELD	INDEX % HELD		QUALITY	PORTFOLIO % HELD	INDEX % HELD
CASH	0	0		CASH	0	0
GOVERNMENT	45	64		GOVERNMENT	45	64
AGENCY	10	11		AGENCY	10	11
PASS-THRU	0	0		AAA	10	2
INDUSTRIAL	15	7		AA	20	9
ELECTRIC / GAS	4	7		A	0	9
TELEPHONE	14	3		BAA	15	5
FINANCE	8	8		OTHER	0	0
INTERNATIONAL	5	0				
OTHER	0	0				

COUPON	PORTFOLIO % HELD	INDEX % HELD		CALL PROVISIONS	PORTFOLIO % HELD	INDEX % HELD
CASH	0	0		NONE (INCL. CASH)	68	68
0 - 7	5	5		WITH FUTURE CALL	29	15
7 - 9	26	23		WITH CURRENT CALL	3	17
9 - 11	21	28				
11 - 13	24	27		PRICE TO CALL	12	20
13 - 15	23	15				
15+	1	2				

```
                          COMPARE SYSTEM
                  DURATION-WEIGHTED DISTRIBUTION
                  ------------------------------
```

```
PORTFOLIO: MULTI DURATION                                    RUN DATE: 11/ 5/87
PRICING DATE:  6/30/87                                       PAGE:        ( 4)
ENDING DATE :  7/30/87
```

	PORTFOLIO				INDEX		
ISSUING SECTOR	MKT VALUE ($000)	% HELD	PARALLEL DURATION (YRS)	CONTRIBUTION TO DURATION (YRS)	% HELD	PARALLEL DURATION (YRS)	CONTRIBUTION TO DURATION (YRS)
CASH	0	0	0.00	0.00	0	0.00	0.00
GOVERNMENT	45544	45	3.97	1.80	64	4.61	2.96
AGENCY	10006	10	3.80	0.38	11	3.19	0.36
PASS-THRU	0	0	0.00	0.00	0	0.00	0.00
CORPORATE	44861	45	5.49	2.44	25	5.14	1.30
INDUSTRIALS	15141	15	4.07	0.61	7	4.98	0.41
ELECTRIC/GAS	3563	4	3.81	0.14	7	5.30	0.38
TELEPHONES	13789	14	8.38	1.15	3	7.38	0.23
FINANCE	7549	8	3.23	0.24	8	3.89	0.28
INTERNATIONAL	4819	5	6.46	0.31	0	0.00	0.00
OTHER	0	0	0.00	0.00	0	0.00	0.00
				4.63			4.62

```
NOTE:  INDEX VALUES ARE AS OF MOST RECENT FRIDAY DATE.
       THIS MAY NOT CORRESPOND TO FOUR FACTOR DURATION
       INDEX VALUES, WHICH ARE PRICING DATE SPECIFIC.
```

COMPARE SYSTEM
PORTFOLIO SUMMARY

PORTFOLIO: MULTI DURATION   RUN DATE: 11/ 5/87
PRICING DATE: 6/30/87   FUNDAMENTALS   PAGE: (5)
ENDING DATE: 7/30/87

PORTFOLIO VS. LBGC

	YIELD TO MATURITY (%)	CURRENT YIELD (%)	QUALITY	COUPON (%)	MATURITY YEARS
	--------	-------	-------	------	--------
PORTFOLIO ASSETS ----------------					
	8.806	9.902	AA	10.661	9.937
LBKL GOV/CORP INDEX -------------------					
	8.310	8.656	AAA	9.100	9.550
DIFFERENCE ----------					
	0.496	1.246		1.561	0.387

                                         COMPARE SYSTEM
PORTFOLIO: MULTI DURATION   PORTFOLIO SUMMARY REPORT   RUN DATE: 11/ 5/87
PRICING DATE: 6/30/87   -----------------------   PAGE: (6)
ENDING DATE: 7/30/87

                                       FOUR FACTOR DURATION

                                       PORTFOLIO VS. LBGC

                                    -----DURATION IN YEARS-----
                                                          PASS
                          YIELD TO   NON- QUAL THRU
                          MATURITY   PARA PARA SPRD SPRD   CONVEXITY
                          --------   ----- ----- ----- ----- ---------

PORTFOLIO ASSETS

                           8.806   4.63 0.80 1.50 0.00   0.10

LBKL GOV/CORP INDEX

                           8.310   4.62 0.67 0.97 0.00   0.10

DIFFERENCE

                           0.496   0.01 0.13 0.53 0.00   -0.00

COMPARE SYSTEM
SENSITIVITY ANALYSIS
0.08 YEAR HORIZON

PORTFOLIO: MULTI DURATION
PRICING DATE: 6/30/87
ENDING DATE: 7/30/87

                                     PORTFOLIO

RUN DATE: 11/ 5/87
PAGE: (7)

TOTAL RETURN COMPONENTS

INTEREST RATE CHANGE BASIS POINTS	INCOME EFFECT	PARALLEL EFFECT (%)	NON-PARALLEL EFFECT (%)	QUALITY SPREAD EFFECT (%)	PASS-THRU SPREAD EFFECT (%)
-400	0.703	16.940	3.136	5.209	0.000
-350	0.705	14.936	2.728	4.636	0.000
-300	0.707	12.971	2.326	4.074	0.000
-250	0.710	11.026	1.930	3.512	0.000
-200	0.712	9.012	1.540	2.908	0.000
-150	0.714	6.806	1.153 *	2.205	0.000
-100	0.716	4.518	0.768	1.460 *	0.000 *
-50	0.718	2.245 *	0.384	0.722	0.000
0	0.721	0.000 **	0.000 **	0.000 **	0.000 **
50	0.723	-2.194 *	-0.380	-0.704	0.000
100	0.725	-4.333	-0.755	-1.390 *	0.000 *
150	0.727	-6.399	-1.125 *	-2.049	0.000
200	0.730	-8.382	-1.487	-2.680	0.000
250	0.732	-10.271	-1.842	-3.277	0.000
300	0.734	-12.061	-2.187	-3.839	0.000
350	0.736	-13.746	-2.524	-4.362	0.000
400	0.738	-15.323	-2.851	-4.844	0.000

** MEAN INTEREST RATE CHANGE
* 10% TO 90% CONFIDENCE INTERVAL

```
                        COMPARE SYSTEM
                    SENSITIVITY ANALYSIS
                      0.08 YEAR HORIZON
                    --------------------
PORTFOLIO: MULTI DURATION          PORTFOLIO VS. LB6C                    RUN DATE: 11/ 5/87
PRICING DATE:  6/30/87                                                   PAGE:        ( 8)
ENDING DATE:   7/30/87
```

TOTAL RETURN DIFFERENCES

INTEREST RATE CHANGE BASIS POINTS	INCOME EFFECT	PARALLEL EFFECT (%)	NON-PARALLEL EFFECT (%)	QUALITY SPREAD EFFECT (%)	PASS-THRU SPREAD EFFECT (%)
-400	0.037	-2.403	0.331	1.148	0.000
-350	0.038	-1.814	0.299	1.120	0.000
-300	0.038	-1.236	0.266	1.091	0.000
-250	0.038	-0.688	0.231	1.053	0.000
-200	0.039	-0.259	0.195	0.961	0.000
-150	0.039	-0.072	0.155 *	0.761	0.000
-100	0.039	-0.018	0.110	0.508 *	0.000 *
-50	0.040	0.002 *	0.059	0.252	0.000
0	0.040	0.000 **	0.000 **	0.000 **	0.000 **
50	0.040	-0.001 *	-0.062	-0.244	0.000
100	0.041	0.002	-0.127	-0.479 *	0.000 *
150	0.041	0.029	-0.193 *	-0.699	0.000
200	0.041	0.089	-0.259	-0.901	0.000
250	0.041	0.193	-0.324	-1.080	0.000
300	0.042	0.346	-0.388	-1.234	0.000
350	0.042	0.554	-0.450	-1.359	0.000
400	0.042	0.820	-0.510	-1.454	0.000

```
** MEAN INTEREST RATE CHANGE
*  10% TO 90% CONFIDENCE INTERVAL
```

COMPARE SYSTEM
TRACKING SUMMARY

PORTFOLIO: MULTI DURATION   RUN DATE: 11/ 5/87
PRICING DATE: 6/30/87   PORTFOLIO VS. LBGC   PAGE: (9)
ENDING DATE: 7/30/87

TABLE OF EXPECTED RETURN DIFFERENCES

| | ------------ M O N T H S ------------ | | | |
	(3)	(6)	(9)	(12)
10% C.L.	0.69	0.81	0.92	1.03
25% C.L.	0.45	.0.57	0.68	0.79
MEAN	0.11	0.22	0.33	0.45
75% C.L.	-0.23	-0.12	-0.01	0.11
90% C.L.	-0.47	-0.36	-0.25	-0.13

Glossary of Key Terms

Accrued interest: the interest earned, but not yet paid, on a bond investment. A bond purchased between coupon payment dates is subject to accrued interest.

Accumulated investment base (AIB): the amount of dollars subject to reinvestment (i.e., coupon receipts plus any interest-on-interest earned).

Active investor: an investor who buys and sells bonds on a regular, ongoing basis. This investor rarely holds a bond until final maturity.

Actual/actual basis: under this approach, accrued interest is calculated on the basis of the actual number of days transpiring since the last coupon payment date and the actual number of days in the interval between the last coupon payment date and the upcoming coupon payment date. The actual/actual basis is used with U.S. Treasury bonds.

Aggregate bond index: a bond index that includes mortgage passthroughs in its composition.

Aggressive investments (or portfolios): investments offering a combination of high risk and high return.

Alpha (α): see *bond alpha*.

Amortized cost: see *book value*.

Annual-pay bond: a bond that makes coupon payments on an annual basis.

Arithmetic mean return: a simple average of a series of individual periodic returns.

Average convexity: see *portfolio convexity*.

Average convexity factor: the average of two or more convexity factors; typically an average of the convexity factors for a rise and a fall in interest rates of similar magnitude (e.g., 200 basis points).

Average duration: see *portfolio duration*.

Average duration risk: see *portfolio duration*.

Average life: see *weighted average maturity*.

Average quality: see *portfolio quality*.

Average quality risk: see *portfolio quality*.

Average return: see *arithmetic mean return* and *geometric mean return*.

Average yield curve risk: the weighted average exposure of a bond portfolio to nonparallel shifts in the yield curve; also see *nonparallel duration* and *maturity (or duration) distribution*.

Balloon payment: the final principal repayment on a sinking fund bond; also termed the *balloon*.

Baseline total return curve: a projected total return curve predicated on the simple assumption of a status quo environment.

Basis point (BP): 1/100th of 1%; 0.0001 in decimal form.

Basis point (BP) add-on: the basis point difference between a 1-year holding-period return and a semiannually compounded expression of the identical 1-year return.

Bear market: a period of rising interest rates and falling bond prices.

Benchmark: a comparative base for performance evaluation. A benchmark can be a broad-based bond index, a customized bond index, or a specific client objective.

Beta (β): see *bond beta*.

Beta-changer: see *market timer*.

Bond: a financial obligation for which the issuer promises to pay the bondholder a specified stream of future cash flows, including periodic interest payments (i.e., coupons) and a principal repayment.

Bond alpha (α): The *Y*-intercept of the least-squares regression line that best represents the relationship between a bond's return and the market return (defining the *Y*-axis as the excess return of the bond vis-à-vis the market return). Positive alpha is the excess return that the bond generates above and beyond the return suggested by the security market line; negative alpha is a shortfall in actual returns vis-à-vis the security market line.

Bond beta (β): The slope of the least-squares regression line that best represents the relationship between a bond's return and the market return. In formula terminology, beta is the covariance of the security and market returns divided by the variance of the market returns. By definition, the market portfolio bears a beta of 1.0. Bonds with betas of less than 1.0 are termed *defensive investments;* bonds with betas of greater than 1.0 are regarded as *aggressive investments*.

Bond index: a composite of bond issues designed to replicate the structure and perfor-

mance behavior of a specific segment(s) of the bond market.

Bond market portfolio: see *market portfolio*.

Bond price: the market value of a bond, expressed either in dollars (e.g., $845.00) or as a percentage of par value (e.g., 84.50).

Bond price sensitivity: the sensitivity of a bond's price to changes in interest rates; in this book, the terms *bond price sensitivity* and *bond price volatility* are used interchangeably.

Bond price volatility: see *bond price sensitivity*.

Bond value: the market value of a bond; see *bond price*.

Book gain: an accounting-based gain that is calculated as the increase in book value over a specified period of time. Additionally, a book gain includes the excess of a bond's sale price over its book value on the date of sale (see *realized gain*).

Book loss: an accounting-based loss that is calculated as the decrease in book value over a specified period of time. Additionally, a book loss includes the excess of a bond's book value on the date of sale over the bond's sale price (see *realized loss*).

Book value: the amortized cost, or cost basis, of a bond investment; calculated as the original purchase price as adjusted for scientific amortization of the bond's premium or discount over the holding period.

Breakeven reinvestment rate (BERR): the reinvestment rate that equalizes the returns between two alternative investments.

Breakeven yield level: the end-of-holding-period yield level that leads to equivalent returns between a longer maturity bond and a shorter maturity counterpart. The longer the maturity (and duration) of the issue involved, the less protection it provides against rising interest rates vis-à-vis its less volatile substitute.

Breakeven yield spread: the end-of-holding-period yield spread that leads to equivalent returns between two alternative investments.

Bull market: a period of falling interest rates and rising bond prices.

Bullet: the intermediate maturity bond in a dumbbell/bullet swap.

Bullet bond: a noncallable bond that repays its entire principal at final maturity.

Bullet-to-dumbbell swap: a swap from an intermediate maturity bond (bullet) into a short maturity:long maturity combination (dumbbell).

Buy-and-hold investor: an investor who purchases bonds and holds them until final maturity.

Buy-and-hold strategy: purchasing bonds and holding them until final maturity; turnover is minimized in such a strategy (0% turnover rate during the holding period).

Call-adjusted yield (CAY): a yield to maturity based on the equivalent price of a noncallable security.

Call option: the right to redeem a security at a prespecified price (strike price) over a specified time period. Corporate bonds typically give the bond issuer a series of call options with progressively lower strike prices over time. The call option(s) may be a refunding call or a cash call.

Call risk: the risk that the issuer will redeem the bond prior to final maturity, forcing the bondholder to reinvest the proceeds in a lower yielding environment.

Call or convexity risk: the risk of unexpected returns attributable to call and convexity features. Noncallable bonds provide incremental returns (positive convexity) whereas callable bonds are susceptible to unpleasant return surprises (negative convexity). A comparison of the *coupon distribution* of a portfolio versus that of a chosen benchmark reveals the call or convexity biases of the portfolio.

Callable bond: a bond that is redeemable prior to final maturity at a prespecified price over a prespecified time period. The bond may have cash call and/or refunding call features.

Capital market line (CML): a plotting of risk:return combinations in a straight-line form. The risk-free rate of interest and the market return form the basis for the line

construction. The standard deviation in total return serves as the risk measure.

Cash call: An early redemption provision in which the debt issue can be paid off with excess cash flow (e.g., from business operations, from asset sales) but cannot be refinanced with new, lower cost debt.

Cash flow yield: the discount rate that equates the present value of a bond's future cash flows to the bond's current market price. Generally applied to sinking fund bonds and mortgage-backed securities. Also termed *discounted cash flow (DCF) yield.*

Compound interest: interest earned on both the principal amount and the reinvestment of coupon cash flows.

Compound interest accumulation: see *accumulated investment base.*

Compound interest factor: the multiplier that translates the present value of an investment into a future value—$(1 + i)^n$; also termed a *future value factor.*

Compounded return: total return expressed in a periodically compounded form.

Compounding: moving from a present value to a future value; the opposite of *discounting.*

Concavity: see *negative convexity.*

Contribution: an additional investment into an existing portfolio or fund.

Convex: cup-shaped away from the origin of the graph.

Convexity: the curvature of the price:yield relationship of a noncallable bond away from the origin of the graph (*convex* to the origin); also see *positive convexity.*

Convexity enhancement swap: a swap into a more positively convex (or a less negatively convex) bond.

Convexity factor: the convexity return per 100BP change in yield.

Convexity returns: price returns in excess of those predicted by the modified duration of a bond (see *positive convexity*); negative price impacts are attributable to *negative convexity.*

Coupon: a periodic interest amount paid to the bondholder by the issuer of the bond.

The coupon payment is typically made semiannually; therefore, the coupon amount is calculated as:

$$\frac{\text{semiannual coupon}}{\text{payment}} = \frac{\text{principal}}{\text{amount}} \times \frac{\text{coupon}}{\text{rate}} \times \frac{1}{2}$$

Coupon distribution: a market value based stratification of a portfolio's coupon structure (e.g., 0–5%, 5–7%, . . . , 14+%); used in assessing a portfolio's call/convexity risk.

Coupon drop: another term for coupon payment; see *coupon*.

Coupon rate of interest: the annual interest rate stated on a bond and paid by the issuer of the bond; also termed the *stated rate of interest*.

Coupon return: the return attributable to coupon receipts and accruals; can be expressed in either dollars or percentages.

Coupon sector swap: a swap into a bond in a more attractively priced coupon sector.

Coupon spread: the yield spread between a high coupon bond and a low coupon bond of similar maturity.

Credit risk: the risk that (1) the issuer is downgraded to a lower quality category and/or (2) the issuer fails to make timely payments of interest or principal.

Crossover price: the price at which a bond's *yield to maturity* and *yield to call* are equal.

Crossover yield: the yield that corresponds to a bond's *crossover price*.

Current-coupon yield curve: the yield curve for the on-the-run, current auction U.S. Treasury issues.

Current yield (CY): the annual percentage coupon return on a bond based on the bond's current market price.

Current yield enhancement swap: a swap into a bond offering additional current yield.

Defensive investments (or portfolios): investments offering a combination of low risk and low return.

Discount: the amount by which a bond's par value exceeds the bond's price.

Discount bond: a bond selling at a price below par value (in dollar terms, less than

$1,000.00; in percentage of par terms, less than 100.00).

Discount interest factor: the multiplier that translates the future value of an investment into its present value equivalent— $1/(1 + i)^n$; also termed a *present value factor*.

Discount rate of interest: the rate of interest at which future cash flows are discounted to the present.

Discounted cash flow (DCF) yield: see *cash flow yield*.

Discounting: moving from a *future value* to a *present value;* the opposite of *compounding*.

Distribution: see *withdrawal*.

Dollar payup: the additional outlay required in a *par-for-par swap* into a higher priced bond.

Dollar takeout: the net cash inflow resulting from a *par-for-par swap* into a lower priced bond.

Dollar-weighted rate of return (DWROR): the internal rate of return for a portfolio of bonds. By nature, this rate of return is influenced by the portfolio size during the performance period and is, therefore, impacted by *contributions* to, and *withdrawals* from, the portfolio.

Dumbbell: the combination of a short maturity bond and a long maturity bond; used in dumbbell/bullet swapping.

Dumbbell/bullet swap: a swap from a short maturity:long maturity combination (*dumbbell*) into an intermediate maturity bond (*bullet*) or vice versa.

Dumbbell-to-bullet swap: a swap from a short maturity:long maturity combination (*dumbbell*) into an intermediate maturity bond (*bullet*).

Duration: the weighted average maturity of a bond's cash flow stream, where the present values of the cash flows serve as the weights; the future point in time at which, on average, an investor has received exactly half of the original investment, in present value terms; a bond's zero-coupon equivalent; the fulcrum of a bond's present value cash flow timeline. Also called *Macaulay's duration*.

Duration contribution: the absolute amount of a portolio's duration that is contributed by the portfolio holdings in a specific market sector (e.g., 1.25 years of the total portfolio duration of 7.50 years); calculated as the sector duration times the sector weighting (based on market values).

Duration-dollars: a duration-weighted dollar concept; found by multiplying the duration of an investment by its market value.

Duration risk: the sensitivity of a bond (or bond portfolio) to parallel shifts in interest rates. Modified Macaulay's duration attempts to describe this risk under conditions of small moves in interest rates. Larger shifts in interest rates introduce additional risk factors, including yield curve risk, call/convexity risk, and sector spread change risk (quality sector, issuer sector, etc.).

Duration to call: the duration of a bond to the first call date; the bond is expected to be prematurely called.

Duration to maturity: the duration of a bond to the final maturity date; the bond is expected to remain outstanding until final maturity.

Duration weight: the percentage contribution of a portfolio's duration that is attributable to the portfolio holdings in a particular market sector; calculated as the sector duration contribution divided by the overall portfolio duration.

Duration-weighted contraction swap: a swap from a long maturity issue into a shorter maturity issue. The swap is risk-neutralized through the use of duration as the risk measure. A duration-weighted contraction swap is undertaken with the expectation of a steepening of the yield curve.

Duration-weighted dumbbell/bullet swap: a swap either from a short maturity:long maturity combination into an intermediate maturity issue (dumbbell-to-bullet swap) or vice versa (bullet-to-dumbbell swap). The swap is risk-neutralized through the use of duration as a risk measure.

Duration-weighted extension swap: a swap from a short maturity issue into a longer maturity issue. The swap is risk-neutralized through the use of duration as the risk measure. A duration-weighted extension swap is undertaken with the expectation of a flattening of the yield curve.

Effective duration: the duration of a bond given its current market price, its call features, and an expected level of future interest rate volatility. Effective duration is bounded by the *duration to call* and the *duration to maturity*. Also termed *adjusted duration, call-adjusted duration,* and *option-adjusted duration*.

Effective interest amortization: see *scientific amortization*.

Effective maturity: the average maturity of a bond, given the potential for early call. For a noncallable bond, the final maturity date serves as the effective maturity. For a callable bond, the effective maturity is bounded by the first call date (shortest potential maturity) and the final maturity date (longest potential maturity); the position within this continuum is a function of the call price, the current market price, and the yield volatility assumed. The effective maturity is positively related to the call price, and is inversely related to the market price and the volatility level.

Efficient frontier: the series of efficient portfolios that covers the risk spectrum.

Efficient market: a market in which all securities are fairly valued by rational, profit-seeking investors who utilize all publicly available information pertaining to the securities in establishing market-clearing prices.

Efficient portfolio: a portfolio that offers the highest level of return for a given level of risk. Alternatively, a portfolio that offers the lowest level of risk for a given level of return. Risk-averse investors always prefer efficient portfolios.

Esoteric security (or sector): A security (or sector) with nontraditional features (e.g., put options, unusual call options, unique sinking fund provisions, currency options, commodity-linked performance). Not understood by the typical market participant; examples include CMOs, IOs, POs, oil index bonds, REALS, and pay-in-kind bonds. Opposite of *generic security (or sector)*.

Expectations theory: a theory asserting that the shape of the yield curve reflects investors' expectations regarding the future trend in interest rates. Expectations of rising rates create a positively sloped yield curve; expectations of falling rates create a negatively sloped yield curve; and expectations of stable rates create a flat yield curve.

Extra-market risk: see *unsystematic risk*.

Face value: see *principal amount*.

Fixed-income security: a financial instrument promising a fixed amount of periodic income over a specified future time span. See *bond*.

Flat yield curve: a yield curve in which short maturity issues, intermediate maturity issues, and long maturity issues trade at similar yields.

Forward rate (FR): the marginal yield between two successive spot rates; a future interest rate implied by the shape of the spot rate curve.

Full price (or full purchase price): the price of a bond, inclusive of accrued interest.

Future value (FV): the value of an investment or cash flow at a specified future point in time.

Future value factor: see *compound interest factor*.

Gain: an increase in wealth from an accounting standpoint; see *book gain*.

General interest rate risk: the risk that the general level of interest rates will change, causing unexpected price appreciations/(depreciations).

Generic security (or sector): a security (or sector) with traditional features. The average market participant understands the structure and mechanics of a generic security (or sector). Examples include U.S. Treasury bonds, federal agency bonds, standard structure corporate bonds, and mortgage passthrough securities. Opposite of *esoteric security (or sector)*.

Geometric mean return: the compounded total return of an investment over a multi-period time frame; an internal rate of return that connects the initial value of an investment to its end-of-measurement-period value.

Gross return: total return before subtracting management fees.

Half-life: the point in time at which exactly half of a bond's principal has been repaid.

Historical total return curve: a total return curve predicated on historical returns.

Holding-period duration: the duration of a bond for a given holding period. The duration figure can be an average for the period or, simply, a duration as of the end of the holding period.

Holding-period return (HPR): the total return on an investment over a specified holding period; also termed a *noncompounded total return*.

Humped yield curve: a yield curve in which intermediate maturity issues trade at higher yields than both short maturity issues and long maturity issues.

Illiquidity: the degree of inability to buy or sell a bond at a fair market price in a timely manner.

Illiquid security: a security that cannot be traded in a timely manner at a fair market price.

Inefficient market: a market in which undervalued securities and overvalued securities can be found.

Inferior investments (or portfolios): investments offering a combination of high risk and low return.

Inflation premium: the component of a nominal interest rate that compensates the investor for expected future inflation. The inflation premium is intended to maintain the purchasing power of an investor.

Interest: the cost of borrowing money (borrower's viewpoint); the compensation for deferring consumption to a future period (lender's viewpoint).

Interest-on-interest: see *reinvestment return*.

Interest rate: the market-clearing price of money as expressed in percentage terms (e.g., 9.50%).

Interest rate anticipation swap: a risk-altering swap that attempts to take advantage of expected future movements in the general level of interest rates.

Internal rate of return (IRR): the discount rate that equates the present value of a bond's future cash flows to the bond's current market price. Examples of IRRs include the *yield to maturity*, the *yield to call* and the *cash flow yield*.

Intra-issuer sector risk: the risk associated with over/(under)exposure to various industries within a given issuer sector; assessed by a comparison to a chosen benchmark.

Intra-issuer sector swap: a swap into a more attractively priced bond within the same issuer sector.

Issue-specific risk: the risk associated with over/(under)exposure to individual issuers or individual issues; assessed by a comparison to a chosen benchmark.

Issue-specific swap: a swap into a more attractively priced bond in the same general issuer category and in the same industry sector (perhaps even the same company).

Issuer sector decision: the decision regarding a bond portfolio's exposure to various issuer sectors (e.g., U.S. Treasuries, federal agencies, industrials, financials, utilities).

Issuer sector risk: the risk associated with over/(under)exposure to various issuer sectors; assessed by a comparison to a chosen benchmark.

Issuer sector swap: a swap into a bond in a more attractively priced issuer sector.

Least-squares regression line: see *regression line*.

Liquidity: the ability to purchase or sell an investment in a timely manner at a fair market price; the ability to recover the principal of a bond in a reasonably short period of time (liquidity preference theory).

Liquidity enhancement swap: a swap into a more liquid security.

Liquidity preference theory: a theory asserting that the shape of the yield curve reflects investors' desires for liquidity; therefore, the yield curve should be modestly upward sloping.

Liquidity risk: the risk that an investment will be difficult to sell at a fair market price in a timely fashion.

Loss: a decrease in wealth from an accounting standpoint; see *book loss*.

Macaulay's duration: see *duration*.

Market portfolio: the portfolio of securities representing the market (e.g., the bond market).

Market return: the total return on the market portfolio over a specified time period.

Market segmentation theory: a theory asserting that the shape of the yield curve is determined by the linking of a sequence of submarkets of supply and demand for funds. The interest rates in each market sector form the composite yield curve.

Market timer: an investor who anticipates general changes in interest rates and adjusts portfolio holdings based on those predilections. This investor maintains a low duration (or low beta) portfolio in periods of rising interest rates and maintains a high duration (or high beta) portfolio in periods of falling interest rates. Also termed a *beta-changer*.

Market value weight: the relative amount of the total portfolio value that is attributable to a specific portfolio member or group of members (e.g., a sector).

Maturity (or duration) decision: the decision with regard to a bond portfolio's average maturity or average duration; that is, the decision regarding the general level of market risk exposure.

Maturity (or duration) distribution: a market value based stratification of a portfolio's maturity (or duration) structure (e.g., 1–2 years, 2–3 years, . . . , 30+ years); used in the assessment of a portfolio's yield curve risk.

Maturity sector swap: a swap into a bond in a more attractively priced maturity sector.

Median: the middle value; the observation above which half of the total observations lie and below which half of the total observations lie.

Modified duration: a mathematically adjusted version of Macaulay's duration; calculated by dividing Macaulay's duration by (1 + YTM/2) for semiannual-pay bonds. Serves as a measure of the sensitivity of a bond's price to changes in interest rates.

Modified duration line: the tangent line to the price:yield curve at a specified market price and a corresponding market yield.

Negative alpha: see *bond alpha*.

Negative convexity: that portion of the curvature of the price:yield relationship for a callable bond that faces the origin of the graph (concave to the origin). In this section of the price:yield curve, the modified duration tangent line lies above the price:yield curve; therefore, relative to duration-suggested price changes, negative return impacts occur. Also termed *concavity*.

Negatively sloped yield curve: a yield curve in which short maturity issues trade at higher yields than progressively longer maturity issues; also termed a *downward-sloping yield curve*.

Net price: the quoted price of a bond, excluding accrued interest.

Neutral portfolios: bond portfolios with average market risk (beta = 1.00).

Neutral (or normal) position: the sector weighting of a specified benchmark portfolio or index; this weighting can be market value based or duration based.

Nominal interest rate: the quoted interest rate; comprised of a real rate of interest, an inflation premium, and a risk premium.

Nominal return: the absolute or stated return.

Nominal (face) value: the stated value of a cash flow.

Noncompounded total return: see *holding-period return*.

Nonparallel (NP) duration: a portfolio average used by Capital Management Sciences to assess a portfolio's exposure to nonparallel shifts in the shape of the yield curve.

Nonparallel shift TR curve: a total return curve emanating from the assumption of a nonparallel change in yields.

Observed duration: the price sensitivity of a bond as observed in real life; calculated as the actual percentage change in price divided by the actual BP change in yield. The observed duration will vary as the result of the magnitude and the direction of the observed yield change.

Par bond: a bond selling at a price equal to par value (in dollar terms, $1,000.00; in percentage of par terms, 100.00).

Par value: see *principal amount*.

Par-for-par swap (or trade): a swap in which the par amount held is unchanged.

Parallel duration: a portfolio average used by Capital Management Sciences to assess a portfolio's average call-adjusted Macaulay's duration.

Percentile ranking: the position of a portfolio's performance relative to a universe of portfolio performances; can range from the 1st percentile (top 1% of the observations) to the 100th percentile (bottom 1% of the observations).

Plain vanilla security (or sector): see *generic security (or sector)*.

Portfolio alpha (α): the Y-intercept of the least-squares regression line that best represents the relationship between a bond portfolio's return and the market return. Alternatively, the portfolio alpha is the excess return that the bond portfolio generates above and beyond the return suggested by the security market line.

Portfolio beta (β): the slope of the least-squares regression line that best represents the relationship between a bond portfolio's return and the market return. In formula terms, the bond portfolio beta is the covariance of the portfolio and market returns divided by the variance of the market returns. By definition, the market portfolio bears a beta of 1.00. Bond portfolios with betas of less than 1.00 are termed *defensive investments;* bond portfolios with betas of greater than 1.00 are termed *aggressive investments*.

Portfolio convexity: the convexity of a portfolio of bonds; calculated as the weighted average convexity of the component securities, where the market values serve as the weights.

Portfolio duration: the duration of a portfolio of bonds; calculated as the weighted average duration of the component securities, where the market values serve as the weights.

Portfolio liquidity risk: the relative ease with which a portfolio's holdings can be traded. Difficulty in finding a liquid market to quickly and efficiently trade the portfolio holdings implies a greater degree of liquidity risk.

Portfolio quality: the weighted average quality of a bond portfolio; calculated by assigning numeric values to quality categories and summing the contributions as weighted by market values or duration weights. Also see *quality distribution.*

Portfolio RCY: the market value weighted average of the RCYs of the individual portfolio members.

Portfolio return: the total return on a portfolio of bonds; derived as the weighted average of the total returns of the component bonds, where the market values serve as the weights.

Positive alpha: see *bond alpha.*

Positive convexity: the incremental price returns garnered by the curvature of the price:yield relationship of a noncallable bond; price returns in excess of those predicted by the modified duration of the bond.

Positively sloped yield curve: a yield curve in which short maturity issues trade at lower yields than progressively longer maturity issues; also termed an *upward sloping yield curve.*

Premium: the amount by which a bond's price exceeds the bond's par value.

Premium bond: a bond selling at a price above par value (in dollar terms, greater than $1,000.00; in percentage of par terms, greater than 100.00).

Present value (PV): the current value of an investment or cash flow; the current market value of an investment; the value of an investment or cash flow as expressed in today's dollars.

Present value factor: see *discount interest factor.*

Price:yield curve: the curve representing the relationship between a bond's price and a bond's yield.

Price return: the return attributable to the capital appreciation or depreciation of an investment; calculated as the change in dollar price; can be expressed in either dollars or percentages.

Price volatility multiplier: the modified duration of a bond as adjusted by a convexity factor; a better predictor of bond price volatility than the modified duration alone.

Principal amount: the underlying stated value of a bond, typically repaid at final maturity; generally, this value is $1,000.00. The principal amount serves as the basis for calculating coupon payment amounts. Also termed the *principal,* the *par value,* or the *face value.*

Proceeds swap (or trade): a swap in which the total amount of dollars invested remains the same; that is, the sale proceeds are fully invested in the newly purchased security.

Product risk: the risk that stems from purchasing unique or esoteric fixed-income products. A full understanding of the cash flow features of the specific security is critical to controlling this risk. A limitation on the amount of holdings of esoteric products is also helpful.

Projected total return curve: a total return curve predicated on expectations or projections of future returns.

Quality distribution: a market value based stratification of a portfolio's quality structure (e.g., U.S. Treasury, federal agency, AAA, AA, A, BBB); used in assessing a portfolio's quality/credit risk.

Quality enhancement swap: a swap into a higher quality bond.

Quality or credit risk: the risk of yield spread changes between various quality sectors as the result of changes in credit perceptions. For an individual bond holding, quality risk entails the risk of a deteriorating ability to meet interest or principal payments and, potentially, default.

Quality sector decision: the decision regarding a bond portfolio's exposure to various quality sectors (e.g., U.S. Treasuries, federal agencies, AAAs, AAs, As, BBBs).

Quality sector swap: a swap into a bond in a more attractively priced quality sector.

Quality spread: the yield spread between a high quality bond and a low quality bond of similar maturity.

Quality spread risk: a portfolio average used by Capital Management Sciences to assess a portfolio's average quality risk exposure.

Quartile: a partition of the universe of observations; four quartiles cover the entire spectrum of observations: 1st quartile (1st–25th percentile); 2nd quartile (26th–50th percentile); 3rd quartile (51st–75th percentile); and 4th quartile (76th–100th percentile).

Real interest rate: the underlying compensation for deferring consumption to a future period; the nominal interest rate adjusted for an inflation premium and a risk premium.

Real return: the total return in excess of the inflation rate.

Realized compound yield: the semiannually compounded total return on a bond, expressed in a percentage form; a yield to maturity adjusted for the actual reinvestment rate realized and the actual sale price of the bond (if sold prior to final maturity).

Realized gain: the excess of a bond's sale price over its book value on date of sale.

Realized loss: the excess of a bond's book value on date of sale over its sale price.

Refunding call: an early redemption provision in which a bond issue can be refinanced with new, lower cost debt.

Regression line: the straight line that best describes the relationship between two variables (e.g., security/portfolio return and market return); also termed the *least-squares regression line*.

Regression line analysis: the use of regression lines to assess the relationship between se-

curity (or portfolio) return and market return.

Reinvestment rate (of interest): the interest earned on the reinvestment of coupon payments.

Reinvestment rate protection swap: a swap into a bond that provides incremental returns should interest rates (and reinvestment rates) subsequently decline.

Reinvestment rate risk: the risk that the actual reinvestment rate falls short of the expected or assumed reinvestment rate.

Reinvestment return: the return attributable to the reinvestment of coupon cash flows; can be expressed in dollars or in percentages; also termed *interest-on-interest*.

Relative duration: the ratio of the duration of a portfolio and the duration of a chosen benchmark; a measure of the relative risk between the portfolio and the benchmark.

Relative return: the return of a bond portfolio relative to the return of a chosen benchmark.

Relative standard deviation (RSD): the ratio of the standard deviation of a portfolio's returns and the standard deviation of a benchmark's returns; a measure of the relative risk between the portfolio and the benchmark.

Return smoothing: the tendency for total return differences to dampen over time, as price returns diminish in relative importance.

Riding-the-yield-curve: rolling up (or down) the yield curve as a result of the passage of time; also see *yield curve roll factor, riding-the-yield-curve swap, rollup, rolldown*.

Riding-the-yield-curve swap: a risk-altering swap that attempts to take advantage of a stable interest rate environment by modestly extending the maturities of issues held. In a positive yield curve environment, the ride or roll down the yield curve (from the passage of time) generates excess total returns.

Risk: the degree of unpredictability in a bond's future returns. Bond risk arises from market (interest rate) risk, purchasing power (inflation) risk, quality/credit risk, call risk, liquidity risk, etc.

Risk-altering swap: a swap that deliberately changes the general market risk exposure of a portfolio holding to take advantage of an anticipated movement in future interest rates.

Risk-averse investor: an investor who demands a higher level of return for incremental risk undertaken.

Risk-neutral investor: an investor who is indifferent with regard to risk, neither seeking it nor avoiding it.

Risk-neutral swap: a swap that maintains a similar degree of general market risk exposure.

Risk-seeking investor: an investor who enjoys risk and accepts incremental risk while expecting the same or lower levels of return.

Risk:return quadrant: one of four sections (I, II, III, IV) of risk:return pairings; can represent *superior investments* (I), *aggressive investments* (II), *inferior investments* (III), or *defensive investments* (IV).

Risk premium: the component of a nominal interest rate that compensates the investor for risks such as credit risk, call risk, liquidity risk, and the risk of higher-than-expected inflation.

Rolldown: the ride down the yield curve, typically expressed in basis points of yield (e.g., 20BP rolldown); also see *riding-the-yield-curve*.

Rollup: the ride up the yield curve, typically expressed in basis points of yield (e.g., 10BP rollup); also see *riding-the-yield-curve*.

SLGC: abbreviation for Shearson Lehman Government/Corporate.

STRIPS: Separately Traded Registered Interest and Principal Securities: zero-coupon bonds that are directly backed by the U.S. Government. STRIPS are pieces of a coupon-bearing U.S. Treasury bond that was stripped to create a set of individual cash flows that are each sold separately and each carry a different CUSIP number.

Scenario-weighted return: a probability-weighted average total return based on expectations regarding potential future outcomes or scenarios.

Scientific amortization: the natural tendency of a bond's price to approach par value (for a bond expected to be called, the bond's price approaches the call price). The bond's premium or discount is amortized as time passes. The initial price and yield determine the rate at which the premium or discount amortization occurs. Holding the yield level constant, the amount of amortization for a given period is the change in price that naturally occurs.

Sector bet: an over/(under)weighting in a market sector purposefully undertaken to enhance the total return of a bond portfolio.

Sector duration: the weighted average duration of the holdings of a specific market sector in a portfolio or index.

Sector swaps: swaps within and between sectors of the fixed-income market; these swaps are designed with total return enhancement as the objective.

Sector weight: the percentage of a portfolio or index that is attributable to a specific market sector; the calculation is typically based on market values.

Security market line (SML): a plotting of risk:return combinations in a straight-line form. The risk-free rate and the market return form the basis for the line construction. Beta serves as the risk measure.

Semiannual-pay bond: a bond that makes coupon payments on a semiannual basis.

Simple interest: interest earned on the principal amount only.

Sinking fund (or sinker): the periodic retirement of a portion of the principal amount of a bond issue. A prespecified schedule determines the timing and the amount of the sinking fund payments.

Specialized or customized bond index: a bond index that is specially tailored according to a client's investment objectives and constraints.

Spot rate (SR): the interest rate on a pure discount security of a specified future maturity date.

Spot rate curve: a plotting of the relationship between spot rates and terms to maturity.

Standard deviation (σ): an expression of the variability in a series of data items; calculated as the square root of the average squared deviation from the mean of the observations. For a large number of observations, approximately 68% of the observations lie within one standard deviation of the mean, approximately 95% of the observations lie within two standard deviations of the mean, and virtually all of the observations lie within three standard deviations of the mean.

Standard deviation in total return: the variability in total return as expressed by the standard deviation risk measure; see *standard deviation*.

Substitution swap: a swap into an identical bond selling at a lower price.

Superior investments (or portfolios): investments offering a combination of low risk and high return.

Systematic (market) risk: the risk stemming from general or systemwide market forces; risk that cannot be diversified away. Also termed *nondiversifiable risk*.

30/360 basis: under this approach, accrued interest is calculated on the basis of a 30-day month and a 360-day year. The 30/360 basis is used with federal agency bonds and corporate bonds.

Term structure of interest rates: see *yield curve*.

Term to maturity: the number of years remaining until the final maturity date.

Theoretical bond price or value: the current value of a bond as derived by discounting its cash flow stream by factors stemming from the spot rate curve.

Theoretical duration: a duration derived through the use of discount factors that emanate from the spot rate curve.

Time value of money: time has a value in monetary terms; a dollar received today has more value than a dollar received at a future point in time because today's dollar can be invested to earn interest over the interim period.

Time-weighted rate of return: the total return for an investor who purchases the fund at the beginning of the performance measurement period, makes no contributions or withdrawals, and holds the fund shares until the end of the performance measurement period; a geometric average of a series of annual returns.

Total return (TR): the change in the total value of an investment over a specified period. For a fixed-income investment, total return is comprised of price return, coupon return, and reinvestment return. Total return can be expressed in either dollars or percentages.

Total return attribution: an analysis of the contributors to total return.

Total return (TR) curve: a plotting of the relationship between the total returns (historical or expected) of a series of bonds and the risk of each of the individual securities, where the risk measure can be the term to maturity, the duration, the beta, the standard deviation in total return, etc.

Total return enhancement swap: a swap into a bond offering greater total return potential.

Total return spread: the total return differential between two bonds (or sectors); typically expressed in basis points.

Transaction cost: the cost of executing a bond transaction as represented by the bid-offer spread on the bond in the marketplace.

Unrealized gain or loss: the difference between a bond's current market value and the bond's current book value.

Unsystematic (diversifiable) risk: the risk attributable to specific portfolio holdings or market sectors. This risk can be diversified away by holding the market portfolio. Also termed *extra-market risk* since it is above and beyond the general degree of risk exposure as described by systematic or market risk.

Variance (σ^2): an expression of the variability in a series of data items; calculated as the average squared deviation from the mean of the observations. Also see *standard deviation*.

Weighted average cash flow (WACF): the average maturity of a bond's cash flow stream, where the nominal values serve as the weights. The WACF is generally expressed either as a future date (e.g., 9/15/94) or as a number of years until the average date (e.g., 7.60 years); also termed *weighted average life.*

Weighted average duration: see *portfolio duration.*

Weighted average life (WAL): see *weighted average cash flow.*

Weighted average maturity (WAM): the average maturity of a bond's principal repayments, where the nominal values serve as the weights. The WAM is generally expressed either as a future date (e.g., 6/30/96) or as a number of years until the average maturity date (e.g., 9.60 years); also termed *average life.*

Withdrawal: a divestment from an existing portfolio or fund.

Yield: see *yield to maturity.*

Yield curve (YC): a plotting of the relationship between bond yields to maturity and terms to maturity.

Yield curve risk: the risk that the yield curve shifts in a nonparallel fashion, creating unexpected price appreciations/(depreciations).

Yield curve roll factor: the basis point change in yield ascribed to a move along the yield curve as a result of the passage of time; see *riding-the-yield-curve.*

Yield-giveup swap: a swap into a lower yielding bond.

Yield-pickup swap: see *YTM enhancement swap.*

Yield spread: the yield differential between two bonds/sectors; typically expressed in basis points.

Yield to average life (YTAL): the discount rate that equates the present value of a bond's future cash flows received through the average life date to the bond's current market price. All principal repayment is assumed to be made on the average life date.

Yield to call (YTC): the discount rate that equates the present value of a bond's future cash flows received through the call date to the bond's current market price.

Yield to maturity (YTM): the discount rate that equates the present value of a bond's future cash flows received through the maturity date to the bond's current market price.

Yield-to-maturity (YTM) enhancement swap: a swap into a higher yielding bond; also termed a *yield-pickup swap.*

Yield value of a 32nd (YV32): the average basis point change in yield that results from repricing a bond 1/32nd point higher and 1/32nd point lower than the bond's current market price.

YV32-weighted contraction swap: same as *duration-weighted contraction swap* except that YV32s are used to risk-neutralize the trade.

YV32-weighted dumbbell/bullet swap: same as *duration-weighted dumbbell/bullet swap* except that YV32s are used to risk-neutralize the trade.

YV32-weighted extension swap: same as *duration-weighted extension swap* except that YV32s are used to risk-neutralize the trade.

Zero-coupon bond: a bond that makes no coupon payments during its life span. The bondholder receives the principal repayment at final maturity; consequently, a zero-coupon bond always trades at a discount until, at final maturity, it reaches par value.

Index